Social Network Engineering for Secure Web Data and Services

Luca Caviglione
National Research Council of Italy, Italy

Mauro Coccoli
University of Genoa, Italy

Alessio Merlo
University of Genoa, Italy & Università Telematica E-Campus, Italy

Managing Director:	Lindsay Johnston
Editorial Director:	Joel Gamon
Book Production Manager:	Jennifer Yoder
Publishing Systems Analyst:	Adrienne Freeland
Development Editor:	Myla Merkel
Assistant Acquisitions Editor:	Kayla Wolfe
Typesetter:	Alyson Zerbe
Cover Design:	Jason Mull

Published in the United States of America by
Information Science Reference (an imprint of IGI Global)
701 E. Chocolate Avenue
Hershey PA 17033
Tel: 717-533-8845
Fax: 717-533-8661
E-mail: cust@igi-global.com
Web site: http://www.igi-global.com

Library of Congress Cataloging-in-Publication Data

Social network engineering for secure web data and services / Luca Caviglione, Mauro Coccoli, and Alessio Merlo, editors.
pages cm
Includes bibliographical references and index.
Summary: "This book provides empirical research on the engineering of social network infrastructures, the development of novel applications, and the impact of social network- based services over the internet"--Provided by publisher.
ISBN 978-1-4666-3926-3 (hardcover) -- ISBN 978-1-4666-3927-0 (ebook) -- ISBN 978-1-4666-3928-7 (print & perpetual access) 1. Online social networks--Security measures. 2. Data protection. I. Caviglione, Luca II. Coccoli, Mauro, 1980- III. Merlo, Alessio, 1966-
HM742.S6287 2013
302.3--dc23

2012051554

British Cataloguing in Publication Data
A Cataloguing in Publication record for this book is available from the British Library.

All work contributed to this book is new, previously-unpublished material. The views expressed in this book are those of the authors, but not necessarily of the publisher.

Editorial Advisory Board

List of Reviewers

Stefania Manca, *Institute for Educational Technology - CNR, Italy*
Manuel Mazzara, *UNU-IIST, Macau and Newcastle University, UK*
Michael J. Moore, *Graduate School of Engineering, Osaka University, Japan*
Tadashi Nakano, *Graduate School of Engineering, Osaka University, Japan*
Francesco Osborne, *University of Turin, Italy*
Alexandros Papanikolaou, *Technological Educational Institute of Larissa, Greece*
Frank Piessens, *IBBT–DistriNet, KU Leuven, Belgium*
Nafees Qamar, *UNU-IIST, Macau*
Maria Ranieri, *University of Florence, Italy*
Tom Reynaert, *IBBT–DistriNet, KU Leuven, Belgium*
Camilo Rueda Calderón, *Pontificiad Universidad Javeriana, Cali, Colombia*
Rula Sayaf, *IBBT-Distrinet, KU Leuven, Belgium*
Tatsuya Suda, *The University Netgroup Inc., Fallbrook, CA, USA*
Michele Tomaiuolo, *University of Parma, Italy*
Ilaria Torre, *University of Genoa, Italy*
Vasileios Vlachos, *Technological Educational Institute of Larissa, Greece*

Table of Contents

Foreword xii

Preface xiv

Section 1
Fundamentals

Chapter 1
On Social Network Engineering for Secure Web Data and Services 1
Luca Caviglione, National Research Council of Italy, Italy
Mauro Coccoli, University of Genoa, Italy
Alessio Merlo, University of Genoa, Italy & Università Telematica E-Campus, Italy

Chapter 2
Identity, Credibility, and Trust in Social Networking Sites: Old Issues, New Mechanisms, and Current Challenges for Privacy and Security 5
Stefania Manca, National Research Council, Italy
Maria Ranieri, University of Florence, Italy

Chapter 3
Access Control Models for Online Social Networks 32
Rula Sayaf, KU Leuven, Belgium
Dave Clarke, KU Leuven, Belgium

Section 2
Applications

Chapter 4
Social Interactions and Automated Detection Tools in Cyberbullying 67
Michael J. Moore, Osaka University, Japan
Tadashi Nakano, Osaka University, Japan
Tatsuya Suda, The University Netgroup Inc., USA
Akihiro Enomoto, University of California, USA

Detailed Table of Contents

Foreword xii

Preface xiv

Section 1
Fundamentals

Chapter 1
On Social Network Engineering for Secure Web Data and Services 1
Luca Caviglione, National Research Council of Italy, Italy
Mauro Coccoli, University of Genoa, Italy
Alessio Merlo, University of Genoa, Italy & Università Telematica E-Campus, Italy

This chapter introduces the topics covered by the book, pointing out the main behaviors and technological characteristics of Online Social Networks (OSNs). Besides, new paradigms to implement novel services and interaction flavors are briefly addressed.

Chapter 2
Identity, Credibility, and Trust in Social Networking Sites: Old Issues, New Mechanisms, and Current Challenges for Privacy and Security 5
Stefania Manca, National Research Council, Italy
Maria Ranieri, University of Florence, Italy

This chapter discusses issues related to identity, credibility and trust management in digital contexts. Also, it showcases an analysis of the current state-of-the-art literature about possible impacts on the security and privacy of the final user. Lastly, the chapter outlines some countermeasures to mitigate the aforementioned threats.

Chapter 3
Access Control Models for Online Social Networks 32
Rula Sayaf, KU Leuven, Belgium
Dave Clarke, KU Leuven, Belgium

This chapter tackles the problem of access control applied to OSNs, also by reviewing both fundamentals of access control and many Access Control Models (ACMs). Besides, the chapter classifies such techniques, also by emphasizing aspects related to privacy. Finally, the chapter proposes requirements for future ACMs for OSNs.

Section 2
Applications

Chapter 4
Social Interactions and Automated Detection Tools in Cyberbullying 67
Michael J. Moore, Osaka University, Japan
Tadashi Nakano, Osaka University, Japan
Tatsuya Suda, The University Netgroup Inc., USA
Akihiro Enomoto, University of California, USA

This chapter deals with cyberbullying, which is the digital version of physical bullying. In detail, the chapter highlights how it can be used as a new vector to conduct attacks over the Web. Moreover, authors also introduce the state-of-the art research to automate cyberbullying detection, and propose future trends and directions.

Chapter 5
Social Networks and Collective Intelligence: A Return to the Agora.. 88
Manuel Mazzara, UNU-IIST, Macau and Newcastle University, UK
Luca Biselli, Independent Researcher, UK
Pier Paolo Greco, Newcastle University, UK
Nicola Dragoni, Technical University of Denmark, Denmark
Antonio Marraffa, Polidoxa.com, Germany
Nafees Qamar, UNU-IIST, Macau
Simona de Nicola, University of Bologna, Italy

This chapter proposes Polidoxa, a solution to deliver: a trust-based search engine algorithm analyzing behavior of users; a trust-based social network; a holonic system for bottom-up self-protection of users. Furthermore, it analyzes the most innovative media, and implications in terms of trust of search engines and OSNs.

Chapter 6
Distributed Social Platforms for Confidentiality and Resilience 114
Enrico Franchi, University of Parma, Italy
Michele Tomaiuolo, University of Parma, Italy

This chapter deals with distributed social networks as an alternative to centralized ones. To this aim, authors advise an enhancement of current OSNs via the adoption of peer-to-peer (P2P) principles, and Distributed Hash Tables (DHTs). The proposed architecture can improve resistance of OSNs against anonymity or censorship issues, authenticable contents, semantic interoperability, and data availability.

Chapter 7
Retrieval of Personal Public Data on Social Networks: The Risks for Privacy 137
Francesca Carmagnola, University of Turin, Italy
Francesco Osborne, University of Turin, Italy
Ilaria Torre, University of Genoa, Italy

This chapter investigates the violation of users' privacy via the diffusion of personal data on different OSNs. In detail, authors exploit the aggregation of data retrieved from different OSNs as a tool to reveal and reconstruct identities. Besides, they propose a search-engine to automate such task, and validate their approach via simulations.

Section 3
Security

Chapter 8
Privacy Issues in Social Networks 162
Alexandros Papanikolaou, Technological Educational Institute of Larissa, Greece
Vasileios Vlachos, Technological Educational Institute of Larissa, Greece
Periklis Chatzimisios, Alexander Technological Educational Institute of Thessaloniki, Greece
Christos Ilioudis, Alexander Technological Educational Institute of Thessaloniki, Greece

This chapter analyzes issues related to privacy of OSNs applications. In particular, this work portraits a variety of methods to violate the privacy schema of many OSNs. Besides, the chapter provides real-world use cases and proposes some countermeasures, as well as the needed research to be done.

Chapter 9
A Graph-Based Approach to Model Privacy and Security Issues of Online Social Networks 184
Luca Caviglione, National Research Council of Italy, Italy
Mauro Coccoli, University of Genoa, Italy
Alessio Merlo, University of Genoa, Italy & Università Telematica E-Campus, Italy

This chapter deals with major security characteristics of OSNs, with emphasis on the sharing of data and objects as a possible vector of attacks. Then, it proposes a novel graph-based approach to model attacks and security breaches, in the perspective of developing proper countermeasures, or simulated analyses.

Chapter 10
Security and Privacy of Online Social Network Applications 206
Willem De Groef, iMinds–DistriNet, KU Leuven, Belgium
Dominique Devriese, iMinds–DistriNet, KU Leuven, Belgium
Tom Reynaert, iMinds–DistriNet, KU Leuven, Belgium
Frank Piessens, iMinds–DistriNet, KU Leuven, Belgium

This chapter focuses on security implication of third-party applications populating a variety of OSNs. Then, it discusses some proposals to manage and mitigate the most relevant issues spawned by the injection of additional components in the main framework of the OSN.

Chapter 11
On the Use of Formal Methods to Enforce Privacy-Aware Social Networking 222
Néstor Cataño Collazos, The University of Madeira, Portugal
Sorren Christopher Hanvey, The University of Madeira, Portugal
Camilo Rueda Calderón, Pontificiad Universidad Javeriana, Colombia

This chapter introduces Poporo, a tool based on formal methods to guarantee privacy-aware social networking, i.e., to guide users to responsibly update their settings. Modeling is also applied to compare different security and privacy policies.

Chapter 12
Web Malware that Targets Web Applications 248
Ammar Alazab, Deakin University, Australia
Jemal Abawajy, Deakin University, Australia
Michael Hobbs, Deakin University, Australia

This chapter focuses on malware targeting Web applications, which are popular building blocks in many OSNs. In particular, the chapter discusses Structured Query Language Injection Attack (SQLIA) and Zeus threats, pointing out how they can evade checks by Intrusion Detection Systems (IDS). The chapter also discusses techniques to detect and prevent such malware.

Compilation of References 265

About the Contributors 293

Index 301

Foreword

Since the birth of the Internet, guaranteeing proper security requirements has been one of the main challenges. Besides, 30 years of evolution have changed in a very impressive way the meaning, and the approach, to this problem. In the beginning, the Internet had to cope with security issues in a scenario where users, programmers, system and network managers were highly skilled. Nevertheless, engineers had to deal with very simple network topologies and few media for handling data. Also, applications had a quite long lifecycle (i.e., telnet has been around for more than 20 years, which is unthinkable for a modern "app", yet is still widely used… sigh). Among the others, the most important fact was the embryonic stage of ideas characterizing the "misuse" of network resources. Nowadays it is quite clear that security is not only related to the technical part of the Internet, but it also includes users' awareness and behaviors. In fact, the world has dramatically changed, and being a security professional, or just an enthusiastic, requires a deep and sound knowledge on the areas that are well depicted in this book. In this perspective, the work is a valuable source of information for people involved in Internet related technologies and services.

The areas covered in this book can be summarized as follows:

- Social networks, which are now places where a lot of individuals exchange/integrate their experiences and create a sort of augmented reality. As it happens in the "real" world, new questions arise. For instance: "How do I trust someone?" "How can I avoid disclosing unwanted personal details?" "How can I prevent data fusion as a way to inherit a deeper knowledge about myself?" "How can I implement a solid access control to my (Web) services?" Answers to these – and more questions – will be easily found in this book, which also covers general and sociological aspects related to Social Networks.
- New "cyber" threats, such as the Cyberbullying, which makes the Web a new arena where aggressiveness takes place, also allowing the bothering and harassing people an easier task (e.g., we do not have to take a car and go somewhere, and keyboards do not require muscle power as needed in a street).
- Collective intelligence and opinion building. A very fragile process that sometimes may have its foundation on inaccurate information or, at its worst, intentionally false data in order to bias the public opinion. However, in the past, it was easier for people to measure trustworthiness, since "sources of information" where very stable (few newspapers, radio channels, and TV broadcasts) and, even if not always reliable in their contents, they had to pass through some sort of editing and approval. On the contrary, in today's scenario, it is very hard to clearly measure the reliability of sources. Thus, in this book some innovative techniques for identifying which information is trusted/un-trusted are presented.

- Issues related to the sharing of wanted/unwanted information. The book covers risks and benefits of having semantic contents widely spread over peer-to-peer social networks, as opposite of having a few centralized systems. Also, it explains how people can be forced to share unwanted personal data, which can be inferred through data fusion and integration.
- Privacy and targeted attacks. The book also offers a robust coverage of the concerns related to privacy and data leakage to help the reader in gaining a better consciousness. This will be of great help either to final users or professionals involved in planning, development, testing, management and deployment of social networks based services and products.

In conclusion, I have found in this book a very interesting and innovative way to discuss and examine the problem of security for Web data and services, avoiding the classical "stacked" approach (i.e., wired/wireless transport data security, host integrity, application testing and so on). Instead, a multidisciplinary methodology is favored, and it has been centered on present most critical aspects, i.e., the human behavior and perception. This is why I would definitely recommend reading it.

Massimo Ianigro
National Research Council of Italy, Italy

Massimo Ianigro *is a Research Technologist and Security Expert of the Institute of Intelligent Systems for Automation – Italian National Research Council. His main interests are in the networking field, with focus on security, Internet services, traffic measurement and management, heterogeneous networks and distributed systems. After receiving a MD in Computer Science with a thesis about mobile robot navigation, he has started working at the CNR in 1992 and he is responsible for the networking infrastructure and telematic services for a large number of users and sites disseminated around the country. He is also a member of the GARR-CERT (Computer Emergency Response Team of the nation-wide network of academic institutions) and he is an expert appointed by Italian law enforcement agencies in many computer forensic cases.*

Preface

Online Social Network (OSN) applications are nowadays accessed by about a billion of users, thus they can be considered a real cultural phenomenon, and one of the most innovative component of the Web 2.0. As a consequence, they have relevant impacts on the society, the economy and the technological pool of the Internet. OSN platforms are not only used for content sharing purposes. Rather, they have demonstrated their effectiveness to support the development of new services or applications, and also to provide a suitable playground for real-time user-to-user interactions. To be effective, the engineering and creation of new frameworks require a capillary research activity, both by the Academia and the Industrial world. In fact, advancements in the field of OSN impose the understanding of new users' behaviors, the development of innovative Web-based interaction paradigms, the modeling of application-specific traffic patterns and network requirements, the creation of highly scalable architectural blueprints, the definition of novel Quality of Service (QoS) and Quality of Experience (QoE) guarantees, and, definitely, a thorough understanding of *security* hazards. To this aim, it must be considered that OSNs store, deliver and manage personal data, and they are tightly coupled with identities of individuals. It must be also underlined that their specificities make the constant cross-pollination between digital and real life a tangible and actual danger, thus making an intimate understanding of *privacy* issues an unavoidable task. Accordingly, the word "*secure*" must be considered with the acceptation of a hyponym embracing security and privacy risks at different levels, i.e., physical, digital, and social. Unfortunately, this requires a highly multidisciplinary effort, ranging from social sciences, to software engineering.

In this perspective, this book entitled *Social Network Engineering for Secure Web Data and Services* tries to capture the state-of-the-art of engineering, development and research, applied to OSNs, having the secure qualification as the founding principle. Its main goal is to consider issues and solutions to prevent security threats, and introduce proper countermeasures to attacks at every level during the design and development of OSN applications (or while relying upon such frameworks). Due to the multidisciplinary nature of the topic, *Social Network Engineering for Secure Web Data and Services* has been architected to be useful to a mixed audience. Specifically, it is intended for professionals and researchers in the area of OSN, software engineering, network and software security specialists, as well as professionals in charge of investigating computer frauds, and behavioral aspects of platforms delivering social network services in a broad sense. To increase its accessibility, the book covers aspects both from the theoretical and practical points of view, without neglecting the vision from social sciences, e.g., in the field of communication, education, and sociality.

To support such vision, our work is composed by 12 chapters written by experts in the relevant field, which have been double blindly reviewed by authoritative peers. When receiving submissions, we decided to discard works not clearly focusing on relevant topics, or not giving real benefits to perspective readers. To better organize the contributions, also making the book accessible to readers with a different understanding on the topic, we grouped the chapters into three sections. Namely: (1) Fundamentals, (2) Applications, and (3) Security.

The first section starts with the chapter "*On Social Network Engineering for Secure Web Data and Services*" introducing the state-of-the-art in the engineering of OSNs infrastructures, the impact of OSN-based services over the Internet, and a possible research roadmap. Then, "*Identity, Credibility and Trust in Social Networking Sites. Old Issues, new Mechanisms and Current Challenges for Privacy and Security*" provides a wide overview of the current literature on identity, credibility and trust, and their implications for privacy and security, from the perspective of social and behavioral sciences. To complete such an introductory path, the work "*Access Control Models for Online Social Networks*" showcases the essential aspects of access control and reviews the classical Access Control Models (ACMs) with emphasis on how they can contribute to enhance privacy of OSNs, and by clearly indicating core requirements for future implementations.

In the second section, the chapter "*Social Interactions and Automated Detection Tools in Cyberbullying*" introduces to Cyberbullies, which are individuals abusing digital media (such as websites, social networking services, blogging, email, instant messaging, chat rooms, and cell phones) to attack victims. This work reviews the state-of-the-art research in automated tools to detect cyberbullying, as well as future perspective for its automated detection. The second contribution is "*Social Networks and Collective Intelligence: A Return to the Agora,*" where authors answer the following questions: "How can information quality be reliably assessed?" "How can sources credibility be fairly assessed?" "How can gatekeeping processes be found trustworthy when filtering out news and deciding ranking and priorities of traditional media?" The answers they provide are enclosed in Polidoxa (from Greek poly – πολύ, meaning "many" or "several" and doxa – δόξα, meaning "common belief" or "popular opinion") offering a trust-based search engine, a social network and a holonic system for bottom-up self-protection and social privacy. Then, "*Distributed Social Platforms for Confidentiality and Resilience*" rethinks the current approach of building social networking systems by using a huge centralized entity owned by a single company. In this vein, authors do propose a solid distributed social networking platform consisting in a novel peer-to-peer blueprint that leverages existing, widespread and stable technologies such as Distributed Hash Tables (DHTs) and BitTorrent. To conclude, "*Retrieval of Personal Public Data on Social Networks. The Risks for Privacy*" analyzes the risks for privacy coming from the distribution of user data over several social networks. Besides, the work concentrates on hazards introduced by the aggregation of user data discovered on different sources into a single more complete profile, which makes possible to infer other information (possibly private).

The third section focuses on security aspects. The chapter "*Privacy Issues in Social Networks*" defines concepts belonging to privacy in social networks, and demonstrates how it can be violated. Also, authors discuss various countermeasures, as well as future research directions in the field of competence. The work "*A Graph-Based Approach to Model Privacy and Security Issues of Online Social Networks*" analyzes how personal information can be exploited to conduct malicious actions, with the aim of introducing a graph-based modeling methodology to elaborate countermeasures or automated checking procedures. The third contribution is "*Security and Privacy of Online Social Network Applications*" where authors point out that basic mechanisms for isolating applications are well understood, but when applied to social-enabled applications will fall short. Then, they identify and discuss the current security and privacy problems related to social applications and their platforms, also by making proposals on how to address such problems. The work entitled "*On the Use of Formal Methods to Enforce Privacy-Aware Social-Networking*" examines the use of formal techniques and verification tools to ensure privacy-aware social networking, where users can predict the consequences of updating their privacy settings. To achieve this goal, they propose a tool called Poporo. The book concludes with "*Web Malware That Targets Web Applications*" investigating the most severe threats affecting Web applications such as the Structure Query Language Injection Attack (SQLIA) and the Zeus threat.

Section 1
Fundamentals

Chapter 1
On Social Network Engineering for Secure Web Data and Services

Luca Caviglione
National Research Council of Italy, Italy

Mauro Coccoli
University of Genoa, Italy

Alessio Merlo
University of Genoa, Italy & Università Telematica E-Campus, Italy

ABSTRACT

Online Social Network (OSN) applications are used every day by millions of people, and have impacts on the society, economy and lifestyle. They also accelerate the development, or the adoption, of new technologies, for instance to support new mobile paradigms. Besides, OSNs are an important building block of the Web 2.0, thus offering new services, such as product placement, advertising and user profiling. Hence, OSNs are valuable frameworks, contributing to the technological pool of the Internet itself. Their attitude of shifting an individual life into a digital space makes OSNs interesting targets for attacks, to disclose personal details, and to force human securities through digital insecurities. In order to be effective, OSN platforms must be properly engineered, also by having privacy and security protection as strict design constraints. To this aim, it is of crucial importance investigating potential new behaviors, Web-based technologies, traffic patterns and innovative security policies. In this perspective, this chapter discusses the state-of-the-art in the engineering of OSNs infrastructures, the key issues, and the research actions needed to effectively advance in the social network engineering for secure Web data and services.

DOI: 10.4018/978-1-4666-3926-3.ch001

INTRODUCTION

In recent years, Online Social Network (OSN) services (Boyd & Ellison, 2007) are becoming a consistent part of the Internet and the World Wide Web (WWW). In fact, they are used every day by millions of people, interacting through such platforms according to different flavors. Specifically:

- By using the OSN in a stand-alone manner from a Web browser, for exploiting social duties, such as, maintaining or establishing relationships according to common interests, real-life partnerships, or for business development;
- By exploiting the social infrastructure as an integrated communication platform, thus for sharing data, exchanging messages, or for audio/video conferencing;
- By syncing their real-world activities and social knowledge with remote peers, making OSNs as the first massive technological enabler for the mobile Internet. We mention, among the others, the sharing of physical locations, contacts and events, photos, and reviews or suggestions about commercial activities or trips. In this case, important components are the hardware equipment of handheld devices, the ubiquitous availability of the Internet, and the introduction of ad-hoc client interfaces making the access to, and the control of, digital alter egos simple and effective;
- By considering the OSN as a third party component. For instance, to share comments relying on such platform as a trusted identity manager, to keep track of visited sites and to declare interests about specific topics or brands;
- By consuming data via the Application Programming Interfaces (APIs) made available by many services to build new applications, or by adopting the OSN as a real development platform.

Consequently, OSNs can be considered one of the most relevant advancements for creating an *Internet of People*, thus making the individual a central entity. However, focusing on "humans", rather than devices or services, is not a complete novel concept. In more details, the World Wide Web Consortium (W3C) put a relevant effort in the creation of a Social Web (W3C, 2010). Notwithstanding, such a vision has been not implemented under its organic guidance, rather it has been progressively built according to ad-hoc OSN platforms and other services, e.g., those for sharing photo or for audio/video communications. As a result, the social organization, with the acceptation of services, APIs, human-to-machine interactions, and business-to-business logics, constitute a very split-space, resulting into mostly overlapped or closed sets of functionalities.

Needless to say, data stored and managed have great potentialities for the following reasons:

1. Performances of OSNs are tightly coupled with the accuracy of data provided by users. As an example, the more a user offers personal details, the better will be the outcome of algorithms used to suggests friends, potential business partners, reconnect with past classmates, or to find people sharing common interests. On the contrary, this can expose individuals to threats similar to those happening in real life, e.g., bullying (accordingly defined as cyber-bullying);
2. The popularity of social applications, jointly with their ubiquitous integration, e.g., via mash-ups, plug-ins and task-specific code snippets, can lead to massive data volumes describing persons, habits, preferences, and personal details; also, these sets of data may be also accessed by malicious applications, thus potentially compromising the privacy of the user;
3. The individual-centric nature of OSNs intrinsically gives a lot of freedom to users. In fact, people are owners of data, and everyone

has different needs when constructing his/her alter ego, thus making information management and privacy settings often delegated to users, which may be circumvented or forced to spread their own data to malicious targets.

Points 1-3 can lead to several hazards, and capture the attention of many bodies, possibly aiming at performing some undesirable actions. In more detail, (1) could bring the attention to single attackers aiming at forcing the digital representation of an individual for small scams or simple curiosity. Then, (2) deals with very appealing data, which can be used both for large-scale fraud activities, or sold to Industries or Companies for business development, employees or competitor profiling purposes, or worst, blackmailing competitors. Lastly, (3) represents an issue per se, since high freedom put in non-skilled hands often leads to dangerous actions. We point out that, even in presence of conscious users, privacy management policies and options are often incompatible, very mixed and confusing.

To summarize, heterogeneities, the lack of long-term standardization efforts, the attractiveness of personal data (e.g., both from the industrial world for marketing purposes, and from attackers for bringing attacks to the next level), make privacy and security a critical aspect to evaluate. At the same time, the aforementioned characteristics make the engineering and management of proper security countermeasures an extremely complex task. Thus, engineering secure data and services belonging to social areas require a multidisciplinary effort, which spans over sociology, relationship issues, cognitive processes, scalability issues, human-machine-interaction, Web 2.0 technologies, ubiquitous availability and dependability.

Proper engineering and research actions can dramatically reduce (or completely prevent, in the best case) the natural vocation of OSN applications in amplifying the effectiveness of classical attacks, e.g., social engineering, multiple profile fusion, user profiling and identity theft (Caviglione & Coccoli, 2011). Additionally, a thorough investigation process can reveal the major effectiveness in state-of-the-art security solutions, which can quickly become outdated or loose effectiveness due to user-generated flaws, lack of unified privacy/security frameworks, threats rooted from the usage of Web technologies, weak security at the network level and interactions with un-authoritative/untrusted third parties or machineries.

Therefore, in order to perform an effective social network engineering for secure data and services, it is important to investigate, among the others, the following aspects: sociological implications of individuals interacting into a digital environment, and their exploitation through engineering approaches; identity credibility and trust issues; modeling including users' dynamics, hazardous behaviors, and definition of schemas to represent security issues; evaluation of current development tools, standard and technologies of OSN applications; the design and deployment of social-enabled frameworks; potential contact points between OSNs and networking, e.g., perform traffic analysis and identification of social service, possibly in relation to network security; application of the OSN paradigm to new scenarios, e.g., e-learning, on-line gaming, application development, and A/V conferencing; understanding and optimizing Web-oriented interaction, protocols, and performances; make the security an imperative requirement, thus by meticulously evaluating general security aspects of OSNs, privacy, authentication, authorization, access control and development of innovative and effective testing tools; implementation of new semantic methodologies and architectural blueprints.

In this vein, efforts both from academics and industrial researchers are needed to fill the gap in the current state-of-the-art literature on data, services and engineering methodologies applied to social networks in a broad sense.

REFERENCES

Boyd, D. M., & Ellison, N. B. (2007). Social network sites: Definition, history, and scholarship. *Journal of Computer-Mediated Communication*, *13*(1), 210–230. doi:10.1111/j.1083-6101.2007.00393.x.

Caviglione, L., & Coccoli, M. (2011). Privacy problems with Web 2.0. *Computer Fraud & Security*, (10): 16–19. doi:10.1016/S1361-3723(11)70104-X.

W3C (World Wide Web Consortium) - Incubator Group Report (2010). A standards-based, open and privacy-aware social Web. Retrieved September, 2012 from http://www.w3.org/2005/Incubator/socialweb/XGR-socialweb-20101206

Chapter 2
Identity, Credibility, and Trust in Social Networking Sites: Old Issues, New Mechanisms, and Current Challenges for Privacy and Security

Stefania Manca
Institute for Educational Technology - CNR, Italy

Maria Ranieri
University of Florence, Italy

ABSTRACT

Over recent years, the notions of identity, credibility and trust in digital contexts have been gaining renewed interest from scholars in different fields (from social studies to engineering and computer science), especially for their consequences for privacy and security. Emerging and urgent questions are: What does the management of online personal data entail? How much personal information are we entitled to share with others? What measures do people usually adopt to protect their identity and privacy? Are they always aware of the risks they may run? What consequences may emerge in the long term if cautions are ignored? These are some of the questions that should be addressed by users, experts and scholars engaged with digital environments, especially social networking sites. This chapter focuses on these issues trying to provide a wide overview of the current literature on identity, credibility and trust, and their implications for privacy and security, from the perspective of social and behavioral sciences. Some measures provided by experts on how to protect against the most common security and privacy threats are also outlined.

DOI: 10.4018/978-1-4666-3926-3.ch002

INTRODUCTION

The rise of social networking sites (SNSs) over the past ten years has been one of the most relevant phenomena among Web 2.0 tools. Although there is no unique way of classifying the current forms of techno-sociability (e.g., Hussein et al., 2009), social networking sites are a particular subset of online social networking, whose distinguishing characteristic is that they "are specifically designed to support and develop friendship and whose overt purpose is to provide a context and appropriate tools for doing so" (Merchant, 2012, p. 4). Typical examples of SNSs are Facebook, Twitter, MySpace or LinkedIn, which are now gaining momentum as shown by recent studies (Rainie et al., 2012). According to a Pew Research Center survey on the use of SNSs in the US (Smith, 2011), two-thirds of adults use tools such as Facebook or Twitter, and declare that they use them mainly to stay in touch with friends and family members, while half use them to connect with old friends they have lost touch with. SNSs are becoming dominant especially among young people with 80% of teens now using many of them (Lenhart, 2009; Lenhart et al., 2011). Internet users' growing interest in SNSs is also confirmed by other studies. According to one of them (Nielsen, 2011), Americans spend more time on Facebook than they do on other websites, and a similar trend is also emerging in Europe.

In the meantime, there is a growing convergence between social networking services and mobile devices. Increased ownership of smartphones and other mobile devices amongst the youth and adult population is well documented today, also in relation to SNS access. At the end of 2010, almost 40% of social media users accessed these tools through their mobile phones and social networking apps were the third most downloaded applications by mobile owners (Nielsen, 2011). This tendency seems to be destined to grow as testified by recent statistics. Indeed, 2011 saw the continued rise of mobile social networking with an increase of about 75% from the previous year both in the US and Europe, and more than half of mobile social networking users' access social media almost every day (ComScore, 2012). Of the various SNSs, Facebook, now the most popular with more than 950 million users, has more than 500 million users that log in through mobile products (Facebook, 2012).

The wide diffusion of these technologies has raised new questions in the public and academic debate about their impact on users' personal and social life. Indeed, a social networking site is a category of websites where individual users create their public or semi-public profiles, list connections with others (friends, followers or buddies) and traverse the site through their own and others' friend lists forming a public networked space (Boyd & Ellison, 2007). The profiles typically include identifiable information about users (e.g., age, gender, interests, etc.) and have unique URLs that can be visited directly. Users can keep their profiles updated posting comments and other information as well as being able to see comments posted by visitors. All these functions generate an online network space where each profile is linked to the profile of the other individuals giving rise to a traversable network of "friends of friends".

If SNSs are changing the way people communicate and interact, at the same time they also generate new risks for security and privacy. The huge amount of personal data now available online raises new challenges on how to protect privacy and guarantee security, especially for young people. However, considering that this is an inescapable global trend, our societies must learn to balance their benefits with their drawbacks, putting a particular emphasis on education as a means to develop media awareness and appropriate socio-technical skills.

With this in mind, this chapter focuses on these issues trying to provide a wide overview of the current literature on identity, credibility and privacy in SNSs, and their implications for trust and security, from the perspective of social and behavioral sciences. In particular, the first section introduces the subject providing some background information on social network theory and SNSs' characteristics. The second section focuses on the main issues of the chapter, offering an insight into the crucial topics debated in the current literature on SNSs and identity, credibility and trust. While analyzing the old and new mechanisms that are reshaping these notions, the consequences for privacy and security will be examined. The third section is dedicated to the new and future trends in the field. Although research on SNSs is still at the beginning, location-based services and content-based image retrieval systems are also emerging in social networking practices posing relevant threats for privacy and security. The chapter concludes with a reflection on how to deal with the complexity characterizing the new techno-social space shaped by SNSs, with specific focus on the role of education and media literacy.

MAIN CONCEPTS: SOCIAL NETWORKS AND SOCIAL NETWORKING SITES

Over recent years, the concept of social network has been gaining growing interest from different research areas (psychology, sociology, anthropology, economics, engineering, etc.) due to its implications within organizations and to the rise of SNSs. However, this notion is not a new one. Since 1940 it has been conceptualized by scholars within the Social Network Analysis (SNA) area (Scott, 1991; Wasserman & Faust, 1994), a research field that was of considerable size in the 70s and that has provided a useful background for the study of online interactions (Garton et al., 1997). Without expecting to be exhaustive, in the following a brief overview of the social network theory with specific reference to the characteristics of SNSs will be presented.

A social network can be defined as a network of individuals. These individuals may be connected to different degrees by certain interpersonal relationships based on informal bonding features, such as values or visions, which provide important support to individuals' personal, professional and social life (Cross & Parker, 2004). A key difference between the social network approach and other research perspectives is that "it is the interaction between people that matters, rather than what individuals think or do on their own" (Haythornthwaite, 1996, p. 127). This leads to putting attention on the various types of relationships that people may maintain in a network with their pairs. These connections are usually called ties and they may range from weak to strong ties depending on the type of exchanges, frequency of contact, duration of the relationship, intimacy, etc. One of the most influential studies on this topic goes back to Granovetter (1973), who first formulated the theory of the strength of weak ties. According to his theory, weak ties are far more valuable than strong ties in so far as the diffusion of information within weak ties is wider, while strong ties are concentrated within the same flow of information.

Another important aspect of social network theory refers to the concept of centralization, which was theorized by Freeman (1979), who pointed out three aspects of this notion: degree of a node (i.e., the number of connections with other actors); control (i.e., the level of dependency of one actor to communicate with other actors); independence (i.e., the minimal extent of connection of an actor to other nodes).

All these ideas that have been conceptualized within the field of social network theory have turned out to be helpful to some extent in studying SNSs. But before going through the specific studies, let us remember some fundamental dates in the short history of these services and provide some preliminary definitions (see Boyd & Ellison, 2007).

Although SNSs are now almost completely embedded in our lives, they only have existed since the late 1990s. SixDegrees.com was the first social networking site to be founded in 1997 and two years later LiveJournal was launched including new features such as guest books and diary pages. Then, in 2001, LinkedIn was established. However, social networking sites did not reach a considerable size until 2002 with the founding of Friendster, to become more and more popular with MySpace and Facebook. In particular, Facebook in 2004 attracted a lot of young adults from the main US universities as it was a closed network addressed only to this audience (for a detailed history of Facebook see Kirkpatrick, 2010).

A wide definition of SNSs comes from Boyd and Ellison (2007), who describe them as "[...] web-based services that allow individuals to (1) construct a public or semi-public profile within a bounded system, (2) articulate a list of other users with whom they share a connection, and (3) view and traverse their list of connections and those made by others within the system" (p. 211). These characteristics are commonly mentioned in the current literature to distinguish these sites from other web-based services that support the creation and the management of other types of online communities. Indeed, as previously stated, the peculiarity of SNSs such as Facebook is that they are applications where networking is the main activity, while the focus of other Web 2.0 tools such as YouTube is mainly on uploading and sharing contents.

SNSs have received attention across a number of research areas. Studies have been carried out on identity presentation and privacy concerns (Boyd & Hargittai, 2010; Waters & Ackerman, 2011), on the relationship between profile and friendship articulation (Wang et al., 2010) and on their implications for civic engagement (Hampton et al., 2011; Park et al., 2009). In the educational field, the focus is on students and teachers' educational uses of social networking sites (Hew, 2011; Yang et al., 2011), with a special emphasis on teacher presence and self-disclosure (Mazer et al., 2007), on appropriate professionalism/behavior (Ferdig et al., 2008) or on professional development (Ranieri et al., 2012).

Generally, literature points out that social networking sites are mainly used as tools supporting existing social relationships and enabling the maintenance of social capital (Ellison et al., 2007). This notion, that has been developed by several authors (e.g., Bourdieu, 1986; Coleman, 1988; Putnam, 1995), refers to "the aggregate of the actual or potential resources which are linked to possession of a durable network of more or less institutionalized relationships of mutual acquaintance or recognition" (Bourdieu, 1986, p. 248). Social capital has a positive role within a community of individuals in so far as it facilitates coordination and cooperation for mutual benefit. Individual benefits come from the exchange of resources, which can take the form of useful information, personal relationships, or the capacity to create and manage groups. Putnam (2000) identified two types of social capital: bridging and bonding. The former is characterized by weak ties based on the exchange of useful information, while the second refers to the benefits that individuals may derive from emotionally close relationships. In the context of Internet studies, the potential of SNSs to expand, enhance and accelerate the individual's social capital with an increase in available information, opportunities, and benefits from this wide and heterogeneous network has been stressed by many recent surveys (Pfeil et al., 2009; Steinfield et al., 2008; Valenzuela et al., 2009). Indeed, SNSs include features which allow people not only to maintain old contacts, but also to create new connections, whose nature may be better described as "latent ties", that are defined as connections "technically possible but not yet activated socially" (Haythornthwaite, 2005, p. 137). The information included in the user's profile may motivate visitors to activate "latent ties", transforming them into the weak ties linked to bridging social capital outcomes. Briefly, although research suggests that SNSs are mainly used to maintain existing social relationships, there is also evidence that "users may use the site to convert latent into weak ties" (Ellison et al., 2011, p. 877).

Taking into consideration these SNS characteristics and the types of ties enabled by social networking sites may help understand the issues emerging from the use of these services and the relative challenges for identity, credibility, trust, privacy and security. In the next section the different issues will be presented in separate paragraphs, though there exist so many conceptual relationships between the notions considered that sometimes it is very hard to draw clear and definite boundaries between them.

MAIN ISSUES IN SOCIAL NETWORKING SITES

Identity

One of the main issues involved in the complex phenomenon of how we carry out our digital lives is that of identity. The concept of identity has always been one of the most controversial in psychological research and literature. Scholars have long argued about the meaning of this term and countless theories have been proposed as definitive approaches to identity (e.g., Buckingham, 2007). On the Internet, identity is mainly constructed and maintained through online discourse. Computer-mediated discourse may take a variety of forms (e.g., e-mail, discussion groups, real-time chat, virtual reality role-playing games), but characteristic to all is that linguistic properties vary depending on the type of messaging system used and the social and cultural context embedding particular instances of use (see Herring, 2001).

Scholars have long debated the implications of being deeply involved in participatory practices on the Internet through its diverse forms of communication environments, also prior to the advent of SNSs. In the seminal text "Life on the Screen: Identity in the Age of the Internet", Sherry Turkle (1997) argues that technical environments such as multiplayer real-time virtual worlds (MUDs), for instance, allowing their users to interact with others with complete anonymity, offer the unprecedented possibility of experimenting by representing themselves as being any gender, orientation, race or profession. This potential psychotherapeutic value, of being free to reveal aspects of their personality which would not otherwise surface, was highly stressed by Turkle, who at the same time cautioned against the risks of mixing virtual and offline life.

Individual identity is always inextricably related to social identity, since individuals always categorize and label themselves and others according to a social perspective. In recent times both individual and social identities have become a fluid and contingent matter, if not a liquid entity (Bauman, 2004). In the new realm of digital media how people represent themselves in the case of instant messaging, chat or social networking, via the use of avatars, e-mail signatures, IM nicknames, etc., raise serious claims about the question whether online identities are more or less honest or truthful than offline ones.

The issue of anonymity, or of false identities, has been seriously challenged by the most recent social networking sites. If most of the SNSs that preceded Facebook allowed users to handle anonymity, Facebook is both in principle and in practice based on real identity. The presence of a (semi) public profile, where people disclose information about themselves, seems to have encouraged individuals to be more honest and truthful about their identity. As clearly stated by David Kirkpatrick, in his well-documented book about the birth and evolution of Facebook, "On Facebook it is important today to be your real self as it was launched at Harvard in February 2004. Anonymity, role-playing, pseudonyms, and handles [...] have little role here. If you invent a persona or too greatly enhance the way you present yourself, you will get little benefit from Facebook.

Unless you interact with others as yourself, your friends will either not recognize you or will not befriend you" (Kirkpatrick, 2010, pp. 12-13).

This means that people have to be willing to share as much information about themselves with others as possible. This has led to a great emphasis on the importance of managing the impression we wish to produce on the others, up to the growing obsession to exploit any opportunity to promote themselves though frequent measures of narcissism (Carpenter, 2012; Ong et al., 2011). This issue has gained great attention also from specialized literature, that has devoted several studies to the issue of impression management in social networking sites, providing detailed analysis on how people self-present in these environments (Rosenberg & Egbert, 2011; Winter et al., 2011; Zwier et al., 2011), also with focus on gender differences (Haferkamp et al., 2012).

At the same time the construction of a network of known people can reduce the amount of unsolicited and undelivered consequences of personal information disclosure. Indeed, one of the most wide-spread phenomena that have arisen as a contemporary effect of this adoption of real names and identities is that of identity theft. Identity theft is a form of stealing someone's identity in which someone pretends to be someone else by assuming that person's identity for personal gain and exploitation, and can include financial, criminal, governmental and medical identity theft. Experts have identified several ways through which social networking users expose themselves to higher risks of identity theft: using low privacy or no privacy settings, accepting invitations to connect from unfamiliar persons or contacts, downloading free applications for use on their profile, etc. (ITRC, 2012). However, though users adopt minimal measures, such as using the highest level of privacy settings that the site allows, using the least amount of information necessary to register for and use the site, or only connecting to people already known and trusted, there are several technical ways to create automated identity theft of real user profiles (Bilge et al., 2009). One of them, called profile cloning, consists of cloning an already existing profile and sending friend requests to the contacts of the victim, thus accessing the sensitive personal information provided by those contacts that accept the friendship requests. Another way, called cross-site profile cloning attack, consists of cloning the identity of a victim in the site where he/she is registered and forging it in a social networking site where he/she is not yet registered; in this way, it is possible to rebuild the social network of the victim by contacting his/her friends that are registered on both the sites. These means have been revealed both effective just for the reasons outlined above: typical users tend to accept friend requests from forged identities that are actually already confirmed contacts in their friend list, and receiving contacts from profilers that exist only once on that particular site do not raise suspicion about the user identity. As we will see in the following, the issue of credibility may become crucial in evaluating true and stolen identities, at least as one of the possible measures to protect against identity frauds.

Credibility

The concept of known identity is also strictly intertwined with the issue of credibility (Rieh & Danielson, 2007). When we try to reflect on this concept, we realize that we are dealing with fluid meanings that are difficult to define. An interesting attempt at reconstructing the semantic evolution of this concept can be found in Metzger and Flanagin (2008), who illustrate that from Aristotle onwards the theme of credibility has been dealt with from different research perspectives also giving different results, so that today a clear-cut and shared definition does not exist. Despite this difficulty, the authors underline that there are several issues involved in the process of assessment of credibility. On the one hand, people need to be able to assess the objective and subjective components of the believability of sources to come to trust their veracity; this implies that individuals have to hone skills and invoke effective tools for assessment. On the other hand, the voices of the communities one belongs to are emerging as the coin of credibility as evidence that the locus of knowledge ownership moves to communities of users. In other cases, institutional or corporate entities are emerging as arbiters of credibility.

All these issues are on stage when especially one confronts the arena of problems that have emerged with the widespread diffusion of multiple sources of information on the Internet and in digital media. Within these environments, notions that were previously kept distinct, like identity, source of information, message and media credibility, are merged together. In particular, the Internet has introduced new significant problems as regards assessment of personal and information credibility/reliability, such as the elements that distinguish online information from that transmitted through traditional channels: if, to cite the renowned adage, "On the Internet, nobody knows you're a dog" (Steiner, 1993), the problem of personal credibility is an emerging phenomenon. This may be of crucial importance, for example, when people confront credibility of service offers or selling of products in large virtual marketplaces such as eBay, where the construction of the seller credibility is the key element of success. eBay's system of rating other members, known as feedback, is one of the most important parts of an eBay account, and good and positive feedback received from past customers serve as a means through which to get more buyers in the future.

As for SNSs, where participants are both consumers and producers of content, mechanisms of establishing credibility through new forms of social approval are emerging, which compensate for the often ambiguous nature typical of digital environments. In the vast amount of information that continuously appears on the home pages of Facebook or Twitter, for instance, users need to select what content to choose to follow or read from the vast pool of potential choices, which other users' updates to subscribe to maximize the relevance, credibility and quality of the information received.

On the Internet there are a great number of guidelines and a huge amount of advice with the aim of establishing social media credibility. Most of them are strictly related to the issue of identity and of self-disclosure about the authorship of shared resources: using real names, real photos, completing profile information, connecting with a "healthy" amount of connections to show that the individual has a network that values his/her presence, communicating and not just broadcasting (Schaffer, 2009). As clearly stated in one of several posts about this issue, "The connection between author and content, transparency, and disclosure of affiliation is even more important online than off" (Lazen, 2012). Interestingly, the same author claims that the use of information about affiliation can both validate and create suspicious interpretation when the profile picture is a company logo: "We only publish posts by people. And corporations are NOT people", he states.

Also specialized literature confirms that both the topical content of information sources and social network structure affect source credibility (Suh & Pirolli, 2011). From this perspective, measures to identify and rank social network users according to their relevance and expertise for a given topic have been proposed, through the combination of the analysis of the link structure of social networks with topic models of the content of messages (Canini et al., 2011). Other measures to assess true identity aim at enabling online personas to cost-effectively obtain credentials that verify the credibility of their identity statements. Among measures of social validation (Jessen & Jørgensen, 2012), that include the large–scale verifications made by others (e.g., comments, Facebook Likes, shares, social bookmarks, ratings, etc.), social tagging is a form of folksonomy that allows users to describe or categorize web resources with text labels freely, in a collaborative manner (Trant, 2009). In this way it is the collective that determines the credibility or authenticity of a person or of a resource. Social tagging may also be used to estimate a given user's credibility by asking their friends if they are legitimate, such as posting facts/assertions on one's SNS profile and ask friends to tag those facts as true or false (Sirivianos et al., 2009). Moreover, in so far as social networking services allow people to tag other people, further forms of social tagging concern the categorization of individuals rather than that of resources. For example, in professional contexts the practice of online people tagging is now emerging as a way to capitalize knowledge within organizations (Cook & Pachler, 2012), and the reliability of the shared knowledge depends on the credibility of people that have been tagged.

Trust

Trust is a complex and abstract concept that has been studied in several fields, from sociology to psychology, economics, organizational science and more recently in computational models of cognitive science (Castelfranchi & Falcone, 2010). Although its value is not disputed for the formation of valuable connections and relationships, there is no unique definition of it and it is difficult to identify the elements that construct it. This is true both for offline and online trust (Wang & Emurian, 2005). In this chapter, we adopt the definition provided by Mayer, Davis and Schoorman (1995), who argue that trust consists of "the willingness of a party to be vulnerable to the actions of another party based on the expectation that the other will perform a particular action important to the trustor, irrespective of the ability to monitor or control that other party" (p. 712). According to this definition, the trustor is willing to believe the trustee and to depend to a certain extent on him.

Understanding the mechanisms that justify the willingness of a person to depend on others is not an easy task. In an attempt to clarify the nature of trust, some scholars in social sciences (Chopra & Wallace, 2003) suggested considering three main dimensions that may influence the trusting beliefs: 1) affective based trust, which is based on the implicit attitude/propensity to trust; 2) institution based trust, which refers to the faith that people have in collective entities; and 3) cognitive based trust, which relies on rapid, cognitive cues or first impressions. This means that different components, from the emotional and cognitive aspects to the institutional ones, may impact on the individual's willingness to accept a vulnerable situation depending on other individuals. Other factors that are crucial for inferring trust are the history between people, a person's background and trustworthiness assessments during a physical meeting. These elements provide a trustor with a belief of trustees' reliability.

When coming to trust online information or online environments such as SNSs, we face similar problems and some specific issues. Online trust has been widely investigated (Wang & Emurian, 2005; Joinson et al., 2010; Krasnova et al., 2010) and studies have shown that the "formation of online trust is a difficult process, but when it is created, it serves to mitigate the perceptions of risk, uncertainty and vulnerability that are associated with the disclosure of personal and identifiable information" (Mesh, 2012, p. 1471). The difficult process of trusting online interactions and environments is determined by the fact that trust may only be based on the information available on the Internet. However, though the information is limited or incomplete and does not include all the aspects that influence the formation of trusting beliefs (Golbeck, 2009), it must be noticed that many SNSs allow users to express information about themselves, their social connections and the way they behave online. Therefore, these services include a certain amount of valuable information about an individual. In particular, three main types of information seem to mediate the presence of individuals in SNSs: 1) personal information (Boyd & Ellison, 2007); 2) the online social context (Donath & Boyd, 2004); and 3) online interactions (Donath, 2008).

Personal information is posted by SNS users to be displayed on their public (or semi-public) profiles. They may include both discursive and visual data, providing direct or indirect cues about an individual. For example, they may incorporate the "profile information" or the "profile photo" as well as links to external resources or multimedia contents such as music, videos, pictures, etc. This data provides identifiable information that influences the perception of others and reduces ambiguity (Tanis & Postmes, 2005). On a conceptual level, identifiable information may vary in degrees as there is a certain identity knowledge (e.g., a legal name and address) that can be used to identify a person uniquely, while some other identity knowledge (e.g., a pseudonym) may not have a similarly effective function (Mesh, 2012). The same is true with pictures which are one of the most compelling features. As stated by Boyd & Heer (2006), they "are the most noticeable component of profile identity performance and active users update their photos regularly to convey various things about themselves" (p. 8). The integration between pictures and other discursive identity knowledge information may be enough to enable trust within computer-mediated communication. Another important factor influencing the trustor's impressions is the general similarity between his/her profile and the trustee's profile: when the profile of the trustee is similar to the trustor's profile, the trustor's impression of the trustee improves. In some ways, "social closeness and taste overlap are required" (Bonhard & Sasse, 2006, p. 84).

The connections that people make and maintain within SNSs generate a social context that offers useful information to assess the quality of a person. Being part of a certain group or being a friend of certain persons may be informative about a user's personal characteristics such as his/her interests, attitudes and preferences. By simply creating certain connections or participating and interacting in a community, the user leaves voluntary and involuntary pieces of not distorted information about him/her-self thus offering valuable cues for other users. This also has consequences for the user's reputation in so far as the willingness to be friend of a certain person entails that that person is relevant for his/her life (Donath & Boyd, 2004). At the same time, there are some issues. As explained before, a variety of strong and weak ties are maintained in SNSs without distinction, so the difficulty to assess users is that connections are often treated equally (Boyd & Heer, 2006). Recently, some procedures to support and improve the social dynamic of SNS have been developed by enriching the description of the relationships or differentiating the different types of connections. For example, LinkedIn requires a person to know the other person that he/she wants to add to his/her network, Google+ introduced the system of 'Circles' that allow users to distinguish between different groups of people within their networks, while Facebook introduced the lists of friends that allow users to set different access to contents for each of them.

However, in order to get a richer picture of the user's profile the number and the types of connections that he/she maintains are not enough. They are helpful indicators of the user's popularity, but further valuable information can be derived from an analysis of the content of the interactions. This brings us to the last possible source of information for inferring trust in SNSs: the analysis of users' interactions. Interactions are more dynamic than profiles and may provide relevant information about the relationship between the user and his/her friends or contacts. For instance, if a user frequently visits a friend's profile with comments, this could indicate that he/she wants to dedicate his/her time to this particular relationship. Comments' length, frequency and content may be considered important indicators to evaluate the relationship (Donath, 2008), although the interpretation of these cues is quite complex. Indeed, in order to assess the relationships between a user and his/her contacts, the time spent on commenting a specific friend, for example, should be compared with the average amount of time that he/she spent on commenting other friends. At the moment, there are no automatic or semi-automatic measures to communicate trust through interactions on SNSs, therefore inferring trust remains one of the most difficult tasks to accomplish on these sites. However, the possibility of rating members provided by certain services such as eBay may help users assess the interactions taking place in these environments and supports the process of online trust building.

Privacy and Security

Generally defined as "the ability to control and limit physical, interactional, psychological and informational access to the self or one's group" (Burgoon et al., 1989, p. 132), privacy is one of the most controversial challenges that has emerged within the global phenomenon of SNSs. Overall, the disclosure of personal data is often a condition to access several online services, but this is particularly true with SNSs as self-disclosure is required "as part of the functionality of the system itself" (Joinson et al., 2010, p. 2). Moreover, huge amounts of personal data are being viewed, compiled and utilized by individuals and organizations, third party data aggregators included. As for the latter, for instance, Facebook applications are third-party systems that interact with the social network, without being part of it and require users to give permission to access their data. Users usually give their consent in so far as these applications provide them with entertainment services to interact within the network, but do not have any control on the extent to which their data is accessed and on how this data is used. Another example concerns the functionality of uploading location-aware photographs from camera phones that requires users to take a certain number of privacy-related decisions about levels of public access related to both security issues and the risk of self and other disclosure (Ahern et al., 2007).

Privacy on SNSs also shows a paradox: people are concerned about their privacy, but at the same time disclose detailed personal information on their profiles (Joinson et al., 2010; Utz & Kramer, 2009). This seems to be consistent with the results that emerged in the first studies about online privacy issues, which demonstrated that though most Internet users express privacy-protectionist attitudes; this rarely translates into consistent behavior (e.g., Fox et al., 2000). For instance, in a study on e-commerce, Metzger (2006) did not find any association between users' privacy concerns or privacy policies and disclosure behavior. The failure of various privacy enhancing technologies in the marketplace also suggests a disjunction between people's stated attitudes and their actual actions to protect their privacy (Acquisti & Grossklags, 2003).

There are different reasons that can explain why there is no evidence of a link between privacy concerns and actual behavior. A first issue relates to the fact that privacy policies are very often overlooked by users, or if users read them they do not fully understand their contents (Milne & Culnan, 2004). Secondly, studies on the relationship between privacy concern and behavior have concentrated on the measurement of reported or intended disclosure rather than actual behavior (e.g., Malhotra et al., 2004), although when actual behavior is considered, the same pattern of results often emerges (e.g., Gideon et al., 2006). Thirdly, the measurement of privacy concerns tends to be generic and it often reflects the distinction between generic privacy concerns and people's interpretation of a specific situation (Palen & Dourish, 2003). Finally, when coming to SNSs the inconsistency between declared privacy concerns and actual behavior might reflect the difficulty of finding a balance between privacy concerns and impression management goals and narcissism.

However, since the main purposes of a SNS are self-presentation and maintaining relationships, and both can be obtained making visible as much information as possible on one's own profile, the question of protecting personal data (biographical information, photos, preferences, etc.) becomes a crucial issue.

The first studies on this topic showed that people were not very aware of the risks of disclosing too much information and that the issue of privacy was mostly apparent. Research into one of the first popular social networking sites, Friendster, describes how members create their profile with the intention of communicating news about themselves to others. Using an ethnographic approach, Boyd (2004) reveals the possibility of unintended consequences when members, who can control what appears on their profile, cannot control what appears on a friend's profile. Crude pictures on a friend's profile caused concern for a teacher when her students asked to "friend" her. This placed her in an awkward position, because allowing students access to her profile would also allow them to view her friends, who she knew to have risqué pictures on their profile. Also the first studies conducted on Facebook highlight that users reveal a lot of information about themselves, and are not very aware of privacy options or who can actually view their profile (Acquisti & Gross, 2006; Dwyer et al., 2007). This has especially profound implications when personal information is posted online by young people (Livingstone, 2008; Livingstone & Brake, 2010).

Indeed, the careless use of public data in SNSs hides several risks. For example, the content that a user posts may be used for illegal purposes such as spam, scripting between different web services, malware, spear-phishing, illegal usage of users profiles (profile-squatting), sexual harassment, identity thefts, personal persecution (stalking), brand or individual image damaging, net bullying and social engineering attacks. Van der Hoeven (2008) distinguishes four types of harm that may arise when privacy protections are compromised: 1) Information based harm: the most obvious example for this category is identity theft, but it can also include harm to the person, which is possible through the acquisition of data or information about the person; 2) Information inequality: this is the case of using behavioral monitoring and analysis techniques for commercial purposes, when the information about past purchases, habits and preferences are used for web marketing and price discrimination, without awareness on the part of the individual. This is a delicate aspect, especially when considering SNSs and the not fully transparent role of third-party data aggregators; 3) Information injustice: when information is taken out of context and used for totally different purposes, this inappropriate use of personal data may have unfair implications. An exemplary case is where prospective employers have begun to search SNSs for personal information on job candidates; 4) Restriction of moral autonomy: when an individual is limited in his/her options for self-representation because of the omnipresence and pervasiveness of personal information, there is a restriction on the choices that the right to privacy protects. For instance, behavioral profiling and advertising can limit individuals' options for self-presentation due to the persistent profiles that may exist across a number of different domains. Another example is the creation of multiple online profiles as a strategy to keep personal data contexts clearly separate (e.g., one profile for friends, one for purchases, and one for professional use).

Each of these types of harm may have direct or indirect impact on individuals. Directly, they may influence people for example via credit card fraud, physical harm or lost possessions; indirect impacts may consist of generating tensions (e.g., in cases of stalking or personal surveillance) or destroying relationships because of the disclosure of personal data. However, privacy risk assessment is not an objective process as privacy is context dependent, so personal information that might seem inherently harmless, when moved to other contexts or combined with other personal information, becomes dangerous (Robinson et al., 2009). For example, the disclosure of certain personal data to a public local body for job placement might be not only harmless but also necessary, while the disclosure of the same data to an unknown Internet service selling uncertain financial products could prove to be seriously dangerous.

With the growing importance of documents and dispositions provided by the several Data Protection and Privacy Commissions (see, for instance, the 2008 International Data Protection and Privacy Commissioners Conference around the theme "Protecting privacy in a borderless world", that have forced SNSs to improve their privacy policies) nowadays SNS providers and IT corporations are developing more sophisticated privacy settings and more usable privacy policy. For example, Microsoft publishes lists of tips for social networking safety. From the Safety & Security Center pages[1] users can download free safety brochures that may help prevent and correct privacy and online safety issues related to social networking. At the same time, SNS users have become more literate and sensible on how to manage privacy settings. Overall, it seems that ongoing commercialization of SNSs and the reports about privacy intrusion are leading to more restrictive privacy settings (Lewis et al., 2008), a movement emphasized also by the increasing percentage of users that have changed their default settings to more restrictive ones (Lenhart, 2009).

This privacy movement has been acknowledged also by specialized literature that emphasizes how people have acquired growing awareness on the dangers of putting lots of sensitive information on their profiles much too enthusiastically. There is indeed a trade-off between opposing motivations, such as impression management and narcissism, and perceived group norms that influence many aspects of user behaviors (smoking and drinking behavior, for example), that ultimately lead to make profiles only visible to certain categories of connections (friends and friends of friends) (Utz & Kramer, 2009). Also longitudinal studies conducted to reveal changes in attitudes towards privacy show that far from being nonchalant and unconcerned about privacy matters, the majority of young adult users of Facebook are engaged with managing their privacy settings on the site at least to some extent, probably due to the increase in public attention to privacy matters, the change of policy of Facebook's default settings, and the prompts the site displayed to users (Boyd & Hargittai, 2010).

If federal laws and protection acts in the US have contributed to making people, and especially teens and young adults, more aware of the risks implied in making profiles visible to everyone, at the same time, according to some scholars, these legal interventions have helped spread that culture of fear that seems to pervade our lives today: "While fear may be an effective technique for prompting the development of skills, the long–term results may not be ideal. The culture of fear tends to center on marginalized populations and is often used as a tool for continued oppression and as a mechanism for restricting access to public spaces and public discourse. To the degree that women are taught that privacy is simply a solution to a safety issue, they are deprived of the opportunities to explore the potential advantages of engaging in public and the right to choose which privacy preferences and corresponding privacy settings on sites like Facebook serve their needs best" (Boyd & Hargittai, 2010). One of the countermeasures adopted by users towards ongoing suggested restricted measures, mostly addressed to children and women, have resulted in conscious violations of the Terms of Service that forbid children under the age of 13 from creating an account, which have been created in response to the Children's Online Privacy Protection Act (COPPA)[2]. A recent survey (Boyd et al., 2011) shows that many parents know that their underage children are on Facebook in violation of the site's restrictions and that they are often complicit in helping their children join the site, probably as a response to the message implicitly sent by COPPA that undermines parents' ability to make choices and protect their children's data.

EMERGING TRENDS AND NEW THREATS: PRIVACY AS THE "ELEPHANT IN THE ROOM"

Location-Based Services

In the intersection between social networking services and mobile devices a new sector, the so-called location-based services (LBS), deserves attention both for the growing number of users and observers of this new phenomenon. Location-aware computing refers to computing that provides a number of tools able to continuously monitor, communicate, and process information about an individual's location with a high degree of spatial and temporal precision and accuracy. Location-based services, which rely on location-aware computing, are applications capable of utilizing the position of a device, and its user, in the provision of a value-added service, such as providing personalized and customizable information, etc. The growing number of mobile phones endowed with location tracking technologies, such as GPS or Assisted GPS, and the increasing availability of Wi-Fi networks, have lead to a widespread adoption of these features.

From this perspective, a number of mobile applications that allow users to locate one another are seriously challenging, among others (e.g., the notion of "uberveillance", introduced by Michael and Michael, 2010), the issues of privacy and security. When applied to social networking, location-based social networking (LBSN) applications are part of a new suite of tools (Fusco et al., 2010). Within the plethora of these tools, one of the most common features enabled by smartphones, for instance, is geotagging, that is the capability to tag people according to images and places easily uploadable in social networking sites.

One of the most common location-based social networking tools is Foursquare, a website for mobile devices, such as smartphones and tablets, where users "check in" at venues the application locates nearby, text messaging or leave comments about the sites visited. Location is based on GPS hardware in the mobile device or network location provided by the application. Each check-in awards the user points and sometimes "badges." These kinds of tools are, according to some scholars, changing the way we see and interpret the physical world we live in. Evans (2011), for instance, argues Foursquare may play an active role in the transformation of experience of the world for users. Relying on the Heideggerian concept of technology as something that brings forth what is absent, thus changing the relationship between the world and humanity, Evans underlines how Foursquare allows users to check-in existing spots on the map but also to create new spots that can be relayed to friends of the user through a message to their mobile device. Thus in this case "LBS allow users to make inscriptions that have power in the world and that operate as both personal and social gazetteers, providing a layer of information to maps that is personally relevant as it records experience of those places from a personal perspective, and as an inscription which others can follow and base their navigational decisions upon when moving through public places" (p. 249). Using the site as an advertisement for certain places or to chart his/her own movements and monitor his/her own social habits and trends, Foursquare is transforming the way its users interact with physical space and at the same time provides users with a navigational tool that is mainly for social and cultural reasons, rather than geographical and navigational.

In another study conducted on the use of PeopleFinder, an application that enables cell phones and laptop users to selectively share their locations with friends, family and colleagues, the authors reported the results on the concerns expressed about the privacy implications associated with this class of software (Sadeh et al., 2009). The objective of the work was to understand people's attitudes and behavior towards privacy while interacting with such applications and to explore technologies that empower users to specify their privacy preferences in an efficient and effective manner. The results show that privacy preferences are a complex issue and depend on a variety of contextual attributes, such as relationship with requester, time of day and area of location. Moreover, the authors highlighted how most users are not good at articulating their privacy preferences, since once defined the latter are rarely modified unless they are given tools that help them better understand how their policies behave in practice.

From a wider perspective about LBSN, the impact upon relationships in society, with a particular emphasis on trust, is another emerging issue that scholars have started to study. In one research project carried out at the University of Wollongong (Fusco et al., 2011), the findings illustrate that most people are willing to share data about their physical locations with persons that they trust (typically family and close friends), whereas they are more reluctant to share their locations with their weak social ties or strangers (co-workers, government agencies and commercial entities). The general results of the study highlight, on the one hand, that LBSN may have unintended consequences that could be disruptive to relationships; on the other hand, LBSN could strengthen relationships because, for instance, providing one's real-time location to a family member or a close friend would act to reaffirm aspects of trust. Anyway, about how this shared date may be misused later or by third parties remains an open issue for most of the people involved in the research.

A further different perspective about these tools is provided by Michael & Michael (2011), who clearly state more of their inconveniences than their advantages:

It is important, however, to point to the possibility that all this monitoring might also mean that we become acutely aware that we are being constantly watched and expected to act in particular ways in particular situations [...]. This could ultimately impact on our own ability to be creative, be different, be diverse and be our own person. It is not only the loss of privacy that is increasingly at risk, but also the wonder of improvisation. We will be playing to a packed theatre instead of being comfortable in our own skins and identities (p. 124).

Content-Based Image Retrieval Systems

Another emerging area widely adopted on the Internet are the so-called content-based image retrieval systems (CBIR), that are based on techniques for retrieving images on the basis of automatically-derived features such as color, texture and shape, rather than the metadata such as keywords, tags and/or descriptions associated with the image (Lew et al., 2006). These systems are also starting to be adopted by SNSs, where inferring geo-location information of users is made possible by recognizing characteristics of objects and places depicted in images associated with profiles.

These techniques, combined with the possibility for users to tag photos with descriptive keywords and also with geographic coordinates, represent a serious risk in terms of security since information about user location and the places he/she visited can be inferred and revealed. For instance, CBIR opens up the possibility of deducing location data from profiles containing images of users' homes. Together with face recognition, that allows the linking of profile data involving the person's physical body, these techniques allow linking of location data through the recognition of common objects in images, thus resulting in several undesired outcomes, such as the phenomena of stalking, unwanted marketing, blackmailing and all other threats associated with unwanted disclosure of location data, or assisting blackmailers looking for specific types of image which might later be used as part of a digital dossier (Hogben, 2007).

Indeed, if precise location can uniquely identify us, satisfying our needs, desires and answering our claims, there are also a number of undesirable effects related to our privacy protection: 1) unsolicited marketing for products or services that are related to one person's location are very frequently sent by unscrupulous businesses; 2) if location is inextricably linked to personal well-being and safety, failing to protect location privacy may lead to harmful events, such as stalking or assault; 3) knowledge about location can be used to extrapolate personal information about an individual, such as personal political views, state of health or personal preferences (Duckham et al., 2007).

Anyway, experts have recommended some measures that users can adopt to protect against these techniques. One of these is to promote and research image-anonymization techniques and best practices. If on the one hand research can invest in algorithms that limit the ability of automatic face recognition by removing identifying information while preserving other aspects of the face such as gender, ethnicity and expression, or in identifying tools that make image obfuscation possible, on the other hand users can link their faces by avoiding usage of identical images across services as well as choosing images which are difficult for algorithms to recognize, i.e., non-frontal images under non-standard illumination, displaying varied facial expressions. Finally, network operators could give similar recommendations to their users and check for compliance (Hogben, 2007).

CONCLUSION

Social networks and their internal mechanisms of socializing and exchanging information, resources and support have been investigated by many scholars, but have recently received renewed attention due to the rapid grow of SNSs. Basically these sites are new web based services that enable the rise of a new public networked arena, where the already existing virtual communities are now reshaping, also prompted by the parallel development of Web 2.0 technologies. Through these new digital tools, individuals are not only consumers of contents who passively receive information, but also producers who actively participate in connecting with other people, creating contents and sharing information. Within this context, SNSs are playing a pivotal role in so far as most Internet users are using them actively engaging with managing personal information on the web and initiating or maintaining connections with others.

At the same time, these kinds of sites are stressing new challenges of old issues that deserve renewed interest. The matters of real identity and personal credibility, for instance, are strictly intertwined with the issue of trust, since this latter plays an important role within social interactions. Trust, indeed, is one of the critical components that have to be taken into consideration when we develop valuable connections and relationships from interactions. The mechanisms which lead to the formation of trust judgments are quite far from being completely understood, especially online. However, as many scholars underline, trust requests the propensity of the trustor to be to some extent vulnerable and to depend on another person. This "willingness towards vulnerability" may raise concerns about security, particularly in virtual interactions and with young people. Security, indeed, has to do with safety and in the absence of sufficient or reliable cues, as may be the case in online transactions, the "willingness towards vulnerability" may threaten personal safety or the exchange of property or goods. But this is only one side of the story. SNS environments provide several and valuable information to draw inferences about trust, while raising new challenges. What is the information to be considered to infer the trustee's credibility? How to assess their reliability? How much information should be disclosed to make people able to infer trust?

This leads to another significant issue: privacy. How to protect our own privacy, or at least reduce interference from outside, has become one of the main challenges in these times of widespread digital connections. What measures can be adopted to face "surveillance" and undesired intrusiveness, for instance, are further questions that users ask experts, policy makers and governments. The debate is marked by a plethora of positions, even opposed. In relation to the challenges posed by Location-Based Services, for instance, scholars list at least three ways to face them (Michael & Michael, 2011). The first one, adopting the "do nothing" approach and take the risk, as suggested by danah Boyd (2011), implies that we stop being obsessed by the consequences of using the new technologies and see how far they might take us and what we might become or transform as a result. The second one refers to the position according to which we let case law determine for us what is legal or illegal based on existing laws, or new or amended laws that might be introduced as a result of LBS challenges. Thirdly, we can rely on and encourage industry regulations that stipulate how LBS applications should be developed and that technical expectations on accuracy, reliability and storage of location data are met. None of these positions is according to these authors mutually exclusive, of course. The final solution may well be at times to introduce industry regulations or codes, at other times to do nothing, and in other cases to rely on legislative amendments despite the length of time it takes to develop these.

Other more radical positions even question the same issue of privacy, as a byproduct of an old culture and society where people have always managed different social identities. As reported by David Kirkpatrick (2010), according to Mark Zuckerberg, the Facebook founder, "The days of you having a different image of your work friends or co-workers and for the other people you know are probably coming to an end pretty quickly" (p. 199). His radical vision of an open and more transparent world has always determined the Facebook privacy policy from its birth, their precise request made to users to create profiles with real names and encouraging them to mix information about their personal, social and work lives. In recent times, however, Facebook, adopting a similar policy to the Circles of Google+, has allowed its users to discriminate between different lists of friends.

Beyond these extreme positions, there is the serious problem of how to help people develop their privacy policies, bearing in mind that privacy is not a static matter, but a dynamic process of managing boundaries that may evolve over time. With this statement in mind, technological research has been suggesting new ways through which to address a balance between privacy and utility through the design of better presence technologies (Biehl et al., 2013), or to find the best compromise between accuracy and amount of information shared and privacy-setting types with differing levels of complexity (Benisch et al., 2011). Helping people to specify privacy and security policies is, on the other hand, strictly related to the fact that better privacy policies cannot be managed simply by static enforcement of rules, but must be seen as a dynamic process of managing boundaries (Sadeh et al., 2009).

From a different perspective, there would be a fourth way, which is to foster individuals' awareness through education and literacy. Some sort of privacy literacy related to SNSs may rely on educational messages that point to potential dangers of public profiles and to establish shared norms. Since adolescents and young adults are especially sensitive to peer pressure, for instance, providing information about the privacy-protecting behavior of peers could also lead to more restricted profiles, especially if campaigns of this kind are based on messages that are delivered by a peer rather than by a teacher or spokesperson (Utz & Kramer, 2009).

Any guideline or decalogue that could be produced should anyway rely on the following considerations. The undesired consequences of "our being online" are often determined not by others or by artifacts, but by us. Of course, others may be willing to deceive us and technologies have their own affordances and properties, but not knowing how artifacts work or ignoring what the web services' policies are or the national laws on privacy are the first threats for our online safety. So, the fourth option to face the issues mentioned in this chapter is the way of people's empowerment, which entails providing individuals with appropriate socio-technical skills and media/digital literacy. As the American scholar Renée Hobbs (2010) points out, digital and media literacy is the ability to: 1) make responsible choices and access information by locating and sharing materials and comprehending information and ideas; 2) analyze messages in a variety of forms by identifying the author, purpose and point of view and evaluating the quality and credibility of the content; 3) create content in a variety of forms for authentic purposes, making use of language, images, sound and new digital tools and technologies; 4) reflect on one's own conduct and communication behavior by applying social responsibility and ethical principles; and 5) take social action by working individually and collaboratively to share knowledge and solve problems in the family, workplace and community and participating as a member of a community. Similarly, Calvani and colleagues (2012) define digital competence as the capacity to be able to explore and face new technological situations in a flexible way, to analyze, select and critically evaluate data and information, to exploit technological potentials in order to represent and solve problems and to build shared and collaborative knowledge, while fostering awareness of one's own personal responsibilities and the respect of reciprocal rights/obligations. In the age of techno-sociability, literacy has also to do with facing digital technologies as well as with the ethical and societal challenges that they raise, such as managing online identity, stating personal privacy policies and being able to select reliable information and cues for trust and credibility.

REFERENCES

Acquisti, A., & Gross, R. (2006). *Imagined communities: Awareness, information sharing and privacy on the Facebook.* Paper presented at the 6th Workshop on Privacy Enhancing Technologies, Cambridge, UK.

Acquisti, A., & Grossklags, J. (2003). *Losses, gains, and hyperbolic discounting: An experimental approach to information security attitudes and behavior.* Paper presented at the 2nd Annual Workshop on Economics and Information Security, College Park, MD.

Ahern, S., Eckles, D., Good, N. S., King, S., Naaman, M., & Nair, R. (2007). Photo sharing: Overexposed? Privacy patterns and considerations in online and mobile photo sharing. In *Proceedings of ACM CHI 2007 Conference on Human Factors in Computing Systems 2007*. New York: ACM Press.

Bauman, Z. (2004). *Identity: Conversations with Benedetto Vecchi*. Cambridge, UK: Polity Press.

Benisch, M., Kelley, P., Sadeh, N., & Cranor, L. (2011). Capturing location-privacy preferences: Quantifying accuracy and user-burden tradeoffs. *Personal and Ubiquitous Computing, 15*(7), 679–694. doi:10.1007/s00779-010-0346-0.

Berendt, B., Gunther, O., & Spiekermann, S. (2005). Privacy in e-commerce: Stated preferences vs. actual behavior. *Communications of the ACM, 48*(4), 101–106. doi:10.1145/1053291.1053295.

Biehl, J. T., Rieffel, E. G., & Lee, A. J. (2013). When privacy and utility are in harmony: Towards better design of presence technologies. *Personal and Ubiquitous Computing, 17*(3), 503-518. doi:10.1007/s00779-012-0504-7

Bilge, L., Strufe, T., Balzarotti, D., & Kirda, E. (2009). All your contacts are belong to us: Automated identity theft attacks on social networks. In J. Quemada, G. León, Y. S. Maarek & W. Nejdl (Eds.), *Proceedings of WWW 2009* (pp. 551-560). New York: ACM Press.

Bonhard, P., & Sasse, M. A. (2006). 'Knowing me knowing you' - Using profiles and social networking to improve recommender systems. *BT Technology Journal, 24*(3), 84–97. doi:10.1007/s10550-006-0080-3.

Bourdieu, P. (1986). The forms of capital. In J. Richardson J. (Ed), *Handbook of theory and research for the sociology of education* (pp. 241–258). New York: Greenwood.

Boyd, D. (2004). *Friendster and publicly articulated social networks.* Paper presented at the SIGCHI Conference on Human Factors and Computing Systems, Vienna, Austria.

Boyd, D. (2011). *The unintended consequences of obsessing over consequences (or why to support youth risk-taking).* Retrieved September 11, 2012, from http://www.zephoria.org/thoughts/archives/2011/07/29/consequences.html

Boyd, D., & Ellison, N. B. (2007). Social network sites: Definition, history, and scholarship. *Journal of Computer-Mediated Communication, 13*(1), 210–230. doi:10.1111/j.1083-6101.2007.00393.x.

Boyd, D., & Hargittai, E. (2010). Facebook privacy settings: Who cares? *First Monday, 15*(8). Retrieved September 11, 2012, from http://www.uic.edu/htbin/cgiwrap/bin/ojs/index.php/fm/article/viewArticle/3086/2589

Boyd, D., Hargittai, E., Schultz, J., & Palfrey, J. (2011). Why parents help their children lie to Facebook about age: Unintended consequences of the 'Children's Online Privacy Protection Act'. *First Monday, 16*(11). Retrieved September 11, 2012, from http://www.uic.edu/htbin/cgiwrap/bin/ojs/index.php/fm/article/viewArticle/3850/3075

Boyd, D., & Heer, J. (2006). *Profiles as conversations: Networked identity performance on friendster.* Paper presented at the 39th Annual Hawaii International Conference of System Sciences (HICSS'06), Kauai, Hawaii.

Buckingham, D. (2007). Introducing identity. In Buchingham, D. (Ed.), *Youth, identity, and digital media* (pp. 1–24). Cambridge, MA: The MIT Press.

Burgoon, J. K., le Poire, B. A., Kelley, D. L., & Parrott, R. (1989). Maintaining and restoring privacy through communication in different types of relationships. *Journal of Social and Personal Relationships, 6*(2), 131–158. doi:10.1177/026540758900600201.

Calvani, A., Fini, A., Ranieri, M., & Picci, P. (2012). Are young generations in secondary school digitally competent? A study on Italian teenagers. *Computers & Education, 58*(2), 797–807. doi:10.1016/j.compedu.2011.10.004.

Canini, K. R., Bongwon, S., & Pirolli, P. L. (2011). Finding credible information sources in social networks based on content and social structure. Paper presented at the *3rd IEEE International Conference on Social Computing*, Boston, MA.

Carpenter, C. J. (2012). Narcissism on Facebook: Self-promotional and anti-social behavior. *Personality and Individual Differences, 52*(4), 482–486. doi:10.1016/j.paid.2011.11.011.

Castelfranchi, C., & Falcone, R. (2010). *Trust theory: A socio-cognitive and computational model.* Chichester, UK: John Wiley & Sons.

Chopra, K., & Wallace, W. A. (2003). *Trust in electronic environments.* Paper presented at the 36th Annual Hawaii International Conference on System Sciences (HICSS'03), Big Island, Hawaii.

Coleman, J. S. (1988). Social capital in the creation of human capital. *American Journal of Sociology, 94*, S95–S120. doi:10.1086/228943.

ComScore. (2012, February 23). *2012 Mobile future in focus*. Whitepaper. Retrieved September 11, 2012, from http://www.comscore.com/Press_Events/Presentations_Whitepapers/2012/2012_Mobile_Future_in_Focus

Cook, J., & Pachler, N. (2012). Online people tagging: Social (mobile) network(ing) services and work-based learning. *British Journal of Educational Technology*, *43*(5), 711–725. doi:10.1111/j.1467-8535.2012.01346.x.

Cross, R., & Parker, A. (2004). *The hidden power of social networks*. Boston, MA: Harvard Business School Press.

Donath, J. (2008). Signals in social supernets. *Journal of Computer-Mediated Communication*, *13*(1), 231–251. doi:10.1111/j.1083-6101.2007.00394.x.

Donath, J., & Boyd, D. (2004). Public displays of connection. *BT Technology Journal*, *22*(4), 71–82. doi:10.1023/B:BTTJ.0000047585.06264.cc.

Duckham, M., Mokbel, M., & Nittel, S. (2007). Special issue on privacy aware and location-based mobile services. *Journal of Location Based Services*, *1*(3), 161–164. doi:10.1080/17489720802089489.

Dwyer, C., Hiltz, S. R., & Passerini, K. (2007). *Trust and privacy concern within social networking sites: A comparison of Facebook and MySpace*. Paper presented at AMCIS 2007, Keystone, CO.

Ellison, N. B., Steinfield, C., & Lampe, C. (2007). The benefits of Facebook 'friends': Social capital and college students' use of online social network sites. *Journal of Computer-Mediated Communication*, *12*(4), 1143–1168. doi:10.1111/j.1083-6101.2007.00367.x.

Ellison, N. B., Steinfield, C., & Lampe, C. (2011). Connection strategies: Social capital implications of Facebook-enabled communication practices. *New Media & Society*, *13*(6), 873–892. doi:10.1177/1461444810385389.

Evans, L. (2011). Location-based services: Transformation of the experience of space. *Journal of Location Based Services*, *5*(3-4), 242–260. doi:10.1080/17489725.2011.637968.

Facebook (2012). *Key Facts*. Retrieved September 11, 2012, from http://newsroom.fb.com/content/default.aspx?NewsAreaId=22

Ferdig, R. E., Dawson, K., Black, E. W., Paradise Black, N. M., & Thompson, L. A. (2008). Medical students' and residents' use of online social networking tools: Implications for teaching professionalism in medical education. *First Monday*, *13*(9). Retrieved September 11, 2012, from http://firstmonday.org/htbin/cgiwrap/bin/ojs/index.php/fm/article/viewArticle/2161/2026

Fox, S., Rainie, L., Horrigan, J., Lenhart, A., Spooner, T., & Carter, C. (2000). *Trust and privacy online: Why Americans want to rewrite the rules*. Pew Internet and American Life Project.

Freeman, L. C. (1979). Centrality in social networks conceptual clarification. *Social Networks*, *1*(3), 215–239. doi:10.1016/0378-8733(78)90021-7.

Fusco, S. J., Michael, K., Aloudat, A., & Abbas, R. (2011). *Monitoring people using location-based social networking and its negative impact on trust: an exploratory contextual analysis of five types of "friend" relationships*. Paper presented at the International Symposium on Technology and Society, Chicago, IL.

Fusco, S. J., Michael, K., & Michael, M. G. (2010). *Using a social informatics framework to study the effects of location-based social networking on relationships between people: A review of literature*. Paper presented at the IEEE Symposium on Technology and Society, Wollongong, Australia.

Garton, L., Haythornthwaite, C., & Wellman, B. (1997). Studying online social networks. *Journal of Computer-Mediated Communication*, *3*(1).

Gideon, J., Cranor, L., Egelman, S., & Acquisti, A. (2006). *Power strips, prophylactics, and privacy, oh my*! Paper presented at the Second Symposium on Usable Privacy and Security, Pittsburgh, PA.

Golbeck, J. (2009). Trust and nuanced profile similarity in online social networks. *ACM Transactions on the Web*, *3*(4). 1–33.

Granovetter, M. S. (1973). The strength of weak ties. *American Journal of Sociology*, *78*(6), 1360–1380. doi:10.1086/225469.

Haferkamp, N., Eimler, S. C., Papadakis, A.-M., & Kruck, J. V. (2012). Men are from Mars, women are from Venus? Examining gender differences in self-presentation on social networking sites. *CyberPsychology. Behavior and Social Networking*, *15*(2), 91–98. doi:10.1089/cyber.2011.0151.

Hampton, K. N., Sessions Goulet, L., Rainie, L., & Purcell, K. (2011). *Social networking sites and our lives. How people's trust, personal relationships, and civic and political involvement are connected to their use of social networking sites and other technologies*. Pew Research Center's Internet & American Life Project.

Haythornthwaite, C. (1996). Social network analysis: An approach and technique for the study of information exchange. *Library & Information Science Research*, *18*(4), 323–342. doi:10.1016/S0740-8188(96)90003-1.

Haythornthwaite, C. (2005). Social networks and Internet connectivity effects. *Information Communication and Society*, *8*(2), 125–147. doi:10.1080/13691180500146185.

Herring, S. C. (2001). Computer-mediated discourse. In Schiffrin, D., Tannen, D., & Hamilton, H. (Eds.), *The handbook of discourse analysis* (pp. 612–634). Oxford, UK: Blackwell Publishers.

Hew, K. F. (2011). Students' and teachers' use of Facebook. *Computers in Human Behavior*, *27*(2), 662–676. doi:10.1016/j.chb.2010.11.020.

Hobbs, R. (2010). *Digital and media literacy: A plan of action*. Knight Commission on the Information Needs of Communities in a Democracy, Aspen Institute, Washington DC. Retrieved September 11, 2012, from http://www.knightcomm.org/digital-and-media-literacy/

Hogben, G. (Ed.). (2007). *Security issues and recommendations for online social networks*. ENISA Position Paper No.1.

Hussein, D., Ghada, A., & Hamad, A. (2009). Classifying Web 2.0 supported applications by pattern of usage: Functional & technical ISSUES. In *MCIS 2009 Proceedings*. Paper 94.

Identity Theft Resource Center. (2012). *ITRC fact sheet 138 - social networking and identity theft*. Retrieved September 11, 2012, from http://www.idtheftcenter.org/artman2/publish/v_fact_sheets/FS_138.shtml

Jessen, J., & Jørgensen, A. H. (2012). Aggregated trustworthiness: Redefining online credibility through social validation. *First Monday*, *17*(1). Retrieved September 11, 2012, from http://www.firstmonday.org/htbin/cgiwrap/bin/ojs/index.php/fm/article/view/3731/3132

Joinson, A. N., Reips, U.-D., Buchanan, T., & Schofield, C. B. P. (2010). Privacy, trust, and self-disclosure online. *Human-Computer Interaction*, *25*(1), 1–24. doi:10.1080/07370020903586662.

Kirkpatrick, D. (2010). *The Facebook Effect: The Inside Story of the Company that is Connecting the World*. New York: Simon & Schuster.

Krasnova, H., Spiekerman, S., Koroleva, K., & Hildebrand, T. (2010). Online social networks: Why we disclose. *Journal of Information Technology*, *25*, 109–125. doi:10.1057/jit.2010.6.

Lazen, M. (2012, April 5). Social media today: Demanding credibility in authorship. *Social Media Today*. Retrieved September 11, 2012, from http://socialmediatoday.com/node/484395

Lenhart, A. (2009). *Adults and social network websites*. Pew Research Center's Internet & American Life Project.

Lenhart, A., Madden, M., Smith, A., Purcell, K., Zickuhr, K., & Rainie, L. (2011). *Teens, kindness and cruelty on social network sites. How American teens navigate the new world of "digital citizenship."*. Pew Research Center's Internet & American Life Project.

Lew, M. S., Sebe, N., Lifl, D. C., & Jain, R. (2006). Content-based multimedia information retrieval: State of the art and challenges. *ACM Transactions on Multimedia Computing, Communications, and Applications*, *2*(1), 1–19. doi:10.1145/1126004.1126005.

Lewis, K., Kaufman, J., & Christakis, N. (2008). The taste for privacy: An analysis of college student privacy settings in an online social network. *Journal of Computer-Mediated Communication*, *14*(1), 79–100. doi:10.1111/j.1083-6101.2008.01432.x.

Livingstone, S. (2008). Taking risky opportunities in youthful content creation: Teenagers' use of social networking sites for intimacy, privacy, and self-expression. *New Media & Society*, *10*(3), 393–411.

Livingstone, S., & Brake, D. R. (2010). On the rapid rise of social networking sites: New findings and policy implications. *Children & Society*, *24*(1), 75–83. doi:10.1111/j.1099-0860.2009.00243.x.

Malhotra, N. K., Kim, S. S., & Agarwal, J. (2004). Internet users' information privacy concerns (IUIPC): The construct, the scale and a causal model. *Information Systems Research*, *15*(4), 336–355. doi:10.1287/isre.1040.0032.

Mayer, R. C., Davis, J. H., & Schoorman, F. D. (1995). An integrative model of organizational trust. *Academy of Management Review*, *20*(3), 709–734.

Mazer, J. P., Murphy, R. E., & Simonds, C. J. (2007). I'll see you on 'Facebook': The effects of computer-mediated teacher self-disclosure on student motivation, affective learning, and classroom climate. *Communication Education*, *56*(1), 1–17. doi:10.1080/03634520601009710.

Merchant, G. (2012). Unravelling the social network: Theory and research. *Learning, Media and Technology*, *37*(1), 4–19. doi:10.1080/17439884.2011.567992.

Mesh, G. S. (2012). Is online trust and trust in social institutions associated with online disclosure of identifiable information online? *Computers in Human Behavior*, *28*(4), 1471–1477. doi:10.1016/j.chb.2012.03.010.

Metzger, M. J. (2006). Effects of site, vendor, and consumer characteristics on Web site trust and disclosure. *Communication Research*, *33*(3), 155–179. doi:10.1177/0093650206287076.

Metzger, M. J., & Flanagin, A. J. (Eds.). (2008). *Digital media, youth, and credibility*. Cambridge, MA: The MIT Press.

Michael, K., & Michael, M. G. (2011). The social and behavioural implications of location-based services. *Journal of Location Based Services*, *5*(3-4), 121–137. doi:10.1080/17489725.2011.642820.

Michael, M. G., & Michael, K. (2010). Towards a state of uberveillance. *IEEE Technology and Society Magazine*, *29*(2), 9–16. doi:10.1109/MTS.2010.937024.

Milne, G. R., & Culnan, M. J. (2004). Strategies for reducing online privacy risks: Why consumers read (or don't read) online privacy notices. *Journal of Interactive Marketing*, *18*(3), 15–29. doi:10.1002/dir.20009.

Nielsen. (2011). *State of the media: The social media report Q3 2011*. NM incite. Retrieved September 11, 2012, from http://blog.nielsen.com/nielsenwire/social/

Ong, E. Y. L., Ang, R. P., Ho, J. C. M., Lim, J. C. Y., Goh, D. H., Lee, C. S., & Chua, A. Y. K. (2011). Narcissism, extraversion and adolescents' self-presentation on Facebook. *Personality and Individual Differences*, *50*(2), 180–185. doi:10.1016/j.paid.2010.09.022.

Palen, L., & Dourish, P. (2003). Unpacking privacy for a networked world. In *Proceedings of CHI '03*. New York: ACM Press.

Park, N., Kee, K., & Valenzuela, S. (2009). Being immersed in social networking environment: Facebook groups, uses and gratifications, and social outcomes. *Cyberpsychology & Behavior*, *12*(6), 729–733. doi:10.1089/cpb.2009.0003 PMID:19619037.

Pfeil, U., Arjan, R., & Zaphiris, P. (2009). Age differences in online social networking – A study of user profiles and the social capital divide among teenagers and older users in MySpace. *Computers in Human Behavior*, *25*(3), 643–654. doi:10.1016/j.chb.2008.08.015.

Putnam, R. D. (1995). Bowling alone: America's declining social capital. *Journal of Democracy*, *6*(1), 65–78. doi:10.1353/jod.1995.0002.

Putnam, R. D. (2000). *Bowling alone: The collapse and revival of American community*. New York: Simon & Schuster. doi:10.1145/358916.361990.

Rainie, L., Lenhart, A., & Smith, A. (2012). *The tone of life on social networking sites*. Pew Research Center's Internet & American Life Project.

Ranieri, M., Manca, S., & Fini, A. (2012). Why (and how) do teachers engage in social networks? An exploratory study of professional use of Facebook and its implications for lifelong learning. *British Journal of Educational Technology*, *43*(5), 754–769. doi:10.1111/j.1467-8535.2012.01356.x.

Rieh, S. Y., & Danielson, D. R. (2007). Credibility: A multidisciplinary framework. In Cronin, B. (Ed.), *Annual review of information science and technology* (Vol. 41, pp. 307–364). Medford, NJ: Information Today.

Robinson, N., Graux, H., Botterman, M., & Valeri, L. (2009). *Review of the European Data Protection Directive*. Santa Monica, CA: RAND Corporation.

Rosenberg, J., & Egbert, N. (2011). Online impression management: Personality traits and concerns for secondary goals as predictors of self-presentation tactics on Facebook. *Journal of Computer-Mediated Communication*, *17*(1), 1–18. doi:10.1111/j.1083-6101.2011.01560.x.

Sadeh, N., Hong, J., Cranor, L., Fette, I., Kelley, P., Prabaker, M., & Rao, J. (2009). Understanding and capturing people's privacy policies in a mobile social networking application. *Personal and Ubiquitous Computing*, *13*(6), 401–412. doi:10.1007/s00779-008-0214-3.

Schaffer, N. (2009). HOW TO: Establish social media credibility in 7 easy steps. Retrieved September 11, 2012, from, http://windmillnetworking.com/2009/09/01/how-to-establish-social-media-credibility-in-7-easy-steps/

Scott, J. (1991). *Social network analysis: A handbook*. Newbury Park, California: SAGE Publications.

Sirivianos, M., Kim, K., & Yang, X. (2009). FaceTrust: *Assessing the credibility of online personas via social networks*. Paper presented at the Usenix Workshop on Hot Topics in Security (HotSec) 2009, Montreal, Canada.

Smith, A. (2011). *Why Americans use social media. Social networking sites are appealing as a way to maintain contact with close ties and reconnect with old friends*. Pew Research Center's Internet & American Life Project.

Steiner, P. (1993, July 5). Cartoon. *The New Yorker*.

Steinfield, C., Ellison, N. B., & Lampe, C. (2008). Social capital, self-esteem, and use of online social network sites: A longitudinal analysis. *Journal of Applied Developmental Psychology*, *29*(6), 434–445. doi:10.1016/j.appdev.2008.07.002.

Suh, B., & Pirolli, P. (2011). *Finding credible information sources in social networks based on content and social structure*. Paper presented at the 3rd IEEE International Conference on Social Computing (SocialCom), Boston, MA.

Tanis, M., & Postmes, T. (2005). Short communication, a social identity approach to trust: Interpersonal perception, groups membership and trusting behaviour. *European Journal of Social Psychology*, *35*(3), 413–424. doi:10.1002/ejsp.256.

Trant, J. (2009). Studying social tagging and folksonomy: A review and framework. *Journal of Digital Information*, *10*(1), 1–44.

Turkle, S. (1997). *Life on the screen: Identity in the age of the Internet*. New York: Simon & Schuster.

Utz, S., & Kramer, N. (2009). The privacy paradox on social network sites revisited: The role of individual characteristics and group norms. *Cyberpsychology: Journal of Psychosocial Research on Cyberspace*, *3*(2), article 1. Retrieved September 11, 2012, from http://www.cyberpsychology.eu/view.php?cisloclanku=2009111001&article=1

Valenzuela, S., Park, N., & Kee, K. F. (2009). Is there social capital in a social network site?: Facebook use and college students' life satisfaction, trust, and participation. *Journal of Computer-Mediated Communication*, *14*(4), 875–901. doi:10.1111/j.1083-6101.2009.01474.x.

Van der Hoven, J. (2008). Information technology, privacy and the protection of personal data. In Weckert, J., & Hoven, J. (Eds.), *Information technology and moral philosophy* (pp. 301–321). Cambridge, MA: Cambridge University Press.

Wang, S. S., Moon, S.-Il, Kwon, K. H., Evans, C. A., & Stefanone, M. A. (2010). Face off: Implications of visual cues on initiating friendship on Facebook. *Computers in Human Behavior*, *26*(2), 226–234. doi:10.1016/j.chb.2009.10.001.

Wang, Y. D., & Emurian, H. H. (2005). An overview of online trust: Concepts, elements, and implications. *Computers in Human Behavior*, *21*(1), 105–125. doi:10.1016/j.chb.2003.11.008.

Wasserman, S., & Faust, K. (1994). *Social network analysis: Methods and applications*. Cambridge, UK: Cambridge University Press. doi:10.1017/CBO9780511815478.

Waters, S., & Ackerman, J. (2011). Exploring privacy management on Facebook: Motivations and perceived consequences of voluntary disclosure. *Journal of Computer-Mediated Communication*, *17*(1), 101–115. doi:10.1111/j.1083-6101.2011.01559.x.

Winter, S., Haferkamp, N., Stock, Y., & Kramer, N. C. (2011). The digital quest for love – The role of relationship status in self-presentation on social networking sites. *Cyberpsychology: Journal of Psychosocial Research on Cyberspace*, *5*(2), article 3. Retrieved September 11, 2012, from http://cyberpsychology.eu/view.php?cisloclanku=2011121801&article=3

Yang, Y., Wang, Q., Woo, H. L., & Quek, C. L. (2011). Using Facebook for teaching and learning: A review of the literature. *International Journal of Continuing Engineering Education and Lifelong Learning*, *21*(1), 72–86. doi:10.1504/IJCEELL.2011.039695.

Zwier, S., Araujo, T., Boukes, M., & Willemsen, L. (2011). Boundaries to the articulation of possible selves through social networking sites: The case of Facebook profilers' social connectedness. *CyberPsychology, Behavior and Social Networking*, *14*(10), 571–576. doi:10.1089/cyber.2010.0612.

ADDITIONAL READING

Amichai-Hamburger, Y., & Vinitzky, G. (2010). Social network use and personality. *Computers in Human Behavior*, *26*(6), 1289–1295. doi:10.1016/j.chb.2010.03.018.

Antheunis, M. L., & Schouten, A. P. (2011). The effects of other-generated and system-generated cues on adolescents' perceived attractiveness on social network sites. *Journal of Computer-Mediated Communication*, *16*(3), 391–406. doi:10.1111/j.1083-6101.2011.01545.x.

Antheunis, M. L., Valkenburg, P. M., & Jochen, P. (2010). Getting acquainted through social network sites: Testing a model of online uncertainty reduction and social attraction. *Computers in Human Behavior*, *26*(1), 100–109. doi:10.1016/j.chb.2009.07.005.

Back, M. D., Stopfer, J. M., Vazire, S., Gaddis, S., Schmukle, S. C., Egloff, B., & Gosling, S. D. (2010). Facebook profiles reflect actual personality, not self-idealization. *Psychological Science*, *21*(3), 372–374. doi:10.1177/0956797609360756 PMID:20424071.

Barnes, S. (2006). A privacy paradox: Social networking in the United States. *First Monday*, *11*(9). Retrieved September 11, 2012, from http://firstmonday.org/htbin/cgiwrap/bin/ojs/index.php/fm/article/view/1394/1312

Bergman, S. M., Fearrington, M. E., Davenport, S. W., & Bergman, J. Z. (2011). Millennials, narcissism, and social networking: What narcissists do on social networking sites and why. *Personality and Individual Differences*, *50*(5), 706–711. doi:10.1016/j.paid.2010.12.022.

Bonhert, D., & Ross, W. H. (2010). The influence of social networking web sites on the evaluation of job candidates. *CyberPsychology, Behavior and Social Networking*, *13*(3), 341–347. doi:10.1089/cyber.2009.0193.

Brandtzæg, P. B. (2012). Social networking sites: Their users and social implications — A longitudinal study. *Journal of Computer-Mediated Communication*, *17*(4), 467–488. doi:10.1111/j.1083-6101.2012.01580.x.

Buffardi, L. E., & Campbell, W. K. (2010). Narcissism and social networking web sites. *Personality and Social Psychology Bulletin*, *34*(10), 1303–1314. doi:10.1177/0146167208320061 PMID:18599659.

Burngarner, B. A. (2007). You have been poked: Exploring the uses and gratifications of Facebook among emerging adults. *First Monday*, *12*(11). Retrieved September 11, 2012, from http://firstmonday.org/htbin/cgiwrap/bin/ojs/index.php/fm/article/view/2026/1897

Carpenter, J. M., Green, M. C., & LaFlam, J. (2011). People or profiles: Individual differences in online social networking use. *Personality and Individual Differences*, *50*(5), 538–541. doi:10.1016/j.paid.2010.11.006.

Chan, T. S. (2010). Social networking site: Opportunities and security challenges. In Dasgupta, S. (Ed.), *Social computing: Concepts, methodologies, tools, and applications* (pp. 1726–1739). Hershey, PA: IGI Global.

Chellappa, R. K., & Sin, R. G. (2005). Personalization versus privacy: An empirical examination of the online consumer's dilemma. *Information Technology Management, 6*(2-3), 181–202. doi:10.1007/s10799-005-5879-y.

DeWall, C. N., Buffardi, L. E., Bonser, I., & Campbell, W. K. (2011). Narcissism and implicit attention seeking: Evidence from linguistic analyses of social networking and online presentation. *Personality and Individual Differences, 51*(1), 57–62. doi:10.1016/j.paid.2011.03.011.

Golbeck, J. (2007). The dynamics of Web–based social networks: Membership, relationships, and change. *First Monday, 12*(11). Retrieved September 11, 2012, from http://firstmonday.org/htbin/cgiwrap/bin/ojs/index.php/fm/article/view/2023/1889

Gonzales, A. L., & Hancock, J. T. (2011). Mirror, mirror on my Facebook wall: Effects of exposure to Facebook on self-esteem. *CyberPsychology, Behavior and Social Networking, 14*(1-2), 79–83. doi:10.1089/cyber.2009.0411.

Hampton, K. N., Sessions Goulet, L., Marlow, C., & Rainie, L. (2012). *Why most Facebook users get more than they give. The effect of Facebook 'power users' on everybody else*. Pew Research Center's Internet & American Life Project.

Hanson, T. L., Drumheller, K., Mallard, J., McKee, C., & Schlegl, P. (2011). Cell phones, text messaging, and facebook: Competing time demands of today's college students. *College Teaching, 59*(1), 23–30. doi:10.1080/87567555.2010.489078.

Hargittai, E. (2007). Whose space? Differences among users and non-users of social network sites. *Journal of Computer-Mediated Communication, 13*(1), 276–297. doi:10.1111/j.1083-6101.2007.00396.x.

Hogeboom, D. L., McDermott, R. J., Perrin, K. M., Osman, H., & Bell-Ellison, B. A. (2010). Internet use and social networking among middle aged and older adults. *Educational Gerontology, 36*(2), 93–111. doi:10.1080/03601270903058507.

James, C., Davis, K., Flores, A., Francis, J. M., Pettingill, L., Rundle, M., & Gardner, H. (2009). *Young people, ethics, and the new digital media. A synthesis from the good play project*. Cambridge, MA: The MIT Press.

Kim, J., & Lee, J.-E. R. (2011). The Facebook paths to happiness: Effects of the number of Facebook friends and self-presentation on subjective well-being. *CyberPsychology, Behavior and Social Networking, 14*(6), 359–365. doi:10.1089/cyber.2010.0374.

Lenhart, A., & Madden, M. (2007a). *Social networking websites and teens: An overview*. Pew Internet and American Life Project Report.

Lenhart, A., & Madden, M. (2007b). *Teens, privacy, & online social networks*. Pew Internet and American Life Project Report.

Lin, K.-Y., & Lu, H.-P. (2011). Intention to continue using Facebook fan pages from the perspective of social capital theory. *CyberPsychology, Behavior and Social Networking, 14*(10), 565–570. doi:10.1089/cyber.2010.0472.

Mauri, M., Cipresso, P., Balgera, A., Villamira, M., & Riva, G. (2011). Why is Facebook so successful? Psychophysiological measures describe a core flow state while using Facebook. *CyberPsychology, Behavior and Social Networking, 14*(12), 723–731. doi:10.1089/cyber.2010.0377.

Mehdizadeh, S. (2010). Self-presentation 2.0: Narcissism and self-esteem on Facebook. *CyberPsychology, Behavior and Social Networking*, *13*(4), 357–364. doi:10.1089/cyber.2009.0257.

Muscanell, N. L., & Guadagno, N. E. (2012). Make new friends or keep the old: Gender and personality differences in social networking use. *Computers in Human Behavior*, *28*(1), 107–112. doi:10.1016/j.chb.2011.08.016.

Nadkarni, A., & Hofmann, S. G. (2012). Why do people use Facebook? *Personality and Individual Differences*, *52*(3), 243–249. doi:10.1016/j.paid.2011.11.007 PMID:22544987.

Nosko, A., Wood, E., & Molema, S. (2010). All about me: Disclosure in online social networking profiles: The case of FACEBOOK. *Computers in Human Behavior*, *26*(3), 406–418. doi:10.1016/j.chb.2009.11.012.

Stefanone, M. A., Lackaff, D., & Rosen, D. (2011). Contingencies of self-worth and social-networking-site behavior. *CyberPsychology, Behavior and Social Networking*, *14*(1-2), 41–49. doi:10.1089/cyber.2010.0049.

Stutzman, F., Capra, R., & Thompson, J. (2011). Factors mediating disclosure in social network sites. *Computers in Human Behavior*, *27*(1), 590–598. doi:10.1016/j.chb.2010.10.017.

Tokunaga, R. S. (2011). Social networking site or social surveillance site? Understanding the use of interpersonal electronic surveillance in romantic relationships. *Computers in Human Behavior*, *27*(2), 705–713. doi:10.1016/j.chb.2010.08.014.

Turkle, S. (2011). *Alone together: Why we expect more from technology and less from each other*. New York: Basic Books.

Utz, S. (2010). Show me your friends and I will tell you what type of person you are: How one's profile, number of friends, and type of friends influence impression formation on social network sites. *Journal of Computer-Mediated Communication*, *15*(2), 314–335. doi:10.1111/j.1083-6101.2010.01522.x.

Utz, S., Tanis, M., & Vermeulen, I. (2012). It is all about being popular: The effects of need for popularity on social network site use. *CyberPsychology, Behavior and Social Networking*, *15*(1), 37–42. doi:10.1089/cyber.2010.0651.

Valkenburg, P. M., Peter, J., & Schouten, A. P. (2006). Friend networking sites and their relationship to adolescents' well-being and social self-esteem. *Cyberpsychology & Behavior*, *9*(5), 584–590. doi:10.1089/cpb.2006.9.584 PMID:17034326.

Vasalou, A., Joinson, A. N., & Courvoisier, D. (2010). Cultural differences, experience with social networks and the nature of "true commitment" in Facebook. *International Journal of Human-Computer Studies*, *68*(10), 719–728. doi:10.1016/j.ijhcs.2010.06.002.

Wilson, K., Fornasier, S., & White, K. M. (2010). Psychological predictors of young adults' use of social networking sites. *CyberPsychology, Behavior and Social Networking*, *13*(2), 173–177. doi:10.1089/cyber.2009.0094.

Wise, K., Alhabash, S., & Park, H. (2010). Emotional responses during social information seeking on Facebook. *CyberPsychology, Behavior and Social Networking*, *13*(5), 555–562. doi:10.1089/cyber.2009.0365.

KEY TERMS AND DEFINITIONS

Credibility: A quality of a person, a message/information or a media, that depends on assessment judgments of reliability based on a certain set of personal and collective criteria. Credibility is related to the issue of identity and trust as it implies the trustworthiness of the shared information.

Identity: In social networking sites it is related to the images that people build of themselves through the quantity of information they share with others, either related to personal information (e.g., age, status, preferences, etc.) and to the actions that they perform in these environments.

Personal Credibility: The process through which we build our image of persons able to obtain trust, respect and being believable. Personal credibility is strictly intertwined with the issue of identity, though it is mostly based on what people do as a consequence of real self-disclosure.

Privacy: The dynamic process through which an individual manages boundaries between what to disclose to other people and what to keep strictly private through conscious or unconscious privacy policy.

Security: In the context of the Internet and social networking sites security regards personal or social safety from risks of intrusion or fraud in the managing of data and interpersonal relationships. The issue may be tackled from a technical perspective, by implementing security engineering systems, and/or developing appropriate socio-technical skills and digital literacy through education.

Social Capital: The overall amount of actual or potential resources available in a durable network of more or less institutionalized relationships of mutual support or recognition. Benefits for individuals may come from the exchange of resources such as information, personal relationships, or capacity of creating groups.

Social Networking Site (SNS): A web service allowing users to create a public or semi-public profile, create lists of friends and traverse their list of connections, forming a public online network community. There are a number of web services enabling people to create a profile and connect, but while the specific activity of SNS is networking, the other types of services are focused on uploading and sharing.

Trust: A mental model involving emotional and cognitive components which brings the trustor to believe in the trustee and depend on him/her. It entails the attitude of the trustor to be vulnerable to the actions of trustee without the possibility of controlling his/her behavior.

ENDNOTES

1. http://www.microsoft.com/security/online-privacy/social-networking.aspx (last accessed 11/09/2012)
2. http://www.ftc.gov/ogc/coppa1.htm (last accessed 11/09/2012)

Chapter 3
Access Control Models for Online Social Networks

Rula Sayaf
KU Leuven, Belgium

Dave Clarke
KU Leuven, Belgium

ABSTRACT

Access control is one of the crucial aspects in information systems security. Authorizing access to resources is a fundamental process to limit potential privacy violations and protect users. The nature of personal data in online social networks (OSNs) requires a high-level of security and privacy protection. Recently, OSN-specific access control models (ACMs) have been proposed to address the particular structure, functionality and the underlying privacy issues of OSNs. In this survey chapter, the essential aspects of access control and review the fundamental classical ACMs are introduced. The specific OSNs features and review the main categories of OSN-specific ACMs are highlighted. Within each category, the most prominent ACMs and their underlying mechanisms that contribute enhancing privacy of OSNs are surveyed. Toward the end, more advanced issues of access control in OSNs are discussed. Throughout the discussion, different models and highlight open problems are contrasted. Based on these problems, the chapter is concluded by proposing requirements for future ACMs.

INTRODUCTION

Online social networks (OSNs) are social networks that are established through web-based services through which people can foster social relationships. Sites such as LinkedIn, Facebook, Google+, MySpace, etc, are therefore type of OSNs (Hafez Ninggal & Abawajy, 2011), but also blogging services, peer-to-peer, collaborative and content sharing sites such as Youtube and Flicker, and social bookmarking services such as CiteULike are also types of OSNs.

Users of OSNs create their own social spaces and upload different types of personal data such as photos, videos, texts, etc. OSNs facilitate easy social interaction by allowing users to establish

DOI: 10.4018/978-1-4666-3926-3.ch003

relationships and connect to other users, who may be friends in the offline world or strangers.

One of the fundamental features of OSNs is the ability to share personal data with others in a relatively privacy-preserving manner. The recent surge of interest in OSNs has been coupled with serious privacy and security concerns, primarily caused by the lack of proper data protection means (Cutillo, Molva, & Strufe, 2009). For instance, users' privacy concerns have affected the popularity of MySpace. Studies have showed that due to lack of privacy control on MySpace, users have abandoned this OSN (Baracaldo, López, Anwar, & Lewis, 2011) and have migrated to other OSNs for their better privacy-preserving means.

Access control mechanisms are employed in OSNs to enable users to control the dissemination of their own data and protect their privacy accordingly (Abiteboul et al., 2005). Other approaches are employed to protect rights and ownership of data, such as digital rights management (Rodriguez, Rodriguez, Carreras, & Delgado, 2009), which we will review later, and watermarking of individual data (Bedi, Wadhai, Sugandhi, & Mirajkar, 2005). Both these approaches and access control models are intended to improve privacy preservation of OSN users.

However, there are many underlying problems in access control mechanisms used in current OSNs. First, only a small percentage of users change the default access control settings to define their own access control policies (Gross & Acquisti, 2005). Second, when these access control mechanisms are used they fail to address the required fine-grained control to avoid privacy violations (Masoumzadeh & Joshi, 2010). The sensitive personal data in OSNs requires a high-level of protection by means of appropriate access control (Gates, 2007). An inherent challenge is how to define an appropriate ACM to regulate access to OSNs' users' data. ACMs should offer a fine-grained control that captures the specific structure and features of an OSN. Mostly, data dissemination is based on relationships represented in the OSN. Therefore, simple access control lists (Cankaya, 2011) and even more advanced classical ACMs fail to satisfy access control requirements of OSN, as they are not based on the specific properties of social relationships.

Recently, various ACMs have been specifically proposed to address OSN privacy-protection requirements. In this chapter we focus on OSN-specific problems and requirements and how those are tackled by different ACMs.

BACKGROUND AND PRELIMINARY NOTIONS

Online Social Networks

A social network (SN) is a set of people connected to each other by social relationships. *Offline Social Networks* refer to real-world social communities. *Online Social Networks* (OSNs) are web-based services that offer the functionality of creating a personal representation of one's self through which one can socialize with others. A *user* is represented in the OSN via a profile to which personal data can be added. An *owner* is a user who adds her data, referred to as *objects,* and can share them with others.

A main feature of OSNs is the articulation of various types of relationships between profiles to facilitate the social communication with others. The social communication includes various activities such as sharing objects, creating groups, organizing online and offline events, etc.

Users in an OSN and their relationships form a *social graph.* Nodes and links in the graph denote users and relationships, respectively (Carminati, Ferrari, & Perego, 2006b). Each pair of users in the graph is connected via a path of links between them. The distance between two users measures the number of links of the shortest path between the two corresponding nodes. The social graph is commonly utilized as an abstraction of OSNs upon which ACMs are formalized.

Access Control Models

An *access control model (ACM)* is a formalization of how policies are composed based on a specific set of features in the system to regulate and authorize access to data. An *access control policy* defines constraints on whether an access request to an object should be granted or denied. In the context of OSNs, a *requestor* initiates a request asking for a specific permission on a specific object from its owner. The owner regulates access to and dissemination of her objects by means of defined access control policies. Once a request is authorized, the specific set of permissions entailed by the policy will be granted to the requestor, who is then referred to as the *accessor. Delegation* is entrusting a user (*delegate*) to act on an object with the authority of the object owner (*delegator*). Delegation of authority is convenient for OSNs where users trust each other to further disseminate their objects over the network.

Access control is a two-fold control, authoritative or prohibitive. Most ACMs formalize authoritative, or positive, policies only by assuming a closed-world model (Samarati & Vimercati, 2001). In the closed-world model a request can only be honored by an existing authoritative policy or else it will be denied. In many cases, conflicting policies and hierarchy-propagated policies (Carminati, Ferrari, Heatherly, Kantarcioglu, & Thuraisingham, 2009) might unexpectedly authorize a request and violate the privacy of the owner. Therefore, prohibitive, or negative, policies are crucial to limit accidental authorizations of positive policies. Positive and negative policies are enforced in access control in a mutual exclusion pattern (Samarati & Vimercati, 2001). This pattern authorizes a request if this request is entailed by a positive policy and not denied by a negative policy. This approach ensures more controlled authorization, contributing to more protection against imprecisely defined access control policies.

For each ACM there should be a specific *enforcement mechanism* to enforce policies in the system. The enforcement mechanism verifies a request and matches it against defined policies to infer an authorization decision with the right permission to be granted. In OSNs a centralized authority, a reference monitor, decentralized authorities or users themselves, can carry out policies enforcement.

Next, we will review the central classical ACMs to establish a sufficient background, before discussing OSN-specific models.

Classical Access Control Models

Access control mechanisms are used in information systems to mitigate security and privacy risks of unauthorized access to data. Those mechanisms vary depending on the underlying structure of the system and the levels of protection needed. The first abstraction of an access control model is the access control matrix (Lampson, 1974). The matrix model describes the system as a protection state by defining a list of access permissions of each subject. A *reference monitor* guards access to objects based on the protection state of the system. A major drawback of this model is the static nature of defining permissions for all the system's subjects. The matrix model lacks abstraction possibilities for groups of subjects and objects. This entails that for each new subject in the system, new lists should be created to guard access to each existing object; the same also applies for each new object in the system. The overhead of changing the protection state limits the applicability of the matrix in large-scale systems. More advanced models expand upon earlier models with specific enhancements to address requirements, identified weaknesses and limitations in expressiveness. These models are more suited to emerging structure and context changes of systems.

Administrative Access Control Models

ACMs can be categorized into three models based on the administration method (Chinaei, Barker, & Tompa, 2009):

1. Mandatory Access Control (MAC) (Bell & LaPadula, 1973) is a central authority system that enforces a lattice-based representation of objects and subjects using specific security or sensitivity levels. System administrators define the security level classifications of subjects and objects to guard access authorizations in the system. A policy constrains access based on the security level of the requestor and the security level of the object to be accessed. MAC models are employed in systems where high security needs to be maintained.
2. Discretionary Access Control (DAC) (United States Department of Defense, 1985), or identity-based access control (IBAC), enables system subjects to decide on how to grant permissions to other subjects in the system without any authority involvement. A subject is entitled to define constraints that should be satisfied by an entity in order to be granted specific access permission. DAC models are employed in systems where subjects are responsible for guarding access to their own objects, e.g., OSNs. Other models such as the model of Carminati, Ferrari, Heatherly, Kantarcioglu, and Thuraisingham (2009) extend the DAC concept by enabling users to also define sets of constraints to filter access requests before granting access.
   DAC and MAC are not mutually exclusive and can be jointly applied, as in the Chinese wall model (Kessler, 1992).
3. Role-Based Access Control (RBAC) is an alternative model for systems that define specific roles of subjects. Roles are abstract descriptions of what subjects are entitled to perform in the system. Access to an object is dependent on the role assigned to the requestor and the permissions associated to this role. Roles can have different positive and negative permissions, if the model defines negative policies. When different roles are assigned to one subject then the authorized permissions might result in conflicts. The main issues of concern in RBAC are how to assign roles to subjects statically and/or dynamically, and how to guarantee that no conflicts will arise. F. Chen and Sandhu (1995) addressed the assignment of non-conflicting roles by applying constraints. In their approach, constraints can be used as invariants in the system or preconditions for an action. For example, mutually exclusive roles can be validated by constraints to check that a user cannot have the two roles assigned at once (F. Chen & Sandhu, 1995). Schaad (2001) argues that the Separation of Duty constraints proposed by F. Chen and Sandhu (1995) could still cause conflicts if users are able to delegate roles. Schaad (2001) proposed a rule-based declarative separation of duty approach to statically and dynamically detect role-assignment constraint conflicts and further prohibit delegation of roles. In principal, separation of roles can be guaranteed (Chen & Li, 2006) based on the requirements highlighted in the work of Clark and Wilson (1987).

Attribute-Based Access Control Models

Attribute-Based Access Control (ABAC) is another kind of access control model. ABAC formally describes policies based on attributes of subjects, objects and other environment-specific data. In comparison with RBAC, ABAC is more flexible by facilitating the definition of rich and fine-grained policies.

Attribute-Based Encryption (ABE) is a more secure version of ABAC. In ABE, attributes are encrypted using a public and a secret key and distributed to users to which the composition of attributes applies. Bethencourt, Sahai, and Waters (2007) employ ABE for a group-based access control. In their Ciphertext-Policy Attribute-based Encryption model, private keys are defined by a set of attributes and embodied in the form of ciphertext. The ciphertext is a two-part component: an encrypted object and a set of attributes involved in the access control policy. For a request to be authorized, the attributes of the requestor must comply with the ciphertext's attribute component. The policies can be expressed in a collision-resistant monotonic access tree structure. This structure allows a user to have access to more than one private key without being able to aggregate the keys or attributes to access data.

Classic policy models are not targeted to a specific type of system. In general, those models are too abstract to be employed in collaborative systems such as OSNs. OSNs systems have a particular structure and type of communication that requires flexible and highly expressive ACMs. Classical models fail to fully address the requirements of OSNs. However, we will discuss later in this chapter some classical models that have been adapted to OSNs. The adaptations basically focus on exerting more dynamic policy definition mechanisms using specific OSN features to support high granularity protection (Tolone, Ahn, Pai, & Hong, 2005).

ACCESS CONTROL IN ONLINE SOCIAL NETWORKS

In this section we provide an extensive overview of the main aspects of access control models as solutions to various privacy-related issues in OSNs. We start off by reviewing the main privacy problems reported in OSNs. We then provide the essential requirements proposed for OSN-specific ACMs. Then we survey the most prominent OSN-tailored ACMs. In the description of each model, we highlight the main contribution of the model and contrast different approaches. Towards the end of the chapter, we discuss the points in which ACMs need to be enhanced to address open privacy issues. We conclude our discussion by proposing more extensive requirements to fulfill the discussed issues of current OSN-specific ACMs, and to be considered in future research in this domain.

Privacy Risks in Online Social Networks

OSNs have grown in popularity and become a worldwide phenomenon (Squicciarini & Sundareswaran, 2009). The main features of fostering relationships and sharing data OSNs attract up to 4 users among each 5 Internet users (The State of Social Media 2011: Social is the new normal, 2012). Nonetheless, those features involve many privacy risks. A risk is defined as the insecurity about a potential negative consequence of a specific action (Havlena & DeSarbo, 1991) that is proportional to the likelihood of the negative consequence (Peter & Tarpey, 1975). Estimating risks is strongly coupled with how users perceive their privacy (Norberg, Horne, & Horne, 2007). The indisputable problem in OSNs is that users fail to correctly estimate privacy risks (Acquisti & Grossklags, 2005) and fail to match them to their actual behaviors in the OSNs (Spiekermann, Grossklags, & Berendt, 2001); this is due to many reasons as we will discuss here.

Acquisti and Grossklags (2005) highlight the following reasons that hinder making proper privacy decisions:

- Incomplete information about the possible accessors that makes the risks involved nondeterministic, especially for external parties accessors.

- "Bounded rationality" (Simon, 1982) limits users ability to rationalize about all available data. Even if a user has access to all data about possible accessors and who should not have access due to all the possible risks, the user's mental model would simplify the quantitative facts when making privacy-related decisions. The inferred decisions might be not very accurate for defining certain policies.
- Social preferences and patterns of data disclosure affect users' decisions. Complete information utilization would not prevent privacy-related decisions from deviating from rationality under those effects.
- Failure in predicting the future preferences and the tendency to compromise in the present to get immediate benefits affects the future privacy status of users.

Users lack proper information about how to make informed privacy decisions (Acquisti & Grossklags, 2005). Therefore, the outcome of the decisions they make using the privacy management tools in current OSNs clashes with their expectations. In Facebook, only about 40% of the privacy settings enable access to data as the owner expects (Lipford, Besmer, & Watson, 2008). The rest of the settings enable more users to access than the owner expects. Users contribute to this discrepancy by acting differently to the privacy concerns they express. Norberg, Horne and Horne (2007) coined the term "privacy paradox" to describe the relationship between users' intentions of disclosure and their actual behavior.

When users grant access to their data, they are concerned about their privacy. However, these concerns are multi-faceted. Users are more concerned about privacy when disclosing to close friends than to strangers (Gross & Acquisti, 2005). This can be explained based on the incomplete information factor about weak ties shared with strangers (Granovetter, 1973). OSNs facilitate the fostering and managing of a large number of weak ties very easily. Reasoning about the incomplete information to estimate privacy risks of weak ties makes those ties one the main reasons behind the difficulty of managing privacy in OSNs (Donath & Boyd, 2004). In addition, trust plays a significant role in disclosure decisions (Norberg, Horne, & Horne, 2007). Estimating trust for weak ties is a challenge that results in privacy risks.

The patterns of data sharing in OSNs further complicate reasoning about privacy. OSN users aim at expanding their social interactions within the network and sharing their objects on a large scale (Squicciarini, Shehab, & Wede, 2010). Indeed, OSNs are designed to encourage users to share. For instance, Facebook is designed to encourage disclosure of as much information as possible (Hu, Gail-Joon, & Jan, 2012). Facebook status textbox encourages users to update the status by showing the text "What's on your mind?" in order to encourage users to write what's on their minds as their status. Facebook users reveal significantly more identifying information about themselves than users in other OSNs (Dwyer, Hiltz, & Passerini, 2007; Gross & Acquisti, 2005). A personal information revelation study states, "Participants are happy to disclose as much information as possible to as many people as possible" (Gross and Acquisti, 2005, p. 2). As the social interactions evolve, more privacy threats arise. Social interactions with friends and friends of friends and so on, might lead to inappropriate disclosure of private information. This is often the case when users are not aware of who can access their objects (Squicciarini, Shehab, & Wede, 2010; Hogben, 2008).

Trying to mitigate privacy risks by limiting interaction on OSNs would not satisfy users' needs. ACMs employed in OSNs should facilitate maximal privacy preservation without hindering interaction. Access control tools in current OSNs are generally simplistic and coarse-grained (Squicciarini, Shehab, & Wede, 2010; Masoumzadeh & Joshi, 2010), which occasionally contributes to the failure of privacy protection required by users. All the reasons mentioned above contribute to specifically making OSNs users the victims of privacy violations (Wang & Sun, 2010).

We will now list the main OSNs challenges and privacy risks reported in the literature:

- Automatic identity theft (Leyla, Thorsten, Davide, & Engin, 2009), where an attacker can fake a profile of a user and establish connections with the victim's friends resulting in accumulating sensitive communication data.
- Economic loss can be caused due to unauthorized access to data of users in OSNs (Tuunainen, Pitkanen, & Hovi, 2009).
- Data aggregation is possible for malicious users and third party applications (Acquist et al., 2007).
- Reputation jeopardy of users, especially for prospective employer (Rosenblum, 2007).
- Hacking and phishing of personal data by third parties (Debatin, Lovejoy, Horn, & Hughes, 2009).
- OSNs profile pictures can be improperly used. For example, a personal profile photo from Facebook was publicly used to announce a death in the media (ABC Media Watch, Filleting Facebook. Australian Broadcasting Corporation (ABC), 29 October 07, 2007).
- OSNs-targeting worms that turns users' machines into zombies on a botnet (New MySpace and Facebook Worm Target Social Networks, 2008).
- Cyberbullying and stalking by acquiring sensitive data about the victim user (Acquisti et al., 2007).
- Unwanted linkability from photos through the tags of other users who are not the owner of the photo (Acquisti et al., 2007).
- Blackmailing users (Gross & Acquisti, 2005).
- Price discrimination (Gross & Acquisti, 2005).
- Selling data to marketing companies (Rosenblum, 2007).
- Sexual predators, especially of kids, through accessing their sensitive data on OSNs (Rosenblum, 2007).
- Face recognition of profile images available on OSNs can result in users being tracked and recognized in other contexts, e.g., traffic cameras (Acquisti et al., 2007).

All of the previously mentioned issues intensify the fundamental necessity of enhancing security and privacy protection mechanisms of OSNs. To address the unforeseen threats, fine-grained ACMs are required to facilitate more control and protection over any type of data disclosed in the OSN (Masoumzadeh & Joshi, 2010). We do not explicitly suggest that access control is a solution to all the above-mentioned threats; however, guarding access to data is the first fundamental step towards privacy protection. Moreover, OSNs providers such as Facebook and MySpace, support access control models to construct better trust basis with the privacy-concerned users (H. Wang & Sun, 2010).

Access Control Models Requirements for OSNs

OSNs can be viewed as group-like and collaborative systems, where various ACMs can be applicable for such systems. Same models include Task-based access control (Thomas & Sandhu, 1994; Thomas & Sandhu, 1998), Team-based access control (Thomas, 1997), and Context-based ACMs (Covington et al., 2001). These models are appropriate for OSNs more than the previously discussed classical models are.

In order to evaluate whether an ACM fits OSNs, we review the essential ACM requirements to effectively address security and privacy in OSN within Web 2.0 (Gates, 2007). An ACM should fulfill the following requirements:

Requirement 1: Relation-based access control is a fundamental requirement to capture the main notion of OSNs. A model should distinguish different types of relationships and grant permissions appropriately (Villegas, Ali, & Maheswaran, 2008).

Requirement 2: Fine granularity is required to control access to every single piece of data disclosed over the OSN.

Requirement 3: Interoperability of access control policies to enable users to save and refer to their policies on different OSNs.

Requirement 4: Sticky policies (Mont, Pearson, & Bramhall, 2003) should be enforced to encapsulate an object and its access control policies in one entity. This guarantees that access to an object is regulated according to the owner's specification, regardless of who is delegated to disseminate this object.

The requirements address different access control aspects; Requirement 1 and Requirement 2 are related to the modeling. Requirement 3 is concerned with linking multiple OSNs frameworks and business models and thus raising issues that are out of access control models scope. The encapsulation of policies with objects in Requirement 4 specifies access control enforcement approach that is not a fundamental part of the access control modeling. Therefore, access control models vary in the degree they address these requirements; most of the models are concerned with Requirements 1 and 2. We will notice the variance in adoption of these requirements in the reviewed OSN-specific ACMs. We will refer to which requirements are satisfied by each model.

It is noteworthy that fine granularity contributes to the complexity of an ACM. This complexity negatively affects users and makes the construction of well-specified policies challenging, which results in privacy violations (Villegas, Ali, & Maheswaran, 2008). Finding models that compromise fine granularity and complexity towards user-friendliness with an acceptable level of privacy-preservation and protection is a challenge.

In the subsequent sections we will review the most common ACMs in the domain. The models are separated into sections based on the most prominent feature of the model.

Rule-Based Access Control Models

In rule-based models (Didriksen, 1997) policies are based on rules that constrain authorization decisions based on various features. In an early OSN-specific ACM, Carminati, Ferrari, and Perego (2006b) capture relationships in a rule-based model. The work views the OSN as a social graph to capture particular relationship features on which the model is formalized. A directed link in the social graph represents a relationship from the initiator of the relationship to the receiver. The depth of a relationship is the length of the path. The notion of depth is used to distinguish between a direct and indirect relationship when the depth is =1 or is >1, respectively. Trust is another feature to distinguish relationships. Trust denotes how much the initiator of a relationship and all the users within the same path trust the receiver of the relationship. The model exploits the Web Ontology Language (OWL) (Oasis Committee. XACML 2.0 Specification., 2012) to represent the OSN and relationships features. Typically, a relationship is represented as an attribute of a *User* class ontology. Since in this model a relationship has many features, it cannot be modeled as an attribute. Using REL-X OWL vocabulary (Carminati, Ferrari, & Perego, 2006a), a relationship is represented as class ontology with features as class properties. Representing the relationship as a separate class makes reasoning about specific relationship properties feasible (Carminati, Ferrari, Heatherly, Kantarcioglu, & Thuraisingham, 2009).

An *access control rule* is the composition of antecedent constraints about an access request, including the to-be-accessed object, and the requestor specifications that entail a specific set of access permissions or prohibitions (Carminati, Ferrari, Heatherly, Kantarcioglu, & Thuraisingham, 2009). The relationship-based access control rules constrain access based on relationship features. Rules have the format:

$$Rule = \left(obj_{id}, Condset\right):$$
$$Condset = \left\{cond_{1},..., cond_{n}\right\}$$

where obj_{id} is the object to be accessed, $cond_i$ is a tuple of a requestor relationship properties specifications, which has the form:

$$Cond = \left(v, rt, D_{\max}, t_{\min}\right)$$

where *v* is the object's owner node, *rt* is the relationship type between the requestor and the object owner, D_{max} is the maximum depth, and t_{min} is the minimum trust. When a request is initiated on a specific object, the requestor's has to prove that the relationship features she owns comply with the condition set of the rule defined. The model translates relationships and rules to logical formulas to easily generate and assert proofs. A rule is expressed as follows:

$$\begin{aligned} & hasSub\left(?rel, ?x\right) \wedge hasObj\left(?rel, v\right) \\ & \wedge hasType\left(?rel, rt\right) \wedge hasDepth\left(?rel, ?\mathrm{D}\right) \\ & \wedge \leq \left(?\mathrm{D}, \mathrm{D}_{\max}\right) \wedge hasTrust\left(?rel, ?t\right) \wedge \geq \left(?t, t_{\min}\right) \end{aligned}$$

where *?x* is the requestor, *?rel* is the relationship between the requestor and object owner.

Access control enforcement here is done at the client-side, inspired by the work of Weitzner, Hendler, Berners-Lee, and Connolly (2006). The model extends the distributed architecture of access control enforcement to be semi-decentralized and thereby overcome the burden of managing certificates. Trusted central nodes save users' data and issue certificates of relationships and trust levels. A signed certificate by both users proves the existence of a direct relationship with a specific trust value. An indirect relationship certificate is a chain of certificates of all relationships in its path; the trust level of this indirect relationship is the accumulated trust value of all sub relationships.

This early work establishes the basis for later OSN-specific access control models. This model conforms to Requirements 1 and 2 by utilizing relationships and enriching the fine granularity of policies with various relationship features. Nonetheless, the rules are limited to relationship properties and do not include other aspects of OSNs such as various user, object, permission, and ownership types.

Role Based Access Control Models

RBAC is applicable in systems in which users can be distinguished and granted access based on different roles. This same distinction of users roles can clearly be realized in OSNs based on the distinction of different relationships users could share with others. Relation Based Access Control (RelBAC) (Giunchiglia, Zhang, & Crispo, 2008) is an RBAC model applicable to OSNs and other applications. RelBAC incorporates relation-based policies as well as role-based policies. This is significant to verify the identity and trust of users as well as relationships for authorization. RelBAC views relationships differently from other relationship-based models, as we will discuss later. In this model, relations do not denote user-to-user relationships; rather, they denote user-to-object relationships. The user-to-object relationship is established when a user is granted a specific permission over an object. RelBAC is formalized in an *Entity Relationship (ER)* diagram of users, objects and permissions. The ER diagram is translated into a *Description Logic (DL)* representation. DL is a knowledge representation logic that facilitates rich system representation (Baader, Calvanese, McGuinness, Nardi, & Patel-Schneider, 2003). Users and objects are modeled as DL atomic concepts and permissions are modeled of as DL roles. The model captures a dynamic organisation of users in terms of a hierarchy of groups and objects in a hierarchy of classes. Both hierarchies are linked to a permission hierarchy by means of n-ary relations; Users, Objects, and Permission hierarchies are denoted by means of subsumption axioms:

$$X_i \subseteq X_j : X_i^J \subseteq X_i^J$$

where X_i, X_j are User, Object, or Permission sets. In a hierarchy where *Friend* is a user type that is a generalization of *Closefriend*, the subsumption is expressed as:

$$Closefriend \sqsubseteq Friend$$

An ontology-based formalization of OSNs (Finin, Ding, Zhou, & Joshi, 2005) lends itself to represent hierarchies using Lightweight Ontologies (Giunchiglia, Marchese, & Zaihrayeu, 2005). The representation captures access control rule instantiations of those permissions/relations. Similarly to the hierarchies, rules are articulated as one the three formulas:

$$C \sqsubseteq P, \; C \equiv P, \text{ or } C \sqsupseteq P$$

where C is a group of users or a class of objects, P is a class of permissions formulated in DL syntax, $\equiv$ is equality operator and $\sqsubseteq, \sqsupseteq$ are subsumption operators. For example, the following rule states that any user from the Friend group is allowed to download all objects of type Film:

$$Friend \sqsubseteq \exists Download.Film.$$

The rule above is user-centric. A rule can also be object-centric. For example, the following rule states that all films can be downloaded by some friend:

$$Film \sqsubseteq \exists Download^{-1}.Friend.$$

This formulation of rules allows the system to dynamically evolve the hierarchies without causing conflicts. Moreover, by using the DL atomic negation and complex concept negation, the model formalizes permission negation and denial of permissions, respectively. In addition, RelBAC employs quantificational constructs to represent n-ary relations between objects, users and permissions. This facilitates the expression of policies of an n-owned object by defining permissions of the owners, which we will discuss later in the chapter. Current OSNs and other ACM do not employ quantification constructs. This is advantageous for limiting the number of re-shares and limiting delegation of trust. Such expressiveness satisfies Requirement 2 of fine granularity.

Many models extend RBAC for OSNs by preserving authorization mechanisms and adapting roles to the OSN-specific entities, users or relationships. RBAC captures a social relationship by representing it in terms of the two roles of the users involved in this relationship. For Tang, Mao, Lai, and Zhu (2009), OSN-specific ACM requirements are used to define relationship-based policies and support sharing objects with different users or groups of users. The authors adapted RBAC to meet those requirements. Their model extends the decentralized management role-based model ARBAC97 (Sandhu, Bhamidipati, & Munawer, 1999) and introduces a server and client to manage roles and permissions, respectively. Upon requesting access to an object, the server managing roles verifies only the roles relevant to the relationship between the requestor and the owner. The owner checks with the client module for the list of permissions that can be granted to a request. A model is required to allow the inherent feature of OSNs users of having multiple relationships and therefore multiple roles. The model reflects this feature by enabling users to have multiple roles assigned to them, one role per relationship. Referring to the relationship path between a requestor and an object's owner implicitly guarantees the separation of roles; yet the authors do not clarify how roles are separated if two users share more than one relationship in different contexts.

Tie-RBAC is another application of RBAC in OSNs (Tapiador, Carrera, & Joaquın, 2011). The notion of tie denotes the composition of a relationship and the two users involved in it. Ties define an automatic system of role-assignment upon establishing a relationship between two users. For instance, when a user establishes a Father-Son relationship with another user, the tie established would assign the roles Father and Son to the initiator and receiver of the relationship, respectively. The access control enforcement in this model is the typical RBAC. Comparably to Tang, Mao, Lai, and Zhu's (2009) model, roles here can be cast on individual users or groups. The model conforms to Requirement 1, while the granularity of policies, Requirement 2, is rather coarse.

Although RBAC extensions to OSNs are able to conform to Requirement 1 and 2, there are other features that can be difficult to explicitly express in such models. Although trust can be implicitly associated with specific roles in a system, it is required to have models where trust can be quantified and used to compose fine-grained policies. Other social graph related aspects, such as a relationship path and distance between users, are not captured in RBAC. Generally, discretionary RBACs are not well suited for OSNs since they burden users with tasks of associating permissions to static roles in different dynamic contexts that are not distinctively separate (Shen & Hong, 2006).

Next, we overview attribute-based models, where a role is decomposed into detailed attributes. These models offer more flexibility in resolving separation of duty constraints.

Attribute-Based Access Control Models

The flexibility of Attribute-Based Access Control models (ABAC) is employed in OSNs for a higher level of expressiveness and finer granularity. To preserve the privacy and anonymity of OSN users, ABACs usually incorporate encryption techniques. For instance, Persona is a decentralized OSN with an effective and privacy preserving application of ABAC (Baden, Bender, Spring, Bhattacharjee, & Starin, 2009). Access control in Persona is a two-fold mechanism that integrates attribute-based encryption, attribute-based access control and encryption. With this mechanism users are entitled to manage and enforce access control policies without the need to trust a central authority. A user manages access to her objects by distributing public keys to other users entitled to access her objects. The act of exchanging keys implicitly captures the notion of trust over relationships in an OSN by connecting to *a group of potential accessors who can access a set of objects with those keys.* The group encryption protocol is based on generating a group key and encrypting it using each member's public key (Wong, Gouda, & Lam, 1998; Naor, Naor, & Lotspiech, 2001). Accessing an object requires the availability of an ABE group key to decrypt a symmetric key with which the object is encrypted. Access permissions and implicit trust can be propagated to indirect relationships such as friend-of-friends via the creation of a group based on another friend's existing group. For instance, if X has defined a group of his 'friends' and Y defines a new group $Y_{X\text{-}friends}$ based on $X_{friends}$ group, then all members of $X_{friends}$ will have access permissions assigned to $Y_{X\text{-}friends}$. The model is not limited to only group-based access, it also facilitates individualistic access control by specifying identity-based access permissions. This multi-faceted accessor specification contributes to the fine granularity of the model, thereby satisfying Requirement 2. The downside is that it does not clearly state how group and individual changes can be captured and adapted to in the dynamic environment of OSNs. In case of a group deletion, the ABE key of the group changes for new encryptions, while previously encrypted objects will still be accessible to the revoked user. Re-encrypting all objects is crucial to overcome this issue and avoid possible privacy threats.

This issue is further addressed in the Encryption-based Access Control in Social Networks with Efficient Revocation (EASiER) (Jahid, Mittal, & Borisov, 2011). EASiER extends ABE and uses a "minimally trusted proxy" to resolve revoked users. The model exploits an effective revocation scheme CP-ABE (Bethencourt, Sahai, & Waters, 2007) to adapt to the dynamic group changes in the OSN. In CP-ABE a ciphertext is a two-part component: encrypted data and components for attributes involved in the ABE key. In order to gain access to an object, a requestor sends part of a ciphertext to the proxy to be decrypted to a form that only an unrevoked user can combine with her attribute keys to decrypt this object. In the revocation scheme of M. Naor and Pinkas (2001), the proxy receives a new key for each revocation without having to commit further changes either to users' keys or to previously encrypted objects. Attribute-based policies facilitate the incorporation of various OSN-related attributes and features, thereby satisfying Requirement 2. The secure proxy-based model is applicable in various OSN structures. The proxy can be a central authority in a centralized OSN, or distributed over the network in a decentralized OSN.

Distinctive authorization based on the validation of specific attributes facilitates anonymous authentication and preserves requestor's identity and privacy. Squicciarini, Trombetta, Bhargav-Spantzel, and Bertino (2007) propose a k-anonymous (Sweeney, 2002) attribute-based access control model to preserve sensitive information about users' access history in distributed systems. The proposed model is not specifically tailored for OSNs, yet, it is applicable with OSN-specific attributes. The main contribution of this model is that a requestor can specify k-anonymous credentials to be submitted if there are at least k other undistinguishable sets. The flow of authorization can be summarized as follows:

1. A policy enforcer sends information about attributes to be submitted to the credential submitter (requestor).
2. Before sending the k-anonymous attributes, the credential submitter runs a private matching protocol to check for k identical sets or asks the enforcer for more information.
3. If the submitter is certain of the existence of k identical sets, then the k-anonymous set is sent to gain access to an object.

The negotiation of the attribute sets facilitates anonymous trust negotiation using a cryptographic based communication in a setting where a submitter cannot be tracked and identified.

It is possible to deploy this model in a decentralized OSN if users are provided with local mechanisms for k-anonymous set generation and for private matching protocols. Despite the privacy preservation of requests and anonymous communication, the model does not explicitly incorporate relationship data of users unless this data is represented in the set of attributes.

In this section we gave an overview of various ABAC models that can be applied in both centralized and decentralized OSNs. The challenge of those models remains in determining which attributes to base policies on.

Trust-Based Access Control Models

Golbeck (2009) defines trust as follows: "trust in a person is a commitment to an action based on a belief that the future actions of that person will lead to a good outcome" (p. 5). Trust plays a key role in relationships between users in OSNs and has a substantial effect on decisions related to authorising access to objects (Golbeck, 2009). In this context, relationships are modeled as edges with a fixed trust value in the social graph (Maheswaran, Tang, & Ghunaim, 2007). As we have seen in the previous sections, many models employ trust as a key constraint in authorising access to objects. Maheswaran, Tang, and Ghunaim (2007) recognize four types of trust modeling:

- Social graph-based trust computation (Xiong & Liu, 2004) similar to trust estimation in the model of Carminati, Ferrari, and Perego (2006b).
- Sensitive trust modeling, where any change in the assessment parameters will be immediately reflected on the trust values.
- Anonymous trust modeling where users anonymously contribute to the ratings of trust (Singh & Liu, 2003).
- Fuzzy trust modeling using fuzzy techniques to combine ratings of users (Aringhieri, Damiani, Di Vimercati, Paraboschi, & Samarati, 2006).

The gravity-based model (Maheswaran, Tang, & Ghunaim, 2007) employs several mechanisms and algorithms for trust computation in OSNs. Trust is established via interactions among users forming positive or negative context-based trust. Independent contexts are modeled in a *Trust Space* where trust calculations are performed in a time-based manner. This trust measure is represented as the distance between two users and can increase or decrease proportionally to the trust value.

Trust-based ACMs are rule-based models that incorporate trust in policy constraints and authorization decisions. Ali, Villegas, and Maheswaran (2007) introduced Social Access Control (SAC) for OSNs. This multi-level security inspired-model (Benantar, 2006) classifies users and objects in hierarchies based on specific trust values. Each user is assigned an average of trust ratings $r(u)$ by community members (Golbeck, 2006; Levien, 2009). The user can minimally change the rated trust value, by a value λ, to reflect her *operating trust level* τ within a session:

$$\tau = \lambda r\left(u\right) \text{ where } 0 \leq \lambda \leq 1.$$

The operating trust level of a user X is cast as the trust level t_0 of objects owned by X. The trust level of an object accessed by a user is reflected as an effective trust level of this user. An important contribution of this model is the use of trust to strongly constrain access to objects. While in other models, the trust value of an accessor is independent of the trust level of the owner in the system, this model strongly couples the trust of the accessor with the trust of the owner by allowing users to only access objects within a limited range of their own trust value; otherwise information leakage is reported.

The model employs trusted nodes to encrypt objects based on social encryption schemes (Shamir, 1979). When the trusted node verifies a key, access is granted to the requestor and no delegation of access is allowed.

Another utilization of trust is found in the Personal Data Access Control (PDAC) model, proposed by Villegas, Ali, and Maheswaran (2008) for sharing data in centralized OSNs and other systems. The model aims to be user-friendly so that users are not overburdened with many decisions and access control criteria. To share personal data/objects, the owner is only required to define thresholds of three trust zones: acceptance, attestation and rejection. The owner also specifies attestation nodes and the constraints under which the attesters can undersign a request. PDAC quantifies the trust of a requestor based on the relationship with and the distance from the owner, thereby conforming to Requirement 1. Analogously to SAC (Ali, Villegas, & Maheswaran, 2007), the social community contributes to the trust quantification formalism. Initially, a user X and the community mutually perform a trust evaluation of X's friends and the zones they belong to from the perspective of X. First, the owner defines the zone her friends belong to, and then the social community contributes to refining the trust and the zones of those friends. The trust degree of a requestor is based on the distance from an owner's object and past context-dependent access experience. The context-dependent access experience is quantified according to the accesses granted to the requestor by the owner and her social neighborhood community. The requestor is classified based on the estimated trust in one of three zones. In comparison with the k-anonymous model (Squicciarini, Trombetta, Bhargav-Spantzel, & Bertino, 2007), although this model does not protect anonymity, it offers more sensitive trust quantification by referring to past access history of a requestor, leading to more accurate authorization decisions.

Authorizations in the model are automatically dependent on the trust zone. A requestor classified in the acceptance zone can automatically access objects of the owner. A rejected zone requestor will be automatically prohibited from accessing an object. An attestation zone requestor needs to be undersigned by the specific attestation nodes. The incorporation of distance, context, and history of access as well as the trust in a requestor by the community enriches the granularity of this model, thereby conforming to Requirement 2. Besides access control, the model implements a tracking mechanism to detect re-sharing of objects and to report data leakage. This mechanism tracks and verifies that the trust constraints of a re-shared object comply with the original owner's constraints.

The Trust-involved Access Control (TAC) model (Wang & Sun, 2010) takes a further step into modeling more complex and fine-grained policies. TAC employs a *trust-involved* and purpose-based model for privacy preservation in OSNs. A purpose defines the reason for accessing a data object (Ni et al., 2010). TAC defines intended purposes P_i over objects to regulate access. Intended purposes include prohibited intended purposes *PIP* and allowed intended purposes *AIP*. The model defines a hierarchy of purposes with generalization and specialization operations and with precedence of *PIP* over *AIP* for conflict resolution. To access an object, an access purpose P_a should specify the access purposes. The purpose P_a is matched against allowed intended purposes P_{ai} of the same object to check whether *AIP* and *PIP* logically implies P_a.

In contrast to Ali, Villegas, and Maheswaran's (2007) model, this model considers both direct and indirect relationships. Access control policies are composed of trust criteria as well as relationship property criteria, which makes the model more protective if trust is not accurately or easily quantified. A policy is defined as a tuple:

$$\left(D, S, R, P, D_{\max}, T_{\min}, 0\right)$$

where D is a data object, S is a subject or a group of subjects requesting access, R is the relationship type between the requestor and the owner, D_{max} is the maximum distance of the relationship path, T_{min} is the minimum trust required, and O is a set of obligations the accessor needs to comply to upon access. For example, the rule "X allows her friends with minimal T trust to access her object O for P purpose, where an accessor is obliged to notify the owner by email" is formulated as:

$$\left(O, X, Friends, P, 1, T, Notify\left(Email\right)\right)$$

Based on the notion of purpose introduced, policies are either negative or positive. Positive policies implicitly authorize the requested permissions and all their subclass permissions in the defined hierarchy. The model can be also classified as relationship-based model as it depends on the relationship type and path length of the relationship as well as other features. This model conforms to Requirements 1 and 2.

The drawback of trust-based models is usability, if users are required to provide input that contributes to trust assessment, such as defining the trust level of objects and zones of access as well as the trust thresholds. Trust-assessment could be problematic in cases where a new user joins and there is no past experience of OSN interaction with this user to assess the trust level.

Next, we discuss other OSN-specific access control models based on other OSN-related features.

Access Control Models in Semantic-Based OSNs

The inclusion of semantic web technologies into frameworks and applications has enhanced data sharing and usage. The semantic web lends itself to OSNs by supporting the fundamental functionality of exchanging and sharing data across the network of users (W3C, 2009b). For instance, tagging systems are employed in MySpace (Feigenbaum, Herman, Hongsermeier, Neumann, & Stephens, 2007). Resource Description Framework (RDF) and Web Ontology Language (OWL) have been employed to represent personal information of users in OSNs since the early work on Friend of a Friend (FOAF) (Brickley & Miller, 2007). FOAF describes the relationships of users in RDF annotations as an effort to contextualize the semantic web in social networks. Another example of semantic web extensions in social networks is the "Like" button of Facebook that links data from the web to Facebook using the Open Graph Protocol.

In relation to access control, semantic web technologies enable a standardized and dynamic means to control and track objects an OSN. Using ontology basic representation in OSNs facilitates the composition of a more fine-grained access control policies (Carminati, Ferrari, & Perego, 2006b). On the structural level, ontology-based models emerged to exploit rule-based policies to protect the semantic-rich data.

Kruk, Grzonkowski, Gzella, Woroniecki, and Choi (2006) present a Distributed FOAF Realm of the previous FOAF Realm work on Kruk (2004). D-FOAF is distributed identity management system for OSN that uses structure-based access rights and delegations based on the FOAF notion. The specificity of the system structure they model (W3C information management system as a case study) is that users do not own objects; rather they have access to certain objects and they can extend the accessibility to these objects by delegating it to others. The model is based on friendship relations of users who belong to different/distributed sub-communities. The proposed structure saves information about the relationship between two nodes without further details about type, context or any other relationship feature. This structure of the social network saves access rights in an ACL attached to a resource, which is referred to as the Social Networked Access Control List. This list also defines access rights delegation using two criteria values, namely, a maximal distance from the user in the networks' graph d_{max} and a minimal friendship level metric $flm\_context_{min}$, which reflects the strength of the relationship. By exploiting these two criteria, the model employs a rudimentary version of trust-based access control. In contrast to other models such as Wang and Sun (2010)'s model, this one does not cover aggregation of policies and how to resolve conflicts of delegations. However, this model conforms to Requirements 1 and 2.

Carminati, Ferrari, Heatherly, Kantarcioglu, and Thuraisingham (2009) address privacy issues of OSNs by proposing an enhanced and extensible ACM that exploits OWL to represent the social network in a knowledge base (SNKB). Analogously to Carminati, Ferrari, and Perego's (2006b), relationships are represented as ontology classes compliantly with W3C specification (W3C, 2009a), which enables n-ary relationships. A relationship here denotes a relation between two users as well as a relation between a user and an object, e.g., *ownership* or *tagged in* relationships. The two relationship types support the definition of more fine-grained policies in comparison with only user-user or user-object relationship types seen in RBACs and other models. Similarly to RBAC models previously discussed, objects, relationships and permissions are depicted in hierarchies, which facilitates the propagation of permissions within the hierarchies.

The model comprises three types of policies:

- **Access Control Policies:** Negative and positive relationship-based policies that define conditions over the type, depth and trust value of a relationship to authorize/deny access.
- **Filtering Policies:** Define conditions to refine user's access to objects or requests to a user's objects.
- **Admin Policies:** Allow the system administrator to specify users or define conditions over users that can define access control and filtering policies.

A Security Authorization Knowledge Base (SAKB) encodes the three types of permissions for the three types of policies, namely access control authorizations, prohibitions and admin authorizations. All are organized by means of ontologies. For policy enforcement, Semantic Web Rule Language (SWRL) first transforms a policy into a rule to be queried by the central authorization enforcement entity against the SAKB. Finally, this model conforms to Requirements 1 and 2.

Ontology modeling of OSNs and ACMs facilitates rich and dynamic representations and flexible control over objects. However, as it is the case in ACMs, there are still specific access control problems that are not addressed. Multiple ownership protection is an important problem that rises in OSNs, yet few of those models address that issue. We will review later in the chapter a model that employs semantic web technologies to extend ontology-based models and addresses this problem.

Relationship-Based Access Control Models

A relationship-based access control model does not base authorization on users' identities. Instead, it only consults the social graph's topological structure to extract relationship-related information between an accessor and an owner of an object to authorize an access request.

Fong (2011) formalizes a general-purpose relationship-based access control model (ReBAC), capturing binary relationships such as Parent-Child. The relationship representation captures direct and indirect relationships, corresponding to requirements stated in Carminati, Ferrari, and Perego (2006b). A relationship *X-Y* is cast as roles of the users involved in it. The work's novelty is in capturing the context-dependency of relationships. This is a contribution to the extent that relationships are separated by organizing contexts into a hierarchical structure, where no two relationships in different contexts can be activated simultaneously. Sharing objects over different contexts is based on this hierarchy structure.

The authors interpret ReBAC as a generalization of RBAC where relationships are represented by roles bound in sessions just as relationships are bound in contexts (Fong, 2011). The context hierarchy is analogous to separation of duties mechanisms in RBAC (Chen & Sandhu, 1995).

The model depicts the OSN as "a collection of assertions of relationships between individuals in a given population" (Fong, 2011, p. 1). The social network system is a formalized relational structure in a social graph:

$$G = \left\langle V, \left\{R_i\right\}_{i \in I} \right\rangle$$

where V is the set of users in the network, I is the set of relationships identifiers, and each R_i is a binary relationship between two users.

A *resource* is one or more objects. An access control policy is modeled as a predicate to exclusively capture the relational information between the owner and the accessor:

$$U \times U \times G\left(U, J\right) \rightarrow \left\{0,1\right\}$$

where U is an owner or an accessor, and *G(U,J)* is the social network, which is a graph of users and relationship identifiers. The predicate takes an owner, an accessor and a social network as parameters and will either authorize or decline the request. The model uses vocabularies defined either by the system and/or the users, such as public, friend-of-friend.

ReBAC exploits modal logic formula to express relationship structure between requestors and owners:

$$\varphi, \Psi ::= \mathrm{T} \mid \mathrm{a} \mid \neg\varphi \mid \varphi \wedge \Psi \mid \langle \mathrm{i} \rangle \varphi \mid \langle -\mathrm{i} \rangle \varphi$$

For example an owner a can grant access to *friends or parents* using the formula (Fong, 2011):

$$\langle \text{friend} \rangle \mathrm{a} \vee \langle \text{parent} \rangle \mathrm{a}$$

This way of composing policies enables the expression of the strength of a relationship required to gain access to an object, for example <friend><best_friend>a (Fong, 2011). It also employs composite relations to express trust delegation (Weeks, 2001; Li, Mitchell, & Winsborough, 2002), for example granting access to friends-of-friends implicitly delegates authority to friends and their friends.

ReBAC is a formalized as a protection system captured as a tuple:

$$\langle J, U, R, C, c_o, policy, owner \rangle$$

where J is a set of relation identifiers, U is a set of users, R is a set of protected resources, C is a set of relationships contexts, c_o the root context in the context hierarchy, *policy* is a function mapping a policy to resource, *owner* is a function that maps a resource to an owner. The access control protection system evolves based on changes in the context hierarchy by means of *state transitions* that are discussed in (Fong, 2011).

A *protection state* is an instantiation of the protection system tuple for request parameters: owner, requestor, active context relationship and social network. The requestor-owner relationship inherits relationships from ancestor contexts. The authorization decision depends on consulting the protection state of a request. The model conforms to requirement 1, but it does not incorporate fine-granular policy definition.

A more recent work by Fong and Siahaan (2011) investigates the representational completeness of relational policies in ReBAC. The investigation reveals that there were policies that could not be defined using ReBAC. To address the incompleteness, this work introduces non-idempotent conjunction and vertex identification mechanisms to avoid cycles in the graph. The extended language can express a family of ReBAC policies that are proven to be representationally complete (Fong & Siahaan, 2011). The extended ReBAC model is proven to be complete in binary relationship systems. This would be a potential limitation for applying ReBAC in OSNs where relationships might be of multiple arity, as we will discuss in the next section. To address multiple ownership in ReBAC, the model has to extend the policy predicates to resolve different relationship contexts between a requestor and the multiple owners.

N-Owned Object Protection/ Relational Data Protection

An *n*-owned object is an object that is owned by and linked to more than one user. Relational data is the data about and generated by an existing relationship between two users, and therefore is owned by the two users. *N*-owned data protection is a fundamental aspect of multi-user systems such as OSNs (Hu, Gail-Joon, & Jan, 2012). In these systems, sharing in not only uni- or bi-directional, it is mostly n-ary directional, causing ownership to become of n-ary as well. A photo owner can share a photo in her OSN with n-users tagged in it, thereby expanding the unary ownership to be n-ary ownership. The original owner should not control such *n*-owned object without involving the other n owners in access control decisions (Squicciarini, Shehab, & Wede, 2010).

Almost all models reviewed earlier in this chapter do not address this issue. A challenge is how to aggregate the owners' preferences and compose their policies defined over one object. Bonatti, De Capitani Di Vimercati, and Samarati (2002) employ algebra for security policies composition. The algebra implementation is based on translating policies of multiple owners to equivalent logic.

In relationship-based models, the policy composition mechanism of n-owners policies has to preserve the original owners' relationship-based constraints. A policy is monotonic if access is never denied upon adding an edge to the social graph and is never granted upon deletion of an edge. On the other hand, anti-monotonic policies do not allow access if the social graph structure is changed. The policy combinators introduced in Anwar & Fong (2010) combine primitive policies to represent complex policies, while preserving monotonic and anti-monotonic policies. More policy composing mechanisms are surveyed in De Capitani Di Vimercati, Foresti, Jajodia, & Samarati (2007).

Another challenge is how to detect the existence of relational data and that an object is *n*-owned. Masoumzadeh and Joshi (2010) employ semantic web technologies and the richness of ontology-based models to define a flexible and fine-grained model to address this challenge. The proposed Ontology-Based Access Control Model for Social Networking Systems (OSNAC) extends many notions of the previously discussed model of Carminati, Ferrari, Heatherly, Kantarcioglu, and Thuraisingham (2009). The main contributions of OSNAC are, the formalization of multiple authorities in OSNs, and, the enforcement mechanism of combined policies of multiple owners. The model extends the OSN knowledge base using a sublanguage of OWL to represent rich RDF graphs representation. The access control policies are queried on the knowledge base via SWRL. The model defines the concept of type "*Annotation*" to represent a relation between more objects; e.g., a comment annotates an object with a note or a tag annotates a photo with a person.

The model defines an Access Control Ontology (ACO) to represent user-object relations as *reified* properties, permissions, and permission authorizations to specific users.

The model formalizes policies for administrators and uses authorizations. These can be either basic or advanced. A basic policy rule defines access authorizations granted by a user or the system to a requestor. Advanced policies define various types of delegation rules based on complex composition of authorizations. This is extended in a formalization of *dependent authorizations*, where an authorization can be inferred based on another authorization. The main core contribution of this model is the *multiple-authority specification* that enables disjunctive or conjunctive forms of multi-authority to authorize permissions for *n*-owned objects.

An access request is a tuple *<s,rsc,p>*, where *s* is the requesting subject, *rsc* is an instance of a reified property to be accessed, and *p* is the requested permission. A request is authorized if there exists an instance of permission *p* in the access control ontology for *s* on *rsc*. Negative policies are not explicitly captured in the model, however, the closed-world assumption here guarantees that if an authorization cannot be inferred by a defined rule then the negation cannot be inferred either. This assumption constrains unintended authorization from being granted; consequently users are not required to explicitly define prohibited permissions. This model conforms to Requirements 1 and 2.

Next we discuss another type of access control model that follows a different approach in addressing some of the issues discussed before.

Voting-Based Models

Users vary in their privacy preferences. When defining access control policies over n-owned objects it is a challenging task to satisfy all owners' preferences. A. C. Squicciarini, Shehab, and Wede (2010) state that this process should be fair to all owners of an object. Their proposed model is focused on how to reflect co-owners policy specifications onto one policy that maximizes the satisfaction of co-owners privacy preferences. In other word, this model focuses on the conjunctive multi-authority introduced in OSNAC. This work is based on the Clark-Tax voting protocol (Clarke, 1971) as it provides a simple mechanism that does not allow users to manipulate their voting. This mechanism aggregates owners' access control policies and promotes truthfulness of users. In this mechanism, an ownership right is granted based on an assessment of the user's truthfulness. To make the process less burdensome, the mechanism learns about the users' privacy preferences in order to estimate preferences of new objects. If the new object is not similar to any existing object then the mechanism cannot predict the privacy preferences.

Aggregation of policies is modeled as a Nash equilibrium problem (Mas-Colell, Whinston, & Green, 1995) wherein users are rewarded with incentives for truthfulness based on the VCG payment model (Groves, 1973). The incentive-based system simply rewards a user i proportionally to the number of n-owned object with n-co-owners:

$$c = m_i + \left(\beta \times m_i\right) \times n$$

where m_i is the credit value assigned to i, $\beta \times m_i$ is the credit assigned to users who accept co-ownership, with $\beta \in [0,1]$. Each co-owner quantifies the benefit value she gets from sharing an object and associates it to her privacy preference g. A collective function outputs the value that maximizes the social values of co-owners:

$$g^* = \arg\max \Sigma_{i=1}^{n} v_i \left(g\right)$$

where $v_i(g)$ is the benefit value a user i gets.

The mechanism can be applied on different types of policies where attributes are based on the social graph, such as distance-based, geographical locations or common user groups (Squicciarini, Shehab, & Wede, 2010). This model does not conform with ACMs requirements because it addresses a specific problem; but it can be integrated with other models.

Web Traveler

Although ACMs enable owners to control access to their objects, this control is limited to the user's own space in the OSN. The lack of proper accountability and audit tools enable users to re-share an object and unlawfully gain ownership, thereby depriving the original owner from access control. The difference with the previously discussed n-owned object problem is that the set of owners of one object keeps on expanding over time. As a result, the previously discussed models are unable to directly address this problem.

Rodriguez, Rodriguez, Carreras, and Delgado (2009) address this issue by using Digital Rights Management in OSNs. In their work, users can control access to data by defining flexible conditions in a Right Expression License. Authorizations are granted based on decentralized verification of the license the requestor owns against the requested permissions.

Squicciarini and Sundareswaran (2009) propose Web Traveler, a model to preserve the owners original access control policies over any access to her objects within the OSN, thereby conforming to Requirement 4. In their model they focus on photos, which are shared in vast amounts in OSNs; 3 billion photos are uploaded on Facebook each month (Facebook Stat Page, 2011). Web Traveler is an image-centric ACM where policies are always linked to images defining who can access, download and upload them. The policy language XACML-like rules (Oasis Committee. XACML 2.0 Specification, 2012), defines five actions/permission over images, view, upload, download, tag, and comment, organized into a hierarchy. Policies are relationship and attribute-based, and can only be defined for an added image if the image does not exist in the system before (Chang, Li, Wang, Mork, & Wiederhold, 1999). If the new image already exists in the system, then the original owner's policies are enforced.

The model utilizes positive and negative policies to limit granted authorizations, and it also prohibits delegation of authority unless the user explicitly allows it. Moreover, the model can be generalized over different data types, given appropriate matching mechanisms. Consequently, the model provides a strict privacy protection of users and their data through all out the OSN.

DISTRIBUTED ACCESS CONTROL FOR OSNS

In centralized OSNs, a central authority is responsible for providing the functionality of managing users' data and enforcing access control. In a decentralized or distributed OSN system, trust in a central authority is not required; rather data management and access control enforcement are distributed and carried out by users themselves, or by parties they trust. Distributed access control enables users to manage their local social networks themselves, and is therefore considered to offer more privacy protection for users.

Ahmad and Whitworth (2011) summarize the social and technical requirements of access control:

- Protect ownership of data.
- Discretionary roles by users.
- Objects classification by users.
- Delegation of access rights.

The authors argue that distributed access control will satisfy these requirements and they develop a mathematical model accordingly.

We add to these requirements that a model should properly represent the social graph information within the decentralized OSN structure. The previously discussed models: Carminati, Ferrari, and Perego's (2006b) model, Tang, Mao, Lai, and Zhu's (2009) model, Baden, Bender, Spring, Bhattacharjee, and Starin's (2009) model, Jahid, Mittal, and Borisov's (2011) model, Kruk, Grzonkowski, Gzella, Woroniecki, and Choi's (2006) model are all applicable in decentralized OSNs as we have noted earlier.

ACCESS CONTROL MODELS FOR EXISTING OSNS

Next, we will overview formalized models of some of the current OSNs to understand the underlying mechanisms behind their access control models and how they can be extended to address related access control and privacy concerns issues.

Facebook-Style Access Control Model

Facebook (Facebook, 2011) is the most widespread OSN in the world and has the largest number of registered users (Facebook Stat Page, 2011). Many researchers have been studying different aspects of this OSN and analyzing its privacy issues and threats (Gross & Acquisti, 2005; Cain, Scott, & Akers, 2009).

In order to better understand the privacy policies and points where refinement is needed, it is essential to refer to the formalization of Facebook access control model by Anwar and Fong (2010). The model formalizes the specific two-phase capability-based (Miller, Yee, & Shapiro, 2011; Dennis & Van Horn, 1966) authorization process in Facebook. To access a specific user's profile or one of her objects, the first phase involves having the capability to access or reach a *search listing* of this user. Facebook provides two means to access a search listing by global name search or by traversing the social graph. Once the search listing is reached and the user's node in the graph is located, the second phase involves the actual access request to this user's profile or object. The second authorization phase is based on consulting access policies. This model formalizes the communication history and relationship topology for authorization decisions. Communication history is captured by means of a *communication automaton*:

$$M = \langle \Sigma, \Gamma, \gamma_0, \delta \rangle$$

where Σ is a finite set of possible communication primitives defined in Facebook, e.g., initiate relationship or accept a relationship, Γ is a finite set of communication states, $\gamma_0 \in \Gamma$ is an initial state, and δ is the transition function, which given a communication state, maps the current system state into a next state. An *adjacency predicate* translates a communication state between two users into an acquaintance relationship. The model defines the *global communication state* as the mapping of each pair of users to their current communication state. The two-phase authorizations are queried against the system's global communication state and the list of policies defined. An authorization decision is based on the social graph and the communication state between an owner and a requestor. The model formalizes four types of policies a user *u* can define:

- Search policies, which define who is authorized to produce a search listing of *u*.
- Traversal policies, which define who is authorized to traverse links of *u*.
- Communication policies, which define who is authorized to communicate via the system defined primitives with *u*.
- Access policies, which define who is authorized to access objects.

Anwar and Fong (2010) state that the model instantiated for Facebook does not capture some aspects of Facebook, such as groups and networks, poking and messaging communication, and the open-world assumption. Rather, the authors instantiate their model to support more policies than the Facebook model does, such as celebrity, clique, stranger, bad company and trusted referral (Anwar & Fong, 2010). However, the *n*-owned object problem is not covered by the extended family of access control model proposed in this work.

Google+ Access Control Model

Google+ (The Google+ Project, 2011) is a more recent OSN. The most prominent feature of Google+ is the notion of circles, which are used by users to define groups of their friends and assign access control policies accordingly. A circle is a set of friends and an extended circle denotes all the members of a user's circles and all the members in their circles, which is analogous to the notion of FOAF. The utilization of circles in Google+, as well as friend lists in Facebook, adds the possibility to specifically select the desired audience allowed to access a specific object. Studies showed that users' mental models about their privacy involve subgroups and communities of their friends (Alessandra, Kristen, & Eytan, Last Updated April 2011.). Correspondingly, circles assist users in comprehending the targeted audience of a disclosed object and to then take an informed decision about the target disclosure audience.

Hu, Gail-Joon, and Jan (2012) formalized a model based on Google+ notion of circles and extended it to address the *n*-owned object or multiparty ownership. In the Circle-based Multiparty Access Control (CMAC) friends can be assigned a certain trust level and then grouped into circles. The model classifies owners in four types of controllers:

- **Owner:** A user who posted an object in her space.
- **Contributor:** A user who posted an object in someone else's space.
- **Stakeholder:** A user who shares partial ownership in an object of another owner or contributor, e.g., a user tagged in a photo.
- **Disseminator:** A user who discloses data not owned by herself.

A positive or negative policy is a tuple:

<O, OT, A, D, E>

where *O* is an owner or a controller of an object, *OT* is the controller type, *A* is set of targeted audience defined in terms of circle/extended circles or everyone, *D* is a data object to be accessed, *E* effect of enforcing the policy by either denying or permitting access. In the model, a permitted access might cause more privacy violations than a denied access. Furthermore, conflicting policies are resolved based on the higher precedence of denied access over permitted access.

Similarly to the voting-based model (Squicciarini, Shehab, & Wede, 2010), CMAC enables owners to express their preferences and then implement a preferences balancing mechanism. Whereas in the model of Squicciarini, Shehab, and Wede, (2010) the objective is to reward users who share, CMAC facilitates the expression of willingness to disclose. The conflict resolution mechanism estimates a *Privacy Risk* counter-proportionally to:

- The trust level of a requestor t_r.
- The number of controllers allowing an access.
- The privacy concerns of controllers estimated from the default privacy setting pc_o.
- The sensitivity of a denied-access-to object s_o.

The privacy risk of a requestor *r*:

$$Pr(r) = (1 - t_r) \times \sum_{o \in controllers_d} pc_o \times s_o$$

To balance disclosing intentions of all controllers, the model utilizes a *sharing loss* estimation function using the same four factors utilized for estimating privacy risk from the controllers who permit an access request:

$$Sl(r) = t_r \times \sum_{o \in controllers_a} (1 - pc_o) \times (1 - s_o)$$

Authorization is a decision based on a trade off (Brickell & Shmatikov, 2008; Li & Li, 2009) between *Sl(r)* and *Pr(r)*:

$$AD = \begin{cases} Permit : \alpha Sl(r) \geq \beta Pr(r) \\ Deny : \alpha Sl(r) < \beta Pr(r) \end{cases}$$

where $0 \leq \alpha, \beta \leq 1$ are preference of privacy risk and sharing loss, such that $\alpha + \beta = 1$.

Given all the *n*-owned models discussed earlier, the contribution of this model lies in its empowering owners to express their disclosure intentions flexibly based on different factors including the history of their privacy preferences. On the other hand, it does not propose a representation of the *n*-owned relational data, in contrast with the work of Masoumzadeh and Joshi (2010). Moreover, defining sensitivity of objects might cause problems if an owner is not aware of how other owners model their sensitivity scale.

OPEN PROBLEMS AND FUTURE RESEARCH DIRECTIONS

OSNs are dynamically changing environments with various types of interactions and relationships. The continuous change and evolution makes it look as if any access control model will be insufficient due to the rapid changes in those environments. Context-dependency is a fundamental aspect of the specific nature of interactions in OSNs. Users tend to rely on contexts of data objects to base their disclosure decisions (Majeski, Johnson, & Bellovin, 2011). Amongst all changing aspects of OSNs, context-dependency contributes to making access control models more dynamic and adaptive given the evolution of contexts in the OSNs. Context-dependent access control models (Covington et al., 2001) are not strongly employed in the literature. In many models though, context-dependency is exploited to varying degrees. In the gravity-based model contexts represent trust spaces (Maheswaran, Tang, & Ghunaim, 2007). While in Ali, Villegas, and Maheswaran (2007)'s model, history of access is context-dependent and plays a role in authorization decisions. In the relationship-based ACM of Fong (2011) relationships are context-dependent. Despite the richness of employing such context-dependent aspects, none of those models formalize context-dependency in all relevant aspects of the ACM. In general, type of users, relationships, history of access, objects, permissions and communication are all aspects that can be context-dependent, which when employed in ACMs would yield a more natural depiction of how users actually think of their social spaces (Majeski, Johnson, & Bellovin, 2011).

Protecting contexts that dynamically change in OSNs is a further complicated issue. Access control models offer protection by means of policies defined with no possibility to dynamically adapt the policies to the changes in the OSN. One work that proposes a privacy-preserving approach through guarding access policies over time is the evolving access control model proposed by Crescenzo and Lipton, (2009). The model implements an extra layer in the ACM to guard privacy settings of users over time. The objective is to maximize the ability to share objects between users while preserving their privacy. An automatic manipulation module manages the visibility settings of objects and maintains the privacy of a user. A data object is not considered to be sensitive on its own, rather an aggregation of user's objects can become at a specific point in time of a sensitive nature depending on changes in relationships, contexts of interaction in the OSN, etc. The model protects sensitive objects and the users' privacy by protecting at least one of the sensitive subset objects by setting it to *private*, thereby mitigating possible privacy violations. The contribution of automatic guarding and changing of policies is novel and promises assistance for users in maintaining a certain level of privacy. For a better employment of this approach, users should be able to specify object's sensitivity criteria in a context-dependent manner. For instance a group of objects is sensitive when disclosed to *friends from work* might be different from the group of objects that are sensitive to be disclosed to *close friends*.

Finally, across the wide spectrum of access control models we can still find gaps in matching users' expectations and requirements for online interaction protection. One of the main issues of why access control models fail is the existence of both offline and online social networks, both of which users rely on to construct their relationships. In specific cases online relationships can complement offline interaction needs. Through facilitating easy communication, online relationships involve more data disclosure when offline social network contact is missing (Dwyer, Hiltz, & Passerini, 2007). Detecting the offline-online SN dependence pattern would enhance users' experience in OSNs and access control privacy protection.

Next, we summarize the requirements we elicited from the review of access control models literature to provide guidelines for future research.

Requirements of Access Control Models for OSNs

Through our review we have discussed open issues that need to be addressed in future work of ACMs. For this reason we propose specific requirements to address those issues of access control models.

We first propose requirements to address general aspects of access control to enhance the overall functionality and efficiency:

A model should formalize policies, type of users, relationships, history of access, objects, permissions and communication in a context-dependent manner to enable dynamic adaptation of access control policies when contexts change.

A model should facilitate potential accessor visibility. When a user composes a policy and verifies it against the possible accessors, this contributes to addressing any inconsistency between whom users think will be accessing their objects and the actual accessors. Such functionality will enable users to make informed decisions about the policies they make.

A model should be able to learn about users' privacy preferences and adapt the defined policies over time according to the learned preferences.

A model should be able to suggest appropriate policies (Majeski, Johnson, & Bellovin, 2011) for new objects or users added to a user's social space to reduce complexity of composing policies for each update in the OSN.

A model should facilitate different fine granularity levels of policy definitions. A user should be able to define policies based on specific sets of features.

A model should be able to maintain the same permissions for the policy targeted-users over time. Normally, a user defines a policy with an intention to allow/prohibit access of a specific set of users, on which the policy criterion applies. This user might require that the policy will always allow/prohibit access to the same set of uses over time. Given the changes in the OSN, e.g., relationships, a user who was at a certain point in time prohibited to access some data might gain access. This might happen without the knowledge of the data owner and hence violates his privacy because the user expects that all users who can/cannot access will always have the same permissions. By definition of access control enforcement, a policy criterion will always be consulted to honor or deny a request without any static allocation that is allowed or not allowed to access. This requirement conflicts with the concept of *dynamic* access control enforcement, yet it has to be possible for a user to opt in for such access control enforcement.

A model should enable control over third party application permissions. In OSNs, users exchange data and communicate over the network. This functionality is not existent with third party applications. Thus permissions of OSN users should be different from permissions of third party applications.

A model should adapt to offline-online social networks dependencies.

Hereafter, we propose requirement to address specific issues of ACMs. Based on the type of the OSN, an access control model should satisfy some or all of the following requirements:

Trust based access control models should assess trust precisely without burdening the user with input that has to be provided for this assessment. In some models users are required to assign trust values for their objects and for friends or other users. While this is an important aspect to capture the user's mental model about trust values of her objects and friends, the model should incorporate as much information as possible from the OSN and the interactions between users to assess trust from. Moreover, the model should provide a normalization approach for the trust values of different users.

A model should enhance control over delegation of authority. Many models utilize the notion of delegation through composite relations (Blaze, Feigenbaum, & Lacy, 1996; Clarke et al., 2002; Li, Grosof, & Feigenbaum, 2003). The downside is that such models do not incorporate fine-grained control to constrain this delegation. For instance, it should be possible to limit how far the delegation of friends-of-friends in the OSN can be propagated. We propose one solution for this challenge by using certificates of delegation proposed in the work of Abadi, Burrows, Lampson, and Plotkin (1993). A certificate proves an authorization of the holder and indicates constraints about how this delegation can be further extended.

A model should define negative and positive policies or else explicitly assume a closed-world model (Samarati & Vimercati, 2001). This is required to guarantee that unintended authorizations are never granted.

A model should properly represent and protect *n*-owned objects.

A model should represent any hierarchies of objects, relationships or permissions to the user. This is required to enable the user to comprehend the consequences of propagated permissions from a higher level to a lower level in the hierarchy. This is essential to mitigate implicit permission casting that a user is not aware of, causing privacy vulnerabilities.

A model should offer specific control over location-based information. In Facebook for instance, location information is added as complementary data to an object. We state that a user should be able to protect this data separately from the object it is attached to.

CONCLUSION

In this chapter we have reviewed the fundamental aspects of access control and the basic essential classical ACMs. We have discussed privacy problems in OSNs and the ACMs requirements to address these problems. We have surveyed the most prominent ACMS and highlighted the main contribution of each model. Throughout the review of ACMs, we indicated the aspects that could be extended. The discussion included models in centralized and decentralized OSNs. Finally, we proposed requirements to address the open problems in current ACMs in order to facilitate fine-grained access control and better privacy preservation in OSNs.

ACKNOWLEDGMENT

The research leading to these results has received funding from the IWT in the context of the SBO project on Security and Privacy for Online Social Networks (SPION).

REFERENCES

Abadi, M., Burrows, M., Lampson, B., & Plotkin, G. (1993). A calculus for access control in distributed systems. *ACM Transactions on Programming Languages and Systems*, *15*(4), 706–734. doi:10.1145/155183.155225

Abiteboul, S., Agrawal, R., Bernstein, P., Carey, M., Ceri, S., & Croft, B. (2005, May). The Lowell database research self-assessment. *Communications of the ACM*, *48*(5), 111–118. doi:10.1145/1060710.1060718

Acquisti, A., Carrara, E., Stutzman, F., Callas, J., Schimmer, K., & Nadjm, M. (2007). *Security issues and recommendations for online social networks*. ENISA.

Acquisti, A., & Grossklags, J. (2005). Privacy and rationality in individual decision-making. *IEEE Security and Privacy*, *3*(1), 26–33. doi:10.1109/MSP.2005.22

Ahmad, A., & Whitworth, B. (2011). *Distributed access control for social networks. Information Assurance and Security (IAS)* (pp. 68–73). IEEE.

Alessandra, M., Kristen, L., & Eytan, A. (Last Updated April 2011.). The PVIZ comprehension tool for social network privacy settings. *UM Tech Report* #CSE-TR-570-11.

Ali, B., Villegas, W., & Maheswaran, M. (2007). A trust based approach for protecting user data in social networks. *In Proceedings of the 2007 conference of the center for advanced studies on collaborative research* (pp. 288–293). New York, NY, USA: ACM.

Anwar, M., & Fong, P. W. L. (2010). *An access control model for Facebook-style social network systems* (Tech. Rep. No. 2010-959-08). Department of Computer Science, University of Calgary, Calgary, Alberta, Canada.

Aringhieri, R., Damiani, E., Di Vimercati, S. D. C., Paraboschi, S., & Samarati, P. (2006, February). Fuzzy techniques for trust and reputation management in anonymous peer-to-peer systems: Special topic section on soft approaches to information retrieval and information access on the web. *Journal of the American Society for Information Science and Technology*, *57*(4), 528–537. doi:10.1002/asi.20307

Ashley, P. (2003). Enterprise privacy authorization language (EPAL 1.1). *W3C Working Group*. Retrieved March, 2012, from http://www.zurich.ibm.com/security/enterprise-privacy/epal/Specification/

Australian broadcasting corporation (ABC). (2007, 29 October). ABC media watch, filleting facebook. Retrieved March, 2012, from http://www.abc.net.au/mediawatch/transcripts/s2074079.htm

Baader, F., Calvanese, D., McGuinness, D., Nardi, D., & Patel-Schneider, P. (2003). *The description logic handbook: Theory, implementation and applications*. Cambridge University Press.

Baden, R., Bender, A., Spring, N., Bhattacharjee, B., & Starin, D. (2009). Persona: An online social network with user-defined privacy. *In Proceedings of the ACM SIGCOMM 2009 conference on data communication* (pp. 135–146). New York, NY, USA, ACM.

Baracaldo, N., López, C., Anwar, M., & Lewis, M. (2011). Simulating the effect of privacy concerns in online social networks (pp. 519-524). *Information Reuse and Integration (IRI)*, IEEE International Conference.

Bauer, L., Ligatti, J., & Walker, D. (2005, June). Composing security policies with Polymer. *SIGPLAN Notices*, *40*, 305–314. doi:10.1145/1064978.1065047

Bedi, R., Wadhai, V.M., Sugandhi, R., & Mirajkar, A.(2005). Watermarking social networking relational data using non-numeric attribute. *International Journal of Computer Science 9*.

Bell, D. E., & LaPadula, L. J. (1973). *Secure computer systems: Volume I – Mathematical foundations, Volume II – A mathematical model, Volume III – A refinement of the mathematical model* (No. MTR-2547).

Benantar, M. (2006). *Access control systems: Security, identity management and trust models* (Benantar, M., Ed.). Springer.

Berendt, B., Gunther, O., & Spiekermann, S. (2005, April). Privacy in e-commerce: Stated preferences vs. actual behavior. *Communications of the ACM*, *48*, 101–106. doi:10.1145/1053291.1053295

Bethencourt, J., Sahai, A., & Waters, B. (2007). Ciphertext-policy attribute-based encryption. In *IEEE symposium on security and privacy* (pp. 321–334). IEEE Computer Society.

Blaze, M., Feigenbaum, J., & Lacy, J. (1996). Decentralized trust management. In *Proceedings of the 1996 IEEE symposium on security and privacy* (pp. 164–173). Washington, DC, USA: IEEE Computer Society.

Bonatti, P., De Capitani Di Vimercati, S., & Samarati, P. (2002). An algebra for composing access control policies. *ACM Transactions on Information and System Security*, *5*(1), 1–35. doi:10.1145/504909.504910

Brickell, J., & Shmatikov, V. (2008). The cost of privacy: Destruction of data-mining utility in anonymized data publishing. In Li, Y., Liu, B., & Sarawagi, S. (Eds.), *KDD* (pp. 70–78). ACM. doi:10.1145/1401890.1401904

Brickley, D., & Miller, L. (2007). FOAF Vocabulary Specification 0.91. Retrieved March, 2012, from http://xmlns.com/foaf/spec/20071002.html (Computer software manual No. November).

Brickley, D., & Miller, L. (2010, January). FOAF Vocabulary Specification 0.97 (Namespace document). Retrieved March, 2012, from http://xmlns.com/foaf/spec/20100101.html

Cain, J., Scott, D. R., & Akers, P. (2009, October). Pharmacy students' Facebook activity and opinions regarding accountability and e-professionalism. *American Journal of Pharmaceutical Education, 73*(6), 104. doi:10.5688/aj7306104

Cankaya, H. C. (2011). Access control lists. In van Tilborg, H. C. A., & Jajodia, S. (Eds.), *Encyclopedia of cryptography and security* (2nd ed., pp. 9–12). Springer.

Carminati, B., Ferrari, E., Heatherly, R., Kantarcioglu, M., & Thuraisingham, B. (2009). A semantic web based framework for social network access control. In *Proceedings of the 14th ACM symposium on access control models and technologies* (pp. 177–186). New York, NY, USA: ACM.

Carminati, B., Ferrari, E., & Perego, A. (2006a). The REL-X vocabulary. *OWL Vocabulary*. Retrieved March, 2012, from http://www.dicom.uninsubria.it/andrea.perego/vocs/relx.owl

Carminati, B., Ferrari, E., & Perego, A. (2006b). Rule-based access control for social networks. In *On the Move to Meaningful Internet Systems 2006: OTM Workshops (2)*, (pp. 1734– 1744). Springer.

Castrucci, A., Martinelli, F., Mori, P., & Roperti, F. (2008). Enhancing Java-ME security support with resource usage monitoring. In *Proceedings of the 10th international conference on information and communications security, 5308* (pp. 256–266). Berlin, Germany: Springer-Verlag.

Chang, E., Li, C., Wang, J., Mork, P., & Wiederhold, G. (1999). Searching near-replicas of images via clustering. In *Proc. SPIE symposium of voice, video, and data communications* (pp. 281–292).

Chen, F., & Sandhu, R. (1995). Constraints for RBAC. In *1st ACM workshop on role-based access control* (pp. 39–46). ACM.

Chen, H., & Li, N. (2006). Constraint generation for separation of duty. In *Proceedings of the eleventh ACM symposium on access control models and technologies* (pp. 130–138). New York, NY, USA: ACM.

Chinaei, A. H., Barker, K. & Tompa, K. (2009). Comparison of access control administration models. *Ubiquitous Communication and Computing Journal (UBICC), 4*(3).

Clark, D. D., & Wilson, D. R. (1987). A comparison of commercial and military computer security policies. In *Proc. Symposium on Security and Privacy 1987* (IEEE Press), 184–193.

Clarke, D., Elien, J.-E., Ellison, C., Fredette, M., Morcos, A., & Rivest, R. L. (2002, February). Certificate chain discovery in SPKI/SDSI. *Journal of Computer Security, 9*(4), 285–322.

Clarke, E. H. (1971). Multipart pricing of public goods. *Star, 11*(1), 17–33.

Covington, M. J., Long, W., Srinivasan, S., Dev, A. K., Ahamad, M., & Abowd, G. D. (2001). Securing context-aware applications using environment roles. In *SACMAT '01: Proceedings of the sixth ACM symposium on access control models and technologies* (pp. 10–20). New York, NY, USA: ACM Press.

Crescenzo, G., & Lipton, R. J. (2009). Social network privacy via evolving access control. In *Proceedings of the 4th international conference on wireless algorithms, systems, and applications* (pp. 551–560). Berlin, Germany: Springer-Verlag.

Cutillo, L., Molva, R., & Strufe, T. (2009). Safebook: A privacy-preserving online social network leveraging on real-life trust. *Communications Magazine, IEEE, 47*(12), 94–101. doi:10.1109/MCOM.2009.5350374

De Capitani Di Vimercati, S., Foresti, S., Jajodia, S., & Samarati, P. (2007). Access control policies and languages in open environments. In *Secure Data Management in Decentralized Systems* (pp. 21–58). Springer. doi:10.1007/978-0-387-27696-0_2

Debatin, B., Lovejoy, J. P., Horn, A.-K., & Hughes, B. N. (2009). Facebook and online privacy: Attitudes, behaviors, and unintended consequences. *Journal of Computer-Mediated Communication, 15*(1), 83–108. doi:10.1111/j.1083-6101.2009.01494.x

Dennis, J. B., & Van Horn, E. C. (1966). Programming semantics for multi-programmed computations. *Communications of the ACM, 9*(3), 143–155. doi:10.1145/365230.365252

Didriksen, T. (1997). Rule based database access control: A practical approach. In *Proceedings of the second ACM workshop on role-based access control* (pp. 143–151). New York, NY: ACM.

Donath, J., & Boyd, D. (2004). Public displays of connection. *BT Technology Journal, 22*, 71–82. doi:10.1023/B:BTTJ.0000047585.06264.cc

Dwyer, C., Hiltz, S. R., & Passerini, K. (2007). Trust and privacy concern within social networking sites: A comparison of Facebook and Myspace. In Hoxmeier, J. A., & Hayne, S. (Eds.), *AMCIS* (p. 339). Association for Information Systems.

Erlingsson, U., & Irm, F. B. S. (2000). IRM enforcement of java stack inspection. In *Proceedings of the 2000 IEEE Symposium on Security and Privacy*, 246–255. IEEE.

Facebook. (2011). Website. Retrieved March, 2012, from http://www.facebook.com.

Facebook Stat. Page. (2011). Website. Retrieved March, 2012, from http://www.socialtechnologyreview.com/articles/50-facebook-stats-every-marketer-should-know

Feigenbaum, L., Herman, I., Hongsermeier, T., Neumann, E., & Stephens, S. (2007, December). The semantic web in action. *Scientific American, 297*, 90–97. doi:10.1038/scientificamerican1207-90

Finin, T., Ding, L., Zhou, L., & Joshi, A. (2005). Social networking on the semantic web. *The Learning Organization, 12*(5). doi:10.1108/09696470510611384

Fong, P. W. L. (2011). Relationship-based access control: protection model and policy language. In *Proceedings of the first ACM conference on data and application security and privacy* (pp. 191–202). New York, NY, USA: ACM.

Fong, P. W. L., & Siahaan, I. (2011). Relationship-based access control policies and their policy languages. In *Proceedings of the 16th ACM symposium on access control models and technologies* (pp. 51–60). New York, NY, USA: ACM.

Gates, C. (2007). Access control requirements for Web 2.0 Security and Privacy. *IEEE Web, 2*, 2–4.

Giunchiglia, F., Marchese, M., & Zaihrayeu, I. (2005). *Towards a theory of formal classification (Tech. Rep.)*. University of Trento.

Giunchiglia, F., Zhang, R., & Crispo, B. (2008). RELBAC: Relation based access control. In *Proceedings of the 2008 fourth international conference on semantics, knowledge and grid* (pp. 3–11). Washington, DC, USA: IEEE Computer Society.

Golbeck, J. (2006). Combining provenance with trust in social networks for semantic web content filtering. In *IPAW'06* (p. 101-108). Springer.

Golbeck, J. (2009). *Trust and nuanced profile similarity in online social networks. TWEB, 3(4)*. ACM.

Granovetter, M. S. (1973, January). The strength of weak ties. JSTOR. *American Journal of Sociology*, *78*(6), 1360–1380. doi:10.1086/225469

Gross, R., & Acquisti, A. (2005). Information revelation and privacy in online social networks. In *Proceedings of the 2005 ACM workshop on privacy in the electronic society* (pp. 71–80). New York, NY: ACM.

Groves, T. (1973). Incentives in teams. *Econometrica*, *41*, 617–631. doi:10.2307/1914085

Hafez Ninggal, M. I., & Abawajy, J. (2011). *Attack vector analysis and privacy-preserving social network data publishing. Trust, Security and Privacy in Computing and Communications (TrustCom)* (pp. 847–852). IEEE.

Hamlen, K. W., Morrisett, G., & Schneider, F. B. (2006). Computability classes for enforcement mechanisms. *ACM Transactions on Programming Languages and Systems*, *28*(1), 175–205. doi:10.1145/1111596.1111601

Havlena, W. J., & DeSarbo, W. S. (1991). On the measurement of perceived consumer risk. *Decision Sciences*, *22*(4), 927–939. doi:10.1111/j.1540-5915.1991.tb00372.x

Hogben, G. (2008). *Security issues and recommendations for online social networks (Tech. Rep.)*. European Network and Information Security Agency.

Hu, H., Gail-Joon, A., & Jan, J. (2012). *Enabling collaborative data sharing in Google+ (Tech. Rep.)*. Arizona State University.

Jahid, S., Mittal, P., & Borisov, N. (2011). EASiER: Encryption-based access control in social networks with efficient revocation. In *Proceedings of the 6th ACM symposium on information, computer and communications security* (pp. 411–415). ACM.

Kessler, V. (1992). On the Chinese wall model. In *Proceedings of the second European symposium on research in computer security* (pp. 41–54). London, UK: Springer-Verlag.

Kruk, S. (2004). FOAF-realm-control your friends' access to the resource. *FOAF Workshop proceedings 186*. Retrieved March, 2012, from http://www.w3.org/2001/sw/Europe/events/foaf-galway/papers/fp/foaf realm/.

Kruk, S., Grzonkowski, S., Gzella, A., Woroniecki, T., & Choi, H. (2006). D-FOAF: Distributed identity management with access rights delegation. *The Semantic Web–ASWC 2006*(4), 140–154.

Lampson, B. (1974). Protection. *ACM SIGOPS Operating Systems Review*, *8*(1), 18–24. doi:10.1145/775265.775268

Levien, R. (2009). Attack-resistant trust metrics. In *Computing with social trust* (pp. 121–132). Springer. doi:10.1007/978-1-84800-356-9_5

Leyla, B., Thorsten, S., Davide, B., & Engin, K. (2009, April). All your contacts are belong to us: Automated identity theft attacks on social networks. In *18th international world wide web conference*. ACM.

Li, N., Grosof, B. N., & Feigenbaum, J. (2003, February). Delegation logic: A logic-based approach to distributed authorization. *ACM Transactions on Information and System Security*, *6*(1), 128–171. doi:10.1145/605434.605438

Li, N., Mitchell, J. C., & Winsborough, W. H. (2002). Design of a role-based trust-management framework. In *Proceedings of the 2002 IEEE symposium on security and privacy* (pp. 114–130). Washington, DC, USA: IEEE Computer Society.

Li, T., & Li, N. (2009). On the tradeoff between privacy and utility in data publishing. In Elder, J. F. IV, Fogelman-Soulie, F., Flach, P. A., & Zaki, M. (Eds.), *KDD* (pp. 517–526). ACM. doi:10.1145/1557019.1557079

Ligatti, J., Bauer, L., & Walker, D. (2005). Enforcing non-safety security policies with program monitors. *Computer Security ESORICS*, *3679*, 355–373.

Lipford, H. R., Besmer, A., & Watson, J. (2008). Understanding privacy settings in Facebook with an audience view. In *Proceedings of the 1st conference on usability, psychology, and security* (pp. 2:1–2:8). Berkeley, CA, USA: USENIX Association.

Maheswaran, M., Tang, H. C., & Ghunaim, A. (2007). Towards a gravity- based trust model for social networking systems. In *Proceedings of the 27th international conference on distributed computing systems workshops* (pp. 24–24). Washington, DC, USA: IEEE Computer Society.

Majeski, M., Johnson, M., & Bellovin, S. M. (2011). *The failure of online social network privacy settings* (Tech. Rep. No. CUCS-010-11). Department of Computer Science, Columbia University.

Mas-Colell, A., Whinston, M. D., & Green, J. R. (1995). *Microeconomic theory - chapter 23*. Oxford University Press. Hardcover.

Masoumzadeh, A., & Joshi, J. (2010). OSNAC: An ontology-based access control model for social networking systems. In *Proceedings of the 2010 IEEE second international conference on social computing* (pp. 751–759). Washington, DC, USA: IEEE Computer Society.

Mika, P. (2005). Ontologies are us: A unified model of social networks and semantics. In Gil, Y., Motta, E., Benjamins, V. R., & Musen, M. A. (Eds.), *The Semantic Web - ISWC 2005* (pp. 522–536). Springer. doi:10.1007/11574620_38

Miller, M. S., Yee, K.-P., & Shapiro, J. (2011). *Capability myths demolished* (Tech. Rep.). Systems Research Laboratory, Johns Hopkins University. Retrieved March, 2012, from http://srl.cs.jhu.edu/pubs/SRL2003-02.pdf.

Mont, M. C., Pearson, S., & Bramhall, P. (2003). Towards accountable management of identity and privacy: Sticky policies and enforceable tracing services. *14th International Workshop on Database and Expert Systems Applications (DEXA'03), September 1-5, 2003, Prague, Czech Republic, (pp. 377-382)*. IEEE Computer Society.

Naor, D., Naor, M., & Lotspiech, J. B. (2001). *Revocation and tracing schemes for stateless receivers. Advances in Cryptology—CRYPTO 2001* (pp. 41–62). Springer.

Naor, M., & Pinkas, B. (2001). Efficient trace and revoke schemes. In *Proceedings of the 4th international conference on Financial Cryptography, 9*(6), 1–20. London, UK: Springer-Verlag.

New Myspace and Facebook worms target social networks. (2008). Website. Retrieved March, 2012, from http://www.darknet.org.uk/2008/08/new-myspace-and-facebook-worm-target-social-networks/

Ni, Q., Bertino, E., Lobo, J., Brodie, C., Karat, C.-M., Karat, J. et al. (2010, July). Privacy-aware role-based access control. *ACM Transactions of Information System Security, 13*(3), 24:1–24:31.

Norberg, P. A., Horne, D. R., & Horne, D. A. (2007). The privacy paradox: Personal information disclosure intentions versus behaviors. *The Journal of Consumer Affairs, 41*(1), 100–126. doi:10.1111/j.1745-6606.2006.00070.x

Oasis committee. XACML 2.0 specification. (2012). Website. Retrieved March, 2012, from http://www.oasisopen.org/committees/tchome.php?wgabbrev= xacmlXACML20

Peter, J. P., Tarpey, S., & Lawrence, X. (1975, June). A comparative analysis of three consumer decision strategies. *The Journal of Consumer Research, 2*(1), 29–37. doi:10.1086/208613

Rodriguez, E., Rodriguez, V., Carreras, A., & Delgado, J. (2009). A digital rights management approach to privacy in online social networks. In *Workshop on privacy and protection in web-based social networks (within ICAIL'09), Barcelona, Spain, 2009*. IDT Series, vol. 3, ISSN 2013-5017.

Rosenblum, D. (2007, May-June). What anyone can know: The privacy risks of social networking sites. *Security Privacy, IEEE, 5*(3), 40–49. doi:10.1109/MSP.2007.75

Samarati, P., & Vimercati, S. D. C. D. (2000). Access control: Policies, models, and mechanisms. In R. Focardi & R. Gorrieri (Eds.), *FOSAD* (LNCS Vol. 2171, p. 137-196). Springer.

Samarati, P., & Vimercati, S. D. C. D. (2001). Access control: Policies, models, and mechanisms. In *Revised versions of lectures given during the IFIP WG 1.7 international school on foundations of security analysis and design on foundations of security analysis and design: Tutorial lectures, 2171* (pp. 137–196). London, UK: Springer-Verlag.

Sandhu, R., Bhamidipati, V., & Munawer, Q. (1999). The ARBAC97 model for role-based administration of roles. *ACM Transactions on Information and System Security, 2*(1), 105–135. doi:10.1145/300830.300839

Schaad, A. (2001). Detecting conflicts in a role-based delegation model. *Seventeenth Annual Computer Security Applications Conference*, 117–126. IEEE Comput. Soc.

Shamir, A. (1979, November). How to share a secret. *Communications of the ACM, 22*(11), 612–613. doi:10.1145/359168.359176

Shen, H.-B., & Hong, F. (2006). An attribute-based access control model for web services. In *Proceedings of the seventh international conference on parallel and distributed computing, applications and technologies* (pp. 74–79). Washington, DC, USA: IEEE Computer Society.

Simon, H. A. (1982). Models of bounded rationality. Trustme: Anonymous management of trust relationships in decentralized P2P systems. In N. Shahmehri, R. L. Graham, & G. Caronni (Eds.), *Peer-to-peer computing* (p. 142-149). IEEE Computer Society.

Spiekermann, S., Grossklags, J., & Berendt, B. (2001). E-privacy in 2nd generation E-commerce: Privacy preferences versus actual behavior. *World Wide Web Internet And Web Information Systems*, 38–47.

Squicciarini, A., Trombetta, A., Bhargav-Spantzel, A., & Bertino, E. (2007). K-anonymous attribute-based access control. *E. International Conference on Information and Computer Security (ICICS'07).*

Squicciarini, A. C., Shehab, M., & Wede, J. (2010, June). Privacy policies for shared content in social network sites. *The VLDB Journal, 19*(6), 777–796. doi:10.1007/s00778-010-0193-7

Squicciarini, A. C., & Sundareswaran, S. (2009, December). Web-traveler policies for images on social networks. *World Wide Web (Bussum), 12*, 461–484. doi:10.1007/s11280-009-0070-8

Sweeney, L. (2002, October). K-anonymity: A model for protecting privacy. *International Journal of Uncertainty. Fuzziness and Knowledge-Based Systems, 10*, 557–570. doi:10.1142/S0218488502001648

Tang, Y., Mao, C., Lai, H., & Zhu, J. (2009, December). Role based access control for social network sites. 2009 *Joint Conferences on Pervasive Computing (JCPC)*, 389–394.

Tapiador, A., Carrera, D., & Joaquin, S. (2011). Tie-RBAC: An application of RBAC to social networks. *Web 2.0 security and privacy*. Oakland, California.

The Google+ project. (2011). Website. Retrieved March, 2012, from https://plus.google.com

The state of social media 2011: Social is the new normal. (2012). Website. Retrieved March, 2012, from http://www.briansolis.com/2011/10/ http://www.briansolis.com/2011/10/state-of-social-media-2011/

Thomas, R. K. (1997). Team-based access control (TMAC): A primitive for applying role-based access controls in collaborative environments. In *Second ACM workshop on role-based access control* (pp. 13–19). ACM.

Thomas, R. K., & Sandhu, R. S. (1994). Conceptual foundations for a model of task-based authorizations. In *7th IEEE computer security foundations workshop* (pp. 66–79). IEEE Computer Society Press.

Thomas, R. K., & Sandhu, R. S. (1998). Task-based authorization controls (TBAC): A family of models for active and enterprise-oriented authorization management. In *Proceedings of the IFIP TC11 WG11.3 eleventh international conference on database security xi: Status and prospects* (pp. 166–181). London, UK: Chapman & Hall, Ltd.

Tolone, W., Ahn, G.-J., Pai, T., & Hong, S.-P. (2005). Access control in collaborative systems. *ACM Computing Surveys*, *37*(1), 29–41. doi:10.1145/1057977.1057979

Tuunainen, V. K., Pitkanen, O., & Hovi, M. (2009). *Users' awareness of privacy on online social networking sites - case Facebook. 22nd Bled eConference eEnablement: Facilitating an Open, Effective and Representative eSociety.* Slovenia: Bled.

United States Department of Defense. (1983). *Trusted Computer System Evaluation Criteria (Orange Book).* D. of Defense.

Verhanneman, T., Piessens, F., De Win, B., & Joosen, W. (2005). Uniform application-level access control enforcement of organization wide policies. In *Proceedings of the 21st annual computer security applications conference* (pp. 431–440). Washington, DC, USA: IEEE Computer Society.

Villegas, W., Ali, B., & Maheswaran, M. (2008). An access control scheme for protecting personal data. In *Proceedings of the 2008 sixth annual conference on privacy, security and trust* (pp. 24–35). Washington, DC, USA: IEEE Computer Society.

W3C. (2009a). *Status for resource description framework (RDF) model and syntax specification.* Retrieved March, 2012, from http://www.w3.org/1999/status/PR-rdf-syntax-19990105/status.

W3C. (2009b). *W3C semantic web activity.* Retrieved March, 2012, from http://www.w3.org/2001/sw/

Wang, C., & Leung, H.-F. (2004). A secure and private Clarke tax voting protocol without trusted authorities. In *Proceedings of the 6th international conference on electronic commerce* (pp. 556–565). New York, NY, USA: ACM.

Wang, H., & Sun, L. (2010). Trust-involved access control in collaborative open social networks. In *Proceedings of the 2010 fourth international conference on network and system security* (pp. 239–246). Washington, DC, USA: IEEE Computer Society.

Weeks, S. (2001). Understanding trust management systems. In *Proceedings of the 2001 IEEE symposium on security and privacy* (pp. 94–105). Washington, DC, USA: IEEE Computer Society.

Weitzner, D. J., Hendler, J., Berners-Lee, T., & Connolly, D. (2006). Creating a policy-aware web: Discretionary, rule-based access for the world wide web. In Ferrari, E., & Thuraisingham, B. (Eds.), *Web and information security* (pp. 1–31). Idea Group Inc. doi:10.4018/978-1-59140-588-7.ch001

Wong, C. K., Gouda, M. G., & Lam, S. S. (1998). Secure group communications using key graphs. *ACM SIGCOMM Computer Communication Review*, *28*(4), 68–79. doi:10.1145/285243.285260

Xiong, L., & Liu, L. (2004, July 8–10). Peertrust: Supporting reputation-based trust for peer-to-peer electronic communities. *IEEE Transactions on Knowledge and Data Engineering*, *16*(7), 843–857. doi:10.1109/TKDE.2004.1318566

ADDITIONAL READING

Abdessalem, T., & Dhia, I. B. (2011). A reachability-based access control model for online social networks. In *Databases and social networks* (pp. 31–36). New York, NY, USA: ACM. doi:10.1145/1996413.1996419

Beato, F., Kohlweiss, M., & Wouters, K. (2009). Enforcing access control in social network sites. *Hot Topics in Privacy Enhancing Technologies (HotPETS)*, 1–11.

Carminati, B., & Ferrari, E. (2008). Access control and privacy in web-based social networks. *Access Control and Privacy in Web-based Social Networks*, *4*(4), 395–415. Emerald Group Publishing Limited.

Carreras, A., Rodrıguez, E., & Delgado, J. (2009). Using XACML for access control in social networks. In *W3C workshop on access control application scenarios.*

Chong, C., Corin, R., Doumen, J., & Etalle, S. (2006). License script: A logical language for digital rights management. *Annales des Télécommunications*, *61*(3), 284–331. doi:10.1007/BF03219910

Danezis, G. (2009). Inferring privacy policies for social networking services. In *Proceedings of the 2nd ACM workshop on security and artificial intelligence* (pp. 5–10). New York, NY, USA: ACM.

Debatin, B., Lovejoy, J. P., Horn, A.-K., & Hughes, B. N. (2009). Facebook and online privacy: Attitudes, behaviors, and unintended consequences. *Journal of Computer-Mediated Communication*, *15*(1), 83–108. doi:10.1111/j.1083-6101.2009.01494.x

Erlingsson, U., & Schneider, F. B. (2000). SASI enforcement of security policies: A retrospective. In *Proceedings of the 1999 workshop on new security paradigms* (pp. 87–95). New York, NY, USA: ACM.

Fernandez, E. B., Marin, C., & Petrie, M. M. L. (2010). Handbook of social network technologies and applications. *Social Networks*, 569–582.

Giunchiglia, F., Zhang, R., & Crispo, B. (2009). Ontology driven community access control. In *1st workshop on trust and privacy on the social and semantic Web Spot2009*. Citeseer.

Joshi, J. B. D., Bertino, E., Latif, U., & Ghafoor, A. (2005). A generalized temporal role-based access control model. *IEEE Transactions on Knowledge and Data Engineering*, *17*, 4–23. doi:10.1109/TKDE.2005.1

Lazarsfeld, P. F., & Merton, R. K. (1954). Friendship as a social process: A substantive and methodological analysis. In Berger, M., Abel, T., & Page, C. (Eds.), *Freedom and control in modern society* (pp. 18–66). New York: Van Nostrand.

Ligatti, J., Bauer, L., & Walker, D. (2005). Enforcing non-safety security policies with program monitors. *Computer Security ESORICS 2005. LNCS, 3679*, 355–373.

Nasirifard, P. (2007). Context-aware access control for collaborative working environments based on semantic social networks. In *Proceedings of the Doctorial Consortium Workshop at Sixth International and Interdisciplinary Conference on Modeling and Using Context (Context'07)*, Roskilde, Denmark, 2007.

Palen, L., & Dourish, P. (2003). Unpacking "privacy" for a networked world. In *Proceedings of the SIGCHI conference on human factors in computing systems* (pp. 129–136). New York, NY, USA: ACM.

Park, J., Sandhu, R., & Cheng, Y. (2011). User-activity centric framework for access control in online social networks. *IEEE Internet Computing*, 1–9.

Squicciarini, A., Paci, F., & Sundareswaran, S. (2010). PriMa: An effective privacy protection mechanism for social networks. In *Proceedings of the 5th ACM symposium on information, computer and communications security* (pp. 320–323). ACM.

KEY TERMS AND DEFINITIONS

Access Control Model (ACM): A formalization of how policies are composed based on a specific set of features in the system to regulate and authorize access to data.

Access Control Policy: Constraints on whether an access request to an object should be granted or denied.

Accessor: An authorized requestor that has been granted the specific set of permissions entailed by the policy.

Delegation: Entrustment in a user (delegate) to act on an object in a certain way with the authority from the object owner (delegator).

Offline Social Networks: Real-world social communities.

Online Social Networks (OSNs): Web-based services that offer the functionality of creating a personal representation of one's self through which one can socialize with others.

Owner: A user who adds her data, referred to as objects, and can share them with others.

Requestor: A user who initiates a request to be granted a specific permission on a specific object from its owner.

Social Network (SN): A set of people connected to each other by social relationships.

User: Any agent that uses the OSN and is represented via a profile of personal data.

Section 2
Applications

Chapter 4
Social Interactions and Automated Detection Tools in Cyberbullying

Michael J. Moore
Osaka University, Japan

Tadashi Nakano
Osaka University, Japan

Tatsuya Suda
The University Netgroup Inc., USA

Akihiro Enomoto
University of California, USA

ABSTRACT

Face-to-Face bullying is a traditional form of bullying in which bullies attack victims through physical, verbal, or social attacks. Cyberbullying is a new form of bullying. Cyberbullies abuse digital media to attack victims (such as attacks through websites, social networking services, blogging, e-mail, instant messaging, chat rooms, and cell phones). Cyberbullying and face-to-face bullying share many similarities. For example, bullies achieve power over a victim in both cyberbullying and face-to-face bullying. On the other hand, cyberbullying has differences from face-to-face bullying that arise from characteristics of digital media such as anonymity and rapid spreading of attacks. This chapter highlights key concerns of cyberbullying stemming from the use of digital media and discusses existing models of face-to-face bullying which may aid in model cyberbullying. This chapter then introduces state-of-the-art research in automated tools to detect cyberbullying. Finally, this chapter concludes with future perspective of research in automated tools to detect cyberbullying.

DOI: 10.4018/978-1-4666-3926-3.ch004

INTRODUCTION

In the digital age, many types of social, educational, and economic interactions are conducted through digital media. Digital media provides the storage and transmission of information in various formats through websites, social networking services, blogging, email, instant messaging, chat rooms, and cell phones. Formats of digital media include text, audio, image, and video data. Although digital media enhance many positive social, educational, and economic interactions by providing ubiquitous access to communication, by increasing the speed of communication, by reaching a broad audience, and by allowing anonymous individuals to interact; digital media also worsen negative social, educational, and economic interactions. Cyberbullying is one such social interaction which is negatively impacting society. Cyberbullying is the abuse of digital media to cause psychological and social harm to a victim(s) (Li, 2007; Kowalski, Limber, & Agatston, 2008; Hinduja & Patchin, 2009; Tokunaga, 2010). Cyberbullies leverage the capabilities of digital media to increase the psychological and social harm caused to victims of cyberbullying.

Cyberbullying is a growing concern with significant psychological and social problems for individuals involved in cyberbullying. For example, cyberbullying has been associated with several recent suicides (Ruedy, 2008; Lewin, 2010; Hinduja & Patchin, 2010). Another significant problem is aggression or violent retaliation by victims of cyberbullying. For example, victims of cyberbullying were eight times more likely to carry a weapon to school (Ybarra, Diener-west, & Leaf, 2007). There are also a variety of other significant psychological and social problems for cyberbullies and victims of cyberbullying which include emotional distress, depression, aggression, poor parent-child relationships, substance abuse, rule-breaking problems, academic difficulties, and delinquency (e.g., detentions, suspensions, or skipping school) (Ybarra & Mitchell, 2004; Ybarra, Mitchell, Wolak, & Finkelhor, 2006; Ybarra et al., 2007; J. Wang, Nansel, & Iannotti, 2011). As digital media use continues to grow, other significant psychological and social problems may also be observed such as eating disorders, chronic illness, running away from home, excessive psychosomatic symptoms, neuroticism, antisocial behavior, criminal conviction, or violent death (Ybarra & Mitchell, 2004; Patchin & Hinduja, 2006; Ybarra et al., 2007; K. Moore, 2011; Englander, 2012).

Face-to-face bullying is a traditional form of bullying in which bullies attack victims through physical, verbal, or social attacks (Olweus, 1991). Unlike cyberbullying, bullies in face-to-face bullying use non-digital media communication to bully (e.g., face-to-face talking, body language, or physical interaction). The key characteristics of face-to-face bullying are (1) the attacks are intentional, (2) the victim of face-to-face bullying perceives damage as the result of the attacks, (3) the attacks occur repeatedly, and (4) the bully has power over a victim to prevent the victim from adequate defense from the attacks (Olweus, 1991). These key characteristics are important for defining cases where face-to-face bullying can lead to significant problems.

Cyberbullying and face-to-face bullying share many similarities but have several differences. One similarity is that both use verbal and social attacks to cause harm to the victim. Another similarity is that both use the same key characteristics (i.e., intentional attacks, perception of harm, repetitive occurrence, and power over the victim) to cause psychological or social harm to victims (Smith et al., 2008; Dooley, Pyzalski, & Cross, 2009). One primary difference is that the participants in cyberbullying socially interact through digital media which introduces different characteristics such as anonymity, rapid spreading of communication, and communication anywhere and anytime. Another difference is that cyberbullies can utilize digital media with new capabilities to create new types of power over a victim and to increase the damage to victims.

Models of cyberbullying and face-to-face bullying are useful for understanding the characteristics of cyberbullying. Since there are similarities between face-to-face bullying and cyberbullying, models from face-to-face bullying in some cases may apply to modeling cyberbullying. One model describes the roles of individuals in cyberbullying. In face-to-face bullying, roles of participants may be a bully, victim, assistant of the bully, defender of the victim, etc. Each of these roles has been associated with various psychological and social characteristics. Another model describes the types of attacks. In face-to-face bullying, there are models for how a bully achieves power over a victim using certain types of attacks such as verbal and social attacks. For example, power over a victim can be achieved by attacking victims who are vulnerable to harm or by forming a group to attack a victim.

Research and development of automated tools to detect cyberbullying potentially reduce the harm caused by cyberbullying. The automated tools analyze characteristics of communications, characteristics about individuals sending the communications, and characteristics about the group and community interactions of the individuals. The automated tools use the various characteristics of cyberbullying to filter the massive amounts of digital media data down into the data which may be potential cyberbullying. Communications which may be cyberbullying can then be automatically blocked to help prevent the potential damage which the communication could have caused. Automated techniques may also complement and enhance other means to combat cyberbullying such as education of youth, counseling of victims, and enforcing laws.

In the remainder of this chapter, we highlight background on roles and attacks in cyberbullying and key concerns stemming from the use of digital media, we introduce state-of-the-art research in automated tools to detect cyberbullying that are being developed, and finally we discuss challenges and future perspective on research in automated tools to detect cyberbullying.

BACKGROUND ON CYBERBULLYING

In this section, we discuss existing research which has characterized the roles of individuals and types of attacks in cyberbullying. Characterization of the roles and attacks is important since cyberbullying can be identified as social interactions which match the characteristics of an attack.

Roles in Cyberbullying

Cyberbullying is a type of social interaction in which individuals participate in certain roles (e.g., a cyberbully and a victim of cyberbullying). In the following, we describe models of roles in cyberbullying. One model defines the role of an individual in cyberbullying from the actions they performed with respect to the cyberbullying. Another model defines individuals as bystanders who choose their role based on a cyberbullying situation.

In the model based on actions of an individual, the roles of individuals include a victim of bullying; a ringleader bully who organizes and initiates bullying; assistant bullies who help the ringleader by attacking the victim or preventing defense by the victim; reinforcers who passively reinforce bullying without actively participating (i.e., by watching, laughing, or encouraging the bullies); outsiders who perform no action for or against bullying; defenders who assist the victim (i.e., by helping the victim, finding help for the victim, or telling the bullies to stop); peer helpers who provide support for the victim (e.g., academic or family peer counselor); reporters who discuss bullying but may not have directly witnessed the bullying; and accusers who identify the bullies (Blias, 2008; Smith et al., 2008; Wang et al., 2010; Sahin, 2012; Law, Shapka, Domene, & Gagne,

2012; Xu, Jun, Zhu, & Bellmore, 2012). Roles may or may not be consistent over time (Taki et. al., 2008). For example, "bully-victims" may in some situations be a bully and in other situations be a victim. Bully-victims are distinguished from both the "bully" and "victim" role since bully-victims have distinct psychological and social characteristics. Victims, bullies, and bully-victims may often have the same role in both cyberbullying and face-to-face bullying (Blias, 2008; Smith et al., 2008; Twyman, Saylor, Taylor, & Comeaux, 2010). On the other hand, a cyberbully may be retaliating in response to being a victim of face-to-face bullying (Ybarra & Mitchell, 2004; Dooley et al., 2009).

In the model based on bystanders, a bullying situation starts with the ringleader bully, the victim, and everyone else as bystanders. The action of a bystander in the situation depends on how the situation progresses (Thornberg, 2007). The specific situation may be critical in determining whether a bullying situation will occur (e.g., bullies may seek specific environments which have certain types of bystanders present and no adult supervision) (Andrews & Chen, 2006). A bystander observing a bullying situation may decide to side with the bully, victim, or neither depending on the actions of the bully, victim, and other bystanders.

Types of Cyberbullying Attacks

Cyberbullying includes a variety of verbal and social attacks. Examples of verbal attacks include physical, racial, or sexual teasing/insults about the victim or threats about stalking, violence, or death of the victim. Examples of social attacks include socially excluding a victim or spreading rumors about a victim to damage the social relationships of the victim.

Cyberbullying attacks can be classified at a high-level based on the technique applied to degrade or threaten the victim (Hinduja & Patchin, 2009; Paragina, Paragina & Jipa, 2011; Bayzick, Kontostathis & Edwards, 2011). Cyberbullying can occur as "bashing" or "flaming" with verbal attacks to degrade or threaten the victim over a short period of time; "harassment" to degrade or threaten the victim over a long period of time; "denigration" to degrade or threaten the victim by spreading false information about a victim; "outing" to degrade or threaten the victim by disclosing personal information of a victim in public; "posing", "impersonation", or "masquerade" by pretending to be the victim and performing negative or embarrassing actions; "excluding" a victim from social activities in digital media to degrade the victim; "trickery" to install viruses onto or take control over the websites, social networking services, blogging, email, instant messaging, chat rooms, or cell phone of a victim; and "flooding" by performing excessive communications to prevent communication by the victim.

Additional Characteristics of Cyberbullying Attacks

Each of the types of attacks has additional characteristics such as the type and format of digital media or being coupled with face-to-face bullying. These additional characteristics can impact the harm caused by the cyberbullying.

Cyberbullying can occur through various types of digital media (i.e., websites, social networking services, blogging, email, instant messaging, chat rooms, and cell phones) (Ybarra & Mitchell, 2004; Li, 2007). For example, cyberbullies may create rumors about a victim, fake accounts with defamatory personal information, or defamatory polling websites. A cyberbully can privately attack with personal messages (e.g., instant messaging, e-mail, or cell phones). Cyberbullies can publicly attack with digital media which are temporary (e.g., chat rooms) or persist for a potentially long period of time (e.g., social networking services, blogging, or websites). There are some studies indicating the type of digital media can impact perceived harm. For example, victims of cyberbullying have been shown to be more harmed by insults in chat rooms compared to insults sent through e-mail (Smith et al., 2008). The media a cyberbully chooses for attacks may be associated with their motivation, such as reactive cyberbullying being associated to attacks through messages and embarrassing images and proactive cyberbullying being associated to attacks through hostile websites (Law et al., 2012).

Cyberbullying can occur through a variety of formats of digital media (i.e., text, audio, image, and video data). Certain formats of digital media cause more damage to victims of cyberbullying. Victims of cyberbullying are more negatively affected by video and images compared to audio phone calls, text messages, or text email (Ybarra et al., 2006; Smith et al., 2008; Slonje & Smith, 2008). For example, victims of cyberbullying were very stressed when asked to send their picture coupled with cyberbullying (Wolak, Mitchell, & Finkelhor, 2007). Image and video cyberbullying may have more impact and in some cases can be more damaging than face-to-face bullying (Slonje & Smith, 2008).

Cyberbullying can also occur coupled with face-to-face bullying. Face-to-face bullying includes physical attacks such as physically harming a victim, damaging the possessions of a victim, removing the clothing of a victim, coercion, or violent criminal acts against a victim (Smith, 2004). Face-to-face bullying can be combined with cyberbullying by, for example, "happy slapping" in which cyberbullies record physical attacks into video and share the videos through digital media (Smith et al., 2008). Cyberbullying may also be an extension of social exclusion by an entire class (e.g., 'ijime' in Japan and 'wang-ta' in Korea) or school (e.g., 'jun-ta' in Korea) (Smith, Cowie, Olafsson, & Liefooghe, 2002; Taki et al., 2008). Cyberbullying coupled with face-to-face bullying is especially of concern, since this has been found to increase the stress caused to victims of cyberbullying (Wolak et al., 2007).

Concerns about Digital Media Characteristics that Worsen Cyberbullying

In the following, we summarize key concerns in cyberbullying which result from the use of digital media. As described above, psychological or social harm of a victim occurs when bullying has certain key characteristics (i.e., intentional attacks, perception of harm, repetitive occurrence, and power over a victim). A cyberbully can use characteristics of digital media to worsen cyberbullying. It is important to characterize what digital media characteristics produce these concerns in order to identify conditions which may produce an environment that does not deter or even encourages cyberbullying.

The perception of harm by a victim may be increased by the ubiquity of communications. Ubiquity of digital media indicates that the digital media can be sent and retrieved anywhere and anytime. Ubiquity is available through mobile devices (e.g., cell phones) and through access to digital media at various locations (e.g., at home). As a result of ubiquity, a cyberbully can attack from anywhere and anytime, and a victim can be attacked anywhere and anytime (Patchin & Hinduja, 2006). For example, the victim may receive cyberbullying attacks even at home and after school. Ubiquity increases the perception of harm by the victim since the victim may feel unable to escape from cyberbullying attacks.

The repetition of attacks to a victim may be increased by the persistence of digital media attacks. Persistence of digital media attack indicates that the digital media can be stored and retrieved at any later time. Persistence in digital media is available through storing digital media in an accessible location which is available for a long period of time (e.g., a website) or by copying the digital media repeatedly over time (e.g., forwarding digital media among individuals).

The persistence can produce the same effect as attacks repeated over time since the victim can view the attack repeatedly (Li, 2007; Dooley et al., 2009). For example, a cyberbullying attack which creates a website with defamatory information about a victim remains available and can cause more harm to a victim since it can be repeatedly viewed by the victim.

The power over a victim may be increased by the spreading and anonymous nature of digital media and by the technical skill of cyberbullies. Spreading of digital media indicates the digital media can reach a broad audience (e.g., digital media can virally spread through retransmission among individuals). A cyberbully can spread an attack by directly recruiting attackers or by publicly posting an attack in which individuals from anywhere can join (Dooley et al., 2009; Lewin, 2010). Spreading of cyberbullying through digital media achieves power over a victim, since cyberbullies can overwhelm the victim with cyberbullying attacks which come from a widespread audience (Kowalski & Limber, 2007; Li, 2007). Anonymity of digital media indicates that a receiver of the digital media does not know who sent the digital media. Anonymity is often easily available in digital media. Some digital media allow their users to be fully anonymous with no identifier. Most digital media allow their users to be pseudo-anonymous with an arbitrary identifier (without relationship to the real identify of the individual). Anonymity achieves power over a victim, since a cyberbully with anonymity may cause stress to a victim and a victim cannot as easily defend or retaliate against a cyberbully who has anonymity (Li, 2005; Kowalski & Limber, 2007; Patchin & Hinduja, 2006). Technical skill of an individual indicates that the individual is capable of using technical skill to manipulate devices or digital media to perform more complex functionality. Technical skill of a cyberbully may also achieve power over a victim. For example, a cyberbully with technical skill in software can take control over the digital media of a victim (e.g., installation of a virus or unauthorized software on devices of a victim) and, for example, acquire sensitive personal information of the victim (e.g., personal communication or passwords) (Dooley et al., 2009) or reduce the power of the victim by blocking mechanisms which a victim uses to defend themselves.

Certain characteristics of digital media can encourage cyberbullying. One such characteristic is dissociation by which a cyberbully is detached from the damage which he or she causes to a victim. Disassociation occurs in digital media since a cyberbully may not see the psychological or social harm caused to the victim (Kowalski & Limber, 2007). This disassociation causes cyberbullying to become relatively impersonal and results in increased aggression and inappropriate behavior (Ybarra & Mitchell, 2004; Patchin & Hinduja, 2006; Li, 2007). Another characteristic of digital media is social status, such as ranking and power of an individual in a social group (e.g., ranking of a student in a class), which a cyerbully may gain through cyberbullying. Social status is often gained by face-to-face bullies (Juvonen, Graham, & Schuster, 2003) and is also perceived as a reason for individuals to cyberbully (K. Moore, 2011). Another characteristic of digital media which may contribute to cyberbullying is lack of supervision. Lack of supervision occurs since there are often no authorities to censor or monitor communications and since digital media are often used in a private context (Patchin & Hinduja, 2006). Cyberbullies can also abuse anonymity to avoid supervision, since anonymity prevents authorities (e.g., parents and school administrators) from identifying the source of cyberbullying (Li, 2007). The lack of supervision frees cyberbullies from social constraints on their behavior (e.g., legal and social punishment) (Patchin & Hinduja, 2006; Li, 2007).

AUTOMATED TOOLS TO DETECT CYBERBULLYING

Automated tools may help detect cyberbullying. In this section, we discuss high level applications of automated tools to detect cyberbullying. Then, we overview research in techniques, such as text analysis, image/video analysis, and social network analysis, which may apply to the detection of cyberbullying.

Application of Automated Tools to Reduce Cyberbullying and Harm Caused by Cyberbullying

Automated tools can be applied by a user to filter potential cyberbullying and can supplement non-automated techniques to combat cyberbullying such as education of youth, counseling of victims, and enforcing laws.

Automated tools to detect cyberbullying can be applied by end-users to automatically filter potential cyberbullying communications. The automated tool scans communications, performs analysis to determine if a communication matches characteristics of cyberbullying, and automatically blocks communications suspected to be cyberbullying. There are several commercial products which advertise the capability of blocking and reporting cyberbullying.

Education is one technique to reduce the potential harm of cyberbullying. This can occur through educating authorities about the existence of and techniques to combat cyberbullying; by educating individuals about how to interact with digital media; educating individuals about how to cope with cyberbullying; and educating individuals about conflict resolution (Reid, Monsen, & Rivers, 2004; D. Wong, 2004; Williams & Guerra, 2007; Ybarra et al., 2007). Education can also be targeted to those with more risk of severe harm, such as youth those with mental or social challenges (Ybarra et al., 2007). Automated tools can enhance education by detecting cyberbullying and providing automated guidance to victims of cyberbullying. For example, the automated tool can automatically inform the victim about techniques to handle detected cyberbullying or inform a cyberbully about the potential negative impact of their actions (Dinakar et al., 2012).

Counseling of individuals affected by cyberbullying is important for reducing psychological and social harm caused by cyberbullying. Automated tools may identify those who is at risk (e.g., identify those who have been attacked by cyberbullying or appear to be distressed) and automatically contact help, such as peers or authorities, for the victim of cyberbullying before the situation becomes more serious (Dinakar et al., 2011).

Laws against cyberbullying are reasonable, since cyberbullying can have severe consequences such as suicide and physical violence (Shariff, 2005; Gillespie, 2006; Ruedy, 2008; Zwart, Lindsay, Henderson, & Phillips, 2011). Automated tools to detect cyberbullying may make these laws more enforceable by identifying cyberbullying and gathering evidence of cyberbullying. Bosse and Stam (2011) demonstrate that adding automated agents into a virtual environment can reduce the occurrence of cyberbullying (e.g., agents which analyze individual behavior, give incentive for good behavior, and penalize cyberbullying). In the simulation by Bosse and Stam (2011), the agents first warn individuals that they may be performing actions which are not allowed and then block individuals from continued actions.

Identifying Attacks through Text Analysis

In the following, we overview existing work which applies automated text analysis to classify digital media in a text format. Cyberbullying attacks may contain specific words since cyberbullies and bully assistants use aggressive content in order to psychologically and socially harm the victim of cyberbullying. Text analysis can be applied to identify the emotional content of textual data (Pang

& Lee, 2008). In the case of detecting cyberbullying, existing research uses text analysis to identify highly aggressive content in digital media and the sender of the aggressive content is considered as a potential cyberbully or bully assistant. Existing research focuses on contents which are formatted as text, since text is more easily processed for emotional content compared to audio, image, or video. Focusing on cyberbullying attacks which are formatted as text may also be important if text is used in conjunction with more damaging formats of digital media such as images or video.

One text analysis technique to identify highly aggressive text is through template matching of the text. The text is considered highly aggressive when the text matches certain sentence patterns, has pronouns (e.g., you, he, or they), has profanity (e.g., derogatory, sexual, or racial terms), or has a large number capital letters (Yin et al., 2009; Bayzick et al., 2011; Bosse & Stam, 2011; M. Moore, Nakano, Enomoto & Suda, 2012). One challenge with aggressive content formatted as text is that words are often intentionally misspelled (e.g., duplicate characters inserted or letters replaced with symbols or numbers). Sood, Antin, and Churchill (2012) suggest using humans to regularly classify messages and to apply Levenshtein Edit Distance to identify misspelling variations of words. The Levenshtein Edit Distance approach identifies what known word is closest to some unknown word by measuring a distance which is determined by word edit operations such as character insertion. Another technique to identify the emotion of text is through matching of emoticon symbols representing emotional content (Mishne, 2005). An example of emoticons is a sequence of keyboard character symbols which represent a facial or emotional expression.

A more general text analysis technique to identify highly aggressive text is through supervised machine learning. To apply supervised machine learning, humans first manually classify a set of messages for aggressiveness which is then used by a machine learning approach to generate statistics about, for example, what words and phrases are associated with cyberbullying. Then, the machine learning approach can classify the aggressiveness of other text not in the training set. Several existing machine learning approaches have been applied to identify highly aggressive text (e.g., a naive Bayes filter, rule-based Jrip, tree-based J48, support vector machines, latent semantic analysis) (Ptaszynski et al., 2010; Reynolds, Kontostathis, & Edwards, 2011; Sood et al., 2012; Dhanalakshmi & Chellappan, 2012; Nahar, Unankard, Li, & Pang, 2012; Dinakar et al., 2012). These machine learning approaches have been compared against each other and machine learning approaches were better able to identify aggressive text and to outperform simple template matching of text (Reynolds et al., 2011; Dinakar et al., 2012). Classification accuracy can be further increased by braking down classification for each role of individuals in cyberbullying, such as a cyberbully, victim of cyberbullying, or defender in cyberbullying (Xu et al., 2012).

Identifying Attacks through Image/Video Analysis

Since cyberbullying through aggressive images and video may be more damaging than face-to-face bullying, it may be appropriate to focus on detecting cyberbullying in image and video formats. There are a broad variety of techniques for analyzing images to determine the characteristics and content of images (Datta, Joshi, Li, & Wang, 2008). Image and video analysis has progressed such that cyberbullying through certain types of image and video may be detectable. Although, there are no existing studies on whether image and video analysis can be used to specifically detect cyberbullying, there is a growing body of work on analyzing images and video which may directly apply to detecting cyberbullying.

One type of cyberbullying is associated with filming video of face-to-face bullying and sharing the video. One area of video analysis which may help to identify these attacks is detection of violent human behavior, such as a fight. To perform the analysis, video frames are processed to determine the position of people in each frame (Lin, Sun, Poovendran, & Zhang, 2010). Then, the types of body motions and relative position and velocity of individuals are processed to classify whether the individuals are participating in activities such as walking, running, or fighting (Lin et al., 2010). The existing work in this area focuses on analysis of surveillance cameras; however, the work is a potential starting point for analysis of videos from cell phones used in cyberbullying.

Another type of cyberbullying is associated with modifying or producing images for the purpose of denigration or impersonation. One area of image analysis which may help to identify these attacks is detection of image or video forgeries in the area of digital forensics. The digital characteristics of images and video may contain characteristics of what part of an image or video was modified (Wang, 2009). However, as modification of images and video may be common in non-cyberbullying communication, a necessary next step may be to determine what impact the change in the image or video has on the content of the image or video.

Characterizing Cyberbullying through Social Network Analysis

As discussed above in concerns about digital media, there are several characteristics of digital media (e.g., ubiquity, persistence, spreading, and anonymity) which may worsen cyberbullying by increasing the perception of harm, by producing a repetitive occurrence, and by increasing power over the victim. Social network analysis can be applied to quantify several characteristics which may be indicators of potential harm of digital media. One representation of a social network is a graph with individuals represented as nodes and relationships between individuals represented as edges. An edge is associated with communications and characteristics of communications between two or more individuals.

Analysis of relationships in a social network can give some indicators to malicious behavior. Relationships have characteristics such as the frequency, time and location of communications, the specific media of communication (e.g., includes pictures or video), and attachment sizes (Hadjidj, Debbabi, Lounis, & Iqbal, 2009). Cyberbullying attacks may be associated with certain relationship characteristics. For example, an individual may suddenly receive an unusually large number of messages from individuals whom they do not usually receive messages, and thus they may be experiencing a flooding attack which utilizes the spreading characteristic of digital media. Or for example, if cyberbullying attacks are associated with individuals in the same physical locality, then the individual may be at greater risk for cyberbullying coupled with face-to-face bullying.

Cyberbullies may gain power over a victim through utilizing a large number of attackers to overwhelm a single victim. Social network analysis can be applied to rank individuals who are most at risk for psychological and social harm as a result of cyberbullying (Nahar et al., 2012). Ranking the individuals helps to target administrator resources towards analyzing cases with the greatest potential for harm. For example, the social network can be used to rank individuals in terms of which individuals are the overall most aggressive (i.e., sends the most cyberbullying attacks) or most victimized (i.e., receives the most cyberbullying attacks) (Nahar et al., 2012).

Cyberbullies may gain power over the victim by utilizing fake accounts to appear as multiple cyberbullies or to gain additional advantage in a social network. One area in social network analysis targets the detection of fake accounts. In one approach, a probabilistic model of honest users is built, and the probabilistic model is applied to detect fake accounts which do not match the model (Danezis & Mittal, 2009). However, such detection may be difficult as fake accounts be used to appear similar to normal accounts (Yang et al., 2011).

Cyberbullies may gain power over the victim by utilizing anonymity. Social network analysis may be used to measure the anonymity of an individual in a social network (Sweeny, 2002; Singh & Zhan, 2007). Social network analysis may be appropriate for measuring anonymity since identifiers in a communication can be arbitrarily produced (e.g., by making alternate accounts for the purpose of cyberbullying). In the case of cyberbullying, anonymity of an individual may be measured as how much social network information is available about the individual and the strength of the interactions of the individual with their social network.

Other Relevant Social Network Analysis

It may be possible to measure other social network characteristics as additional knowledge for detecting cyberbullying and the potential harm of cyberbullying. Existing studies in sociology may be a starting point for identifying other social characteristics relevant to cyberbullying and may be especially relevant in the case of detecting the more harmful cyberbullying coupled with face-to-face bullying. In the following, we describe how the roles of individuals in face-to-face bullying and cyberbullying have been associated with certain group and community characteristics. A group consists of a set of individuals who interact together more frequently and less frequently with others outside of the group. A community consists of all the individuals and groups within a social context (e.g., within a class or within an online social website). These various characteristics of groups and communities can produce additional social network analysis to enhance the classification of the role of individuals within the groups.

Characteristics of groups have been correlated with whether an individual is likely to be a bully or victim in face-to-face bullying. Group similarity describes how similar the individuals in a group are with each other. Bullies (i.e., ring-leader, reinforcers, and assistants) have been associated with having friendships with other bullies (Haselager, Hartup, Lieshout, & Riksen-walraven, 1998; Huttunen, Salmivalli, & Lagerspetz, 2006) and victims have been associated with lacking friendships with bullies (Mouttapa, Valente, Gallaher, Rohrbach, & Unger et al., 2004). Group size describes the relationship network to which an individual is strongly connected. Bullies, defenders, and victims have been associated with having respectively more, fewer, or lacking an extensive relationship network (Huttunen et al., 2006; Sahin, 2012). Group cohesion refers to the strength of the relationships between the members of a group. Victims and bully-victims have been associated as lacking close friends (Veenstra et al., 2005; Wong, 2009). Having strong relationships appears to prevent victimization and psychological and social harm caused by being a victim (Pakaslahti & Keltikangas-järvinen, 2001; Huttunen, et al., 2006). Group rank is the popularity of a group relative to other groups in a social context. In Björkqvist et al. (2001), individuals of a class list groups in their class, and the order in which individuals listed the groups of a class was considered to be the rank of the group (e.g., a popular group is often listed first and thus has the highest rank). Aggressive males and females have been associated with a high group rank (Björkqvist et al., 2001).

An individual may also have characteristics of popularity within a group or community (e.g., in a class). Rank of an individual within their group can be measured similarly to rank of a group within a class (Björkqvist et al., 2001). Aggressive individuals, such as bullies and defenders, had a high rank within their group and community (Pellegrini, Bartini, & Brooks, 1999; Björkqvist et al., 2001; Pakaslahti & Keltikangas-järvinen, 2001; Juvonen et al., 2003). Victims and bully-victims often have low community popularity (Juvonen et al., 2003; Felipe, García, Babarro, & Arias, 2011;

Sahin, 2012). Centrality is a measure of how well connected an individual is in a community which may correlate with the popularity of the individual. Bullies and defenders have been associated with higher network centrality (Gest, Graham-bermann, & Hartup, 2001; Xie, Farmer, & Cairns, 2003).

Enhancing Analysis through Psychological and Physical Characteristics of Individuals

Psychological and physical characteristics of individuals can be used to enhance the detection of the role of an individual in cyberbullying (Dadvar & Jong, 2012). The characteristics may be available through, for example, individual profiles which provide information about the individual. In the following, we describe individual characteristics and their association to roles in cyberbullying.

Psychological characteristics of victims may apply to enhancing detection of the more harmful cyberbullying coupled with face-to-face bullying. Victims of face-to-face bullying have been associated with characteristics of being passive, physically weak, mentally weak, anxious, low in self-esteem, hyperactive, or poor at handling aggressive reactions (Smith, 2004; Reid et al., 2004). In addition, victims of face-to-face bullying may also be individuals who are from ethnic or racial minorities, do not fit gender stereotypes, or have mental or physical challenges (Reid et al., 2004; Wong, 2009). As a result of face-to-face bullying, victims of face-to-face bullying may also exhibit depression, anxiety, social phobias, somatic complaints, and withdrawal. Identifying these specific characteristics of victims may enhance detection of cyberbullying. For example, classification of cyberbullying attacks can be broken down based on what characteristic of a victim they target such as attacks targeting sexual, racial/cultural, or intellectual characteristics of a victim (Dinakar et al., 2012). Breaking down the classification leads to higher accuracy in identifying attacks since the criteria for matching a certain type of attack, such as words/phrases which are racial attacks, are more specific.

Knowledge about the ages of individuals can be used to enhance the detection of cyberbullying. The classification of cyberbullying can similarly be enhanced by breaking down the classification by ages of individuals (Dadvar & Jong, 2012). Another consideration is the usage of age to determine the potential harm of cyberbullying. The relative ages of a cyberbully to a victim of the cyberbully can be an indicator for potentially more harmful cyberbullying. A relatively older cyberbully may have more mental capacity than a relatively younger victim of cyberbullying (e.g., an adult cyberbullying a child) and thus may gain power over a victim and cause more distress to the victim of (Ybarra & Mitchell, 2004; Wolak et al., 2007). Also, youths are more likely to be victims of cyberbullying since they are more likely to believe threats, may not be able to evaluate the true threat, lack experience or education necessary to manage cyberbullying, and thus are more likely to be distressed by cyberbullying (Ybarra et al., 2006; Stacey, 2010).

Knowledge about the gender of individuals can be used to enhance the detection of cyberbullying. The classification of cyberbullying can similarly be enhanced by breaking down classification tasks by gender (Dadvar & Jong, 2012). Both males and females perform cyberbullying (Ybarra & Mitchell, 2004; Patchin & Hinduja, 2006; Tokugana, 2010; Wang et al., 2010); however, the method of cyberbullying can vary. Gender may be associated with the types of attacks received, such as boys being attacked by hate messages and females being attacked by name-calling (Rivers & Noret, 2009). Gender may also be related to the likelihood of the role of an individual in cyberbullying. Males have been reported to more likely be both face-to-face bullies and cyberbullies (Li, 2005; Li, 2006). Females have been reported to more frequently be the targets of cyberbullying (Ybarra & Mitchell, 2007).

Other Relevant Psychological and Physical Characteristics of Individuals

It may be possible to measure other psychological and physical characteristics of individuals as additional knowledge for detecting cyberbullying and the potential harm of cyberbullying. Existing studies in psychology on face-to-face bullying may be a starting point for identifying other psychological and physical characteristics which may be associated with specific roles in cyberbullying. Bullies in face-to-face bullying have been associated with aggressiveness, a positive attitude towards violence, disruptiveness, unfriendliness, less empathy for their victims, and negative relationships (Smith, 2004; Pakaslahti, & Keltikangas-järvinen, 2001). Similarly, cyberbullies have been found to have a positive towards violence and a desire for dominance (Williams & Guerra, 2007; Ven, 2011). However, in cyberbullying, since there are other techniques available to achieve power over a victim, cyberbullies may have less physical, mental, or social strength than their victims (Vandebosch & Cleemput, 2008). Bully-victims in face-to-face bullying have been associated with the most risk for psychological (e.g., aggression, hyperactivity, and depression), school, and social problems in comparison to an individual who is only a bully or only a victim (Juvonen et al., 2003; Felipe et al., 2011). However, in cyberbullying, the bully-victim may not be associated with the same characteristics, such as depression, as a face-to-face bully-victim (Wang et al., 2010). These other psychological and physical characteristics of individuals may help to enhance the accuracy of future tools to detect cyberbullying.

FUTURE RESEARCH DIRECTIONS IN DEVELOPING AUTOMATED TOOLS TO DETECT CYBERBULLYING

In this section, we briefly overview several open issues in developing automated tools to detect cyberbullying.

Automated Tools to Process a Variety of Cyberbullying Attacks

Existing automated tools may be difficult to extend to a wide variety of attacks. In existing work, machine learning is applied to build an automated tool to classify whether cyberbullying is in digital media (Hadjidj et al., 2009; Dadvar & Jong, 2012; Dinakar et al., 2012). The machine learning performs a supervised learning task with human-classified digital media examples of cyberbullying and non-cyberbullying. The wide variety of types of digital media (i.e., websites, social networking services, blogging, email, instant messaging, chat rooms, and cell phones), types of cyberbullying attacks (e.g., verbal or social attacks), and adaptation of attacks by cyberbullies makes it difficult to develop tools to identify all potential attacks. In the case of machine learning, this may require a very broad set of human-classified examples, which may or may not be feasible.

Existing psychology and sociology studies in characteristics of cyberbullying may provide hints for generalizing automated tools. Cyberbullying has been associated with certain characteristics and automated tools can focus on detecting these characteristics as intermediate knowledge for cyberbullying detection. Such characteristics include characteristics of digital media used to perform attacks, psychological and physical characteristics of individuals participating in an attack, and group and community characteristics of individuals participating in an attack.

Automated Tools to Rank the Severity of Cyberbullying

Existing automated tools to detect cyberbullying have not been evaluated against all the key characteristics of bullying, such as intentional attack, perceived damage, repeated occurrence, and power over a victim. Current research focuses on identifying the existence of an attack. An open issue is how to detect the severity of cyberbullying by identifying whether the victim of cyberbullying perceives damage, whether the victim experiences some repetitive occurrence, and whether the cyberbully achieves power over a victim. Psychosocial studies have been conducted to identify characteristics of more harmful cyberbullying. One potential direction is to develop automated tools for detecting characteristics associated with more harmful cyberbullying.

Automated tools can rank the potential for perceived damage based on certain characteristics of cyberbullying, such as the format of digital media, relative ages of individuals, or being coupled with face-to-face bullying. Existing work in image and video analysis may be able to detect cyberbullying through more harmful image and video formats. Text analysis may also apply to identifying the potential existence of images or video used in cyberbullying attacks. Certain types of images and videos may be indicators of face-to-face bullying, and thus detecting the existence of video and images may be particularly important for advancing the effectiveness in detecting severe cases of cyberbullying. However, such analysis in the context of detecting harmful cyberbullying remains an open issue.

Automated tools can also rank the power over a victim based on characteristics of digital media usage, such as spreading, anonymity, and technical skill. Social network analysis may provide techniques to detect the spreading and anonymity of cyberbullying. Computing security may provide techniques to detect power over a victim through technical skill such as detecting flooding of the devices of a victim, identity theft to impersonate a victim, or unauthorized access and control of the digital media of a victim. Although such techniques are promising, the effectiveness of these techniques in detecting harmful cases of cyberbullying remains an open issue.

Automated Tools with Limited Digital Media Characteristics

Automated tools may require detailed characteristics about digital media in order to accurately determine whether the digital media contain cyberbullying. However, the characteristics of the digital media may be limited according to who applies the automated tool. In the case that an individual applies an automated tool, the individual may not be able to apply group or community analysis techniques since they may only have access to their own communications. In the case that a digital media provider (e.g., provider of Internet access or digital media services) applies an automated tool, the digital media provider may not have access to data or characteristics of data due to privacy concerns. Characteristics of the digital media may also be limited as a result of anonymity. If an individual attacks anonymously, then the profile of the individual may be unavailable and the group and community characteristics of the anonymous individual are likely to appear different from their true group and community characteristics. An open issue is to develop alternative methods to detect cyberbullying when certain characteristics of digital media are unavailable.

CONCLUSION

This chapter discussed existing research on face-to-face bullying and cyberbullying. We also discussed automated tools to detect cyberbullying. Automated tools can detect cyberbullying by analyzing the data (e.g., text, images, audio, and video) in digital media, the communication characteristics of digital media, the psychological and physical characteristics of individuals, and the group and community characteristics of the individuals. Existing research has developed several automated tools for detecting cyberbullying attacks; however, there are still several open issues.

The automated tools to detect cyberbullying discussed in this chapter may also apply to detecting other abuses of digital media such as detecting aggression in work places (Harvey, Treadway, & Heames, 2007), adult predators sexually harassing youth (Kontostathis, Edwards, & Leatherman, 2009), spamming (Dhanalakshmi & Chellappan, 2012), cyberstalking (Pittaro, 2007), terrorism (Ressler, 2006), impersonation of individuals, or unauthorized gathering of private information.

Another promising direction is to model social interactions among individuals in order to understand how the social interactions of individuals may lead to cyberbullying behavior. Ochoab et al., (2011) conducted simulations of software agents which have abstract representations of individual differences (e.g., language, location, and use of technology) and form groups with similar individuals. In the simulation, the agents interact socially and social behavior, such as social exclusion, emerges. The simulation model may be extended and used to identify strategies to combat certain types of cyberbullying (Ochoab et al., 2011).

REFERENCES

Andrews, G. J., & Chen, S. (2006). The production of tyrannical space. *Children's Geographies, 4*(2), 239–250. doi:10.1080/14733280600807120

Bayzick, J., Kontostathis, A., & Edwards, L. (2011, June). *Detecting the presence of cyberbullying using computer software*. Paper presented at the ACM Web Science, Koblenz, Germany.

Björkqvist, K., Österman, K., Lagerspetz, K. M. J., Landau, S. F., Caprara, G. V., & Fraczek, A. (2001). Aggression, victimization, and sociometric status: Findings from Finland, Israel, Italy, and Poland. In Ramirez, J. M., & Richardson, D. S. (Eds.), *Cross-cultural approaches to research on aggression and reconciliation* (pp. 111–119). Hauppauge, NY: Nova Science.

Blias, J. J. (2008). *Chatting, befriending, and bullying: Adolescent internet experiences and associated psychosocial outcomes*. (Doctoral thesis). Queen's University, Canada.

Bosse, T., & Stam, S. (2011). A normative agent system to prevent cyberbullying. In *Proceedings of at the International Conferences on Web Intelligence and Intelligent Agent Technology* (pp. 425-430). Los Alamitos, CA: IEEE Computer Society.

Dadvar, M., & Jong, F. D. (2012). Cyberbullying detection: A step toward a safer internet yard. In *Proceedings of the 21st International World Wide Web Conference* (pp. 121-125). New York, NY: Association for Computing Machinery.

Danezis, G., & Mittal, P. (2009, February). *SybilInfer: Detecting sybil nodes using social networks*. Paper presented at the 16th Annual Network & Distributed System Security Symposium, San Diego, CA.

Datta, R., Joshi, D., Li, J., & Wang, J. Z. (2008). Image retrieval: Ideas, influences, and trends of the new age. *ACM Computing Surveys, 40*(2), 5: 1-60.

Dhanalakshmi, R., & Chellappan, C. (2012). Mitigating e-mail threats - a web content based. In S. I. Ao, O. Castillo, C. Douglas, D.D. Feng, & J. Lee (Eds.), *Proceedings of the International Multi Conference of Engineers and Computer Scientists* (pp. 632-637). Hong Kong, China: International Association of Engineers.

Dinakar, K., Jones, B., Havasi, C., Lieberman, H., & Picard, R. (in press). Commonsense reasoning for detection, prevention, and mitigation of cyberbullying. *ACM Transactions on Interactive Intelligent Systems*.

Dinakar, K., Jones, B., Lieberman, H., Picard, R., Rose, C., Thoman, M., & Reichart, R. (2011, June). *You too?! Mixed-initiative LDA story matching to help teens in distress*. Paper presented at the Sixth International AAAI Conference on Weblogs and Social Media, Dublin, Ireland.

Dooley, J. J., Pyzalski, J., & Cross, D. (2009). Cyberbullying versus face-to-face bullying: A theoretical and conceptual review. *The Journal of Psychology, 217*(4), 182–188. doi:10.1027/0044-3409.217.4.182

Englander, E. K. (2012). Spinning our wheels: Improving our ability to respond to bullying and cyberbullying. *Child and Adolescent Psychiatric Clinics of North America, 21*, 43–55. doi:10.1016/j.chc.2011.08.013

Felipe, M. T., García, S. D. O., Babarro, J. M., & Arias, R. M. (2011). Social characteristics in bullying typology: Digging deeper into description of bully-victim. *Procedia - Social and Behavioral Sciences, 29*, 869-878.

Gest, S. D., Graham-bermann, S. A., & Hartup, W. W. (2001). Peer experience: Common and unique features of number of friendships, social network centrality, and sociometric status. *Social Development, 10*(1), 23–40. doi:10.1111/1467-9507.00146

Gillespie, A. A. (2006). Cyber-bullying and harassment of teenagers: The legal response. *Journal of Social Welfare and Family Law, 28*(2), 123–136. doi:10.1080/09649060600973772

Hadjidj, R., Debbabi, M., Lounis, H., & Iqbal, F. (2009). Towards an integrated email forensic. *Digital Investigation, 5*(3-4), 124–137. doi:10.1016/j.diin.2009.01.004

Harvey, M., Treadway, D. C., & Heames, J. T. (2007). The occurrence of bullying in global organizations: A model and issues associated with social/emotional contagion. *Journal of Applied Social Psychology, 37*(11), 2576–2599. doi:10.1111/j.1559-1816.2007.00271.x

Haselager, G. J. T., Hartup, W. W., Lieshout, C. F. M. V., & Riksen-walraven, J. M. A. (1998). Similarities between friends and nonfriends in middle childhood. *Child Development, 69*(4), 1198–1208.

Hinduja, S., & Patchin, J. W. (2009). *Bullying beyond the schoolyard: Preventing and responding to cyberbullying*. Thousand Oaks, CA: Corwin Press.

Hinduja, S., & Patchin, J. W. (2010). Bullying, cyberbullying, and suicide. *Archives of Suicide Research, 41*(3), 206–221. doi:10.1080/13811118.2010.494133

Huttunen, A., Salmivalli, C., & Lagerspetz, K. M. J. (2006). Friendship networks and bullying in schools. *Annals of the New York Academy of Sciences. Understanding Aggressive Behavior in Children, 794*, 355–359.

Juvonen, J., Graham, S., & Schuster, M. A. (2003). Bullying among young adolescents the strong, the weak and the troubled. *Pediatrics, 112*(6), 1131–1137. doi:10.1542/peds.112.6.1231

Kontostathis, A., Edwards, L., & Leatherman, A. (2009, May). *ChatCoder: Toward the tracking and categorization of internet predators*. Paper presented of the Text Mining Workshop held in conjunction with the Ninth Siam International Conference on Data Mining, Sparks, NV.

Kowalski, R. M., & Limber, S. P. (2007). Electronic bullying among middle school students. *The Journal of Adolescent Health, 41*(6), S22–SS30. doi:10.1016/j.jadohealth.2007.08.017

Kowalski, R. M., Limber, S. P., & Agatston, P. W. (2008). *Cyber bullying: The new moral frontier*. Oxford, UK: Blackwell Publishing Ltd. doi:10.1002/9780470694176

Law, D. M., Shapka, J. D., Domene, J. F., & Gagné, M. H. (2012). Are cyberbullies really bullies? An investigation of reactive and proactive online aggression. *Computers in Human Behavior*, *28*(2), 664–672. doi:10.1016/j.chb.2011.11.013

Lewin, T. (2010, May 5). Teenage insults, scrawled on web, not on walls. *New York Times*. Retrieved October 1, 2012, from http://www.nytimes.com/2010/05/06/us/06formspring.html.

Li, Q. (2005, April). *Cyberbullying in schools: Nature and extent of Canadian adolescents' experience*. Paper presented at the Annual Meeting of the American Educational Research Association, Montreal, Canada.

Li, Q. (2006). Cyberbullying in schools: A research of gender difference. *School Psychology International*, *27*(2), 157–170. doi:10.1177/0143034306064547

Li, Q. (2007). New bottle but old wine: A research of cyberbullying in schools. *Computers in Human Behavior*, *23*(4), 1777–1791. doi:10.1016/j.chb.2005.10.005

Lin, W., Sun, M., Poovendran, R., & Zhang, Z. (2010). Group event detection with a varying number of group members for video surveillance. *IEEE Transactions on Circuits and Systems for Video Technology*, *20*(8), 1057–1067. doi:10.1109/TCSVT.2010.2057013

Mishne, G. (2005, August). *Experiments with mood classification in blog posts*. Paper presented at the Workshop on Stylistic Analysis of Text for Information Access, Salvador, Brazil.

Moore, K. N. (2011). *Cyberbullying: An exploratory study of adolescent girls' perspectives on technology's impact on relationships*. (Doctoral Thesis). State University of New Jersey Rutgers.

Moore, M. J., Nakano, T., Enomoto, A., & Suda, T. (2012). Anonymity and roles associated with aggressive posts in an online forum. *Computers in Human Behavior*, *28*(3), 861–867. doi:10.1016/j.chb.2011.12.005

Mouttapa, M., Valente, T., Gallaher, P., Rohrbach, L. A., & Unger, J. B. (2004). Social network predictors of bullying and victimization. *Adolescence*, *39*(154), 315–335.

Nahar, V., Unankard, S., Li, X., & Pang, C. (2012). Sentiment analysis for effective detection of cyber bullying. *Web Technologies and Applications*, *7235*, 764–774. doi:10.1007/978-3-642-29253-8_75

Ochoa, A., Ponce, J., Jaramillo, R., Ornelas, F., & Hernández, D. Eliasa, A., & Hernández, A. (2011, December). *Analysis of cyber-bullying in a virtual social networking*. Paper presented at the 11th International Conference on Hybrid Intelligent Systems, Malacca, Malaysia.

Olweus, D. (1991). Bully/victim problems among schoolchildren: Basic facts and effects of a school based intervention program. In Pepler, D. J., & Rubin, K. H. (Eds.), *The development and treatment of childhood aggression* (pp. 411–448). Mahwah, NJ: Lawrence Erlbaum Associates, Inc.

Pakaslahti, L., & Keltikangas-järvinen, L. (2001). Peer-attributed prosocial behavior among aggressive/preferred, aggressive/non-preferred, non-aggressive/preferred and non-aggressive/non-preferred adolescents. *Personality and Individual Differences*, *30*(6), 903–916. doi:10.1016/S0191-8869(00)00082-9

Pang, B., & Lee, L. (2008). Opinion mining and sentiment analysis. *Foundations and Trends in Information Retrieval*, *2*(1-2), 1–135. doi:10.1561/1500000011

Paragina, F., Paragina, S., & Jipa, A. (2011, April). *The cyberbullying and the educational resources*. Paper presented at the 7th International Scientific Conference eLearning and Software for Education, Bucharest, Romania.

Patchin, J. W., & Hinduja, S. (2006). Bullies move beyond the schoolyard: A preliminary look at cyberbullying. *Youth Violence and Juvenile Justice*, *4*(2), 148–169. doi:10.1177/1541204006286288

Pellegrini, A. D., Bartini, M., & Brooks, F. (1999). School bullies, victims, and aggressive victims: Factors relating to group affiliation and victimization in early adolescence. *Journal of Educational Psychology*, *91*(2), 216–224. doi:10.1037/0022-0663.91.2.216

Pittaro, M. (2007). Cyber stalking: An analysis of online harassment and intimidation. *International Journal of Cyber Criminology*, *1*(2), 180–197.

Ptaszynski, M., Dybala, P., Matsuba, T., Masui, F., Rzepka, R., & Araki, K. (2010, March). *Machine learning and affect analysis against cyberbullying*. Paper presented at the the Linguistic and Cognitive Approaches to Dialog Agents Symposium, Leicester, United Kingdom.

Reid, P., Monsen, J., & Rivers, I. (2004). Psychology's contribution to understanding and managing bullying within schools. *Educational Psychology in Practice*, *20*(3), 241–258. doi:10.1080/02667360420002518l7

Ressler, S. (2006). Social network analysis as an approach to combat terrorism: Past, present, and future research. *The Journal of the Naval Postgraduate School Center for Homeland Defense and Security*, *2*(2).

Reynolds, K., Kontostathis, A., & Edwards, L. (2011, December). *Using machine learning to detect cyberbullying*. Paper presented at the 10th International Conference on Machine Learning and Applications and Workshops, Honolulu, HI.

Rivers, I., & Noret, N. (2009). 'I h8 u': Findings from a five-year study of text and email bullying. *British Educational Research Journal*, *36*(4), 643–671. doi:10.1080/01411920903071918

Ruedy, M. C. (2008). Repercussions of a MySpace teen suicide: Should anti-cyberbullying laws be created. *North Carolina Journal of Law and Technology*, *9*(2), 323–346.

Sahin, M. (2012). The relationship between the cyberbullying/cybervictmization and loneliness among adolescents. *Children and Youth Services Review*, *34*, 834–837. doi:10.1016/j.childyouth.2012.01.010

Shariff, S. (2005). Cyber-dilemmas in the new millennium: School obligations to provide student safety in a virtual school environment. *McGill Journal of Education*, *40*(3), 467–487.

Singh, L., & Zhan, J. (2007, November). *Measuring topological anonymity in social networks*. Paper presented at the IEEE International Conference on Granular Computing, Silicon Valley, CA.

Slonje, R., & Smith, P. K. (2008). Cyberbullying: Another main type of bullying? *Scandinavian Journal of Psychology*, *49*, 147–154. doi:10.1111/j.1467-9450.2007.00611.x

Smith, P. K. (2004). Bullying: Recent developments. *Child and Adolescent Mental Health*, *9*(3), 98–103. doi:10.1111/j.1475-3588.2004.00089.x

Smith, P. K., Cowie, H., Olafsson, R. F., & Liefooghe, A. P. D. (2002). Definitions of bullying: A comparison of terms used, and age and gender differences, in a fourteen-country international comparison. *Child Development*, *73*(4), 1119–1133. doi:10.1111/1467-8624.00461

Smith, P. K., Mahdavi, J., Carvalho, M., Fisher, S., Russell, S., & Tippett, N. (2008). Cyberbullying: Its nature and impact in secondary school pupils. *Journal of Child Psychology and Psychiatry, and Allied Disciplines*, *49*(4), 376–385. doi:10.1111/j.1469-7610.2007.01846.x

Sood, S. O., Antin, J., & Churchill, E. F. (2012). *Using crowdsourcing to improve profanity detection* (Technical Report, SS-12-06). Retrieved from http://www.aaai.org/ocs/index.php/SSS/SSS12/paper/download/4256/4698

Stacey, E. (2008). Coping with the cyberworld: Student perspectives on cybersafe learning environments. In Schubert, S., Davies, G., & Stacey, E. (Eds.), *LYICT 2008: ICT and Learning in the Net Generation* (pp. 224–236). Kuala Lumpur, Malaysia: Open University Malaysia.

Sutton, J., & Smith, P. K. (1999). Bullying as a group process: An adaptation of the participant role approach. *Aggressive Behavior*, *25*, 97–111. doi:10.1002/(SICI)1098-2337(1999)25:2<97::AID-AB3>3.0.CO;2-7

Sweeny, L. (2002). K-anonymity: A model for protecting privacy. *International Journal on Uncertainty, Fuzziness and Knowledge-based Systems*, *10*(5), 557–570. doi:10.1142/S0218488502001648

Taki, M., Slee, P., Hymel, S., Pepler, D., Sim, H., & Swearer, S. (2008). A new definition and scales for indirect aggression in schools: Results from the longitudinal comparative survey among five countries. *International Journal of Violence and School*, *7*, 1.

Thornberg, R. (2007). A classmate in distress: Schoolchildren as bystanders and their reasons for how they act. *Social Psychology of Education*, *10*(1), 5–28. doi:10.1007/s11218-006-9009-4

Tokunaga, R. S. (2010). Following you home from school: A critical review and synthesis of research on cyberbullying victimization. *Computers in Human Behavior*, *26*(3), 277–287. doi:10.1016/j.chb.2009.11.014

Twyman, K., Saylor, C., Taylor, L. A., & Comeaux, C. (2010). Comparing children and adolescents engaged in cyberbullying to matched peers. *Cyberpsychology, Behavior, and Social Networking*, *13*(2), 195–199. doi:10.1089/cyber.2009.0137

Vandebosch, H., & Cleemput, V. K. (2008). Defining cyberbullying: A qualitative research into the perceptions of youngsters. *Cyberpsychology & Behavior*, *11*, 499–503. doi:10.1089/cpb.2007.0042

Veenstra, R., Lindenberg, S., Oldehinkel, A. J., Winter, A. F. D., Verhulst, F. C., & Ormel, J. (2005). Bullying and victimization in elementary schools: A comparison of bullies, victims, bully/victims, and uninvolved preadolescents. *Developmental Psychology*, *41*(4), 672–682. doi:10.1037/0012-1649.41.4.672

Ven, T. M. V. (2011). *Motivations behind cyber bullying and online aggression: Cyber sanctions, dominance, and trolling online*. (Master's thesis). Ohio University.

Wang, J., Nansel, T. R., & Iannotti, R. J. (2010). Cyber and traditional bullying: Differential association. *The Journal of Adolescent Health*, *48*, 415–417. doi:10.1016/j.jadohealth.2010.07.012

Wang, W. (2009). *Digital video forensics*. (Doctoral thesis). Dartmouth University.

Williams, K. R., & Guerra, N. G. (2007). Prevalence and predictors of internet bullying. *The Journal of Adolescent Health*, *41*, S14–S21. doi:10.1016/j.jadohealth.2007.08.018

Wolak, J., Mitchell, K. J., & Finkelhor, D. (2007). Does online harassment constitute bullying? An exploration of online harassment by known peers and online-only contacts. *The Journal of Adolescent Health, 41*(6), S51–S58. doi:10.1016/j.jadohealth.2007.08.019

Wong, A. H. (2009). *The prevalence of ethnicity-related victimization in urban multiethnic schools*. (Master's Thesis). University of Toronto.

Wong, D. S. W. (2004). School bullying and tackling strategies in Hong Kong. *International Journal of Offender Therapy and Comparative Criminology, 48*(5), 437–453. doi:10.1177/0306624X04263887

Xie, H., Farmer, T. W., & Cairns, B. D. (2003). Different forms of aggression among inner-city African–American children: Gender, configurations, and school social networks. *Journal of School Psychology, 41*(5), 355–375. doi:10.1016/S0022-4405(03)00086-4

Xu, J., Jun, K., Zhu, X., & Bellmore, A. (2012). Learning from bullying traces in social media. In *Proceedings of the Conference of the North American Chapter of the Association for Computational Linguistics: Human Language Technologies*. Stroudsburg, PA: The Association for Computational Linguistics.

Yang, Z., Wilson, C., Wang, X., Gao, T., Zhao, B. Y., & Dai, Y. (2011). Uncovering social network sybils in the wild. In *Proceedings of the ACM SIGCOMM Internet Measurement Conference* (pp. 259-268). New York, NY: Association for Computing Machinery.

Ybarra, M. L., Diener-west, M., & Leaf, P. J. (2007). Examining the overlap in Internet harassment and school bullying: Implications for school intervention. *The Journal of Adolescent Health, 41*(6), S42–S50. doi:10.1016/j.jadohealth.2007.09.004

Ybarra, M. L., & Mitchell, K. J. (2004). Youth engaging in online harassment: Associations with caregiver–child relationships, Internet use, and personal characteristics. *Journal of Adolescence, 27*(3), 319–3360. doi:10.1016/j.adolescence.2004.03.007

Ybarra, M. L., Mitchell, K. J., Wolak, J., & Finkelhor, D. (2006). Examining characteristics and associated distress related to internet harassment: Findings from the second youth internet safety survey. *Pediatrics, 118*(4), e1169–e1177. doi:10.1542/peds.2006-0815

Yin, D., Davison, B. D., Xue, Z., Hong, L., Kontostathis, A., & Edwards, L. (2009, April). *Detection of harassment on Web 2.0*. Paper presented at the Content Analysis in the Web 2.0, Madrid, Spain.

Zwart, M. D., Lindsay, D., Henderson, M., & Phillips, M. (2011). *Teenagers, legal risks and social networking sites*. Victoria, Australia: Monash University.

ADDITIONAL READING SECTION

Andrews, G. J., & Chen, S. (2006). The production of tyrannical space. *Children's Geographies, 4*(2), 239–250. doi:10.1080/14733280600807120

Beran, T., & Li, Q. (2007). The relationship between cyberbullying and school bullying. *Journal of Student Wellbeing, 1*(2), 15–33.

Blias, J. J. (2008). *Chatting, befriending, and bullying: Adolescent internet experiences and associated psychosocial outcomes*. (Doctoral thesis). Queen's University, Canada.

Datta, R., Joshi, D., Li, J., & Wang, J. Z. (2008). Image retrieval: Ideas, influences, and trends of the new age. *ACM Computing Surveys, 40*(2), 5: 1-60.

Dinakar, K., Jones, B., Havasi, C., Lieberman, H., & Picard, R. (in press). Commonsense reasoning for detection, prevention, and mitigation of cyberbullying. *ACM Transactions on Interactive Intelligent Systems*.

Dinakar, K., Jones, B., Lieberman, H., Picard, R., Rose, C., Thoman, M., & Reichart, R. (2011, June). *You too?! Mixed-initiative LDA story matching to help teens in distress*. Paper presented at the Sixth International AAAI Conference on Weblogs and Social Media, Dublin, Ireland.

Englander, E., Mills, E., & McCoy, M. (2009). Cyberbullying and information exposure: User-generated content in post-secondary education. *International Journal of Contemporary Sociology*, *46*(2), 215–230.

Hinduja, S., & Patchin, J. W. (2010). Bullying, cyberbullying, and suicide. *Archives of Suicide Research*, *41*(3), 206–221. doi:10.1080/13811118.2010.494133

Huttunen, A., Salmivalli, C., & Lagerspetz, K. M. J. (2006). Friendship networks and bullying in schools. *Annals of the New York Academy of Sciences. Understanding Aggressive Behavior in Children*, *794*, 355–359.

Kowalski, R. M., Limber, S. P., & Agatston, P. W. (2008). *Cyber bullying: The new moral frontier*. Oxford, UK: Blackwell Publishing Ltd. doi:10.1002/9780470694176

Li, Q. (2008). A cross-cultural comparison of adolescents' experience related to cyberbullying. *Educational Research*, *50*(3), 223–234. doi:10.1080/00131880802309333

Lin, W., Sun, M., Poovendran, R., & Zhang, Z. (2010). Group event detection with a varying number of group members for video surveillance. *IEEE Transactions on Circuits and Systems for Video Technology*, *20*(8), 1057–1067. doi:10.1109/TCSVT.2010.2057013

Moore, K. N. (2011). *Cyberbullying: An exploratory study of adolescent girls' perspectives on technology's impact on relationships*. (Doctoral Thesis). State University of New Jersey Rutgers.

Olweus, D. (1996). Bullying at school: Knowledge base and an effective intervention program. *Annals of the New York Academy of Sciences*, *794*, 265–276. doi:10.1111/j.1749-6632.1996.tb32527.x

Patchin, J. W., & Hinduja, S. (2006). Bullies move beyond the schoolyard: A preliminary look at cyberbullying. *Youth Violence and Juvenile Justice*, *4*(2), 148–169. doi:10.1177/1541204006286288

Sahin, M. (2012). The relationship between the cyberbullying/cybervictmization and loneliness among adolescents. *Children and Youth Services Review*, *34*, 834–837. doi:10.1016/j.childyouth.2012.01.010

Salmivalli, C. (1999). Participant role approach to school bullying: Implications for interventions. *Aggressive Behavior*, *25*, 97–111.

Smith, P. K., Mahdavi, J., Carvalho, M., Fisher, S., Russell, S., & Tippett, N. (2008). Cyberbullying: Its nature and impact in secondary school pupils. *Journal of Child Psychology and Psychiatry, and Allied Disciplines*, *49*(4), 376–385. doi:10.1111/j.1469-7610.2007.01846.x

Sood, S. O., Antin, J., & Churchill, E. F. (2012). *Using crowdsourcing to improve profanity detection* (Technical Report, SS-12-06). Retrieved October 1, 2012, from http://www.aaai.org/ocs/index.php/SSS/SSS12/paper/download/4256/4698

Sutton, J., & Smith, P. K. (1999). Bullying as a group process: An adaptation of the participant role approach. *Aggressive Behavior*, *25*, 97–111. doi:10.1002/(SICI)1098-2337(1999)25:2<97::AID-AB3>3.0.CO;2-7

Taki, M., Slee, P., Hymel, S., Pepler, D., Sim, H., & Swearer, S. (2008). A new definition and scales for indirect aggression in schools: Results from the longitudinal comparative survey among five countries. *International Journal of Violence and School*, *7*, 1.

Thornberg, R. (2007). A classmate in distress: Schoolchildren as bystanders and their reasons for how they act. *Social Psychology of Education*, *10*(1), 5–28. doi:10.1007/s11218-006-9009-4

Tokunaga, R. S. (2010). Following you home from school: A critical review and synthesis of research on cyberbullying victimization. *Computers in Human Behavior*, *26*(3), 277–287. doi:10.1016/j.chb.2009.11.014

Wolak, J., Mitchell, K. J., & Finkelhor, D. (2007). Does online harassment constitute bullying? An exploration of online harassment by known peers and online-only contacts. *The Journal of Adolescent Health*, *41*(6), S51–S58. doi:10.1016/j.jadohealth.2007.08.019

Xu, J., Jun, K., Zhu, X., & Bellmore, A. (2012). Learning from bullying traces in social media. In *Proceedings of the Conference of the North American Chapter of the Association for Computational Linguistics: Human Language Technologies*. Stroudsburg, PA: The Association for Computational Linguistics.

Ybarra, M. L. (2004). Linkages between depressive symptomatology and Internet harassment among young regular internet users. *Cyberpsychology & Behavior*, *7*(2), 247–257. doi:10.1089/109493104323024500

Ybarra, M. L., & Mitchell, K. J. (2007). Prevalence and frequency of internet harassment instigation: Implications for adolescent health. *The Journal of Adolescent Health*, *41*(2), 189–195. doi:10.1016/j.jadohealth.2007.03.005

KEY TERMS AND DEFINITIONS

Automated Tools to Detect Cyberbullying: Computing techniques and software for analyzing communications to determine whether the communications are being used for cyberbullying.

Cyberbullying: The abuse of digital media to cause psychological and social harm to others.

Face-to-Face Bullying: A traditional form of bullying in which bullies attack victims through physical, verbal, or social attacks.

Power over a Victim: The ability of a cyberbully to prevent the victim from adequate defense from the attacks. The ability can be increased by capabilities of digital media such as ubiquity and rapid spreading.

Roles in Cyberbullying: Individuals how participate in cyberbullying take on certain social roles. Examples of roles include a cyberbully who attacks a victim or a defender who helps a victim.

Social Attacks: Socially excluding a victim or spreading rumors about a victim to damage the social relationships of the victim.

Verbal Attacks: Physical, racial, or sexual teasing/insults about the victim and include threats about possible harm (e.g., stalking, violence, or death of the victim).

Chapter 5
Social Networks and Collective Intelligence:
A Return to the Agora

Manuel Mazzara
UNU-IIST, Macau & Newcastle University, UK

Nicola Dragoni
Technical University of Denmark, Denmark

Luca Biselli
Independent Researcher, UK

Antonio Marraffa
Polidoxa.com, Germany

Pier Paolo Greco
Newcastle University, UK

Nafees Qamar
UNU-IIST, Macau

Simona de Nicola
University of Bologna, Italy

ABSTRACT

Nowadays, acquisition of trustable information is increasingly important in both professional and private contexts. However, establishing what information is trustable and what is not, is a very challenging task. For example, how can information quality be reliably assessed? How can sources' credibility be fairly assessed? How can gatekeeping processes be found trustworthy when filtering out news and deciding ranking and priorities of traditional media? An Internet-based solution to a human-based ancient issue is being studied, and it is called Polidoxa, from Greek "poly" (πολύ), meaning "many" or "several" and "doxa" (δόξα), meaning "common belief" or "popular opinion." This old problem will be solved by means of ancient philosophies and processes with truly modern tools and technologies. This is why this work required a collaborative and interdisciplinary joint effort from researchers with very different backgrounds and institutes with significantly different agendas. Polidoxa aims at offering: 1) a trust-based search engine algorithm, which exploits stigmergic behaviours of users' network, 2) a trust-based social network, where the notion of trust derives from network activity and 3) a holonic system for bottom-up self-protection and social privacy. By presenting the Polidoxa solution, this work also describes the current state of traditional media as well as newer ones, providing an accurate analysis of major search engines such as Google and social network (e.g., Facebook). The advantages that Polidoxa offers, compared to these, are also clearly detailed and motivated. Finally, a Twitter application (Polidoxa@twitter) which enables experimentation of basic Polidoxa principles is presented.

DOI: 10.4018/978-1-4666-3926-3.ch005

INTRODUCTION

In the democratic city state of ancient Greece, the "agora" (from Greek: 'Αγορά, "gathering place" or "assembly") was the place where citizens used to meet, discuss, exchange information and make important decisions about the future of society. In this place, the concept of public sphere was born: in fact it was considered another kind of space, a sort of empty space next to the private one. The citizens used to meet there and considered it not a personal but a common space. It was by virtue of this effort that the perfect model of a democratic city was born: the agora was the meeting place of the assembly of citizens: in the public square each person is equal no one is subjected to any other. The agora was the political place of a multitude, composed by different parts but similar at the same time, all with the same rights. It was a place where discussions occurred without violence, force and abuses. Hannah Arendt in Vita Activa (Vita Activa, 1958) identified in this Greek model of cities the highest forms of citizenship: every Athenian citizen, in person and not through representation, when a serious risk and danger occurred, used to go in the agora and discuss the highest issues, committing themselves to put into practice what has been said. This was a political system based on equality of knowledge, information exchange and decision making fairness. Nowadays, the mechanism by which information is spread across (and consequently how decisions are made) has had a significant change in nature. In fact, the majority of people retrieve their information from major TV stations, radio and newspapers. The weakness of this mechanism is that it is a one-way information, not a cross-flow one. This means that citizens have lost their ability to interact with the decision making process. Consequently, the concept of "agora" is lost in favour of a different mechanism.

These days the average citizen gets access to information mainly by watching TV, especially the main national channels. Radio, newspapers and magazines represent a secondary source of information but they are hardly comparable to the power of TV. In particular, reading takes time and it does not suit well the hectic life style of modern times. As a consequence, information obtained by reading books can be considered quite negligible for an adult citizen with an average level of education. Another major problem comes from the fact that the majority of the world population speaks just its native language while some information is not always accessible in that language. Furthermore, to have a complete unbiased (or at least, multi-biased) source of information, it would be quite useful to access documents coming from diversified sources in different languages. According to the A.C. Nielsen Co., the average American citizen watches more than 4 hours of TV each day (or 28 hours/week, or 2 months of nonstop TV-watching per year). In a 65-year life span, that person will have spent 9 years watching TV. The percentage of Americans regularly watching TV while eating dinner is 66%, while 49% say they simply watch too much of it. These are very alarming numbers and they may raise health concerns, but the authors believe that there is an even bigger issue behind them. Accessing information mainly or exclusively from TV, as the common experience (plus statistics) shows, is obscuring the potential of other sources of information like radio, newspapers, magazines, books, the Internet or a community of trusted contacts. These other sources are generally able to provide a much wider opinion range. Indeed, we are not really able to access unbiased sources, but we could get what we call a "multi-biased source" at least. A more heterogeneous set of different viewpoints, which then could stimulate human critical thinking and cognitive interpolation is desirable.

Gatekeeping Process

The fundamental problem with TV news is that the information streaming is simply unidirectional, i.e., there is no possibility for the audience to interact with the process in any way. This is clearly the opposite principle with respect to that of the agora. The final result obtained from mass media passes through many levels of organizational processing on its way to the audience and, at each step the original data is filtered – reduced in length, edited and so on. Each step in the process could be identified as a gate, through which the data must pass before reaching the final users. Consequently, this situation is known as gatekeeping (White, 1950; Mccombs & Shaw, 1972. See Figure 1). Gatekeeping is generally a very effective mechanism to ensure that an irrelevant or misleading piece of information will not reach the general public. It determines a *quality assurance* process and an expert evaluation similar to what happens in conferences/journals peer-reviewed system. However, there is also a potential drawback: with TV and its gatekeeping mechanism, the audience is not able to provide real time feedback, and this may cause misunderstandings and lack of active interaction. Furthermore, people are not able to decide their information source or the type of content or express the will to expand some topics either. This means that mass media tend to "set the agenda," i.e., the list of items that people will be discussing. This theory is known as agenda-setting theory (McCombs, Shaw, 1972 & McCombs, 2004) and asserts that mass media have a large influence on audiences, choosing which stories have to be considered newsworthy and how much prominence and space they are given. Agenda-setting theory's main postulate is salience transfer *(ibidem)*. Salience transfer is the ability of a mass media to transfer relevant issues from their news media agendas to public agendas. Thus, the power of the media may lie not in its ability to determine people's opinions, but rather in its role of determining what issues will be considered important enough to discuss. Whatever is not appearing on the main media simply does not exist. This has a quite subtle consequence. The German political scientist Elisabeth Noelle-Neumann has defined an important theory called the spiral of silence theory (Noelle-Neumann, 1974). This theory asserts that a person is less likely to voice an opinion on a topic if he/she feels that idea belongs to a minority. This is for fear of reprisal or isolation from the majority. Thus, TV news can easily transfer this feeling to the watcher who is following the news from his home, maybe at a time of the day when the attention is not at its peak. As stated earlier, 66% of Americans regularly watch television while eating dinner and this is the time when news are usually broadcasted (McCombs & Shaw, 1972). A relevant social experiment emphasizing the fragility of the person in a mass society when he is confronted with the contrary opinion of a majority, and the tendency to conform even if this means to go against the person's basic perceptions, was made by Asch (Asch, 1955). Entman also described the spectator's condition very well in

Figure 1. Gatekeeping

World

his article "How the media affect what the people think," where he explains how media contribute to what people think precisely by affecting what they can think about (Entman, 1989).

In some cases, the fact that information goes through gatekeeping (i.e., every journalist has to go through several levels of approval (like director, editor, company shareholders) before the information is released to the public) could lead to situations that are unfavourable to the final "consumer." Consider, for example, the case in which news agencies are purchased and they become part of a larger business, where providing information may not be the main core business or in addition they could be affected by the company's position on the Stock Market. Example of this has been the concern that Reuters' objective reporting may be affected by recent merging with Thomson Corporation, owning 53% of the company, in contrast with the 15% limitation to share ownership historically imposed by its constitution to preserve freedom and integrity of the agency. More information on this concern can be found on the BBC website (http://news.bbc.co.uk/2/hi/business/6656525.stm).

Once the gatekeeping process has been understood, its potential risks and limitations have to be accepted together with its advantages. Now, if we consider how the main channels and news agencies are more and more centralized (like every other business), it is not difficult to realize how the whole mass media communication sector has the potential to be put under control in the future, especially in some countries where the democratic process is considered weaker (Maurer & Kolbitsch, 2006).

Outline and Contributions

This work contributes with several principles and technicalities to build a social platform to achieve collective intelligence via information sharing among trusted contacts. It also presents a Twitter-based implementation of a subset of these principles. Trust modeling, social networks, collective intelligence, algorithms and the relative motivations supported by literature in communication sciences are a quite inedited interdisciplinary blend, which has not been really investigated so far. We intend to pursue our investigation and expand our knowledge on this topic.

The chapter is structured as follows: after an introduction on the problems and motivations which led to this research, an overview on traditional media, search engines and social networks is presented and a synopsis is offered. What Polidoxa is and how its trust model works is then detailed. Specifically, the concept of trust is investigated under different perspectives and as a function of several parameters. Privacy and security, among others, are also considered. The relevant concept of "immunity" is also investigated. Finally, a Twitter-based implementation is presented as a first proof-of-concept prototype of the Polidoxa platform.

TRADITIONAL MEDIA

The mechanism by which traditional media (like TV, radio and newspapers) intrinsically operate, is to allow only passive actions, i.e., reading, watching and listening to specific contents according to the opinion of some expert or authority, which should guarantee the quality of information. The audience here does not control the medium content, the agenda setting, and the choice of experts and commentators in charge of presenting the facts. This means that the media owner (the publisher) indirectly chooses who the experts are and controls who says what. Indeed, in a globalized world, media from different cultural, political or religious background, present quite different interpretations of facts coming from different "experts." With so many sources of information and no shared and agreed evaluation parameters to decide who is an expert and on what, citizens are left in confusion. Even when, for fairness (or in Latin "*par condicio*"), experts from different parts are involved in the discussion, the user has still no chance to intervene in the process. The only freedom and choice given to the audience is switching the media, or that specific channel, off. The communication model is consequently unidirectional and it relies on three rigid rules: Gatekeeper, Speaker, and Audience, as shown in Figure 1.

INTERNET AND SEARCH ENGINES

Given the limitations of the traditional media, it is necessary a look into new media to identify how the gap could be filled. Since Internet offers an open platform to exchange information and can be considered a paradigm shift similar to the one that was brought by the Gutenberg's invention of mechanized press, it seems to be a valid target for this research.

With the arrival of Internet, the limitations of traditional media (i.e., offering only the passive actions of reading, watching and listening) can be overcome. It is indeed possible for users to control the information they achieved, choose the content to read and how to interact with other users or bloggers. It is also possible to choose the timing for accessing the information and by doing so, the tendency of watching the news while dining, which coincides with the weakest time for a critical thinking process, can be avoided. Internet has the full potential to reverse (or at least minimize) the process, avoiding the agenda-setting theory issues or the spiral of silence condition. However, to exploit this potential, users need some know-how: given the limited control on the information on the Web, it is possible to find very good pieces of so-called "alternative journalisms" as well as any kind of hoax.

Internet is not a passive media like TV; users are expected to be active and critical thinking is stimulated. However, users have to be educated to use the media. The potential of Internet could be seriously reduced in the future, if focal nodes will be set under control with the same gatekeeping process discussed for the traditional media. Again, gatekeeping is effective at ensuring quality but it limits feedback process and critical thinking. To the best of our knowledge, search engines like Google or social networks like Facebook are, for most users, the starting point of the majority of their research. So the important question is: how can we be sure that these nodes are trustworthy? Let us briefly analyse the main characteristics of these two powerful instruments in the hands of Internet users.

Search Engines

Today the most popular and used search engines on the market allow users to search over nothing less than trillions of different documents. Such a possibility was totally unthinkable only 20 years ago. However, results coming from these engines are mainly commerce-oriented and purely based on a quantitative algorithm that has significant margins of improvements in terms of results quality. For example, simply typing in Google bar "economic crisis in Europe" we are offered millions of links and their order is purely decided on the basis of the most linked pages, which tells nothing about the specific user needs, which are different from one person to another. There are two critical aspects of Google ranking: first, pages coming from popular newspapers are top ranked apart from their content; second, privileged ads slots can be bought, again independently from their content. Consequently, gatekeeping process is still an open issue and Google could be influenced as easily as TV channels. Furthermore, the communication model is still unidirectional. Given the enormous amount of information available on the Web and the typical user profile and effort put into the search, vast amount of information remains, in fact, inaccessible for users. Therefore, this communication model remains not very different from the one offered by traditional media, i.e., the

Gatekeeper (databases and ranking algorithm), Speaker (result page), Audience (users). The major lack in this model is the fact that the audience has no chance to self-configure the ranking algorithm and therefore being able to influence the content and the order of the search results (apart from minor flexibility given by the use of advanced search features). The way in which the search engine presents the results still remains a black box for the average user. Overall, it could be said that "what is not found on the first page of Google results does not exist." Considering how powerful a medium like Internet is, we would expect users to be somehow able to interact with it in a much more proactive way.

SOCIAL NETWORKS

Social networks service like Facebook have a focus on collecting and sharing users' data (family, friends, pictures etc...) and personal interests/information. These days, they have massive numbers of users accounting worldwide for an incredible amount of hours of usage. If we disregard all the private information posted on Facebook, which are irrelevant for people outside your closest group, the platform can be proactively used to share quality information. Indeed, social networks are very different from search engines, because of the way the source of information can be controlled by users. A generic user, for example, can follow a specific trusted friend or hide information coming from (or going to) untrusted users, who seem to post information considered irrelevant. Unfortunately, even with Facebook, users are not able to rank information since all posts are only shown chronologically. Users are not able to set content alerts to be informed only about specific topics. Another issue is that users cannot enrich their posts by linking pieces of information that are not on the Internet, although this is becoming less and less relevant as all the other media are also posting their contents on the Web.

Being Facebook supported by advertising, this information is more critical in term of quantity, rather than quality. The way Facebook is structured does not consequently promote or improve critical thinking, learning, comprehension and discussion among its users. Mechanisms such as "like," for example, are structured for giving just a quick evaluation, which, as a consequence, may be simply an accelerated feeling, not moderated by critical thinking. According to a Nielsen's Company research, people are spending more and more time on social networks. Global average time spent is in fact about five and half hours per month and this number is increasing, with Facebook currently dominating its position as a destination.

Social networking is globally expanding and it is likely to deeply influence the way people will interact with other people in the future, promoting connections able to go beyond the classical geographical limits (Mazzara, Marraffa, Biselli, & Chiarabini, 2011). At the same time, social networks have some other interlinked privacy and security issues that are discussed hereunder.

TRUST, PRIVACY, AND SECURITY IN SOCIAL NETWORKING

Massive use-based growth of social networks such as Facebook, LinkedIn, and MySpace --with millions of users everyday-- play an indispensable role in our daily-life. Nonetheless, dissemination of unverified (dis)information on such social networking sites can affect individuals as well as religious, ethnic and geographically dislocated communities. Such a factor alludes to intentional- or unintentional sharing of information where people are pulled into fierce debates as well as conflicts. This is actually a "wild expansion" of social networks (in terms of data) that has paved the way to share personal opinions along with possibly forged facts favouring a specific group. Albeit social networks proclaim several benefits and competitive features, they are not exempt from subtle data leakages and facts misinterpretations. This further means that there is no independent source to confirm the validity of given facts and figures. They also lack in specifying and implementing appropriate security and privacy procedures to protect users' data. For example, our whole Facebook album is exposed to a stranger after a comment from a friend in our network. Also, how our stored information can be manipulated is one of the unknown aspects. Several famous personalities across the globe have been the victims of intruders and attackers on such social networks. Ordinary users are generally unaware of such intricacies unless they encounter certain inconveniences against which they report loss of data and misuse of their accounts. Such victims are large in numbers and they need coordinated efforts to deal with their issues.

Yet another and implicit aspect of users' data may as well be sold by a social network to a third party. An outcome can also be compromising data integrity and confidentiality (irrespective of the intentional or unintentional move) due to flexibly implemented security mechanisms or inadequate security policies. These issues are encouraging to underpin the state-of-the-art trust, security and privacy, and the collaborative ability among users of such social networks. The alluded issues have been already approached in various ways such as Safebook (Cutillo, Molva, & Önen, 2011), which offers a so-called replacement to Facebook using P2P network in a more decentralised way. Safebook puts a special emphasis on the privacy of its users with regards to the application provider and shields against malicious users or intruders. Ding, Cruz, and Li (2009) attempted to model a feature social network called friend suggestion. Their approach is based on high level Petri nets, but extended with channels to formally model social networks. Another recent added challenge to security and privacy is in mobile social networks, which require user's location and preferences. Issues reported in mobile social networks can be found in Beach, Gartrell, and Han (2009) such as direct anonymity issues and eavesdropping, spoofing, replay and wormhole attacks. This lack of security and privacy does not surprise at all, since social network applications do not take into account security and privacy by design.

To the authors' interest, trust and a cohesive collaboration environment are vital to understand and enhance social networks' security and collaboration on the available information. To this end, use of formal methods in terms of analysing and reasoning security and privacy properties based on the proposed trust model are justified as they allow simulating patterns and systems existing in nature. For example, using formal methods one can unambiguously specify pattern of social relationships and then reason about it. For instance, Fong, Anwar, and Zhao (2009) have provided a formalized model of Facebook access control mechanism and reported it as a Discretionary Access Control (DAC).

Our proposed construction of formal models for modelling trust in social networks requires a rigorous treatment by using novel concepts and then by allowing formal reasoning over the constructed models. However, before constructing trust model one should think of access control mechanism to be applied. For example, access control mechanism and a security policy play the role of backbone in such systems which can be taken into account to construct formal models. For instance, DAC can only be used where the user of a computer system is fully aware of the consequences of a granted permission and revoking it, which is just not the case in Facebook. It is pertinent to note that although Facebook offers DAC it eventually fails to handover all the control to its users. Thus, a greater portion of the information is beyond the control of users, and actually the information is centrally administered -- just as in Role-Based Access Control (RBAC). Centrally administered security policies result in exposing users' photo albums or a wall post, and similarly falsely suggesting a friend outside one's network.

The notion of trust is equally applicable to social networks. For example, Bonneau, Anderson, and Church (2009) suggested having privacy suites that can be chosen from the user's privacy settings. These suites would be specified by friends or trusted experts, with the possibility to be modified by its user if necessary. One of the reasons to opt for such an option roots back to the problem that users lack an understanding of privacy settings. For example, Facebook presents 61 settings on 7 different configuration pages, and LinkedIn has 52 settings on 18 Pages (*ibidem*). Thus, given a trust model between a user's friends and other experts, one can reduce the security and privacy threats in social networks. However, those are unformalized trust models and incomparable to our approach in that they do not study and embed the mechanism in addition to applying access control. Our extended focus is also to monitor the information flow on these social networking sites and to address users' needs accordingly from media perspectives.

SYNOPSIS

In synthesis, our research identified the following:

- **Traditional Media:** The content is controlled by the gatekeeper.
- **Web and Search Engines:** The content is controlled by the gatekeeper, but users can decide the topic. However, the requested content has to be stored in the corporation databases and this content has to appear reasonably high in the engine ranking to be accessible to the average user.
- **Social Networks:** The content is not controlled by any central authority or gatekeeper, but it is controlled by the specific user belonging to a contacts' network. The major feature of a user's network is trustworthiness of the content.

POLIDOXA AND TRUST

The advent of social networks may give rise to a paradigm shift in communication provided that a number of issues are solved. Our objective are those of combining the potential of search engines to quickly retrieve information and the ability of controlling its source, which is typical of social platforms. Polidoxa (from Greek "poly," (πολύ), meaning many or several and "doxa" (δόξα), meaning "common belief" or "popular opinion") is a platform which aims at introducing the concept of "trust" in social networks to improve information quality and general knowledge. In social sciences "trust" is defined as a situation where one party is willing to rely on the actions of another party (Mayer, Davis, & Schoorman, 1995).

More formally, let us define a set U of users; the function trust is defined as follows:

$$Trust : \left(A \in U, B \in U\right) \rightarrow \left[0, 99\right]$$

That means, the trust of a user A for user B is expressed by a natural number between 0 and 99. For example, *Trust (Alice, Bob) = 99* means that Alice consider Bob a very trustable individual. It is worth noting that this function is not transitive, i.e., it can be that *Trust (Bob, Alice) = 0.*

At the moment, social networks like Facebook or LinkedIn allow only information to be shown chronologically or being filtered in some very basic way. There is no notion/acknowledgement of "trust" between users and different contacts have similar relevance. Polidoxa is instead based on the principle that immediate contacts have more influence, while the others see a reduction of their influence which is proportional to their distance. Even direct contacts are not all at the same level, but users can decide a "trust" score and this score will change over time according to their activities. Polidoxa is based on the principle of collective/ swarm intelligence which is the normal way of operating between colonies of insects living in collaborative communities (Maurer & Kolbitsch, 2006; Joslyn, Rocha, Smith, Johnson, Rasmussen, & Kantor, 1998).Trust is the key to information and Internet has an enormous potential to fix the issue of information trustworthiness.

Multi-Dimensional Trust

In the previous section trust was considered to be a mono-dimensional entity. In reality, trust between individuals is not a mono-dimensional entity, but a multi-dimensional one. Multi-dimensional trust can be formally defined as follows (*U* is a set of users and *T* is a set of topics):

$$MTrust : \left(A \in U, B \in U, t \in T\right) \rightarrow \left[0, 99\right]$$

That means, the trust of a user *A* for user *B* regarding a topic t is again expressed by a natural number between 0 and 99. For example, *Trust (Alice, Bob, football) = 99* means that Alice consider Bob a very trustable individual. It is worth noting that this function is not transitive, i.e., it can be that *Trust (Bob, Alice, football) = 0* while, at the same time, it can be *Trust (Bob, Alice, fashion): 99.*

A given topic *t* directly defines a projection of trust over a user's contacts.

$$Experts : \left(A \in U, t \in T\right) \rightarrow P\left(U\right)$$

For example, for Alice Bob, Ken, and John are football experts and their opinion is highly valuable:

Experts (Alice, football) = {Bob, Ken, John}

Once a subjective set of experts for a given user and topic has been individuated, a number of analyses can be performed on these experts, for example opinion mining.

Opinion Mining and Collective Intelligence

Although other researchers have used swarm intelligence techniques to get high quality data from web communities, applying swarm intelligence algorithms to social networks to achieve collective intelligence is an open research domain. One of the most promising investigations is described in "Swarm Intelligence for Analysing Opinions in Online Communities" by the University of Erlangen-Nuremberg in Germany. In this work, text mining techniques are combined to ant colony metaheuristic algorithm to perform opinion mining. This research can be divided in two major parts: 1) opinion mining and 2) use of ant colony for swarm opinion forecast. The main goal of this work is to distinguish between "positive," "negative" and "no opinion." The method consists in separating the words in each sentence and calculating the relative frequencies. At that point, polarity of each post is calculated. The results of this work are presented in Figure 2.

Once opinion mining has been performed, an algorithm inspired by the ant colony metaheuristic can be used. The actual implementation of the algorithm consists in using posts polarity as ant pheromones. In this way, ants can predict next post polarity. More details about ant algorithm will be given in the following sections.

Figure 2. Opinion mining

Class	Precision	Recall
Positive	62.96%	62.52%
Negative	86.35%	86.05
No Opinion	81.65%	81.07%

Quarantine and Trust as a Function of Distance

Trust is not only a multi-dimensional, but also a multi-level concept. Google+ (https://plus.google.com/), for example, evaluates only the first degree of separation between contacts. Polidoxa, instead, aims at evaluating the whole network of contacts, assuming knowledge sharing as being important even when coming from indirect sources. The assumption is that immediate contacts have more influence, while other contacts from different levels see a reduction of their influence, which is somehow proportional to their distance. Every user of Polidoxa has an inner circle of first contact users which he/she likes to follow and are considered information sources and generators. Whoever is not in this immediate set of trusted sources belongs to "the rest of the world," a grey mass of users about whom he/she does not have any information. Polidoxa aims at offering a second list of users, i.e., a "selection" of people from "the rest of the world" which has the potential to become relevant and trustworthy by the user. This list of people will be kept initially in a "quarantined mode," i.e., under observation and the user will be able to pick up some (or all) of those and bring them into the set of direct contacts. How do these candidates are selected from the system among the (potentially) millions of users? It is well-known that every person in the world is separated on average by anybody else by six steps; at least in western urban world. This fact is well known as the "Six degrees of separation theory" or "Small-world experiment" (Travers & Milgram, 1969). Thus, how can the "most trustable" persons in the system be suggested to the users? A mathematical model of "trust transitivity" needs to be developed. How does trust decrease when we pass from one level of separation to the next one? This issue is not entirely solved at the moment and several possible solutions are under consideration. The most obvious, simple, but imprecise solution is defining the inferred trust as decreasing in a linear way.

Let us define a function expressing the distance between two users:

$$Dist : \left(A \in U, B \in U\right) \rightarrow N$$

Now, let us suppose we have (with *k=99* in this case):

$Dist(A,B) = x$

then

$Trust\ (A, B) = k \text{ for } x=1$
$Trust\ (A, B) = 1/x * k \text{ for } x>1$

This means that first level contacts have here a value trust of 99 and the indirect contacts see their trust decreasing in a linear way. Of course, this is a simplification since the direct contact trust can be in fact set by the user (in practice this *k* is changing over time, see the following sections to understand how further parameters are implied in this change).

However, this solution is imprecise because we know by experience that trust is not a linear relationship, i.e., the contacts a person has at the third or even fourth level, have a value which is generally close to zero while direct contacts or contacts of contacts are very valuable. Other better possibilities are expressed in Figure 3.

Figure3. Trust definition

$\text{TRUST}(u,v) = \alpha(d(u,v))$	
Linear	$\alpha(x) = \frac{1}{x}$
Quadratic	$\alpha(x) = \frac{1}{x^2}$
Gravitational	$\alpha(x) = \frac{1}{4\pi x^2}$

We are evaluating another ranking system based on a trust relationship inspired to a Kepler-Newton modelling system. During our life time we in fact trust our parents, relatives, friends, or even people we do not know, creating our solar system. We add "new planets" which we critically found compatible to the beliefs of our mental galaxy. Our contact links are based on a non-linear relationship, where the quality of trust increases when it gets closer to our beliefs, knowledge, commitment etc. Research in this area has been already developed at McGill University, Canada (Maheswaran, Tang, & Ghunaim, 2007). The Inverse Square Law on which the idea is based is shown in Figure 4. We can make a simpler analogy between this idea and how forces distribute over a sphere. By defining the intensity i of the *Trust* as: $i = T/A$ where *T* is *Trust* and *A* the area of the sphere, i.e., our social network, we *get* $i = T/A = k*T/(4\pi x^2)$ with x the radius. Thus, if $x2 > x1$ *then* $i2 < i1$ which means the more the contact is distant, the less powerful the trust is.

SOCIAL NETWORKS, SWARMS, AND COLLECTIVE INTELLIGENCE

A platform like Polidoxa, based on a community of a potentially significant number of members (the humankind) has the potential of becoming a "Swarm," using an analogy inspired by the concept of "swarm intelligence" found in nature (Beni & Wang, 1989). We have studied, at a micro scale level, whether swarm intelligence can help parts of Polidoxa algorithms and, at macro scale level, whether new interesting aspects can emerge regarding intelligence and knowledge sharing coming from the online Polidoxa community. Swarm intelligence in nature has been primarily investigated regarding the achievement of goals like, for example, finding optimal paths to food and other tasks of relevant importance for a community of social insects. Recently this concept has inspired the exploration of new algorithms to solve optimization problems, for example the "Travelling Salesman Problem" (Kuo, Horng, Kao, Lin, Lee, Chen, Pan, & Terano, 2010). As stated earlier, from the point of view of the

Figure 4. Inverse square law

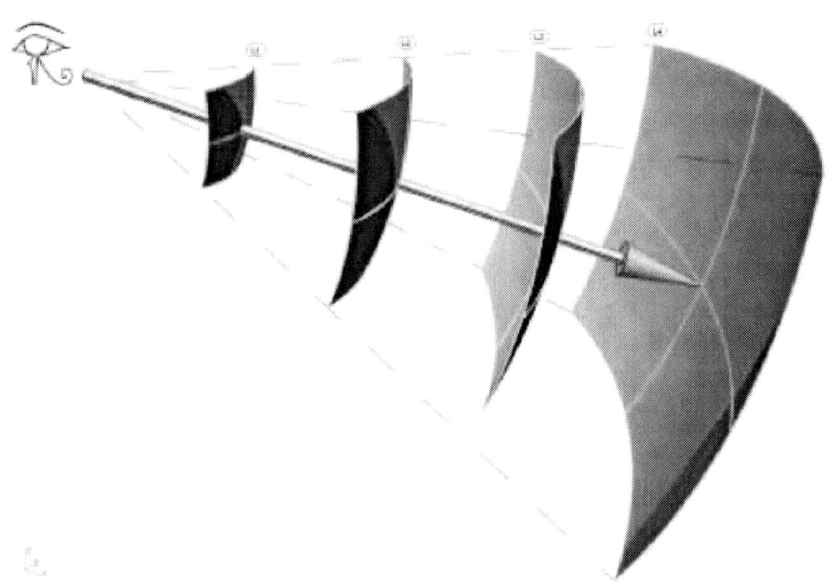

communication issue, Polidoxa's main goal is the improvement of information quality, general knowledge and discussion. Although this cannot be formulated as an optimization problem (there is simply no ideal optimum), swarm intelligence can be still exploited as it will be presented in next sections.

At a macroscale level, is there any analogy between Polidoxa and a swarm intelligent system? In nature, swarms, as systems, have some common characteristics, which have been analysed by (Dorigo & Birattari, 2007):

- They are composed by many individuals.
- These individuals are identical, or in some cases, they have some small variations.
- The single individual has only local knowledge of the system.
- The overall result of the system is the interaction between the independent agents or interacting with the environment in a stigmergic way.
- The resulting system is self-organizing.

In the next paragraphs the concept of stigmergy, which was introduced in this above list, will be analysed in more details. In nature, swarm intelligence can emerge from members with limited intellectual capabilities *per se* (such as communities of ants, termites, bees, etc.), interacting in an in direct and asynchronous way. However, the potential performance of a community made by individuals having higher intelligence is still an open issue. The idea that an online community made of human groups can exhibit an intelligent behaviour has been investigated by some authors (Luo, Xia, Yoshida, & Wang. 2009). It was concluded that these communities have their own characteristics, which are different from "Team Intelligence" and "Business Intelligence," normally the target of "intelligence modeling." This is because in a team, only a small number of participants are involved. Furthermore, in business there is normally a hierarchy, scarce flexibility and openness, which are instead characteristics of online communities, where there is more freedom and participation may not be constant. New participants can bring in new ideas and creativity to the online community they join, as well as interpretations, for example regarding facts. The process is of course bidirectional, because incoming knowledge is also outcoming knowledge, back to the members. The obvious consequence of this bidirectional flow is that the gatekeeping process is no longer necessary to choose the topics which are relevant for the mass. The system will self-organize in search of relevant issues and news. Luo, Xia, Yoshida, and Wang (2009), have started to study what community intelligence is and when it can emerge, defining it as the result of a "triple interwoven network of knowledge network, human network and media network (technological network)."

Polidoxa platform, being potentially based on a large number of members, can be affected by the "swarm effect" and consequently show collective intelligence, due to the interaction, knowledge transfer and exchange between a massive number of participants belonging to different networks. Although this system can ideally perform like a neural network in a brain, the authors recognize that being communities focused on interests, opinions, etc, the concept of a "global brain" (Russel, 1993) may not suitable for online communities and the expression of "supernetworks," networks of networks, may be more appropriate (Nagurney & Wakolbinger, 2005).

As a community of users, Polidoxa will be based on a network of humans, a media network, the web and a knowledge network. Knowledge will be stored on the Web and it will be re delivered to the individuals, in a way which is very similar to the performance of stigmergic systems (Dorigo, Bonabeau, & Theraulaz, 2000). It can then be concluded that Luo, Xia, Yoshida, and Wang's model can indeed fit and describe how Polidoxa can perform and how a stigmergic behaviour can emerge from the collective intelligence of this online community.

A Stigmergic Behavioural System as in Swarms

As previously anticipated, the concept of "Stigmergy" (Dorigo, Bonabeau, & Theraulaz, 2000) has been regarded as significant in shaping the Polidoxa platform. The idea is inspired by Social Insect colonies, which are huge communities. To communicate they use a "face to face" communication system without the intervention of a centralized artificial medium (Miller, 2010). This system guarantees that information will never be centralized by a small colony subset. The knowledge sharing process works bottom-up, following the principles of democracy as described regarding the Agora. This principle seems to work efficiently in insects' communities. Every time the information is passed on, the receiver checks who the sender is. If some information is ambiguous, the receiver stops the information flow and sends other insects to control which information is actually the correct one. As previously analysed, the human way to transfer and share information is different and it is normally influenced at best, or filtered, at worst, by mass media (TV, radio, newspaper, books, education system, etc.). Humans communicate in an unreliable way because they almost entirely rely upon mass media, bypassing every democratic principle and accepting a top down sharing of information. From a technical point of view, while a very strict group of people may have the potential to control mass information, this is impossible with the insects' communication model, which does not permit a centralized control. Consequently, the authors believe that insect colonies behaviour may inspire Polidoxa mechanism to work efficiently without any necessary centralized control, apart from technical assistance.

If Polidoxa aims at working like a stigmergic system, social interaction and networking are enhanced by the "collective intelligence," which will be superior to the sum of knowledge of individuals, as analysed in previous chapter. As a result of this, Polidoxa can consequently offer a platform for discussion which may contribute at elevating users' higher level of knowledge, criticism and consciousness (open source projects like Wikipedia, assuming there are no administrators, are examples of successful stigmergic systems). They work in a similar way to how social insect colonies build up a complex system to tell each other where to locate sources of food or picking up materials. Wikipedia is based on a collaborative system, without any external instruction, guidance or hierarchy. In the same way, Polidoxa users, as a colony of brains, can (a) share information, (b) interact with it, (c) generate discussion, (d) enhance the service itself, (e) redefine how it will work in the future, etc. This happens as in a self-organizing system, which facilitates cooperative team work. This evolution from chaotic groups to self-organized users groups without any central guidance, will help in redefining of how information can be delivered, offering a real alternative to the traditional media top-down approach. The limitations imposed by the lack of users' guidance and hierarchy to meet the community goals, are possibly overcome by introducing a Holonic System functionality in Polidoxa.

How Polidoxa as a Holonic System Addresses the Lack of Hierarchy

The concept of a holonic system, first coined by Koestler (1968), can be expressed in engineering terms as that of a system that is made up of autonomous units who are themselves (sub)systems, all acting in a cooperative way (Brennan, 2001). Although subject to the system's supra-hierarchy called holarchy, self-reliant units are characterised by a degree of independence, that aims at self-sustaining, stability and efficient use of resources (Calabrese, 2011). The intrinsic duality of a holonic system, being simultaneously a "whole" and a "part" brings in a potentially new approach in how to implement the aims of the Polidoxa Platform.

An example of a holonic system and its duality is the human body; being it a whole system whose physical boundaries could be set as the skin that "senses" many, although not all the external "signals," it transfers these signals to the brain which interprets them and instructs the specialised sub-systems (such as organs, muscles, etc.) to perform the required action(s). The Holon, seen as a self-contained autonomous and cooperative entity, can be described also as a dissipative system in thermodynamics. A dissipative system (an Open System) is capable of exchanging energy and matter and interacts with the outer environment by means of its surroundings; any exchange of energy and/or matter results in the modification of its internal energy. These exchanges can be considered stimulus and they will produce a response that is managed by higher-level components "super-holons" and is transferred to lower-level components "sub-holons." A holonic system is represented in Figure 5.

If the stimulus that the Super-Holon detects from the external environment through suitable sensors can be of different nature, and not all may be beneficial, it is of primary interest to understand and implement how it is it possible to prevent malicious stimulus to affect the holon. This challenging task requires that stimulus, or Users from now on, are recognised as genuine ones after being quarantined before gaining access. Any recognised malicious user will then be expelled from the system and prevented from re-entry even if it changes "identity." The following paragraphs provide a methodological approach towards the holonic quarantine.

Invited Users or Self-Candidacy Users

Polidoxa aims at redefining the Trust, and Trust defines acceptance among users. Polidoxa is based on a holonic system which acts as a whole system and, simultaneously, as a cooperating set of sub-systems. Users' attempts to gain entry to the Polidoxa platform need to be recognised not only as non-malicious, but they have to comply with the goals of (a) being self-sustaining, (b) increase system's stability and (c) make efficient use of available resources (of the Polidoxa users' community). Quarantine is believed to be an effective way for any user to be accepted by the Polidoxa community; quarantine is performed by peers (other Polidoxa users) who are fully specialised and so capable of recognising a similar pair.

A very interesting example of such peer-reviewed activity is offered once again by nature. Studies on ants' communities demonstrated that once a colony member has been infected, its nestmates perform a grooming activity toward the affected pair with the ultimate goal of guarantee-

Figure 5. A holonic system composed by a super-holon, a lower level holon and a further lower-level sub-holons; when stimulated by the outer environment the holon produces responses to sub-holons and then to the outer environment

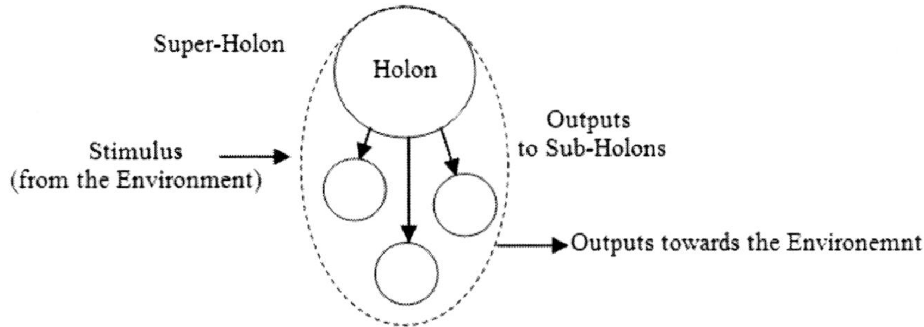

ing the survival of the whole colony (Konrad et al., 2012). The tasks can be broken down in few steps and the ants behave in such a way that they 1) share part of the fungal infection in order lower its concentration from the severely affected individual to non-lethal values, 2) transfer (sharing) of low infection levels triggers the immune system of the grooming group and speeds up the healing process of the affected individual 3) the immunizing agent acts as a marker for the recognition of future occurrences of the infection. By doing so the community is preserved from identical future infections because the immunization information has become part of common knowledge (*ibidem*).

Social contact to pathogen-exposed individuals, or malicious users, enables immunisation of the entire colony, the Polidoxa community, and this is applied to Polidoxa. A sequence of steps would be as follows: a) each user intervenes in quarantining a new user and is (or should be) capable of recognising any potential threat, b) acts to remove the malicious pathogen, c) keep memory of it and shares the information for social immunisation, and d) the malicious user is marked and permanently banned from any future re-entry attempt.

Trust as a Function of Network Activity

As shown previously, trust changes as a function of distance. Furthermore, trust changes over time as a function of network activity. The following parameters have been individuated as being relevant to update trust:

- For each user, the number of likes related to his posts: user popularity.
- For each user, the ratio #Likes/#Dislike (with #A cardinality of set A) for that user.
- Rate of activities (share, comments, like, dislike) on a posted item within a temporal interval.
- Number of private messages between the user and another user.
- For each post of the user, the number of comments coming from another user.
- Number of user comments to posts coming from another user.
- Followers list.
- Users that belong to subscribed groups.
- Each group to which the user belong, number of the published posts on that group.
- List of configurable keywords.
- Favourite sites/blogs list.
- Post labels.
- Post frequencies.
- RSS feed's list of the user and of all the first grade user's contacts –i.e., people directly connected with him – (configurable in case of extension to more than one level).

Table 1 synthesizes how trust has to be calculated at given time intervals.

All these parameters can be used to identify malicious users and non-trustworthy information in the style of Immune Network Systems but this goes beyond the scope of this work.

Table 1. How trust has to be calculated at given time intervals.

Dynamic Parameters Depending on Activities and Degree of Separation
1: Evaluate ***like* and *dislike***: the more 'like' an article gets, the more important it is
2: Evaluate **comments in *like* thread**
3: Evaluate **amount and frequency of *share* function within a temporal interval**: a high frequency within a temporal interval is an indicator of hot and important news
4: Evaluate the **number of comments** of the post
5: Evaluate the **number of private messages** exchanged with the poster
6: Evaluate **keywords, labels match**
7: Evaluate **if the poster belongs to a shared group** and **the activities on that group**
8: Evaluate **the freshness** of a document/article/post

POLIDOXA@TWITTER

Polidoxa@Twitter (Chamot, 2012) is the implementation of a simplified version of the Polidoxa's principles on top of the Twitter platform. Twitter (https://twitter.com) has many of the described characteristics of social networks like Facebook and LinkedIn. It has a simplicity which makes it a very good case study to experiment the ideas presented in this work, without worrying about unnecessary complications: information as it is presented in Facebook and LinkedIn is structured and varied (text, pictures, videos etc...); Twitter instead enables its users to send and read only text-based posts of up to 140 characters (the "tweets"). This makes easier to collect and store them for analysis purposes. Having Twitter mostly text information, only text-based analysis is necessary (no picture recognition or particular data analysis etc.…). Since the number of tweets exchanged in a given timeframe is much higher than the number of Facebook or LinkedIn posts, it is therefore faster to create a collection of relevant data (news). Furthermore, tweets messages contain *hashtags* which are important to make the analysis more effective and efficient.

The remaining of this section will present an overview of the current prototype. Describing the implementation details is far out of the scope of this work and it would require a dedicated treatment. The prototype has been developed as a Twitter application that provides services to collect, store and analyze information gathered from Twitter. From a functional point of view, the architecture of the system can be divided into three main components: a *front-end application* acting as interface between the user and a *back-end application* that implements the data model and all the relative Polidoxa services. The *back-end application* interacts with a mysql *database* in which all the data is stored. The *front-end application* provides an access control model based on two different user roles: administrator and normal user. Let us focus on the functionalities offered to a normal user.

In order to use the Polidoxa application, each user must authenticate using his/her Twitter account, as shown in Figure 6.

If the authentication succeeds, then the user is redirected to a registration form that has to be filled in to complete the registration. See Figure 7.

Figure 6. User authentication

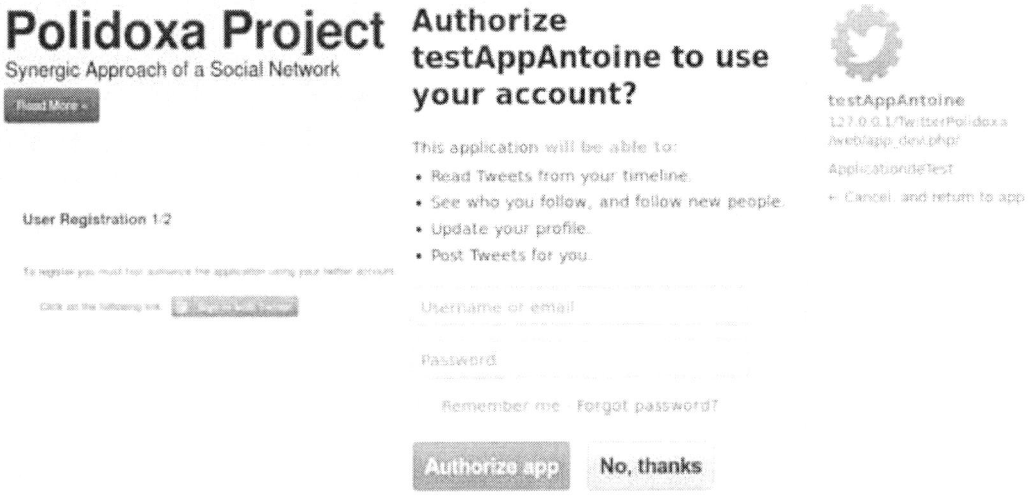

Figure 7. User registration form

Finally, the application checks whether the twitter account has not been already registered. In case of success, a validation email is sent to the user with a link to validate the account. After validation, the registration is completed and the user can finally log-in.

Figure 8. Static trust setup

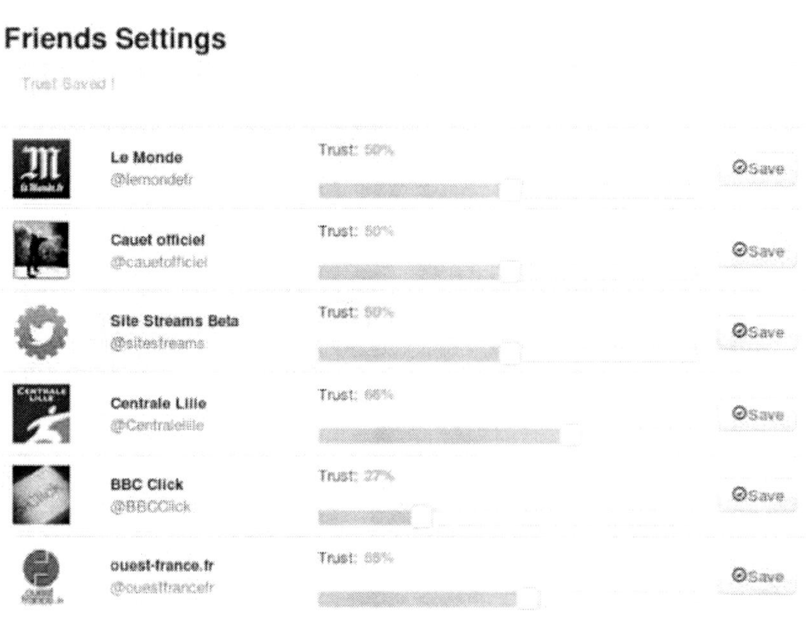

Static Trust

Each user's contact in a Polidoxa@twitter network is associated with a static parameter representing the trust value defined by the user for his/her relationship with that particular contact. Trust is a percentage with a default value of 50%. The user can update this value at any time (Figure 8). Tweets are initially visualized/ranked/ordered according to this value.

Dynamic Trust

Contacts that have a specific activities history have to be considered more relevant and have an automatic offset/boost of their trust values (for example a person with a default of 50% after some activity could rise to 55% and then 60%). The dynamic trust is used to order result on the basis of the user network activities. This network activity information has been collected and stored in a back-end database. The dynamic trust is calculated for each contact using the formula shown in Figure 9.

Figure 9. Trust formula

$$Dynamic\_Trust = Static\_Trust + \alpha_F * Nbr\_favorites + \alpha_R * Nbr\_retweets + \alpha_M * Nbr\_mentions + \alpha_{FF} * Nbr\_FridayFollows + \alpha_C * Results\_count$$

The formula contains the following parameters:

- **Static Trust:** User-defined value in the range 0,…,10.
- **Nbr_favorites:** Number of tweets sent by the contact and favoured by the user. This number is multiply by a coefficient chosen by the administrator.
- **Nbr_retweets:** Number of tweets sent by the contact and retweeted by the user. This number is multiply by a coefficient chosen by the administrator.
- **Nbr_mentions:** Number of tweets sent by the user containing mentions referring this friend. This number is multiply by a coefficient chosen by the administrator.
- **Nbr_FridayFollows:** Number of tweets sent by the user containing FridayFollows referring this friend. This number is multiply by a coefficient chosen by the administrator.
- **Results_count:** Number of tweets belonging to the friend matching the given search. This number is multiply by a coefficient chosen by the administrator.

The first four parameters are related to the activity occurring between the user performing the search and each of his/her contact. The idea is to give more importance to those contacts with whom the user interacted more. The last parameter is instead not specific to a contact but to a search: it corresponds to the number of matching items when a query is performed.

In order to decrease the dynamic trust value, the network activity of each user does not take into account items older than one full year. Therefore, if a user has not been interacting with a contact for some time, this will result in a decrement of the dynamic trust.

The coefficients appearing in the formula above can be set at any time only by the system administrator. This can be done throughout a dedicated interface, as shown in Figure 9.

The result of a search is displayed to the user as shown in Figure 10. The number of results is given at the top of the list of tweets. This list is composed of ordered tweets. For each of them the trust value is shown at the top right corner. Only the first 50 results are loaded. If the user scrolls down then the next 50 are added and so on, until no more results are available.

Figure 10. Configuration of coefficients for dynamic trust

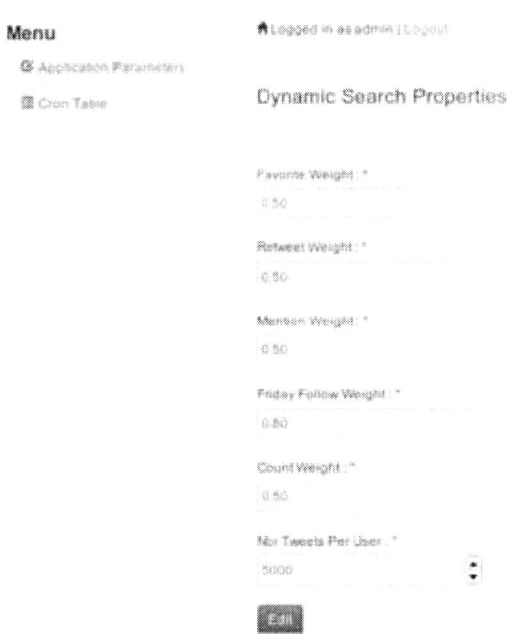

Searches can be configured by means of the parameter search menu (Figure 11). Three basic functionalities have been developed in the current version of the prototype: (1) one field allows to switch between static and dynamic trust (to order tweets); (2) a number of fields let the user specify the time range of the search; (3) finally, the last option gives the possibility to restrict the search to some specific friends only.

Static vs. Dynamic

In this section a simple example is discussed to show how searches based on static and dynamic trust differ and how (and why) they actually generate different results. The example is based on database content which has been used to test the application. The content is not actually based on a prolonged and real use of the tool, but still it is realistic and it provides enough evidence to draw our conclusion.

Figure 10 shows the results of the search of the keyword "apple" under static trust. In particular, the static trust setup is the one depicted in Figure 8. As the screen-shot in Figure 10 shows, the results coming from the newspaper Twitter account "ouest-france" are the first displayed. This is because the source is considered the most trustworthy by the user itself (55% of trust). The results are then ordered according to the static trust previously configured (Figure 8).

Let us assume now that the user decides to switch from static to dynamic trust in the search parameters and he/she runs the same search again. The result of the experiment is shown in Figure 12.

In this case the first result of the search is a tweet coming from "TechCrunch" and showing a trust value of 56.02%. This is due to the fact that the Twitter account associated with this user had more interactions with this account (accordingly to the formula showed above). Thus, despite the fact that the user might think that "ouest-france" is more trustworthy than "TechCrunch," his/her activities on the network show exactly the contrary. This ia a very interesting aspect showing how Polidoxa can provide informed recommendations

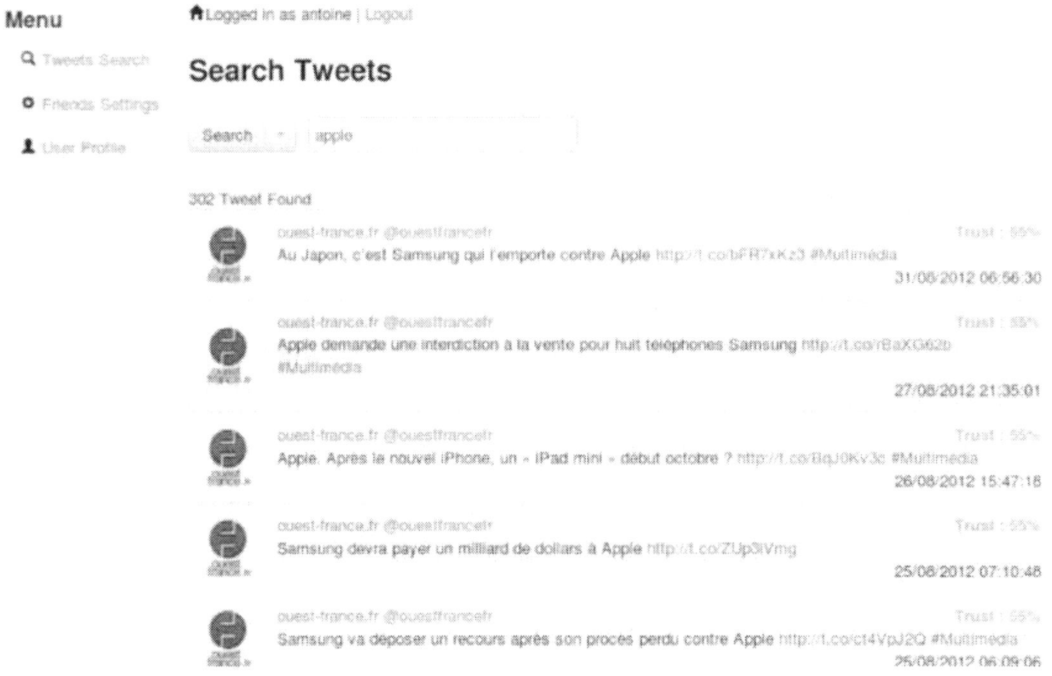

Figure 11. Static trust: search results

Figure 12. Configuration of search parameters

based on social network analysis, in particular on interactions a users had with his network.

Overall and in the middle-run, this mechanism tends to correct users' judgment (which sometime can be biased) by adapting the trust value according to accountable actions (retweets, mentions, etc) and not to personal judgment only. Analysis and simulation to show evidence of this specific fact are left as future works. For now, we would like to point out how the major impact of dynamic trust seems to be its potential to correct users' biased judgment by making use of recorded and undisputed interactions/activities data. See Figure 13.

RELATED WORKS

In this section we compare the Polidoxa idea with Google and Grouplens. PageRank is the parameter used by Google and it is based on the links received by a page and on the "authority" of certain pages. Thus, when a page is linked by another page with "authority," this gives more relevance to the page itself. The important question here is: how can we decide about the authority of a page? This is not clear and Google says nothing about it. One who works in SEO (Search Engine Optimization) —

Figure 13. Dynamic trust: search results

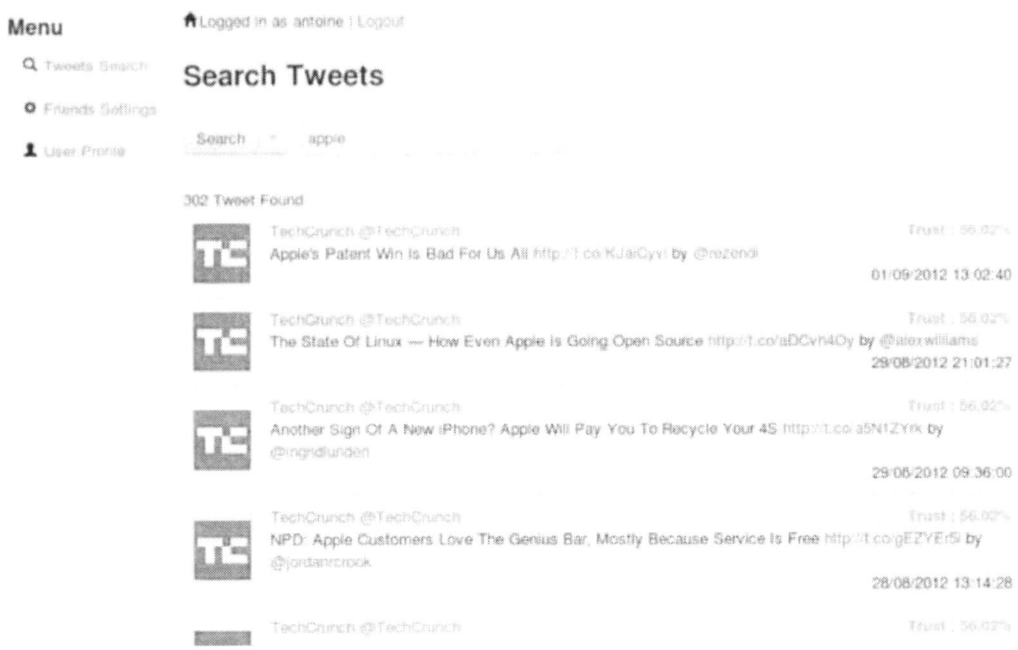

like one of the authors does — knows very well that "inlinks evaluation" (evaluation of links coming from other pages) is a process which lasts for months. This means that a page with qualitatively valuable information actually needs months to acquire some "authority." With Polidoxa, everything instead depends on the network's activity, without a delay of months but actually minutes. Relevance of information for Google is decided in a "black box" with a non-transparent process, and it can therefore be manipulated by SEO specialized agency (an online marketing branch which has the goal of bringing a page or document in search engines ranking top position). Polidoxa aims at offering a simple answer to this issue since relevance of information is determined by users'social network and it cannot be influenced by SEO agency. Polidoxa introduces a trust ranking algorithm where:

1. The user assigns a trust parameter (a numeric value/percentage) to each of his/her first level contact.
2. The user's first level network determines a dynamic trust parameter on the basis of its activity (e.g., retweet, FF…).

Potentially (but not implemented here), users' indirect links (contacts of contacts) can also influence dynamic trust on the basis of their activity; in this case, how much the trust value is influenced would depend on the actual distance, according to some exponentially inverse law (as discussed in this work).

Users have now a unique instrument for searching information which values more their direct connections, without limiting the use of traditional media or search engine. As a consequence, users are more willing to use their critical thinking when reading news and they are motivated to think about the sources and the process of news creation and dissemination. Indeed, all the filters created by the so-called "subject matter experts" of Grouplens (http://www.grouplens.org/biblio) are, in reality, not very transparent. For example, who decides who is an expert? Furthermore, an "expert" can be easily manipulated. With Polidoxa the "subject matter experts" are instead precisely decided by the users and not by an unknown, not better defined, external entity.

Polidoxa gives users the possibility of configuring their searches and the related ranking. It does not limit the general network activity but it gives the user a chance of monitoring the specific activity of his/her trusted network. The fundamental idea is that we tend to trust more the people we know and with these people we usually discuss more, get more feedback, interact more, etc. However, the possibility to follow famous people we do not directly know but, for some reason we trust, is not prevented. This is because a user may want to follow a distant person who is considered a role/spiritual model. Certainly, also in this virtual trusted network all the persuasion/influence mechanisms may still be valid and alter the trust relationship in a not obvious way. These aspects are described in detail by Cialdini (2000).

Polidoxa users have the opportunity to be aware of the activity of the trusted network but still have to use their critical thinking to evaluate the information. This should give the opportunity to the "deep Web" (all that information not crawled by search engines) to eventually reach the Web surface. The Polidoxa ranking increases the quality of information, facilitates the discussion and could improve the lifestyle of participants simply exchanging information and sharing knowledge. Looking at the data of seo-scientist.com (http://www.seo-scientist.com) we discover that about 80% of the users just click the first three results given by a search engine. As a consequence, ranking of information is of extreme importance and offering a trust ranking based on the users activities is fundamental to offer qualitatively better results because that means improving the first three positions according to the user priorities and preferences. With Polidoxa the user and his/her trusted network influences the ranking and everybody has the chance to receive a customized and configurable ranking.

FUTURE WORKS

A Polidoxa based news search engine is a promising idea to explore. The engine would be based on a configurable ranking algorithm. Users will be able to choose the sources from which the engine should retrieve the topics and ranking criteria may also be selected. The trustworthy social network allows following the information posted exclusively by trusted users on specific topics, which can be set. Other approaches can be found on the market, such as Google+, that support choices based on other people opinions. Polidoxa extends this idea by proposing a built-in search engine and by organizing people in a trustworthy social network where news positively evaluated by linked contacts, have a higher priority than the ones evaluated by indirect contacts. The higher the degree of separation, the lower the priority. The major difference with the Google algorithm is that Pagerank evaluates the link relationships of a document by looking at the entire Web, while Polidoxa evaluates the link relationships of the network community, giving more importance to the network activities within a shorter relational distance.

CONCLUSION

This chapter contributes with several principles and technicalities to build a social platform to achieve collective intelligence via information sharing among trusted contacts. It also presents a Twitter-based implementation of a subset of these principles. Trust modeling, social networks, collective intelligence, algorithms and the relative motivations supported by literature in communication sciences are a quite inedited interdisciplinary blend, which has not been really investigates so far. We intend to pursue our investigation and move the human knowledge further on this topic

The fact that people tend to passively receive TV information without verifying it has been emphasized. The gatekeeping process of traditional media, although generally considered a safe and quality assuring medium, poses new risks when control over the information is becoming more and more centralized. Internet has an enormous potential to fix this issue, but the current instruments commonly used like Google and Facebook lack the most important concept in this field: they do not embed the notion of individual trustworthiness of a source. Polidoxa, instead, connects local knowledge making it accessible for everybody and it is conceived to promote public awareness and discussion in total freedom, like in an open piazza. Polidoxa is based on our philosophy:

We believe first in what we can directly verify, then in what our closest contacts have verified. We doubt about what people we do not know say about things we have never seen (it does not matter if this is coming from official sources) until our network of trusted contacts allows us to trust it because it has been verified directly by them.

Today we tend not to verify mainstream information and this has the potential to become a growing issue in the future. Polidoxa may be an answer to this problem.

The same principles on which Polidoxa is based (collective intelligence, collaboration, stigmergy) apply to the full implementation of the system too. We are indeed looking for potential collaborators interested in developing aspects of this project both at the theoretical/algorithmic level and at the software engineering/implementation level. We believe that only collective intelligence can create platforms for the exploitations of collective intelligence itself. We believe that cooperation, knowledge sharing between individuals and quality of life in general, can all be significantly improved by taking inspiration from nature.

ACKNOWLEDGMENT

The idea of Polidoxa slowly emerged among friends and its basic principles have been discussed and experimented over time with information sharing via other experimental platforms or, sometime, just emails. This topic has been discussed with several friends and colleagues before taking shape. All of them contributed substantially to the idea or the realization. We want to thank, in particular, Georgios Papageorgiou, Luca Chiarabini, Giuseppe Marraffa, Luca Ermini, Matteo Dall'Osso, Fabrizio Casalin and Chiara Succi. We also want to thank members of the Reconfiguration Interest Group and the Dependability Group at Newcastle University and the people involved in the EU FP7 DEPLOY Project (Industrial deployment of system engineering methods providing high dependability and productivity). A big acknowledgment to Antoine Chamot from DTU (for having collaborated in the implementation of the first prototype). Finally, colleagues and friends at UNU-IIST, Macau cannot be forgotten. This work has been partially supported by the SAFEHR project funded by Macao Science and Technology Development Fund.

REFERENCES

Arendt, H. (1958). *Vita activa. The human conditon*. University of Chicago Press.

Asch, S. (1955). Opinions and social pressure. *Scientific American*, *193*, 31–35. doi:10.1038/scientificamerican1155-31

Auletta, K. (2010). *Googled: The end of the world as we know it*. London, UK: Virgin Book.

Beach,A., Gartrell, M., & Han, R. (2009). Solutions to security and privacy issues in mobile social networking. *CSE*, (4), 1036–1042.

Beni, G., & Wang, J. (1989). *Swarm intelligence in cellular robotic systems. Proceed. NATO Advanced Workshop on Robots and Biological Systems*. Tuscany, Italy

Bonabeau, E., Dorigo, M., & Theraulaz, G. (1999). *Swarm intelligence: from natural to artificial systems*. Oxford University Press.

Bonneau, J., Anderson, J., & Church, L. (2009). Privacy suites: Shared privacy for social networks. *SOUPS 2009, Proceedings of the 5th Symposium on Usable Privacy and Security*.

Brennan, R. W. (2001). Holonic and multi-agent systems in industry. *The Knowledge Engineering Review*, *16*(04), 375–381. doi:10.1017/S0269888901000200

Calabrese, M. (2011), *Hierarchical-granularity holonic modelling*. (PhD Thesis). University of Milan, Italy.

Carr, N. (2010). *The shallows: What the internet is doing to our brains*. W. W. Norton & Co.

Chamot, A. (2012). *Prototype implementation of a social network application for the Polidoxa project*. (Master's thesis). Technical University of Denmark.

Christakis, N. A., & Fowler, J. H. (2009). *Connected: The surprising power of our social network and how they shape our lives*. New York: Little, Brown and Co.

Chun, W. H. K., & Keenan, T. W. (2005). *New media, old media: A history and theory reader*. Routledge.

Cialdini, R. (2000). *Influence: Science and practice*. Boston, MA: Allyn & Bacon.

Cutillo, L. A., Molva, R., & Önen, M. (2011). *Safebook: A distributed privacy preserving online social network* (pp. 1–3). WOWMOM. doi:10.1109/WoWMoM.2011.5986118

Ding, J., Cruz, I., & Li, C. (2009). *A formal model for building a social network*. SOLI.

Dorigo, M., & Birattari, M. (2007). Swarm intelligence. *Scholarpedia*, *2*(9), 1462. doi:10.4249/scholarpedia.1462

Dorigo, M., Bonabeau, E., & Theraulaz, G. (2000). Ant algorithms and stigmergy. *Future Generation Computer Systems*, *16*(9), 851–871. doi:10.1016/S0167-739X(00)00042-X

Entman, R. M. (1989). How the media affect what people think: An information processing approach. *The Journal of Politics*, *51*(2), 347–370. doi:10.2307/2131346

Fong, P. W. L., Anwar, M. M., & Zhao, Z. (2009). *A privacy preservation model for facebook-style social network systems* (pp. 303–320). ESORICS. doi:10.1007/978-3-642-04444-1_19

Joslyn, C., Rocha, L., Smith, S., Johnson, N. L., Rasmussen, S., & Kantor, M. (1998). Symbiotic intelligence: Self-organizing knowledge on distributed networks driven by human interaction. In Adami, C. (Eds.), *Artificial life VI*. Cambridge, MA: MIT Press.

Koestler, A. (1968). *The ghost in the machine*. New York: Macmillan.

Konrad, M., Vyleta, M. L., Theis, F. J., Stock, M., Tragust, S., Klatt, M., & Cremer, S. (2012). Social transfer of pathogenic fungus promotes active immunisation in ant colonies. *PLoS Biology*, *10*(4), e1001300. doi:10.1371/journal.pbio.1001300

Kuo, I., Horng, S., Kao, T., Lin, T., Lee, C., Chen, Y., & Terano, T. (2010). A hybrid swarm intelligence algorithm for the travelling salesman problem. *Expert Systems: International Journal of Knowledge Engineering and Neural Networks*, *27*(3), 166–179. doi:10.1111/j.1468-0394.2010.00517.x

Luo, S., Xia, H., Yoshida, T., & Wang, Z. (2009). Toward collective intelligence of online communities: A primitive conceptual model. *Journal of Systems Science and Systems Engineering*, *18*, 203–221. doi:10.1007/s11518-009-5095-0

Maheswaran, M., Cheong Tang, H., & Ghunaim, A. (2007). Towards a gravity-based trust model for social networking systems. *Distributed Computing Systems Workshops, International Conference on, 0:24, 2007.*

Maurer, H., & Kolbitsch, J. (2006). The transformation of the web: How emerging communities shape the information we consume. *Journal of Universal Computing Science*, *12*(2), 187–213.

Mayer, R. C., Davis, J. H., & Schoorman, F. D. (1995). An integrative model of organizational trust. *Academy of Management Review*, *20*(3), 709–734.

Mazzara, M., Marraffa, A., Biselli, L., & Chiarabini, L. (2011). The Polidoxa Shift: a New Approach to Social Networks. *Journal of Internet Services and Information Security (JISIS)*, *1*(4), 74–88.

Mazzara, M., Marraffa, A., Biselli, L., & Chiarabini, L. (2011). Polidoxa: A synergic approach of a social network and a search engine to offer trustworthy news. In *International Workshop on TRUstworthy Service-Oriented Computing (INTRUSO 2011)*. Copenhagen, Denmark.

Mccombs, M. (2004). *Setting the agenda: The mass media and public opinion*. New York: Blackwell Publishing.

Mccombs, M., & Shaw, D. (1972). The agenda-setting function of mass media. *Public Opinion Quarterly*, *36*, 176–187. Chicago, IL: University of Chicago Press. doi:10.1086/267990

Miller, P. (2010). *Smart swarm: Using animal behaviour to organise our world*. Collins.

Nagurney, & Wakolbinger, T. (2005). Supernetworks: An introduction to the concept and its applications with a specific focus on knowledge supernetworks. *International Journal of Knowledge, Culture and Change Management.*

Noelle-Neumann, E. (1974). The spiral of silence: A theory of public opinion. *The Journal of Communication*, *24*, 43–51. doi:10.1111/j.1460-2466.1974.tb00367.x

Parikka, J. (2010). *Insect media. An archaeology of animals and technology*. University of Minnesota Press.

Rosalind, T. (1992). *Literacy and orality in Ancient Greece*. Cambridge, MA: Cambridge University Press.

Russell, P. (1983). *The global brain: Speculations on the evolutionary leap to planetary consciousness*. Boston, MA: Houghton Mifflin.

Sampson, T. D. (2012). *Virality. Contagion theory in the age of networks*. University of Minnesota Press.

Shuangling, L., Haoxiang, X., Taketoshi, Y., & Zhongtuo, W. (2009). Toward collective intelligence of online communities: A primitive conceptual model. *Journal of Systems Science and Systems Engineering*.

Steven, J. (2002). *Emergence: The connected lives of ants, brains, cities and software*. Penguin.

Travers, J., & Milgram, S. (1969). An experimental study of the small world problem. *Sociometry*, *32*, 425–443. doi:10.2307/2786545

White, D. M. (1950). The gate-keeper: A case study in the selection of news. *The Journalism Quarterly*, *27*, 383–390.

ADDITIONAL READING

Bruno, N. (2010). Tweet first, verify later? How real-time information is changing the coverage of worldwide crisis events'. Reuters Institute for the study on journalism. Retrieved from http://reutersinstitute.politics.ox.ac.uk/fileadmin/documents/Publications/fellows__papers/2010-2011/tweet_first_verify_later.pdf

Clayman, S., & Reisner, A. (1998). Gatekeeping in action: Editorial conferences and assessments of newsworthiness. *American Sociological Review*, *63*, 178–199. doi:10.2307/2657322

Fidler, R. (1997). *Mediamorphosis: Understanding new media*. Thousand Oaks, CA: Pine Forge.

Griffith, B. (2003). High-tech multitasking: Fan chat is message to media'. *The Boston Globe,* 21, December: C10.

Haesen, R., Baesens, B., Martens, D., De Backer, M., & Holvoet, T. (2006). Ants constructing rule-based classifiers. Technical report. Katholieke Universiteit Press, Leuven.

Jenkins, I. H., & Thornurn, D. (Eds.), *Democracy and New Media* (pp. 365–372). Cambridge, MA: MIT Press.

Katz, E., & Lazarsfeld, P. F. (1956). *Personal influence: The part played by people in the flow of mass communication's*. Glencoe: Columbia Press.

Lewis, J. (1992). A history of Ancient Greece. The glory that was Greece. The agora., International World History Project. Retrieved August 23, 2012, from http://history-world.org/agora.htm

Livingston, S., & Lance Bennett, W. (2003). Gatekeeping, indexing, and live-event news: Is technology altering the construction of news? *Political Communication*, *20*, 363–380. doi:10.1080/10584600390244121

McQuail, D. (2010). *Mass communication theory* (6th ed.). London, UK: Sage.

Morozov, E. (2011). *The net delusion: The dark side of internet freedom*. PublicAffairs. doi:10.1017/S1537592711004026

Walsh, P. (2003). The withered paradigm: The web, the expert and the information hegemony.

KEY TERMS AND DEFINITIONS

Agora: The central spot in ancient Greek city-states. The literal meaning of the word is "gathering place" or "assembly." The agora was the centre of athletic, artistic, spiritual and political life of the city.

Collective Intelligence: A shared or group intelligence emerging from the collaboration and/or competition of many individuals.

Gatekeeping: The process through which information is filtered for dissemination, whether for publication, broadcasting, the Internet, or some other mode of communication.

Holonic System: A system composed of autonomous units who are themselves (sub) systems, all acting in a cooperative way.

Social Network: A service (generally web-based) allowing individuals to construct a (semi) public profile and to define a set of other users with whom they share a privileged first-level connection. Among first-level connections messaging and other forms of interactions are possible.

Stigmergy: A mechanism of indirect coordination between agents or actions. The principle is that the trace left in the environment by an action stimulates the performance of a next action, by the same or a different agent. In that way, subsequent actions tend to reinforce and build on each other, leading to the spontaneous emergence of coherent, apparently systematic activity.

Trust: A measurement/metric of the degree to which one user trusts the activities of another.

Chapter 6
Distributed Social Platforms for Confidentiality and Resilience

Enrico Franchi
University of Parma, Italy

Michele Tomaiuolo
University of Parma, Italy

ABSTRACT

Social networking sites have deeply changed the perception of the web in the last years. Although the current approach to build social networking systems is to create huge centralized systems owned by a single company, such strategy has many drawbacks, e.g., lack of privacy, lack of anonymity, risks of censorship and operating costs. These issues contrast with some of the main requirements of information systems, including: (i) confidentiality, i.e., the interactions between a user and the system must remain private unless explicitly public; (ii) integrity; (iii) accountability; (iv) availability; (v) identity and anonymity. Moreover, social networking platforms are vulnerable to many kind of attacks: (i) masquerading, which occurs when a user disguises his identity and pretends to be another user; (ii) unauthorized access; (iii) denial of service; (iv) repudiation, which occurs when a user participates in an activity and later claims he did not; (v) eavesdropping; (vi) alteration of data; (vii) copy and replay attacks; and, in general, (viii) attacks making use of social engineering techniques. In order to overcome both the intrinsic defects of centralized systems and the general vulnerabilities of social networking platforms, many different approaches have been proposed, both as federated (i.e., consisting of multiple entities cooperating to provide the service, but usually distinct from users) or peer-to-peer systems (with users directly cooperating to provide the service); in this work the most interesting ones were reviewed. Eventually, the authors present their own approach to create a solid distributed social networking platform consisting in a novel peer-to-peer system that leverages existing, widespread and stable technologies such as distributed hash tables and BitTorrent. The topics considered in detail are: (i) anonymity and resilience to censorship; (ii) authenticatable contents; (iii) semantic interoperability using activity streams and weak semantic data formats for contacts and profiles; and (iv) data availability.

DOI: 10.4018/978-1-4666-3926-3.ch006

INTRODUCTION

Nowadays, millions of people of any age and gender regularly access Online Social Networks (OSNs) and spend most of their online time social networking. According to Boyd and Ellison (2008), teenagers have a clear understanding of privacy related issues; however, the same does not apply to some adults that (*i*) did not even use email and other basic Internet services before the social networking revolution (Stroud, 2008) and (*ii*) not only have limited computer-related technical skills, but they also lack risk consciousness about privacy issues. Moreover, many people are becoming uncomfortable with the presence of their employers in the same social networking systems, because some personal data may leak in their corporate environment due to privacy configuration errors (Skeels & Grudin, 2009).

However, privacy threats can also come from the service providers. In fact, even if the social networking systems are greatly dissimilar in their user base and functionality, they are almost always centralized systems. Because of their centralized nature, a simple browser-based user experience is possible and, moreover, many algorithms, e.g., friend suggestion, are far easier and more efficient to implement.

A minor drawback is that scaling centralized systems to tens or hundreds of millions of users is not an easy task. At any rate, while we consider this drawback as a minor one from a technical point of view, since the problem can be solved providing enough resources, it becomes a huge social drawback, because for most companies advertisement is the main source of income and, consequently, they have strong motive to make it as precise as possible, typically mining user provided data. This behavior poses serious threats to privacy and data protection issues. In fact, many social networking systems have very demanding terms of service, essentially asking their users a non-exclusive, transferable, sub-licensable, royalty-free, worldwide license to use content that they submit (Facebook, 2011; Twitter, 2011).

Moreover, social networking sites guide their users into "walled gardens," without giving users full control over their own information because such information constitutes much of their company value (Shankland, 2011; Berners-Lee, 2010).

A second feature of centralized systems is that service providers are in the position to effectively perform a-priori or a-posteriori censorship, or to disclose all the information they have, no matter how private, to other entities. They can perform such actions either motivated by selfish interests or forced under legal terms and other forms of pressure.

Considering that: (*i*) no single centralized entity can withstand the operative costs of a large scale social networking system without a solid business-plan; (*ii*) most business plans are based on targeted advertisement; and (*iii*) even if a service provider would be fair with its user's data, it would remain vulnerable to legal requests to disclose such data, we favor a P2P approach.

In the first place, P2P systems essentially achieve automatic resource scalability, in the sense that the availability of resources is proportional to the number of users. This property is especially desirable for media sharing social networking systems, considering the exceptionally high amount of resources needed.

Moreover, regarding censorship issues, a P2P system essentially solves them by design. Without a central entity, nobody is in the position of censoring data systematically, nor may be held legally responsible for the diffusion of censorable data: the sole owners and responsible of the data are the users themselves. However, P2P systems, and especially those based on a Distributed Hash Table (DHT), may be liable to attacks meant to disrupt the system functionality (Urdaneta et al., 2011); in this particular scenario the severity of such attacks may be mitigated using the social network itself as source of human trust relationships, which make Sybil attacks harder to succeed (Lesniewski-Laas, 2008; Yu et al., 2006). Privacy, on the other hand, is typically solved using key systems and cryptography.

In the rest of this work, first we introduce some background information regarding: (*i*) how P2P systems have been successfully used to provide censorship-resistant systems, although without social focus; (*ii*) how DHTs work, which are their main weaknesses and how they can be overcome; and (*iii*) how the apparently contrasting requirements of social networking systems (privacy and information sharing) can be reconciled in a distributed system, using modern cryptographic techniques. Then, we introduce the security requirements of a social platform and the main attacks it is susceptible to. Eventually, we present the most widely known distributed social platforms, both in the general context of social networking and in the more reduced context of micro-blogging; then we discuss Blogracy, a distributed social networking platform we have built with features relevant to micro-blogging, such as: (*i*) anonymity and resilience to censorship; (*ii*) authenticatable contents; (*iii*) semantic interoperability using activity streams and weak semantic data formats for contacts and profiles; and (*iv*) data availability.

BACKGROUND

The P2P community has a long and successful history of solutions to issues regarding various aspects of system and information security, in particular anonymity and privacy. Part of the attentions that have been devoted to the subjects is relative to the intrinsic characteristics of the P2P medium, especially when used for file sharing, where often published data is public by default and consequently security by obscurity is not even a plausible illusion. Moreover, although the main focus of P2P systems was and is information sharing, early legal disputes, involving popular services like Napster, made clear the importance of privacy and anonymity. Eventually, the attacks that P2P systems had to withstand were not only of legal nature, but also directed against their object storage and search infrastructures (Biddle et al., 2002), and consequently security became a very important topic in the community.

These ideas led to the construction of uncensorable and resilient information sharing systems such as Freenet. The idea was that because of their distributed nature, such systems would be movable targets for traditional attackers. We present the main results in that area in Subsection "Decentralized and anonymous content publishing."

The most widespread P2P systems are implemented using a Distributed Hash Table (DHT), i.e., a decentralized distributed system providing the interface of a traditional hash table, but where the data is distributed among the participants of the distributed system. DHTs work well in practice; still there are a number of vulnerabilities that have to be considered when basing a system over a DHT. They are discussed in subsection "Vulnerabilities of Distributed Hash Tables."

Modern distributed social platforms are strongly influenced by the earlier efforts. However, the duality between information sharing and privacy is even more evident. In fact, a privacy-aware social platform should be able to deliver the information to each of the intended recipients and to none of the other users. Unfortunately, in an open file sharing context, access to the data transiting on the P2P medium cannot usually be restricted, leaving cryptography as the only viable solution. The problem is that the set of recipients needs to be set on a *per-datum* basis. Access may be limited to the members of a circle of personal acquaintances, or authorized subscribers of a news channel. The problem regards also other distributed information storage and retrieval systems and is similar to the one faced by broadcasters of copyrighted materials, who need to distribute protected content over potentially untrusted channels. In this kind of settings, a broadcaster (e.g., a pay-per-view television) would want to be able to send a ciphered content over a public channel, making it readable only by a dynamically selected subset of all receivers. Nowadays, the more promising solution to this kind of issues is Attribute-Based Encryption, which we present in Subsection "Attribute-Based Encryption."

Decentralized and Anonymous Content Publishing

Clarke et al. (2001; 2002) developed Freenet, which is one of the first and more complete implementation of distributed information storage and retrieval systems. It is essentially a cooperative distributed file system. Freenet is intended to pave the way for a non-censorable and secure global information storage system characterized by: (*i*) privacy and anonymity of information producers and consumers; (*ii*) data location independence; and (*iii*) lazy replication. Freenet is currently implemented as an adaptive peer-to-peer network, where each node provides both (*i*) a local datastore, which is made available to the network for reading and writing, and (*ii*) a dynamic routing table, which associates some nodes with the keys they are thought to hold, on the basis of some heuristics. The system is able to manage two kinds of keys, that are (*i*) content-hash keys, calculated as the SHA-1 hash of the file content, or (*ii*) signed-subspace keys, which are the hash of a namespace, concatenated with the hash of the user's public key that defines the namespace. A signed-subspace key may be associated directly with a content file, or it may be associated with an index file, listing references to some other files, in the form of content-hash keys. Anonymity is obtained through a mix-net scheme. The routing algorithm operates over different kinds of networks, with both "OpenNet" connections (which may involve any node of the network) and "DarkNet" connections (which have to be defined explicitly and are only known to friend nodes). In either case, the protocol is not reliable, i.e., it operates as a "best effort" system and offers no guarantee that a shared file is eventually found. Moreover, it has not been fully analyzed nor evaluated on a very large network. One of the simplest ways to access Freenet is via FProxy, a software which allows users to browse "freesites," i.e., web sites that store their contents on Freenet instead of a web server. Various popular forum systems are built on Freenet, including Frost, FMS, FreeTalk, but the solution for filtering the large amount of spam coming from anonymous sources, without opening the door for censorship, is not yet clear.

OsirisSPS (Serverless Portal System) (http://www.osiris-sps.org/) is a framework for creating community-oriented web sites and forums distributed over a peer-to-peer network. It uses a Kademlia DHT for portal distribution and a reputation mechanism for site administration; unfortunately, its source code has not yet been published. The system is anonymous and prevents any association between a user ID and his real identity or network location. User posts are signed and private messages are encrypted. Content is distributed and replicated over multiple nodes, and can be accessed from participating nodes even when they are off-line. Reputation management is one of the most distinguishing aspects of the program: each user is free to rate other users on the basis of their contribution to the portal, and, consequently, each local node is able to process the pages and remove the negative contents (possibly spam or disturbing messages). Other than so-called Anarchists portals, the system allows Monarchists portals, where some users are appointed as administrators and are the only ones able to rate and control other users' contributions. To simplify access to the portals, a web gateway, named Isis, has been developed. An Isis system does not store information locally, but instead forwards all requests over the Osiris network. Since anonymity cannot be guaranteed for this kind of access, Isis is limited to read-only operations.

Various *anonymization services* are available, which can also be integrated into more complex applications as an underlying communication network layer. The technologies vary from relatively simple proxies, which protect users' communications from unauthorized spilling and decouple their actions in the network from their actual network locations, to mix-net schemes based on multiple relays and various envelops and encryption layers. The latter services are often built as some variation of Chaum's (1981) mix-net scheme, which inspired also the more famous Onion routing scheme used by Tor (Goldschlag et al., 1999) and the one used by I2P (Zzz & Shimmer, 2009).

From the early experiences on anonymous sharing of resources, some mechanisms were abstracted and developed along some common guidelines. This is the case of Distributed Hash-Tables (DHT), which has become a common component of many modern distributed systems. DHTs associate values with keys, similarly to regular hash-tables, however, the storage of all key-value pairs is distributed among all nodes of the system. In popular peer-to-peer applications, in particular, the Kademlia DHT is an established choice, considering that it is used in the major file-sharing platforms, including eMule and BitTorrent.

Another option is Pastry, which is a realization of the same DHT general concept. In Pastry, however, the key space is assumed circular. Pastry has become the basis of a number of content sharing platforms, thanks to the early work which lead to the realization of PAST, a distributed file system with automatic replication and reliable routing. Castro et al. (2002) built Scribe, an application level multicast infrastructure on top of the Pastry DHT, which was used in a number of projects for peer-to-peer collaboration and dissemination of information. Scribe creates and manages multicast groups on top of Pastry. Any Scribe node can create a group, providing a group ID and some credentials to be used for access control. Other nodes can then join the group or send multicast messages, which are delivered to all members. Multicast messages are delivered by some forwarder nodes, which form a multicast tree. Forwarder nodes themselves are not required to be part of the group; instead, they automatically become forwarders if they are on the Pastry route of some new member of the group, when it sends a join request. The delivery mechanism is described as best-effort, without strong guaranties about actual delivery and arrival order of messages. However, some extensions are suggested to obtain stronger reliability, including automatic fault detection and hailing of the multicast tree, sequential numbering of messages and replication of information sources. Simulation results suggest the basic mechanism achieves acceptable delay and link stress when compared to IP multicast, with good load balancing among the nodes of the network.

Vulnerabilities of Distributed Hash Tables

Although DHT-based systems overcome the weakness of a single point of failure, there are some well-known and important vulnerabilities in DHT-based systems:

- Sybil attacks, or node insertion attacks, where multiple nodes are created in the network, each of them representing fictitious identities but all belonging to a single user.
- Routing attacks, which collectively use Sybil nodes to inject ad-hoc entries in the routing table of other nodes and thus disrupt the correct message routing procedure.
- Eclipse attacks, which use routing attacks to partition the network in distinct connected components, with the ultimate goal of separating a set of victim nodes from the rest of the overlay network.
- Storage attacks, where Sybil nodes are used to provide bogus responses to queries.
- Publish attacks, based on index poisoning, where essentially some bogus content is deliberately spread to the index nodes

responsible for other files or keywords; publish and Sybil attacks are in a sense orthogonal; in fact, publish attacks can exploit Sybil nodes, if available, but can even misguide good nodes to spread false information.

Many of the proposed countermeasures to securing P2P networks are based on some notion of "trust" among peers. Depending on the approach they use to evaluate and manage trust relationships among peers, those countermeasures can be divided in two main groups: (*i*) credential and policy based, (*ii*) reputation based. Each of them has some context where it can be applied more successfully, though introducing additional complexity and other aspects of security concern. Relying on a Certification Authority means providing it with the power to issue and retract certificates, thus possibly open the way to masquerading attacks, like in the recent cases involving Comodo and Diginotar (Pranata et al., 2011), or even detain or generate all the current private keys of the platform principals, which in turn means accessing all protected resources. Reputation systems, on the other hand, need to carefully balance the necessity to exclude rogue nodes from the platform operations, with the risks related to bogus feedbacks and collusions to confuse or subvert the evaluation of peers' reputation. Cheng and Friedman (2005), for example, propose a general asymmetric reputation algorithm, resistant to Sybil nodes.

Another approach that is possible is to rely on the structural redundancy of DHT systems, to exclude rogue nodes. Some solutions are proposed, as an application of consensus algorithms to peer-to-peer networks, including the classical Byzantine agreement. This solution is proved to work if less than 1/3 of the n nodes are "traitors" ($n > 3t$, where t is the number of traitors). Thus, the Byzantine protocol alone may not succeed in blocking attackers, if those are allowed to create an arbitrary number of Sybil nodes. Moreover, the complexity of the agreement protocol, where the number of messages depends exponentially on the network cardinality (Tanenbaum, 2006), makes it completely inapplicable on the scale of a global peer-to-peer network, but only to sub-networks.

Along with other similar research works, Lesniewski-Laas (2008) and Yu et al. (2006) propose to exploit the users' social graph to increase resistance against Sybil attacks. Viswanath et al. (2010) analyze various protocols of this type and compare them with previous general community detection algorithms, which all search for a cluster of interconnected nodes around a trusted node. Interestingly, they suggest that networks with such a community structure could be particularly vulnerable to specialized Sybil attacks.

Concluding, while being subject to a number of possible attacks, some DHT systems have proved robust enough to continue their operation, mainly thanks to their intrinsic redundancy. In Kademlia implementations, for example, the stable nodes tend to remain longer in the routing tables, thus exhibiting some resistance to the malicious behavior of new rogue nodes introduced into the network. Also, the severity of Sybil attacks can be reduced if nodes are not able to arbitrarily choose their own identifiers, and if the number of nodes running in the same local network is constrained. Cholez, Chrisment, and Festor (2010) propose to compare the theoretical distribution of node IDs after a lookup process, demonstrated to be geometrical, with real node IDs, to detect large Sybil attacks. Urdaneta et al. (2011) provide a detailed analysis of threats to DHTs, together with some proposed countermeasures. While underlining the existing vulnerability to Sybil attacks, authors conclude that *current DHT deployments are not specifically designed to tolerate the presence of malicious nodes. However, most of them are based on Kademlia, which provides relative security by using data replication and a redundant routing mechanism similar to wide paths.*

Attribute-Based Encryption

In social networking and micro-blogging applications it is often desirable to make some content available to a restricted audience, only. Access may be limited to the members of a circle of personal acquaintances, or authorized subscribers of a news channel. Exploiting traditional public key cryptography and multicast group key management, it is possible to deliver a secret session key to intended recipients of confidential messages. This requires rekeying users periodically, with a computational complexity and message overhead which is linear with *N*, the cardinality of the group. As an alternative solution, group members can be organized in a multicast tree, reducing the cost of rekeying to *log(N)* (Canetti, 1999).

Another recently emerging approach is to publish content, possibly on an insecure medium, which can be decrypted only by users with proper attributes, as required by the content publisher's policy. These Attribute-Based Encryption protocols are effectively an extension of the Identity-Based Encryption (IBE) protocol, proposed as a theoretical concept by Shamir (1984). The first practical implementation was described by Boneh and Franklin (2001). In an IBE system, any unique identifier (e.g., e-mail address or OpenId url) can function as a public key. This possibility largely reduces the need for public key infrastructure to distribute certificates. In fact, in IBE schemes users can calculate the public key corresponding to any other identifier they know, after acquiring at startup just a single set of public configuration parameters. To decrypt the received message, instead, the recipient has to download his own private key from a central authority, the Private Key Generator (PKG). This operation is usually done only once, so that the central authority is not required to be constantly online. This contrasts with traditional public-key infrastructures, in which private keys are chosen randomly, and their corresponding public keys have to be certified. On the other hand, a PKG is more sensitive than a traditional Certificate Authority (CA) in that, if the master private key is compromised, then it can be used to generate the actual private keys of all users. In fact, key escrow is an inherent property of IBE systems. A traditional Certification Authority, if compromised or obliged to, at worst can forge new certificates and certificate revocation information; i.e., it will make future usage of the system insecure, but it will not necessarily be able to read all messages encrypted with previously assigned keys.

After the creation of a working IBE system, advances were made quite rapidly in the field. Sahai and Waters (2005) introduced the concept of Fuzzy-IBE, providing IBE schemes with an error-tolerance which proves handy for encryption using biometrics. Sahai and Waters also introduced Attribute-Based Encryption (ABE). In an ABE system, both the user' private credential and the cipher-text are associated with a set of attributes. A user can decrypt the cipher-text only if the attributes of his private credential match those of the cipher-text. Based on ABE, Goyal et al. (2006) proposed a key-policy attribute-based encryption (KP-ABE) scheme. Soon after, Bethencourt et al. (2007) constructed the first cipher-text-policy attribute-based encryption (CP-ABE). In CP-ABE, the user is provided with a private credential which attests a set of attributes, while an access policy is embedded directly into cipher-texts. The attributes associated with a user's private credential need to satisfy the access policy of the cipher-text, for the user being able to decrypt the cipher-text. The definition of KP-ABE systems is reversed with respect to CP-ABE systems. In KP-ABE, an access policy is embedded into a user private credential, while cipher-texts are associated with a set of attributes. The attributes of the cipher-text need to satisfy the access policy of the user, for the user being able to decrypt the cipher-text. In both schemes, the required overlapping of attributes can be defined as a k-of-n function, i.e., at least k attributes out of n in the policy have to be matched. For instance, the common AND or OR operators can be defined as functions with $k=n$ or $k=1$, respectively. Moreover, both KP-ABE and CP-ABE allow users to delegate a subset of their own authorized access permissions, or attributes, to other users, thus facilitating the management of group membership, particularly in those cases where a unique group manager cannot be supposed to be continuously available or being able to manage a large group membership.

SECURITY IN DISTRIBUTED SOCIAL NETWORKING SYSTEMS

In the previous section, we gave some context regarding P2P systems, their main low-level security issues and typical solutions. Both the issues and the countermeasures are rather technical. On the other hand, we have an intuitive understanding of the main security requirements of a generic information system, which can also be extended on a social networking system. Nonetheless, in this Section we briefly describe such requirements to avoid ambiguity. Eventually, in the second part of this Section, we focus on the typical vulnerabilities of a social networking platform, with special regards for those affecting a distributed one (e.g., in a distributed setting everything occurs on an insecure medium, while in the typical business environment most operations are performed on an intranet, that has higher security guarantees with regards to eavesdropping).

Security Requirements of OSNs

The users of information systems have various types of security requirements, including: confidentiality, integrity, accountability, availability and anonymity. The same security requirements can be applied to social networking platforms as well. In this Subsection, we provide a short overview of these security requirements and how they apply to the context of online social networks.

Confidentiality. Any private datum stored by service providers or communicated to other users by the means offered by the social networking platform should remain confidential. Related information (such as when the communication occurred or when a specific datum was stored or even when any datum was stored) should remain confidential as well, since eavesdroppers may be able to infer information about a user's activities not only from the content of the messages exchanged, but also from the pattern of message flow on the system. Users may also want to keep their physical and network location confidential. Users should be allowed to decide if their presence (including fine-grained profile data, attributes, contacts) will be available through public directories. Platform security policies, on the other hand, may apply different rules to users who chose to be completely anonymous or operating under a pseudonym, possibly reversible by some privileged authority. Audit logs are important for accountability. But since they list all of a user's important activities on the platform, their content must remain confidential and accessible only to authorized administrators.

Integrity. Social platforms must protect users from unauthorized modification of their profile and messages. The integrity of shared resources and of the whole infrastructure must also be protected from unauthorized modifications. Intentional attacks against a user's communications can be made by changing the content, source or destination of a message, replacing or deleting an entire message, replaying an old message. The integrity of user communications in social platforms also relies on the features of lower-level protocols (e.g., TLS or plain sockets).

Accountability. Each user should be authenticated and audited, maintaining a log of all relevant events, in order to hold him accountable for his own actions. Each log record should at least include the name of the user responsible for the event, time, type and result of the event.

The rules applying to the management of audit logs greatly vary in different legal and social contexts. Audit logs must also be protected from lower level failures. Accountability is important for protecting the resources of the system and also for building trust among users. A formally correct user, according to security policies, could still intentionally attempt at deception or spread false information, *bona fide*. Additional auditing may be helpful, especially if reputation is valued in the community. In communities where reputation is held into account, the social networking infrastructure should protect it from various threats, including masquerading attacks.

Availability. Especially in the case of professional communities, the social networking infrastructure should ensure high availability of both data and services. The social platform should be able to handle the requests of scores of visitors and regular users, or risk suffering common denial of service threats. Shared resources should be available and allocated according to a fair policy, or at least to a graceful degradation of service quality. The infrastructure should be able to detect and recover from various failures. In some cases, users may be directly involved in the recovery process. Ensuring confidentiality, integrity and accountability requires additional computational resources, disk space and network capacity, thus influencing the system availability.

Identity and anonymity. In social networking platforms, accountability of users always needs to be balanced with privacy requirements. In some cases, users may be asked to provide their real world identities, while in other cases only their virtual identities are relevant. Especially in the first case, the platform should provide means to keep profile information secret from other users, while still maintaining a form of reversible anonymity, if necessary for legal or other accountability reasons. The policy of collection and use of audit information must be available to users in a comprehensible form. In human communities, anonymity is important in allowing the adoption of unpopular viewpoints, lifestyles and behaviours. On the other hand, anonymity makes the development of trust among users difficult or impossible.

Security Threats to OSNs

Social networking platforms are susceptible to different types of attacks. For better analyzing these attacks, it is useful to identify the main abstract components of a generic social networking platform, corresponding to different functional aspects of those systems. We identify four main components:

- The social networking component, which manages and protects access to the users' personal profiles and the social relationships among users.
- The content management component, which manages and protects access to all user generated content, including personal status updates, comments, links to other content, photos and multimedia galleries.
- The infrastructure services component, which provides the basic infrastructure services needed to run the social networking platform, including storage and replication services for content and profiles, information indexing and routing, management of users' online presence.
- The communication and transport component, encapsulating basic inter-networking and ad-hoc networking functionalities.

Attacks can be directed to each of the different layers we mentioned; some attacks may target more than one layer or there may be attack variants targeting different levels, but with roughly the same logic.

Moreover, we can differentiate between two different kinds of attackers: (*i*) *intruders,* i.e., users accessing the system without proper authorization, or (*ii*) *insiders*, i.e., regular users or entities participating in the systems operations, assuming malicious behaviors. From the user's point of view, malicious behavior can also be attributed to the service provider. In the rest of this subsection we review the main kinds of attack.

Masquerading. When a rogue user disguises his identity and claims the identity of another user, the former is said to be masquerading. Masquerading may be attempted by an attacker either during a conversation or while registering his own profile, for deceiving other users or the whole social networking platform. Simple impersonation, by cloning the victim's profile from the same platform or by porting profile data from a different platform, may easily lead the attacker to gain trust from the victim's contacts. Especially in communities where reputation is valued, masquerading can damage the user whose identity has been stolen, as it can damage other users eventually deceived. Sometimes, masquerading is the first step to gain access to infrastructure services and resources to which the attacker is not entitled. Another possibility is that the attacker is pretending to be another user in order to shift the blame for any liable action. A particular type of masquerading occurs when a rogue platform pretends to be a legitimate social networking platform, misleading unsuspecting users, with the goal to acquire sensible information (phishing) or engaging in other harmful activities.

Unauthorized access. Users who have not been granted adequate permissions for accessing some services and resources, may attempt to circumvent the security mechanisms and policies of the system and gain unauthorized access. In a social networking platform, any user who has access to some profiles and messages can harm their legitimate owners. Accessing data without proper authorization allows also an untrusted user to produce such harm. The collection of existing data is the basis of profiling attacks. These data may also supply some knowledge for secondary data collection from a wide range of different sources, including other OSNs. Remote access can also occur at system level. In this case the attacker may directly gain control of all resources.

Denial of Service (DoS). The services and communications at the infrastructure level can be disrupted by common denial of service attacks. Social networking platforms are also susceptible to all the conventional denial of service attacks aimed at the underlying operating system or communication protocols. In addition to attacking the whole infrastructure of a social networking platform, users can also launch denial of service attacks against specific users, especially in a distributed platform. For example, repeatedly sending messages or other spam may place undue burden on the recipient users and their systems. Malicious users can also intentionally distribute false or useless information to prevent other users from completing their social activities.

Repudiation. In general, repudiation occurs when a user, after having performed some action, later denies that action having happened (at least under his responsibility). Repudiation can be intentional or even accidental. It can also be the result of a misunderstanding, when users have a different view of events. In any case it can generate important disputes. In a sense, nothing can prevent a user from repudiating one of his actions. But a social networking platform can eventually help resolving disputes by providing needed evidence, if it maintains a sufficiently detailed log of events. For users who value their reputation, the availability of such evidence may constitute a valid deterrent.

Eavesdropping. The attempt to observe the flow and possibly the content of confidential messages is one of the most classical security threats. Apart from reading the content of messages, which may require cryptanalysis, an eavesdropper may gather useful information by simply observing the pattern of messages and their recipients, for example inferring the type of services being requested. To eavesdrop on other users, an attacker may also exploit the infrastructure and communication services of the platform, e.g. through unauthorized access.

Alteration. When a user signs up a social networking service, he starts exposing his profile and content to the platform. An attacker may tamper with the profile and content data published by the victim, with all the messages he communicates to other users and all data used on the infrastructure services. Alteration can also be conducted by the service operator, which provides the facilities for online social networking and may take control of published data. Alteration may take the particular form of filtering, or censorship, when applied systematically for removing undesired content from the OSN.

Copy and replay. Each action in a social network may be subject to copy and reply. In this type of security threat, an attacker attempts to intercept some data and clone it, for retransmitting it later. The interceptor may successfully copy and replay a message, a complete profile or any other data. If those data are not associated with a signature and a timestamp, the repeated reception of such copies may pass unnoticed and accepted as a legitimate action.

Social engineering. In a social networking application, a common attack is to psychologically manipulate a user into performing misguided actions. It is similar to a confidence trick or a traditional fraud, but by means of computer-based communications and online social networking, typically to gain access to confidential information. In most cases the victim and the attacker never acknowledged each other directly in real life. In its essence, "social engineering" is associated with social sciences and is defined in general as an act of psychological manipulation. But recently its usage is becoming increasingly important among computer professionals.

DISTRIBUTED SOCIAL NETWORKING SYSTEMS

In the Introduction, we argued that many of the problems relative to social networking platforms are related to their centralized nature. We believe that a viable solution is to distribute the platform, so that no single entity: (*i*) has to withstand the costs; (*ii*) is responsible for the data (both legally and operatively); and (*iii*) owns the whole system. The distribution can occur in two radically different ways:

1. **Federation:** In a federated system, multiple entities cooperate to provide the service. Each of them provides access to the whole system to a subset of its users. The system is perceived as a whole because each of the federated providers keeps information synchronized with the other providers. The users are free to choose a provider they trust (both from a technical reason and from legal/moral ones). Notice that many existing systems already work this way: e.g., emails are a federated service, where multiple servers cooperate. However, a social networking platform has a much higher interactivity with respect to emails. Notice that in federated systems it is still possible that a user is also a service provider (for himself). For instance, it was not uncommon among UNIX users to have their own SMTP server. Nowadays, spam and the consequent strategies such as white/gray-listings made this approach less popular.
2. **Peer-to-Peer (P2P):** In a P2P system, *every* user is also a service provider. The whole system is built around this idea, which can be interpreted as a limit case of federated system. The traditional distinctions between servers and clients are blurred; every node both provides services to and requests them from the other nodes. We favor this approach

because it maps well the very structure of social networks that are made of interacting nodes.

In the rest of this section, we review some of the most popular distributed social networking systems, both federated and P2P. Eventually, we present Blogracy, a P2P system we built to overcome the issues of confidentiality and resilience in social networking systems.

Federated Social Networking Systems

Among the federated social networking systems, one of the best known is Diaspora (http://joindiaspora.com/). Diaspora is being implemented in Ruby and released as open source. Users can participate in the network by setting up their own server, which is named a "pod," and can host the content produced by various users. Otherwise they can exploit already existing pods which can host their content and their social connections. User relations and information flows are asymmetrical, i.e., a user's content is only distributed and disclosed to authorized followers. Diaspora servers communicate by means of an ad-hoc federation protocol and the standard Salmon protocol (http://www.salmon-protocol.org/) for comments. They exchange semantically annotated messages in various situations, including: discovery of information about hosted users, notification of acceptance for sharing information, publication and possible retraction of posts, publication and possible retraction of comments and "like" flags (either from the user or from others) on one of the user's post, private conversations and messages, profile information. The security model being proposed for implementation is still under discussion, but would probably include encryption of a single post trough a session key. The session key has to be sent individually to the audience of the post; thus, it needs to be encrypted repeatedly, using the public key of each intended recipient.

Another attempt in a similar direction is StatusNet (http://status.net/), formerly known as Laconica. StatusNet is an open source project providing similar functionalities to those found on Twitter. It is implemented in PHP and adheres to the OStatus standard protocol for the interconnection of various servers. The first deployment was the identi.ca micro-blogging service. Among the most interesting features, StatusNet shows quite strong interoperability with other networks:

- Ability to send updates via (*i*) the XMPP protocol, (*ii*) SMS, (*iii*) the Salmon protocol.
- Support for the OpenID authentication.
- Compatibility with Twitter at the API level.
- Integration, in various ways, with both Twitter and Facebook.

Apart from automatic management of URL-shortening, StatusNet also handles various semantic contents associated with posts, including: (*i*) geolocation and maps; (*ii*) attachments and links to external resources; (*iii*) both hash-tags and bang-tags for groups. From the security point of view, StatusNet essentially relies on a profile URI, which needs to be based on a secure transport for assuring authenticity and confidentiality of exchanged data. The OStatus and Salmon protocols allow additional levels of security, but still require a secure transport at handshake.

Peer-to-Peer Social Networking Systems

PeerSoN (Buchegger & Datta, 2009; Buchegger et al., 2009) is a system designed to provide encryption, decentralization and direct data exchange in the field of social networks, dealing with privacy and connectivity issues. The implementation is based on a two-tier architecture. The first tier is based on a Distributed Hash Table (DHT) and handles the look-up functionalities; basically it allows to find users and data over the social network. Unfortunately, the originally chosen DHT implementation, OpenDHT, later became overloaded and unusable and had to be switched off (Buchegger et al., 2009). As a consequence the PeesSoN prototype is presently run as a centralized service, for testing and evaluation. With regards to security and encryption, the first prototype of PeerSoN is designed around a Public Key Infrastructure (PKI). Given the centralized or hierarchical nature of PKI, this solution hardly matches the needs of a decentralized network. In fact, Buchegger et al. (2009) hint at some studies being conducted for removing a centralized PKI and for developing a more efficient approach, but the result is not yet clear, as the initial focus has not been oriented on the encryption and privacy issues, but to make online social networks distributed.

A more interesting part of the system design is the description of prototype protocols. In PeerSoN each user has a unique ID, possibly computed as a hash of the user's email. In the DHT, various values are associated with this ID, representing the various locations or machines used by the user to connect to the network, and the status of each location, connected or not. Then, to check for updates from a particular user, the filename of his index file is used as a key in the DHT, and corresponding locations possessing the file are returned, associated with the version number of the stored index file. It is worth noticing that this protocol is a bit different from common file sharing, where a hash of the file content, and not its name, is used as its DHT key. The index file contains a list of newly generated content, which has to be searched for and downloaded in a similar way. Another possibility, which is considered by the PeerSoN system, is the direct pushing of new content to supposedly interested peers. Some measures are suggested to avoid receiving spam and other undesired or malicious content, especially on constrained devices and connections. In particular, gray and black lists are cited, but without providing any detail about adopted reputation mechanisms.

Safebook (Cutillo et al., 2009) is based on a DHT and a network of socially close peers, defined Matryoshka. Peers in a user's Matryoshka are trusted and support the user by anonymizing communications and replicating content and profile information. Safebook exploits a more traditional certification authority. In fact, a user's public key cannot be calculated from his identity, and all public/private key pairs are generated locally by the peers.

LifeSocial (Graffi et al., 2010) is a prototype developed over FreePastry for DHT indexing and PAST for data replication. It is composed of various mandatory modules, for managing profile, friends, groups and photos. Additional modules are available for chat and whiteboard functionalities.

Blogracy is our own fully distributed P2P micro-blogging platform, based on Bittorrent. Its main focus is: (*i*) anonymity and resilience to censorship; (*ii*) authenticatable contents; (*iii*) semantic interoperability using activity streams and weak semantic data formats for contacts and profiles; and (*iv*) data availability. More details are given in the "Design and Features of Blogracy" Subsection of the present chapter.

Distributed Propagation of Feeds and Updates

Xu et al. (2010, 2010b) described Cuckoo as a decentralized and socio-aware online micro-blogging service. It follows a hybrid approach consisting of: (*i*) a structured overlay network, Pastry, and a gossip protocol for disseminating micro-news among users with the same interests; and (*ii*) support for centralized dedicated services, like Twitter, which in fact still store users' profiles and other data. The peer-to-peer infrastructure is mainly motivated by the goals of reducing bandwidth and storage space on the server side. On this basis, Cuckoo nodes maintain information about social relations, i.e., friends, neighbors, followers and followees. Friend nodes help each other to balance load, thus creating a sort of virtual node. Notifications are dealt with direct push, in the case of normal users, or with gossip propagation, in the case of celebrities and broadcasters.

FeedTree (Sandler et al. 2005) is an RSS feed distribution service based on peer-to-peer subscription mechanisms. RSS (Real Simple Syndication) is an XML-based feed format used by websites to list novel content: its basic functioning requires interested subscribers to query a server periodically, according to a typical pull approach, thus significantly increasing the load of popular websites. FeedTree proposes a transition towards pushing RSS items over a peer-to-peer network, distributing the load over the nodes of a group multicast tree. For this purpose, FeedTree exploits Pastry and Scribe. To allow a smoother adoption of the service, various levels of integration with existing software are proposed. The easier one includes a "republishing" engine running close to the web-server, sifting new content for peer-to-peer distribution, and a FeedTree proxy running on the client machine, receiving feeds pushed over the peer-to-peer network and providing them directly to the traditional RSS client.

Perfitt and Englert (2010) describe Megaphone as a micro-blogging system, based on an optimized, trustworthy peer-to-peer network. In fact, nodes are enabled to sign and encrypt each piece of content they publish, making it verifiable and confidential for subscribers. The basic distribution mechanism is based on Scribe multicast trees. Thus, a subscriber node has to know in advance the node ID of the posters to follow, or at least it has to be able to generate it. The poster's node ID corresponds exactly to a Scribe multicast group ID. In Megaphone, the node ID is a hash of its public key, and the couple of public/private keys is generated autonomously by each node. The follower is supposed to obtain the poster's public key via an out of bound mechanism, like an email or a web page, in the process of discovery and acquaintance with the poster. Each message can be encrypted with a secret session key, which is suggested to be changed on a daily basis. The session key is itself ciphered with the public key of each follower. All of these copies of the session key are then packaged together and distributed as a message over the multicast channel. Since the scalability of such a mechanism has quite clear limitations, an alternative solution, based on delegation, is briefly described in the original work. Thus, to improve its scalability towards large micro-blogging environments while preserving confidentiality, the Megaphone system should be adapted to this kind of delegation, which however requires additional join requests and some different but important interaction of the poster node with each subscriber.

Other Social Networking Systems

SCOPE (Mani et al. 2010) is a prototype for spontaneous peer-to-peer social networking. The main aim of the system is to create ad-hoc social networks based on proximity, i.e., exploiting wireless network infrastructure and services available in the user's local place. The system is composed of a number of modules, together providing all needed functionalities. One module is designed for social services, i.e., for the management of user profiles, social contacts and groups. Another module uses a DHT to provide distributed storage. A module based on P2PSIP (Bryan et al. 2006) is responsible for the management of sessions, for real-time applications. Then, specialized modules are dedicated to service advertisement and discovery (yellow pages) and for other tasks. The network itself is organized in a typical hybrid peer-to-peer architecture, with peers distinguished as super nodes and client nodes. While super nodes provide all the important services of the network, including lookup, routing, session management and DHT-based storage, instead, client nodes are supposed to have highly constrained computational resources and bandwidth, and thus are only able to connect to super nodes and exploit the needed services.

Persona (Baden et al., 2009) is designed as a set of social networking services. It uses an interesting Attribute-Based Encryption protocol for protecting access to users' content. It allows each user to create various groups of "friends," by assigning proper attribute credentials. Content can then be associated with a publication policy and made available only to a restricted audience.

Design and Features of Blogracy

While many authors argue for the distribution and openness of social networking and micro-blogging services, few usable implementations exist, either in the field of federated networks or as fully distributed solutions. However, most of the systems and studies described in the previous Section shall be carefully considered since they provide some theoretical foundations and some viable solutions to particular issues, even when they remain at the level of abstract algorithms, simulations and theoretical analysis.

Moreover, all these efforts led to the definition of open formats and protocols which are common ground for the interoperability and distribution of social networking applications. On the basis of existing or proposed solutions, we therefore present a new system, which we named Blogracy (http://www.blogracy.net/) (Franchi & Tomaiuolo, 2012). In the following paragraphs, we describe its main distinguishing features and how they relate to other existing systems and abstract architectures.

Our new system is built incrementally over popular services; in fact, from the very beginning, we chose to leverage existing and widespread networks for file sharing, and providing to those enormous communities specific features for micro-blogging applications and for publishing personal activity streams.

From an architectural point of view, Blogracy is built upon a peer-to-peer file-sharing mechanism and two logically separated DHTs. Users in Blogracy have a profile and a semantically meaningful activity stream, which contains their actions in the system (e.g., add a post, tag a picture, comment a video). One DHT maps the user's identifier with his activity stream, which also contains a reference to the user's profile and references to user generated content (e.g., posts, comments). These references are keys of the second DHT which are then resolved to the actual files, delivered using the underlying peer-to-peer file-sharing mechanism. These basic file sharing techniques are well tested and in widespread use. In particular, it is common practice to associate files (or file parts, or chunks) with their hash, and using the hash itself to identify a file, to share or download. A quite similar technique was found also in Freenet, as well as most of the following networks.

For all practical purposes, individual users of large networks have to be associated with numerical identifiers or unique strings, since names used in real life are hardly unique. In a typical Trust Management scheme, a user's public key is used directly to represent the user, so that all contents produced by the user can be easily verified against his public key, which is also his own main identifier. Alternatively, a cryptographic hash of the public key can be used (Li, 2000), without loss of security, and this is exactly the scheme adopted in Blogracy, the hash function being the same as the one used by the DHT.

However, anonymity is an issue also at the lower network level. In fact, if file locations are expressed as plain network addresses, these can be easily associated with a particular person or entity which can be called for taking legal responsibility of shared materials or expressed ideas, if they are deemed illegal or censored for any reason.

The users' network addresses, in particular, are typically published in DHT entries associated with shared files. This kind of issues applies to a number of contexts but, since they are essentially related to a lower network level, they are best solved at that very level. In fact, various anonymizing technologies exist, ranging from simple proxies, to complex networks. The latter includes the famous Tor (Dingledine et al., 2004), a network based on the onion routing protocol, but with centralized management, and I2P (Zzz & Schimmer, 2009), also based on a variation of the mix-net scheme, but completely distributed.

Being mainly a platform for resilient micro-blogging, Blogracy is designed to assure new contents are published and distributed as widely as possible, exploiting the most popular and effective file-sharing infrastructure available today. While contacts are not published by default, actually there's no restriction about access to posts. However, since the core sharing system is completely agnostic with respect to published content, data can be easily encrypted with any cryptographic algorithm, either symmetric or asymmetric, including attribute-based encryption. In fact, Blogracy supports attribute-based encryption. Similarly to Persona, Blogracy privacy model uses attribute credentials for protecting access to sensible content, creating a sort of very flexible personal circles of contacts, i.e., parametrized roles to be assigned to users for granting a certain set of access rights. The encryption scheme is based on the CP-ABE protocol (Bethencourt et al., 2007). A practical and quite simple alternative, which could be easily added to the system, is to encrypt sensible posts with a secret session key, and then encrypt this session key with the public key of each intended reader. This approach would be similar to Megaphone, and it would scale till medium-sized groups, which would probably cover a significant number of use cases.

Considering individual security threats, Blogracy is designed to show resilience against censorship and centralized control over published data. Its completely distributed architecture and the replication of popular data, typical of file sharing systems, provide resistance against DoS attacks. Moreover, traditional signatures and timestamps, together with CP-ABE, are used as means to protect against eavesdropping, alteration, copy and replay, repudiation, unauthorized access. Conversely, it opposes limited resistance against masquerading and some form of social engineering, exactly for the absence of any centralized control.

FUTURE RESEARCH DIRECTIONS

While a number of distributed social networking systems have been proposed, many underlying mechanisms and also various aspects of the high level architecture are yet object of analysis and research. Many of these systems, for example, use some DHT component for basic indexing. However, the robustness of DHTs, and in particular their resistance to Sybil and pollution attacks, is still being discussed. The approaches to this issue vary (Urdaneta et al., 2011), but in general in distributed social networking systems the presence of a global authentication authority is not always possible or desirable. Distributed mechanisms for reputation and trust may contrast with the requirement for anonymous operation, but are still possible under the assumption of secure pseudonyms (Li, 2000). Social relationships of trust among human users can also be used to make the DHT more robust (Lesniewski-Laas, 2008; Yu et al., 2006).

Open peer-to-peer overlay networks usually guarantee a certain level of anonymity, since usually they do not require any registration or authentication. However, the network addresses involved in the network operations may be traced, and the association with a responsible person may be inferred. Anonymizing infrastructures exist, ranging from simple proxies to global mix-net networks, but their availability, operation cost and resilience to technical and legal threats are not yet adequate for all use cases (Dingledine et al., 2004). Fully distributed, automatically and dynamically reconfiguring schemes would better scale to the needs of global peer-to-peer networks (Zzz & Schimmer, 2009).

On the issue of the confidentiality of personal data, solutions for sharing data only for a limited audience may be adapted from other fields. For example, the problem of broadcasting copyrighted material has some similarities with our problem. However, typical solutions were devised with a smaller number of entities in mind, and suffer from scalability problems, especially in the case of rekeying. New cryptographic schemes may be applied, but they need to be generalized for appliance in open networks. For example, ABE encryption schemes are promising (Bethencourt et al., 2007), but they need to work in an open, multi-authority scenario (Lewko & Waters, 2011), possibly maintaining the confidentiality of exchanged credentials and policies, like with oblivious commitments (Li & Li, 2006).

In distributed social networking platforms, the responsibility of storing all data is shared among users. For this reason, it is necessary to ensure a minimum level of data availability even for users with sparse social relations. Rzadca et al. (2010) discuss how data availability in a P2P social application should be modeled and modeling the systems and they estimate expected performances. Such studies are expected to become more common because they avoid the likelihood to deploy a system that cannot work.

Newer social networking systems should interoperate with the other existing systems, including social networking sites, micro-blogging platforms and all other existing forms of social information systems. Although some standardization efforts are being conducted – including Portable Contacts, Activity Streams, OpenSocial, FOAF –, (*i*) their acceptance is not yet adequate, (*ii*) the standards are not yet stable enough and (*iii*) their implementations are not yet completely compatible.

Finally, in distributed social platforms, algorithms for friend discovery are still an argument of research. This issue is related to the intrinsically distributed nature of those systems, where information about users is not available to a single central entity, but is available only to local contacts. Moreover, the issue is complicated when profile data is kept confidential, and disclosed only after some acknowledgement between the users. In those cases, the algorithms and the studies about Automated Trust Negotiations (Winsborough & Li, 2002) may help to define patterns and strategies for facilitating the creation of trust relationships.

CONCLUSION

Although the current approach to build social networking systems is to create huge centralized systems owned by a single company, such strategy has many drawbacks, regarding: (*i*) privacy and anonymity of users; (*ii*) risks of *a priori* or *a posteriori* censorship; (*iii*) ownership and use-rights of the users data; (*iv*) interoperability with other systems; and (*v*) costs of the infrastructure, especially when it has to support media files.

In this chapter, we discussed the main security and functional requirements of a social networking platform, that are: (*i*) confidentiality, i.e., the interactions between an user and the system must remain private unless explicitly public; (*ii*) integrity, i.e., unauthorized modifications to profiles and other user generated content must not occur; (*iii*) accountability, i.e., authorized modifications must be traceable; (*iv*) availability; (*v*) identity and anonymity. Such requirements can be violated by various threats and attacks, such as (*i*) masquerading, which occurs when a user disguises his identity and pretends to be another user; (*ii*) unauthorized access; (*iii*) denial of service; (*iv*) repudiation, which occurs when a user participates in an activity and later claims he did not; (*v*) eavesdropping; (*vi*) alteration; (*vii*) copy and replay; (*viii*) social engineering.

In order to overcome both the intrinsic defects of centralized systems and the general vulnerabilities of social networking platforms, many different approaches have been proposed, either as federated (i.e., consisting of multiple entities cooperating to provide the service, but usually distinct from users) or peer-to-peer systems (with users directly cooperating to provide the service) and in this work we have reviewed the most popular.

Eventually, we briefly discussed our own approach to create a solid distributed social networking platform consisting in a novel peer-to-peer system that leverages existing, widespread and stable technologies such as DHTs and BitTorrent. Blogracy is a micro-blogging social networking system, and consequently we gave priority to the features more important for micro-blogging, such as: (*i*) anonymity and resilience to censorship; (*ii*) authenticatable contents; (*iii*) semantic interoperability using activity streams and weak semantic data formats for contacts and profiles; and (*iv*) data availability. Although Blogracy is not yet feature-complete, we have created a working prototype, implementing all core functionalities as a layer over a well-tested distributed file sharing system.

REFERENCES

Baden, R., Bender, A., Spring, N., Bhattacharjee, B., & Starin, D. (2009). Persona: An online social network with user-defined privacy. In *Proceedings of the ACM conference on Data communication, SIGCOMM '09*, (pp. 135–146). ACM.

Berners-Lee, T. (2010, December). Long live the web: A call for continued open standards and neutrality. *Scientific American Magazine*. Retrieved September 26, 2012, from http://www.scientificamerican.com/article.cfm?id=long-live-the-web

Bethencourt, J., Sahai, A., & Waters, B. (2007). Ciphertext -policy attribute-based encryption. In *IEEE Symposium on Security and Privacy* (pp. 321-334). IEEE Computer Society.

Biddle, P., England, P., Peinado, M., & Willman, B. (2002). The Darknet and the future of content distribution. In *Lecture Notes in Computer Science, Vol. 2696. Proceedings of the 2002 ACM Workshop on Digital Rights Management* (pp. 155–176). Berlin: Springer / Verlag.

Boneh, D., & Franklin, M. (2001). Identity based encryption from the Weil pairing. Extended abstract in *Lecture Notes in Computer Science, Vol. 2139. Advances in Cryptology – Crypto 2001* (pp. 231–229). Berlin: Springer / Verlag.

Boyd, D., & Ellison, N. B. (2008). Social network sites: Definition, history, and scholarship. *Journal of Computer-Mediated Communication, 13*(1), 210–230. doi:10.1111/j.1083-6101.2007.00393.x

Buchegger, S., & Datta, A. (2009). A case for p2p infrastructure for social networks - opportunities & challenges. In *Proceedings of Sixth International Conference on Wireless On-Demand Network Systems and Services, WONS 2009* (pp. 161–168).

Buchegger, S., Schiöberg, D., Vu, L., & Datta, A. (2009). PeerSoN: P2P social networking: Early experiences and insights. In *Proceedings of the Second ACM EuroSys Workshop on Social Network Systems* (pp. 46–52). ACM.

Canetti, R., Thomas, J., Garay, J., Itkis, G., Micciancio, D., Naor, M., & Pinkas, B. (1999). Multicast security: A taxonomy and some efficient constructions. In *Proceedings of INFOCOM '99, Eighteenth Annual Joint Conference of the IEEE Computer and Communications Societies* (vol. 2, pp. 708-716). IEEE Computer Society.

Castro, M., Druschel, P., Kermarrec, A.-M., & Rowstron, A. (2002). Scribe: A large-scale and decentralized application-level multicast infrastructure. *IEEE Journal on Selected Areas in Communications, 20*(8), 1489–1499. doi:10.1109/JSAC.2002.803069

Chaum, D. L. (1981). Untraceable electronic mail, return addresses, and digital pseudonyms. *Communications of the ACM, 24*(2), 84–90. doi:10.1145/358549.358563

Cheng, A., & Friedman, E. (2005). Sybilproof reputation mechanisms. In *Proceedings of the 2005 ACM SIGCOMM workshop on Economics of peer-to-peer systems, P2PECON '05* (pp. 128-132). ACM.

Cholez, T., Chrisment, I., & Festor, O. (2010). Efficient DHT attack mitigation through peers' ID distribution. In *Proceedings of the 2010 IEEE International Symposium on Parallel & Distributed Processing, Workshops and Phd Forum, IPDPSW* (pp. 1-8).

Clarke, I., Miller, S., Hong, T., Sandberg, O., & Wiley, B. (2002). Protecting free expression online with Freenet. *Internet Computing, IEEE, 6*(1), 40–49. doi:10.1109/4236.978368

Clarke, I., Sandberg, O., Wiley, B., & Hong, T. (2001). Freenet: A distributed anonymous information storage and retrieval system. In *Designing Privacy Enhancing Technologies* (*Vol. 2009*, pp. 46–66). Lecture Notes in Computer Science Berlin: Springer / Verlag. doi:10.1007/3-540-44702-4_4

Cutillo, L. A., Molva, R., & Strufe, T. (2009). Safebook: A privacy preserving online social network leveraging on real-life trust. In *IEEE Communications Magazine*, ser. *Consumer Communications and Networking, 47*(12), 94–101. IEEE Computer Society.

Dingledine, R., Mathewson, N., & Syverson, P. (2004). Tor: The second-generation onion router. In *Proceedings of the 13th conference on USENIX Security Symposium, SSYM'04* (pp. 21–21). San Diego, CA: USENIX Association.

Facebook (2011). *Facebook statement of rights and responsibilities*. Retrieved September 26, 2012 from http://www.facebook.com/terms.php

Franchi, E., & Tomaiuolo, M. (2012). Software agents for distributed social networking. In *Proceedings of the 13th Workshop Dagli Oggetti agli Agenti, WOA 2012* (pp. 1–5).

Goldschlag, D., Reed, M., & Syverson, P. (1999). Onion routing. *Communications of the ACM, 42*(2), 39–41. doi:10.1145/293411.293443

Goyal, V., Pandey, O., Sahai, A., & Waters, B. (2006). Attribute-based encryption for fine-grained access control of encrypted data. In *ACM Conference on Computer and Communications Security* (pp. 89–98). ACM.

Graffi, K., Groß, C., Mukherjee, P., Kovacevic, A., & Steinmetz, R. (2010). LifeSocial.KOM: A P2P-based platform for secure online social networks. In *Proceedings of the 10th IEEE International Conference on Peer-to-Peer Computing, IEEE P2P'10* (pp. 554–558). IEEE Computer Society.

Leskovec, J., Lang, K. J., Dasgupta, A., & Mahoney, M. W. (2008). Statistical properties of community structure in large social and information networks. In *Proceeding of the 17th International Conference on World Wide Web* (pp. 695–704).

Lesniewski-Laas, C. (2008). A Sybil-proof one-hop DHT. In *Proceedings of the 1st workshop on Social network systems* (pp. 19–24). ACM.

Lewko, A., & Waters, B. (2011). Decentralizing attribute-based encryption. In *Advances in Cryptology – EUROCRYPT 2011* (*Vol. 6632*, pp. 568–588). Lecture Notes in Computer Science Springer. doi:10.1007/978-3-642-20465-4_31

Li, N. (2000). Local names in SPKI/SDSI. In *Proceedings of the 13th IEEE workshop on Computer Security Foundations, CSFW '00*. IEEE Computer Society.

Mani, M., Nguyen, A., & Crespi, N. (2010). Scope: A prototype for spontaneous P2P social networking. In *Proceedings of the 8th IEEE International Conference on Pervasive Computing and Communications Workshops, PERCOM* (pp. 220–225). IEEE Computer Society.

Perfitt, T., & Englert, B. (2010). Megaphone: Fault tolerant, scalable, and trustworthy P2P microblogging. In *Proceedings of the Fifth International Conference on Internet and Web Applications and Services, ICIW'10* (pp. 469–477). IEEE Computer Society.

Pranata, I., Skinner, G., & Athauda, R. (2011). A distributed community approach for protecting resources in digital ecosystem. In *International Conference on Advanced Computer Science and Information System, ICACSIS* (pp. 95–100).

Rzadca, K., Datta, A., & Buchegger, S. (2010). Replica placement in p2p storage: Complexity and game theoretic analyses. In *Proceedings of the International Conference on Distributed Computing Systems* (pp. 599–609). IEEE Computer Society.

Sahai, A., & Waters, B. (2005). Fuzzy identity based encryption. In *Advances in Cryptology – Eurocrypt 2005* (*Vol. 3494*, pp. 557–557). Lecture Notes in Computer Science Springer. doi:10.1007/11426639_27

Sandler, D., Mislove, A., Post, A., & Druschel, P. (2005). Feedtree: Sharing web micronews with peer-to-peer event notification. In *Peer-to-Peer Systems IV* (*Vol. 3640*, pp. 141–151). Lecture Notes in Computer Science Berlin: Springer / Verlag. doi:10.1007/11558989_13

Shamir, A. (1984). Identity-based cryptosystems and signature schemes. In *Lecture Notes in Computer Science, Vol. 196. Advances in Cryptology: Proceedings of CRYPTO 84* (pp. 47–53). Berlin: Springer/Verlag.

Shankland, S. (2010). *Facebook blocks contact exporting tool*. Retrieved September 26, 2012, from http://news.cnet.com/8301-30685_3-20076774-264/facebook-blocks-contact-exporting-tool/

Skeels, M., & Grudin, J. (2009). When social networks cross boundaries: A case study of workplace use of Facebook and Linked-In. In *Proceedings of the ACM 2009 international conference on Supporting group work* , *09*, 95–104. doi:10.1145/1531674.1531689

Stroud, D. (2008). Social networking: An age-neutral commodity — Social networking becomes a mature web application. *Journal of Direct. Data and Digital Marketing Practice*, *9*(3), 278–292. doi:10.1057/palgrave.dddmp.4350099

Tanenbaum, A. S., & Steen, M. V. (2006). *Distributed systems: Principles and paradigms* (2nd ed.). Prentice Hall.

Twitter (2012). *Twitter terms of service*. Retrieved September 26, 2012, from http://twitter.com/tos

Urdaneta, G., Pierre, G., & Steen, M. V. (2011). A survey of DHT security techniques. *ACM Computing Surveys*, *43*(2), 1–49. doi:10.1145/1883612.1883615

Viswanath, B., Post, A., Gummadi, K. P., & Mislove, A. (2010). An analysis of social network-based Sybil defenses. *ACM SIGCOMM Computer Communication Review*, *40*(4), 363–374. doi:10.1145/1851275.1851226

Winsborough, W. H., & Li, N. (2002). Towards practical automated trust negotiation. In *Proceedings of the Third International Workshop on Policies for Distributed Systems and Networks* (pp. 92–103). IEEE Computer Society.

Xu, T., Chen, Y., & Fu, X. (2010). Twittering by cuckoo: Decentralized and socio-aware online microblogging services. In *Proceedings of the ACM SIGCOMM 2010 Conference* (pp. 473–475). ACM.

Xu, T., Chen, Y., Zhao, J., & Fu, X. (2010). Cuckoo: Towards decentralized, socio-aware online microblogging services and data measurements. In *Proceedings of the 2nd ACM International Workshop on Hot Topics in Planet-scale Measurement* (pp. 4:1–4:6). ACM.

Yu, H., Kaminsky, M., Gibbons, P., & Flaxman, A. (2006). Sybilguard: Defending against sybil attacks via social networks. *ACM SIGCOMM Computer Communication Review*, *36*(4), 267–278. doi:10.1145/1151659.1159945

Zzz, & Schimmer, L. (2009). Peer profiling and selection in the I2P anonymous network. In *Proceedings of PET-CON 2009* (pp. 1–12). Dresden, Germany.

ADDITIONAL READING

Acquisti, A., & Gross, R. (2009). Predicting social security numbers from public data. *Proceedings of the National Academy of Sciences of the United States of America*, *106*(27), 10975–10980. doi:10.1073/pnas.0904891106

Agarwal, A. *Security update & new features*. Retrieved September 26, 2012, from http://blog.dropbox.com/index.php/security-update-new-features/

Andrews, D. C. (2002). Audience-specific online community design. *Communications of the ACM*, *45*(4), 64–68. doi:10.1145/505248.505275

Bergenti, F., Franchi, E., & Poggi, A. (2011). Agent-based social networks for enterprise collaboration. In *2011 IEEE 20th International Workshops on Enabling Technologies: Infrastructure for Collaborative Enterprises* (pp. 25–28). IEEE Computer Society.

Bergenti, F., Franchi, E., & Poggi, A. (2012). Enhancing social networks with agent and semantic web technologies. In *Collaboration and the semantic web: Social networks, knowledge networks, and knowledge resources* (pp. 83–100). Hershey, PA: IGI Global. doi:10.4018/978-1-4666-0894-8.ch005

Bilge, L., Strufe, T., Balzarotti, D., & Kirda, E. (2009). All your contacts are belong to us: Automated identity theft attacks on social networks. In *Proceedings of the 18th international conference on World wide web* (pp. 551-560).

Bonneau, J., Anderson, J., Anderson, R., & Stajano, F. (2009). Eight friends are enough: Social graph approximation via public listings. In *Proceedings of the Second ACM EuroSys Workshop on Social Network Systems* (pp. 13-18).

Boyd, D. M., & Ellison, N. B. (2007). Social network sites: Definition, history, and scholarship. *Journal of Computer-Mediated Communication, 13*(1), 210–230. doi:10.1111/j.1083-6101.2007.00393.x

Burt, R. S. (1992). *Structural holes: The social structure of competition*. Cambridge, MA: Harvard University Press.

Chvatal, V. (1979). A greedy heuristic for the set-covering problem. In *Mathematics of Operations Research* (pp. 233-235).

Cohen, B. (2003). Incentives build robustness in BitTorrent. In *Proceedings of Workshop on Economics of Peer-to-Peer systems* (pp. 68-72).

Contractor, N. S., & Monge, P. R. (2003). Using multi-theoretical multilevel models to study adversarial networks. In *Dynamic Social Network Modeling and Analysis* (pp. 324–344). Workshop Summary and Papers.

Ellison, C., Frantz, B., Lampson, B., Rivest, R., Thomas, B., & Ylonen, T. (1999). SPKI certificate theory. *IETF RFC 2693*.

Falkner, J., Piatek, M., John, J. P., Krishnamurthy, A., & Anderson, T. (2007). Profiling a million user DHT. In *Proceedings of the 7th ACM SIGCOMM Conference on Internet Measurement, IMC '07*, (pp. 129-134). ACM.

Fitzpatrick, B., & Lueck, J. (2010). The case against data lock-in. *Communications of the ACM*, *53*(11), 42. doi:10.1145/1839676.1839691

Franchi, E., & Poggi, A. (2011). Multi-agent systems and social networks. In *Business Social Networking: Organizational, Managerial, and Technological Dimensions*. Hershey, PA: IGI Global. doi:10.4018/978-1-61350-168-9.ch005

Gaudin, S. (2011). Have LinkedIn's security woes permanently damaged the social network? *ComputerWorld*. Retrieved September 26, 2012, from http://www.computerworld.com/s/article/9228122

Huber, M., Mulazzani, M., Kitzler, G., Goluch, S., & Weippl, E. (2011). Friend-in-the-middle attacks exploiting social networking sites for spam. *IEEE Internet Computing*, *15*(3), 28–34. doi:10.1109/MIC.2011.24

Irani, D., Webb, S., Pu, C., & Li, K. (2011). Modeling unintended personal-information leakage from multiple online social networks. *IEEE Internet Computing*, *15*(3), 13–19. doi:10.1109/MIC.2011.25

Li, N., & Grosof, B. (2000). A practically implementable and tractable delegation logic. In *Proceedings of the 2000 IEEE Symposium on Security and Privacy* (pp. 29-44). IEEE Computer Society.

Li, N., Grosof, B. N., & Feigenbaum, J. (2003). Delegation logic: A logic-based approach to distributed authorization. *ACM Transactions on Information and System Security*, *6*(1), 128–171. doi:10.1145/605434.605438

Li, N., Zhang, N., & Das, S. K. (2011). Preserving relation privacy in online social network data. *IEEE Internet Computing*, *15*(3), 35–42. doi:10.1109/MIC.2011.26

Morris, R., & Thompson, K. (1979). Password security: A case history. *Communications of the ACM*, *22*(11), 594–597. doi:10.1145/359168.359172

Nielsen (2011). *State of the media: The social media report*. Retrieved September 26, 2012, from http://blog.nielsen.com/nielsenwire/social/

Oechslin, P. (2003). Lecture Notes in Computer Science: *Vol. 2729. Making a faster cryptanalytic time-memory trade-off* (pp. 617–630). Springer.

Rabkin, A. (2008). Personal knowledge questions for fallback authentication: Security questions in the era of Facebook. In *Proceedings of the 4th symposium on Usable privacy and security* (pp. 13-23).

Rivest, R. L., & Lampson, B. (1996, September 15). *SDSI - A simple distributed security infrastructure*. Retrieved September 26, 2012, from http://people.csail.mit.edu/rivest/sdsi11.html

Shear, M. D., & Vick, K. (2008, September 18). Hackers access Palin's personal e-mail, post some online. *washingtonpost.com*.

Steiner, M., En-Najjary, T., & Biersack, E. W. (2007). A global view of Kad. In *Proceedings of the 7th ACM SIGCOMM conference on Internet measurement, IMC '07* (pp. 117-122). ACM.

Wang, F., Moreno, Y., & Sun, Y. (2006). Structure of peer-to-peer social networks. *Physical Review E: Statistical, Nonlinear, and Soft Matter Physics*, *73*(3), 1–7. doi:10.1103/PhysRevE.73.036123

Wasko, M., & Faraj, S. (2005). Why should I share? Examining social capital and knowledge contribution in electronic networks of practice. *Management Information Systems Quarterly*, *29*(1), 35–57.

Zhang, C., Sun, J. J., Zhu, X. Y., & Fang, Y. G. (2010). Privacy and security for online social networks: Challenges and opportunities. *IEEE Network*, *24*(4), 13–18. doi:10.1109/MNET.2010.5510913

KEY TERMS AND DEFINITIONS

DarkNet: In general a hidden or obscure network. It may include some web-like infrastructure and content or any other collaborative information systems. Independently of its mechanisms and goals, its distinguishing feature is to be clandestine, in the sense that it is known and accessible only to the acknowledged members of a certain community.

Distributed Hash Table (DHT): A mechanism for distributing data among peers in an overlay network. The network may have responsibility for managing actual data storage or simply indexing. Usually a DHT allows to efficiently search for a key, for retrieving and storing corresponding values on the proper node. In fact, the domain of possible keys is subdivided among the nodes, and each node is responsible for a certain subspace. Typically the complexity of the search is logarithmic against the network cardinality.

Pseudonymity: A mechanism for allowing users to operate under a pseudonym, or a "false name." It is used by people to avoid disclosing their real name and in particular their legal identity. Pseudonymity has being used long before the Internet, but it has acquired particular importance for users operating in global computer networks. The pseudonymity mechanisms available on the Internet may vary in the degrees of anonymity they provide. In fact, pseudonyms may range from unlinkable identifiers, like those provided by some remailer systems, to easily linkable names, where the association with the particular user (or the legal entity) they represent is publicly available.

Social Engineering: In information security, social engineering is an attack meant to psychologically manipulate a user into performing misguided actions. Exploiting computer-based communications and online social networking systems, it aims at obtaining confidential information, by means of confidence tricks. Social engineering is similar to frauds attempted in more traditional contexts, but is becoming increasingly important among computer professionals. The victim and the attacker need not to know each other in their real lives, and in fact often they never acknowledged each other directly.

Social Network: Social structure made of agents (individuals) that are connected by relationships.

Social Networking System: A software system that allows users to manipulate a representation of their online social networks and to interact with the other users in the system, especially collaboratively discussing user-produced resources (e.g., posts, pictures).

Sybil Node: A node of a peer-to-peer network belonging to an attacker, i.e. an entity which operates to subvert the network operation. Usually a large number of Sybil nodes are generated, possibly using a limited number of actual computers, to collaborate and alter reputation, routing, indexing and/or any other functionality of the peer-to-peer network.

Trust Management: A system for the symbolic representation, creation and management of social trust. In particular, trust can be used for controlling access to protected resources. A request for accessing a resource is accepted only if accompanied with sufficient credentials, according to a local policy. Trust, quantified as a set of access rights, can be further delegated to other agents, creating trust networks. A chain of credentials may be used to represent the trust flow, from the resource manager to the agent requesting access. Automated Trust Negotiation allows to automate trust building, guiding the disclosure of credentials according to privacy policies and negotiation strategies.

Chapter 7
Retrieval of Personal Public Data on Social Networks:
The Risks for Privacy

Francesca Carmagnola
University of Turin, Italy

Francesco Osborne
University of Turin, Italy

Ilaria Torre
University of Genoa, Italy

ABSTRACT

In this chapter, the authors analyze the risks for privacy coming from the distribution of user data over several social networks. Specifically, they focus on risks concerning the possibility to aggregate user data discovered on different sources into a single more complete profile, which makes possible to infer other data, likely set as private by the user. In order to show how it is possible to human users as well as to software agents crawling social networks, identifying users, linking their profiles and aggregating their data, the authors describe the prototype of a search engine they developed. The authors also present a simulation analysis to show the retrievability of user data by using a combination of people search engines and they provide statistics on the user perception on this issue.

INTRODUCTION

Online Social Networks (OSNs) allow people to publish and share information about themselves and to connect to the other members of the network. In recent years the participation in OSNs has rapidly increased. Among the top 100 most popular websites in 2102 in America, 84 are OSNs[1].

Despite the great variety of existing social networks, people using these systems share the common expectation of providing a virtual representation of themselves aimed at contacting or

DOI: 10.4018/978-1-4666-3926-3.ch007

being contacted by other people belonging to the network (e.g., Facebook, Classmates, Twitter), meeting new friends (e.g., Friendster, Orkut), finding new jobs or carrier opportunities (e.g., Linkedln), sharing interests (e.g., MySpace), receiving or providing recommendations (e.g., Tribe), and so on. OSNs offer people the opportunity to establish new relationships and to interact with other people, even if far. They offer tools to foster online collaboration and facilitate the rise of new initiatives and business relationships.

Despite these interesting opportunities, there are several critical aspects. Because of the false "sense of intimacy" in social networks, people tend to be less selective in choosing the individuals to interact with and to disclose personal information more easily than in traditional relationships. Thus, a huge and heterogeneous amount of user data is scattered over social networks, including contact information, identifiable data (often published together with photographs of the subject, of her/his relatives and friends), interests, as well as political and sexual orientation, information such as current and previous schools and career, drinking and drug habits, incomes, etc[2]. This behavior is very common among the so-called "digital natives." Young people seem to be more relaxed in publishing intimate details of their life on the Web than "digital immigrants" (Prensky, 2004). The result is a huge amount of personal data published in OSNs with the user consent, given by accepting the policies of the social network upon registration.

However, the uncontrolled dissemination of user data can cause damages to users[3]. In this context, the security and privacy of sensitive user information becomes a relevant issue to deal with (Ahn et al., 2011). Most of the risks are due to the lack of transparency and to the ambiguity of the data processing policy and services terms of use. Even though the Privacy Guarantees of 70 Counties (within the International Data Protection and Privacy Commissioners conference around the theme "Protecting privacy in a borderless world"[4]) have forced OSNs to improve their privacy policies, the risk of losing the control of user data and the risk that data are shared with unauthorized third parties is still high.

Third party systems can obtain authorization from users to access their profiles for some services, gather personal private information and then use such data for different goals, that unlikely match those desired by the users, such as for marketing analyses and for advertising.

Anyone on OSNs can collect personal data and use them for purposes such as direct personal attacks, discriminations or to take on the identity of another individual (identity theft).

Recently, the profiles in OSNs are also used for *social media job hunt* that is for recruiting and evaluating a candidate for a job position. A research conducted between December 2011 and January 2012[5] showed that two out of three companies use social network profiles to evaluate and select human resources. This makes even more important to pay attention to the personal information scattered over social networks.

The focus of this contribution is specifically on the risks associated to the possibility of collecting and aggregating user data on OSNs. A paradox is that while on OSNs, and in general on social systems, users have the impression to be virtual, thanks to the multiple identities that they can easily change whenever they want, actually, following the pieces of personal information scattered across different social systems, it is possible to reconstruct their real identity. The collection and aggregation of scattered user data produces a new profile, which is more complete than the starting ones, and this richer profile may allow the inference of personal data, set as private by the user.

Moreover, it is worth noting that the insertion of data, comments and photos over time makes social systems historical repositories of the users' activities and personal data, which often do not disappear even when the subject wishes it. The removal of the user account is rarely accompanied by a complete removal of all user-generated content (posts, comments, audio-video, etc.). What typically happens is that the profile is deactivated, resulting in the maintenance of a hidden copy of the data. Moreover, data that are indexed by search engines can be available even after their removal: this is a violation of Directive 95/46/EC as individuals are deprived of an effective mean to control the spread of their data.

In order to show how it is possible to human users as well as to software agents crawling social networks, identifying users and aggregating their data, in this chapter we describe the prototype of a vertical search engine, called CS-UDD (Cross-System User Data Discovery), that can be used to retrieve and aggregate personal public user data distributed on OSNs. The CS-UDD has been designed as a search service for software agents that query it in order to personalize their services (Carmagnola et al., 2009; 2010). Afterwards, we have also developed a prototype for human users. It can be used as a people search engine, but also as a tool for monitoring one's own public data on OSNs.

Collecting and aggregating user data are not always negative tasks for users. Technologies and standards for user data portability and representation have been developed quite in order to make easier the automatic exchange of user data, which can be useful to users, for example to skip the replication of registration procedures, to access different services by using mechanisms for single sign on, to obtain personalized services, etc. Nevertheless, users have to be aware about what data are public and the possible use of their aggregated data.

After describing the CS-UDD, the chapter will present a simulation analysis of user data collection by using the CS-UDD together with other people search engines. The objective is to use a real example in order to show the possibility to identify users on different social networks, to aggregate the user data discovered on various systems into a single profile and to infer new data about the user. The final aim of the analysis is showing that risks for user privacy do not concern only unauthorized access to private user data (criticalities related to the OAuth protocol, to the setting of visibility/privacy options, to the automatic propagation of authorizations, etc.): it often hides behind the public data.

In the last part of the chapter, we report a study we did with the support of the CS-UDD. Using a sample of subjects with real accounts on OSNs, we estimated the retrievability of their personal data and analyzed the perception of these subjects about the privacy problem related to the spreading of personal data and to the possibility of retrieving them.

The contribution is organized as follows. We first discuss the issue of privacy in OSNs. Then we describe the CS-UDD. Next, we present a simulation analysis of user data discovery on different OSNs, followed by a study about retrievability of user data and about the perception of privacy among OSNs users. Finally we conclude the chapter providing future directions of research.

Data Sharing and User Privacy in Social Network Systems

As introduced above, several types of information about a user can be published in a OSN, such as age and gender, education, employment history, sexual and political interests, photos and videos, contacts, geographical location, personal interests, etc.

Exchanging such data between applications may be valuable in several areas and for different purposes. For example, the exchange of user data between applications results useful to save users from repeating the boring process of filling in similar forms for different services (Vassileva, 2001). Systems partaking in the process of user data exchange can enrich their own profiles or can enrich repositories of user profiles (Heckmann, 2006). Berkovsky et al. (2008) propose a framework to import and integrate user data from other recommender systems. The authors underline that even though several obstacles exist to user data integration, such as different representation formats, different context of acquisition, privacy risks, etc., user models mediation can be useful to support personalization services.

Despite benefits, there are many critical points and risks related to the dissemination of user data on OSNs (Chen et al., 2009; Zheleva & Getoor, 2009; Krishnamurthy & Wills, 2009, Caviglione & Coccoli, 2011). First of all we sketch the modalities to acquire private user data, then we describe possible uses of such data and finally we present other risks derived from the manipulation and combination of public data.

Retrieval of Private User Data

1. Visibility of private data depending on errors or constraints in privacy settings. The user can involuntary make some information visible by ignoring or misusing the privacy settings. In some cases, a portion of information is visible by default. Sometimes the user is allowed to make private only part of his/her data because the OSN does not offer the possibility to completely restrict access to all the data.
2. Changing of privacy policies. a social network can change its privacy policy, resulting that data and content that were posted with restrictive privacy settings may become visible (Gross & Acquisti, 2005).
3. OSN business model based on user data. The user's desire is the possibility of easily managing and controlling the visibility of their data in OSNs (Cheek & Shehab, 2012), however this contrasts the business model of most OSNs. Indeed, even if social systems are free, users are indirectly required to pay by allowing the reuse of their data stored in personal profiles on social networks. For most systems, the data contained in user profiles and the number of unique users (combined with the frequency of usage) are the only real assets they own. This is a further stimulus for the collection, processing and use of user data, resulting in additional risks to users' privacy.
4. Authorized access to private user data performed by third-party applications. On the one hand third-party systems require access to OSN user data for providing users with additional services. On the other hand, OSN must also respect its members' privacy by preventing the disclosure of sensitive information in the data they provide. Satisfying both concerns is, for OSN, quite challenging (Li et al., 2011). For example, Facebook applications are third-party systems that interact with the social network, without being part of it and require users the authorization to access their data. Users provide their consent since these applications are aimed at making the social network more attractive by offering services and amusing methods for interacting with contacts in the social network. Examples of such applications are games, online polls and quizzes. Often users allow third-party applications to access their profiles since they do not fully perceive the extent of the permissions being granted, due to the lack of transparency of the permission policies and due to the prevention to use the service, if the user does not provide all the requested authorizations.
5. User's contacts may spread information and data about other users without their explicit permission. It is common that people talk about or tag other users.
6. Users may be the involuntary bridge to private data of their contacts. Depending on the privacy settings of users, once third-party applications have received permission from a primary user, they can gain access to the personal information of users' contacts without their explicit permission. In fact, social networks do not necessarily guarantee the security of the information that has been

uploaded to a profile, even when those posts are set to be private. For example, Facebook's Privacy Policy states that: "We cannot guarantee that only authorized persons will view your information. We cannot ensure that information you share on Facebook will not become publicly available. We are not responsible for third-party circumvention of any privacy settings or security measures on Facebook."[6] Moreover it was shown (Catanese et al., 2011) that with a well-built crawler it is possible to collect large samples of these networks comprising millions of connections among users.

Another way to access the personal information of a person by using her/his contacts is through the so-called "friend injection," that is attackers that add themselves as friends on behalf of the victim and thus infiltrate the target's closed network, or through "application injection," that is by installing, and controlling a custom third-party application (Huber et al., 2011).

Uses of Personal User Data

1. Third-party applications may use personal data they have collected for different goals, such as marketing analyses and to allow advertisers to better target their ads. This is valuable for them since targeted advertisements are more likely to result in a purchase than non-targeted ones. Notice, however, that third-party applications can gather user data and information also through electronic tracking of users' actions on the Web, such as page viewed, click-through, etc.
2. Beside the uses described above, others are illegal practices and can be even dangerous for users. Examples of illegal purposes are spam, scripting between different web services, malware (Mazur et al., 2009; Luo et al., 2009), spear-phishing, illegal usage of users profiles (profile squatting), sexual harassment, identity theft, personal persecution (stalking), brand or individual image damaging, net bullying and social engineering attacks (Hogben, 2007; Lindamood et al., 2009).
3. Other times, private subjects may search for information about users for non-illegal purposes, such as for knowing about the author of a post, for checking the validity of an information source, for recruiting and evaluating a candidate for a job position. A research carried on between December 2011 and January 2012 showed that two out of three companies use social network profiles to evaluate and select new human resources as well as to complete the candidates' curriculum vitae[7].

A recent survey by the authors of Reppler,[8] an advanced social media monitoring service, has investigated how job recruiters screen job candidates on social networks.[9]

The survey, which was conducted on a sample of 300 hiring professionals, showed that more than 90% of recruiters and hiring managers have visited a potential candidate's profile on a social network as part of the screening process. The most used social networks are Facebook (76%), Twitter (53%) and LinkedIn (48%). In most cases, recruiters look at social networking sites after they receive an application (47%).

On the one hand, 69% of recruiters have rejected a candidate based on content found on his/her social networking profiles, such as content and pictures drawing the user while drinking and using drugs (19%), false statement about the qualification (13%), inappropriate photos (11%), inappropriate comments (11%), negative comments about a previous employer (11%), poor communication skills (11%), disrespect of confidential information from a previous employer (7%). On the other hand, 68% of recruiters declared that they have hired a candidate based on information in social networking sites, such as a positive impression of their personality and organizational fit (39%), creative ideas (36%), solid communication skills (33%), good references posted by others (34%).

Risks Derived from the Manipulation and Combination of Personal Public Data

1. A relevant issue concerning user privacy in social networks is that disparate pieces of information about an online identity can be easily combined from multiple networks (Irani et al., 2011). Indeed, collecting and aggregating user data scattered across different OSNs produces a new profile, which is more complete than the starting one. Moreover this richer profile may allow the inference of new user data, which was not public, originally. This is what typically happens when using people search engines on the Web. They can browse the entire Web or be focused on specific social systems or specific domains. The first kind of engine is more frequent. Examples are yoName, Wink, Pipl, Snitch.Name, 123people and Folowen. They usually require the user name and last name. Some of them, as Wink and Pipl, permit also to enter other data for making the query more precise, such as the user gender, country, etc. The CS-UDD prototype we developed is similar to them since it allows as well specifying some input data, but it is focused on browsing specific OSNs (it will be presented in the next section).
2. A further worrying issue about user privacy concerns Content-Based Image Recognition (CBIR). Geolocalizing users and places is enhanced by using these techniques, that make possible recognizing characteristics of objects and places depicted in images associated with profiles (Gudivada & Raghavan, 1995). In addition to these techniques, many social systems enable users to publish geo-located content in real time, thus combining real-time location-reporting capabilities with traditional social network functionality. Foremost examples are Facebook, Foursquare, Twitter, Google Latitude, Flickr, Gowalla, Loopt, and MyTown. In these systems users can post their location update or tag photos with descriptive keywords and also with geographic coordinates. This may represent a serious risk in terms of security since information about user location and the places he/she visited can be inferred and revealed.
   Moreover, users can also report location information of other individuals, who have little or no control over the published data (Vicente et al., 2011).
3. A kind of risk that differs from those above concerns the lack of user's control about data update. Typically, in social systems data are updated directly by the user while, third-party applications - that collect users data without their explicit consent and control - data may be outdated, with the result of fostering the spread of false user information in the net.

The risk of outdated data is also due to the difficulty of deleting the user account and the related data. Often, social networks simply allow to "deactivate" accounts. Other times the deletion requires complicated, multi-step processes that can stretch over the course of days (or weeks). The consequence is that users stop using accounts, while maintaining them. For example, deleting a Facebook account is a difficult task. When a user tries to cancel his/her account, this is simply deactivated and it can be reactivated as soon as the user logs again into the system. In case a user wishes to permanently delete the account, a request to Facebook is required. However, Facebook does not immediately delete the account, and if at any time before it is permanently deleted the user logs in, the deletion request will be cancelled. It is also difficult to remove the Facebook account of a deceased person. This can be done only following an official request by a family member.

A similar procedure is performed by Flickr. When an account is deleted, photos, metadata and comments are stored on servers for 90 days, but are not longer publicly accessible. After this period, Flickr will remove the content from the server, providing the complete elimination of the personal information. If an account is reactivated within this period of 90 days, the account, as well as all the content, is restored.

A system where the deletion of the account is almost impossible is Skype. Once created, a Skype account cannot be deleted and no change of the Skype Name is allowed. However, the user can remove all the personal data contained in the Skype profile. In this way the user cannot be found by using the personal information provided to Skype (but he/she can still be found via the Skype Name).

In contrast to delete a Facebook or a Skype account, deleting a Twitter account is relatively easy. The user's request for the account deletion puts it in a "queue" for permanent deletion. However, this takes up to a month for the account and information to disappear entirely from their system. Deleting a MySpace account is simple as well. Once a deletion request is provided, an email is sent to the user. When the user gets the email, a confirmation is required and then the account is immediately deleted. The same process is performed by LinkedIn and StumbleUpon. Instead Google allows a user to choose whether deleting only some of the services and information associated with it, or if deleting the entire account.

Anyway, it is clear that, even if the user permanently deletes his/her account from all social systems, there may be copies of the account stored by third-party systems and data and copies of the profile webpage collected and indexed by search engines. The consequence is that the account can never be completely removed and the user cannot be aware of this.

A way for users to control their data on the Web is using OSNs aggregators. However, in this case the perspective is different from people search engines since social network aggregators are aimed at organizing and simplifying the user's social networking experience by aggregating content posted on several social networks into a single dashboard. Content may include user profile data and also streaming data such as messages, posts, tweets, etc. The aggregation is done by API applications, which must be provided by the user with his/her user id and password of the social media to be syndicated. Examples of such systems are Doozly, Sobees, Alternion, FriendFeed, Meevr, Vinehub, Flavors.me, Profilactic.

Aggregators (e.g. Guy et. al, 2008), recommenders and personalized services represent the other face of data sharing, since they are examples of opportunities offered by using standards and protocols for user data exchanging and searching. Recently, many Web data portability solutions have been proposed. One of the most challenging projects is Dataportability, which had the original aim of allowing users to control their own data, shared over different Internet-based applications. More recently, the organization has achieved the further goal of advocating open standard representation of data to make web data portability a reality. There are numerous open standards that work in this direction, such as OpenID, OAuth, microformats, FOAF, APML, RDFa, SIOC, SKOS.

THE CS-UDD PROTOTYPE: AN OVERVIEW

Cross-System User Data Discovery (CS-UDD) is the name of a project we have been working on to develop techniques for retrieving and aggregating user data distributed on social networks (Carmagnola et al., 2009; 2010). These techniques can be used to develop web search services being queried by systems, but also people search engine for OSNs being queried by persons and as a tool for monitoring one's personal data on social networks.

In this contribution, the description of the mechanisms used by the CS-UDD to identify users and to infer private attributes is aimed to make people more aware about the possible risks coming from crossing user data from different OSNs. In the next section, the CS-UDD will be used in a simulation on user data search, carried out by using the CS-UDD together with other people search engines.

Given a user to be searched and a variable set of known user data (user attributes), the prototype works as a crawler, browsing social networks' websites, retrieving profiles that match the input user attributes and correlating the user data within them. Each discovered user profile is returned with a Certainty Factor (CF), ranging from 0 to 1, expressing the confidence that the profile belongs to the searched user. CS-UDD does not return only user profiles, but also user attributes, they too returned with an estimated CF.

The approach for the identification and retrieval of user data on different OSNs is based on the following concepts:

- The user identity is a collection of attributes.
- Replicated user data on different profiles in social systems can be used to match the profiles in order to evaluate if the profiles are compatible and thus if they can potentially belong to the same user.
- The greater the number of matching attributes in two profiles, the higher the probability that the two profiles belong to the same user.
- The more specific such attributes are, the higher the probability the two profiles belong to the same user.
- The more persistent the compared attributes are, the lower is the probability the profiles belong to the same user in case the attributes do not match.
- If two profiles have both high probability to belong to the same user, except for a very small set of attributes, a correct prediction of the non-compatible user attributes can be done anyway, by computing a value that is compatible with both the profiles (for example, by extending the values range).

This process can become recursive. Indeed, the new user data discovered with this technique can be reprocessed to find even other alternative identities of the same user. For example, when discovering that the user has some specific features, the search can be expanded to include profiles with such features on the same or on different social networks. This can lead to find identities the user thought not attributable to him and also identities that can be fake fraudulent profiles.

In the following we provide some details about the techniques used by the CS-UDD, based on the concepts mentioned on top of this section.

The basic concept of the approach is that the "user identity" can be seen as a collection of properties. Each of them contributes to identify the user with different strength. Among the user's properties, the persistent features (e.g., name and birth date) are the most relevant when disambiguating one individual from another (Windley, 2005). The national personal number (e.g., SSN, NIN, etc.), being unique for each person, would clearly be sufficient to identify users. In its absence, and in absence of any other recognition mechanism, the approach adopted by the CS-UDD for identifying users on OSNs is based on matching the attributes of the searched user (input profile) with the attributes of the profiles stored on OSNs. In this way it is possible to estimate a degree of similarity between the input profile and the retrieved profiles. If two profiles have the same attributes, the probability they belong to the same owner is high. Thus it could be even possible to link profiles which do not expose name and surname, but which expose and share other significant and/or numerous attributes.

The tricky issue is defining the algorithm to estimate the probability that two profiles belong to the same user, given a set of shared attributes. To this aim, we defined a number of indicators and we used them in the algorithm to *weight* the contribution of each shared attribute to the probability of the user identification. The main indicators are: the *persistency* of the compared attributes, the *frequency* of the attribute's values and the *specificity* of the attributes (especially of the user nicknames).

- Persistent attributes are user features that do not change over time. Attributes can be placed on a scale of persistency, with the higher value assigned to birth date and to the national personal code. Other persistent attributes are the name and gender, followed by others that rarely change, such as the country, the e-mail, the homepage, etc. The persistency of an attribute is a significant parameter especially when two attributes do not match. It results in a very high probability that the profiles belong to different persons. Generalizing this concept, we compute the *variability* of an attribute including in this indicator not only persistency but also attributes which may vary in profiles belonging all to the same person because of errors or falseness. The variability is defined as a measure of frequency of variations of the attribute and is used within a logarithmic function expressing an inverse relation between the frequency of variations and the weight associated to that shared attribute.
- Frequency of the shared value's attribute is an indicator that evaluates if the value of the attribute shared by the profiles is frequent in the given population or not. If it is not frequent, the matching of the attribute in the two profiles is more significant than when it is frequent. Thus, it receives a higher weight. As the above indicator, this one also is used within a logarithmic function which expresses an inverse relation between the frequency of the attribute's value and the weight associated to that shared attribute.
- Specificity of the attribute is an indicator applied to nicknames. The idea of considering the nickname specificity in the algorithm for profile matching is that, given two profiles with the same nickname, the probability they belong to the same user is much higher if the matching nickname is rare and complex. People tend to be conservative in choosing nicknames, and thus it is very likely that they use the same nickname (or a similar nickname) on different systems. This behavior is very critical with regard to user privacy since it is an easy way for searchers to connect two remote and unrelated profiles.

After the matching phase described above, the set of profiles selected by using the mentioned indicators are *cross-linked*, *clustered* and *heuristics* are applied to refine the estimation of match and to extract the attributes included in the matching profiles.

In this way, attributes that are replicated on different profiles are used for estimating the probability of match between the profiles and to allow accessing the other attributes that are different in the matched profiles.

Example of User Data Discovery by Exploiting CS-UDD and Other People Search Engines

To exemplify the possible risks for user privacy hiding behind public data, we simulate a case of social media job recruiting. As said before, two out of three companies systematically use social network profiles to evaluate and select new human resources.[10]

Specifically, we simulate the case of a recruiter who wishes to explore social networking systems to discover more information about a candidate (target user *U*) who submitted an application.

Given this goal, a possible way can be querying different engines and using the results returned by the queries as input to refine the query on the same or another search engine.

In our example, we perform a recursive search by:

Step 1: Exploiting *CS-UDD* to identify the target user *U* on different social networks.
Step 2: Using the data retrieved through *CS-UDD* as input to perform a new search on the CS-UDD and to query two people search engines: *123people* and *Pipl.*
Step 3: Checking the retrieved profiles by analyzing the retrieved data and following the retrieved links.
Step 4: Expanding the search to the social network of U (people related to U) in order to find further information about *U*.

In this way, the search process becomes a learning process where each new acquired piece of information is used to expand the search and to infer data.

In Figure 1 we show the flow chart of the search process and in the subsequent pages we provide details about the retrieved, aggregated and inferred data. Notice that since the analysis is based on real profiles, we turn the information that can identify the user (first name, surname, nicknames, birth date) into symbols (x, y, z, b etc.) and blur them in the screenshots.

Step 1

CS-UDD is provided with an initial set of *U*'s attributes: full name *x y*, city *Turin,* gender *female* (Figure 2, left side). CS-UDD crawls a set of social networks (e.g., Facebook, MySpace, Skype, Flickr and Netlog) and retrieves a set of profiles matching the input attributes (three profiles on Facebook: f1, f2, f3, one on MySpace:m1, one on Netlog:n1 and three on Skype: s1, s2, s3), as displayed on the right side of the figure.

Among the retrieved profiles, it suggests, as probable profiles owned by the *U*, the profiles with a CF over a threshold (the bold ones in Retrieved Profiles section of the figure). Moreover, it returns a set of new *U*'s *attributes* derived from the retrieved profiles by applying a set of rules (see the Discovered Attributes section of the figure): *U*'s age: *25*, birth date: *13/04/1987*, province: *Piemonte*, country: *Italy* and profession: *student*.

Another set of relevant data extracted from the retrieved profiles concerns *U*'s *nicknames*. Most of profiles on OSNs use nicknames as identifier of the profile. Typically, nicknames are used in the URL of the user profile. In our example, considering the four suggested profiles (the bold ones in Figure 2), three different *U*'s nicknames can be found:

nick1 (profile on Netlog, with CF=1): Corresponds to *xy* (first name last name).
nick2 (profile on MySpace, with CF=1): Corresponds to *xy87* (first name last name birth year).
nick3 (profile on Skype, with CF=0.87): Corresponds to *x_y* (first name_last name).

Facebook uses nicknames only as identifier of the profile in the URL. In the example it corresponds to *xy*.

Step 2

Recursive Search on the CS-UDD

U's attributes discovered in Step 1 are used as input for a new search on the CS-UDD, as shown in Figure 1. The output of the new search differs from the previous one in two ways: some of the profiles retrieved in Step 1 are discarded (f2 and

Figure 1. Flow chart of the search process

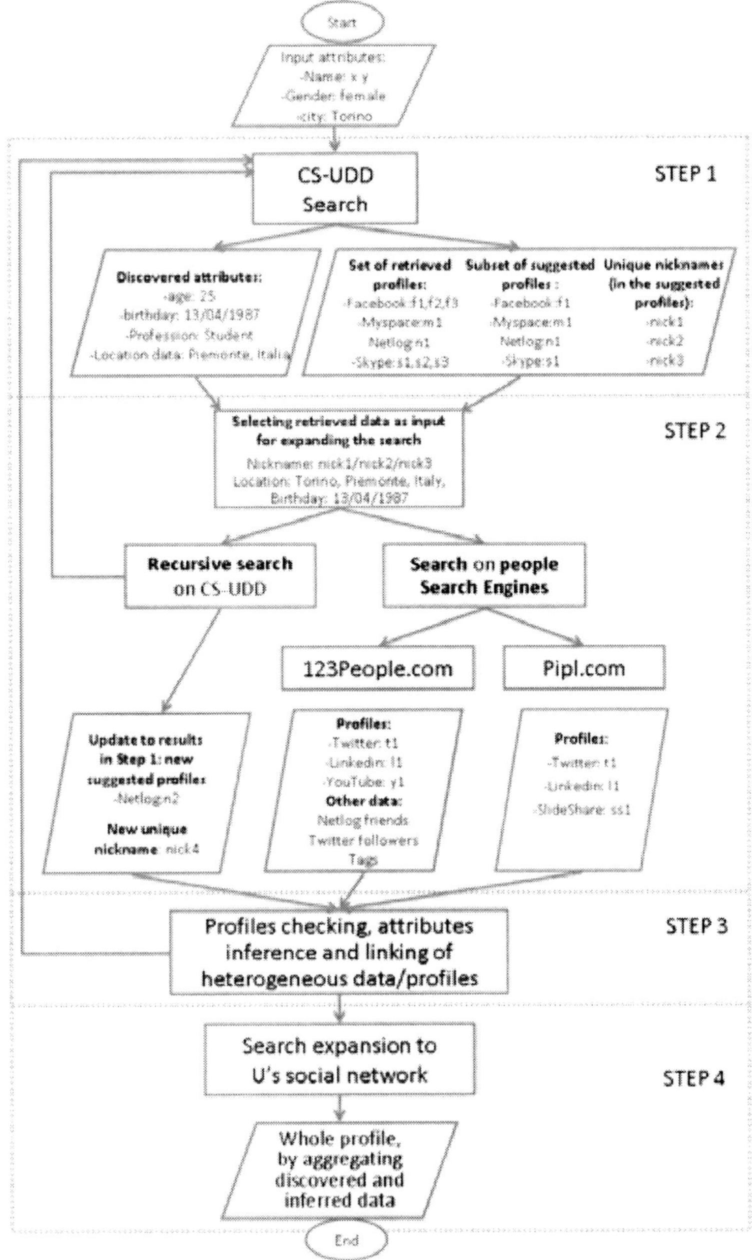

s3) since their attributes do not match the new input data; on the other hand a new profile is retrieved on Netlog (n2), matching *U*'s first name, city and the birth date attribute discovered in Step 1. n2 profile uses a nick different from the three ones above and provides new *U*'s attributes:

love status: *engaged to qx* (name of boyfriend), fancy: *man* and native language: *italian*.

nick4 (profile on Netlog, with CF=0.73): Corresponds to *z* (string of characters with no reference to other *U*'s attributes).

Figure 2. Search performed on the CS-UDD: input and output data

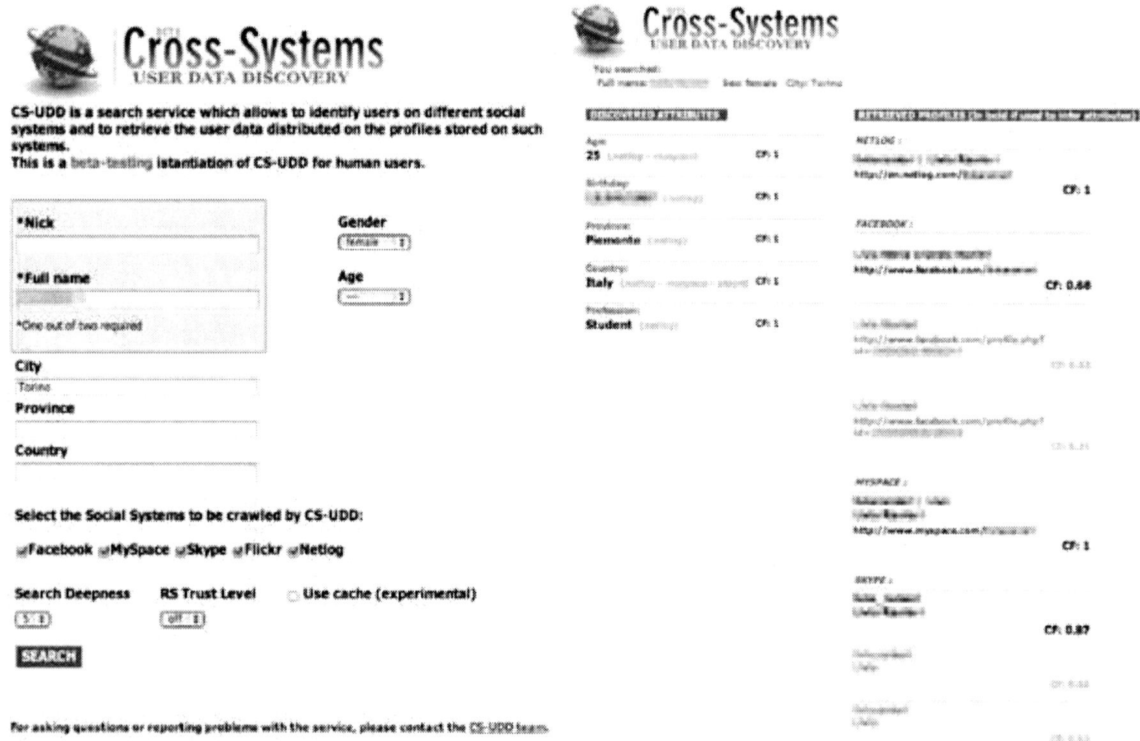

It is worth noting that, even though this profile does not provide *U*'s surname or the nickname, it has been identified by CS-UDD as belonging to *U* with a good CF by exploiting some references to personal data. The discovery of this profile demonstrates the possibility of linking unrelated profiles, such as the official user profiles and her/his personal and informal profiles, with serious risks for privacy.

Search on People Search Engines

123People and *Pipl* are people search engines that perform horizontal search by crawling the Web and returning the whole amount of information matching the search request. This kind of search engines is useful since they extend the search to plenty of social systems and repositories. The drawback is that many results they provide are not relevant to the searcher.

As an example, querying *123People* by providing it with *U*'s name *x* and *U*'s last name *y*, returns 17 profiles. Instead, by providing *123People* with nicks extracted by using the CS-UDD, makes the result more precise.

123People retrieves profiles on Twitter (t1), Linkedin (l1), YouTube (y1) and also on other less popular social systems such as Klout.com (a service which measures the user influence on social networks, also collecting a set of SN ID for a given user). Moreover it retrieves new attributes: *Netlog friends*, *Twitter followers* and the user's *tags*. *Pipl* retrieves the same profiles t1 and l1 and also a new profile on SlideShare (ss1).

Step 3

The goal of this step is to identify the profiles belonging to *U* and the heterogeneous information referring to *U* among the whole amount of data retrieved in the previous steps. To get this result, the recruiter has to explore each profile returned in the previous steps and use strategies to find relations with *U* and connections with other retrieved data.

While exploring profiles, the recruiter can use various types of data to make inferences allowing the finding of similarities and connections among them. The most relevant and easy-to-grasp data that a human searcher can use to this aim are:

- Photos and videos (useful not only to associate *U* to a profile, when the recruiter knows her/him, but also to find connections between profiles).
- Explicit relations between profiles (i.e., a user profile including links to other profiles owned by that person).

Other analyses that can be performed are:

- Cloud analysis of *shared friends* between profiles.
- Location-based analysis, comparing profiles by exploiting all the information regarding location: birth place, school's location, place of work, tags on photos, etc.

In order to guide the selection of the profiles to be explored, a useful support comes from the CF associated to profiles and attributes returned by the CS-UDD. In particular they are useful if the searcher does not personally know the target user.

This is the case in our example. The recruiter does not know the face of *U*, thus he starts the exploration from the profiles suggested by the CS-UDD: f1, m1, n1, s1 and n2.

Three profiles among the suggested ones have photos that allow them to say that they belong to the same subject. Two of them have CF=1. Consequently also the third profile gets a CF=1.

Differently, the second profile discovered on Netlog, n2, does not have photos. However, looking at the friends cloud, it is possible to find a set of friends in common with n1, where the list of friends is visible. Given that the birth date and city are the same, it seems very probable that n2 belongs to the same user *U*.

Analyzing the profiles, it is likely that n1 is an old and perhaps forgotten profile, given that the profession is "student" while other profiles say "journalist." This is confirmed by the profile on Linkedin, l1, which provides several explicit links to other resources related to *U:* her *Twitter account*, her *blog* and the *web page of her company* and other information concerning the *history of U*: schools, jobs, professional experiences, etc.

Step 4

The exploration in Step 3 has produced a set of profiles and data that refer to *U*. The investigation can be further expanded to profiles of people who have relations with *U* (*U*'s friends, relatives, followers, etc.).

The analysis on the retrieved profiles shows that *U* does not manage privacy with coherency. Looking at Facebook profile, she demonstrates to pay attention to privacy, since only little information is public, however, the other profiles have more public data. One possible reason may be that older accounts are often neglected by the user and become more vulnerable. Moreover, different OSNs have different policies and procedures for privacy management.

Just as an example of the amount of data that can be obtained by exploring the user's *social graph*, we briefly describe an analysis performed from *U*'s tweets and followers on Twitter.

Looking at tweets it is easy to discover people with the same family name. Following the link, it is possible to start a new search with the new user U_1 related to U, and it is easy to find U_1's Facebook account. U_1 is less reserved than U and publishes a diary with several photos, including photos with U and descriptive tags that specify also the geographic coordinates of the place in the pictures: *secondary school*, U's *house at Christmas*, U_1's *holiday house,* etc.

Moreover, if the searcher has a friend in common with U or with U_1, (s)he has access to larger sets of information. It is even possible for him/her to add tags to posts and photos owned by friends and by friends of friends. This demonstrates the uncontrollability of data referring to each person.

Concluding the search and aggregating all the collected data, the searcher can build a detailed profile of *U*, which includes information about:

- **Personal Data:** Name and Surname (*x, y*), Age (*25*), Birth date (*13/04/1987*), Gender (*f*), City home (*Torino*), Country home (*Italy*).
- **Nicknames:** *xy*, *xy87*, *x_y*, *z* (unsafe behavior: using as passwords nicks used for other accounts).
- **Contacts:** (Email on linkedin: *x.y@)gmail.com*).
- **URLs:** Accounts on various social systems and Personal blog.
- **Education:** Degree, School (name, URL, etc.), Education field, Titles and Certificates.
- **Interests:** Hobbies, Sexual Orientation, Favourite groups.
- **Work:** Current project, Past projects, Field, Companies.
- **Artefacts:** Publications, Reviews, Videos, Images.
- **Activities:** Posts, Tweets, Comments, Ratings, Tags (provide a global picture of U's personality).
- **Status:** Current activity (*online*, *away*, etc. on the social network), Current mood, Current place, Love status (*engaged to qx*: name of the boyfriend).
- **Photos:** Personal photos, Other's photos.
- **Known People:** Friends, Relatives (e.g. U_1), Partner (*qx*).

Further data can be *inferred* by exploring *U*'s numerous profiles on OSNs and the profiles of *U*'s relatives and friends: Estates (inferable, in the example, from tagged photos), Social status, Current location (out of home, alone, etc.), Habits, U's defects and qualities (acquired by exploring U's friends and relatives profiles, posts, tweets, etc.).

EXPERIMENTAL ANALYSIS ON THE RETRIEVAVILITY OF USER DATA

In this section we report the study we did to investigate how users perceive the risks for privacy on social networks and how the use of an application like CS-UDD could be useful to monitor the *retrievability* of users' public data, relieving this problem (Carmagnola et al. 2013).

Many issues about the relationships between users, social networks and privacy issues are topical today. Are people aware of privacy risks when they enter personal information on a social network? Do they care about it? How do they react when a search engine finds out data supposed not to be recoverable? How is it possible to raise awareness on possible risks for privacy when dealing with social networking systems?

Our hypothesis was that, using the techniques described before, it would be possible to automatically find a fair number of attributes and social network profiles for an appreciable percentage of people. Moreover we wanted to search for a correlation between the number of social networks used by a person and the ability to retrieve his/her data.

To this purpose, we implemented a two-part test to evaluate both the retrievability of the user data and the perception of the privacy problem.

Study Sample

The sample included 101 subjects, 65 female and 36 male, ranging from 19 to 35 years old, recruited according to availability sampling strategy. Subjects are students of the School of Literature and Philosophy at the University of Turin attending the classes of "Basic computer science" and "HTML laboratory." Considering the average age of the sample and the course of study they were attending, we assume that they all have medium skill with digital technologies and social networks. Experimental subjects were introduced to the purpose of the test; that is, to what extent the retrievability of their private data scattered on social networks is simple or difficult. Moreover, they were required to perform a search on the CS-UDD using their real data as input for the search. Finally, users were told that they would have to confirm or deny the profiles that CS-UDD returns and to fill in a questionnaire.

User Data Retrievability

In the first part of the test, each subject involved in the study was required to provide some basic data (name, age and city) in a simplified version of the beta-testing instantiation of CS-UDD for human users. In contrast to the standard version displayed in Figure 2, this interface does not allow to set the deepness of the search and to select which social networks to crawl. By default, the OSNs crawled are Facebook, Netlog, MySpace and Skype. We selected this specific set of OSNs since we wanted to include both very used systems as Facebook and Skype[11] and also less popular (even declining) ones as MySpace and Netlog. This allowed us to study how the different peculiarities of these systems affect the retrievability of user data.

Input data entered by subjects were used by the CS-UDD to start the search, which returned profiles and attributes discovered in the mentioned OSNs. After the search, subjects were requested to review the results and check a "right" or "wrong" button for every returned profile and attribute. This information allowed us to compute the precision of the returned data. Notice that no user data was saved by the system, and the results were managed as aggregated data, replacing the profiles name with a random code, which cannot be traced back to the original. Furthermore subjects had to provide their informed consent for data processing.

Since subjects were required to address every returned profile and attribute as "right" or "wrong," we were able to compare the retrieved attributes and profiles with the true ones by means of the two standard metrics in Information Retrieval: Precision and Recall. Precision is the percentage of retrieved objects that are relevant and Recall is the percentage of relevant objects that are retrieved on the total (the total number of profiles owned by the subject on the mentioned OSNs is asked him/her in the second part of the test).

As stated before, the results of the CS-UDD are associated with a CF. This value can be used by a human user or an application to decide which data are to be trusted and used.

- For the discovered user attributes, we obtained a precision ranging from 94% to 97.1% depending on the CF associated to the attribute. This confirms that user attributes can be retrieved with a very high precision by cross checking different information even in noisy places like social networks.
- For the retrieved profiles, if we limit the computation to profiles retrieved with a CF of 1, we obtain 83% Precision and a 27% Recall, while if we consider the results for any returned CF, we obtained a value of 77% for Recall and 58% for Precision. Precision and Recall have an inverse relationship.

These results show that user profiles can be retrieved with a probability ranging from 27% to 77%. Details can be found in the paper mentioned above. This value is very high considering that the input query is limited to a small set of user attributes. Moreover, the correctness (precision) is even higher, both for the profiles and for the specific user attributes.

One can observe that the retrievability of user data is highly connected with the setting of privacy options: users that are more aware of privacy risks tend to set their data as private and therefore their data can be found with less success. However, the contribution of our study is to show that this behavior is not sufficient to maintain user data private. As we illustrated in the previous sections and as we confirmed with this analysis, user data can often be retrieved even when the users are aware of privacy risks and manage to protect their privacy.

In particular, our study revealed that there are some factors that influence the retrievability of user data. Two relevant factors that we report here are 1) the occurrence of profiles abandoned and not deleted by users and 2) the number of accounts on several OSNs.

1. Occurrence of profiles abandoned and not deleted. As in other fields, people tend to follow trends. In OSNs people often create accounts on the current top social network and then leave it even when it is no longer popular. This gives rise to a "cemetery" of not used profiles that can be used to extract any kind of data. Therefore, since these data are usually out of date, it is easy to find in them some incorrect information. As Figure 3 shows, subjects that declare to have found a forgotten profile through CS-UDD (see question 4) are characterized by a Precision and Recall of retrieved profiles, respectively 24% and 12% higher than the Precision and Recall of those who did not find any forgotten profile. This may suggest that forgotten profiles can be found easily since old social networks may have less strict privacy policies, or policies may have changed during the years, or simply users were less concerned about the privacy problem and did not set personal data as private.
2. Another factor we analyzed in the mentioned study is the number of social networks currently used.

Results are displayed in Figure 4. As the top shows, 78% of the users of the sample use one or two social networks (namely, has an account on one or two OSNs and use them at the same time). The average number of social networks for user is 1.6±0.84. The most popular network is Facebook, used by 80% of the test sample. MySpace and Netlog are far less popular today, but still very useful for finding particular attributes or cross-confirming some of them.

Figure 3. Relation between abandoned and not deleted profiles and precision and recall of retrieved profiles

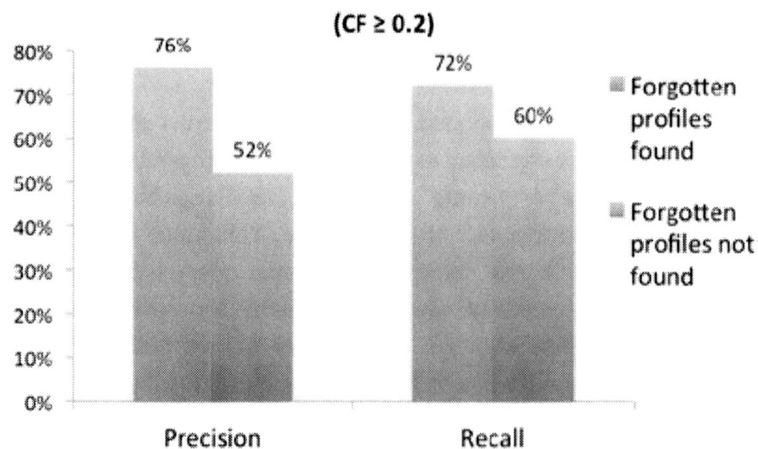

Using a high number of social networks increases the probability to find at least some public data and allows applications like the CS-UDD to cross-check the data, improving the precision of the identification process.

The top of Figure 5 shows to what extent the Precision of both attributes and profiles increases with the number of social networks used at the same time by the user. In particular, when the number of social networks used is at least two, we obtain a significant boost in the Precision of the retrieved profiles. This comes from the cross-linking and clustering techniques used by the CS-UDD, which allows to cross-check the different profiles data. Therefore, it is more likely to find at least one user profile if a person has many of them in different social networks.

User Perception of the Risk

In the second part of the study, subjects were required to answer a questionnaire aimed to investigate their perception about the privacy problems related to the spreading of their public data in social networks.

Below we report the questionnaire. It should be noted that while the first three questions were asked to the full sample of 101 people, the remaining questions were necessarily limited to the people (91 users) who actually declared to use at least one social network.

Figure 4. On the top: number of social networks used. On the bottom: percentage of users for each social network

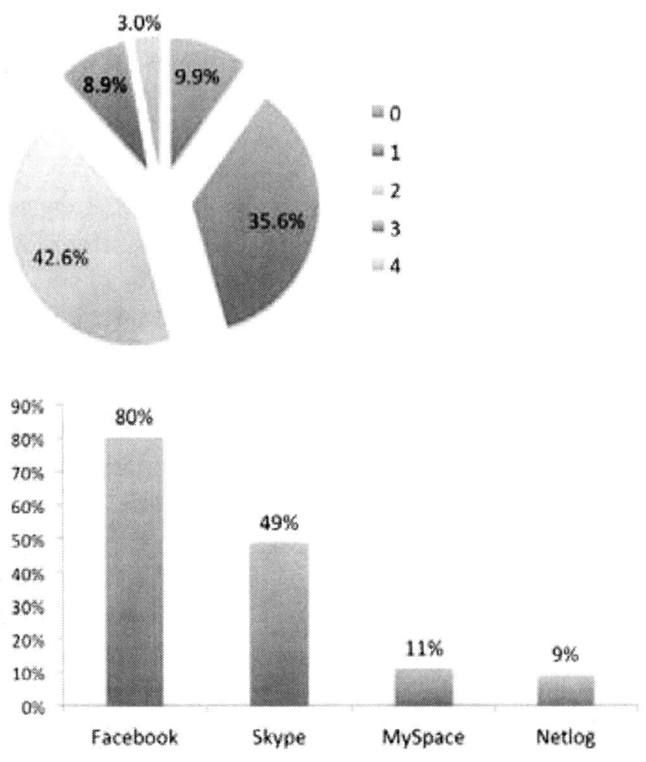

Figure 5. On the top: the search precision as a function of the number of social networks used. On the bottom: the shift in the perception of the risk depending on the search results

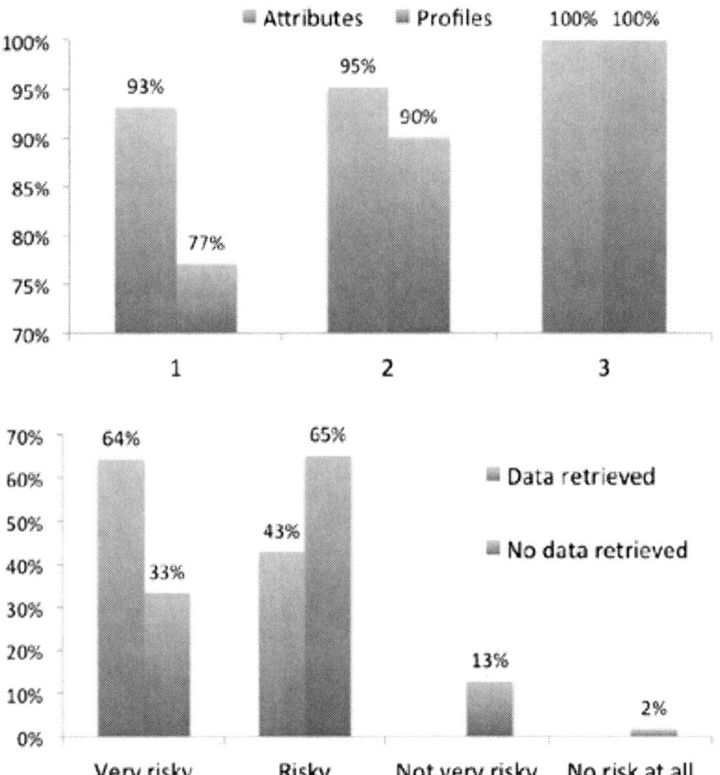

Questionnaire

1. In your opinion, how severe are the risks for privacy when using a social network?
   a. **Very risky:** 38.6%
   b. **Risky:** 52.5%
   c. **Not very risky:** 7.9%
   d. **No risk at all:** 1%
2. Have you ever used a people search engine (such as 123people)?
   a. **Yes:** 19.8%
   b. **No:** 80.2%
3. Have you ever used a profiles aggregator; that is, a service which merges your profiles from multiple social networks?
   a. **Yes:** 12.9%
   b. **No:** 87.1%
4. Did you find any profiles you forgot to have?
   a. **Yes:** 20.9%
   b. **No:** 79.1%
5. Did you find any personal data you thought not to be retrievable?
   a. **All:** 17.6%
   b. **Some:** 3.3%
   c. **At least one:** 9.9%
   d. **Not one:** 69.2%
6. Before the test, did you know that the retrieved data were public or did you think they were private (namely visible only to your contacts)?
   a. **All Private:** 12.9%
   b. **Some private and some public:** 70.3%
   c. **All public:** 16.8%
7. Are you going to edit your public data after seeing the CS-UDD search results?
   a. **Yes:** 25.3%
   b. **No:** 74.7%

It is interesting to report that the privacy issue is perceived as relevant from more than 90% of the subjects. The majority of users never used a people search engine or a user profiles aggregator system. This may reveal that people in the sample consider different social networks as separate entities. Indeed, even if they care about protecting their personal data on a single social network, they often don't know that gathering information from different sources makes possible to access many personal information and to define a more complete personal profile.

Answers to question number 4 show that the issue of forgotten profiles is quite common. More than 20% of people in our sample found a forgotten profile by searching with the CS-UDD. Of course, users cannot protect data they do not know being public. Therefore, since today it is quite common for many different online services to ask for a wide variety of data, forgotten sources of information are a risk for privacy.

Question 5 addresses the problem of keeping track of personal data: more than 30% of users in the sample found personal data they thought not to be retrievable. This may be due to forgotten profiles as well as to the fact that social networks often do not allow users to clearly see which data are public and which are private. People who had at least one forgotten profile were more likely to find data they thought not to be retrievable on the Web. Finding unexpected personal data may be the real spring that makes the user want to fix her or his social network privacy settings. We found that the 57% of the people who found these data decided to try to face the privacy risk problem and modifying their online personal data, against 11% of the people who did not find any of them.

Question 6 highlights how much the average user is oblivious to the status of her/his data. More than 83% of the sample thought that some of the data we retrieved was private, while all the data returned by this prototype were public. Luckily, it seems that after trying the CS-UDD one fourth of the sample decided to fix their personal data (question 7).

The bottom of Figure 5 shows how the awareness of the vulnerability of personal data may change the perception of the privacy risks. Users who found unexpected personal data during the test are significantly more worried about their privacy on social networks. The difference between the two groups is statistically significant, with $p = 0.007$. However it seems that even when users wish to improve the control over their public data when using social networks, they lack proper user-friendly tools. Most social networks offer confusing and over complex set of options that the typical social networks user does not know how to manage. Indeed, after this evaluation, many subjects who never thought deeply about this issue came to ask advices about how to secure their data on different social networks. Even if in most cases it was possible to secure them with the desired granularity, the process was far from being trivial.

Given this context it seems to be relevant to supply every person with the possibility of keeping track of her/his data. Search engines, like the CS-UDD, can be useful tools for this task.

CONCLUSION

In recent years, OSNs have greatly increased the number of their users. People provide these systems with a virtual representation of themselves for different purposes, for example to contact or being contacted by other people belonging to the network, meeting new friends, finding new jobs or career opportunities, sharing interests, receiving or providing recommendations, etc.

In social networks it is possible to find a great deal of information about users, such as biographical information (education, employment history, etc.), age and gender, sexual and political interests, photos and videos, contacts, geographical location and personal interests.

Due to the nature of such systems, people show the tendency to disclose personal information more easily than in traditional relationships, underestimating the risks related to the uncontrolled dissemination of their personal data. For example, the user data discovered on social systems can be aggregated into a single profile, which is more informative than the initial data set. This happens because new data about the user can be inferred by merging different pieces of information. Moreover, content posted by other people (such as tags, comments, etc.) as well as CBIR techniques, can be used to acquire new information about the user and his/her life.

This chapter has presented and discussed the risks associated with the possibility of collecting and aggregating user data in OSNs showing how simple it is for human users, as well as for software agents, to identify users and aggregate their data by exploiting public data scattered in OSNs. The objective is to show that risks for user privacy do not concern only unauthorized access to private user data but may concern public data as well.

To this purpose, we have described the prototype of a search engine, named CS-UDD (Cross-System User Data Discovery), which can be used to retrieve and aggregate personal public user data distributed on OSNs. We have designed the CS-UDD as a search service for software agents that query it in order to personalize their services. We have also developed a prototype for human users that can be used as a people search engine, but also as a tool for monitoring one's own public data on OSNs.

To exemplify the possible risks for user privacy that hide behind public data when a recursive method of search is applied, we simulated a case of a social media job recruiter who searches for information about a possible candidate for a position. The use case has exemplified how easily public data in OSNs can be used to create a complete user profile which can be used to evaluate a person.

Finally, we have reported the results of a study we did with real accounts on OSNs to evaluate both the retrievability of the system and how users perceive the risks for privacy on social networks.

Among the results, the study has demonstrated that privacy issue is perceived as relevant for more than 90% users and that the awareness of the vulnerability of personal data does increase the perception of privacy risks. Furthermore, we show that one of the most important risk factor is to have at least one forgotten profile. Given these results it seems to be relevant to provide people with suitable means for keeping track of their data in OSNs. Search engines, like the CS-UDD, can be useful tools for this task.

In the future we plan to improve the search engine CS-UDD by refining its capability of retrieving and aggregating user data distributed on social networks. Specifically, we aim at optimizing the performance of the algorithm to estimate the probability that two profiles belong to the same user, given a set of shared attributes. To this purpose, pattern matching and text mining techniques for extending the search also to attributes with images, photos and open fields will be adopted. Moreover, we plan to implement the CS-UDD as a web service for applications that offer personalized services, such as recommender systems (Resnick & Varian, 1997), which require knowing user data to accomplish their task.

REFERENCES

Ahn, G. J., Shehab, M., & Squicciarini, A. (2011). Security and privacy in social networks. *IEEE Internet Computing*, *15*(3), 10–12. doi:10.1109/MIC.2011.66

Berkovsky, S., Kuflik, T., & Ricci, F. (2008). Mediation of user models for enhanced personalization in recommender systems. *User Modeling and User-Adapted Interaction*, *18*(3), 245–286. doi:10.1007/s11257-007-9042-9

Carmagnola, F., Osborne, F., & Torre, I. (2009). *Cross-systems identification of users in the social web*. Paper presented at the IADIS International Conference WWW/Internet, Rome, Italy.

Carmagnola, F., Osborne, F., & Torre, I. (2010). *User data distributed on the social web: How to identify users on different social systems and collecting data about them*. Paper presented at the International Workshop on Information Heterogeneity and Fusion in Recommender Systems, within the International Conference on Recommender Systems, Barcelona, Spain.

Carmagnola, F., Osborne, F., & Torre, I. (2013). A study with real users on factors influencing identification and information leakage. Paper under revision. *Journal of Information Science*. SAGE Publications.

Catanese, S., Meo, P. D., Ferrara, E., Fiumara, G., & Provetti, A. (2011). *Crawling Facebook for social network analysis purposes*. Paper presented at the International Conference on Web Intelligent, Mining and Semantics, WIMS 2011, Sogndal, Norway.

Caviglione, L., & Coccoli, M. (2011). Privacy problems with Web 2.0. *Computer Fraud & Security*, (10): 16–19. doi:10.1016/S1361-3723(11)70104-X

Cheek, G., & Shehab, M. (2012). *Privacy management for online social networks*. Paper presented at the 22th International World Wide Web Conference, Lyons, France.

Chen, B., Kifer, D., LeFevre, K., & Machanavajjhala, A. (2009). Privacy-preserving data publishing. *Foundations and Trends in Databases*, *2*(1-2), 1–167. doi:10.1561/1900000008

Enisa Europa. (2013). Website. Retrieved September 9, 2012, from http://www.enisa.europa.eu/

Facebook. (2013). Website. Retrieved September 9, 2012, from http://www.facebook.com/note.php?note_id=%20322194465300

Gross, R., & Acquisti, A. (2005). *Information revelation and privacy in online social networks*. Paper presented at the ACM workshop on Privacy in the electronic society, WPES '05. New York, NY, USA.

Gudivada, V. N., & Raghavan, V. V. (1995). Content-based image retrieval systems. *IEEE Computer*, *28*(9), 18–31. doi:10.1109/2.410145

Guy, I., Jacovi, M., Shahar, E., Meshulam, N., Soroka, V., & Farrell, S. (2008). *Harvesting with SONAR: the value of aggregating social network information*. Paper presented at the 26th annual SIGCHI conference on Human factors in computing systems, Florence, Italy.

Heckmann, D. (2006). *Ubiquitous user modeling. Dissertations in Artificial Intelligence,* vol. 297. DISKI. IOS Press.

Hogben, G. (2007). *Security issues and recommendations for online social networks. Position Paper*. ENISA, European Network and Information Security Agency.

Huber, M., Mulazzani, M., Weippl, E., Kitzler, G., & Goluch, S. (2011). Friend-in-the-middle attacks: Exploiting social networking sites for spam. *IEEE Internet Computing*, *15*(3), 28–34. doi:10.1109/MIC.2011.24

Irani, D., Webb, S., Li, K., & Pu, C. (2011). Modeling unintended personal-information leakage from multiple online social networks. *IEEE Internet Computing*, *15*(3), 13–19. doi:10.1109/MIC.2011.25

Krishnamurthy, B., & Wills, C. (2009). *On the leakage of personally identifiable information via online social networks*. Paper presented at the 2nd ACM Workshop on Online Social Networks. New York: ACM.

Li, N., Zhang, N., & Das, S. K. (2011). Preserving relation privacy in online social network data. *IEEE Internet Computing*, *15*(3), 35–42. doi:10.1109/MIC.2011.26

Lindamood, J., Heatherly, R., Kantarcioglu, M., & Thuraisingham, B. (2009, April). *Inferring private information using social network data*. Paper presented at the 18th international conference on World Wide Web, Madrid, Spain.

Luo, W., Liu, J., Liu, J., & Fan, C. (2009). *An analysis of security in social network*. Paper presented at the 6th IEEE International conference on dependable, automatic and secure computing, Chengdu, China.

Mazur, Z., Mazur, H., & Mendyk-Krajewska, T. (2009). Security of internet transactions. *Internet-Technical Development and Applications, 64*, 243–251. doi:10.1007/978-3-642-05019-0_26

Prensky, M. (2004). The emerging online life of the digital native. Retrieved August 05, 2012, from http://www.marcprensky.com/writing/Prensky-The_Emerging_Online_Life_of_the_Digital_Native-03.pdf

Reppler. (2013a). Website. Retrieved September 9, 2012, from http://www.reppler.com/

Reppler. (2013b). Managing your online image across social networks. Retrieved September 9, 2012, from http://blog.reppler.com/2011/09/27/managing-your-online-image-across-social-networks

Resnick, P., & Varian, H. (1997, March). Recommender systems. *Introduction to special section of Communications of the ACM, 40*(3).

Vassileva, J. (2001). *Distributed user modelling for universal information access*. Paper presented at the 9th International Conference of Human–Computer Interaction, New Orleans, Louisiana, USA.

Vicente, C. R., Freni, D., Bettini, C., & Jensen, C. S. (2011). Location-related privacy in geo-social networks. *IEEE Internet Computing, 15*(3), 20–27. doi:10.1109/MIC.2011.29

Windley, P. (2005). *Digital identity*. Sebastopol, CA: O'Reilly Media, Inc.

Zheleva, E., & Getoor, L. (2009, April). *To join or not to join: The illusion of privacy in social networks with mixed public and private user profiles*. Paper presented at the 18th International conference on World Wide Web, Madrid, Spain.

ADDITIONAL READING

Acquisti, A., & Gross, R. (2009). Predicting social security numbers from public data. Retrieved October 19, 2012, from http://www.heinz.cmu.edu/~acquisti/ssnstudy/

Anderson, J., Diaz, C., Bonneau, J., & Stajano, F. (2009). *Privacy preserving social networking over untrusted networks*. Paper presented at the 18th International conference on World Wide Web the 2nd ACM SIGCOMM Workshop on Online Social Networks, Barcelona, Spain.

Antón, A., Bertino, E., Li, N., & Yu, T. (2007). A roadmap for comprehensive online privacy policy management. *Communications of the ACM, 50*(7), 109–116. doi:10.1145/1272516.1272522

Aroyo, L., Dolog, P., Houben, G. J., Kravcik, M., Naeve, A., Nilsson, M., & Wild, F. (2006). Interoperability in personalized adaptive learning. *Education Technology Society, 9*(2), 4–18.

Balduzzi, M., Platzer, C., Holz, T., Kirda, E., Balzarotti, D., & Kruegel, C. (2010). Abusing social networks for automated user profiling. In *Proceedings of the 13th International Symposium on Recent Advances in Intrusion Detection* (pp. 422–441). Springer.

Barker, K., Askari, M., Banerjee, M., Ghazinour, K., Mackas, B., & Majedi, M. …Williams, A. (2009). *A data privacy taxonomy*. Paper presented at the 26th British National Conference on Databases, Birmingham, UK.

Benevenuto, F., Rodrigues, T., Cha, M., & Almeida, V. (2009, November). *Characterizing user behavior in online social networks*. Paper presented at the 9th ACM SIGCOMM conference on Internet measurement conference (IMC '09). Chicago, Illinois, USA.

Bonneau, J., & Preibusch, S. (2009). *The privacy jungle: On the market for data protection in social networks*. Paper presented at the 8th Workshop on the Economics of Information Security (WEIS 2009), University College London, England.

Brusilovsky, P., & Maybury, M. T. (2002). From adaptive hypermedia to the adaptive web. *Communications of the ACM*, *45*(5), 30–33. doi:10.1145/506218.506239

Carmagnola, F., & Cena, F. (2009). User identification for cross-system personalisation. *Information Sciences*, *179*(1-2), 16–32. doi:10.1016/j.ins.2008.08.022

Carmagnola, F., Cena, F., & Gena, C. (2011). User model interoperability: A survey. *User Modeling and User-Adapted Interaction*, *21*(3), 285–331. doi:10.1007/s11257-011-9097-5

Dolog, P., & Schäfer, M. (2005). *A framework for browsing, manipulating and maintaining interoperable learner profiles*. Paper presented at the 10th International Conference on User Modeling, Edinburgh, Scotland, UK.

Dwyer, C., Hiltz, R., & Passerini, K. (2007). *Trust and privacy concern within social networking sites: A comparison of Facebook and MySpace*. Paper presented at the 13th Americas Conference on Information Systems, Keystone, Colorado, USA.

He, J., Chu, W., & Liu, Z. (2006). *Inferring privacy information from social networks*. Paper presented at the IEEE International Conference on Intelligence and Security Informatics, San Diego, California, USA.

Heatherly, R., Kantarcioglu, M., Lindamood, J., & Thuraisingham, B. (2009). *Preventing private information inference attacks on social networks*. Technical Report UTDCS-03-09, University of Texas at Dallas.

Krishnamurthy, B., & Wills, C. (2008). *Characterizing privacy in online social networks*. Paper presented at WOSN: Workshop on Online Social Networks, Seattle, WA, USA.

Labitzke, S., & Taranu, I. H. (2011). What your friends tell others about you: Low cost linkability of social network profiles. *Proceedings of the International ACM Workshop on Social Network Mining and Analysis* (pp. 51-60). ACM.

Leonardi, E., Houben, G.-J., van der Sluijs, K., Hidders, J., Herder, E., Abel, F., & Heckmann, D. (2009). *User profile elicitation and conversion in a mashup environment*. Presented at the International Workshop on Lightweight Integration on the Web, in conjunction with the 9th Int. Conference on Web Engineering, San Sebastian, Spain.

Musiał, K., & Kazienko, P. (2012). Social networks on the Internet. *World Wide Web (Bussum)*, *15*, 1–42.

Oreilly, T. (2005). what is web 2.0. design patterns and business models for the next generation of software. Retrieved August 5, 2012, from http://www.oreillynet.com/pub/a/oreilly/tim/news/2005/09/30/what-isweb-20.html

Privacy Rights Clearinghouse. (1995, revised 2012). Fact sheet 18: Privacy and the Internet: Traveling in cyberspace safely. Retrieved August 5, 2012, from http://www.privacyrights.org/fs/fs18-cyb.htm

Richter Lipford, H., Besmer, A., & Watson, J. (2008). *Understanding privacy settings in Facebook with an audience view*. Paper presented at the 1st Conference on Usability, Psychology, and Security. USENIX Association, San Francisco, CA, USA.

Van Der Sluijs, K., & Houben, G. (2006). A generic component for exchanging user models between web-based systems. *International Journal of Continuing Engineering Education and Lifelong Learning*, *16*(1-2), 64–76. doi:10.1504/IJCEELL.2006.008918

Wu, L., Majedi, M., Ghazinour, K., & Barker, K. (2010, March). *Analysis of social networking privacy policies*. Paper presented at the 2010 EDBT/ICDT Workshops (EDBT '10). Lausanne, Switzerland.

Zheleva, E., & Getoor, L. (2011). Privacy in social networks: A survey. In *Social network data analytics* (pp. 277–306). Springer. doi:10.1007/978-1-4419-8462-3_10

KEY TERMS AND DEFINITIONS

Information Retrieval and Aggregation: Methods and techniques to search for information and data and to combine the retrieved results.

People Search Engines: Vertical search engines designed to retrieve information and data about people.

Social Web: A collaborative platform where people participate in content creation.

User Data Discovery: Retrieval of unknown user data.

User Privacy: Personal and private life.

User Profiles: Set of data and information about a subject, usually edited by the subject her/himself.

User Profiling: Process of building a user profile, usually carried out by third-parties (human agents or software agents).

ENDNOTES

1. Popularity is based on traffic data provided by Alexa Internet, Inc. (www.alexa.com), an Amazon company specialized in website analysis and site audit (July, 2012).
2. Gross and Acquisti have analyzed the data entered by a sample of 4000 Facebook users and found that a significant proportion of them revealed their birth date (84%), the mobile phone number (40%), the courses they have attended (42%), their political ideas (53%) and their sexual orientation (59%) (Gross & Acquisti, 2005).
3. See reference "Enisa Europa (2013)."
4. The conference was held in Strasbourg, in October 2008.
5. Research led by Recruiting & Social Network, Lorenzo Pulici, HR & Communication Specialist, December 2011, January 2012.
6. See reference "Facebook (2013)."
7. Research led by Recruiting & Social Network, Lorenzo Pulici, HR & Communication Specialist, December 2011, January 2012.
8. See reference "Reppler (2013a)."
9. See reference "Reppler (2013b)."
10. Research led by Recruiting & Social Network, Lorenzo Pulici, HR & Communication Specialist, December 2011, January 2012.
11. While Skype is not properly a social network it does have many characteristics similar to them when it comes to privacy problems. Indeed Skype users do connect in a network of contacts and are encouraged to build a public profile as complete as possible to make it retrievable by others.

Section 3
Security

Chapter 8
Privacy Issues in Social Networks

Alexandros Papanikolaou
Technological Educational Institute of Larissa, Greece

Vasileios Vlachos
Technological Educational Institute of Larissa, Greece

Periklis Chatzimisios
Alexander Technological Educational Institute of Thessaloniki, Greece

Christos Ilioudis
Alexander Technological Educational Institute of Thessaloniki, Greece

ABSTRACT

The inherent human need for communication and socialization is the reason for the ever-increasing use of social networking services. Social networks are a very powerful communications tool that also has the ability of aggregating large volumes of information. However, if this user-related information is exploited in certain ways, it can have harmful consequences on user privacy. This chapter defines what privacy is in the context of social networks, demonstrates how user privacy can be violated, and supports these claims with examples of real incidents. Furthermore, it presents various countermeasures, as well as directions for future research with the common goal of the protection of user privacy.

INTRODUCTION

The evolution of the Internet and the computer technologies in general, have given birth to the so-called Web 2.0, which features user-centered design, participatory information sharing, interoperability and collaboration, as well as a rich collection of web applications. A Web 2.0 site allows users to interact and collaborate, generate and/or publicize content or knowledge in a virtual community. Given this social aspect of Web 2.0, it focuses on three main aspects: a) Information management, which deals with finding, evaluating and administrating the content, b) relationship management that involves the creation and maintenance of contacts and c) self-management

DOI: 10.4018/978-1-4666-3926-3.ch008

that deals with the presentation of personal information (Pekárek & Pötzsch, 2009). Generally speaking, Web 2.0 follows the Web-as-a-Platform model, where a user requires only a web browser to access various web applications, regardless of Operating System type (e.g., Microsoft Windows, Linux, MacOS X), without the need of specific client software, thus loosening the dependency on a particular desktop computer.

Perhaps two of the most representative examples of Web 2.0 are social networks and collaborative workspaces. Social networks are virtual societies where users create and manage their profiles, communicate, interact and establish connections with other users, view their connections' profiles and traverse through their connections' contacts. Examples of the most popular social networks are Facebook, Twitter and LinkedIn. Collaborative workspaces provide the required infrastructure to facilitate collaboration and knowledge sharing among users or user groups. File-sharing systems, online collaborative editors, wikis and so on are some examples; Google Docs, for instance, is a popular and free collaborative workspace available to all Google subscribers. Both of these communities feature some common functionality, such as the organization of contacts in groups/workspaces, the ability to monitor a user's activity or be notified (usually via e-mail) when a certain event or user activity occurs. Examples of other communities that have emerged through Web 2.0 are Mobile Social Networks (namely, social networks where the individuals connect to each other through their mobile phones and/or tablets) and cloud communities (such as Dropbox for file storage and Amazon EC2 for computational power).

As the popularity of such online communities increased, counting hundreds of thousands of users, privacy concerns arose. The notion of privacy is rather polymorphic and depends heavily on the context it is found in, as well as on the individual himself (Nissenbaum, 2004). Generally speaking, privacy is directly related to the protection of personal data, whereas confidentiality is the prevention of information disclosure to certain individuals or groups. Hence, privacy is a subset of confidentiality. There are three main rights that social network users should demand, in order to be able to protect their privacy (Opsahl, 2010):

- **The right to informed decision-making:** That is, the users should have access to a clear user interface that allows them to control who accesses their data and how this data is used. In addition, they should be able to see who and when accesses their data, as well as which parts of their data get accessed, and not just control full access in a "yes/no" manner. What is more, it would be desirable to have an alert raised when legal or administrative processes have been invoked, in order to acquire information about a given user.
- **The right to control:** The social network service (SNS) must ensure that users retain control over the way their data is used and disclosed. For example, a third-party application should not be able to gather any personal information about a user through their friends, unless the user specifically allows it to do so. However, there are additional difficulties in achieving this goal, due to the basic functionality of the Web that facilitates copying, linking and distributing any kind of information on a massive scale. Furthermore, sometimes this is almost impossible to control, like in the case of a digital photograph showing more than one person that is also possessed by some of them (e.g., a group of friends); it only suffices for one of them to disclose it to the social network service, in order for the latter to be able to associate all the individuals with the depicted event or location (e.g., through face recognition software).

- **The right to leave:** The users must retain the right to be able to discontinue the use of a particular social network service and have all of their profile-related data deleted (or exported in a usable format – data liberation), rather than denying access to the "deleted" data. This was actually one of the main criticisms of certain popular social network services that caused quite a lot of discomfort among their users (Websites 'keeping deleted photos', 2009).

Moreover, since participation to such collaborative environments is available to anyone, it may occur that certain actions of a given individual may damage other individuals' reputation in an irreversible manner. These collaborative environments are software designed by humans; however, both software and human users are susceptible to errors, which may have harmful consequences if they occur.

Privacy is important because it helps people maintain their individuality. Controlling the publicity of information about themselves essentially helps them in defining themselves and in a free country they would certainly not have to answer questions about the choices they make or the information they share.

The purpose of this chapter is to study the privacy aspects in social networks and present the latest developments and challenges. It will initially present the importance of the privacy problem in social networks, followed by suitable definitions of privacy in the context of social networks. The various threats and attacks on privacy in social networks will be presented, followed by the available countermeasures that deal with the protection of privacy. Finally, the chapter will conclude with open problems and directions for future research on the user privacy in social networks.

PRIVACY IN SOCIAL NETWORKS

In the context of social networks, privacy is not only related to the information content a user creates through uploading and interacting with other users. In order to explain this better, we first need to acquire some more information about the structure of a social network. A social network can be represented by a graph, the so-called social graph, where nodes (or vertices) represent users and edges represent social relations/interactions/information flows. A social graph may be undirected, thus showing mutual interactions and/or relationships (e.g., friendship) or directed, thus exhibiting sort of a one-way relationship (e.g., "following" someone in Twitter or "friending" someone in Facebook). Graphs possess many other exploitable properties and they are being studied by Graph Theory. Once such a network has been generated, another form of privacy that becomes evident is link privacy; namely, who is connected to whom. Certain social networking services allow their users to see all the links of any user in the network, such as Livejournal or enforce a more constrained access policy (ability to see only his friends' lists and/or friends of friends' lists), such as LinkedIn.

Privacy in social networks also suffers from design conflicts as there are inherent contradicting goals between security and privacy, as well as between usability and sociability (Zhang, Sun, Zhu, & Fang, 2010). There is a universally-applicable trade-off between security and functionality that can be visualized in the form of weighting scales: The more "weight" of the one property that gets added to the scales, the more the scales lean towards this side. Hence, for a search query to be both efficient and accurate, as much personal data as possible should be made available to it, thus increasing the probability of privacy breaches to occur. An example of sociability is the so-called social traversal (or social graph exploration), where a user browses through the social connections of other users (any restrictions in this case depend solely on the security policy that the social network service enforces). However, disclosure of the existence of certain relationships may cause discomfort to the individuals involved, for instance, cases where one of the connections in a user's friends list (say, an old classmate) has been engaged in some sort of unlawful and/or criminal activity, or two professionals employed in rival companies are in each other's friends list or connections to specific individuals and/or groups that reveal a particular political/religious/sexual preference or social activity. In addition, although in real life a social connection that has remained "inactive" for a long period of time is "deleted" in some sense, in social networks it requires the user's intervention to be removed and before this happens it may affect him in some way. Furthermore, contact maintenance in social networks can be a rather time-consuming process due to the existence of a large number of contacts and it therefore does not motivate users to perform it, which causes a user's connections not to accurately reflect their social activity.

Unfortunately, even if security and privacy settings exist, their default configurations tend not to be as tight as possible, in an attempt to provide the users with a nice experience, without requiring them to spend a good deal of time configuring their account. An important part of this intended rich user experience are the various social applications on social networking platforms that complicate things even more, since these applications require access to various parts of user profile information. It is also quite reasonable for users to want to control the information about their friends that is available to social applications, in order to protect themselves from having their profile information being inferred through their friends' profile attributes (Hu, Ahn, & Jorgensen, 2012). What is more, various privacy issues originating from loose security settings are usually discovered after the social network service under question has gained popularity, meaning that some damage has already been done. Although the majority of social network sites offer some sort of information access control options to the users (essentially, the ability to apply a security policy), they may need to be revised to deal with new and unforeseen privacy issues, the majority of which emerge from newly-introduced functionality. The transition from the old security policy scheme to the newer one will most probably introduce new privacy control options, which may not be fully compatible with the existing settings and may either require all privacy control options to be reset to their initial values or set the new options to potentially unwanted default values. Needless to say, the ability of a user to correctly understand and adjust his privacy settings to achieve the desired effect is of vital importance. In addition, upon any change in the available privacy options, the user will need to review all his privacy settings from scratch, so as to verify their consistency with the intended security policy and adjust them accordingly. A positive step towards this direction is the "view as..." feature introduced by certain social networking services, such as Facebook and Google+. This functionality allows a user to visualize what profile information is viewable by other users, by being able to explore his profile as somebody else.

Malicious software (malware) can be employed for automating the collection of user-related data. Once a fake profile has been constructed, the malware can be launched and it will start sending requests to other users (based on the way it has been programmed to do so). In most cases, it will successfully achieve the goal of creating an extended list of contacts and extracting any kind of information from them, that would otherwise be impossible for an external user to acquire. A very popular example was the Koobface worm (an anagram of "Facebook") that targeted several popular social networking sites, including Facebook. It featured a rather rich malevolent functionality and activity that included the collection of user profile data (Costoya & Flores, 2009).

As it has already been mentioned, social networks implement different mechanisms for controlling users' privacy, depending on the features and functionality they offer. It is therefore self-explanatory that a universal privacy-controlling scheme cannot be applied. Instead, the various privacy-controlling models must first be extensively reviewed and analyzed so as to identify potential vulnerabilities threatening users' privacy and then correct any detected flaws. Ideally, before the social network service offers new functionality, it should be adequately analyzed with respect to user privacy and only then put into practice. This security analysis is usually a time-consuming process, which contradicts the marketing side of the social network that tries to increase its use and lure new members into it by advertising "attractive" features and functionality.

Another issue worth emphasizing: who are we actually trying to protect our privacy from? There are two main categories of adversaries: Internal and external. The former are legitimate participants of the social network, but have malicious intentions/purposes, for instance, a malicious user, a malicious third party accessing the network infrastructure (e.g., an eavesdropper) or even a malicious social network provider. The latter are not legitimate participants of the social network but can launch attacks on the social network's infrastructure (Zhang et al., 2010). Typically, an internal adversary is considered to be potentially more harmful than an external due to the extended access to resources.

Social networks usually implement some sort of relationship-based access control mechanisms, where access to user resources is granted according to the relationships established in the network. It is therefore important to devise suitable mechanisms to protect relationship privacy. This can be achieved either by developing suitable protocols from scratch (Mezzour, Perrig, Gligor, & Papadimitratos, 2009), or by tailoring existing cryptographic schemes to offer such functionality (Carminati & Ferrari, 2009). What is more, the protection of link privacy enhances user anonymity in cyber-space, since relationship-related inferences cannot be made.

THREATS, VULNERABILITIES AND COUNTERMEASURES FOR PROTECTING PRIVACY IN SOCIAL NETWORKS

Digital Dossier Aggregation

Threats and Risks

The various user profiles that are created and exist on social networks can easily be abused. Processing and mass storage of private data from "strangers" may cause a series of problems. Each user's personal profile usually contains information that can be disclosed to third parties, leading to the public exposure of sensitive private data. A simple example is the collection of all geographical locations a user has been "tagged" in ("tagging" is a feature which allows a user to link other users to a given profile object, such as a digital photograph). Additionally, a more frequent and equally important threat is the disclosure of the name, the surname or even a digital photograph by simply searching through a social network.

Unfortunately, even if the user changes or even deletes some profile information, it is quite likely that this information has also been stored and recorded "elsewhere." Hence, the already-recorded personal data of a given individual have the potential of being turned against them and become rather dangerous for themselves (Pilkington, 2007; Fuller, 2006).

Countermeasures

Protection against storage and processing of profile data from third parties is a combination of techniques and good practices.

It would be particularly beneficial for the social network users to be thoroughly informed about the various dangers lurking in the use of any social network and what are the characteristics of correct and safe use. A significant number of social networking services have already started to adopt various private data protection policies. A characteristic example is hiding the user's postal code. It would be equally effective for the users to withhold additional private data such as home address, phone number, etc.

Moreover, social networking services should be aligned with the existing legal framework in countries where extensive use of such services is observed. The current European legal framework does not fully cover the dangers that exist regarding the protection of private data in social networks from third-party processing and storage. The enforcement of a user certification/authentication service would contribute significantly to the prevention of user impersonation by illegitimate third parties, thus protecting users from having their personal information accessed by unauthorized parties.

Secondary Data Collection

Threats and Risks

Apart from the various personal data and information about their personality that users disclose through social networks, they also produce a large amount of additional information by using the actual social network infrastructure. In particular, whenever a user logs into a social networking site, the site administrator automatically obtains additional information, such as the amount of time the user remained logged into the service, their IP address, the history of profiles the user may have visited, even the various messages (in the form of chat or personal messages) a user has either sent or received. Furthermore, given that users may log into the social network service from different geographical locations (home, work, places related to leisure-time activities), as well as through different devices (desktop, laptop, tablet), they made it possible for the social network providers to associate large amounts of additional data with their profiles.

As the popularity of social networking services increases on a daily basis, as well as the number of their subscribers, any disclosure of private data to third parties, who are interested in exploiting it accordingly (e.g., for advertising purposes), is rather disconcerting.

Countermeasures

Protecting the users from leakage of their private data and information is imperative. Social networking services should make available to their users appropriate authorization and access control mechanisms, in order for them to be able to effectively control access to their profile data. Namely, every user should have the ability to configure what profile information the users of the same social network could access. For instance, it would be possible for given personal data to be accessed only by their friends, their family or specific users of the service. By appropriately configuring these settings, the users will be able to create a more secure environment throughout their social networking sessions.

More importantly, the social networks should promote a set of guidelines that will trigger the users' awareness about the security of their personal data, so as to configure their profiles in the best possible way for protecting their privacy.

Portable social networks are a defense against the threat of secondary data collection. They offer to the user the ability to transfer profile information, as well as account and privacy settings. In particular, a user will not be required to re-enter username, password, email address, re-compose friend lists and re-configure access to profile information.

Finally, it is absolutely necessary to present to users the social network's security policy in a simple and clear manner, so that they will be able to understand the way user data is collected and processed by third parties. That is, to describe the purpose of the data collection by third parties, who are the ones who can access the various data and whether there is a way for accessing and/or modifying this data.

Face Recognition

Threats and Risks

Participation to social networking services is usually accompanied by the users' tendency for mass uploading of digital photographs depicting not only themselves, but also their friends in personal moments. In May 2007, quite an astonishment was caused when Facebook made public some of its statistical data, mainly because they had surpassed their expectations. In particular, until that time, the company had in its possession 1.7 billion personal digital photographs belonging to its users and 2.2 billion users had been tagged in their friends' photographs. These extremely large numbers confirmed the popularity and spread of the social networks on the one hand, and the massive amount of stored photographic material on the other. The existence of face recognition algorithms that become both faster and more efficient as they evolve, made the parallel comparison of a large number of digital photographs possible (Cheng, 2007; Phillips et al., 2006). Hence, the possibility of correctly identifying a given individual who uses an alias/pseudonym and/or false information is evident. In addition, it is very easy for non-authorized third parties to collect information and digital photographs about a given person and use them in a malevolent manner. Unfortunately, face recognition is one of the greatest threats against privacy, due to the possibility of personal data disclosure. Such data cannot be protected by law, as the current legal framework does not cater for protecting the users' real identity from being revealed through social networks. An equally important example could be to reveal the linking of a dating service fake user profile to another profile in any other social network.

Countermeasures

Special care should be taken in dealing with this threat against privacy, involving the disclosure of the users' physical identities. User awareness and training on the risks and dangers behind the publication of any photographic material, either by themselves or by their friends is a fundamental protection measure. Uploaded pictures may also contain additional information that can reveal a given place/location, or allow the identification of another person. Furthermore, pictures may reveal other people's private data, especially when they are tagged with additional meta-data.

Once again, the legal framework in each country needs to clarify the user rights for the protection of their privacy with respect to their participation in social networking services.

Content-Based Image Retrieval (CBIR)

Threats and Risks

Obtaining data through the contents of an image is an application based on a set of methods that acquire, process, analyze, and perceive images through a set of digital data and produce additional information. This application does not focus on the image's meta-data (tags, keywords), but rather on its real data, such as colors, shapes, surfaces, etc. These applications were mainly created for use in the field of criminology. The extraction of evidence through the contents of an image is a developing technology that collects and matches characteristics and properties, thus leading to the required results (Chen, Roussev, Richard III, & Gao, 2005). Despite the guidelines that were given to social networks, as well as the various privacy settings that were made available to the users regarding the uploaded profile images, the users proved out to be rather uninformed on the matter. There are several instances of users who are totally unaware of the existence of this application and the consequences it may have and continue to upload large amounts of photographic material.

Similar to the threat of disclosure and identification of natural persons through images is the disclosure and linking of information regarding geographical location data. It is quite possible that through the processing of an image, the place of residence of a user is revealed and then being followed, blackmailed, or targeted for spam advertising. Unfortunately, the majority of users will not think about these threats.

Countermeasures

To start with, users of social network services must first realize that a profile image may link the various social networking sites a user is a member of. A simple measure that users can take against CBIR is not to upload images where their facial characteristics are clearly visible. Furthermore, it would be desirable to upload different profile photographs in each social network they are members of. An additional protective measure is the use of image processing tools that convert the photographs to other forms, such as caricatures, which will certainly prevent automated analysis. The use of the "CAPTCHA" technology, according to which the user is asked to type a not so easily legible phrase, can prevent the creation of fake/forged accounts by social robots. Moreover, tight default privacy settings on the user's profile regarding who can tag them in their pictures are a good practice against this threat. Finally, users should be particularly careful about the photographs they upload, and most importantly their content, if they desire the best possible protection of their privacy.

Linkability from Image Meta-Data, Tagging, and Cross-Profile Information

Threats and Risks

Several social networking services allow user photographs to be uploaded or tagged by third parties, sometimes without even their consent. It is quite possible that a user may tag almost anything, even someone without an account on a given social networking service (in which case the user is usually notified by an e-mail, containing an invitation to join the social network). Regardless of how careful a user may be, their private information may still be disclosed through a friend's uploaded picture or tag. An additional threat regarding uploaded pictures involves the actual picture's meta-data, such as geo-location information (Schoen, 2007).

Collecting information about a given user profile is quite an easy task. However, combining the information found in several profiles a user may have in different social networks can yield useful additional information. For instance, a LinkedIn or Twitter account that has a more "professional" orientation, if combined with an e.g., Facebook account used mainly for entertainment/leisure, can significantly enrich a user profile (Acquisti et al., 2007).

Countermeasures

The greatest problem in this category is the inability of users to control the right of their own publicity. In particular, users sometimes upload pictures containing additional persons apart from themselves, however without any sort of approval of the involved parties. The availability of three possible settings regarding third-party tagging is quite an effective solution to the problem:

- **Open:** The user can be tagged by anyone, without requiring any prior approval.
- **Controlled:** The user to be tagged has to approve the request.
- **Disabled:** The user cannot be tagged by anyone.

Of course, for offering real protection, this setting should default to "disabled" for new users.

The use of freely-available tools for removing meta-data information from digital photographs is highly recommended, before uploading them to social networking sites.

Difficulty of Complete Account Deletion

Threats and Risks

Several times, users become members of a given social networking site, but at some later point wish to discontinue their membership and completely delete their profile from the site under question. How possible is the complete deletion of profile data, though? It may look to be a simple and straightforward process, but it actually is a rather complicated one. To start with, users can delete primary profile data, such as e-mail address, uploaded photographs, etc. On the contrary, secondary data such as comments on other users' profile or pictures tagged by third parties remain and are not deleted. Apart from cases where such a deletion is not possible (due to its destructive effect on the social network's integrity), the security policy of the given service may explicitly require backup information to be preserved for a certain period of time. Users are therefore unable to fully control their personal data and delete it whenever they wish to do so.

Countermeasures

The first point of action would certainly be to create all the required tools with which the users will be able to deactivate and fully delete their accounts. Furthermore, the terms and conditions of social networking sites should present in a simple and comprehensive way their policy on private data.

The users have, of course, to play their part by adjusting the default privacy settings, in an attempt to have better control over their accounts. It would also be desirable for the social network sites to manage their users' private data in a transparent way.

Another useful piece of information is how long backup copies of a user profile are retained for, once deletion of the given profile has been requested. The option for account deletion exists; nevertheless users cannot be certain that their profile data will actually be deleted.

Threats Directly Related to Privacy

"Traditional" threats appearing in the Internet are also found in social networking sites and can have quite harmful consequences. Examples of such threats are spam attack (SNS Spam), user data collection from different social networks (SNS Aggregators), as well as malware spread. What is more, threats relating to the users' digital identities are equally important. Several examples of fake profile creation have surfaced leakages of user-related information and data, as well as phishing. That is, attempting to acquire personal and/or private information (such as usernames & passwords and credit card numbers) by masquerading as a trustworthy entity). Social threats inside social networks are another phenomenon that is gaining ground. Corporate espionage through social engineering, repeated and intended malevolent acts with the use of technology (bullying), intimidating behaviors (stalking) are some of the most common examples (Gross & Acquisti, 2005).

To sum up, it is worth emphasizing that proper user awareness and training, appropriate measures for protecting the users, the configuration of related settings, the cautious use of social networks are some simple, but also quite effective pre-emptive measures.

PRIVACY MODELS AND MECHANISMS FOR SOCIAL NETWORKS

Trust in Social Networks

Trust is a vital determinant for sharing information, both for real-world relationships, as well as for their digital counterpart. In a social network, a user establishes various levels of trust with the social network's entities that mainly fall into two main categories: the social network itself and the rest of the peers, namely the users.

Trusting the social network itself relates to the degree of confidence a user has regarding how the social network service will use and/or protect the profile information. Hence, a high level of such trust may lead to the creation of a user profile containing real information (name, home address, profession); alternatively, it may lead to large amounts of information-rich content being uploaded, such as photographs, comments and posts about various activities. Nevertheless, in a social network the willingness to share information does not automatically translate into new social interaction, namely the formation of new social relationships (Dwyer, Hiltz, & Passerini, 2007).

Trust among users is mainly established through "friendship" connections, the formation of which is rather complex, as it is influenced by a large set of factors. They are quite similar to real-world friendship relationships in the sense that they will most probably not be formed with random individuals, but will rather require some more information about the parties involved or a recommendation by an already-trusted third party. Examples of the factors that may affect it include experiences and past relationships with the other party, information and/or gossip about their opinions, actions, decisions and so on. In the digital world, additional information is readily available, such as number of friends/followers, number and identities of common friends and membership in groups. It is worth pointing out that the aforementioned factors do not only affect the formation of such a relationship, but also its maintenance.

Once a trust relationship has been established between two users, communication and interaction options increase (ability to send personal messages, to make comments and "like" an object). Given that these quantities are measurable, they can be exploited so as to establish a good indicator about the relationship of these two individuals. This communicational behavior is called *behavioral trust* and it can further be divided into *conversational trust* and *propagation trust* (Adali et al., 2010). Conversational trust increases when the involved parties have long, balanced and frequent conversations, since it indicates that there is a tight connection between these two users. Propagation trust exists when a node propagates information from another node and the more frequent the propagation, the stronger the trust is.

A significant part of the information being posted by users in a social network involves news feeds, which need to be filtered out before becoming useful information for a given individual. One way for achieving this is by ranking this information according to the source's level of trust. Mazzara, Marraffa, Biselli, and Chiarabini (2010) implemented such a tool that consisted of a news search engine and a trusted social network. The news search engine featured a configurable ranking algorithm, which could be customized to the user's taste, by setting the sources it should scan for news. Further customization was also possible that included the ability to set priorities and topics of interest. The ranking algorithm would also take into consideration the trust level of the source, before presenting the results to the user. A pleasant "side-effect" of this approach was the ability to fight the so-called *web spam* problem. Malicious entities (spammers) that either broadcasted false news/information or attempted to add bias to news/opinions by selective broadcasting would simply be excluded by the trusted community.

Despite the lengthy user agreement licenses and the related liabilities, social network users are by no means forced to enter their real personal details in their profile. As a result, a significant number of user accounts in social networking services are fake. For instance, Facebook was estimated to have more than 83 million fake profiles (8.7% of its 995 million global users), of which 46 million were duplicate profiles, 23 million were "user-misclassified" profiles (e.g., for organizations) and 14 million were "undesirable" profiles, mainly used for sending spam to other Facebook users (Sweney, 2012). Some of these duplicate profiles were created by privacy-aware users who wanted to limit their principal account's information leakage and linkability. In such cases, the owner of the multiple profiles may choose to leverage the trust level for each additional account by adding them (or some of them) to the friends list.

Collaborative Privacy Management

The difficulty of controlling privacy in shared content has already been mentioned and the following scenario is a very characteristic instance of this problem: Alice and Bob are friends in real life and they are also connected through a friendship relationship in a social network. Eve is one of Bob's colleagues and is also a friend of Bob in the social network. Suppose that Alice uploads personal photographs of her and Bob attending some sort of a social activity (e.g., a party) and Bob may or may not be tagged in it (he is still in the photograph, though!). The challenge in this case is that Bob would like to somehow control who can see the photographs uploaded by Alice that he is also in. However, he does not have full control over these photographs as he is not the owner of them (they belong to Alice) and he also does not want to prevent Alice from uploading any photographs that include him. Such binary yes/no decisions are either too loose or too restrictive and are undesirable in most cases.

One way for facing the abovementioned problem is through *collaborative privacy management* (Squicciarini, Xu, & Zhang, 2011). The users are initially classified into concerned parties (content-owners and co-owners) and viewers (content-viewers). A content-owner is the one who uploads and owns privacy-sensitive content. A co-owner is a concerned party whose personal information is revealed in a content-owner's shared content. A content-viewer is simply one who can access online material posted by content-owners that does not concern them with respect to privacy issues, but obeys the basic access limitations imposed on the content by the content-owner (e.g., accessible from everyone, from friends, from friends of friends). The online content that can be posted by a content-owner, but concerning a stakeholder can be of any form (photograph, video, text), as long as it contains private information of others that can be identified through searching and/or tagging.

In a scenario like the one mentioned above, the following user requirements are identified (Squicciarini, Xu, & Zhang, 2011):

- A content-owner should be able to invite tagged-users as a co-owner to co-manage privacy-content.
- A co-owner should be aware of the creation of privacy-content that concerns him or her.
- A co-owner should be able to request the control over the privacy-content from the content-owner who created the privacy-content. The control includes the ability to delete, update, and tag the content.
- A co-owner should be able to specify the accessibility of private-content by content-

viewers. Possible access privileges include the ability to view, modify and comment on given privacy-content.

Effectively, this model enables each user of the social network to describe additional relationships between friends and files that can pose privacy concerns. Of course, this is a rather simplistic approach. More sophisticated models require the stakeholder to consult other stakeholders (e.g., through online voting) before specifying viewers' access permissions to an object (Squicciarini, Shehab, & Paci, 2009).

It is worth pointing out that for such models to work, the content owner has to identify the involved individuals, so that they can be notified and set their access preferences for the given content. Nevertheless, there may be cases where an individual in a group photograph does not have a user account in the given social network at the time the photograph was posted. Therefore, privacy issues may occur at some later stage, if the person under question establishes a friendship relationship with the content owner. What is more, under certain circumstances this may be infeasible, such as in the case of a photograph with several people in the background (e.g., at a party or at a music concert). In addition, such models that require the user to constantly review online content posted by other users may cause discomfort and/or ruin the intended pleasant user experience in the social network, especially when there is a large number of active uploaders within one's friends list. Approaches that can automate this process have already been proposed (Squicciarini & Shehab, 2010); however, they rely on the content owner having (correctly) tagged the relevant content. Furthermore, whenever a social networking service enhances the available privacy settings, its users must review all their privacy settings from scratch, so as to ensure that they comply with the security policy they wish to apply to their profile information.

FUTURE RESEARCH DIRECTIONS

Social networks are a recent development for people to communicate, work and entertain themselves. To date, all advancements in the area of Informatics and Communications Technologies, apart from the obvious and important benefits that have brought in, they have also introduced significant security issues. Most of these problems are usually controlled or confronted successfully in time, with the development of suitable tools and security mechanisms. The following are some indicative examples:

- The appearance of malicious software in the '80s was faced with the development of anti-virus software, which led to the creation of a rather profitable industry.
- The initial design of the Internet, in particular the IPv4 protocol that implements the main packet routing functionality does not include any provision for the containment of malicious acts, such as eavesdropping, data manipulation, data source/destination authentication and so on. Such issues were initially faced by the development of new applications, like Virtual Private Networks (VPN), Secure Sockets Layer (SSL), Intrusion Detection/Prevention Systems (IDS/IPS) and then by redesigning the whole protocol so that the aforementioned security issues were cured, thus leading to version IPv6.
- The initial operating systems for personal computers had no provision for multi-user and inter-networking functionality, which lead to the appearance of many and difficult to control security issues. Newer operating systems were developed with multiple inherent security mechanisms, thus making them able to successfully confront even unknown threats.
- Older and very popular programming languages did not consider security as a

necessary non-functional requirement of the produced code. Similarly, most programming courses did not include training on secure code development, network security, etc. Contemporary programming languages have built-in characteristics for avoiding programming errors that lead to vulnerabilities and security holes. Moreover, the widely-adopted software engineering methodologies consider the executable code's security an absolute requirement. In addition, almost all computer science courses offered by universities include information systems security in their syllabus.

Based on the above, it is anticipated that in social networks, which were recently established as an alternative communication platform, similar security issues will arise. Empirical data so far confirms this hypothesis, since major security issues have emerged. Characteristic examples involve the creation of malicious software specially tailored for social networking environments. The exploitation of security vulnerabilities, combined with simple social engineering techniques can lead to a significant spread of malicious software, rendering "traditional" anti-virus software useless. The above were made more obvious in the case of Samy Kamkar, who developed MySpace worm that infected more than 1 million computers in less than 24 hours by exploiting a simple XSS (Cross-Site Scripting) vulnerability (Kamkar, 2005). This malware did not have any devastating consequences, as it simply added Samy Kammar to the list of friends. However, it demonstrated the size of the problem and the impact it can have on social networks. Similar incidents can be found in the literature, such as the Koobface worm (Villeneuve, 2010). This worm was designed to run on several well-known social networking sites, such as Bebo, Facebook, Friendster, Fubar, Hi5, MySpace, Netlog, Tagged, Twitter and Yearbook, although its greatest spread was noticed in Facebook. The goal of its creators was to form a large botnet, aiming at significant financial rewards via a Pay-Per-Install (PPI) manner. Such services are usually offered in the underground market to cyber-criminals who wish to gain control of a large number of computers, in order to use them for criminal activities. The total amount of money they amassed was close to 2 million dollars. The German researcher Jan Droemer lead to the exposure of the Koobface developers: Stanislav Avdeyko (leDed), Alexander Koltyshev (Floppy), Anton Korotchenko (KrotReal), Roman P. Koturbach (PoMuc) and Svyatoslav E. Polichuck (PsViat or PsycoMan), whose activity originated from St. Petersburg, a fact that allowed them to escape arrest, because of the problems in the cooperation between the Western and Soviet democracies.

Social networking platforms are also a valuable means for being informed about and commenting on daily news. They usually spread news significantly faster than conventional media, even electronic ones (Papic & Noonan, 2011). Consequently, they have also been used by activists or politicians as a powerful and important communications tool to promote their views. An exchange of opinions through social networking platforms is certainly beneficial for society. In certain cases, however, they are used for spreading slander and libel against key personalities. Several fake accounts are usually employed for misleading unsuspecting users, in an attempt to increase the number of related posts, thus increasing their credibility. Fortunately, in several cases the source of such information was successfully tracked, in addition to the fake accounts(Ratkiewicz, Conover, Meiss, Gonçalves, Flammini, et al., 2011; Ratkiewicz, Conover, Meiss, Gonçalves, Patil, et al., 2011; Mustafaraj & Metaxas, 2010).

Users with many friends can be exploited by legal companies for product promotion or by criminal groups for sending spam messages. Several incidents have been recorded where user accounts with a large number of contacts have been created manually through the exploitation of low-pay individuals from Asian or Eastern European countries (Motoyama, McCoy, Levchenko, Savage, & Voelker, 2011). A variant of this fraud can be achieved by automated software, the so-called *socialbots*, which were able to convince 35.65% of unsuspecting users to accept friendship requests (Boshmaf, Muslukhov, Beznosov, & Ripeanu, 2011; Wagner, Mitter, Körner, & Strohmaier, 2012). Since the aforementioned percentage is rather large, it is absolutely necessary to continue research on automated spambot detection (Boshmaf et al., 2011).

Social networks are a particularly effective communication tool, not only for normal users, but also for various *hacktivists*. The recent actions of "Anonymous" triggered a lot of discussions on the ways for tracking the offenders through the fake identities they maintain in social networks. The Chief Executive Officer of HFGary Federal, Aaron Barr, attempted to gather information about their friends' characteristics (e.g., age, home location, common friends) using inductive reasoning, but his results were proved to be highly-contradicting (Anderson, 2011). It was also proved that known companies in the field of information security offer to their customers services that include data collection through fake account profiles in social networks and the injection of false information, so as to inflict damage upon their competitors. How the existing legal framework deals with such acts is something that needs to be further looked into. As it was expected, his initiative triggered reactions from hacktivist communities, with rather unpleasant results for him and the companies he was working for (Anderson, 2011).

Recent data reveal the size of the adoption of social networks. A characteristic fact is that Facebook constitutes the largest digital image repository, with 30,000,000,000 images in total and 14,000,000 new images every day (Hogben, 2009). These figures largely exceed those of similar Internet services, such as Flickr. The number of images is something that can easily be counted and evaluated, whereas it is clearly much harder to estimate the significance and the value of the indirectly-generated information, such as the contacts each user has and their importance for the wider social network.

The simplistic approach that the number of contacts (or *edges*, as they are called in Graph Theory) is the main criterion, has not proved to be particularly useful. Metrics such as *betweenness centrality*, *closeness centrality* and *eigenvector centrality* provide much more important information, such as the node's weight in the social network or the frequency at which a node appears in the geodesic distance (i.e., shortest distance) in the information traffic. Nodes exhibiting increased values in those metrics are obviously of high importance in social networks. In most social networking platforms this information could have high marketing value, as nodes with high centrality values have high advertising value, since they can accelerate the transmission of information etc. Consequently, software developers of related applications could benefit from the privileged position of these nodes in the network, in order to promote their services in the best possible way. This practice that could be considered analogous to the "word of mouth" model has been studied by various researchers (Dellarocas, 2001) and has been found to be far more efficient than the traditional and more expensive techniques for promoting products and services, which is mainly the reason for the increased popularity it has gained during the past few years. The use of social networks renders this technique particularly effective, since electronic communication is almost immediate and with many more recipients, compared to the traditional face-to-face exchange of words in real time. The use of social networks may be equally effective in political debates or during campaign period. It is quite common to perform a related analysis on social networks for locating individuals who seem to have a significant influence (Livne, Simmons, Adar, & Adamic, 2011), as well as spreading false news, in order to damage a candidate's reputation or image. Researchers have come up with methods for locating the source of related rumors and determine whether it is a slandering campaign or not (Ratkiewicz, Conover, Meiss, Gonçalves, Flammini, et al., 2011), something that is possible if the nodes that started the broadcasting of malevolent news are located in the graph. However, containing the malevolent news becomes impossible once it has been reproduced by a certain number of users. For this reason, it is quite useful to be able to locate the nodes with the highest centrality, as they can accelerate or slow down the spreading of malicious applications, fake news, slander and so forth.

Furthermore, epidemiologic studies reveal the importance of these nodes regarding the potential to contain the spread of malware. In particular, as far as the spreading of malware is concerned, Facebook's topology that follows power law distribution, contributes in the spreading of malware epidemics. These problems are known to the social networking companies and are faced in their greatest extent with the use of internal security applications, such as the Facebook Immune System that attempts to contain related attacks. On the other hand, there are some who focus on the physical threats that may emerge from social networks, insisting that there is a correlation between the use of social networking services and the increase in incidents of sexually transmitted diseases. The relevant statements of Prof. Peter Kelly (Facebook 'linked to rise in syphilis', 2010), although they have been widely reproduced, do not seem to be supported by the rest of the academic community.

Graph theory in general and social networks in particular form a very important field of application for operations collecting information on social relationships and contacts of members belonging to an organization or group. Security services/agencies and especially secret services increased the use of graph theory, particularly after the unfortunate incidents of 9/11, since researchers like Valdis Krebs (Krebs, 2001) demonstrated the effectiveness that the analysis of suspects' connections may have, as well as the visualization of the obtained results. Even though certain security services had initiated similar projects, like Able Danger in 1998, these projects were classified and due to political opposition did not have the required co-operation with related services, thus failing to achieve their objectives, although they exhibited some positive results. Historically, the use of Graph Theory for the analysis of suspects' contacts initially occurred in World War II (Gutfraind, 2010). Since in social networks certain unlawful activities commence, it is quite a worrying thought if robust social network topologies emerge in the future, where the removal of even their fundamental members will have any effect on the overall function of the social network (Gutfraind, 2010). In case where contemporary activist (or hacktivist) movements such as the "Anonymous" had followed similar structures instead of a hierarchical model, it would have been significantly more difficult to contain their activity, given that many of their topmost members were arrested by the prosecuting authorities in a relatively small time interval (Olson, 2012).

The prosecuting authorities, as well as individual researchers and security experts employed different techniques for analyzing graphs with a variety of success rates. Aaron Barr claimed that it would be possible to identify certain Anonymous members by tracking and analyzing their digital trails in e.g., Facebook, Twitter and IRC (Anderson, 2011). His claims remained unproved; however, some of his main ideas can be applicable. Researchers have managed to determine the exact details of nodes by analyzing the edges and the structure of the network, based on the principle of network homophily (Macskassy & Provost, 2003) or in the behavioral patterns of their nodes (Henderson, Gallagher, Li, Akoglu, Eliassi-Rad, Tong, et al., 2011). In any case, it is important to know that very interesting and very precise correlations may emerge regarding a user's friends. Research has shown that especially in offensive behaviors it is quite effective to track suspects and closely monitor them based on relationships they may have with already branded villains (Macskassy & Provost, 2005). In the past, such procedures were rather hard, time-consuming, and required a significant effort on behalf of the prosecuting authorities, in order to locate and analyze the behavior of known villains' contacts. Currently, by exploiting social networks it is relatively simple to record the social and/or professional relationships of the villains, so as to broaden the set of potential suspects that should be further investigated.

The problem of user privacy is expected to remain the main problem in social networks during the next few years. Traditional techniques for ensuring privacy that are used in almost all other information systems applications (such as the use of strong cryptographic algorithms) have limited effectiveness in social networks. Even though the majority of the current social networks use various techniques for preserving and securing user privacy, there are many techniques for violating it and acquiring access to data that could reveal important information about the relationships of the nodes in a social network. These techniques are mainly based on the principle that the more nodes of the social network are exposed and disclose the true identities of their neighboring nodes namely, their friends, the more the overall social network's privacy decreases. In other words, revealing a node's neighbors contributes to the increase of the network's *node coverage* and therefore to the disclosure of user connections to a skillful adversary. There are several approaches for maximizing the node coverage, using the least possible number of nodes. Malevolent practices of this research involve the disclosure of a user's friends, either for blackmailing purposes through the unveiling of harmful information about the user's social circle, or for cases where employers or prosecuting authorities wish to acquire information about the contacts of a prospective employee or a suspect. It is a rather disconcerting fact that in most cases it is not even required to violate the victim's account, but rather to convince a sufficient number of their friends to use third-party applications of the given social networking platform. Given that in social networks such as Facebook more than 90% of the users have used these applications, it is quite probable that they have already exposed themselves by having involuntarily revealed their contacts (Korolova, Motwani, Nabar, & Xu, 2008).

So far, the term "social network" focuses primarily on social networking platforms, such as Facebook, Twitter, MySpace, LinkedIn, etc. These examples are clearly the most characteristic, however it is worth investigating whether older systems meant for supporting user communication should be regarded as instances of social networks. For example, e-mail supports user communications for decades, nevertheless the isolation of the specific characteristics of the communication patterns, their analysis using Graph Theory and the extraction of useful conclusions regarding the detection of spam messages were relatively recent achievements (Moradi, Olovsson, & Tsigas, 2012).

Moreover, Massively Multiplayer Online Role Playing Games (MMORPG) that have become quite popular lately could be regarded as members of the social networks family. In such games, a large number of users interact with the virtual environment and/or among them, in order to complete various missions/objectives. Figures as high as 13 million players have been recorded so far in some of these games, and, therefore, the sociality that users develop among them is an important aspect of the game. Users may simply co-ordinate themselves to accomplish group missions, as well as for exchanging or buying various inventory items, by using some sort of virtual money. It is also quite possible that certain rare or special items can only be acquired after buying virtual credit with real money, through electronic payments. This resulted in having malevolent users trying to get access to the players' accounts through illegal means (hacking), in order to use their monetary credit to their own benefit, or sell/transfer it to other players. Effectively, we have come up against with rather complex legal matters regarding the case of trading virtual goods using real money, as well as whether stealing virtual goods constitutes a crime and how could their owner possibly be compensated after having suffered such a virtual theft. Another complex issue is the determination of the real value of virtual goods, as it is difficult to estimate the value of both the time and effort a user has spent in order to create a high-level virtual character, if he becomes victim of a skillful adversary's unlawful actions, who may either sell the account for making illegal profit, or simply destroy the player for his own pleasure and satisfaction.

Social networks cover basic human needs for communication and information, as their popularity denotes. They are still in a relatively primitive stage and consequently various security and privacy issues are anticipated. On-going research on matters relating to security and privacy issues in social networks will help them mature and be adopted by even more people, as it occurred with other cutting-edge technologies in the past, such as cellular telephones and the Internet.

CONCLUSION

Social networks have gained great popularity during the past few years, as they can satisfy people's need for communication and socialization in the digital era. However, due to their currently "immature" state, as well as deficient security analysis and design, they suffer from serious security issues, the most important of which is probably the threats on user privacy. On the one hand, providers of social networking services want to collect as much information as possible about their subscribers, in order to exploit it and make a financial profit out of it (for instance, using it for marketing and/or advertising purposes). On the other hand, the majority of the users is unaware of the serious implications some of their actions may have on their privacy, such as uncontrolled "tagging" or excessive uploading of personal digital photographs. Data mining techniques and privacy preserving mechanisms are in a constant arms race. However, in order to ensure user privacy in social networks, additional steps need to be taken. Firstly, the legal framework has to be updated, so as to reflect the requirement for user privacy. Once this has been established, social network service providers should be given guidelines on user privacy and be asked to abide by them that will include offering more control over private information to users. Last but not least, user awareness and training is an equally important defensive measure for protecting their real-life privacy through the virtual world of social networking.

REFERENCES

Acquisti, A., Carrara, E., Stutzman, F., Callas, J., Schimmer, K., & Nadjm, M. (2007). *Security issues and recommendations for online social networks (Position Paper No. 1). European Network and Information Security Agency*. ENISA.

Adali, S., Escriva, R., Goldberg, M. K., Hayvanovych, M., Magdon-Ismail, M., Szymanski, B. K., et al. (2010). Measuring behavioral trust in social networks. In *IEEE International Conference on Intelligence and Security Informatics (ISI)* (pp. 150-152). Vancouver, BC, Canada.

Anderson, N. (2011, February 11). *(Virtually) face to face: How Aaron Barr revealed himself to anonymous*. Ars Technica. Retrieved May 15, 2012, from http://arstechnica.com/tech-policy/2011/02/virtually-face-to-face-when-aaron-barr-met-anonymous/

Anderson, N. (2011, February 14). Spy games: Inside the convoluted plot to bring down wikileaks. *Ars Technica*. Retrieved May 15, 2012, from http://arstechnica.com/tech-policy/2011/02/the-ridiculous-plan-to-attack-wikileaks/

Boshmaf, Y., Muslukhov, I., Beznosov, K., & Ripeanu, M. (2011). The socialbot network: When bots socialize for fame and money. In *Proceedings of the 27th annual computer security applications conference* (pp. 93-102). Orlando, Florida. ACM.

Carminati, B., & Ferrari, E. (2009, November 11-14). Enforcing relationships privacy through collaborative access control in web-based social networks. In *5th international conference on collaborative computing: Networking, applications and worksharing* (pp. 1-9). Washington, DC.

Chen, Y., Roussev, V., Richard, G. III, & Gao, Y. (2005). Content-based image retrieval for digital forensics. In Pollitt, M., & Shenoi, S. (Eds.), *Advances in digital forensics* (*Vol. 194*, pp. 271–282). Springer. doi:10.1007/0-387-31163-7_22

Cheng, J. (2007, May 30). Facial recognition slipped into Google's image search. *Ars Technica*. Retrieved May 15, 2012, from http://arstechnica.com/uncategorized/2007/05/facial-recognition-slipped-into-google-image-search/

Costoya, J. B. J., & Flores, R. (2009). *The heart of KOOBFACE. C&C and social network propagation* (White Paper). Trend Micro. Retrieved from http://www.trendmicro.com/cloud-content/us/pdfs/security-intelligence/white-papers/wp the-heart-of-koobface.pdf

Dellarocas, C. (2001). Analyzing the economic efficiency of eBay-like online reputation mechanisms. In *Proceedings of the 3rd ACM Conference on Electronic Commerce* (pp. 171-179). Tampa, Florida: ACM Press.

Dwyer, C., Hiltz, S. R., & Passerini, K. (2007). Trust and privacy concern within social networking sites: A comparison of Facebook and MySpace. In *Proceedings of the Thirteenth Americas Conference on Information Systems*, Keystone, Colorado.

Facebook 'linked to rise in syphilis'. (2010). *The Telegraph*. Retrieved September 11, 2012 from http://www.telegraph.co.uk/technology/facebook/7508945/Facebook-linked-to-rise-in-syphilis.html

Fuller, A. (2006, January 20). Employers snoop on Facebook. *The Stanford Daily*. Retrieved May 15, 2012, from http://archive.stanforddaily.com/?p=1019651

Gross, R., & Acquisti, A. (2005). Information revelation and privacy in online social networks. In *ACM workshop on privacy in the electronic society* (pp. 71–80). Alexandria, VA, USA: ACM. doi:10.1145/1102199.1102214

Gutfraind, A. (2010). Optimizing topological cascade resilience based on the structure of terrorist networks. *PLoS ONE*, *5*(11), e13448. doi:10.1371/journal.pone.0013448

Hasib, A. (2009). Threats of online social networks. *International Journal of Computer Science and Network Security*, *9*(11), 288–293.

Henderson, K., Gallagher, B., Li, L., Akoglu, L., Eliassi-Rad, T., Tong, H., & Faloutsos, C. (2011). It's who you know: Graph mining using recursive structural features. In *Proceedings of the 17th ACM SIGKDD International conference on knowledge discovery and data mining* (pp. 663-671). San Diego, California: ACM.

Hogben, G. (2009). Security issues in the future of social networking. In *W3C Workshop on the Future of Social Networking*, Barcelona, Spain. Position Paper.

Hu, H., Ahn, G.-J., & Jorgensen, J. (2012). Multiparty access control for online social networks: Model and mechanisms. *IEEE Transactions on Knowledge and Data Engineering*, 99.

Kamkar, S. (2005). *Technical explanation of the MySpace worm*. Retrieved May 15, 2012, from http://namb.la/popular/tech.html

Korolova, A., Motwani, R., Nabar, S. U., & Xu, Y. (2008). Link privacy in social networks. In *Proceedings of the 17th ACM conference on Information and knowledge management* (pp. 289-298). Napa Valley, California: ACM.

Krebs, V. (2001). Connecting the dots – tracking two identified terrorists. Retrieved September 11, 2012, from http://www.orgnet.com/prevent.html

Livne, A., Simmons, M. P., Adar, E., & Adamic, L. A. (2011). The party is over here: Structure and content in the 2010 election. In *Proceedings of the Fifth International Conference on Weblogs.*

Macskassy, S. A., & Provost, F. (2003). A simple relational classifier. In *Proceedings of the Second Workshop on Multi-Relational Data Mining (MRDM-2003) at the Ninth ACM SIGKDD International Conference on Knowledge Discovery and Data Mining (KDD-2003)* (pp. 64-76). Washington, DC.

Macskassy, S. A., & Provost, F. (2005). Suspicion scoring based on guilt-by-association, collective inference, and focused data access. In *International Conference on Intelligence Analysis*.

Mazzara, M., Marraffa, A., Biselli, L., & Chiarabini, L. (2010). The Polidoxa shift: A new approach to social networks. *Journal of Internet Services and Information Security (JISIS)*, *1*(4), 74–88.

Mezzour, G., Perrig, A., Gligor, V. D., & Papadimitratos, P. (2009, December 12-14). Privacy-preserving relationship path discovery in social networks. In *8th international conference on cryptology and network security* (pp. 189-208). Kanazawa, Japan.

Moradi, F., Olovsson, T., & Tsigas, P. (2012). Towards modeling legitimate and unsolicited email traffic using social network properties. In *Proceedings of the Fifth Workshop on Social Network Systems (SNS '12)* (pp. 9:1-9:6). Bern, Switzerland: ACM.

Motoyama, M., McCoy, D., Levchenko, K., Savage, S., & Voelker, G. (2011, August). Dirty jobs: The role of freelance labor in web service abuse. In *Proceedings of the USENIX security symposium*. San Francisco, CA.

Mustafaraj, E., & Metaxas, P. (2010). From obscurity to prominence in minutes: Political speech and real-time search. In *Websci10: Extending the frontiers of society on-line*. Raleigh, NC, US.

Nissenbaum, H. F. (2004). Privacy as contextual integrity. *Washington Law Review (Seattle, Wash.)*, *79*(1), 119–157.

Olson, P. (2012). *We are anonymous: Inside the hacker world of lulzsec, anonymous, and the global cyber insurgency*. Little, Brown and Company.

Opsahl, K. (2010). *A bill of privacy rights for social network users*. Retrieved May 15, 2010, from https://www.eff.org/deeplinks/2010/05/bill-privacy-rights-social-network-users

Papic, M., & Noonan, S. (2011, February). *Social media as a tool for protest*. Retrieved May 15, 2012, from http://www.stratfor.com/weekly/20110202-social-media-tool-protest?utmsource=SWeekly&utmmedium=email&utmcampaign=110203&utmcontent=readmore&elq=8a864881cc2546359a7360759ab0cfb3

Pekárek, M., & Pötzsch, S. (2009). A comparison of privacy issues in collaborative workspaces and social networks. *Identity in the Information Society*, *2*(1), 81–93. doi:10.1007/s12394-009-0016-4

Phillips, P., Scruggs, W., Toole, A., Flynn, P., Bowyer, K., Schott, C., & Sharpe, M. (2006). *FRVT 2006 and ICE 2006 large-scale results (NISTIR No. 7408). Gaithersburg, MD 20899*. USA: National Institute of Standards and Technology.

Pilkington, E. (2007, July 16). Blackmail claim stirs fears over Facebook. *The Guardian*. Retrieved May 15, 2012, from http://www.guardian.co.uk/international/story/0,2127084,00.html

Ratkiewicz, J., Conover, M., Meiss, M., Gonçalves, B., Flammini, A., & Menczer, F. (2011). Detecting and tracking political abuse in social media. In *Proceedings of the 5th International Conference on Weblogs and Social Media (ICWSM)*. Barcelona, Catalonia, Spain: The AAAI Press.

Ratkiewicz, J., Conover, M., Meiss, M., Gonçalves, B., Patil, S., Flammini, A., & Menczer, F. (2011). Truthy: Mapping the spread of astroturf in microblog streams. In *20th international conference companion on world wide web* (pp. 249-252). Hyderabad, India: ACM New York, NY, USA.

Schoen, S. (2007, July 20). Harry Potter and digital fingerprints. *Deep Links News*. Retrieved May 15, 2012, from https://www.eff.org/deeplinks/2007/07/harry-potter-and-digital-fingerprints

Squicciarini, A. C., & Shehab, M. (2010). Privacy policies for shared content in social network sites. *The VLDB Journal*, *19*, 777–796. doi:10.1007/s00778-010-0193-7

Squicciarini, A. C., Shehab, M., & Paci, F. (2009). Collective privacy management in social networks. In *Proceedings of the 17th International World Wide Web Conference* (pp. 461–484). New York: ACM Press.

Squicciarini, A. C., Xu, H., & Zhang, X. (2011). CoPE: Enabling collaborative privacy management in online social networks. *Journal of the American Society for Information Science and Technology*, *62*(3), 521–534.

Sweney, M. (2012). Facebook quarterly report reveals 83m profiles are fake. *The Guardian*. Retrieved September 11, 2012, from http://www.guardian.co.uk/technology/2012/aug/02/facebook-83m-profiles-bogus-fake

Villeneuve, N. (2010, November). *Koobface: Inside a crimeware network* (Technical Report No. JR04-2010). Munk School of Global Affairs.

Wagner, C., Mitter, S., Körner, C., & Strohmaier, M. (2012). When social bots attack: Modeling susceptibility of users in online social networks. In *Making sense of microposts* (pp. 41-48).

Websites 'keeping deleted photos'. (2009). Article. Retrieved from http://news.bbc.co.uk/2/hi/8060407.stm

Zhang, C., Sun, J., Zhu, X., & Fang, Y. (2010). Privacy and security for online social networks: Challenges and opportunities. *IEEE Network*, *24*(4), 13–18. doi:10.1109/MNET.2010.5510913

ADDITIONAL READING

Carminati, B., & Ferrari, E. (2011). Collaborative access control in online social networks. In *Proceedings of the 7th International Conference on Collaborative Computing: Networking, Applications and Worksharing (CollaborateCom)* (pp. 231-240). IEEE.

Chen, X., & Shi, S. (2009). A literature review of privacy research on social network sites. In *International Conference on Multimedia Information Networking and Security (MINES '09)* (vol. 1, pp. 93-97).

Chester, S., & Srivastava, G. (2011). Social network privacy for attribute disclosure attacks. In *International Conference on Advances in Social Networks Analysis and Mining (ASONAM '11)* (pp. 445-449). Washington, DC, USA: IEEE Computer Society.

Cutillo, L. A., Molva, R., & Strufe, T. (2009). Safebook: Feasibility of transitive cooperation for privacy on a decentralized social network. In *Third IEEE International WoWMoM Workshop on Autonomic and Opportunistic Communications (AOC 2009)* (pp. 1-6). Kos, Greece.

Felt, A., & Evans, D. (2008). Privacy protection for social networking platforms. In *Web 2.0 Security and Privacy 2008 (in conjunction with 2008 IEEE Symposium on Security and Privacy)*. The Claremont Resort, Oakland, California.

Fletcher, D. (2010). How Facebook is redefining privacy. *Time Magazine*. Retrieved September 11, 2012 from http://www.time.com/time/magazine/article/0,9171,1990798,00.html

Fong, P., Anwar, M., & Zhao, Z. (2009). A privacy preservation model for facebook-style social network systems. In *Proceedings of the 14th European conference on Research in computer security* (pp. 303-320). Springer-Verlag.

Golbeck, J. (2005). *Computing and applying trust in web-based social networks*. (Unpublished doctoral dissertation). University of Maryland at College Park College Park, MD, USA.

Gross, R., & Acquisti, A. (2005). Information revelation and privacy in online social networks. In *Proceedings of the 2005 ACM Workshop on Privacy in the Electronic Society (WPES '05)* (pp. 71-80). New York, NY, USA: ACM.

Guha, S., Tang, K., & Francis, P. (2008). NOYB: Privacy in online social networks. In *Proceedings of the First Workshop on Online Social Networks (WOSP '08)* (pp. 49-54). New York, NY, USA: ACM.

Hu, H., Ahn, G.-J., & Jorgensen, J. (2011). Detecting and resolving privacy conflicts for collaborative data sharing in online social networks. In *Proceedings of the 27th Annual Computer Security Applications Conference (ACSAC '11)* (pp. 103-112). ACM.

Krishnamurthy, B., & Wills, C. E. (2008). Characterizing privacy in online social networks. In *Proceedings of the First Workshop on Online Social Networks (WOSP '08)* (pp. 37-42). New York, NY, USA: ACM.

Luo, B., & Lee, D. (2009). On protecting private information in social networks: A proposal. In *Workshop on Modeling, Managing, and Mining of Evolving Social Networks, in conjunction with IEEE ICDE* (pp. 1603-1606).

Squicciarini, A. C., Shehab, M., & Wede, J. (2010). Privacy policies for shared content in social network sites. *The VLDB Journal, 19*, 777–796. doi:10.1007/s00778-010-0193-7

Zhang, C., Sun, J., Zhu, X., & Fang, Y. (2010). Privacy and security for online social networks: Challenges and opportunities. *IEEE Network, 24*(4), 13–18. doi:10.1109/MNET.2010.5510913

Zhou, B., Pei, J., & Luk, W. (2008). A brief survey on anonymization techniques for privacy preserving publishing of social network data. *ACM SIGKDD Explorations Newsletter, 10*(2), 12–22. New York, NY, USA: ACM. doi:10.1145/1540276.1540279

KEY TERMS AND DEFINITIONS

Graph Theory: The field of science dealing with the study of graphs, which are mathematical structures used to model pairwise relations between objects from a certain collection.

Network Homophily: The tendency of individuals with similar characteristics to associate with one another.

Privacy: The protection of personally identifiable information that can either be obtained directly from stored data, or indirectly through processing of data.

Socialbot: A type of (ro)bot that controls a social media account. It is automated software that imitates the behavior of a real user (posting messages, sending friend requests, etc.) and tries to convince other users to connect with it, aiming to extract as much information as possible from their profile data, or it may even have malicious intentions, such as the interception of passwords.

Social Graph: A structure that represents every user of the social network as a node and their pair-wise relationships as edges connecting these nodes.

Social Network/Online Social Network/ Social Network Service: A web-based service that allows users to create a profile, form virtual relationship connections with other users (friendship), traverse the connections of another user and interact through various activities, such as sending private messages, uploading digital photographs, posting public comments, remarking other users' content ("like" feature), taking part in online games and so on.

Tagging: A social network's functionality by which a user is allowed to link other users to a given profile object, such as a digital photograph (for instance, indicating the names of the persons shown in the photograph).

Chapter 9
A Graph-Based Approach to Model Privacy and Security Issues of Online Social Networks

Luca Caviglione
National Research Council of Italy, Italy

Mauro Coccoli
University of Genoa, Italy

Alessio Merlo
University of Genoa, Italy & Università Telematica E-Campus, Italy

ABSTRACT

With millions of users, Online Social Networks (OSNs) are a huge cultural phenomenon. Put briefly, they are characterized by: i) an intrinsic sharing of personal information, ii) a rich set of features to publish, organize and retrieve contents, especially for emphasizing their social organization, iii) the interaction with a heterogeneous set of devices, e.g., ranging from desktops to mobile appliances, and iv) the mix of Web-based paradigms and sophisticated methodologies for processing data. However, if not properly implemented, or without effective security policies, i) – iv) could lead to severe risks in terms both of privacy and security. In this perspective, this chapter analyzes the major peculiarities of OSN platforms, the preferred development methodologies, and usage patterns, also by taking into account how personal information can be exploited to conduct malicious actions. Then, a graph-based modeling approach is introduced to reveal possible attacks, as well as to elaborate the needed countermeasures or (automated) checking procedures.

DOI: 10.4018/978-1-4666-3926-3.ch009

INTRODUCTION

Online Social Networks (OSNs) have changed the way people communicate and share their personal information. Also, they are a key advancement for pursuing the vision of developing an Internet of People (IoP), rather than a straight internetwork of nodes. Even if revolutionary, OSNs are not based on completely novel concepts. Specifically, the World Wide Web Consortium (W3C), when detailing the model at the basis of the Social Web (W3C, 2010), envisaged the introduction of a core set of people-centric services. Nowadays, such functionalities are partially implemented within the most popular OSN platforms, rather than in a unified manner as originally planned by the W3C. As a consequence, the current social vocation of the Web has not been developed according to a precise standard, or under an organic guidance. Rather, it has grown (and continues to evolve) around features introduced by the different OSN providers. As a result, social tools are constrained to provide functionalities for task-specific duties, for instance to share photos in an OSN aiming at entertainment, or to publish resumes or portfolios in platforms designed to support business development. To summarize, the overall OSN geography is substantially split, populated by different frameworks delivering services in a non-uniform, redundant and mostly incompatible manner.

But the evolution of Application Programming Interfaces (APIs), jointly with the availability of agreed data representation models, and the creation of business partnerships, allow cross-platform interaction. Among the others, we mention the OpenGraph (OGP, 2012) template for depicting personal relations, thus enabling developers to handle user identities in a portable way. For the case of OSNs relying upon Web technologies, integration mainly takes benefit from the maturity of the *mash-up* approach, which facilitates the aggregation of different Web service providers to produce brand new contents. Another important factor accounting for the success of OSNs is the support of the *anywhere-anytime* paradigm. Yet, it introduces further heterogeneities, since OSNs are accessed from desktops, home appliances, gaming consoles, and mobile devices, e.g., smartphones and tablets. Moreover, this leads to an additional layer of complexity, since some devices exchange data with the OSN by using Web facades (even if tweaked for reduced screen sizes and resolutions), while others do have ad-hoc client-interfaces. In this case, the use of Web views can reduce the necessity of having different server-side implementations, but many applications do use an additional tier of Web-services and specific data models or protocols. As a result, accessing an OSN from different devices implies the use of several technologies, a broad variety of network requirements, traffic behaviors, and security mechanisms. The exploitation of social interactions over the Internet is done via a complex mix of services, technologies, programming methodologies, protocols, usage patterns, and incoherent designs, especially concerning Graphical User Interfaces (GUIs). Besides, to increase the interactivity of pages composing the OSN and to support real-time communications and feedbacks, the usage of specific programming methods within the users' browsers reduce the boundaries between the client and the server. We mention, among others, the *XMLHttpRequest* Javascript object, which enables a constant data movement by using long-held HTTP connections. Thus, the composite nature of the aforementioned scenario has also a huge impact in terms of *privacy* and *security* levels offered by OSN applications (Caviglione & Coccoli, 2011). In fact, many providers offer a variety of privacy management policies or security options, leading to possible attacks, misconfigurations or other hazardous conditions. These aspects should be also jointly considered with specific users' behaviors regarding the disclosure of critical information (e.g., family details reducing the strength of password recovery mechanisms based on secrets), and the pondered reduction of security policies of their accounts (e.g., for accessing to popular, but untrusted, applications or increase their visibility within the OSN). Eventually, the knowledge stored within an OSN can amplify the effectiveness of *social engineering* attacks, thus making privacy management a critical aspect. In addition, OSNs enable new exploits, e.g., multiple profile fusion, user profiling, identity theft and cyber bullying (Honjo et al., 2011). To recap, due to their thorough and composite knowledge about individuals, jointly with the highly fragmented technological composition, OSNs dramatically rise the minimal degree of data protection and security requirements.

In this perspective, to properly guarantee a safe usage, and to not endanger the technological infrastructure in charge of delivering the OSN service, privacy and security management techniques must be carefully designed, engineered, and implemented. Such aspects are of crucial importance to build a safe environment both for users and providers. Furthermore, it is imperative to take into account both the "richness" of data, and the freedom of choices of users, which should drive the entire lifecycle of the OSN development. Unfortunately, it is a very complex task, since it involves a highly multidisciplinary effort, ranging from sociology, relationship issues, cognitive processes, trust management, scalability considerations, human-machine-interaction, Web 2.0 technologies, ubiquitous availability and dependability. In more detail, issues to be considered when designing (or evaluating) the security and privacy scheme of an OSN are, among the others:

- Many platforms offer features to publish and share a rich variety of personal information, e.g., physical locations, pictures and textual entries. Additionally, many OSNs enable individuals to perform actions revealing their relationships with other people or their habits. Therefore, users can be easily profiled, and their activities can be also tracked across the Web. As a result, it is possible to collect very precise sets of information, which can be used to empower attacks based on the *social engineering* approach or massive profiling campaigns.
- The increasing diffusion of ad-hoc client interfaces for accessing an OSN, especially to guarantee mobility support, leads to situations where different devices (e.g., gaming consoles, mobile phones, desktops and set-top-boxes belonging to the same user) concurrently exchange data. On one hand, this particular behavior must be taken into account to avoid session hijacking. On the other hand, the huge volume of sensitive data, constantly moved from different devices to ensure a proper degree of synchronization, must be properly secured.
- OSN services are increasingly integrating features of mobile devices. This is, for instance, the case of Global Positioning System (GPS) information, which, if not properly handled, can result into breaches in the privacy or in the physical security of a user. Additionally, mobile devices are usually battery-operated, thus new attacks based on their limited amount of power can be effectively routed via OSN applications.
- Despite their peculiar nature, about the majority of OSN applications are Web services. In fact, earlier works (see, e.g., Boyd & Ellison, 2007) defined such platforms as Social Networking Sites (SNS). Thus, they are vulnerable to classic attacks such as traffic sniffing, server side misconfigurations, and request forgeries, to mention some. This is also valid when considering specific portions of the overall infrastructure, e.g., the database or the network, which can be endangered by attacks like the Structured Query Language (SQL) injection or a Distributed Denial of Service (DDoS), respectively. Therefore, techno-

logical implications must be clearly considered when developing an OSN-based service.

In this vein, this chapter analyzes the major features of OSN platforms, and the most popular development technologies, in order to introduce a graph-based modeling framework aiming at revealing possible attacks. Such an analysis tool could be adopted to elaborate proper countermeasures, as well as to implement checking procedures, possibly in an automated way.

The contributions of the chapter are: *i*) the review of the major issues concerning security and privacy of OSNs, *ii*) the demonstration of how attacks can be empowered by means of social data, *iii*) the development of a novel graph-based methodology for the systematic investigation of security aspects, and *iv*) the formalization of several prototypal hazards in order to showcase the effectiveness of the approach proposed in *iii*).

The remainder of the chapter is structured as follows: firstly we investigate the related work dealing with security issues of OSNs. Next, we review the features and the technological foundation of the most popular platforms, as to provide the needed background and motivations. Then, we introduce the graph-based modeling framework, as well as different real-world examples, as to prove the effectiveness of the approach. Lastly, we conclude the chapter.

RELATED WORK

As hinted, one of the key consequences of the "social" vocation of OSNs is the relevant volume of data belonging to individuals, which can be easily retrieved through the Internet. As a result, *privacy* is one of the major concerns when developing/managing/utilizing this kind of applications. Nevertheless, it is tightly coupled with *security*, thus such concepts must be jointly analyzed. In fact, attacks are mostly performed to gain access to private data, for instance to conduct other crimes, such as scams. Additionally, the overall security layer could be endangered, or forced, by using personal details as attack tools. As a possible example, we mention, retrieving answers to secret questions (e.g., via discovering the birthdate or place of birth), as well as, the creation of fake profiles, which can bypass the trust mechanisms implemented by the OSN platform (if any). Summarizing, the individual-centric flavor of OSNs recursively influences security and privacy.

Then, it is important to quantify the amount of privacy and security breaches affecting an OSN platform. In this perspective, McCallister et al. (2010) discovered that hazards are somewhat proportional to a metric defined as Personal Identifiable Information (PII). Put briefly, PII can be roughly defined as the amount of information about a user, which is sufficient to distinguish or trace his/her identity (e.g., name, social security number, date and place of birth, or biometric records in some particular cases). The PII could also include any information that is *linked* - or *linkable* - to an individual, such as medical, educational, financial, and employment information. In more details, the adjective "linked" refers to personal information associated to other data about the same user (according to some semantic or logical criteria). Conversely, the information is stated as "linkable" if it could be possible to build a logical association with other information belonging to the same individual. Such properties also grant recognizing users across different OSNs, for instance to take advantage of specific platform-dependent issues. Additionally, even if not classified as PII, there are other possible details, which can lead to hazards, e.g., physical locations. The trivial workaround of securing a profile could be not enough. In fact, due to the networked nature of social relationships and the intrinsic percolation of data, privacy threats can propagate and impact over peers. In this respect,

Baracaldo et al. (2011) developed an agent-based model to evaluate the effects of privacy decisions taken by a single individual. An interesting survey of vulnerabilities of the most popular OSN platforms has been compiled by Bilge et al. (2009). A broader review has been done by Joshi and Kuo (2011), which examine the more common threats of OSNs, with emphasis on de-anonymization, social phishing and neighborhood attacks. Also, their work showcases some privacy protection techniques such as, link prediction (Krishnamurthy & Wills, 2008) and anonymization (Wondracek et al., 2010; Narayanan & Shmatikov, 2009). A more detailed review of the current state-of-the-art literature on privacy (and security) of OSN platforms can be found in the work of Sattikar and Kulkarni (2011), where they selected 28 references in order to analyze: users' behavior in the choice of privacy settings, and the potential disclosure of privacy threatening information, the interaction among multiple data sources, the impact of users' age when publishing sensitive information, and risks associated with the availability of APIs for the access to data stored within an OSN. In this perspective, Sun et al. (2010) introduce proper countermeasures to guarantee data privacy and access control policies when accessing private data stored on potentially untrusted storage sites.

However, privacy is not the only concern when utilizing OSN services. In fact, they also inherit many security issues of the standard Web applications populating the Internet, even if exacerbated by the aforementioned "social" considerations. In this respect, Gao et al. (2011) classified the most common attacks in four main typologies: privacy breaches (as mentioned earlier), viral marketing (e.g., spam and phishing), network (e.g., Sybil and traffic-sniffing attacks), and malware attacks (e.g., worms). We point out that such attacks also depend on the technology at the basis of the communication infrastructure, the OSN, and the information management framework (see Caviglione [2011] for an analysis of possible exploits to OSN applications when accessed through wireless links). Adjusting the underlying technology could prevent many attacks, or at least, reduce their effectiveness. In this respect, many Researchers envisage the decentralization of the OSN providers (Yeung et al., 2009; Jahid et al., 2012), for instance by adopting the peer-to-peer (P2P) communication paradigm, especially to overcome problems arising from the storage of information in centralized servers. Such a class of future Distributed OSN (DOSN) architectures could be able to manage personal data of users almost independently from the OSN service provider (see, e.g., Zhang et al. [2010] for a comparison between the centralized and distributed architectural blueprints). Besides, recent experiences documenting the development of working prototypes are the Safebook system (Cutillo et al., 2011), and the Peerson project (Buchegger et al., 2009).

When a complete redesign is not possible or should be avoided, security could be enforced via client-side tools, or third party specific applications. As an archetype, this is the case of the "flyByNight" application, which has been introduced by Lucas and Borisov (2008). In a nutshell, it is an external component that can be plugged into Facebook to provide an enhanced degree of encryption (by means of a public key algorithm) in order to protect the privacy of messages exchanged between users. A similar tool is None Of Your Business (NOYB), developed by Guha and Francis (2008). Luo et al. (2009) propose the FaceCloak browser extension to protect privacy within Facebook via a proper decoupling mechanism. Basically, it publishes fake information on the OSN, but stores sensitive information in encrypted form on a separate and more secure location.

As a consequence of their almost unlimited popularity, many OSNs are also used as real development platforms, able to run and deliver sophisticated applications or games. Yet, the support of additional features, sometimes provided by untrusted bodies, can be a non-negligible source of hazards. In fact, pluggable components could hide viruses or trojans. On the contrary, also a "clean" application can be hazardous. This is mainly due to the need of accessing a variety of personal information, which can lead to unintended leaks. In this vein, Felt and Evans (2008) studied the 150 most popular Facebook applications and found that almost all of them require the access to private user data, even if not necessary for their correct behavior. Another interesting aspect is related to the effects of *socialbot* attacks, which exploit automated operations (also owing to the availability of rich sets of APIs for accessing the OSN) to perform attacks, build fake profiles or perform scams (see, e.g., Wagner et al. [2012] and references therein).

For what concerns issues belonging to specific technologies, we decide to focus on the Web-centric nature of OSNs. Even if many ad-hoc client interfaces for mobile devices have been developed, they are still Web applications. In fact, many implementations use embedded "Webviews," which are standard features of modern Graphical User Interfaces (GUIs). Thus, OSNs are largely overlapped with the Web 2.0, which imposes users to adopt different strategies to protect their privacy, as well as to avoid the undesired disclosure of data. At the same time, OSN providers should offer an appropriate technological support, also to monitor the disclosed information. As an example, Gates (2007) has identified *four* technical requirements for access control mechanisms, especially suited to support additional constraints imposed by OSN. We point out that this reflects into a new relation-centric enabling to overcome the actual user-centered model currently used to rule personal information. For the sake of completeness, we review such access control mechanisms:

- **Relationship-Based:** The data owner can control the release of their personal information according to the specific data receiver, rather than its role, as it happens in mechanisms like the RBAC (Ferraiolo & Kuhn, 1992; Sandhu et al., 1996), or the improved version with attributes (Kuhn et al., 2010).
- **Fine-Grained:** In addition to being relationship-based, access control must be also available in a fine-grained format, for instance, to protect individual blog entries, particular personal information, or specific photos.
- **Interoperability:** Any access control system that is developed should be interoperable between multiple sites. Ideally, the access control policies and relationship groups defined by the user should migrate with the user, and should be inherited from site to site, rather than be redeveloped for each individual site.
- **Sticky Policies:** Policies that are created by a user do not only need to be interoperable through different sites, but should also follow the protected data accordingly.

Therefore, it is of crucial importance being able to model at least the most critical aspects of an OSN, also in the perspective of engineering the needed countermeasures. However, at the best of authors' knowledge, there is still a lack in the literature about the modeling of such issues, especially jointly addressed with the OSN scenario. A partial exception is the work presented by Laorden et al. (2010), which is a description of a collection of security aspects, and a set of possible attacks aiming at reducing the performance of computer systems. Thus, it is not fully focused on the topic of this chapter.

A REVIEW OF FEATURES AND TECHNOLOGIES OF OSN APPLICATIONS

In order to comprehend the proposed graph-based model, we introduce the features offered by the most popular OSN platforms, and we also briefly review some core technologies used to implement popular services.

OSN Features

According to the general description introduced in the seminal work by Boyd and Ellison (2007), OSN services allow users to: *i*) define a public profile subject to some access control mechanisms, *ii*) establish a neighborhood of "friends," and *iii*) access to peers' profiles, to interact and also to find new relations. We point out that terms like "friends" are not uniquely accepted, and could vary according to the specific OSN implementation (e.g., while Facebook defines contacts as friends, Twitter, which is based on an asymmetrical relationship, calls them follower/following). Therefore, in the rest of this chapter, we will specify the terminology when possible doubts arise. Interested readers could also investigate the work of Zhang et al. (2010), which developed a more fine-grained approach, classifying users activities into *four* areas: *personal* information space, *social* connection space, *communication*, and *search* (e.g., exploring connections). Yet, this level of details is not required for the definition of our model. The exploitation of activities *i*) – *iii*) is done through specific functionalities offered by the OSN platform. To give an understanding of the proposed graph-based approach, and to emphasize how a given feature or procedure could be subtly used to conduct attacks, we do introduce the major characteristics available in the most popular OSNs, e.g., Facebook, Google+, Twitter, and Diaspora.

Creation of a user account: In order to join the service, the individual is prompted to create a personal account. Typically, the procedure requires using a valid email address, along with some personal details. In many OSNs, the use of real name is highly encouraged but not mandatory. In fact, sharing the real name increases the performance of the OSN, for instance in terms of searching individuals. A relevant exception is made by Google+, which enforces people to be verifiable.

Development of a user profile: This entity contains about the totality of the information belonging to a user and it is uniquely bind to the user account. To this aim, users are requested to add personal information such as, e.g., a thumbnail picture, the birthdate, brief information about the education, current or past jobs. Such data are mostly optional, and vary according to the specific purpose of the OSN. For instance, in services aiming at re-join real-life people, such information could be valuable. On the contrary, in services like Twitter or those driven by specific interests, such knowledge could be negligible.

Posting of contents: User-generated information could be very broad and highly influenced both by the scope and the design of the specific OSN. This action is commonly ruled by the "share your thoughts" paradigm. Thus, a user can publish URLs, multimedia material such as photo, video, audio, and textual entries. Again, a peculiar OSN is Twitter, where posting is limited to 140-character long textual messages, called tweets. However, they can be used to embed links to external resources. An important additional service offered by many OSNs (or, in specific cases, by third parties) is the hosting facility. In fact, user-generated contents are directly stored and managed by the OSN framework itself. Recently, they can be also enriched with geographic information, which can be manually inserted or automatically retrieved from the GPS embedded in many portable devices.

Definition of network of contacts (or friends): In order to effectively interact, users are requested to add peers. This operation can be done according to different basis: e.g., real-world existing relationships, common interests, and business partnerships. In the majority of OSNs, interaction is usually bidirectional or mutual. For what concerns Twitter, relationships are asymmetric, i.e., a user A following B does not imply the vice versa. The so-established network is ruled by a set of *privacy options*, which roughly defines "who can view what." Many OSNs have a per-user degree of granularity, but this approach is scarcely exploited by consumers, since it tends to not scale when in presence of a large number of contacts. A more scalable but coarse-grained one is to join contacts in to clusters defined *groups* or *circles*, according to the Facebook or Google+ jargon, respectively. Contacts may not be only limited to physical entities, but can also represent groups or social pages (e.g., belonging to a brand). As regards *privacy* options, the *default* levels are not usually restrictive enough. The available degrees of freedom vary from a service to another, but often enabled to selectively block individuals and coherent set of actions (e.g., photo sharing, and denying/granting the access to well-defined portions of the profile).

Performing interaction with peers: This may happen through a variable set of functionalities such as: commenting, tagging or mentioning friends in posts and pictures, sending private messages to another user or group, real-time chat and integration with third party services, manipulating other users' contents (e.g., re-post in Facebook or Google+, re-twitting in Twitter), rating or recommend entries. In addition, users can browse the public part of the OSN for exploring connections and searching new contacts. The search can be based on identification of people, as well as, on keywords or tags. Additionally, many other high level activities such as, creating pages, and sharing applications like games, could be performed. We point out that, such functionalities imply granting the access to and the control of some portions of the user profile.

Recalling that OSNs form a very heterogeneous space, we can note that the aforementioned features are largely implemented by many services, but with many discrepancies, and with scope-specific tweaks. This is, for instance, the case of Foursquare where about the totality of the interactions is ruled through geographical information. In this perspective, Akre et al. (2009) present an exhaustive analysis of the different features of a variety of OSN, and also emphasize their impact in terms of security and privacy.

OSN Technologies

To effectively comprehend privacy and security boundaries, and how they can be forced, it is also mandatory to evaluate the influence of implementation internals. In fact, the space of insecurities of an OSN must not be separated from the underlying technologies. To this aim, Caviglione et al. (2012) elaborated a *taxonomy*, where the space grouping all the possible hazards is generated via a base composed by three elements, namely, *user*, *social* and, *technological*. By considering flaws of different spaces, OSN developers and attackers can prevent/produce a new class of threats. As a paradigmatic example, we mention the option of mixing social engineering with documented vulnerabilities of specific software modules. To better understand the assumptions of the proposed modeling approach, we give a concise description of the main technological aspects that can lead to insecurity. For the sake of clarity, we focus only on Web and networking issues.

Owing to their strict requirements in terms of scalability and Quality of Experience (QoE) guarantee, OSNs must rely on complex hardware and software platforms. Still, their architectural blueprint is based on the client-server Web model. Hence, an OSN potentially suffers from the vulnerabilities affecting the Web (Joshi et al., 2001; Criscione et al., 2009). Besides, they are further amplified due to the usage of web-services as public interfaces, making possible to switch the OSN into an attack platform (Jun & Wooyong, 2003). To give a more thorough background, we list the most risky vulnerabilities of Web applications.

Specifically, we refer to the Open Web Application Security Project (OWASP) (OWASP, 2012), which publishes a "*ten top-risky vulnerabilities for Web applications*." The latest available release reports the following hazards:

1. **Injection:** Such flaws, like the SQL and Lightweight Directory Access Protocol (LDAP) injections, occur when untrusted data is sent to an interpreter as a part of a query or a command. This can induce misbehaviors within the interpreter, resulting into the execution of unintended commands or the access to unauthorized data.
2. **Cross-Site Scripting (XSS):** They occur when an application sends untrusted data without performing proper validation and escaping procedures. This enables attackers to execute scripts in the victim's browser, e.g., to perform session hijacking, or browser redirection.
3. **Broken Authentication and Session Management:** Authentication and session management are often not correctly implemented, allowing attackers to arbitrarily assume identities by compromising passwords, keys, and session tokens.
4. **Insecure Direct Object References:** A direct object reference is caused by permitting the access to a reference of an internal implementation object, such as a file, a directory, or a database key. Hence, attackers can manipulate these references to access data without proper authorizations.
5. **Cross-Site Request Forgery (XSRF):** It forces a logged-on victim's browser to send a forged HTTP request, including the victim's session cookie and any other automatically included authentication information.
6. **Security Misconfiguration:** Good security practices require having proper configurations defined and deployed for the application, the software libraries, network devices, and the application/Web/database servers. Settings must be checked and updated, since products could not be shipped with secure defaults.
7. **Insecure Cryptographic Storage:** Many Web applications do not protect with appropriate encryption or hashing sensitive data, e.g., authentication credentials. Then an attacker can gain information to conduct scams such as identity thefts.
8. **Failure to Restrict URL Access:** About the totality of Web frameworks evaluates the access rights of a URL only just before rendering protected links and buttons. This "lazy" mechanism could enable attackers to forge URLs for accessing to hidden pages.
9. **Insufficient Transport Layer Protection:** Applications could fail to authenticate, encrypt, and protect the confidentiality and integrity of sensitive network traffic. The main flaws are due to weak algorithms, and expired or invalid certificates.
10. **Unvalidated Redirects and Forwards:** When a user needs to be redirected to external contents (e.g., pages or sites), applications often determine the destinations without checking the trust of the target. As a result, if a proper validation is not performed, users can be routed to phishing or malware sites.

Other technology-related security aspects deal with the user-side part of the OSN, and spans from hardware to software. In fact, many people access to an OSN via Web browsers or ad-hoc client interfaces, which substantially recall the *thin client* philosophy. The latters are tailored to maximize the resources available within each appliance, e.g., built-in cameras, GPS or specific GUIs. In this perspective, also the protocol stack can play a role, since it can have reduced functionalities or erratic behaviors. Then, the OSN could be used to route attacks specifically tweaked for a given class of devices and vulnerabilities. We mention, among the others, the malicious stimulation of handheld devices to drain the battery (Caviglione & Merlo, 2012). Nevertheless, to cope with the more demanding users, OSNs continue to release new features, especially in the field of interactivity, which require client side software technologies such as JavaScript (JS) or the usage of the Asynchronous Javascript And XML (AJAX) programming paradigm. In this way, OSNs guarantee the real-time update of contents, and make the social interaction more effective. In this respect, additional hazards are nested within the traffic patterns produced by Web-based OSN services characterized by well-defined and exploitable characteristics. One of the most common insecurity is the use of HTTP rather than HTTPS for the transmission of data between clients and servers. This could be dangerous when OSNs are accessed from devices using non-protected (or weakly protected accesses, such as those employing Wired Equivalent Privacy - WEP) channels. Therefore, attacks based on traffic sniffing become trivial, i.e., utilizing a common network analyzer such as Wireshark (Wireshark, 2012) or *tcpdump* can suffice.

Due to their Web nature, the *page* is the core component, which is composed by the *main object* containing the HTML source, and *in-line object(s)*, i.e., those linked within the hypertext. Through specific traffic inspection tools all the objects populating the OSN pages can be gathered; for instance, to reconstruct the network of individuals of a user. However, also HTTP traffic with encryption exposes some exploitable features. Actually, OSN applications are characterized by well-defined traffic patterns, especially in terms of throughput (see, e.g., Caviglione [2009] for a general investigation of many Web 2.0 services delivered through satellite environments). In fact, some real-time-like features such as, e.g., updating status in Facebook, mentions in Twitter, Instant Message (IM) notifications, are based on scripts continuously polling a centralized entity. Such actions lead to repetitive traffic templates, commonly moved through long-held HTTP connections rather than performing additional requests. These behaviors can be easily revealed by calculating the Power Spectral Density (PSD) of the traffic trace. This sort of "fingerprint" could be used to discover OSN-related activities within encrypted flows, and to perform malicious actions such as Denial of Service (DoS) attacks to a target machine (since conversation endpoints are usually not encrypted).

The Graph-Based Model

In this section we introduce the graph-based modeling approach to describe and evaluate privacy and security of OSNs. To prove its effectiveness, we use our framework to describe issues of a toy application. Such reference scenario has been designed to be general enough to capture about the totality of real-world platforms. In addition, as to emphasize the tightly coupling between user's behavior and specific implementation choices, we will also apply the model to describe technology-dependent attacks. We underline that the basic formalism, as well as some examples, have been partially borrowed from our past efforts in modeling threats of OSNs. Interested readers can find more details in Caviglione et al. (2012).

In order to reveal possible privacy and security hazards of an OSN, we need a proper layer of abstraction. To this aim, we reduce the OSN as a set of *associations* between *users* and *social objects*, e.g., messages, pictures and videos. From a security point of view, each user shares personal information via objects, also specifying their visibility. Therefore, the social activities performed within an OSN can be considered as a user-driven combination of associations defining relationships between users and objects. Besides, they are not limited to "owned" objects; hence, it is also possible to manipulate other users' objects under specific constraints (e.g., friendships). We introduce the following *three* basic associations:

1. **User-to-User (e.g., Friendship):** It defines a trust relationship between pairs of users, allowing them to share private (or with restricted visibility) information by means of suited objects. Such information is generally publicly available to all friends of both users.
2. **User-to-Object (e.g., Tagging):** It connects users with a given object as to define logical relationships among user and proper objects. This could be, for instance, the outcome of a user tagging a peer into a photo. Since this operation is usually "public," the target of the tag could be interested in reverting or preventing this kind of action.
3. **Object-to-Object (e.g., Posting):** It is executed by a user on an object belonging to another user. A typical example is the posting of an object on a friend's public profile. This operation usually makes the object visible to friends populating the target's neighborhood, and is mainly used to relate objects for creating logical interactions (e.g. to declare events and a places).

We point out that, in our approach, each object must be associated at least to one user (i.e., the owner), and each user must own at least one object (i.e., the user profile). The process of building and destroying associations is subject to the security policies implemented by the OSN. However, such enforcements are seldom sufficient to avoid misuses, and their correct application is often delegated to the user. For instance, let us consider possible hazards affecting previous associations. For the case 1), policies in many OSNs do not allow to keep a friendship relationship reserved, e.g., Twitter. Regarding case 2), it is not always feasible for a user to prevent peers creating user-to-object associations involving himself/herself. Commonly, a user may remove the association only when notified. Lastly, for the case 3), there are no simple policies to block in advance a friend to post on a user wall. Summing up, current privacy and security policies are not restrictive, non-standardized, and too much user-dependent. Investigating differences of how each OSN enforces associations is out of the scope of this chapter. Rather, we only focus on general security-relevant aspects of OSN to assess the impact of potential vulnerabilities that may lead to violations.

A Graph-Based Model for OSNs

To develop our model, we decided to abstract popular OSNs like Facebook and Google+, maintaining enough generality to represent a wide variety of real-world services. To this aim, we introduce a formalization, in which users, objects and associations are represented as *nodes* and *arcs* of a *graph*. Both can be modified upon the execution of valid user actions. For each OSN, a specific set of operations and rules must be defined, including proper constraints. Their successful achievement will result in a modification of the graph by means of associations.

Given **U** as the set of users within an OSN, **O** the set of admissible objects, $u, u_1, u_{2, \dots} \in$ **U** and $o, o_1, o_2, \dots \in$ **O**, we define the following basic relations:

- **Friendship(u1,u2):** To create a friendship-based association between two users; it basically models a user-to-user association.
- **Owner(u,o):** To declare the ownership association between object *o* and user *u* (i.e., the builder). This relation is useful to decide who has full control over an object.
- **Assignment(u,o):** To state that user *u* is related to object *o*, as a result of a linking operation performed by another user (e.g., a friends). In other words, it maps a user-to-object association.
- **Connection(o1,o2):** To state that two objects are related, due to operations made by their respective owners. It defines an object-to-object association.

  We point out that each object may be built and destroyed by a user, and each user can delete a previously established friendship relation, or remove a tag. On the contrary, in all current OSNs a user is an independent entity, which cannot be driven by other peers. Then, to be efficient, security policies of an OSN must ensure such basic assumptions, i.e., preventing malicious users to force remote peers in performing unwanted actions. Based on definitions *a*) – *d*), typical operations in an OSN can be overlaid on top of the previous relations. Therefore, by using a Prolog-like syntax, we define the following operations:

- **Message (u1, o, UList): Owner (u1, o):** Allows to send a public message to friend/non-friend users. It is general enough to represent both the delivery of an object or a message. For instance, it can be used to capture the transfer of a photo, a video or an audio file, as well as an event. Roughly, it is a high-level primitive offering a basic communication channel between users of the same OSN.
- **ChatMessage (u1, o, u2): Owner (u1, o), Friendship (u1, u2):** Allows to send a private chat message (i.e., o) between friends. Accordingly, it is a sub-type of *i*), and specifies the action of communicating only among users which are in a friendship relationship.
- **Tagging (u1, o, u2): Owner (u1, o), Friendship (u1, u2):** Allows to tag the user u_2 on an object o belonging to the user u_1. This operation relates friends with an object, by means of a strict rule. In fact, it imposes the ownership over the object o, as well as, the friendship relation. Even if many OSNs make tagging possible under slacker constraints, we adopt the most compelling situation in order to assess security implications under the more restrictive conditions.
- **Update (u,o): Owner (u,o):** Allows to update the status of an object (e.g., the public profile). This operation does not involve other users, and it is assumed as independent from the state of the OSN.
- **Posting (u,o1,o2): Owner(u,o1), Owner (u2,o2), Friendship (u1,u2):** Allows to post an object o_1 (e.g., a picture) on another object o_2 (e.g., the public profile of another user). In a nutshell, it allows building logic relations between objects, which generally reflect the social background of friends. Also in this case, we consider the more restrictive use case, imposing the friend relationship between the objects' owners.

Figure 1 depicts the graphs corresponding to the aforementioned operations. If successful, each one will modify the state of the related graph. The positive outcome is generally evaluated against the OSN security policy, which should discriminate the legality of a successful operation. In this case, we can reasonably assume that the output graph is likewise legal.

In a more general perspective, a *final* graph can be viewed as an *ordered sequence* of single-operation graphs. To model and understand issues in privacy and security, it is important to discriminate the order of operations leading to that graph in its final form. For instance, a graph resulting from the execution of several operations may have (not) security implications according to their temporal schedule. Thus, it is of paramount importance to capture the order both of operations and associations. In our proposed formalization, is sufficient to add a timestamp value to each action, which can be used to produce an ordering relation among operations. As an example, Figure 2 shows a graph of: *i*) a chat message from u_1 to u_2, *ii*) a tagging of user u_2 on o_1 performed by u_1, *iii*) a posting of o_2 on o_3, and *iv*) a message-based conversation among u_2, u_3 and u_4. According to timestamps operations/associations can be arranged to produce the ordered sequence that builds the graph in its final form.

The proposed approach can be used to implement common security rules characterizing the

Figure 1. Graph modeling of basic OSN operations

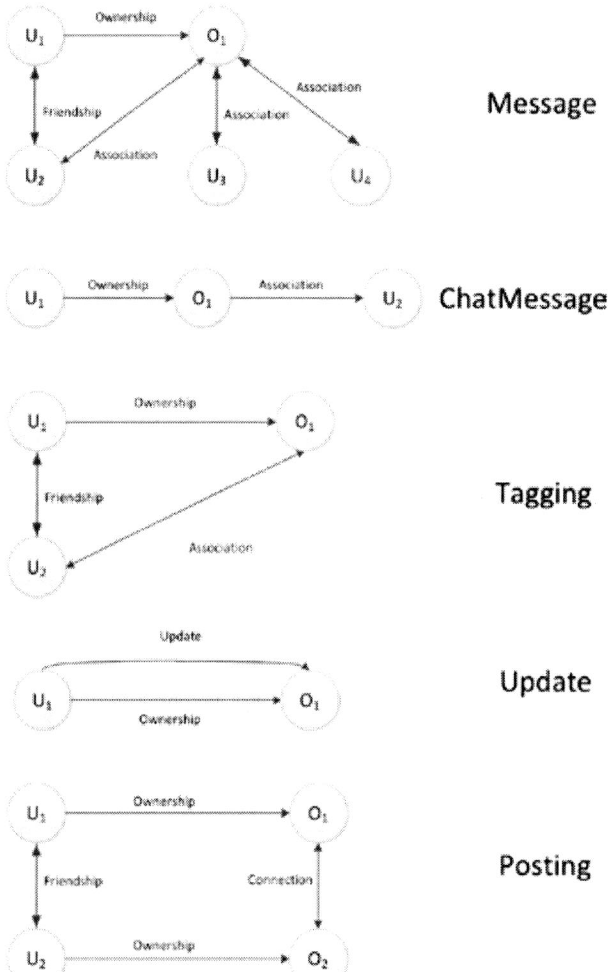

most popular OSNs. Specifically, they will limit the impact of each user on the graph. In detail:

- Users are allowed to modify the graphs only by invoking constrained operations, i.e., the right hand side of each operation, as defined in *i*) – *v*). For instance, by default the user u_1 cannot force the user u_2 to add u_3 as a friend.
- Users have a limited impact on the graph, since they are only allowed to access objects they own or they are associated with, according to the operational constraints.
- Users have a limited view of the whole graph: for instance, a user cannot get access to object not owned or without a connection occurred through tagging or posting operations.

The proposed method is simple yet powerful, making the definition on new operations and constraints easy. In particular, additional operations can be introduced by defining *rules* with a new *left-hand* side part, while new *constraints* can be defined by properly modifying the *right-hand* side. As an example, let us consider the need of

Figure 2. An example of an OSN graph

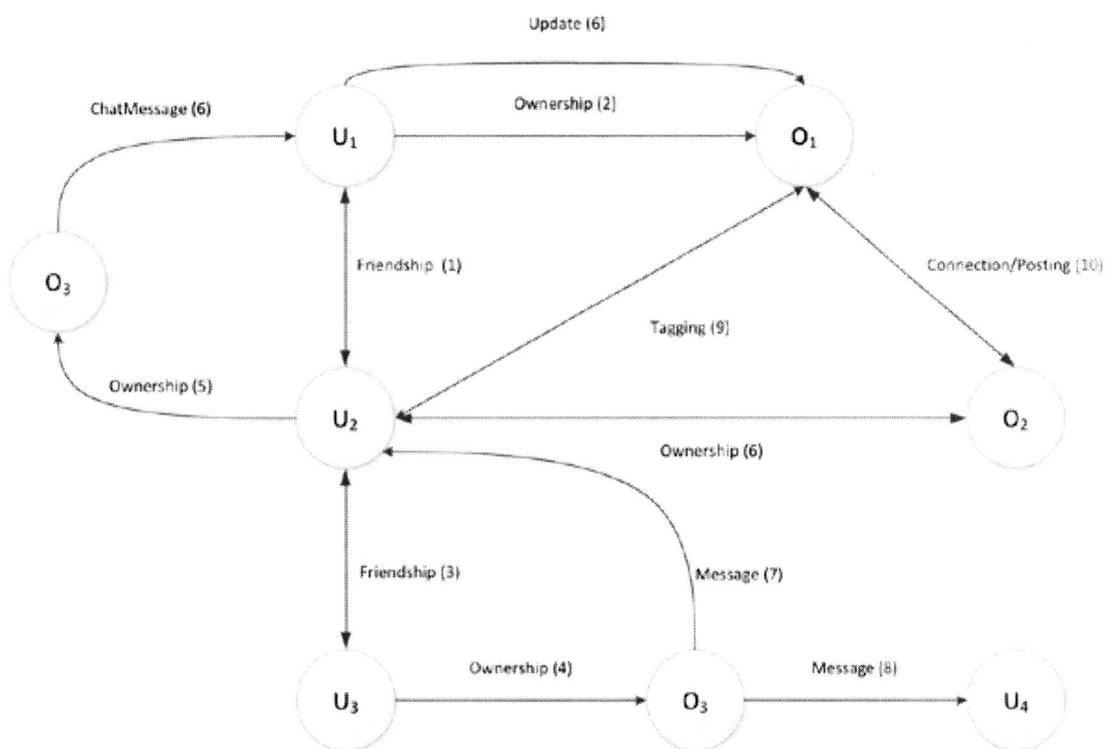

introducing an operation for inviting friends to a social event. Hence, it is sufficient to define a new operation, e.g.:

invitation(u1,o,u2):-Assigned(u1,o), Friendship(u1,u2)

where the right-hand side defines the new operation, while the left-hand one introduces the proper constraints.

Modeling Security and Privacy Issues with the Graph-Based Approach

To prove the effectiveness of the proposed approach, in this section we introduce different attacks that can be done against an OSN. In order to model realistic behaviors, we do assume the user as the more vulnerable element of the OSN. Therefore, forcing an individual to perform legal operations is the most straightforward way for an attacker to create unwanted relations, associations and connections. This leads to valid OSN graphs, even if not reflecting real social connections between users, thus allowing malicious ones to violate both privacy and security of legal ones. Since in our model objects join users, they correspond to vulnerability points that can be exploited to force legal users to modify their social connections, by inadvertently execute operations.

As a first example, we want to showcase how our framework can be used to capture attacks exploiting weaknesses of the technological pool of an OSN platform. Specifically, we deal with the case of an OSN implementing objects via HTML, which is the most diffuse scenario. Thus, all objects may potentially convey some OWASP vulnerabilities like XSS or SQL injection. For instance, with reference to the graph in Figure 2, let us suppose that user u_2 is an attacker aiming at stealing, via a chat message, the session cookie of user u_1. User u_2 may embed some JS code to forward the cookie of u_1 to an external server, resulting into an XSS attack. In fact, the browser of u_1 could automatically execute the JS code, or require an input from the user. Besides, u_2 can get the "valid" cookie (i.e., the one granting the access to the OSN) since access to messages is granted only prior authentication. The success of the previous attack may lead u_2 to be misrecognized as u_1, so to gain the ability to perform legal operations on the graph in his stead, like updating u_1 profile. The corresponding graph is shown in Figure 3.

Another common vulnerability of Web 2.0 applications is the SQL injection, so its proper formalization is of crucial importance. In this vein, we investigate its exploitation and the related alteration to the OSN graph. Yet, we need to make some preliminary assumptions on the database used by the toy OSN. Let us suppose that relationships belonging to posted objects are stored in a table called "Post," which contains three elements, i.e., one is the OSN user, while the others are the two objects. Trivially, if user u_1 posts object o_1 on object o_2, the following query will be executed:

```
INSERT INTO Post VALUES (u1,o1,o2)
```

Let us also suppose that user indicates (at least) the second object to post in an HTML format, and that no checks are made on such input (we point out that missing or insufficient checks are one of the most diffuse security holes). The malicious user u_1 may substitute o_2, with the following string:

```
o2); INSERT INTO Post VALUES (u2,o1,o3
```

Figure 3. Impact of a successful XSS attack

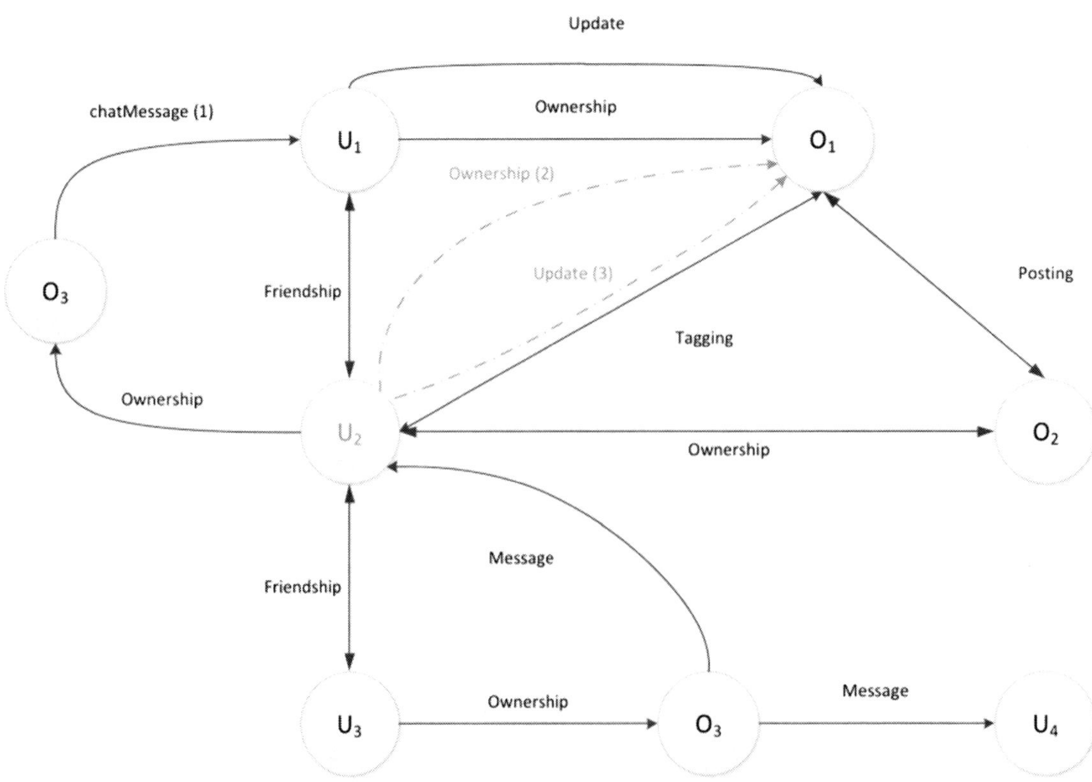

thus forcing the execution of two post queries instead of one. This will result into a posting operation executed by an unaware user u_2. Figure 4 depicts the impact of such attack on the OSN graph.

Other relevant risks are rooted within the support of multiple sessions (that is important for using mobile appliances), which enables the same user to be concurrently connected from different devices to the OSN (*à-la multihoming*). To this aim, the OSN accepts users logged for an indefinite time frame, making the platform a fertile ground for XSRF attacks. For example, let us consider a user u_4 connecting to an OSN via a smartphone. Let us also suppose that a malicious user u_2 discovers the mobile phone number of u_4 by digging information in the public profile, aiming to force u_4 to inadvertently become friends. Since the command request for adding a friend is publicly available to OSN application developers, u_2 may send a message via SMS or MMS, embedding a link with an "add friend" command to u_4. As u_4 goes through the link, the operation is executed without any further confirmation, due to the fact that the session is open and OSN applications do not require re-authentication. As a result, a valid "*add friend*" operation is executed by u_4. The corresponding graph is depicted in Figure 5.

We highlight that in this case, there is no identity theft as in the previous case. From the OSN perspective, the user u_4 is actually performing the "add friend" operation.

Another threat affecting mobile devices is due to intrinsic limitations imposed by the use of batteries, or the adoption of a specific billing plan for accessing the Internet. Regarding the first point, battery in current smartphones is exposed to a non-negligible consumption due to the execution of concurrent applications (see, e.g., Caviglione and Merlo [2012] for a specific analysis of the most important battery draining

Figure 4. Impact of a successful SQL Injection attack

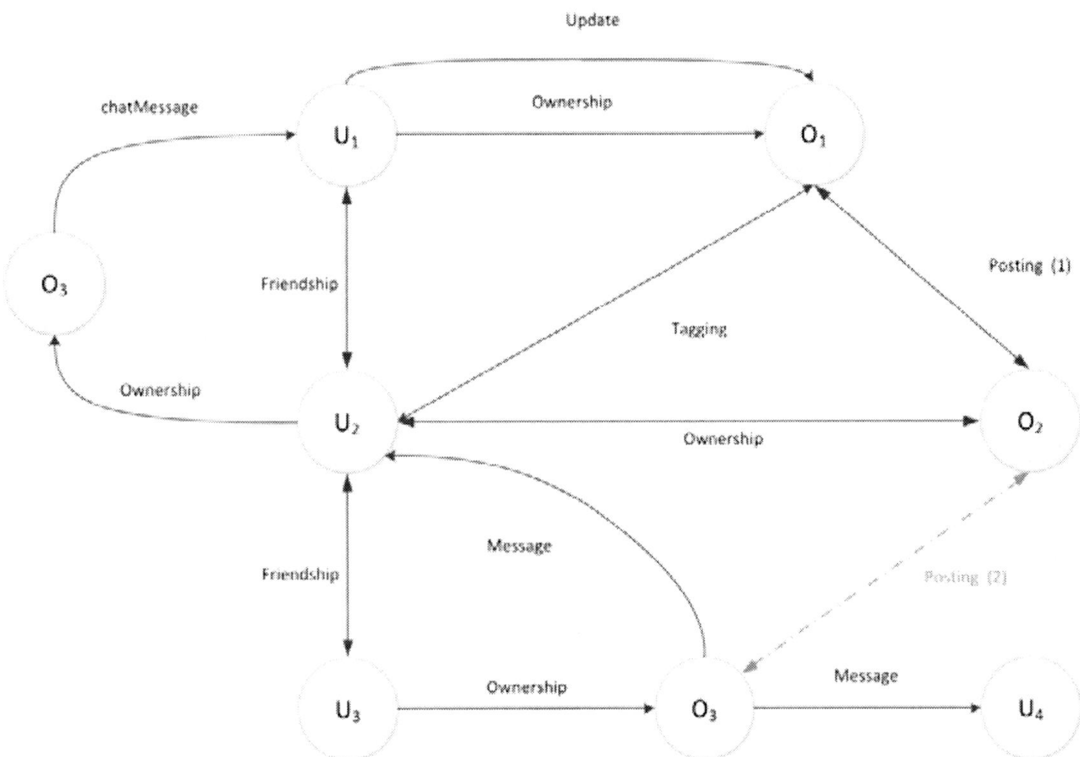

Figure 5. Impact of a successful XSRF attack

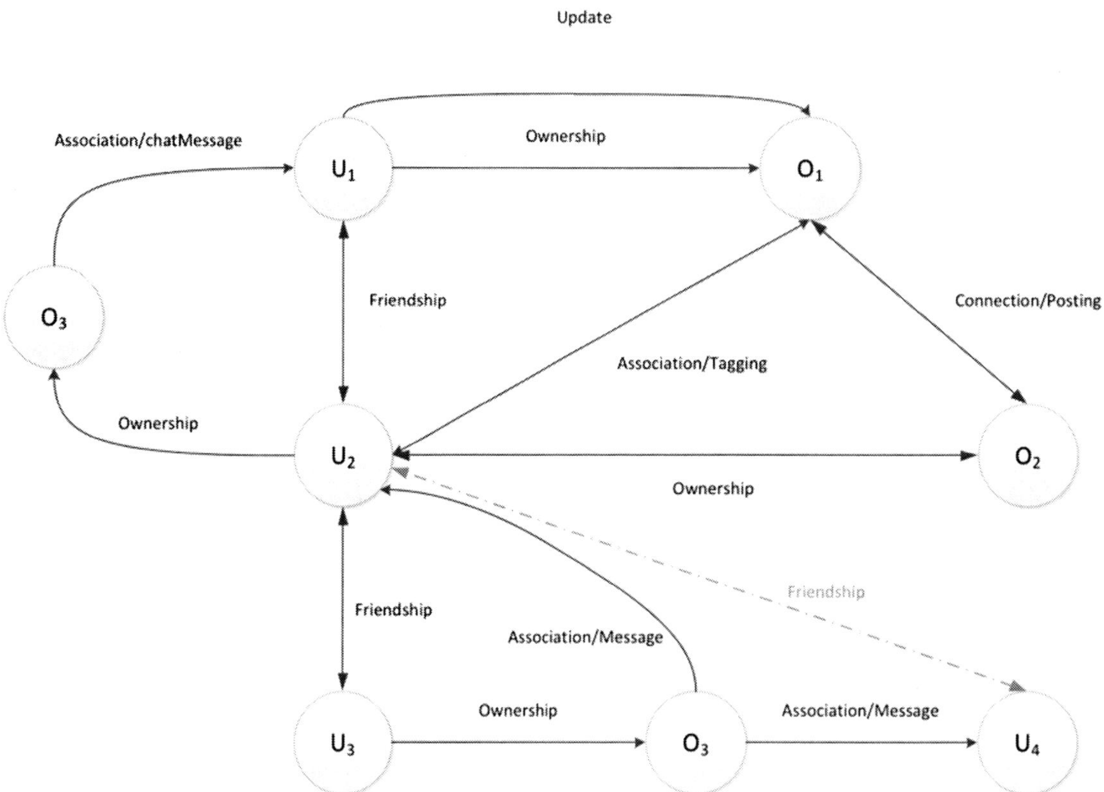

attacks). Concerning access limitations, Internet connectivity is often granted by a cellular network, which is typically billed with a fixed-volume-rate policy. Thus, by considering restrictions imposed by mobile appliances, the multiple session issue may be exploited for battery or subscription consumption attacks. For instance, with reference to the example in Figure 5, an attacker may silently force a user to post different objects by means of his/her smartphone. This would require object to be uploaded from the mobile phone to the OSN. In this case, by means of a malicious message, the user may be forced to upload photos stored in the smartphone to profiles of his/her contacts. In this case, the continuous and unaware posting could lead to consumption of both battery and allotted traffic. Figure 6 shows the impact on the OSN graph. Note that a more sophisticated attack may post object and then delete them, making the attack almost silent.

To enlighten the flexibility of our formalism, finally, let us consider a broken authentication attack, which aims at retrieving valid credentials of users in order to impersonate them. Also in this case, OSNs facilitate the successful execution of these hazards, due to the high number of information available, which can be discovered through suitable operations involving OSN graphs. A typical scenario is when the attacker can exploit a password retrieval service, where a user is challenged on secret information. A malicious entity can try to discover users on the network and to access password retrieval services on their behalf. This can be achieved by using objects acting as "honeypots" (Krawetz, 2004), and the corresponding graph is shown in Figure 7, where u_3 is the malicious user and u_2 performs a tagging operation on the friend u_1.

As a final remark, in all the presented attacks, graphs are transformed through a valid set of

Figure 6. Battery and subscription drain attack

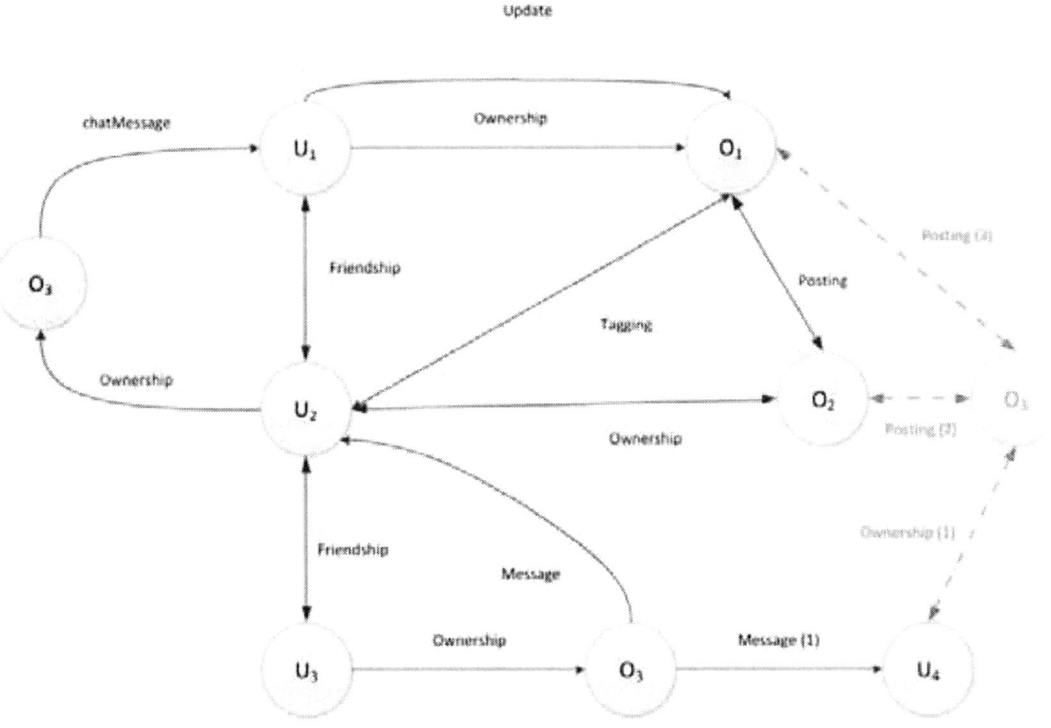

Figure 7. Information retrieval via broken authentication attack

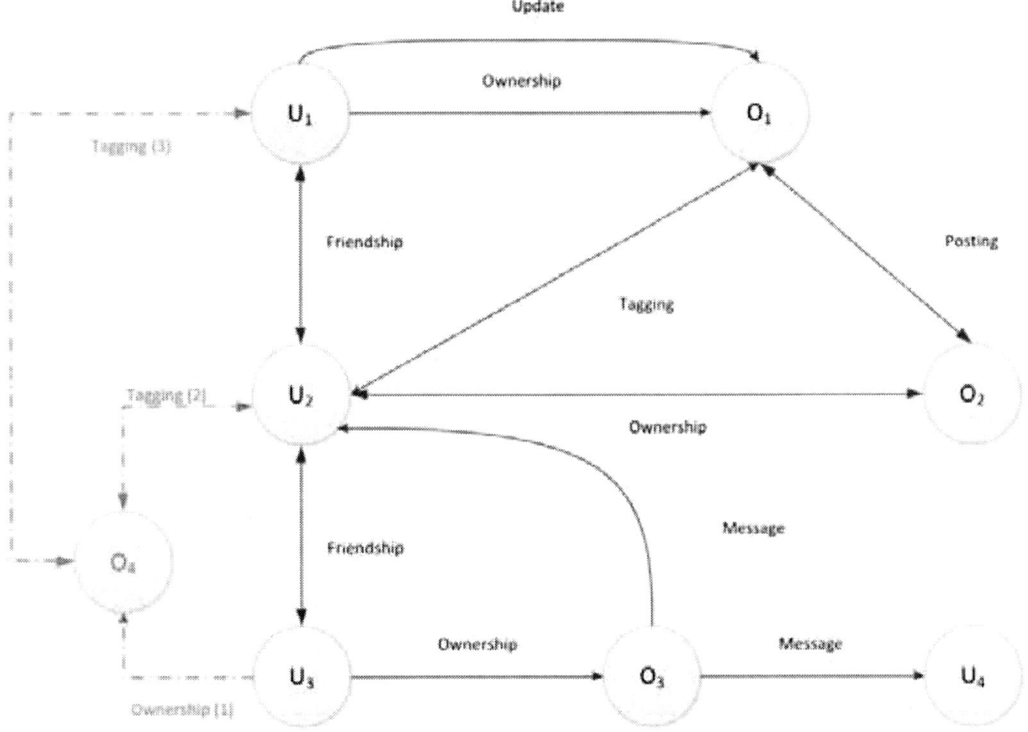

operations, making the discovery of malicious behaviors from the OSN security system very hard. In fact, OSNs usually check for anomalous patterns (e.g., a high number of posting/tagging from a user in a short period of time), but they have no chances to unveil low traffic and sparse attacks. Furthermore, due to the high average number of operations executed on an OSN, it is hard for a generic user to get aware of forced and unwanted operations like those explained in this section. However, the formalization can be used for an off-line analysis (e.g., during the design phase) or to build optimized and focused on-line checking procedures.

CONCLUSION

As a consequence of their popularity and the amount of sensitive data managed, OSNs have many hazards in terms of privacy and security. In this chapter we reviewed the main characteristics of the most popular platforms, the preferred development methodologies, and usage patterns, also by taking into account how personal information can be exploited to conduct malicious actions. Then, we introduced a graph-based modeling approach to reveal possible attacks, as well as to elaborate the needed countermeasures or (automated) checking procedures. To prove the effectiveness of the proposed approach we also modeled some attacks via a general toy OSN application. Future work aims at enriching the number of use-cases, and to produce a prototypal implementation of automated checking software both for revealing breaches and misuses in an on/off line fashion.

REFERENCES

Akre, V., Rizvi, A. H., & Arif, M. (2009). Online social networks - an interface requirements analysis. In *Proceedings of the 2009 IEEE International Symposium on Signal Processing and Information Technology* (pp. 550–556).

Baracaldo, N., Lopez, C., Anwar, M., & Lewis, M. (2011). Simulating the effect of privacy concerns in online social networks. In *Proceedings of the International Conference on Information Reuse and Integration (IRI 2011)* (pp. 519–524).

Bilge, L., Strufe, T., Balzarotti, D., & Kirda, E. (2009). All your contacts are belong to us: Automated identity theft attacks on social networks. In *Proceedings of the 18th International Conference on World Wide Web (WWW '09)* (pp. 551–560).

Boyd, D. M., & Ellison, N. B. (2007). Social network sites: Definition, history, and scholarship. *Journal of Computer-Mediated Community, 13*(1), 210–230. doi:10.1111/j.1083-6101.2007.00393.x

Buchegger, S., Schiöberg, D., Vu, L.-H., & Datta, A. (2009). Peerson: P2P social networking: Early experiences and insights. In *Proceedings of the 2nd ACM EuroSys Workshop on Social Network Systems* (pp. 46–52).

Caviglione, L. (2009). Can satellites face trends? The case of Web 2.0. In *Proceedings of the International Workshop on Satellite and Space Communications (IWSSC'09).*

Caviglione, L. (2011). Extending HTTP models to Web 2.0 applications: The case of social networks. In *Proceedings of the 4th IEEE International Conference on Utility and Cloud Computing (UCC)* (pp. 361–365).

Caviglione, L., & Coccoli, M. (2011). Privacy problems with Web 2.0. *Computer Fraud & Security*, (10): 16–19. doi:10.1016/S1361-3723(11)70104-X

Caviglione, L., Coccoli, M., & Merlo, A. (in press). A taxonomy-based model of security and privacy in online social networks. *International Journal of Computational Science and Engineering.*

Caviglione, L., & Merlo, A. (2012). Energy impact of security mechanisms in modern mobile devices. *Network Security*, (2): 11–14. doi:10.1016/S1353-4858(12)70015-6

Criscione, C., Salvaneschi, G., Maggi, F., & Zanero, S. (2009). Integrated detection of attacks against browsers, web applications and databases. In *Proceedings of the European Conference on Computer Network Defense (EC2ND 2009)* (pp. 37–45).

Cutillo, L. A., Molva, R., & Onen, M. (2011). Safebook: A distributed privacy preserving online social network. In *Proceedings of the 2011 IEEE International Symposium on a World of Wireless, Mobile and Multimedia Networks* (pp.1–3).

Felt, A., & Evans, D. (2008). Privacy protection for social networking platforms. In *Proceedings of Web 2.0 Security and Privacy (W2SP 2008).*

Ferraiolo, D. F., & Kuhn, D. R. (1992). Role based access control. In *Proceedings of the 15th National Computer Security Conference* (pp. 554–563).

Gao, H., Hu, J., Huang, T., Wang, J., & Chen, Y. (2011). Security issues in online social networks. *IEEE Internet Computing*, *15*(4), 56–63. doi:10.1109/MIC.2011.50

Gates, C. E. (2007). Access control requirements for Web 2.0 security and privacy. In *Proceedings of the Workshop on Web 2.0 Security & Privacy (W2SP 2007).*

Guha, S., Tang, K., & Francis, P. (2008). NOYB: Privacy in online social networks. In *Proceedings of the 1st Workshop on Online Social Networks (WOSN 2008)* (pp. 49–54).

Honjo, M., Hasegawa, T., Hasegawa, T., Suda, T., Mishima, K., & Yoshida, T. (2011). A framework to identify relationships among students in school bullying using digital communication media. In *Proceedings of the 3rd IEEE International Conference on Privacy, Security, Risk and Trust (PASSAT), and 2011 3rd IEEE International Conference on Social Computing (SOCIALCOM)* (pp. 1474–1479).

Jahid, S., Nilizadeh, S., Mittal, P., Borisov, N., & Kapadia, A. (2012). DECENT: A decentralized architecture for enforcing privacy in online social networks. In *Proceedings of the IEEE International Conference on Pervasive Computing and Communications Workshops* (pp. 326–332).

Joshi, J. B. D., Aref, W. G., Ghafoor, A., & Spafford, E. H. (2001). Security models for web-based applications. *Communications of the ACM*, *44*(2), 38–44. doi:10.1145/359205.359224

Joshi, P., & Kuo, C.-C. J. (2011). Security and privacy in online social networks: A survey. In *Proceedings of the IEEE International Conference on Multimedia and Expo* (pp. 1–6).

Jun, X., & Wooyong, L. (2003). Sustaining availability of web services under distributed denial of service attacks. *IEEE Transactions on Computers*, *52*(2), 195–208. doi:10.1109/TC.2003.1176986

Krawetz, N. (2004). Anti-honeypot technology. *IEEE Security & Privacy*, *2*(1), 76–79. doi:10.1109/MSECP.2004.1264861

Krishnamurthy, B., & Wills, C. E. (2008). Characterizing privacy in online social networks. In *Proceedings of the Workshop on Online Social Networks* (pp. 37–42).

Kuhn, D. R., Coyne, E. J., & Weil, T. R. (2010). Adding attributes to role based access control. *IEEE Computer*, *43*(6), 79–81. doi:10.1109/MC.2010.155

Laorden, C., Sanz, B., Alvarez, G., & Bringas, P. G. (2010). A threat model approach to threats and vulnerabilities in on-line social networks. *Advances in Intelligent and Soft Computing*, *85*, 135–142. doi:10.1007/978-3-642-16626-6_15

Lucas, M. M., & Borisov, N. (2008). FlyByNight: Mitigating the privacy risks of social networking. In *Proceedings of 7th ACM Workshop on Privacy in the Electronic Society (WPES 2008)* (pp. 1–8).

Luo, W., Xie, Q., & Hengartner, U. (2009). FaceCloak: An architecture for user privacy on social networking sites. In *Proceedings of the International Conference on Computational Science and Engineering, (CSE '09)* (vol. 3, pp. 26–33).

McCallister, E., Grance, T., & Scarfone, K. A. (2010). Guide to protecting the confidentiality of personally identifiable information (PII). Retrieved September, 2012, from http://csrc.nist.gov/publications/nistpubs/800-122/sp800-122.pdf

Narayanan, A., & Shmatikov, V. (2009). Deanonymizing social networks. In *Proceedings of the 30th IEEE Symposium on Security and Privacy* (pp.173–187).

OGP - OpenGraph Protocol. (2012). Website. Retrieved September, 2012, from http://ogp.me

OWASP – The Open Web Application Security Project Homepage. (2012). Website. Retrieved September, 2012, from http://www.owasp.org

Sandhu, R. S., Coyne, E. J., Feinstein, H. L., & Youman, C. E. (1996). Role-based access control models. *IEEE Computer*, *29*(2), 38–47. doi:10.1109/2.485845

Sattikar, A. A., & Kulkarni, R. V. (2011). A review of security and privacy issues in social networking. *International Journal of Computer Science and Information Technologies*, *2*(6), 2784–2787.

Sun, J., Zhu, X., & Fang, Y. (2010). A privacy-preserving scheme for online social networks with efficient revocation. In *Proceedings of the 2010 IEEE INFOCOM* (pp.1–9).

W3C (World Wide Web Consortium) - Incubator Group Report (2010). A standards-based, open and privacy-aware social web. Retrieved September, 2012, from http://www.w3.org/2005/Incubator/socialweb/XGR-socialweb-20101206

Wagner, C., Mitter, S., Strohmaier, M., & Körner, C. (2012). When social bots attack: Modeling susceptibility of users in online social networks. In *Proceedings of the Workshop Making Sense of Microposts (#MSM2012)* (pp. 41–48).

Wireshark, the Worlds Foremost Network Analyzer (2012). Website. Retrieved September, 2012, from http://www.wireshark.org

Wondracek, G., Holz, T., Kirda, E., Antipolis, S., & Kruegel, C. (2010). A practical attack to deanonymize social network users. In *Proceedings of the 2010 IEEE Symposium on Security and Privacy* (pp. 223–238).

Yeung, C. A., Liccardi, I., Lu, K., Seneviratne, O., & Berners-Lee, T. (2009). Decentralization: The future of online social networking. *W3C Workshop on the Future of Social Networking.* Position Paper.

Zhang, C., Sun, J., Zhu, X., & Fang, Y. (2010). Privacy and security for online social networks: Challenges and opportunities. *IEEE Network*, *24*(4), 13–18. doi:10.1109/MNET.2010.5510913

ADDITIONAL READING

Brentham, J. (2002). TCP/IP lean (Web servers for embedded systems). CMPBooks.

Haifeng, Yu., Gibbons, P. B., Kaminsky, M., & Feng, X. (2010). SybilLimit: A near-optimal social network defense against sybil attacks. *IEEE/ACM Transactions on Networking*, *18*(3), 885–898. doi:10.1109/TNET.2009.2034047

Hongyu, G., Jun, H., Tuo, H., Jingnan, W., & Yan, C. (2011). Security issues in online social networks. *IEEE Internet Computing*, *15*(4), 56–63. doi:10.1109/MIC.2011.50

Jagatic, T. N., Johnson, N. A., Jakobsson, M., & Menczer, F. (2007). Social phishing. *Communications of the ACM*, *50*(10), 94–100. doi:10.1145/1290958.1290968

Rosenblum, D. (2007). What anyone can know: The privacy risks of social networking sites. *IEEE Security & Privacy*, *5*(3), 40–49. doi:10.1109/MSP.2007.75

Ruiz Vicente, C., Freni, D., Bettini, C., & Jensen, C. S. (2011). Location-related privacy in geo-social networks. *IEEE Internet Computing*, *15*(3), 20–27. doi:10.1109/MIC.2011.29

Stajano, F., & Wilson, P. (2011). Understanding scam victims: Seven principles for systems security. *Communications of the ACM*, *54*(3), 70–75. doi:10.1145/1897852.1897872

Chapter 10
Security and Privacy of Online Social Network Applications

Willem De Groef
iMinds–DistriNet, KU Leuven, Belgium

Dominique Devriese
iMinds–DistriNet, KU Leuven, Belgium

Tom Reynaert
iMinds–DistriNet, KU Leuven, Belgium

Frank Piessens
iMinds–DistriNet, KU Leuven, Belgium

ABSTRACT

An important recent innovation on social networking sites is the support for plugging in third-party social applications. Together with the ever-growing number of social network users, social applications come with privacy and security risks for those users. While basic mechanisms for isolating applications are well understood, these mechanisms fall short for social-enabled applications. It is an interesting challenge to design and develop application platforms for social networks that enable the necessary functionality of social applications without compromising both users' security and privacy. This chapter will identify and discuss the current security and privacy problems related to social applications and their platforms. Next, it will zoom in on proposals on how to address those problems.

INTRODUCTION

Today social networking sites are ubiquitous and inseparable from the digital world. They host an important part of the online communication and contain the majority of people's personal information that is available on the World Wide Web. The monetary worth of this huge amount of information is ever increasing, resulting in mind-blowing market values.

Ever since Facebook launched their application development environment, social application platforms – together with their applications itself - are ubiquitous in the context of social network-

DOI: 10.4018/978-1-4666-3926-3.ch010

ing sites. Almost every major social networking site nowadays provides means to consult personal user data from their social graph. Third-party social applications spread through the online communities and the popularity of these social applications keeps increasing. Support for such third-party applications is an important contributor to the overall success of social network sites (Pham, 2011).

Typical for these social-aware applications, is that the code provider typically is a third stakeholder, different from the social network site and the end user. Because an application has access to social data, also the application provider itself gets access. Given the growing amount of privacy-sensitive social data on social network sites, this becomes more and more an undesirable situation.

In this chapter we will focus on these privacy and security problems in the context of *online social network applications*. In this context, third-party application are typically developed in client-side scripting languages like JavaScript – which will be executed in the user's browser - often in combination with server-side technologies like PHP or Java – fueling the back-end part of the application.

The first objective of this chapter is to introduce the details — both the architectural and technological - of the previous and current social application platforms. The second objective is to identify three different categories based on these security/privacy related problems. The third objective is to examine what recent scientific literature tries to do in order to address those problems.

BACKGROUND

According to Facebook, people install such applications more than 20 million times per day, day after day (Facebook, 2011). However, the use of such applications comes with privacy and security risk for the social network users.

Trusting Facebook, Google, and other big social network providers to respect your privacy, is hard to avoid when using social networking sites. Trusting each third-party application developer to respect the policies, imposed by the social network providers and to respect the user's privacy, is less justified.

An investigation conducted by the *Wall Street Journal*, published October 18, 2010, claimed that nearly every popular Facebook application was leaking – in some way or another – privacy-sensitive information to other parties, such as Internet tracking companies and advertising companies (Steel & Fowler, 2010).

The basic isolation mechanisms for applications fall short for social-enabled applications: they need more fine-grained control both of the access that these applications have to information, as well as how this information is used after access has been granted. There have been various reported incidents of information leakages by social applications. Mills (2008) report on some applications allowing to peak into the social graph because they are vulnerable for a peephole vulnerability that allowed anyone to view private information. Other applications unintentionally leak private social data – while some even do this on purpose (Steel & Fowler, 2010; Kelly, 2008).

Hence, it is an interesting software engineering challenge to design an application platform for social networks that enables the rich functionality of social applications, but mitigates both security and privacy risks as much as possible.

SECURITY AND PRIVACY OF ONLINE SOCIAL NETWORK APPLICATION PLATFORMS

This section will cover two main implementation models for social network application platforms. Next it will dig into the different security and privacy issues resulting from the design choices made in each implementation model. Finally, it will survey three proposals for more privacy-enhanced social application platforms.

Implementation Models

There exist roughly two different architectures for the implementation of social web applications. The earliest implementation model supports deployment of applications on the social network site infrastructure itself. In this so-called *gadget paradigm*, the application is described in an XML specification and embedded within the social network site infrastructure. This XML file will be loaded, converted and displayed in the context of the social network site in order to deploy the application. In this paradigm, the social network site has total control over the application's code and inserts the social data where needed. The social network site plugs the augmented code of the application in its own code. This approach allows the social network site to exercise a reasonable level of control over the application, as it can freely modify the code.

The growing trend amongst current social network sites, however, is to roll out a different approach: the social network site offers an API to query its data over HTTP. Using protocols such as OAuth, a user can delegate access to his social data to an application provider. The social application can then query the social network API over HTTP. As a consequence of this so-called *distributed paradigm*, social applications no longer have to be integrated in the social network site infrastructure itself.

The benefit for application providers is twofold. First, developers are no longer restricted to the site-specific technologies offered by the social network site. Second, the provider has complete control over its application code. One of the benefits of this paradigm shift for the social network site is the removal of the complex conversion process for the XML specifications. However, this second model comes with additional security and privacy risks.

In this section of the chapter, we will describe the two main architectures for supporting social applications in more detail, as it is the crucial stepping-stone to identify the security and privacy threats.

Gadget Approach

Facebook launched their application development platform on May 24, 2007. In the months after the release, Facebook introduced the Facebook Markup Language (FBML) and Facebook JavaScript (FBJS). FBML is an extension of HTML and provides special tags to extract user-specific data from the social graph. A tag like <fb:name uid="12345"/> can be used to extract the name of the user with id 12345 from the social graph and embed it within the HTML page rendered in the browser. FBJS is a limited, safe subset of standard JavaScript. Facebook can rewrite this subset of JavaScript in such a way that it is safe to embed the application directly into the wrapping Facebook page, without the risk of the wrapping page being compromised by the application's JavaScript e.g., by leaking private information embedded within the page. With these two programming tools in hand, developers could start to design third-party applications for Facebook.

In this setting, applications are in fact simple documents – containing both FBML and FBJS – that have to be transmitted to Facebook in order to become a real social application. When a user wants to use an application, she browses to the application page inside Facebook. Facebook will then translate the FBML tags of the application and convert the FBJS to regular JavaScript. The result is a combination of regular HTML and JavaScript that is embedded in the corresponding Facebook page. Figure 1 illustrates the working of the original FBML/FBJS approach of Facebook applications.

Figure 1. Architectural overview of the gadget approach using FBML and FBJS

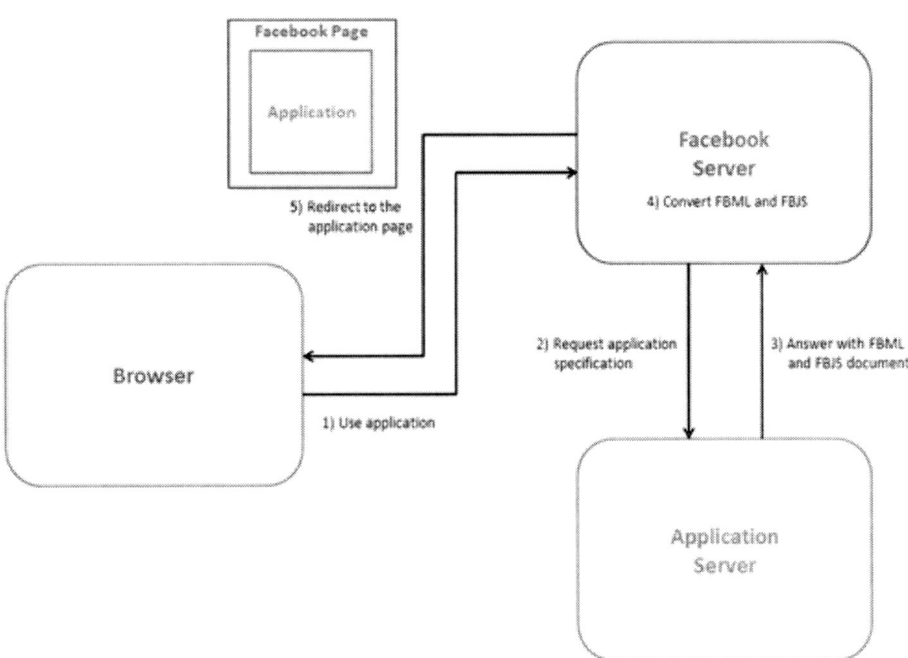

Recently, Facebook decided to change the strategy behind their application platform (Beard, 2010). They chose to shift their focus from the rather static FBML/FBJS to a more distributed approach, in order to give developers the opportunity to create more dynamic applications using regular JavaScript and HTML instead of FBJS and FBML. In April 2010, Facebook launched their Graph API, a RESTful API to extract data from the social graph. The strategy behind this RESTful concept is that it works with simple HTTP requests towards the Facebook servers, based on a unique social-entity-id. Facebook responds with the desired information in the accessible JSON[1] format.

This new strategy allows application developers to design applications that are less interleaved with the Facebook platform internals. Applications can get the desired social information directly from the server. Thus, Facebook is no longer needed as a proxy between the application server and the user, injecting the social context into the application page on the fly.

In a more distributed approach, the application is typically hosted on a server under its own domain name. When the application is accessed as a page in the context of Facebook, this domain is loaded inside an iframe in the Facebook page. This separates the DOM of the wrapping Facebook page from the DOM of the application page, providing enough protection for the sensitive Facebook data.

Together with the introduction of the distributed approach, Facebook made its authorization policy more fine-grained. In the early days, users had only two privacy options for applications: allow the application to access all personal data, or deny it to use any data. Since April 2010, applications have to ask different kinds of permissions from the user, to access different kinds of information. This approach provides more transparency, and allows the user to make a better, well-consistent decision.

Unlike Facebook, other important social networking sites, such as Google, MySpace, Yahoo and Netlog, united their efforts to provide a uniform interoperable social application platform. The specifications of this platform were called OpenSocial and were launched in November 2007. At first sight, the OpenSocial standards are a promising competitor for the aforementioned Facebook platform.

An OpenSocial platform is quite similar to the Facebook platform as it also supports two different strategies to develop applications interacting with a social network, although less separated than those of the Facebook platform. The first strategy is a rather static approach in which the application is provided in an XML file as illustrated in Figure 2. This is called the gadget setting of an application. The XML file is converted and embedded in a wrapping page from the social networking site, similar to Facebook's FBML/FBJS approach. In this setting, applications can make calls to the wrapping social network using a JavaScript API. This strategy of directly embedding applications in a wrapping social networking site page poses the same security problems as in the Facebook platform. For this reason, the OpenSocial gadget strategy is often combined with the use of Caja (Capabilities JavaScript)[2], which is used in the same way as FBJS on the Facebook Platform.

As a second strategy, OpenSocial also provides a RESTful API to communicate with the social networking site. Under this model, applications operate under a separate domain or are contained in an iframe inside the social networking site. It is completely similar to the working of Facebook's Graph API in combination with the iframe setting.

Gadgets are the oldest form of embedded third-party applications in websites. As Facebook is deprecating the gadget approach, our focus will be more on the OpenSocial specification of gadgets. The general idea behind this approach is not complex. The application developer makes his application available somewhere online in a document version. Figure 2 shows how this is typically done using the XML format. In this document, the application developer provides a set of preferences and meta-information on how to run the application. As we can expect, the largest part of the document consists of the application's HTML (or FBML) and limited JavaScript.

The social networking site transforms this document later on into an application that is embedded inside the wrapping page.

Now imagine that we want to add some social context to our application. We could, as an example, change the code in Figure 2 from a simple gadget into a simple social gadget, by making the greeting personal. The corresponding

Figure 2. XML specification of a basic OpenSocial gadget

```
<Module>
  <ModulePrefs title="Hello World!">
    <Require feature="opensocial-0.8" />
  </ModulePrefs>
  <Content type="html" view="canvas">
    <![CDATA[
    <!-- HTML and JS content be here, just as if this were the
    <body> content of a web site -->
    <script type="text/javaScript">alert(\'Helloworld!\')</script>
    <h2>Hello world!</h2>
    ]]>
  </Content>
</Module>
```

XML file in Figure 3 shows that it is enough to use JavaScript code to request the nickname of the current viewer. The JavaScript API provides much more social data requests besides the one illustrated in the example. The OpenSocial JS API supports also these JavaScript API calls. All OpenSocial implementing partners are supposed to implement the OpenSocial APIs. Hence the XML specification of the very basic social application in Figure 3 is portable across all OpenSocial supporting platforms. A developer can specify one application in the OpenSocial XML format, post it somewhere online and point to it from different OpenSocial supporting social networking sites.

It is important to notice that in the gadget setting, there is no need for user authentication: because the user is already logged in with the social networking site and the application is running directly inside the page of the same social networking site, the user's identity and information can easily be transmitted to the application, without the need of extra user-authentication. It is the responsibility of the social networking site to ask the user to explicitly allow the application to access her personal data.

Distributed Approach

The distributed approach is a newer strategy to provide the necessary framework for third-party applications. In this approach, the developer hosts the application under its own domain name. Whenever the application is accessed inside the context of the social networking site, it is simply loaded into an iframe inside that social networking site and its way of operation doesn't change a bit. To support the social setting of this kind of applications that have no direct connection with the social networking site, the platform typically provides REST APIs. These APIs provide a HTTP interface to access social data. The REST-requests can be issued from the application server, from a browser or from anywhere else. Facebook and OpenSocial call their REST API, respectively, Graph API and OpenSocial REST API.

In contrast to the gadget approach in which no explicit authentication and authorization from the user are needed because the application runs inside the social networking site, the distributed approach requires an authentication procedure. Both Facebook and OpenSocial use the OAuth2.0 protocol to authenticate a user. This procedure allows a

Figure 3. XML specification of an OpenSocial Gadget

```
<Module> <ModulePrefs title="Hello World!">
    <Require feature="opensocial-0.8" />
  </ModulePrefs> <Content type="html">
<![CDATA[
    <script type="text/javaScript">
    function onViewerInfoLoaded(response) {
      alert('Welcome ' +
        response.get('viewerInfo').getData().getField('nickname'));}
    function loadViewerInfo(){
      var req = opensocial.newDataRequest();var extraParams = {};
      extraParams[opensocial.DataRequest.PeopleRequestFields.PROFILE_
        DETAILS] = ['nickname', opensocial.Person.Field.THUMBNAIL_URL];
      req.add(req.newFetchPersonRequest(opensocial.IdSpec.PersonId.
        VIEWER, extraParams), "viewerInfo");
      req.send(onViewerInfoLoaded);}
     gadgets.util.registerOnLoadHandler(loadViewerInfo);</script> ]]>
 </Content> </Module>
```

user to give the application access to her private data without having to hand out her credentials. Facebook adds a fine-grained permission model on top of the basic user authentication. We give the authentication and authorization procedure for the Facebook platform.

- The user loads the homepage of the application in his browser either directly under its domain name or inside an iframe in the context of the social networking site.
- The starting page of the application contains JavaScript code to guide the user through the authentication and authorization procedure with the social networking site. This can be done by automatically redirecting the user's browser to a URL like https://www.facebook.com/dialog/oauth?client_id=YOUR_APP_ID&redirect_uri=YOUR_URL&scope=email,friends_likes&response_type=token.
- If the user is not yet logged in to Facebook, he logs in.
- Then he grants the requested access rights to the application.
- Facebook generates an access token for this user and this application, appends this token to the *redirect_url* and redirects the browser back to the application YOUR_URL#accesstoken.
- The application server saves the access token, and redirects the browser to the starting page of the application.

With this access token the application can start to issue the requests for social data to the social application platform. After successfully finishing the OAuth2.0 procedure, the following request, GET https://graph.facebook.com/me/email?&access_token=accesstoken will return the e-mail address of the user who did the authorization procedure. The OpenSocial procedure is similar, apart from a far more coarse-grained permission model. In Facebook there are many different permissions, providing the user with a certain transparency. OpenSocial only provides one specific permission: allow or deny the application to access all of your data.

Issuing these REST-requests with JavaScript from within the browser, poses a problem concerning the Same-Origin Policy of the browser. A certain origin – a triplet consisting of domain name, port, and protocol – is not allowed to access data from another origin. For example, the application running under the domain www.yourapplication.com will not be allowed to directly access data coming from www.socialnetworkingsite.com. The use of JSONP[3], a standard technique to circumvent the Same Origin Policy in many situations, solves this problem.

Security and Privacy Issues

The current state of the art design of social application platforms raises several risks concerning the user's privacy-sensitive information when using third-party applications. This section addresses some of the most important issues concerning these privacy risks, both on architectural and on implementation level. As the distributed approach gains popularity and even seems to replace the gadget approach, we mainly focus on the distributed approach for the rest of this chapter.

Due to the growing popularity of social application platforms and the growing support for APIs to access social data, addressing the security issues of exposing social data to third party applications becomes important. A key problem is the total loss of control by the social network site whenever sensitive information reaches the application provider. Once a social application obtains sensitive information, it is impossible for the social network site to revoke access to information or to enforce any restrictions on where the information can or may flow to. As evidenced by Steel & Fowler (2010), Mills (2008), and Spencer (2008), this problem has become a real-world threat for social application users.

In this section of the chapter we will illustrate these security issues present in the two common implementation models for social applications discussed in the previous section.

Privacy Protection Policy

In the original privacy policy of almost all social networking sites, an application has the same view of the social network as its users. Under the pressure of the public opinion, some big social networking sites like Facebook and Google+ were forced to improve their original privacy policy. Nowadays, social networking sites tend to ask the user to agree with giving the application permission to access her data and put the responsibility of privacy protection in the hands of the end user. This strategy legally protects the social networking sites, as the user explicitly shares her data with the application. However, it can be hard for users to make a well-considered decision, especially since there is a lot of social pressure involved with using social applications.

It is important to note that OpenSocial still doesn't work with a fine-grained permission model, neither for their gadget approach nor their distributed approach, but implementers could always decide to enhance this model within their implementation.

Leaking of Social Data

The first important consequence of the current architecture of social network platforms is the fact that once the sensitive data has reached the application server, neither the user nor the social networking site can control the flow of the data anymore (see Figure 4). This is because of the fact that the application itself is running on servers out-of-control of the social networking site. The application providers have total control of all incoming information – received because the application's user allowed it. Although the application developer is legally prohibited to pass the sensitive data to third parties, there are currently no technically mechanisms to enforce this

Figure 4. Distributed social application platform design

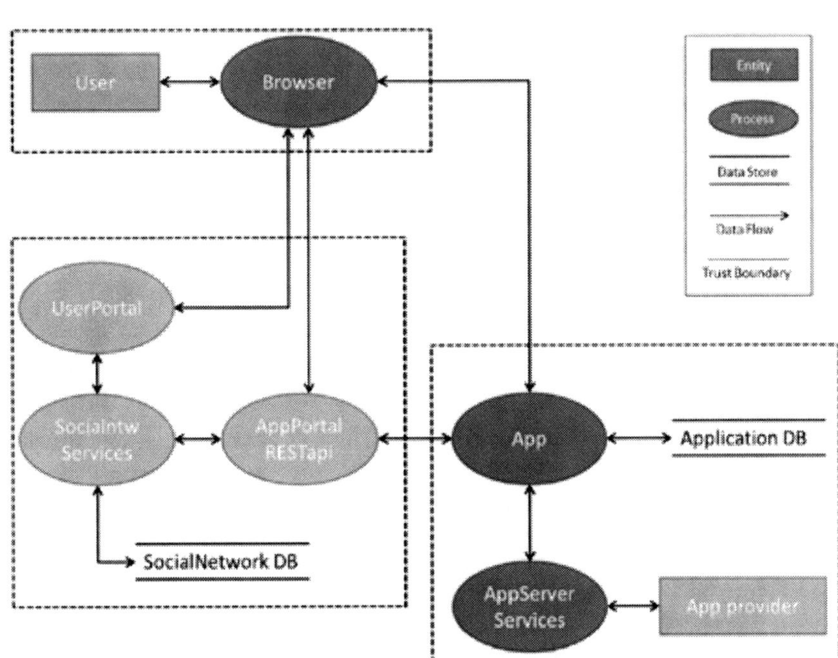

partly because the source code of the application is mainly invisible for the end-user.

A *Wall Street Journal* investigation claimed that nearly every popular Facebook application leaked, in some way or another, sensitive private information to other parties, such as Internet tracking companies and advertising companies (Steel & Fowler, 2010). This transfer of personal information happened without the knowledge of the users. Of course, the companies behind the applications were quick to minimize the impact. They promised to fix the bug that caused the privacy breaches and after a short time of quarantine their applications were still running.

The article showed that most application developers do not hesitate to make money by selling the private information of their users. The article also showed that it is extremely difficult to verify whether every application sticks to the privacy policies - let alone to legally pursue the developers behind it in case of fraudulent behavior. Finally, it also showed that social networking sites and country laws imposing rules and policies upon third-parties are a good way to protect the privacy when there are adequate control mechanisms to verify their compliance with those rules, which is definitely not the case for the current architecture.

Issues with Access Tokens

In the current distributed design of social application platforms, access tokens play an important role in protecting the user's privacy. With a valid access token, any third-party can authenticate a request. It can even spoof that a request was allowed from a specific user. A crucial factor in the use of these access tokens appears to be their lifetime.

Facebook Access Tokens

As described earlier, a Facebook access token is the result of a successful OAuth2.0 user authentication process. Facebook keeps an access token valid for about 60 minutes. After they expire, the application has to redirect the user back to the OAuth2.0 authentication procedure to renew the access token. For convenience, Facebook remembers that the user already granted a certain set of permissions to the application and the user's permission is given implicitly when authenticating. Facebook remembers this set of granted permissions as long as the application is present in the set of applications in the profile of the user. Thus, only when a user runs an application for the first time (or after she removed the application from her applications list), she is required to grant explicitly her permissions; all consecutive times, Facebook will implicitly grant the same permissions.

In order to protect the privacy of Facebook's users, RESTful data requests are only answered when the user is – at the same time of the request – logged in to Facebook. Obviously, Facebook also requires the user to be logged in during any explicit or implicit authentication procedure. So in theory, an application has access to the user's data during the time that the user is logged in to Facebook and until at most one hour after she stopped using the application. After that time, the application would need to renew the access token, however to obtain this token it would have to redirect the browser of the user back to the OAuth2.0 endpoint of the Facebook platform, and this is not possible. Because the user has stopped running the application, code is no longer present in the browser and the application has no longer the possibility of redirecting the user.

Strangely, Facebook offers one violation of this principle. Let us recall the scope parameter in the example of the Facebook OAuth2.0 procedure. When an application developer puts the *offline_access* permission in scope and the user grants this permission, the access token doesn't expire and the data can be accessed even when the user is not logged in to Facebook. This means that her data is accessible for the application provider, any time from now on until she actively removes the application from her profile page.

OpenSocial Access Tokens

An OpenSocial access token, by default, doesn't come with an expiration date. It is up to the implementing OpenSocial container to manage the validity of access tokens. However, OpenSocial standards provide a way to refresh the access token. The application simply has to send the longer-life refresh token that comes together with an access token. The container will respond with a new short-life access token.

OpenSocial's mechanisms to protect the privacy of users are much weaker. The OpenSocial framework doesn't provide any granularity for the permissions included in its access token. It is up to the implementing containers to manage different granularities of permissions. In practice this means that OpenSocial applications often have access to the same kind of data that the user has access to. This contains the user's private data and all the data that other people share with the user.

In contrast to the Facebook platform, where a user always has to go through an explicit or implicit OAuth2.0 procedure before the application acquires an access token, OpenSocial has an alternative built in to circumvent this OAuth2.0 procedure. OpenSocial provides code for getting the security token from inside the gadget setting without any user interaction. This means that an OpenSocial gadget can obtain an access token, even without directing a user through the OAuth2.0 procedure. This can be dangerous because the access token provides the opportunity to access all private information of the user, as we discussed before. First of all, the user doesn't know that she provided the gadget with an access token that gives access to her complete profile. On top of that, there isn't a proper mechanism to revoke the access that is given to the third parties holding this access token.

There can be another privacy problem in an OpenSocial implementation: let's assume that an access token has a lifetime of 20 minutes after the last time it was used. This means that by generating dummy requests every 15 minutes an application developer can keep this token valid for eternity. This makes things worse – in contrast to the Facebook platform – because a user doesn't have to be online to get the answer to a REST-request from the OpenSocial platform. Finally wrapping everything together, this means that once you played a game, the application developer behind this game possibly has an access token that provides access to all of your social data. The access token can be used indefinitely and there is no clear way to revoke it.

Conclusion

We can conclude that the current design of social application platforms is far from privacy friendly. Personal sensitive information can leak away through third-party applications without the user knowing when and to whom this information is sent. On top of that it is not always very clear how to revoke the access rights once granted to third-party applications. The situation is even worse for static data like an e-mail address. Once the user granted permission to an application to read her e-mail address, there is nothing the user or her favorite social networking site can do to restrict its further spreading over the Internet.

As opposed to Facebook – that performed some updates of its platform under pressure of its users to provide a certain legally justified user privacy towards third-party applications – OpenSocial has not yet included these privacy improvements in their design.

Privacy-Enhanced Social Application Platforms

Although the subject is on the verge of scientific study, there are already some suggestions for privacy-enhanced social application platforms in the academic literature. This last section summarizes these different strategies that partially solve the privacy issues discussed above.

This section will survey and compare three different approaches. A first approach was to anonymize social data before handing it over to the application provider. Another idea was to apply concepts from information flow analysis on social applications to contain and regulate information flowing in and out of the application. The third we will discuss is a countermeasure to prevent access tokens from ever leaving the browser.

Privacy-by-Proxy

Already in the early days of the integration of third-party applications with social networking sites, Felt and Evans (2008) uncovered the privacy problems concerning these applications and came up with a solution. As their work already got published in 2008, they based their research on the first Facebook approach, the FBML/FBJS strategy. Although the limitation of their solution to the gadget approach is currently outdated, it was justified in 2008 and is therefore worth to be studied. Being the first to address privacy problems with social application platforms, they did pioneering work both in studying the state of the art in those days and in proposing a solution for the problem. They focused in their work on the Facebook approach, although they argued that it would also work in the OpenSocial gadget approach.

Felt and Evans (2008) propose an implementation for a privacy-enhanced social application platform based on what they call *privacy-by-proxy*. In the gadget approach, the social networking site always hosts the application inside its own page, and it performs a translation from FBML and FBJS to regular HTML and JavaScript. Hence the social networking site acts as a proxy between the application's code and the visualization towards the user.

Felt and Evans (2008) propose to encrypt user ids in order to anonymize the contents of the social graph. The applications are only allowed to work with this anonymized data. They also extend the markup language to include tags that allow working with these anonymized ids. For example, <uval id="[$id]" field="birthday" /> would put the birthday of the user on the screen, based on her anonymized id. Upon the request for the friends of a certain user, an application gets a list of anonymized ids. This way an application can only work with an anonymized social graph. It is very important that de-anonymized data doesn't return to the application server. Because their solution works in the gadget approach, the social networking site has the possibility to statically check – i.e., before it has the chance to get executed – whether the contained JavaScript (FBJS) doesn't leak any data.

This implementation needs one more element to make it completely secure. There has to be a limitation in the set of tags that are translated in the application of a certain user. It is necessary to de-anonymize the birthday of a friend. However, the social networking site should not de-anonymize the birthday of a stranger, because in that case an evil application developer could install its own application and create an extra page in which he exhaustively de-anonymizes his whole database. Felt and Evans (2008) solve this problem by only de-anonymizing data from users that appear on a certain contact list. This list summarizes all people with whom the user has had some sort of interaction.

Felt and Evans (2008) tested their implementation, and only a small minority of the popular Facebook applications of those days would stop working. This proved that the approach was both secure and maintained the important functionality of third-party applications. However, since Facebook and OpenSocial introduced their distributed approach, the social networking site lost its role as proxy between the application and the user. Hence it can no longer translate the tags in a privacy concise way or prevent the private data from being leaked to the application server, as the application server can request personal data directly.

xBook

Singh, Bhola, and Lee (2009) came up with a different, more complex solution addressing the privacy issues concerning social third-party applications – called xBook. It is an architectural framework that combines a social networking site with untrusted third-party applications. It provides a container in which the third-party applications are deployed. That way the xBook framework can monitor and regulate all information streams that pass through the third-party application.

As xBook is a complete architecture that contains both the client side and server side implementation of the third-party applications, it has the possibility to impose strong regulation mechanisms. In order to do this, third-party applications are split up into different components. The subdivision of the components is based on their interaction with third parties and handling of private data. For example: one client side component renders the application's pages in the web browser together with the privacy sensitive data; while another client side component is in charge of communicating with a third-party server. In this setting the second component doesn't have access to the private information contained in the first component. The only way that components can send data to each other is by using xBook as a mediator.

Upon installation of the application, a manifest is presented to the user stating which data will be accessed and shared with which third parties. During operation, xBook verifies that the different components – forming the application – keep to the policy. This strategy gives xBook a powerful mechanism to regulate information streams and make data transfers explicit to the user. The same ideas are implemented for the server side components as well. xBook mediates all inter-component communication and because each component has its own responsibility, it knows where and how private data leaks out of the system.

xBook works in a very rigid way: it addresses all the privacy related issues, discussed in the first part of this chapter. However, the framework comes with some disadvantages. First of all, it is a complex system. It has to statically or dynamically check whether the components behave like they are assumed to behave. For example, a component that has access to private information cannot make calls to third-party servers. This strategy involves the use of JavaScript libraries like Caja or alike for the client side components, and statically checking its compliance. It also requires a server side labeling method to prevent that data leaks unnoticed out of the framework. On top of all these control mechanisms the application server components also run inside of the social networking site's framework, consuming server resources. Finally, even when a social networking site decides to provide the servers and implement all the control mechanisms, it is very unlikely that third-party applications will be happy to provide all their code, even that of the server side, to the social network.

We can conclude that xBook is a theoretically excellent solution for the privacy issues addressed in this chapter. However, disadvantages of xBook are its complexity and possibly the unwillingness of third-party developers to make applications for the framework.

PoX

The third example of a privacy-enhanced social application platform that can be found in the literature is called PoX (Egele, Moser, Kruegel, & Kirda, 2011). It is based on a client-side-proxy idea. The design focuses on providing a privacy-secure environment when using the applications in the distributed approach. The fact that applications can request privacy-sensitive information from the social networking site without the users even being aware of it, poses a major privacy issue in the distributed setting. The third-party application only needs the right access token to get access to the desired information.

PoX introduces a client-side-proxy that mitigates this kind of unnoticed data exchanges by preventing that the access token ever leaves the browser. Without this access token, no third-party can get private data from the social networking site; hence all data exchanges have to pass through the client-side-proxy in the browser. Applications have to request data to the client-side-proxy in the browser of the user. Based on policies – set by the client in an access control list (ACL) – PoX decides whether to forward the request to the social networking site and send the data back to the application server or whether it ignores the request. In this design the user herself can monitor and regulate which personal data are transmitted to third-party applications and which data have to remain confident.

In detail, PoX consists of (1) a plug-in for the browser that filters the access token from the HTTP stream and (2) some code running inside a hidden iframe in the browser. This code uses a technique known as 'long polling' to configure the server-to-client communication. When the application is loaded, the PoX code that resides in the browser makes an HTTP request to the application server and tries to fetch a kind of dynamic webpage. As long as the application doesn't need information, it stalls the response to this request. Once it needs extra personal information, the server generates a response containing the data request. The PoX code decides whether it should forward the request. If yes, it forwards the social networking site's answer to the request and the system goes back into the stalling modus.

In contrast to xBook, PoX is a very lightweight privacy protection mechanism. Despite this relatively simple design it reaches a lot of its goals. With PoX, a user can manage her privacy settings according to her own wishes, and enforce on her own that those wishes are respected. However, both xBook and PoX suffer from the same problem, as the user can still be misled by a third-party application. Imagine for example the case in which a user makes a mistake and trusts an evil third-party application, and she grants access to her personal data. In both designs the third-party application can send this sensitive data to another third-party server out of the control boundary of xBook and PoX. Because of this one-time mistake, the user has lost her information and has no way of revoking the access rights of that information.

FUTURE RESEARCH DIRECTIONS

The three examples found in literature and described earlier, each provide a different interesting point of view on the subject. However, none of them completely solves the earlier listed issues. The approach of Felt and Evans (2008) shows some interesting aspects of anonymization, but unfortunately the social application platforms have evolved a lot since the publication: the solution doesn't work anymore for the distributed approach. Both xBook and PoX map better on the current state-of-the-art social application platforms, but they do not prevent that social data leaks away to servers beyond the control of the user or the social networking site. These findings suggest that there is no privacy enhanced social application platform that maps on the current state of the art and still prevents sensitive data to leak away.

In the distributed approach to social application platforms, maintaining privacy guarantees is essentially an information flow problem (Sabelfeld & Myers, 2003). Third party code gets access to sensitive information and should be prevented from leaking that information to inappropriate channels.

Fortunately, the information flow security community has made significant steps forward over the past decade. In particular, several static and dynamic approaches to enforce information flow security in JavaScript-like languages have been proposed (Hedin & Sabelfeld, 2012; Hedin & Sabelfeld, 2012; Austin & Flanagan, 2012; Chugh, Meister, Jhala, & Lerner, 2009; Bielova, Devriese,

Massaci, & Piessens, 2011; Devriese & Piessens, 2010). Hence, we believe that a promising avenue for future work is the application of these enforcement mechanisms to social applications.

CONCLUSION

The two largest social application platforms – the Facebook platform and the OpenSocial standards – both support the distributed approach to integrate third-party applications within their framework. The OpenSocial gadget approach poses some serious security and privacy risks, so it is questionable whether it will be around for a long time. A support for this claim can be found in the deprecation of Facebook's gadget approach in January 2012.

Apart from the privacy violations identified in the OpenSocial gadget approach, these social application platforms are far from being privacy-friendly. Third-party applications typically have far more access to the user's social data than strictly needed to function, effectively violating the principle of least-privilege and posing privacy threats.

Several privacy-enhanced social application platforms are developed, but none of them seems to completely solve the issues for the most common distributed approach. A promising future direction is to develop such a privacy-enhanced platform using novel enforcement mechanisms recently developed in the information flow security community.

ACKNOWLEDGMENT

This research is partially funded by the Research Fund KU Leuven, the EU-funded FP7 projects NESSoS and WebSand and by the IWT-SBO project SPION. Dominique Devriese holds a Ph.D. fellowship of the Research Foundation – Flanders (FWO).

REFERENCES

Austin, T. H., & Flanagan, C. (2012). Multiple facets for dynamic information flow. In *Proceedings of the ACM SIGPLAN-SIGACT Symposium on Principles of Programming Languages (POPL).*

Beard, E. (2010, April 21). *A new data model.* Retrieved October 6, 2012, from http://developers.facebook.com/blog/post/2010/04/21/a-new-data-model/

Bielova, N., Devriese, D., Massaci, F., & Piessens, F. (2011). Reactive non-interference for a browser model. In *Proceedings of the International Conference on Network and System Security (NSS).*

Chugh, R., Meister, J. A., Jhala, R., & Lerner, S. (2009). Staged information flow for JavaScript. In *Proceedings of the ACM SIGPLAN Conference on Programming Language Design and Implementation (PLDI)* (pp. 50-62).

Devriese, D., & Piessens, F. (2010). Noninterference through secure multi-execution. In *Proceedings of the IEEE Symposium on Security and Privacy* (pp. 109-124).

Egele, M., Moser, A., Kruegel, C., & Kirda, E. (2011). PoX: Protecting users from malicious Facebook applications. In *Proceedings of the IEEE International Conference on Pervasive Computing and Communications Workshops (PERCOM).*

Felt, A., & Evans, D. (2008). Privacy protection for social networking platforms. In *Proceedings of the Workshop on Web 2.0 Security and Privacy (W2SP).*

Hedin, D., & Sabelfeld, A. (2012). Information-flow security for a core of JavaScript. In *Proceedings of the IEEE Computer Security Foundations Symposium (CSF).*

Mills, E. (2008, June 26). *Facebook suspends app that permitted peephole.* Retrieved October 6, 2012, from http://news.cnet.com/8301-10784_3-9977762-7.html

Pham, A. (2011, September 9). Article. *LA Times*. Retrieved October 6, 2012, from http://latimesblogs.latimes.com/entertainmentnews-buzz/2011/09/sims-social-surpasses-farmville-as-second-largest-facebook-game.html

Sabelfeld, A., & Myers, A. C. (2003). Language-based information-flow security. *IEEE Journal on Selected Areas in Communications (JASC)*, 5–19. doi:10.1109/JSAC.2002.806121

Singh, K., Bhola, S., & Lee, W. (2009). xBook: Redesigning privacy control in social networking platforms. In *Proceedings of the USENIX Security Symposium* (pp. 249-266).

Spencer, K. (2008, May 1). *Identity 'at risk' on Facebook*. Retrieved October 6, 2012, from http://news.bbc.co.uk/2/hi/programmes/click_online/7375772.stm

Steel, E., & Fowler, G. A. (2010, October 18). Facebook in privacy breach: Top-ranked applications transmit personal IDs, a journal investigation finds. *The Wall Street Journal*. Retrieved October 6, 2012, from http://online.wsj.com/article/SB10001424052702304772804575558484075236968.html

ADDITIONAL READING

Fogie, S., Grossman, J., Hansen, R., Rager, A., & Petkov, P. D. (2007). *XSS attacks: Cross site scripting exploits and defense*. Syngress.

Hawker, M. D. (2010). *The developer's guide to social programming: Building social context using Facebook, Google Friend Connect, and the Twitter API*. Addison-Wesley Professional.

LeBlanc, J. (2011). *Programming social applications: Building viral experiences with OpenSocial, OAuth, OpenID, and distributed web frameworks*. O'Reilly Media.

Zalewski, M. (2011). *The tangled web*. No Starch Press.

KEY TERMS AND DEFINITIONS

Application Provider: The stakeholder that provides the software of an application, as opposed to other stakeholders such as the end-users of the software or the owner of the infrastructure that runs the software.

Gadget: In the context of this chapter, a gadget is a piece of software that runs in the context of an online social network, and is hosted on the online social network infrastructure.

Information Flow Analysis: The analysis of how inputs to a program influence the outputs of that program, in order to put bounds on the information that can be deduced about private inputs by observers that can only observe public outputs.

JavaScript: A prototype-based dynamic scripting language originally developed by Netscape to support scripting of their web browser. JavaScript was later standardized as ECMAScript, and all major web browsers today support a variant of the language.

Online: Social Network (OSN): An online platform where users can publish public or semi-public profile information, form relationships with other users, and interact in a variety of ways with these relations and with the general public.

Representational State Transfer (REST): An architectural style for distributed software systems that emphasizes uniform, stateless and cacheable software interfaces.

Social Application: In the context of this chapter, a social application is a third-party provided software application that runs in the context of, or in interaction with an online social network, and that makes use of the profile and relationship information that is present in that online social network.

ENDNOTES

1 JSON (JavaScript Object Notation) is a textual representation – based on open standards – of JavaScript objects, designed for human-readable data interchange across the Internet.

2 Caja is a technology to automatically convert JavaScript into a safe subset, based on the concepts of object-capability. The technology is primarily used to run third-party JavaScript code within a sandbox.

3 JSONP is a method to request data from a cross-origin domain. It is primarily used as a browser-independent method to circumvent the same-origin policy.

Chapter 11
On the Use of Formal Methods to Enforce Privacy-Aware Social Networking

Néstor Cataño Collazos
The University of Madeira, Portugal

Sorren Christopher Hanvey
The University of Madeira, Portugal

Camilo Rueda Calderón
Pontificiad Universidad Javeriana, Colombia

ABSTRACT

This chapter discusses the use of formal techniques and formal verification tools to ensure privacy-aware social networking; hence users of social-networking sites can predict what the consequences of updating their privacy settings are. A formal methods approach is presented for modeling and comparing social-network privacy policies, and for checking whether a user's privacy policy can coexist with other policies within a social networking site. The authors present the Poporo tool implementing the approach. Poporo builds on a predicate calculus definition for social networking written in B that models social network content, people in the network, friendship relations, and privacy policies that are modeled as permissions to access content. Several examples of privacy-awareness social networking are also shown using Poporo.

INTRODUCTION

In recent years, on-line social network services in the form of web-sites such as Facebook, MySpace, LinkedIn and Hi5 have become popular tools that allow users to publish content, share common interests and keep up with their friends, family and business connections. A typical social network user profile features personal information (e.g. gender, birthday, family situation), a continuous stream of activity logged from actions taken on the site (such as messages sent, status updated,

DOI: 10.4018/978-1-4666-3926-3.ch011

games played) and media content (e.g. personal photos and videos). The web offers numerous services that suit users' needs based on information extracted from personal profiles. The privacy of this information has become a significant concern. Users may upload media they wish to share with specific friends, but do not wish to be widely distributed to their network as a whole. Some examples of privacy issues are, users can gain access to a photo album of an unknown user simply because a friend is tagged in one of the images or because the user has no control over what an application used by another user with access to one's content can share. Back-doors also exist to facilitate casual connections such as allowing an unknown user to gain access to profile information simply by replying to a message he or she has sent.

Furthermore, social networking sites have conflicting goals. Although respecting the privacy of their client base is important, they must also grow and expand the connections between their users in order to be successful. This is achieved by allowing users to connect over common interests by exposing content through less restrictive policies. Social-networking policies are constantly changed to grant users more control over who can access user's content. This constant change leaves users in the dark on what actually their policies entail, which is exacerbated by the fact that users find stipulating detailed privacy settings to be challenging (Bonneau, Anderson, & Church 2009). Additionally, it is not always possible to trust the social networking site to uphold users' policies as became evident from Facebook privacy breaches in 2009 (Pepitone, 2011) when Facebook changed its privacy policies without informing its users, resulting in content from private groups being made public. Such a breach called for a mechanism for independently checking compliance of new policies to existing policies.

However, privacy means something different to everyone. Based on the diverse types of privacy rights and violations, it is evident that technology has a dual role in privacy: new technologies give rise to new threats to privacy rights, at the same time, new technologies can help preserve privacy. Formal methods can address privacy issues, but privacy raises new challenges, and thus new research opportunities, for the formal methods community (Tschantz & Wing, 2009).

With the explosion of the Internet, privacy is finally getting serious attention by the scientific community. More and more personal information about us is available online. For example with cloud computing and social networks, we further entrust third parties with the storage and management of private information in places unknown to us. We are making it easier for others to find out about our personal habits, tastes, and history.

Data privacy refers to the evolving relationship between technology and the legal right to, or public expectation of privacy in the collection and sharing of data about one's self. Privacy concerns exist wherever uniquely identifiable data relating to a person or persons are collected and stored, in digital form or otherwise. In some cases these concerns refer to how data is collected, stored, and associated. In other cases the issue is who is given access to information. This includes whether an individual has any ownership rights to data about them, and/or the right to view, verify, and challenge that information.

In the context of social networking sites (SNS) from a user's perspective, privacy is enforced through a privacy policy, which is a statement that discloses some or all of the ways a system gathers, uses, discloses and manages the user's data. Personal information can be anything that can be used to identify an individual, not limited to but including; name, address, date of birth, marital status, contact information or any content shared by a user within a SNS. From the perspective of the SNS system, it is a statement that declares a policy on how it collects, stores, and releases personal information. It informs the user what specific information is collected, and whether it is kept confidential or shared with partners and if so, how.

A user's privacy policy defines a set of other users within the SNS, the members of which can be granted access to some content. With the concept of user defined lists, a user can specify which list of users they wish to share said content with and which set of users must never be granted any access privileges over the content. A user might have multiple conflicting policies regarding content sharing. This is due to the flexibility required within social networking sites when it comes to content sharing. A look at trends in current social networking sites shows that a user can either use a pre-defined policy or define a new one, every time they want to share some content. For example, when using Facebook, a user may add some content to the social networking site and then wish to share it. When sharing, the user's default policy is set to the policy last defined by the user; the user then either selects this policy or defines a new policy on-the-fly.

Due to the ability of users to define multiple privacy policies within a social networking site, it is necessary to provide them with the ability to compare these policies and check whether they comply with each other. Users continuously change their policy based on the type and context of the content they are sharing. Users constantly add plug-ins to the social networking site and associate them with their online profiles within these social networking sites. These plug-ins are then granted access to a user's information and content within the social networking site. The users then use these plug-ins to create and share content or consume other user's content. Therefore it is paramount for a user to be able to compare their privacy policy against the transmission policy of a plug-in to ensure it won't breach said policy. Social networking sites are constantly evolving providing their users with more functionality. This change, at times, takes the form of changing the interaction paradigm or the privacy policy paradigm within the social networking site. To aid users the social networking site will update a user's privacy policy to reflect the new policy paradigm. A user must be able to confirm that the new policy adheres to their original policy. Based on the above there exist four major kinds of privacy breaches that a user might need to compare privacy policies for compliance to avoid:

1. **SNS Privacy Breach:** The SNS might make changes to the internal mechanisms of the system which change how and to who some content is transmitted or might change the way privacy policies and defined thereby leaving the user open to privacy breaches.
2. **User Privacy Breach:** Wherein a user inadvertently breaches their own privacy by not realizing that consequences of their own actions due to a lack of understanding of the internal working of the SNS.
3. **User to User Privacy Breach:** Wherein a user might unintentionally breach another user's privacy policy due either sharing that user's content or due to the automated transmission policy adopted by the SNS, e.g., Tagging content of someone can make it visible to an unintended audience.
4. **Application Privacy Breach:** A user might use an application or plug-in developed by a third party developer which might not adhere to either the user's privacy policy or the policy enforced by the SNS.

There is at present no system in place within SNSs, such as Facebook, to allow the user to compare the consequences of their actions to those of a pre-existing policy. In addition to the above shortcoming, policy enforcement is only employed when sharing some content explicitly. The privacy issue raised by such selective policy enforcement is, are there other actions a user might perform which alter the set of users the said content is visible to. For instance, in Facebook, a user might tag some content thereby making it visible to all the "friends" of the tagged user, a comment on some content by a user might make the content visible to the user's friends. Therefore there is a need for policy comparison and compliance every time a user performs an action that might alter the set of privileges over the content in question.

This chapter describes a formal methods approach that addresses the concerns stated above, presenting a mechanism to formally model privacy policies of social-networking sites, for reliably restricting their content, and for verifying whether a user's privacy can coexist with other policies in the network. We introduce the Poporo tool that implements this approach (Cataño, Hanvey, & Rueda, 2012).

The Poporo tool builds upon Matelas[1], a predicate calculus abstract definition for social networking, modeling social-network content, privacy policies, social-network friendship relations, and how these affect the policies with regards to content and other users in the network (Cataño & Rueda, 2010). Matelas has been written in B (Abrial, 1996) and refined (Hoare & Sanders, 1986; Abrial, 1984) into a close-to-code programming library implementing the core functionality needed for social networking.

Poporo also builds upon a translation from B into JML (short for Java Modeling Language) specifications (Cataño, Wahls, & Rueda, 2012), and upon a translation of JML specifications into Yices (Cataño, Rueda, & Hanvey, 2011). JML is a model-based language for specifying the behavior of Java classes (Breunesse, Cataño, Huisman, & Jacobs, 2005; Leaves, Baker, & Ruby, 2006). Yices is an SMT (Satisfiability Modulo Theories) solver (Dutertre & Moura, 2006) that provides support for checking satisfiability of formulae containing un-interpreted function symbols.

The chapter first defines privacy in the context of social networking sites. Next, it introduces the privacy concerns faced by social networking site users. It identifies the kinds of privacy breaches that might occur and their sources. Next, in 'Background' we present a section on existing work on privacy in social networks and their shortcomings, identifying the extensions required for each body of work to contribute to solving the problem. Next we introduce the Poporo tool and how it makes use of existing technologies. We describe Matelas, the B to JML and JML to Yices translators. The chapter describes an efficient and comprehensible way of defining privacy policies on a per user basis. Next we describe how these policies are checked for compliance against existing policies. We demonstrate how the tool can account for the different types of privacy breaches identified. The tool has been incorporated into Facebook as a plug-in. This process has been presented to demonstrate the real world applications of such a formal methods based approach to privacy. We conclude with a discussion on the work presented and possible future directions for research.

BACKGROUND

Privacy of data has been a pressing issue in the context of multiple domains. Anonymization techniques such as differential privacy (Dwork, 2006) and k-anonymization (Bayardo, 2005) have been successfully applied to prevent privacy breaches during data collection and analysis. Differential privacy is a technique that incorporates the concept of auxiliary information into preventing breaches. Data is often collected from different sources. Such data is at times sensitive to the individual providing it and must therefore be kept private. The data must also be made available for analysis to external entities. To prevent privacy breaches such data is scrubbed, i.e., all identifiable markers, such as name, etc., are removed leaving behind data that is useful yet untraceable. In Dwork (2006), the author suggests that although information might be scrubbed, it is possible for an adversary to gather additional information that is not part of the dataset to identify a specific user's data. That is, given a data set, an adversary, i.e., an entity attempting to gather private information, might be in possession of some auxiliary information that makes the data entries identifiable. For example, a dataset containing ages and salaries within an organization might be made available having the names of the employees scrubbed. Now if the adversary is aware of the ages of specific employees their salary information would be identifiable. Differential privacy provides techniques to effectively alter the dataset set in a way where although every entry is altered, as a whole, it doesn't alter the results of any analysis that might be conducted over the dataset. Therefore even with axillary information the entries are no longer identifiable. The altering of data or content within a social networking site is not always feasible as social networks deal with specific data entities as opposed to the collection of all content within the network.

Within k-anonymization techniques attributes are suppressed or generalized until each row is identical with at least k-1 other rows. At this point the database is said to be k-anonymous. Such techniques attempt to address similar privacy issues as those stated in context of differential privacy. Here the approach differs for differential privacy in that, data or information is not altered but rather some the data entities returned as an answer to a query are withheld of additional entities are added. Using this technique an adversary cannot ascertain which data entities are true and which are fabricated. In Sadeh et al. (2009), Gandon and Sadeh (2004), and Norman Sadeh et al., several frameworks are presented to deal with privacy concerns in location aware services. These frameworks rely on various anonymization techniques like the one above. These techniques have shown great success in location-based social networking services. These frameworks primarily rely on altering the content the user is sharing based on the policy defined by the user. Such techniques though successful in certain domains of social networking are not generalizable to all social networks. As stated earlier in various contexts, the identity of the owner of some content within a social networking site can be of paramount importance.

In Anderson et al. (2009), the authors argue that the inability of social networking sites to protect their users from external entities has led to sensitive private information being made public. They propose an architecture that builds a social network out of smart clients and an untrusted central server. The proposed architecture removes control from the developers and places it with the users. Such an approach makes users responsible for their own privacy policy definition. As stated earlier privacy policy definition is not always a straight forward process. There exists a need for an easy to understand mechanism for privacy policy definition before such an approach can be implemented.

In Backstrom et al. (2007), the authors adopted a graph based approach to studying social network privacy. In such an approach the nodes of the graph represent users of other entities within the network and the edges represent the relationships that occur. They studied the effectiveness of anonymization practices in preserving privacy. They described a family of attacks over such a network. Even from a single anonymized copy of a social network, it was found to be possible for an adversary to learn whether edges exist or not between specific targeted pairs of nodes, i.e., the social relationships within the network were prone to privacy breaches. This further iterates the shortcomings of anonymization techniques for ensuring privacy.

In Gilbert and Karahalios (2009), the authors presented their work on the strength of social ties and varying degrees of these ties that exist. A social tie is defined as a connection between two users within the social networking site. The authors argue that not all such social ties are of the same strength and that they vary from a close connection to a distant acquaintance. The authors presented a predictive model that maps social media data to tie strength. Such a predictive model would allow for the automated generation of privacy policies based on the strength of existing ties. Although at over 85% accuracy, such a mechanism is not yet feasible.

Formal methods (FM) consist of a set of techniques and tools based on mathematical modeling and formal logic used to specify and verify requirements and designs for computer systems. Formal methods are widely used today in several fields of software development from avionics, train control systems to financial and networking situations. Formal Methods primarily deal with defining a mathematical description of the software system under development by describing what the behavioral patterns of the system should be. It is also possible to transform a specification into a design, and ultimately into an actual implementation, that is correct by construction. As systems become more complicated, and safety, security and privacy become more important issues, the use of formal methods in system design offers another level of insurance.

Formal methods differ from other methodologies for designing systems through the use of formal verification schemes, that is, the basic principles of the system must be proven correct before they are accepted (Bowen, 1993). Traditionally extensive testing is carried out to verify behavior, but testing is capable of only finite conclusions. Such methods of testing can only show the situations where a system won't fail, but cannot say anything about the behavior of the system outside of the testing scenarios. In contrast, using formal methods, once a theorem is proven true it remains true, thereby guaranteeing the system's behavior. Formal methods help to identify errors in reasoning which would otherwise be left unverified but do not fix bad assumptions in the design.

Tschantz and Wing (2009) focus on the dual role of technology when it comes to privacy, how new technologies raise privacy concerns and how advances in technology can help people to enforce privacy and appropriately deal with breaches when they occur. They discuss the various groups of actions which can result in privacy violations based on the work presented by (Solove, 2006). These violations are categorized into invasions, information collection, information processing, and information dissemination. Invasions and information collection deal with how a user's content is acquired by an entity. In the context of social networking sites, the users themselves add data to the network, after which the data is shared with other entities such as other users or third party applications. Information processing deals with how the information is treated within the system. Within the system the information can be scrubbed, i.e., any identifiable information, such as names, etc., is removed. Within social networking sites this is unfeasible as users need to retain ownership of their content and the ability to share the content. The most paramount in the context of social networking sites is information dissemination, i.e., how the content added by a user is shared within the network. Herein it is necessary for the users to be able to define policies for such sharing, referred to as their privacy policy. The authors call for the use of Formal Methods as a technology to provide for everything from foundational formalizations of privacy to practical tools for checking for privacy violations.

Tschantz and Wing (2009) called for the use of Formal Methods as a technology to provide for everything from foundational formalizations of privacy to practical tools for checking for privacy violations. They define how formal methods can be used to alleviate the privacy concerns plaguing online social networking sites as follows:

- **Modeling a system:** Traditionally one models a system, its environment and the interactions between the two, while simply making assumptions about the environment in which the system operates. We cannot make assumptions about an adversary (an external system or person that might cause a privacy breach) in the way we might about other failures and must therefore include the adversary as part of the system's environment. Privacy involves three entities: the data holder, an adversary, and the data subject. Here we notice the inherent difference between security and privacy:

1. In security, the entity in control of the system also has an inherent interest in its security.
2. In privacy, the system is controlled by the data holder, but it is the data subject that benefits from privacy.

Due to this inherent difference it is not effective to apply existing security policy enforcing mechanisms to privacy policies. Privacy requires modeling different relationships among the (minimally) three entities. Complications arise because relationships do not necessarily enjoy simple algebraic properties and because relationships change over time.

- **Abstraction and Refinement:** Methods that successively refine a high-level specification to a lower-level one, until executable code is reached, rely on well-defined correctness preserving transformations.
- **Policy Composition and Conflicting Requirements:** Whether different components of a system might be governed by different policies or if one system might be governed by more than one policy, we must also provide methods of compositional reasoning. Consider two components, A and B, and privacy policies, P1 and P2, if A satisfies P1 and B satisfies P2, we must be able to define rule concerning the composition of A and B with respect to P1, P2, and P1 $\wedge$ P2.

Trustworthy computing requires balancing privacy with security, reliability, and usability. These properties can at time have conflicting requirements and we need to have a formal understanding of the relationships among these properties. For example, we want auditability for security, to determine the source of a security breach. However, auditability is at odds with anonymity, a desired aspect of privacy. To achieve reliability, especially availability, we often replicate data at different locations; replicas increase the likelihood that an attacker can access private data and make it harder for users to track and manage their data. These trade-offs have been studied and formalized to gain a better understanding of the system.

The MOBIUS infrastructure (Barthe, Grégoire, Jensen, & Pichardie, 2008), put forth by Gilles Barthe et al., is a possible approach for ensuring that third party or external applications being added to the social networking site will not breach a user's privacy. It targets the verification of embedded frameworks that could run third party applications that are checked against a privacy policy modeling platform. MOBIUS draws heavily from foundational proof carrying code (Appel, 2001), so it avoids any commitment to a particular type system and the use of a verification condition (VC) generator. In foundational proof carrying code, the code provider must give both the executable code plus a proof in the foundational logic that the code satisfies the consumer's safety policy. Foundational proof carrying code generates VCs directly from the operational semantics so making the proofs more complicated to produce. There exists the possibility that the proof provided might not correspond to the application in question. These proofs might be altered to pass inspection while the application might breach the privacy policies specified. Additionally, every time an application is updated or altered the entire certification and proving process needs to be carried out once again. In the context of social networking sites, which are constantly evolving and changing, this might not be feasible. There is need for a mechanism which is more efficient and can allow for user's to check whether the application adheres to their privacy policy as opposed to checking the application against the system policy as MOBIUS does.

The need for establishing and enforcing privacy policies has been recognized within the research community with considerable work concentrated on Enterprise level implementation of privacy policies. IBM's Enterprise Privacy Authorization Language (EPAL) and the OASIS eXtensible Access Control Markup Language (XACML) are tailor made languages developed for the definition and enforcement of privacy policies. In EPAL and XACML, a policy consists of one or more Rules. A Rule specifies the condition under which an entity can be granted access to some data. These conditions are specified over specific attribute using functions over values. The rules and conditions must also contain a description of which rule or policy applies to a specific request. This format of policy specification raises problems in the context of SNS as it is too restrictive, requiring the specification of rules relating each user to each content and they do not provide the flexibility for specifying multiple generalizable policies.

George Danezis (2009) proposes the definition of a framework for privacy policies based on social context of user and user content. The framework presented uses an approach based on graph theory drawing context from previous actions performed within the social network. The framework uses a three pronged approach wherein, first, user contexts are inferred by studying the social graph surrounding a user and inferring the possible contexts within which an action may occur. Next every future action must be assigned to a context based on the social graph, e.g., people that are 'tagged' as part of an action. Once an action is assigned a context, the privacy policy for this context is applied with appropriate publishing of content to various users. This form of inferring privacy policies was found to be easier for users, as it automates the process of publishing content. Though easier, it leaves the user susceptible to privacy breaches as they have less control over to whom their content is accessible.

Brunel, Cuppens, Cuppens, Sans, and Bodeveix (2007) define a formal policy specification language for contextual awareness and policy definition. They define access control as a set of rules allowing a user to gain access through the Information System. The policy depends on the subject performing the action and on what he is accessing. Contextual permissions depend on the system environment at the time of the action, i.e., the framework associates the access-privilege conditions that must be satisfied according to the system state.

THE POPORO TOOL

The Poporo tool attempts to address the concerns presented regarding privacy in online social networks. The Poporo tool provides a mechanism for the definition of privacy policies within a Matelas based social network. The tool then compares a user's current privacy policy against a pre-existing one to verify whether a user's privacy policy can coexist with other policies in a social network. Poporo's architecture is presented in Figure 1.

Figure 1. Poporo's formal verification framework

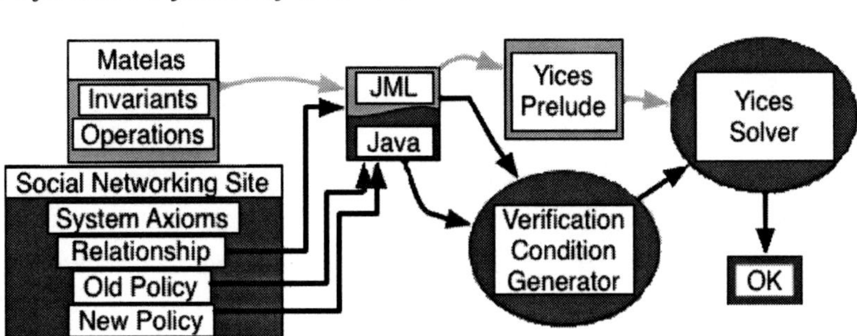

Poporo relies on Matelas, a predicate calculus model for social-networking written in B. Matelas models access permissions as invariants, and B enabled tools can generate proof obligations to ensure that networking operations adhere to these invariants. The operations or events defined in this model define the components which as used to define privacy policies. Most online social networks are built on Java or Java based technology platforms. It is necessary for the Matelas model to be accessible and understood by such platforms. Therefore, the Matelas is translated into the Java Modeling Language (JML) which is a model-based language for specifying the behavior of Java classes. This translation is performed through custom built translators (Cataño, Wahls, & Rueda, 2012).

The definitions of the social networking operations generated by translating the Matelas model into JML are then translated into the Yices Input Language. The primary motivation for mapping the JML model into Yices is to be able to use an efficient solver to verify the JML model for social networking, i.e., the Yices SMT Solver. The JML definitions are translated into the Yices Input Language via translation rules defined in Cataño, Rueda, and Hanvey (2011). The definitions of the social networking operations in the Yices Input Language are referred to as the Yices Prelude. This Yices prelude is used to verify privacy policies for compliance (whether a policy can coexist with another).

A social networking site (SNS) can include user defined privacy policies and a set of axioms about the behavior of the site. A privacy policy is defined as the consequences of a set of actions performed by a user within the social networking site; more specifically a policy is defined as what access permissions are awarded to which users. A privacy policy is defined in Java incorporating the operations defined in Matelas to represent the actions performed. A user of the social networking site can decide to upgrade an old privacy policy into a new policy by imposing a relationship between the variables and actions defined within the policies. Poporo defines the relationship between the old and the new policy as JML specifications. The privacy policy definitions in Java/JML feed into the verification condition generator, which reads the policies in Java/JML and generates verification conditions in the Yices Input Language. These verification conditions define the conditions that must be satisfied to ensure that a new privacy policy is correct and compliant with existing policies. The verification condition generator accepts the Java/JML policy. The verification condition generator is based on weakest pre-condition calculus and makes use of the Yices prelude in conjunction with lambda calculus to generate the verification conditions.

Poporo uses the Yices solver as its back-end proving engine. Yices is an SMT (Satisfiability Modulo Theories) solver that provides support for checking satisfiability of formulae containing uninterpreted function symbols. The verification condition generated by the verification condition generator along with the Yices prelude are then passed to the Yices solver, which determines whether all the verification conditions are satisfied and in turn whether the privacy policies are compliant and the user's privacy maintained.

Matelas

When using a formal methods approach to privacy aware social networking it is necessary to define the internal working of a social network. The definition of a social network must be modeled formally using existing specification languages. The model is meant to capture the various operations that might be executed within the social network along with any system axioms that the network might define. These system axioms state the necessary rule that ensure the correct working of the social network. For instance, a system axiom might state that the user that adds some content to the network must be granted all the access privileges over said content. Within the

Poporo tool this formal social networking model is described as Matelas.

Matelas is a full model for social-networking that has been introduced in Cataño and Rueda (2010). It models social-networking privacy policies as access permissions to network content. Matelas is written in the B language (Abrial, 1996). The B model declares operations for manipulating network content (text, video, photographs, etc.).

Box 1 presents a simplified B model for social networking taken from Cataño and Rueda (2010). The machine SOCIAL_NETWORK declares two sets, PERSON and RAWCONTENT, representing the set of all possible persons and the set of all possible content in the network respectively. Variables "person" and "rawcontent" are the sets of all persons and content that are actually in the network, and "content" is a relation mapping people to their own content.

A common operation in social networking websites is publishing content to people. The operation "transmit_rc" is used to publish the raw-content "rc" from the page of "ow" (the owner of "rc") to the page of "pe." Operation "transmit_rc" is a preconditioned B substitution. Preconditioned substitutions denote substitutions under a particular precondition. If the operation "transmit_rc" is invoked when its precondition (following PRE) is true, the meaning of the operation is the meaning of its substitution (the code following THEN). The operation is not guaranteed to achieve any result if invoked when its precondition is false.

Box 1. B machine for social networking

```
MACHINE SOCIAL_NETWORK
  SETS
      PERSON; RAWCONTENT
  VARIABLES
      person, rawcontent, content
  INVARIANT
       person ⊆ PERSON ∧ rawcontent ⊆ RAWCONTENT ∧
      content ∈ person↔ rawcontent ∧ dom(content) = person ∧ ran(content) =
rawcontent
  INITIALISATION
       person:= ∅ || rawcontent:= ∅ || content:= ∅
OPERATIONS
transmit_rc (ow, rc, pe) ≅
       PRE
            rc ∈ rawcontent ∧ ow ∈ person ∧ pe ∈ person ∧ ow ≠ pe ∧ pe
↦ rc ∉ content
       THEN
            ANY prs WHERE prs ⊆ person
            THEN
             content:= content ∪ {pe ↦ rc} ∪ prs ⊗ {rc}
            END
       END
END
```

In the definition of "transmit_rc," "pe ↦ rc" represents the pair of elements "(pe, rc)." The construct ANY models unbounded choice substitution: it gives the implementer the opportunity to choose any value for the bound variable "prs" that satisfies the WHERE condition "prs ⊆ person." This gives a refining or implementation machine the flexibility to additionally transmit the content "rc" to all of a yet unspecified set of people.

In addition to "transmit_rc," Matelas defines methods for creating content, creating users, editing content, commenting on content and removing content from the network. Matelas introduces the concept of user-defined lists, that is, a set of users in the social-network that share the same privileges over a particular user's content. The operation "transmit_list_rc" in Box 2 publishes the raw content "rc" from the page of "ow" to the pages of any "pe" in the list name. A list is composed of three parts, the creator of the list ("listowner"), the set of its members ("listpe"), and the content of the list (listrc). The operation "transmit_list_rc" adds the content "rc" to the content of every member of list name, and associates the content "rc" with the list name for future reference.

In Facebook, the most standard lists are friends, friends of friends and public (every user of Facebook). A user can also group users together based on some common context such as work colleagues, family, or students. The user then selects a list when sharing some content, requiring the social networking site to ensure that only the intended audience is granted privileges over the content. Additionally, the user might select a list but would like to hide the content from a sub-list, e.g. a user might want to share some content with some colleagues but not with any superior. This functionality is implemented in Matelas through methods for creating and deleting lists, adding members to an existing list, transmitting to a list or a restricted sub-list. The creator of a list (called its owner) can specify any policy over the list or can transmit its content to other users.

Translating B Policies to JML Specifications

As most social networking sites are built on a Java based platform, it is necessary for any formal methods approach to include a mechanism for the tools based on the approach to be compatible with such platforms. This is paramount for the approach to be applicable in a real world environment. Therefore the formal social networking model defined must be translated into a Java compatible

Box 2. B machine for transmitting to a list of users

```
transmit_list_rc (ow, rc, name) ≅
   PRE
    rc ∈ rawcontent∧ow ∈ person∧name ∈ LIST
   THEN
   SELECT
    ow ∈ran(list_owner) ∧ name ∈dom(listpe) ∧
    list_owner(name) = ow ∧ ow = owner (rc) ∧ rc ∉ listrc[{name}]
   THEN
     content:= content∪ (listpe[{name}] ⊗{rc})
     listrc:= listrc∪{name ↦ rc}
    END
```

format. To this end it is necessary to translate the Matelas model in B to predicates understood by Java based platforms.

The translation from B machines to the Java Modeling Language (JML) is based on the work and approach in Cataño, Wahls, and Rueda (2012). The approach has been implemented as The B2Jml tool (Cataño, Wahls, Rivera, & Rueda, 2012), which is integrated into the Poporo tool and is used to translate Matelas social-networking privacy policies to JML.

Box 3 presents the output of applying the B2Jml tool to the B model in Box 1. In JML, model and ghost fields are both specification-only. That is, they exist in JML but they do not exist in the Java code. A significant difference is that model fields are an abstraction of the mutable part of an object's state, while ghost fields can be used to represent immutable data. Classes JMLEqualsSet and JMLEqualsToEqualsRelation (in the org.jmlspecs.models package) are built-in to JML and represent mathematical sets and relations, respectively. The invariant is an assertion that all instances of the class must satisfy in all visible states[2], and the initially clause is an assertion that the initial values of the fields must satisfy. In the specification of the transmit_rc method, the normal_behavior case guarantees that if the

Box 3. A partial JML translation of the social networking machine

```
//@ model import org.jmlspecs.models.*;
public abstract class SOCIAL_NETWORK {
/*@ public model JMLEqualsSet<Integer> person;
    public model JMLEqualsSet<Integer> PERSON;
    public model JMLEqualsSet<Integer> rawcontent;
    public model JMLEqualsSet<Integer> RAWCONTENT;
    public model JMLEqualsToEqualsRelation<Integer, Integer> content;

    public initially person.isEmpty() && rawcontent.isEmpty() && content.isEmpty();
    public invariant person.isSubset(PERSON) && rawcontent.isSubset(RAWCONTENT)
        && (new util.Relation(person, rawcontent)).has(content)
        && content.domain().equals(person) && content.range().equals(rawcontent);
@*/
/*@ public normal_behavior
       requires rawcontent.has(rc) && person.has(ow) && person.has(pe) &&
                 !ow.equals(pe) && !content.has(pe,rc);
       ensures (\exists JMLEqualsSet<Integer> prs; prs.isSubset(person);
                  content.equals(\old(content.union(
                     JMLEqualsToEqualsRelation.singleton(pe, rc)).union(
                        ModelUtils.cartesian(prs, JMLEqualsSet.singleton(rc))))));
   also public exceptional_behavior
       requires !(rawcontent.has(rc) && person.has(ow) && person.has(pe) &&
                   !ow.equals(pe) && !content.has(pe, rc));
       signals (Exception) true; @*/
   public abstract void transmit_rc(Integer rc, Integer ow, Integer pe);
}
```

requires clause (pre-condition) is satisfied, no exception will be thrown, only the locations listed in the assignable clause can be modified by the method, and the post-state will satisfy the ensures clause (post-condition). Within an ensures clause, expressions in \old are evaluated in the pre-state, while all other expressions are evaluated in the post-state. The exceptional_behavior case specifies that the method will throw an exception and no locations will be modified if its pre-condition is satisfied.

Translating JML Policies into Yices

A formal methods approach requires a prover/solver to check whether the model defined for social networking is correct and the various operations defined within the model satisfy the system axioms defined. Within the Matelas B Model it is possible to perform these checks via B-enabled tools. The JML model on the other hand requires to be re-checked for satisfiability. Therefore the JML model must be translated into a format recognized by the chosen prover/solver.

Poporo's primary motivation for translating JML generic types into Yices input language is to be able to use Yices' SMT solver to check satisfiability of the JML model for social networking obtained as a translation from Matelas. In the following, we present parts of the translation from JML to Yices (Cataño, Rueda, & Hanvey, 2011). JML's sets and relations are implemented as the bit-vectors jmlset and jmlrel predicates along with operations for manipulating elements of these types. JML logical operators such as ==>, &&, and || are translated into Yices logical predicates imp, and, and or respectively. JML existential (universal) quantifiers are naturally mapped to the predicate exists (forall) of Yices. JML abstract model variables modeling carrier sets, e.g. "PERSON" and "RAWCONTENT," are translated to global variables of type jmlset. The mapping of JML normal and exceptional post-conditions into Yices relies upon the use of lambda expressions that capture the semantics of the JML specifications.

Two predicates in Yices implement the mapping of JML method specifications. The first predicate models the pre-condition part of the JML method specification and the second models the post-condition part of it. Function precondition-transmit-rc in Box 4 implements the normal pre-condition of method transmit_rc in Yices of the normal_behavior part of the JML specification in Box 3. The function makes use of predicate jmlset-is-member, which checks for the existence of an element in a set in Yices, and the standard Yices function mk-tuple that constructs a pair of elements. Function postcondition-transmit-rc in Box 4 implements the exceptional_behavior part of the JML specification. Poporo defines (not shown here) functions jmlrel-product-set-singleton that implements the cross product between a general set with a singleton set, jmlrel-add-element that adds a pair of elements to a relation, jmlrel-is-equal that checks for equality between two relations, and jmlrel-union that unites two relations.

JML frame conditions, modeled with the aid of the assignable clause of JML, are re-written as method post-conditions stating that every variable except for the ones mentioned in the assignable specification maintain its value from the pre-state to the post-state of the method. The pre-state of a method is the state on entry to it and its post-state is the state on exit from it.

Social Networking Policy Definition

Poporo accepts an old policy, a new policy, and a JML relation between these policies (provide by) from the social-networking site (SNS). Poporo is based on the system axioms enforced by Matelas that are modeled as machine invariants in B. So, any privacy policy within Poporo must adhere to Matelas' invariants. A SNS enforces privacy by obligating users to adhere to a set of system

Box 4. Yices' translation for JML spec for transmitting content

```
(define precondition-transmit-rc::(-> jmlset jmlset jmlrel
                                       (-> int int int bool))
 (lambda(rawcontent::jmlset person::jmlset content::jmlrel)
  (lambda(ow::int rc::int pe::int)
   (and (jmlset-is-member rawcontent-carrier rc)
           (jmlset-is-member rawcontent rc)
           (jmlset-is-member person-carrier ow)
           (jmlset-is-member person ow)
           (not (= ow pe))
           (not (jmlrel-is-member content (mk-tuple pe rc)))))))
 (define postcondition-transmit-rc::(-> jmlset jmlset jmlrel
            (-> jmlset jmlset jmlrel  (-> int int int bool)))
 (lambda(rawcontent-prestate::jmlset person-prestate::jmlset
                                    content-prestate::jmlrel)
  (lambda(rawcontent::jmlset person::jmlset content::jmlrel)
   (lambda(ow::int rc::int pe::int)
    (exists(prs::jmlset)
     (and (jmlset-is-subset prs person-prestate)
            (jmlrel-is-equal content
            (jmlrel-union (jmlrel-add-element content-prestate
                                           (mk-tuple pe rc))
           (jmlrel-product-set-singleton prs rc)))
           (= rawcontent-prestate rawcontent)
           (= person-prestate person)))))))
```

axioms defined by the developers of the SNS. These axioms state the most fundamental rules regarding access privileges or permissions in the SNS. User-defined policies must always satisfy these axioms. A user-defined policy introduces actions to be undertaken when content is shared among users of the network. For instance, a policy might state that a particular content can be shared by all the member of a particular list of users of the SNS.

Poporo translates user-defined policies into Java code. A user-defined privacy policy can stipulate that when a user "ow" publishes certain content "rc" to the pages of users in list "friends," then the policy definition would be as below, where create_account creates users accounts, upload_principal adds network content and transmit_tolist shares content with a specified list of users.

```
Policy(){
   create_account(ow, rc);
   upload_principal(rc, ow);
   create_list(friends, ow);
   transmit_tolist(rc, friends);
 }
```

A user might want to ensure that the content they are sharing is shared with a subset of an existing list of users. Such a policy might stipulate that when a user "ow" publishes certain content "rc," it must be added to the page of all users in list "friends" that don't belong to a list "work." The policy definition would be as below.

```
Policy(){
   create_account(ow, rc);
   upload_principal(rc, ow);
   create_list(friends, ow);
   create_list(work, ow);
   transmit_tolist_restricted(rc,
    friends, work);
 }
```

An example of a transmission policy adopted by an application which allows a user to share their existing content is shown below. Here create_account creates users accounts, upload_principal adds network content transmit_tolist shares content with a specified list of users and grant_view_perm grants a specific user, "pe," view access to the content.

```
NewPolicy(){
   create_account(ow, rc);
   upload_principal(rc, ow);
   create_list(friends, ow);
   transmit_tolist(rc, friends);
   create_account(pe, rcpe);
   grant_view_perm(pe, rc);
 }
```

A NewPolicy as described right above might then be compared to one of the old policies to check whether in breaches them. It is necessary for a policy to contain all the relevant actions, pertaining to the content, performed by a user as the Poporo tool is not aware of the context in which the content is being shared. It is therefore necessary to inform the tool that the content in question was uploaded to the network by a user who previously created an account and the content is being shared with a list of users which was also previously created.

In the context of Facebook, the old policy might model the policy that a user defines when sharing some content, e.g., who is the intended audience of a user's photograph. The new policy might impose a new policy on the same kind of content, e.g. who is the intended audience of user's photographs uploaded to the network on the week-ends. The SNS might further define a new policy by changing the structure of a policy definition, in which case it is necessary to compare the definition with the old policy to avoid a breach like the one in Pepitone (2011).

Due to this required flexibility, it is not possible to use policy definition languages such as IBM's Enterprise Privacy Authorization Language (EPAL) and the OASIS eXtensible Access Control Markup Language (XACML). These languages require the definition of rules that specify the condition under which an entity can be granted access to some data. These rules relate to specific attributes of the content in question. In the context of SNS, these attributes might be the kind of content (status update, photograph, video) or might be the place and time when adding the content to the SNS. In either case it is not feasible to specify a global rule based on the context of the content as users constantly change their policy needs. When looking at context, G. Danezis proposed a framework for privacy policies based on context. The drawback of this approach was the inability for a system to truly gauge context.

The Verification Condition Generator

The verification condition generator (VCGen) takes the user-defined policy Java program and calculates a weakest precondition predicate based on the program instructions, which can be assignments, conditionals, variable declarations, or calls to predefined Matelas methods. We show some of the weakest precondition rules below, where "m.P" and "m.Q" are the precondition and the post-condition of method "m" respectively.

Assg: WP(x=E, Q) = WP(E,Q[x\result])

Seq: WP(S;T, Q) = WP(S, WP(T,Q))

MCall: WP(m(y), Q) = m.P $\wedge$ m.Q[x\y] $\Rightarrow$ Q

The VCGen parses Java the program statement by statement generating a verification condition "VCi" for every statement "Si." "VCi" take the form shown below, where "ri" is the pre-condition of instruction "Si" and "ti" is its post-condition. The consolidated VC is passed to the Yices SMT solver and is checked for satisfiability. If "Si" is a method call (MCall), "VCi+1" represents the property "Q" (calculated through a weakest precondition rule) that the method post-condition "ti" must verify. See Box 5.

$$VC = \mathop{\mathrm{I}}_{t=1}^{t=N} VCi$$

In Leino (2005), Rustan Leino introduces the concept of conservative and liberal weakest preconditions so as to reduce redundancy in the computation of VCs. He defines the weakest precondition of passive statements, that is, statements that do not alter the state of the system. This in combination with static single assignment (SSA) (Srinivasan, & Grunwald, 1991) has been incorporated to suit our purpose. SSA is a property of an intermediate representation (IR), which says that each variable is assigned exactly once with existing variables in the original IR being split into versions. A similar structure to VCs has already been incorporated into Poporo.

Comparing Policies

Poporo checks the compliance of a new policy with an old policy. The new policy can stipulate that the user may share content with a list of users that is known to be a subset of the list of users specified by the old policy. The relation among social-networking variables (the lists) is represented as a JML property and it is translated to Yices. The Yices property is combined with the Yices verification conditions (VCs) obtained for the translation of both policies, and is then passed to the Yices solver. If the VCs and the translation of the JML relationship are satisfiable, then the new and the old policies comply with Matelas. During the process of verification of a privacy policy, the Yices solver generates a post-state of the execution of each policy. The Poporo tool then checks whether the post-state for the new policy is a subset of the post-state for the old policy. More concretely, it checks whether access permissions after the execution the new policy are a subset of the access permissions after the execution of the old policy. If it is the case, the new policy complies with the old policy. Revisiting the kinds of privacy breaches identified earlier, we show how the Poporo tool is effective in identifying these possible breaches.

SNS Privacy Breach

Let us take a real world example of privacy breaches that occurred when Facebook updated the format of their privacy policies (Pepitone, 2011). The policy update granted users with more control over their content, but it reset all previi-

Box 5.

```
(define VCi:: bool
 (let ((ri:: bool (precondition-Si prestate-vars))
(ti:: bool (postcondition-Si prestate-vars poststate-vars)))
(and ri (implication ti VCi+1))))
```

ously defined policies to their default value, i.e. public. The old policy stipulates that a user "ow" can publish content to a list called "friends"[3]. The new policy stipulates that the same user "ow" can publish to the "public" list.

```
OldPolicy(){
    create_account(ow, rc);
    upload_principal(rc, ow);
    create_list(friends, ow);
    transmit_tolist(rc, friends);
 }

NewPolicy(){
    create_account(ow, rc);
    upload_principal(rc, ow)
    create_list(public, ow);
    transmit_tolist(rc, public);
}
```

The Poporo tool needs to know the actual relationship between the lists "friends" and "public" to be able to compare them. We know that any list is a subset of the "public" list. Poporo uses JML to express the relationship between "friends" and "public." The JML property expressing this relation is written as "ensures friends.isSubset(public)"[4] that tells Poporo that "friends" is a subset of "public." Poporo generates the VCs for the old and the new polices independently, and combines these VCs with the VC generated from the JML property to calculate a consolidated VC. Poporo uses Yices to check that the policies satisfy Matelas invariants (the system axioms) and to generate the post-state of the system after executing each policy. Poporo then extracts the set of access permissions (the privacy policy settings) from the post-state of the execution of each policy separately. These access permissions are compared. If the set of access permissions generated by the new policy is not a subset of the access permissions generated by the old policy the tool concludes that the new policy violates the old policy.

The set of access permissions after the execution of the old policy and new policies are presented below. The new policy grants access permissions (the bits 1) to a larger set of users as compared to the old policy. Thus, the Poporo tool informs the user that his new policy violates the original policy. See Box 6.

User Privacy Breach

Let us assume, a user has created three lists within the SNS regarding the users they work with. A list "colleagues" which contains users that they work with who fall on the same or lower level within the organizational hierarchy (peers), a list "superiors" which contains users who are higher than the user in the organizational hierarchy (bosses) and a list "employees" which is made up of all the users in the organization.

The user has defined a policy which states that when they share some content it must only be shared with the users in the list "colleagues." To this effect the user defines a policy as shown below. This policy is referred to as the Old Policy. In this policy first a user "ow" is created with some required content "rc." "ow" refers to the user in question who is defining their policy. Next

Box 6.

```
(=viewpOLD 0b0000000000000000100000000000000000000001000000000100000000000001)
(=editpOLD 0b0000000000000000000000000000000000000001000000000000000000000001)
(=viewpNEW 0b0000000100010000010000110000001000000001000000000100010000000001)
(=editpNEW 0b0000000000000000000000000000000000000001000000000000000000000001)
```

the policy adds some "content" to the network via the upload_principal() operation allocating ownership to "ow." Then the policy creates a list "colleagues" before transmitting "content" to the users in list "colleagues."

Now, the users defines a New Policy, wherein when they share some content it must be shared with the list "employees" but hidden from the list "superiors." This policy might be the policy defined by the user the next time they share some content or the policy adopted by an external plug-in being used by the user. To this effect the policy is defined as shown below. This policy is referred to as the New Policy. In this policy first a user "ow" is created with some required content "rc." "ow" refers to the user in question who is defining their policy. Next the policy adds some "content" to the network via the upload_principal() operation allocating ownership to "ow." Then the policy creates lists "employees" and "superiors" before transmitting "content" to the users.

```
OldPolicy(){
    create_account(ow,rc);
    upload_principal(content,ow);
    create_list(colleagues,ow);
    transmit_tolist(content,
     colleagues);
}

NewPolicy(){
    create_account(ow, rc);
    upload_principal(content,ow)
    create_list(employees,ow);
    create_list(superiors,ow);
    transmit_tolist_restricted
     (content, employees, superiors);
}
```

The list "employees" is the union of two lists, "colleagues" and "superiors." In JML, this is expressed as "ensures employees.equals(superiors.union(colleagues))." Likewise the first example, Poporo generates the VCs for the old and the new polices and combines the VCs with the VC generated from the JML property. Poporo then extracts the set of access permissions from the post-state of each policy. The set of access permissions after the old and new policies are shown below. The new policy grants access permission (the bits in 1) to a subset of users of the old policy. Poporo thus informs the user that the new policy complies with the original policy. See Box 7.

User to User Privacy Breach

Let us assume a user has defined a policy which states that when they are associated with some content, i.e. tagged in some content, it must only be shared with the users in the list "close_friends." To this effect the user defines a policy as shown below. This policy is referred to as the Tagged-Policy. In this policy first a user "ow" is created with some required content "rc." "ow1" refers to the user in question who is defining their policy. Next the policy adds some "content" to the network via the upload_principal() operation allocating ownership to "ow1." Then the policy creates a list "close_friends" before transmitting "content" to the users in list "close_friends."

Now, another user defines a Policy, wherein when they share some content it must be shared with the list "work." The content they are sharing is linked to the previous user by tagging user "ow1" in it. To this effect the policy is defined as shown below. This policy is referred to as the NewPolicy. In this policy first a user "ow2" is created with some required content "rc." "ow2" refers to the user in question who is defining their policy. Next the policy adds some "content" to the network via the upload_principal()operation allocating ownership to "ow." Then the policy creates lists "work" before transmitting "content" to the users in said list.

Box 7.

```
(=viewpOLD 0b0000000000000100000000000000000000000001000000000000000000010001)
(=editpOLD 0b0000000000000100000000000000000000000001000000000000000000010001)
(=viewpNEW 0b0000000000000000000000000000000000000001000000000000000000010001)
(=editpNEW 0b0000000000000000000000000000000000000001000000000000000000010001)
```

```
TaggedPolicy(){
    create_account(owl, rc);
    upload_principal(content,owl);
    create_list(close_friends,owl);
    transmit_tolist(content, close_
friends);
}

NewPolicy(){
    create_account(ow2,rc);
    upload_principal(content,ow2)
    create_list(work,ow);
    transmit_tolist(content,work);
}
```

Since we need to check compliance to “ow1”’s policy, the tool assumes the second policy to belong to user “ow1” as well. Therefore the tool thinks “ow1” and “ow2” refer to the same user. If we were to assume that the list “work” is a subset of the list “close_friends,” the JML property would be written as “ensures work.isSubset(close_friends) && ow1 == ow2.” The set of access permissions after the execution of the old policy and new policies are presented below. As the new set of access permissions is a subset of the permissions granted by the old policy, the Poporo tool informs the user that his new policy complies with the original policy. See Box 8.

Application Privacy Breach

Let us assume a user has defined a policy which states that when they share some content, it must only be shared with the users in the list “close_friends.” To this effect the user defines a policy as shown below. This policy is referred to as the OldPolicy. In this policy, first a user “ow” is created with some required content “rc.” “ow” refers to the user in question who is defining their policy. Next the policy adds some “content” to the network via the upload_principal() operation allocating ownership to “ow.” Then the policy creates a list “close_friends” before transmitting “content” to the users in list “close_friends.”

Next, the user uses an external plug-in, which allows a user to edit content which has been previously uploaded and shared. Now, the application defines a Policy, wherein a user edits some content. The content being edited is effectively deleted and replaced with new content. To this effect, the policy is defined as shown below. This policy is referred to as the NewPolicy. In this policy, first a user “ow” is created with some required content “rc.” “ow” refers to the user in question who is defining their policy. Next, the policy adds some “content” to the network via the upload_principal() operation allocating ownership to “ow.” Then the policy creates lists “close_friends” before trans-

Box 8.

```
(=viewpOLD 0b0000100000000000010000000010000000000001000000000000000000000001)
(=editpOLD 0b0000100000000000010000000010000000000001000000000000000000000001)
(=viewpNEW 0b0000100000000000000000000000000000000001000000000000000000000001)
(=editpNEW 0b0000100000000000000000000000000000000001000000000000000000000001)
```

mitting "content" to the users in said list. Next the policy defines the action of editing content via the edit_owned_not_required().

```
OldPolicy(){
    create_account(ow,rc);
    upload_principal(content,ow);
    create_list(close_friends,ow);
    transmit_tolist(content, close_
friends);
}

NewPolicy(){
    create_account(ow,rc);
    upload_principal(content,ow)
    create_list(close_friends,ow);
    transmit_tolist(content, close_
friends);
    edit_owned_not_
required(content,ow,new_content);
}
```

Since the same list is used in both policies it is not necessary to provide the Poporo tool with a relationship between the two policies. The set of access permissions after the execution of the old policy and new policies are presented below. As the new set of access permissions is a subset of the permissions granted by the old policy, the Poporo tool informs the user that his new policy complies with the original policy. See Box 9.

With the ever-growing complexity of social on-line relationships, trust in the social-network sites is more crucial now than ever before. The complex social relations and connections that exist in SNS make it hard for users to identify what a large global policy entails. Rather, a user with multiple policies regarding specific content can have greater control over their content. This in turn raises the issue of non-compliance between policies over similar content. It is not possible to trust on-line SNS to ensure the privacy of a user's content, as even they might inadvertently breach privacy policies as observed on numerous occasions. The Poporo tool allows users to define multiple policies within a SNS environment and then compare these policies against a pre-existing or global policy on the fly when sharing content. Additionally a user can ensure that an action they perform concerning some content complies with the privacy policy they initially shared the content under. This helps alleviate some of the privacy concerns raised within online SNS.

REAL WORLD APPLICATION

As is abundantly evident, social networking sites have become an integral part of a user's online identity. These users actively share content with other users. As has been illustrated earlier, privacy concerns exist with possible breaches from multiple sources. The presented framework along with the tools implemented based on said framework, attempt to alleviate these concerns. The presented frameworks along with the tools have been demonstrated to work for various scenarios in an offline theoretical environment. It is paramount for the framework and tools to work in a real-world environment in conjunction with a real social networking site (SNS). Therefore as a case study, the Poporo tool was incorporated as a plug-in into Facebook.

Box 9.

```
(=viewpOLD 0b00000000000000000100000000100000000000000001000000000000000000000001)
(=editpOLD 0b00000000000000000100000000100000000000000001000000000000000000000001)
(=viewpNEW 0b00000000000000000100000000100000000000000001000000000000000000000001)
(=editpNEW 0b00000000000000000100000000100000000000000001000000000000000000000001)
```

As of May 2012, Facebook has over 900 million active users making it by far the most popular SNS online today. Facebook incorporates a lot of the system axioms defined within Matelas, though not all. This made Facebook an ideal choice for applying Poporo to a real-world SNS. To account for these additional axioms necessary for ensuring privacy we incorporated Poporo as a plug-in.

Facebook provides an API allowing developers to build plug-ins to access user data once said user has authorized the plug-in. Based on this API, a plug-in was built. The Poporo Facebook plug-in asks a user to grant access to the personal information, restricted to name and email address. It further asks a user to grant access to all their 'friend list.' 'Friend lists' refer to all the list of users created by the user in question along with any auto-generated list associated with the user's profile.

When a user accesses the plug-in via Facebook, if it is their first time accessing the plug-in, they are asked to authorize the Poporo plug-in to access their information else are redirected to the Poporo interface.

Next the user defines their Old policy and the actions defining the New policy. The Old policy is composed of the list of users they wish to share the content with and the list of users they wish to hide the content from. The New Policy is comprised of the action they wish to perform, be it sharing (transmitting), editing content, commenting on content, etc. The plug-in accepts as input the various fields described above and generates the appropriate policy the actions represent. Next the plug-in generates the required JML code relating the various variables of the two policies. In the example presented earlier, it was necessary for the JML relation to be defined by the user. In this plug-in the Poporo tool has access to the present state of the network, i.e. from the information collected from Facebook. Using this information, the plug-in can automatically define any and all relationships that exist between the variables.

The policies generated along with the JML specification is passed onto the Poporo tool. The user is then informed whether their New policy (actions) would breach their Old policy.

FUTURE RESEARCH DIRECTIONS

Social networking has become an integral part of peoples' online lives. Information from online profiles allows developers to provide users with a tailor made experience when using web-services. Users find it hard to balance their privacy needs due to their lack of understanding on how a service might use their information. Therefore a mechanism to define and ensure the privacy policies to which people adhere is needed.

In the context of the presented chapter, some of the more predominant trends of how users interact with social networking sites are presented. With the ever-increasing number of connections (friends), users of social networking sites increasingly rely on grouping mechanisms to define different groups of other users to share specific kinds on content with. These grouping mechanisms, such as friend's lists in Facebook, or friend's circles in Google+, allow a user to organize their friends into groups associated with specific activities or kinds of content. Since these groups grow, and because they are not exclusive of each other, it is necessary to allow a user to define more fine-grained privacy policies within these social networks. The user must be able to specify global privacy policies based on context and content to prevent sharing with an unintended recipient. There is also a need for a mechanism to check a policy against these global policies within the social networking site environment. Future work on Poporo would include the implementation of such a tool for Facebook or Google+ (being the larger social networks today).

Another trend is brought about with the advent of smart mobile devices such as smart-phones and tablets. Users increasingly interact with their social network through these devices on the move. Users use these devices to share content, be it status updates, their location or images of where they are or with whom they are. Users have little or no control over who these applications share their content with. This is due to the physical limitations of these devices as they cannot offer the user the full functionality offered via the social networking site. These applications therefore claim to access the users' privacy policy from the social network and use it when sharing content. The developers of such applications are unknown to the social networking site and might share no trust relationship with the network. Therefore, it is necessary for a user to have a mechanism for checking an application transmission policy against their global privacy policies. Future work on the Poporo tool would need to address these needs as well.

The major hindrance in the implementation of such a tool within the context to existing social networking sites is the lack of a standard model for privacy enforcement within such networks. Additionally these sites do not offer the developers of such tools easy access to a user's privacy policy. This requires a user to redefine their policies within a tool such as Poporo. This introduces the possibility of human error while a user is duplicating their policies.

CONCLUSION

Trust and usage may determine what people are willing to share in a social-network site (SNS). With the ever-growing complexity of social on-line relationships, trust in the social-network sites is more crucial now than ever before. The complex social relations and connections that exist in SNS make it hard for users to identify what a large global policy entails. Rather, a user with multiple policies regarding specific content can have greater control over their content. This in turn raises the issue of non-compliance between policies over similar content. It is not possible to trust on-line SNS to ensure the privacy of a user's content, as even they might inadvertently breach privacy policies as observed on numerous occasions. To overcome this problem, we have presented our formal approach to privacy in social networks and the implementation of this approach as the Poporo tool to enforce compliance of privacy policies across social networks.

The presented approach was based on the incorporation of the Matelas model for social networking. The Matelas model defines a core social networking application which models system axioms and operations. The operations have all been formally verified against the system axiom, defined in the model as invariants. This verified model provided a stable platform for the development of the Poporo tool.

The rules and mechanism defined in the JML to Yices translator, present an approach to check the satisfiability of JML specification by mapping JML specifications into the input language of Yices, and using Yices solver to perform the checking. The Matelas model was translated in to the Yices input language and made up the Yices prelude as described in the structure on the Poporo tool. This prelude fed in to the Yices SMT solver and the Verification condition generator.

It is imperative for the users of social networking sites, to be aware of how their content is shared with other users. Due to the flexibility user's desire within a social networking site, automated policy definition and strict policy definition, through current policy definition languages, are both unfeasible and undesirable. The Poporo tool provided users with a mechanism to define privacy policies on the fly, in an easy to understand format. These privacy policies were defined as Java methods using Matelas operations. Users explicitly state the list of users they wish to share the content with, the list of users they wish to hide the content from and the action they are performing within the social network. Defining privacy policies based on actions is easier for a novice user to comprehend, as users get more familiar with the network and the tool they can then increase the complexity of the privacy policies to suit their needs. Privacy policies defined in this format feed into the verification condition generator where they are checked for compliance with Matelas invariants and with any pre-existing policy the user might have specified.

This verification condition generator (VCGen) draws on weakest precondition calculus to generate verification conditions. The custom built VCGen presented was built specifically for the Poporo tool. The constant improvements made to the VCGen allowed us to improve the VCGen's efficiency. Different formats for VCs, input and output were defined and the most efficient adopted. The VCs generated are passed on to the Yices SMT solver to check their satisfiability. Subsequently, the VCs are passed on the policy compliance module to ensure that a newly defined policy adheres to a pre-existing one.

The Poporo tool allows users to define multiple policies within a SNS environment and then compare these policies against a pre-existing or global policy on the fly when sharing content. Additionally, a user can ensure that an action they perform concerning some content complies with the privacy policy they initially shared the content under. This helps alleviate some of the privacy concerns raised within online SNS.

The examples give the reader an in-depth look at the functioning of the Poporo tool. It was the study of examples like the ones presented that allowed us to determine where the tool lacked refinement and it allowed us to identify bugs within the system. The example presented, though it might look simple, represents a majority of privacy policies a user of a SNS might define. The correct working of such examples and the efficiency demonstrated helps raise confidence in the Poporo tool.

Privacy being is of utmost importance when it comes to online social networks, the Poporo tool provides users with a tool to check privacy policies and compare such policies for compliance. The Poporo tool has been demonstrated to be effective and reliable in ensuring privacy as demonstrated. The performance of the current version of the tool was found to be acceptable at most tasks taking under three minutes to perform. Due to the lack of similar tools for policy comparison it was not possible to compare Poporo's performance against any benchmarks.

The Poporo tool was implemented in an online environment where it had to deal with real world scenarios as a case study. This case study has demonstrated the application of the Poporo tool within a real social networking site. Such a deployment allowed us to gauge the ease with which such a tool might finally be deployed. SNS provide developers with an easy to use API for connecting their plug-ins to the social network and gather authorized information from their users. It also made evident the shortcomings of such an approach. The API are restrictive as the SNS wishes to protect the privacy of their users. It only allows the plug-in limited access to online information. For a tool like Poporo to truly make an impact it necessary for the tool to be incorporated into the SNS system itself as opposed to an external plug-in. Though their remains work to be done to further extend the plug-in to incorporate policies defined by multiple users, it is evident that a tool such as Poporo would greatly benefit users of online SNS.

The formal methods based approach presented along with the accompanying Poporo tool has proven to be effective in both an offline and online environment. Such an approach provides for the flexibility required within a social networking site with users constantly updating their privacy policies and with social networking sites constantly changing to fulfill user demands.

REFERENCES

Abrial, J. R. (1984). The mathematical construction of a program. *Science of Computer Programming*, *4*(1), 45–86. doi:10.1016/0167-6423(84)90011-X

Abrial, J. R. (1996). *The B-book: Assigning programs to meanings*. Cambridge University Press. doi:10.1017/CBO9780511624162

Abrial, J. R., & Hallerstede, S. (2007). Refinement, decomposition and instantiation of discrete models: Application to event-B. *Fundamentae Informatica*, *77*, 1–24.

Anderson, J., Diaz, C., Bonneau, J., & Stajano, F. (2009). Privacy-enabling social networking over untrusted networks. In *Proceedings of the 2nd ACM workshop on Online social networks, 2009*.

Appel, A. W. (2001). *Foundational proof-carrying code. Logic in Computer Science* (pp. 247–256). LICS.

Backstrom, L., Dwork, C., & Kleinberg, J. (2007). Wherefore art thou r3579x?: Anonymized social networks, hidden patterns, and structural steganography. In *Proceedings of the 16th international conference on World Wide Web 2007*.

Barthe, G. A., Grégoire, B., Jensen, T., & Pichardie, D. (2008). *The MOBIUS proof carrying code infrastructure. Formal Methods for Components and Objects (FMCO)* (pp. 1–24). Berlin, Germany: Springer-Verlag. doi:10.1007/978-3-540-92188-2_1

Bayardo, R. J. (2005). Data privacy through optimal k-anonymization. *International Conference on Data Engineering (ICDE)* (pp. 217-228).

Bonneau, J., Anderson, J., & Church, L. (2009). Privacy suites: Shared privacy for social networks. *Symposium on Usable Privacy and Security*. ACM.

Bowen, J., & Stavridou, V. (1993). *Safety critical systems, formal methods and standards*. Computer Lab International. doi:10.1049/sej.1993.0025

Breunesse, C., Cataño, N., Huisman, M., & Jacobs, B. (2005). Formal methods for smart cards: An experience report. *Science of Computer Programming*, *55*(1-3), 53–80. doi:10.1016/j.scico.2004.05.011

Brunel, J., Cuppens, F., Cuppens, N., Sans, T., & Bodeveix, J.-P. (2007). Security policy compliance with violation management. *ACM Workshop on Formal methods in Security Engineering (FMSE)* (pp. 31-40). New York, NY, USA: ACM.

Cataño, N., Hanvey, S., & Rueda, C. (2012). *The Poporo tool*. Retrieved October 5, 2012, from http://poporo.uma.pt/~ncatano/Projects/wespfm/PoporoTool/poporo.php

Cataño, N., & Rueda, C. (2010). Matelas: A predicate calculus common formal definition for social networking. In M. Frappier (Ed.), *ABZ. 5977* (pp. 259-272). Québec: Lecture Notes in Computer Science.

Cataño, N., Rueda, C., & Hanvey, S. (2011). Verification of JML generic types with Yices. In *Proceedings of 6th Colombian Congress of Computing (6CCC)* (pp. 1-6). Manizales, Colombia: IEEE Xplore Digital Library.

Cataño, N., Wahls, T., Rivera, V., & Rueda, C. (2012). *The B2Jml tool*. Retrieved October 5, 2012, from http://poporo.uma.pt/~ncatano/Projects/favas/B2JML.html

Cataño, N., Wahls, T., & Rueda, C. (2012). Translating B machines to JML specifications. *Symposium on Applied Computing, Software Verification and Testing track (SAC-SVT)*. Trento, Italy: ACM.

Danezis, G. (2009). Inferring privacy policies for social networking services. In *Proceedings of the 2nd ACM workshop on Security and Artificial Intelligence* (pp. 5-10). Chicago, Illinois, USA: ACM.

Dutertre, B., & Moura, L. M. (2006). *A fast linear-arithmetic solver for DPLL(T). Computer Aided Verification* (pp. 81–94). CAV. doi:10.1007/11817963_11

Dwork, C. (2006). Differential privacy. *International Colloquium on Automata, Languages and Programming (ICALP)* (pp. 1-12).

Gandon, F. L., & Sadeh, N. M. (2004). Semantic web technologies to reconcile privacy and context awareness. *Journal of Web Semantics*, *1*(3), 241–260. doi:10.1016/j.websem.2003.07.008

Gilbert, E., & Karahalios, K. (2009). Predicting tie strength with social media. In *Proceedings of the 27th international conference on Human factors in computing systems* (pp. 187-196).

Hoare, J. H., & Sanders, J. W. (1986). Data refinement refined. *European Symposium on Programming* (pp. 187-196).

Leaves, G. T., Baker, A. L., & Ruby, C. (2006). *Preliminary design of JML: A behavioral interface specification language for Java* (pp. 1–38). Software Engineering Notes.

Leino, R. (2005). Efficient weakest preconditions. *Information Processing Letters (IPL)*, 281–288. doi:10.1016/j.ipl.2004.10.015

Pepitone, J. (2011). *Facebook settles FTC charges over 2009 privacy breaches*. Retrieved October 5, 2012, from http://money.cnn.com/2011/11/29/technology/facebook_settlement/index.htm?iid=HP_LN

Sadeh, N., Hong, J., Cranor, L., Fette, I., Kelley, P., & Prabaker, M. (2009). Understanding and capturing people's privacypolicies in a mobile social networking application. *Journal of Personal and Ubiquitous Computing*, *13*, 401–412. doi:10.1007/s00779-008-0214-3

Solove, D. J. (2006). A taxonomy of privacy. *University of Pennsylvania Law Review*, *154*(3), 477–560. doi:10.2307/40041279

Tschantz, M. C., & Wing, J. M. (2009). *Formal methods for privacy* (pp. 1–15). Formal Methods, FM.

ADDITIONAL READING

Agarwal, R., & Srikant, R. (2000). Privacy-preserving data mining. In *Proceedings of the 2000 ACM SIGMOD international conference on Management of data* (pp. 439-450).

Anderson, A. (2005). *A comparison of two privacy policy languages: EPAL and XACML. Technical report*. Sun Microsystems Laboratories.

Barth, A., Mitchell, J. C., & Rosenstien, J. (2004). Conflict and combination in privacy policy languages. In *Proceedings of the 2004 ACM workshop on Privacy in the electronic society*.

Culnan, M. J. (2000). Protecting privacy online: Is self-regulation working? *Journal of Public Policy & Marketing*, *19*(1), 20–26. doi:10.1509/jppm.19.1.20.16944

Karjoth, G., & Schunter, M. (2002). A privacy policy model for enterprises. In *Proceedings of Computer Security Foundations Workshop*.

Warren, S. D., & Brandeis, L. D. (1890). The right to privacy. *Harvard Law Review*, *4*(5), 193–220. doi:10.2307/1321160

Yee, G. (2004). Privacy policy compliance for web services. In Proceedings of IEEE International Conference on Web Services.

KEY TERMS AND DEFINITIONS

Formal Methods: A set of techniques and tools based on mathematical modeling and formal logic used to specify and verify requirements and designs for computer systems.

Inter-Policy Compliance: Ensuring a given complies with a pre-existing one.

Privacy-Aware Social Networking: It allows users of social-networking sites to predict or foresee the consequences or effects of changing privacy settings.

Privacy Policy: A set of conditions applied over content transmission ensuring transmission to the intended set of users only.

Social Networks: Online networks allowing for the sharing of content and information between multiple users.

ENDNOTES

1. Mattress in French.
2. That is, the invariant need not hold while a method is executing, but must be re-established by the time that the method terminates.
3. The policies shown here have been simplified for ease of comprehension.
4. The JML ensures clause specifies method post-conditions.

Chapter 12
Web Malware that Targets Web Applications

Ammar Alazab
Deakin University, Australia

Jemal Abawajy
Deakin University, Australia

Michael Hobbs
Deakin University, Australia

ABSTRACT

Web applications have steadily increased, making them very important in areas, such as financial sectors, e-commerce, e-government, social media network, medical data, e-business, academic an activities, e-banking, e-shopping, e-mail. However, web application pages support users interacting with the data stored in their website to insert, delete and modify content by making a web site their own space. Unfortunately, these activities attracted writers of malicious software for financial gain, and to take advantage of such activities to perform their malicious objectives. This chapter focuses on severe threats to web applications specifically on Structure Query Language Injection Attack (SQLIA) and Zeus threats. These threats could adopt new obfuscation techniques to evade and thwart countermeasures Intrusion Detection Systems (IDS). Furthermore, this work explores and discusses the techniques to detect and prevent web application malware.

INTRODUCTION

Malware is a very broad term that describes a kind of malicious software (Valli & Brand, 2008). However, numerous definitions have been proposed to define malware. For example, malware is software that harmfully attacks the software of others (Kramer & Bradfield, 2010). For the purpose of this research, malware is defined as any piece of code or string that causes harm to information systems without a user's permission.

Recent trends in web application malware have become a major threat and they are increasing in complexity and evolving rapidly as systems

DOI: 10.4018/978-1-4666-3926-3.ch012

provide more opportunities for more automated activities. Furthermore, the damages caused by web application malware to individuals and businesses have dramatically increased in 2010 (RSA, 2011).

Today, writers of malicious software (malware) either develop sophisticated techniques to conceal their attacks or constantly change their method of attack to evade detection software. New study identifies a new attack that infected nearly 300,000 web pages, with the infection containing malicious code that revealed client information and directed clients to a fake web site (Jie et al., 2010). However, this type of attack event was just one of a series of malicious activities targeting web applications. Research has indicated that fraud detection has steadily increased over recent years (BitDefender, 2010).

Even though attackers who achieve unauthorized access to financial systems cause huge losses to the financial sector, there is not one single technique that can stop them. However, a threat that was once utilized by individual criminals is now the focus of major organised crime crossing international boundaries and jurisdictions. A report by the Australian government warns that attacks will become more prevalent as more persistent techniques are adopted (RSA, 2011).

Generally, an attacker develops new and sophisticated techniques to target and hack the web application. The result is that attackers gain access to the data of other users. To prevent web application attacks, different approaches have been suggested but they do have limitations. Indeed, some of these approaches have yet to be implemented and in the approaches that have been, most cannot prevent or detect every single type of attack.

There are several different types of malware. These include viruses, worms, Trojan horses, spyware, rootkits and backdoors, etc. This chapter will focus on malware that specifically targets web applications using SQLIAs. This research will make the following contributions:

- Significant investigation exploring new evasion techniques used by hackers to compromise web applications.
- Exploration of existing detection and prevention techniques against SQL injection.

BACKGROUND

Web applications are applications that run over a network (such as the internet or an intranet) that enable a website to become dynamic by making connections within the database. The high level system component of a web application is shown in Figure 1. Included in web application architec-

Figure 1. Web application architecture

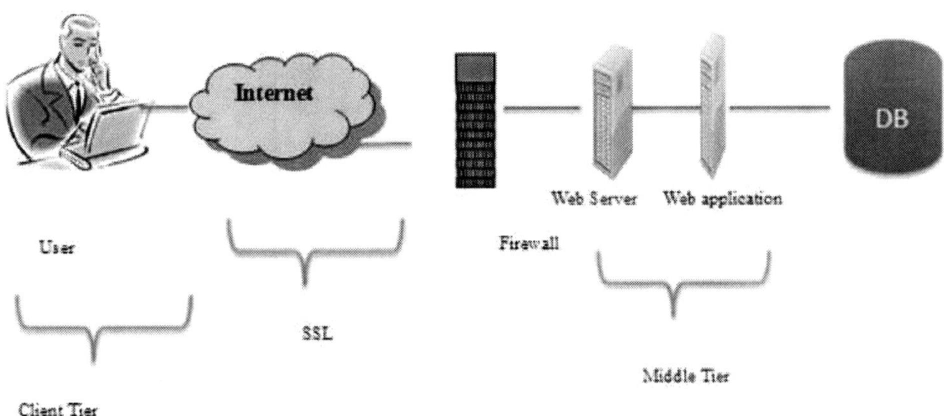

ture are browsers, a network, a web server, a web application and a database.

Figure 2 explains the web application process model in detail. Firstly, the client requests either a static or dynamic page. Secondly, the web browser passes this request through the firewall to the web server. Thirdly, the web server handles this request based on initial configuration such as HTTP, HTTPS, etc. The web server can also handle these requests by "decoding" the webpage. Fourthly, the web server passes this request to the web application server. Next, the web application passes these requests to the database. In addition, the web application processes commands and verifies security access to the database through middleware such as Java Database Connectivity (JDBC), Structured Query Language for Java (SQLJ), Java Data Object (JDO), Open Database Connectivity (ODBC), etc. and makes the logical decisions. After verifying database access, the web application server sends the Structured Query Language (SQL) request to the database server. Finally, the database server manipulates this request by allowing storage, deletion, or updating of the data. Depending upon the SQL query, it sends back the results to the application server.

Generally, web applications use query statements to generate strings to interact with the database. Usually, these queries are generated by web application servers such as ASP, JSP and PHP. A string contains both the query itself and its parameters which are usually the user name and password. Then, the string is forwarded to the database server for checking as a single SQL statement. If the received string is compromised

Figure 2. Web application model works

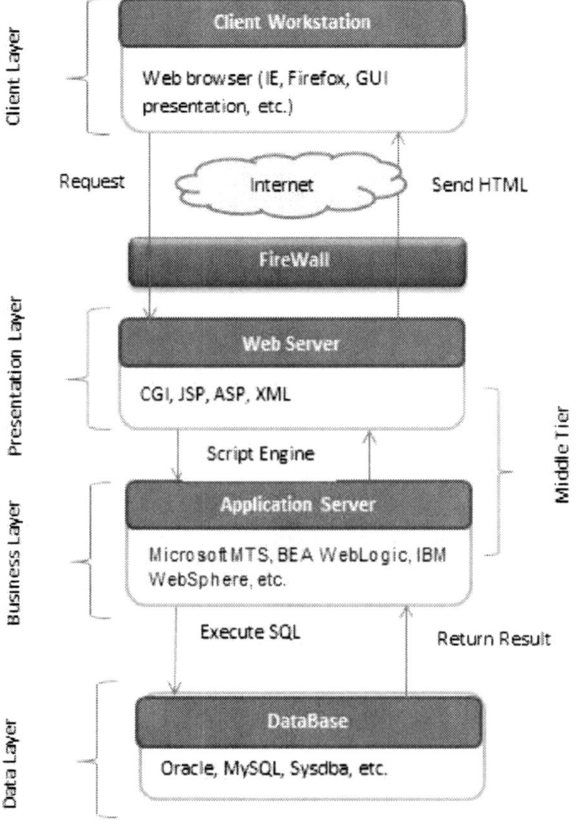

or injected, it will cause data leakage. Therefore, it is important to protect the web application from illegal access.

Web applications are infamous for security vulnerabilities that can be utilised by writers of malware, and also by hackers. The global accessibility of web applications is a serious problem which renders them vulnerable to attack. One of the most known and widespread threats to web applications is SQLIAs (Bisht, Madhusudan, & Venkatakrishnan, 2010).

Web applications offer a great opportunity to access the database through the internet (Peng, Chen, Chung, Roy-Chowdhury, & Srinivasan, 2010), which has provided the required service to customers. However, these advantages have raised a number of security vulnerabilities from improper code that have resulted in Structured Query Language Vulnerabilities (SQLV) that give hackers the ability to influence the Structured Query Language (SQL) a web application passes to the back-end of a database. The insertion of malicious code into strings to gain unauthorized access to a database is used to either retrieve information or destroy the database (DB) where all the data is sensitive.

Web application security generally focuses on identifying vulnerabilities and malicious strings within web applications layers. Firewalls and a Secure Sockets Layer (SSL) protect information transferred between the site and client, but do not protect information against web application hackers because it is built on top of the web application infrastructure (Yu, Aravind, & Supthaweesuk, 2006). Therefore, it is easy to append data and commands into a SQL statement. Even normal users can attempt direct connections to the database through specific ports by bypassing the security mechanism (Vella, 2007).

WEB APPLICATION ATTACK

Web applications are designed to assist any client to connect to the Database (DB) through a user's web Brower. However, if the user's input is not handled correctly, the web application can be left vulnerable to a malicious attack.

In addition, attackers develop tools to look for popular vulnerabilities to launch attacks against web applications. This availability of tools, and the existence of motivations to launch attacks, makes web applications a critical area to study. According to the report of Common Vulnerabilities and Exposures (CVE), the numbers of web-related vulnerabilities increased from 2005 to 2010 (Corporation, 2010).

Moreover, web applications use Rapid Application Development (RAD) to accelerate building complex web application systems but this makes web applications more vulnerable to attacks. According to the Open Web Application Security Project (OWASP), the top ten application security risks are presented in Table 1 (OWASP, 2010). This table shows all of the popular web application attacks.

Another report from the Web Application Security Consortium's Statistics Project (WACSP) stated that in 2010, the popular vulnerabilities in web application found by penetration testers were (Gordeychik 2010). See Table 2.

We note the improper input handling is equal to 14.65% and insufficient authentication is equal to 13.38% which helps to increase SQL injection.

The result is that a SQL injection attack (SQLI) dominates all other vulnerabilities and is still the best known type of attack. It has risen from number two in 2007 to number one in 2010 according to Open Web Application Security (OWASP, 2010).

Furthermore, the WHID announced that the Web Application Security Consortium's Statistics Project revealed the weaknesses that are exploited by various attack methods (http://

Table 1. Attack methods in web applications

No.	Web Application Security Risks	When does it occur?	Impact
1	Injection	The hacker sends a malicious string as a query statement to the database.	Data loss, data stolen, modified, deleted, corruption or denial of access
2	Cross-Site Scripting (XSS)	Attacker executed malicious code in the user's browser	Redirect users to malicious web sites, the result sensitive information
3	Broken Authentication and Session Management	When a session ID is visible due to leaks in the authentication process	Attacker could do anything with the victim's privileged accounts
4	Insecure Direct Object References	When An attacker changes the URL parameters	Compromises all the data
5	Cross-Site Request Forgery (CSRF)	Attacker sends fake HTTP requests to trick a victim into submitting them via image tags.	Loss or modified data
6	Security Misconfiguration	Attackers try to find unused pages, unprotected files and unprotected directories, etc. to reach for sensitive data.	The web application could be completely compromised without knowledge. All data could be stolen or modified
7	Insecure Cryptographic Storage	Here attackers don't break the cryptographic, but disclose something else to get the original text.	Lost data such as health records, credentials, personal data, credit cards, etc.
8	Failure to Restrict URL access	Simply changes the URL to a privileged page	Attacker can do anything the victim can do
9	Insufficient Transport Layer Protection	The attacker simply monitors network traffic (like an open wireless or neighbourhood cable modem network), and observes an authenticated victim's session cookie. Attacker then replays this cookie and takes over the user's session.	Phishing, resulting in a stolen account
10	Invalidated Redirects and Forwards	Attacker redirects links to invalidate and trick victims into clicking it. Victims will probably click on it, with the security mechanism bypassed.	Redirections such as these may attempt to install malware or trick victims into disclosing passwords or other sensitive information

Table 2. Web vulnerabilities

Web Application Vulnerability	Percentage
Improper output handling	22.29%
Insufficient anti automation	15.29%
Improper input handling	14.65%
Insufficient authentications	13.38%
Unknown	8.92%
Application misconfiguration	6.37%
Insufficient process validation	6.36%

projects.Webappsec.org/Threat-Classification) and further research has identified an increase in professional criminals using a combination of attacks (Gordeychik, 2010).

WEB APPLICATION VULNERABILITIES EXPLOITED

Web applications use Rapid Application Development (RAD) to accelerate building complex web application system; unfortunately this makes web applications more vulnerable to attacks. A web application has many features and characteristics which could lead to infection of SQLAs: (i) the input query strings contain usernames and passwords; it may inject with malicious code; (ii) Dynamic query statements also help SQLAs; (iii) SQL queries don't contain any information about the source; (iv) in addition, the problem of SQL injection is the integrity of information fl t (Jie, Phan, Whitley, & Parish, 2010). Furthermore, malicious application writers use combination attacks such as botnets, hacking tool kits and web application vulnerabilities to make cybercriminals more resilient and powerful than ever before.

Today, most industries are moving toward the use of web applications. Even though the features of web applications make them convenient to support and maintain, many of these same features also make them vulnerable to attack. As a result, attackers target web applications to access the database through SQLIAs because this type of attack can compromise the confidentiality and integrity of information in the databases, resulting in the theft of confidential data and the breaking of data integrity or affecting the availability of the web application.

The Open Web Application Security Project (OWASP) revealed that many web application vulnerabilities cause input validation problems. This means the process of checking all the input in an application before using it for the input of the client (OWASP, 2010). However, this is a weakness and can lead to SQL attacks. SQLIAs are not only introduced via any user inputs but also any external strings or outside input that malicious writer uses to build a query string like cookies, a web application variable or a server variable. Attackers have various techniques to employ to find vulnerabilities based on the input source that can be used to cause a database to crash, steal data, or to deface the web. These vulnerabilities can breach the security mechanism that is designed to prevent, detect and recover (Anderson & Moore, 2007) if there is a threat to a web application. In the case of vulnerabilities, there is a lack of enforced security mechanisms, a lack of configuration of security mechanisms and a lack of antivirus detection systems. See Figure 3.

However, the main problem causing web application vulnerabilities are insufficient input validation to exploit invalidate in web applications, the hacker need to inject a malicious string into web applications (Anderson & Moore, 2007). The most commonly used methods hackers use to inject web applications are:

- **Parameter Tampering:** These rely on the browser; the attacker changes the parameters in Uniform Resource Locator (URL) to bypass the security mechanism. For example in online shopping when the developer use hidden field to store item product statues, attackers take advantage from this hidden file and change the information such as shown in the following example:

  <input type="hidden" id="321" name= "cost" value="2.00">

In the above example the attacker can change the cost of a product to lowering cost.

- **Cookie Poisoning:** The attacker puts a malicious string into cookies to submit to web application. Web browsers submit the request using GET or POST methods. If the method GET is used, it means all parameters and values will display in the browser. The result is hackers can tamper this query statement. For example the following URL is submitted: http://www.website.com/

Figure 3. Relation between threat, vulnerabilities, and mechanisms

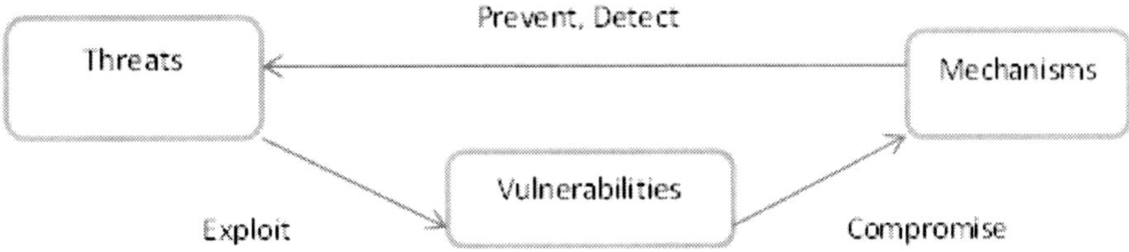

page.asp?UserId=6543&value=1, the hacker can modify the URL parameters (User ID and value) in order to add another account like http://www.website.com/example.asp?UserID=1243&value=9999

In general, hackers develop advanced techniques that compromise a database using SQL statements to steal information from a database that help to compromise web application successfully.

WEB APPLICATIONS THREAT

Recent trends in web application malware have become a major threat and are increasing in complexity as systems provide more opportunities for automated activities. Furthermore, damages caused by malware to individuals and businesses have also significantly increased in the last few years (RSA, 2011).

SQLIAs are one of the biggest threats to web applications. New evasion techniques allow attackers to take control of a database on an application. The result increasingly causes financial fraud, website defacement, denial of service and possibly the manipulation of data.

The general use of the Internet has made it increasingly difficult to find a high level of security because most web applications work as distributed systems and are built on multiple heterogeneous technologies. In addition, hackers increasingly target web applications because they connect with databases that contain sensitive data. The threats related to database security include (Connolly, Begg, & Strachan 1996)

1. Loss of confidentiality when information can be accessed by someone who shouldn't access it.
2. Loss of privacy which refers to exposure of personal information.
3. Loss of integrity which may be due to corrupt data since unauthorized individuals make the integrity loss happen.
4. Loss of availability which means the services or systems cannot be reached due to Denial-of-Service attacks.
5. However, Connolly *et al* also define risk as any effect that might damage a database with the system crashing being the end result. This threat can be classified as:
   a. **Interruption:** An attempt to destroy an asset or make it unusable.
   b. **Interception:** The database becomes unavailable.
   c. **Modification:** For example, a hacker can change the values in a database.
   d. **Fabrication:** A hacker can insert records into an existing database.

SQL INJECTION ATTACKS (SQLIA)

In order to demonstrate the web application threat, we conducted a second study of a SQL Injection Attack. In this section, I will define SQL, SQL injection, and provide examples of a SQL injection, plus various SQL injection vulnerabilities and evasion methods.

Structured Query Language (SQL)

SQL stands for Structured Query Language. It was defined by ANSI (American National Standards Institute) and has also been adopted as a standard by ISO (International Organization for Standardization). SQL is standard language for accessing and manipulating relational database systems (w3schools, 2011).

SQL is divided into three parts: the Data Manipulation Language (DML), Data Definition Language (DDL) and Data Control Language (DCL).

- **DML:** Used to perform, SELECT statement, change existing data - UPDATE statement, create new records holding data - INSERT INTO statement and delete data - DELETE statement.
    - ***SELECT:*** Used for retrieving information from one or more tables in the database and displaying it. The syntax of the SELECT statement is given below:

      SELECT [DISTINCT|ALL] *|column_expression][,...] FROM table_name [alias][,...]

      [WHERE condition] [GROUP BY column_list][HAVING condition]
    - ***INSERT:*** Used for adding new data rows in a table. The syntax of the INSERT statement is given here: INSERT INTO Table_name [(column_list)] VALUES (data).
    - ***UPDATE:*** Used for updating data rows in a table. The syntax of the *UPDATE* statement is given: UPDATE table_name SET column_name1 = data_value1.
- **DDL:** DDL statements are used to build and change the structure of tables, records, fields, and other objects in the database.
    - ***CREATE:*** Creates an object inside the database, the syntax of the CREATE TABLE is CREATE [TEMPORARY] TABLE *[table name]* (*[column definitions]*) *[table parameters]*;
      ALTER TABLE <table name>
    - ***DROP:*** Removes an object from database DROP TABLE <table name>;.
    - ***DCL:*** Statements.
    - ***GRANT:*** Gives user's privileges select, insert, update, or delete on the database.
    - ***REVOKE:*** Withdraw user's privileges select, insert, update, or delete on the database.

SQL Injection Attack (SQLIA) is a type of attack on a web application that occurs when an attacker inputs malicious strings as parameters in legitimate SQL statements (Torrano-Gimenez, Perez-Villegas, & Alvarez, 2010). The SQLIA allows the hacker to gain complete access to the database server resulting in a serious threat to the web application.

Impact of SQL Injection Attacks

SQL injection is a serious threat that can cause the following:

1. **Web Defacements:** Zone-H is a web site that records web site defacements (http://www.zone-h.org/news/id/4735). This site has recorded the web applications that have been hacked over the years using SQL injection vulnerabilities. Records show that there were 33,920 attacks in 2010 and 57,797 attacks in 2009 (Almeida, 2010).
2. **Financial Fraud:** Attacks have been responsible for loss of credentials to fraudsters.
3. **Spoof:** To impersonate a user in order to manipulate a database that allows an attacker to intercept the database.
4. **Tampering:** Updating or deleting data in a database without authorization.
5. **Authentication Bypass:** When the hacker logs onto the web application without a valid username and password.
6. **Information Leakage:** When an application reveals sensitive data, such as technical details of the web application. The result is the theft of sensitive data, such as credit card information and user identities (driver's license number, birth date, passport number, social security numbers, etc.) and user-specific information (passwords, username).

7. **Denial of Service (DoS):** This can occur when the hacker deletes or modifies the database. The end result is the unavailability of the website. This means legitimate users are unable to access or use the web application. For example, if the attacker enters input as "; SHUTDOWN; - -" The query will be: "SELECT * FROM username WHERE userTable=' '; SHUTDOWN; --'and password='whatever";

The result of the above SQL statement means the database will be shut down and a DoS attack will be conducted on the web application because the database becomes unavailable. The '--' character sequence means the comment and the character ";" is the end of one query and the beginning of another SQL statement, which is used to stop the database service.

Example of SQL injection

The code in Box 1 shows a JSP login page that is vulnerable, leading to a SQLIA.

The above code is a simple web application that contains a SQL injection. In this example, the web developer uses input parameters to login using two parameters: username and password, in order to dynamically build an SQL statement. They check the username and password at the login stage against the database as shown in Table 1.

When a user logs in with their user name and password in a web browser, the request is submitted as a dynamic URL, such as http://<mysite>/show.jsp?login=username&pass=password, and sent to the web server. The web server checks the parameters of the login username and the password against the database. If they match, then the account information is returned. Otherwise, a null set is returned by the database and the authentication fails. If the SQLA input "user1'--"as the user name "x" as the password, the database server returns the recode despite the password being incorrect because the database server ignores the statement after the comment "--".

From this example, it follows that the problem is in the structure of the query syntax used by programmers.

SQL Injection Vulnerabilities

A SQL injection attack exploits vulnerabilities in input validation to execute a malicious statement in the database. The problems of SQLI become complicated if the database server doesn't use

Box 1.

```
String username = request.getParameter ("username");
String password = request.getParameter ("password");
Statement stmt = connection.createStatement();
String sql = new String(SELECT password FROM Tableusers WHERE Username=";//
sql query to retrieve 6.values from the secified table
sql += username + "' AND password=" + password;
stmt = Conn.prepareStatement(sql)
ResultSet Rs = stmt.executeQuery() //execute query
if (Rs != null)
displayAccount(Rs); // Show Information
else
sendAuthFailed(); // Authentication failed
```

Table 3. Result of attack type

Attack Type	Result
Unauthorized data access	Allows the SQLIA to trick the web application in order to obtain information from the database that is not supposed to be returned or is not allowed to be seen by this user.
Authentication bypass	Allows the attacker to access the database-driven application and observe data from the database without presenting proper credentials.
Database modification	Allows the attacker to change the database by insert, modify, or destroy data content.

privileged accounts to connect to the database. In this case it is applicable to use the database server to run operating system commands.

Vulnerabilities in web applications allow malicious users to obtain unlimited access to private and confidential information from any database-driven applications written for web applications. This occurs when end user input is a malicious string that literally evades characters embedded in SQL statements. The results are shown in Table 3.

Detection and Prevention Techniques

Researchers have proposed several methods for detection and prevention to assist developers and Anti-Virus (AV) vendors to find defects in defensive coding.

Static Analysis: Pixy (Barnes, Marateo, & Ferris, 2007) is an open source prototype implementation aimed at detecting SQL injection, cross-site scripting, or command injection based on flow-sensitive, inter procedural and context-sensitive data flow analysis. In addition, Pixy uses literal analysis to improve the rightness and precision of its results.

Combined Static and Dynamic Analysis: AMNESIA (Halfond, Orso, & Manolios, 2006) is a technique that combines dynamic and static for preventing and detecting web application vulnerabilities at runtime. AMNESIA uses static analysis to generate different types of query statements. In the dynamic phase, AMNESIA interprets all queries before they are sent to the database and validates each query against the statically built models. In other words, AMNESIA stops all queries before they are sent to the database and validates each query statement against the AMNESIA models. However, the primary limitation in AMNESIA according to Ramaraj et al. (IndraniBalasundaram & Ramaraj, 2011), is a technique that depends on the accuracy of its static analysis for building query models to successfully prevent SQL injection. Furthermore, AMNESIA doesn't consider certain types of code obfuscation or query development techniques that could make this step less precise and result in both false positives and false negatives.

Moreover, Martin, Livshits, and Lam (2005) proposed Program Query Language (PQL) that uses static analysis and dynamic techniques to detect vulnerabilities in web applications. In static analysis, information flow techniques detect when malicious input has been used to generate a SQL query statement which are then flagged as SQLIA vulnerabilities. According to Ramaraj et al. (IndraniBalasundaram & Ramaraj, 2011) the limitation of this approach is that it can only detect known patterns of SQLIA.

Taint Based Approaches: Huang et al. (2004) proposed WebSSARI (Web application Security via Static Analysis and Runtime Inspection) to: a) statically validate existing web applications and legacy web application code without any extra effort for programmer; and b) automatically protect potentially defective code. In this model, static analysis is applied to validate infected runs versus given conditions for sensitive formulations.

Code Checkers: This is based on static analysis of web applications that can reduce SQL injection vulnerabilities and detect type errors. For instance, the JDBC-Checker (Gould, Su, & Devanbu, 2004) is a tool used to check code for statically validating the accuracy of dynamically-generated

SQL queries. However, researchers have also developed particular packages that can be applied to make SQL query statements safe (McClure & Krüger, 2005). These techniques are good but they need extra effort from programmers to build query statements using Application Programme Interfaces (APIs), especially for legacy web applications due to a lack of information about the programmers' intent.

Tainted Data Tracking: This method was proposed by Halfond et al. (Halfond et al., 2006) and is based on track tainted-ness of data. It specifically checks for dangerous content that comes from user input. According to Nguygen-Tuong et al. (2005), this can be done via instrumenting the run time environment or the interpreter of the back-end scripting language so when a SQL statement is sent to the database server, its syntax tree is examined first. However, this approach does not provide any way to check the accuracy of the input validation routines (Bandhakavi, Bisht, Madhusudan, & Venkatakrishnan, 2007). That programs that do use incomplete input checking routines may still pass these checks yet remain vulnerable to injection attacks (Bisht et al., 2010).

Static Analysis: Static analysis uses a statistical approach with data and uses a flow analysis to detect tainted data. This method is not efficient because it can lead to false positives and scalability issues.

Table 4 summarizes the results for detection and prevention techniques against the different types of SQLIA attacks as presented in Section 3.6 and 3.7. Most of these techniques failed to detect stored procedure and new evasion techniques because these techniques focus on queries generated within the application. Only four techniques, Candid, AMNESA, SqlCheckS and parse tree address SQLA attacks based on stored procedure because these techniques use database layer to interpret a SQL statement in a web application layer in the same way as it interprets a database layer.

Table 4. Summary of results for detection and prevention techniques against types of SQLIA

Techniques	Prevent	Detect	Tautology	Illegal	Union	Piggy-Backed	Store Procedure	Timing	Evasion Tech
Candid (Bisht, et al., 2010)	YES	NO	YES	YES	YES	YES	YES	YES	NO
AMNESA (Halfond & Orso, 2006)	YES	YES	YES	YES	YES	YES	YES	YES	NO
CSSE (Pietraszek & Berghe, 2006)	YES	YES	YES	YES	YES	YES	NO	YES	NO
IDS (Valeur, Mutz, & Vigna, 2005)	YES	NO	YES	YES	YES	YES	NO	YES	NO
Dynamic Taint Propagation for Java (Haldar, Chandra, & Franz, 2005)	YES	NO	YES	YES	YES	YES	NO	YES	NO
SqlCheckS (Su & Wassermann, 2006)	YES	NO	YES	YES	YES	YES	YES	YES	NO
Using parse tree validation to prevent SQL injection attacks (Buehrer, Weide, & Sivilotti, 2005)	YES	NO	YES	YES	YES	YES	YES	YES	NO
WebSSARI (Huang, et al., 2004)	NO	YES	YES	YES	YES	YES	NO	YES	NO

CASE SCENARIO: THE ZEUS BOTNET THREAT

Crime tool kit exposes a widespread a variety of attack vectors. Many different attack kits are presented with a range of exploits and a wide array of attack vectors. Advancing in amount of crime tool kit increase the probability for success attack on web application, because there are a more chances that the hacker discovers the web application vulnerability. There are different crime tool kits existing on underground marketplaces.

In order to demonstrate the web application threat, we conducted a study of Zeus Malware. The Zeus Trojan is also called Zbot, NTOS, WSNPOEM, or PRG, and is currently the most dangerous category of financial malware in circulation, both in terms of infection size and effectiveness. Furthermore, it is the biggest and most sophisticated threat to internet security. The Zeus Trojan is estimated to be responsible for about 90% of banking fraud worldwide (RSA, 2011) and guilty of 44% of the world's banking malware infections (Trusteer, 2009). Symantec Corporation describes it as "Zeus, King of the Underground Crimeware Toolkits."

The Zeus Trojan software, which comes with a friendly interface toolkit, is available in underground online forums for $1,500 – $20,000 USD. Currently, it is causing serious problems because it enables cybercriminals to configure and create malicious software to affect user systems, and allows them to take control of a compromised computer to harm the data, log keystrokes, and execute unauthorized transactions in online banking. Reports and studies (Trusteer, 2009) show that since last year, Zeus has been embroiled in more than half of the banking malware infections in the world.

The Zeus Trojan carries a very light footprint and is designed to steal sensitive data stored on computers or transmitted through web browsers. Once infected with Zeus, the computer sends the stolen data to a bot command and control (C&C) server via encrypted HTTP POST requests where the data is stored. It also allows cybercriminals to inject content into a bank's web page as it is displayed in the infected computer browser in real time. It is setup so stolen data is sent to a "drop server" controlled by an attacker called a botmaster and allows cybercriminals to control the infected systems remotely. To compound this problem, Zeus is highly dynamic and applies obfuscation methods such as polymorphic and metamorphic encryption in a network of bots. In each infection, it automatically re-encrypts itself to create a new signature that defeats signature-based detection that makes the signature difficult to comprehend. The Windows Zeus is increasingly hard to stop as it can successfully evade commercial detection engines and is able to hide malicious features such as string and API function calls. The Zeus Trojan is still developing and has versions and new plug-in releases that can also infect the latest operating systems such as Windows 7 and Vista systems (Binsalleeh et al., 2010).

According to numerous research labs and hacker forums, the Zeus botnet has recently combined (RSA, 2011) with the new release of the 2010 'Spy Eye Trojan' source code to create more sophisticated bots and take the threat to a new level. This new toolkit is reportedly available for purchase in the underground market and version 1.4.1 was published in January 11, 2011. This new version combines two versions of a control panel used for committing fraud and managing compromised systems. These trends indicate that self-learning and self-updating by observing system anomalies and behaviour patterns is much warranted in malware detection systems of the future.

According to Trend Micro (Micro's, 2009), the Zeus attack continues to persist due to the following file compression variant: Compressed or packed for executable (UPX), used compression software that is capable of encrypting actual.EXE application code. The result makes applications difficult to analyze.

Furthermore, Zeus has Rootkit capabilities, which allows variants to hide themselves and their malicious routines from users in order to perform stealth routines. Also, Zeus has varying social engineering techniques and has an effective "business model" which means an attacker can develop the software and create crime toolkits, then sell the kits through an established network of money mules to transfer money.

Figure 4 shows how attackers compromise a web application. Firstly, an attacker deploys a malicious string to the web application servers. Secondly, once a malicious application is published on a legitimate site, the user clicks a link on the infected website. Thirdly, after the user clicks on the infected web site, the website redirects the user to the malicious kit. Fourthly, once the user is redirected to the malicious kit that contains the botnet, the users' enter their personal identification on the infected web site. Fifthly, the Trojan reports for a new bot to the C&C (control and command server). Finally, the C&C sends instructions to the Trojan to observe the user, especially the user's access to an e-bank system or financial institution.

FUTURE RESEARCH DIRECTIONS

Researchers have proposed a wide range of techniques to address malware on web applications. However, many of these solutions have limitations that affect their performance and practicality. There are a number of reports showing SQL injection is steadily increasing and that clients are still confused when choosing the appropriate tools because of the difficulty in integrating information vulnerabilities. For example, one of the most common solutions is based on signature detection that has proven unsuccessful due to the development of new evasion techniques by hackers. Most SQL query statements are legitimate keywords that can be displayed if the user makes a HTTP request. The result is a high rate of false positives.

Researchers have been proposing anomaly-based detection systems to overcome the limitation of signature-based detection systems. The main feature of an anomaly-based detection system is its ability to detect unknown attacks (i.e. Zero day attack). Nevertheless, most intrusion detection systems used today are signature-based, with a few anomaly based detection systems used. The

Figure 4. A malicious upload to a web application

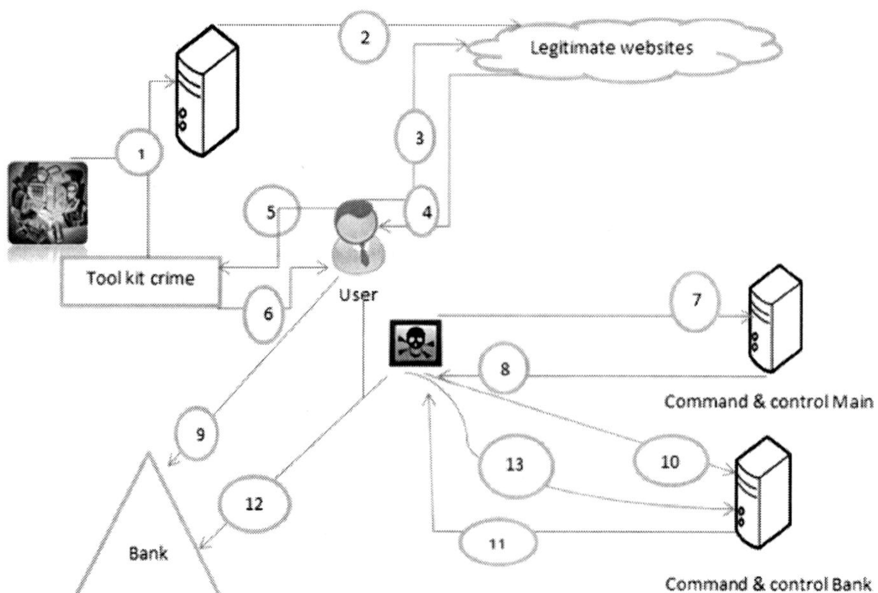

reason for this is signature-based detection systems are easier to implement, easier to set up and more manageable than anomaly-based detection (Bolzoni, 2009; Kruegel & Toth, 2003).

However, the weakness of exiting mechanism to deal of these threats, calling for new mechanisms to detect advance threats that target web application.

In general, prevention and detection web malware is an active research field in both industry and academia, and there are many solutions and tools that have been implemented. Unfortunately not all of them guarantee a high level of security on web applications. Focus should be on the development of a mechanism that is easy to implement, with no modification of code needed, yet is efficient and has a high performance rate for existing web applications

CONCLUSION

Increasingly, web applications are developed over the internet. Securing these web applications is becoming increasingly important as they hold critical security features. The malicious writer takes advantage of a web application vulnerability to promote his attack. These attacks can target the financial and non-financial sectors such as Facebook, Twitter, Gmail, and Yahoo! and against cloud application such as Salesforce and Google Apps. On the other hand, the new generation of the crime toolkits have ability to evade from exiting detection by Polymorphism and Dynamic injection to web page. Additionally, hackers are always trying different and new techniques to hack into your computer system.

Preventing attacks is not a sufficient solution in itself and intrusion detection systems in web applications are necessary, otherwise hackers will repeatedly attack web applications until they find vulnerability. Also, the current exiting detection system and the traditional firewalls are not enough solution to protect your computer system from the latest challenges. Web application protection is still necessary to protect against advanced zero day threat. Therefore, Security awareness and user education are important steps that really help to prevent most of the online attacks.

REFERENCES

Anderson, R., & Moore, T. (2007). Information security economics–And beyond. *Advances in Cryptology-CRYPTO, 2007*, 68–91.

Bandhakavi, S., Bisht, P., Madhusudan, P., & Venkatakrishnan, V. (2007). CANDID: Preventing sql injection attacks using dynamic candidate evaluations. *ACM Conference on Computer and Communications Security* (pp. 12-24).

Barnes, K., Marateo, R. C., & Ferris, S. P. (2007). Teaching and learning with the net generation. *Innovate Journal of Online Education, 3*(4).

Binsalleeh, H., Ormerod, T., Boukhtouta, A., Sinha, P., Youssef, A., Debbabi, M., & Wang, L. (2010, 17-19 August). *On the analysis of the Zeus botnet crimeware toolkit.* Paper presented at the Privacy Security and Trust (PST).

Bisht, P., Madhusudan, P., & Venkatakrishnan, V. (2010). CANDID: Dynamic candidate evaluations for automatic prevention of SQL injection attacks. *ACM Transactions on Information and System Security, 13*(2), 1–39. doi:10.1145/1698750.1698754

Buehrer, G., Weide, B. W., & Sivilotti, P. A. G. (2005). *Using parse tree validation to prevent SQL injection attacks.* Paper presented at the Proceedings of the 5th international workshop on Software engineering and middleware. Lisbon, Portugal.

Corporation, M. (2010). Common vulnerabilities and exposures. Retrieved April, 2011, from http://cve.mitre.org/

Gould, C., Su, Z., & Devanbu, P. (2004). JDBC checker: A static analysis tool for SQL/JDBC applications. In *Proceedings of the 26th International Conference on Software Engineering.*

Halfond, W. G. J., & Orso, A. (2006). Preventing SQL injection attacks using AMNESIA. In *Proceedings of the 28th International Conference on Software Engineering.*

Halfond, W. G. J., Orso, A., & Manolios, P. (2006). Using positive tainting and syntax-aware evaluation to counter SQL injection attacks. In *Proceedings of the 14th ACM SIGSOFT International Symposium on Foundations of Software Engineering.*

Huang, Y.-W., Yu, F., Hang, C., Tsai, C.-H., Lee, D.-T., & Kuo, S.-Y. (2004). *Securing web application code by static analysis and runtime protection.* Paper presented at the Proceedings of the 13th international conference on World Wide Web, New York, NY, USA.

IndraniBalasundaram, & Ramaraj. (2011). An approach to detect and prevent SQL injection attacks in database using web service. *International Journal of Computer Science and Network Security, 11*, 197–205.

Jie, W., Phan, R. C. W., Whitley, J. N., & Parish, D. J. (2010). Research on Multi-Level Security Framework for OpenID. In *Third International Symposium on Electronic Commerce and Security.*

Kramer, S., & Bradfield, J. C. (2010). A general definition of malware. *Journal in Computer Virology, 6*(2), 105–114. doi:10.1007/s11416-009-0137-1

Martin, M., Livshits, B., & Lam, M. S. (2005). Finding application errors and security flaws using PQL: A program query language. *ACM SIGPLAN Notices, 40*(10), 365–383. doi:10.1145/1103845.1094840

McClure, R. A., & Krüger, I. H. (2005). SQL DOM: Compile time checking of dynamic SQL statements. In *27th International Conference on Software Engineering.*

Nguyen-Tuong, A., Guarnieri, S., Greene, D., Shirley, J., & Evans, D. (2005). Automatically hardening web applications using precise tainting. *Security and Privacy in the Age of Ubiquitous Computing*, 295-307.

OWASP. (2010). The top 10 most critical web application security risks. Retrieved April 2011, from owasp.org

Peng, C. S., Chen, S. K., Chung, J. Y., Roy-Chowdhury, A., & Srinivasan, V. (2010). Accessing existing business data from the World Wide Web. *IBM Systems Journal, 37*(1), 115–132. doi:10.1147/sj.371.0115

Pietraszek, T., & Berghe, C. (2006). Defending against injection attacks through context-sensitive string evaluation. In Valdes, A., & Zamboni, D. (Eds.), *Recent advances in intrusion detection (Vol. 3858*, pp. 124–145). Springer. doi:10.1007/11663812_7

RSA. (2011). The current state of cybercrime and what to expect in 2011. USA: EMC corporation.

Su, Z., & Wassermann, G. (2006). *The essence of command injection attacks in web applications.* Paper presented at the Conference record of the 33rd ACM SIGPLAN-SIGACT symposium on Principles of programming languages. Charleston, South Carolina, USA.

Torrano-Gimenez, C., Perez-Villegas, A., & Alvarez, G. (2010). WASAT-A new web authorization security analysis tool. *Web Application Security*, 39-49.

Trend Micro. (2009). 2009's most persistent malware threats. Retrieved February 3, 2011, from http://us.trendmicro.com/imperia/md/content/us/trendwatch/researchandanalysis/2009s_most_persistent_malware_threats__march_2010_.pdf

Trusteer. (2009). Banking malware Zeus sucessfully bypasses anti-virus detection. Retrieved March, 2011, from http://www.ecommerce-journal.com/news/18221_zeus_increasingly_avoids_pcs_detection

Valeur, F., Mutz, D., & Vigna, G. (2005). A learning-based approach to the detection of SQL attacks. In Julisch, K., & Kruegel, C. (Eds.), *Detection of intrusions and malware, and vulnerability assessment* (*Vol. 3548*, pp. 533–546). Springer. doi:10.1007/11506881_8

Valli, C., & Brand, M. (2008). *The malware analysis body of knowledge*. MABOK.

Vella, K. J. (2007, Jun 11). Web applications: What are they? What about them? Retrieved 2011, from http://www.windowsecurity.com/articles/Web-Applications.html?printversion

W3schools. (2011). Introduction to SQL. Retrieved April, 2011, from http://www.w3schools.com/sql/sql_intro.asp

Yu, W. D., Aravind, D., & Supthaweesuk, P. (2006). *Software vulnerability analysis for web services software systems*.

ADDITIONAL READING

Alazab, M., Venkataraman, S., & Watters, P. (2010). Towards understanding malware behaviour by the extraction of api calls. *Cybercrime and Trustworthy Computing Workshop*.

Alazab, M., Ventatraman, S., Watters, P., Alazab, M., & Alazab, A. (2011). *Cybercrime: The case of obuscated malware*. Paper presented at the 7th International Conference on Global Security, Safety & Sustainability. Thessaloniki, Greece.

Clarke, J. (2009). *SQL injection attacks and defense*. Syngress.

Stuttard, D., & Pinto, M. (2011). *The web application hacker's handbook: Finding and exploiting security flaws*. Wiley.

KEY TERMS AND DEFINITIONS

Authentication: The techniques that use to verify and identity of users to the Web application and website, typically based on a username and password.

Buffer Overflow: A buffer overflow attack happens when attackers overload systems to damage the execution stack of a web application. In this attack the attacker sending malicious input to web application, an attacker can cause the web application to execute arbitrary code causing damage over all the system.

Cross-Site Request Forgery (CSRF): A type of attack on web application that takes advantage of a lack of authorization of Web application. This attack permits an attacker to perform malicious commands without user's knowledge. In this attack the attackers cheating an internet user into clicking on a malicious link which is planned to perform a malicious activity on behalf of the users. For example, a user's may click on a malicious link. Once the users clicked on this linked.The linked redirect the user to illegitimate web site that forces the victim to transfer money from the victim's bank account to an attacker's bank account.

Cross-Site Scripting (XSS): A type of attack on web application which occurs when an attacker inserts malicious string or code into a hyper link that appears in legitimate web site. When internet user clicks on this link, the embedded programming is submitted as part of the client's Web request and can execute on the user's computer. The result from this is permitting the attacker to gain critical information.

Insecure Cryptographic Storage: Cryptographic Storage regularly occurs when the developers encrypt the information wrongly. As the web application encrypts sensitive information in a database to avoid revelation to end users. Though, the database is having functionality to decrypt queries against the sensitive information. The system should have been configured to allow only back end applications to decrypt them, not the front end web application. Otherwise, allowing the hackers to attack the database to steal all the critical information.

Security Misconfiguration: A type of attack on web application which occurs when an attacker exploit configuration weaknesses found in web applications. Many web applications have unnecessary features, such as default username. These features may help an attacker to lunch his activities in order to get access to personal information.

SQL Injection Attack (SQLIA): A type of attack on web application which occurs when an attacker inputs malicious strings as parameters in legitimate SQL statement. The SQLIA allow the hacker to gain complete access to the database server a serious threat to the web application.

Web Application Vulnerability: Any weakness in web application architecture, web application design, web application configuration, web application code. That permits an attacker to comprise a web application.

Web Malware: Malicious software intended to harm an internet users system without the user's permission. "Malware" is the general term that describes the various kinds of threats to the computer system.

Compilation of References

Abadi, M., Burrows, M., Lampson, B., & Plotkin, G. (1993). A calculus for access control in distributed systems. *ACM Transactions on Programming Languages and Systems, 15*(4), 706–734. doi:10.1145/155183.155225

Abiteboul, S., Agrawal, R., Bernstein, P., Carey, M., Ceri, S., & Croft, B. (2005, May). The Lowell database research self-assessment. *Communications of the ACM, 48*(5), 111–118. doi:10.1145/1060710.1060718

Abrial, J. R. (1984). The mathematical construction of a program. *Science of Computer Programming, 4*(1), 45–86. doi:10.1016/0167-6423(84)90011-X

Abrial, J. R. (1996). *The B-book: Assigning programs to meanings*. Cambridge University Press. doi:10.1017/CBO9780511624162

Abrial, J. R., & Hallerstede, S. (2007). Refinement, decomposition and instantiation of discrete models: Application to event-B. *Fundamentae Informatica, 77*, 1–24.

Acquisti, A., & Gross, R. (2006). *Imagined communities: Awareness, information sharing and privacy on the Facebook*. Paper presented at the 6th Workshop on Privacy Enhancing Technologies, Cambridge, UK.

Acquisti, A., & Grossklags, J. (2003). *Losses, gains, and hyperbolic discounting: An experimental approach to information security attitudes and behavior*. Paper presented at the 2nd Annual Workshop on Economics and Information Security, College Park, MD.

Acquisti, A., Carrara, E., Stutzman, F., Callas, J., Schimmer, K., & Nadjm, M. (2007). *Security issues and recommendations for online social networks (Position Paper No. 1). European Network and Information Security Agency*. ENISA.

Acquisti, A., & Grossklags, J. (2005). Privacy and rationality in individual decision-making. *IEEE Security and Privacy, 3*(1), 26–33. doi:10.1109/MSP.2005.22

Adali, S., Escriva, R., Goldberg, M. K., Hayvanovych, M., Magdon-Ismail, M., Szymanski, B. K., et al. (2010). Measuring behavioral trust in social networks. In *IEEE International Conference on Intelligence and Security Informatics (ISI)* (pp. 150-152). Vancouver, BC, Canada.

Ahern, S., Eckles, D., Good, N. S., King, S., Naaman, M., & Nair, R. (2007). Photo sharing: Over-exposed?: Privacy patterns and considerations in online and mobile photo sharing. In *Proceedings of ACM CHI 2007 Conference on Human Factors in Computing Systems 2007*. New York: ACM Press.

Ahmad, A., & Whitworth, B. (2011). *Distributed access control for social networks. Information Assurance and Security (IAS)* (pp. 68–73). IEEE.

Ahn, G. J., Shehab, M., & Squicciarini, A. (2011). Security and privacy in social networks. *IEEE Internet Computing, 15*(3), 10–12. doi:10.1109/MIC.2011.66

Akre, V., Rizvi, A. H., & Arif, M. (2009). Online social networks - an interface requirements analysis. In *Proceedings of the 2009 IEEE International Symposium on Signal Processing and Information Technology* (pp. 550–556).

Alessandra, M., Kristen, L., & Eytan, A. (Last Updated April 2011.). The PVIZ comprehension tool for social network privacy settings. *UM Tech Report* #CSE-TR-570-11.

Ali, B., Villegas, W., & Maheswaran, M. (2007). A trust based approach for protecting user data in social networks. *In Proceedings of the 2007 conference of the center for advanced studies on collaborative research* (pp. 288–293). New York, NY, USA: ACM.

Anderson, J., Diaz, C., Bonneau, J., & Stajano, F. (2009). Privacy-enabling social networking over untrusted networks. In *Proceedings of the 2nd ACM workshop on Online social networks, 2009.*

Anderson, N. (2011, February 11). *(Virtually) face to face: How Aaron Barr revealed himself to anonymous.* Ars Technica. Retrieved May 15, 2012, from http://arstechnica.com/tech-policy/2011/02/virtually-face-to-face-when-aaron-barr-met-anonymous/

Anderson, N. (2011, February 14). Spy games: Inside the convoluted plot to bring down wikileaks. *Ars Technica.* Retrieved May 15, 2012, from http://arstechnica.com/tech-policy/2011/02/the-ridiculous-plan-to-attack-wikileaks/

Anderson, R., & Moore, T. (2007). Information security economics–And beyond. *Advances in Cryptology-CRYPTO, 2007,* 68–91.

Andrews, G. J., & Chen, S. (2006). The production of tyrannical space. *Children's Geographies, 4*(2), 239–250. doi:10.1080/14733280600807120

Anwar, M., & Fong, P. W. L. (2010). *An access control model for Facebook-style social network systems* (Tech. Rep. No. 2010-959-08). Department of Computer Science, University of Calgary, Calgary, Alberta, Canada.

Appel, A. W. (2001). *Foundational proof-carrying code. Logic in Computer Science* (pp. 247–256). LICS.

Arendt, H. (1958). *Vita activa. The human conditon.* University of Chicago Press.

Aringhieri, R., Damiani, E., Di Vimercati, S. D. C., Paraboschi, S., & Samarati, P. (2006, February). Fuzzy techniques for trust and reputation management in anonymous peer-to-peer systems: Special topic section on soft approaches to information retrieval and information access on the web. *Journal of the American Society for Information Science and Technology, 57*(4), 528–537. doi:10.1002/asi.20307

Asch, S. (1955). Opinions and social pressure. *Scientific American, 193,* 31–35. doi:10.1038/scientificamerican1155-31

Ashley, P. (2003). Enterprise privacy authorization language (EPAL 1.1). *W3C Working Group.* Retrieved March, 2012, from http://www.zurich.ibm.com/security/enterprise-privacy/epal/Specification/

Auletta, K. (2010). *Googled: The end of the world as we know it.* London, UK: Virgin Book.

Austin, T. H., & Flanagan, C. (2012). Multiple facets for dynamic information flow. In *Proceedings of the ACM SIGPLAN-SIGACT Symposium on Principles of Programming Languages (POPL).*

Australian broadcasting corporation (ABC). (2007, 29 October). ABC media watch, filleting facebook. Retrieved March, 2012, from http://www.abc.net.au/mediawatch/transcripts/s2074079.htm

Baader, F., Calvanese, D., McGuinness, D., Nardi, D., & Patel-Schneider, P. (2003). *The description logic handbook: Theory, implementation and applications.* Cambridge University Press.

Backstrom, L., Dwork, C., & Kleinberg, J. (2007). Wherefore art thou r3579x?: Anonymized social networks, hidden patterns, and structural steganography. In *Proceedings of the 16th international conference on World Wide Web 2007.*

Baden, R., Bender, A., Spring, N., Bhattacharjee, B., & Starin, D. (2009). Persona: An online social network with user-defined privacy. In *Proceedings of the ACM conference on Data communication, SIGCOMM '09,* (pp. 135–146). ACM.

Bandhakavi, S., Bisht, P., Madhusudan, P., & Venkatakrishnan, V. (2007). CANDID: Preventing sql injection attacks using dynamic candidate evaluations. *ACM Conference on Computer and Communications Security* (pp. 12-24).

Baracaldo, N., López, C., Anwar, M., & Lewis, M. (2011). Simulating the effect of privacy concerns in online social networks (pp. 519-524). *Information Reuse and Integration (IRI),* IEEE International Conference.

Barnes, K., Marateo, R. C., & Ferris, S. P. (2007). Teaching and learning with the net generation. *Innovate Journal of Online Education, 3*(4).

Barthe, G. A., Grégoire, B., Jensen, T., & Pichardie, D. (2008). *The MOBIUS proof carrying code infrastructure. Formal Methods for Components and Objects (FMCO)* (pp. 1–24). Berlin, Germany: Springer-Verlag. doi:10.1007/978-3-540-92188-2_1

Bauer, L., Ligatti, J., & Walker, D. (2005, June). Composing security policies with Polymer. *SIGPLAN Notices*, *40*, 305–314. doi:10.1145/1064978.1065047

Bauman, Z. (2004). *Identity: Conversations with Benedetto Vecchi*. Cambridge, UK: Polity Press.

Bayardo, R. J. (2005). Data privacy through optimal k-anonymization. *International Conference on Data Engineering (ICDE)* (pp. 217-228).

Bayzick, J., Kontostathis, A., & Edwards, L. (2011, June). *Detecting the presence of cyberbullying using computer software*. Paper presented at the ACM Web Science, Koblenz, Germany.

Beach,A., Gartrell, M., & Han, R. (2009). Solutions to security and privacy issues in mobile social networking. *CSE*, (4), 1036–1042.

Beard, E. (2010, April 21). *A new data model*. Retrieved October 6, 2012, from http://developers.facebook.com/blog/post/2010/04/21/a-new-data-model/

Bedi, R., Wadhai, V.M., Sugandhi, R., & Mirajkar, A.(2005). Watermarking social networking relational data using non-numeric attribute. *International Journal of Computer Science 9*.

Bell, D. E., & LaPadula, L. J. (1973). *Secure computer systems: Volume I – Mathematical foundations, Volume II – A mathematical model, Volume III – A refinement of the mathematical model* (No. MTR-2547).

Benantar, M. (2006). *Access control systems: Security, identity management and trust models* (Benantar, M., Ed.). Springer.

Beni, G., & Wang, J. (1989). *Swarm intelligence in cellular robotic systems*. *Proceed. NATO Advanced Workshop on Robots and Biological Systems*. Tuscany, Italy

Benisch, M., Kelley, P., Sadeh, N., & Cranor, L. (2011). Capturing location-privacy preferences: Quantifying accuracy and user-burden tradeoffs. *Personal and Ubiquitous Computing*, *15*(7), 679–694. doi:10.1007/s00779-010-0346-0

Berendt, B., Gunther, O., & Spiekermann, S. (2005). Privacy in e-commerce: Stated preferences vs. actual behavior. *Communications of the ACM*, *48*(4), 101–106. doi:10.1145/1053291.1053295

Berkovsky, S., Kuflik, T., & Ricci, F. (2008). Mediation of user models for enhanced personalization in recommender systems. *User Modeling and User-Adapted Interaction*, *18*(3), 245–286. doi:10.1007/s11257-007-9042-9

Berners-Lee, T. (2010, December). Long live the web: A call for continued open standards and neutrality. *Scientific American Magazine*. Retrieved September 26, 2012, from http://www.scientificamerican.com/article.cfm?id=long-live-the-web

Bethencourt, J., Sahai, A., & Waters, B. (2007). Ciphertext -policy attribute-based encryption. In *IEEE Symposium on Security and Privacy* (pp. 321-334). IEEE Computer Society.

Bethencourt, J., Sahai, A., & Waters, B. (2007). Ciphertext-policy attribute-based encryption. In *IEEE symposium on security and privacy* (pp. 321–334). IEEE Computer Society.

Biddle, P., England, P., Peinado, M., & Willman, B. (2002). The Darknet and the future of content distribution. In *Lecture Notes in Computer Science, Vol. 2696. Proceedings of the 2002 ACM Workshop on Digital Rights Management* (pp. 155–176). Berlin: Springer / Verlag.

Biehl, J. T., Rieffel, E. G., & Lee, A. J. (2013). When privacy and utility are in harmony: Towards better design of presence technologies. *Personal and Ubiquitous Computing*, *17*(3), 503-518. doi:10.1007/s00779-012-0504-7

Bielova, N., Devriese, D., Massaci, F., & Piessens, F. (2011). Reactive non-interference for a browser model. In *Proceedings of the International Conference on Network and System Security (NSS)*.

Bilge, L., Strufe, T., Balzarotti, D., & Kirda, E. (2009). All your contacts are belong to us: Automated identity theft attacks on social networks. In J. Quemada, G. León, Y. S. Maarek & W. Nejdl (Eds.), *Proceedings of WWW 2009* (pp. 551-560). New York: ACM Press.

Binsalleeh, H., Ormerod, T., Boukhtouta, A., Sinha, P., Youssef, A., Debbabi, M., & Wang, L. (2010, 17-19 August). *On the analysis of the Zeus botnet crimeware toolkit*. Paper presented at the Privacy Security and Trust (PST).

Bisht, P., Madhusudan, P., & Venkatakrishnan, V. (2010). CANDID: Dynamic candidate evaluations for automatic prevention of SQL injection attacks. *ACM Transactions on Information and System Security, 13*(2), 1–39. doi:10.1145/1698750.1698754

Björkqvist, K., Österman, K., Lagerspetz, K. M. J., Landau, S. F., Caprara, G. V., & Fraczek, A. (2001). Aggression, victimization, and sociometric status: Findings from Finland, Israel, Italy, and Poland. In Ramirez, J. M., & Richardson, D. S. (Eds.), *Cross-cultural approaches to research on aggression and reconciliation* (pp. 111–119). Hauppauge, NY: Nova Science.

Blaze, M., Feigenbaum, J., & Lacy, J. (1996). Decentralized trust management. In *Proceedings of the 1996 IEEE symposium on security and privacy* (pp. 164–173). Washington, DC, USA: IEEE Computer Society.

Blias, J. J. (2008). *Chatting, befriending, and bullying: Adolescent internet experiences and associated psychosocial outcomes.* (Doctoral thesis). Queen's University, Canada.

Bonabeau, E., Dorigo, M., & Theraulaz, G. (1999). *Swarm intelligence: from natural to artificial systems.* Oxford University Press.

Bonatti, P., De Capitani Di Vimercati, S., & Samarati, P. (2002). An algebra for composing access control policies. *ACM Transactions on Information and System Security, 5*(1), 1–35. doi:10.1145/504909.504910

Boneh, D., & Franklin, M. (2001). Identity based encryption from the Weil pairing. Extended abstract in *Lecture Notes in Computer Science, Vol. 2139. Advances in Cryptology – Crypto 2001* (pp. 231–229). Berlin: Springer / Verlag.

Bonhard, P., & Sasse, M. A. (2006). 'Knowing me knowing you' - Using profiles and social networking to improve recommender systems. *BT Technology Journal, 24*(3), 84–97. doi:10.1007/s10550-006-0080-3

Bonneau, J., Anderson, J., & Church, L. (2009). Privacy suites: Shared privacy for social networks. *SOUPS 2009, Proceedings of the 5th Symposium on Usable Privacy and Security.*

Boshmaf, Y., Muslukhov, I., Beznosov, K., & Ripeanu, M. (2011). The socialbot network: When bots socialize for fame and money. In *Proceedings of the 27th annual computer security applications conference* (pp. 93-102). Orlando, Florida. ACM.

Bosse, T., & Stam, S. (2011). A normative agent system to prevent cyberbullying. In *Proceedings of at the International Conferences on Web Intelligence and Intelligent Agent Technology* (pp. 425-430). Los Alamitos, CA: IEEE Computer Society.

Bourdieu, P. (1986). The forms of capital. In J. Richardson J. (Ed), *Handbook of theory and research for the sociology of education* (pp. 241–258). New York: Greenwood.

Bowen, J., & Stavridou, V. (1993). *Safety critical systems, formal methods and standards.* Computer Lab International. doi:10.1049/sej.1993.0025

Boyd, D. (2004). *Friendster and publicly articulated social networks.* Paper presented at the SIGCHI Conference on Human Factors and Computing Systems, Vienna, Austria.

Boyd, D. (2011). *The unintended consequences of obsessing over consequences (or why to support youth risk-taking).* Retrieved September 11, 2012, from http://www.zephoria.org/thoughts/archives/2011/07/29/consequences.html

Boyd, D., & Hargittai, E. (2010). Facebook privacy settings: Who cares? *First Monday, 15*(8). Retrieved September 11, 2012, from http://www.uic.edu/htbin/cgiwrap/bin/ojs/index.php/fm/article/viewArticle/3086/2589

Boyd, D., Hargittai, E., Schultz, J., & Palfrey, J. (2011). Why parents help their children lie to Facebook about age: Unintended consequences of the 'Children's Online Privacy Protection Act'. *First Monday, 16*(11). Retrieved September 11, 2012, from http://www.uic.edu/htbin/cgiwrap/bin/ojs/index.php/fm/article/viewArticle/3850/3075

Boyd, D., & Heer, J. (2006). *Profiles as conversations: Networked identity performance on friendster.* Paper presented at the 39th Annual Hawaii International Conference of System Sciences (HICSS'06), Kauai, Hawaii.

Boyd, D., & Ellison, N. B. (2007). Social network sites: Definition, history, and scholarship. *Journal of Computer-Mediated Communication, 13*(1), 210–230. doi:10.1111/j.1083-6101.2007.00393.x

Brennan, R. W. (2001). Holonic and multi-agent systems in industry. *The Knowledge Engineering Review*, *16*(04), 375–381. doi:10.1017/S0269888901000200

Breunesse, C., Cataño, N., Huisman, M., & Jacobs, B. (2005). Formal methods for smart cards: An experience report. *Science of Computer Programming*, *55*(1-3), 53–80. doi:10.1016/j.scico.2004.05.011

Brickell, J., & Shmatikov, V. (2008). The cost of privacy: Destruction of data-mining utility in anonymized data publishing. In Li, Y., Liu, B., & Sarawagi, S. (Eds.), *KDD* (pp. 70–78). ACM. doi:10.1145/1401890.1401904

Brickley, D., & Miller, L. (2007). FOAF Vocabulary Specification 0.91. Retrieved March, 2012, from http://xmlns.com/foaf/spec/20071002.html (Computer software manual No. November).

Brickley, D., & Miller, L. (2010, January). FOAF Vocabulary Specification 0.97 (Namespace document). Retrieved March, 2012, from http://xmlns.com/foaf/spec/20100101.html

Brunel, J., Cuppens, F., Cuppens, N., Sans, T., & Bodeveix, J.-P. (2007). Security policy compliance with violation management. *ACM Workshop on Formal methods in Security Engineering (FMSE)* (pp. 31-40). New York, NY, USA: ACM.

Buchegger, S., & Datta, A. (2009). A case for p2p infrastructure for social networks - opportunities & challenges. In *Proceedings of Sixth International Conference on Wireless On-Demand Network Systems and Services, WONS 2009* (pp. 161 –168).

Buchegger, S., Schiöberg, D., Vu, L., & Datta, A. (2009). PeerSoN: P2P social networking: Early experiences and insights. In *Proceedings of the Second ACM EuroSys Workshop on Social Network Systems* (pp. 46–52). ACM.

Buckingham, D. (2007). Introducing identity. In Buchingham, D. (Ed.), *Youth, identity, and digital media* (pp. 1–24). Cambridge, MA: The MIT Press.

Buehrer, G., Weide, B. W., & Sivilotti, P. A. G. (2005). *Using parse tree validation to prevent SQL injection attacks.* Paper presented at the Proceedings of the 5th international workshop on Software engineering and middleware. Lisbon, Portugal.

Burgoon, J. K., le Poire, B. A., Kelley, D. L., & Parrott, R. (1989). Maintaining and restoring privacy through communication in different types of relationships. *Journal of Social and Personal Relationships*, *6*(2), 131–158. doi:10.1177/026540758900600201

Cain, J., Scott, D. R., & Akers, P. (2009, October). Pharmacy students' Facebook activity and opinions regarding accountability and e-professionalism. *American Journal of Pharmaceutical Education*, *73*(6), 104. doi:10.5688/aj7306104

Calabrese, M. (2011), *Hierarchical-granularity holonic modelling.* (PhD Thesis). University of Milan, Italy.

Calvani, A., Fini, A., Ranieri, M., & Picci, P. (2012). Are young generations in secondary school digitally competent? A study on Italian teenagers. *Computers & Education*, *58*(2), 797–807. doi:10.1016/j.compedu.2011.10.004

Canetti, R., Thomas, J., Garay, J., Itkis, G., Micciancio, D., Naor, M., & Pinkas, B. (1999). Multicast security: A taxonomy and some efficient constructions. In *Proceedings of INFOCOM '99, Eighteenth Annual Joint Conference of the IEEE Computer and Communications Societies* (vol. 2, pp. 708-716). IEEE Computer Society.

Canini, K. R., Bongwon, S., & Pirolli, P. L. (2011). *Finding credible information sources in social networks based on content and social structure.* Paper presented at the 3rd IEEE International Conference on Social Computing, Boston, MA.

Cankaya, H. C. (2011). Access control lists. In van Tilborg, H. C. A., & Jajodia, S. (Eds.), *Encyclopedia of cryptography and security* (2nd ed., pp. 9–12). Springer.

Carmagnola, F., Osborne, F., & Torre, I. (2009). *Cross-systems identification of users in the social web.* Paper presented at the IADIS International Conference WWW/Internet, Rome, Italy.

Carmagnola, F., Osborne, F., & Torre, I. (2010). *User data distributed on the social web: How to identify users on different social systems and collecting data about them.* Paper presented at the International Workshop on Information Heterogeneity and Fusion in Recommender Systems, within the International Conference on Recommender Systems, Barcelona, Spain.

Carmagnola, F., Osborne, F., & Torre, I. (2013). A study with real users on factors influencing identification and information leakage. Paper under revision. *Journal of Information Science*. SAGE Publications.

Carminati, B., & Ferrari, E. (2009, November 11-14). Enforcing relationships privacy through collaborative access control in web-based social networks. In *5th international conference on collaborative computing: Networking, applications and worksharing* (pp. 1-9). Washington, DC.

Carminati, B., Ferrari, E., & Perego, A. (2006). The REL-X vocabulary. *OWL Vocabulary*. Retrieved March, 2012, from http://www.dicom.uninsubria.it/andrea.perego/vocs/relx.owl

Carminati, B., Ferrari, E., & Perego, A. (2006). Rule-based access control for social networks. In *On the Move to Meaningful Internet Systems 2006: OTM Workshops (2)*, (pp. 1734– 1744). Springer.

Carminati, B., Ferrari, E., Heatherly, R., Kantarcioglu, M., & Thuraisingham, B. (2009). A semantic web based framework for social network access control. In *Proceedings of the 14th ACM symposium on access control models and technologies* (pp. 177–186). New York, NY, USA: ACM.

Carpenter, C. J. (2012). Narcissism on Facebook: Self-promotional and anti-social behavior. *Personality and Individual Differences*, *52*(4), 482–486. doi:10.1016/j.paid.2011.11.011

Carr, N. (2010). *The shallows: What the internet is doing to our brains*. W. W. Norton & Co.

Castelfranchi, C., & Falcone, R. (2010). *Trust theory: A socio-cognitive and computational model*. Chichester, UK: John Wiley & Sons.

Castro, M., Druschel, P., Kermarrec, A.-M., & Rowstron, A. (2002). Scribe: A large-scale and decentralized application-level multicast infrastructure. *IEEE Journal on Selected Areas in Communications*, *20*(8), 1489–1499. doi:10.1109/JSAC.2002.803069

Castrucci, A., Martinelli, F., Mori, P., & Roperti, F. (2008). Enhancing Java-ME security support with resource usage monitoring. In *Proceedings of the 10th international conference on information and communications security, 5308* (pp. 256–266). Berlin, Germany: Springer-Verlag.

Catanese, S., Meo, P. D., Ferrara, E., Fiumara, G., & Provetti, A. (2011). *Crawling Facebook for social network analysis purposes*. Paper presented at the International Conference on Web Intelligent, Mining and Semantics, WIMS 2011, Sogndal, Norway.

Cataño, N., & Rueda, C. (2010). Matelas: A predicate calculus common formal definition for social networking. In M. Frappier (Ed.), *ABZ. 5977* (pp. 259-272). Québec: Lecture Notes in Computer Science.

Cataño, N., Hanvey, S., & Rueda, C. (2012). *The Poporo tool*. Retrieved October 5, 2012, from http://poporo.uma.pt/~ncatano/Projects/wespfm/PoporoTool/poporo.php

Cataño, N., Rueda, C., & Hanvey, S. (2011). Verification of JML generic types with Yices. In *Proceedings of 6th Colombian Congress of Computing (6CCC)* (pp. 1-6). Manizales, Colombia: IEEE Xplore Digital Library.

Cataño, N., Wahls, T., & Rueda, C. (2012). Translating B machines to JML specifications. *Symposium on Applied Computing, Software Verification and Testing track (SAC-SVT)*. Trento, Italy: ACM.

Cataño, N., Wahls, T., Rivera, V., & Rueda, C. (2012). *The B2Jml tool*. Retrieved October 5, 2012, from http://poporo.uma.pt/~ncatano/Projects/favas/B2JML.html

Caviglione, L. (2009). Can satellites face trends? The case of Web 2.0. In *Proceedings of the International Workshop on Satellite and Space Communications (IWSSC'09)*.

Caviglione, L. (2011). Extending HTTP models to Web 2.0 applications: The case of social networks. In *Proceedings of the 4th IEEE International Conference on Utility and Cloud Computing (UCC)* (pp. 361–365).

Caviglione, L., & Coccoli, M. (2011). Privacy problems with Web 2.0. *Computer Fraud & Security*, (10): 16–19. doi:10.1016/S1361-3723(11)70104-X

Caviglione, L., Coccoli, M., & Merlo, A. (in press). A taxonomy-based model of security and privacy in online social networks. *International Journal of Computational Science and Engineering*.

Caviglione, L., & Merlo, A. (2012). Energy impact of security mechanisms in modern mobile devices. *Network Security*, (2): 11–14. doi:10.1016/S1353-4858(12)70015-6

Chamot, A. (2012). *Prototype implementation of a social network application for the Polidoxa project.* (Master's thesis). Technical University of Denmark.

Chang, E., Li, C., Wang, J., Mork, P., & Wiederhold, G. (1999). Searching near-replicas of images via clustering. In *Proc. SPIE symposium of voice, video, and data communications* (pp. 281–292).

Chaum, D. L. (1981). Untraceable electronic mail, return addresses, and digital pseudonyms. *Communications of the ACM, 24*(2), 84–90. doi:10.1145/358549.358563

Cheek, G., & Shehab, M. (2012). *Privacy management for online social networks.* Paper presented at the 22th International World Wide Web Conference, Lyons, France.

Chen, F., & Sandhu, R. (1995). Constraints for RBAC. In *1st ACM workshop on role-based access control* (pp. 39–46). ACM.

Chen, H., & Li, N. (2006). Constraint generation for separation of duty. In *Proceedings of the eleventh ACM symposium on access control models and technologies* (pp. 130–138). New York, NY, USA: ACM.

Chen, B., Kifer, D., LeFevre, K., & Machanavajjhala, A. (2009). Privacy-preserving data publishing. *Foundations and Trends in Databases, 2*(1-2), 1–167. doi:10.1561/1900000008

Cheng, A., & Friedman, E. (2005). Sybilproof reputation mechanisms. In *Proceedings of the 2005 ACM SIGCOMM workshop on Economics of peer-to-peer systems, P2PECON '05* (pp. 128-132). ACM.

Cheng, J. (2007, May 30). Facial recognition slipped into Google's image search. *Ars Technica.* Retrieved May 15, 2012, from http://arstechnica.com/uncategorized/2007/05/facial-recognition-slipped-into-google-image-search/

Chen, Y., Roussev, V., Richard, G. III, & Gao, Y. (2005). Content-based image retrieval for digital forensics. In Pollitt, M., & Shenoi, S. (Eds.), *Advances in digital forensics (Vol. 194*, pp. 271–282). Springer. doi:10.1007/0-387-31163-7_22

Chinaei, A. H., Barker, K. & Tompa, K. (2009). Comparison of access control administration models. *Ubiquitous Communication and Computing Journal (UBICC), 4*(3).

Cholez, T., Chrisment, I., & Festor, O. (2010). Efficient DHT attack mitigation through peers' ID distribution. In *Proceedings of the 2010 IEEE International Symposium on Parallel & Distributed Processing, Workshops and Phd Forum, IPDPSW* (pp. 1-8).

Chopra, K., & Wallace, W. A. (2003). *Trust in electronic environments.* Paper presented at the 36th Annual Hawaii International Conference on System Sciences (HICSS'03), Big Island, Hawaii.

Christakis, N. A., & Fowler, J. H. (2009). *Connected: The surprising power of our social network and how they shape our lives.* New York: Little, Brown and Co.

Chugh, R., Meister, J. A., Jhala, R., & Lerner, S. (2009). Staged information flow for JavaScript. In *Proceedings of the ACM SIGPLAN Conference on Programming Language Design and Implementation (PLDI)* (pp. 50-62).

Chun, W. H. K., & Keenan, T. W. (2005). *New media, old media: A history and theory reader.* Routledge.

Cialdini, R. (2000). *Influence: Science and practice.* Boston, MA: Allyn & Bacon.

Clark, D. D., & Wilson, D. R. (1987). A comparison of commercial and military computer security policies. In *Proc. Symposium on Security and Privacy 1987* (IEEE Press), 184–193.

Clarke, D., Elien, J.-E., Ellison, C., Fredette, M., Morcos, A., & Rivest, R. L. (2002, February). Certificate chain discovery in SPKI/SDSI. *Journal of Computer Security, 9*(4), 285–322.

Clarke, E. H. (1971). Multipart pricing of public goods. *Star, 11*(1), 17–33.

Clarke, I., Miller, S., Hong, T., Sandberg, O., & Wiley, B. (2002). Protecting free expression online with Freenet. *Internet Computing, IEEE, 6*(1), 40–49. doi:10.1109/4236.978368

Clarke, I., Sandberg, O., Wiley, B., & Hong, T. (2001). Freenet: A distributed anonymous information storage and retrieval system. In *Designing Privacy Enhancing Technologies (Vol. 2009*, pp. 46–66). Lecture Notes in Computer ScienceBerlin: Springer / Verlag. doi:10.1007/3-540-44702-4_4

Coleman, J. S. (1988). Social capital in the creation of human capital. *American Journal of Sociology, 94*, S95–S120. doi:10.1086/228943

ComScore. (2012, February 23). 2012 Mobile future in focus. *Whitepaper.* Retrieved September 11, 2012, from http://www.comscore.com/Press_Events/Presentations_Whitepapers/2012/2012_Mobile_Future_in_Focus

Cook, J., & Pachler, N. (2012). Online people tagging: Social (mobile) network(ing) services and work-based learning. *British Journal of Educational Technology, 43*(5), 711–725. doi:10.1111/j.1467-8535.2012.01346.x

Corporation, M. (2010). Common vulnerabilities and exposures. Retrieved April, 2011, from http://cve.mitre.org/

Costoya, J. B. J., & Flores, R. (2009). *The heart of KOOBFACE. C&C and social network propagation* (White Paper). Trend Micro. Retrieved from http://www.trendmicro.com/cloud-content/us/pdfs/security-intelligence/white-papers/wp the-heart-of-koobface.pdf

Covington, M. J., Long, W., Srinivasan, S., Dev, A. K., Ahamad, M., & Abowd, G. D. (2001). Securing context-aware applications using environment roles. In *SACMAT '01: Proceedings of the sixth ACM symposium on access control models and technologies* (pp. 10–20). New York, NY, USA: ACM Press.

Crescenzo, G., & Lipton, R. J. (2009). Social network privacy via evolving access control. In *Proceedings of the 4th international conference on wireless algorithms, systems, and applications* (pp. 551–560). Berlin, Germany: Springer-Verlag.

Criscione, C., Salvaneschi, G., Maggi, F., & Zanero, S. (2009). Integrated detection of attacks against browsers, web applications and databases. In *Proceedings of the European Conference on Computer Network Defense (EC2ND 2009)* (pp. 37–45).

Cross, R., & Parker, A. (2004). *The hidden power of social networks.* Boston, MA: Harvard Business School Press.

Cutillo, L. A., Molva, R., & Önen, M. (2011). *Safebook: A distributed privacy preserving online social network* (pp. 1–3). WOWMOM. doi:10.1109/WoWMoM.2011.5986118

Cutillo, L., Molva, R., & Strufe, T. (2009). Safebook: A privacy-preserving online social network leveraging on real-life trust. *Communications Magazine, IEEE, 47*(12), 94–101. doi:10.1109/MCOM.2009.5350374

Dadvar, M., & Jong, F. D. (2012). Cyberbullying detection: A step toward a safer internet yard. In *Proceedings of the 21st International World Wide Web Conference* (pp. 121-125). New York, NY: Association for Computing Machinery.

Danezis, G. (2009). Inferring privacy policies for social networking services. In *Proceedings of the 2nd ACM workshop on Security and Artificial Intelligence* (pp. 5-10). Chicago, Illinois, USA: ACM.

Danezis, G., & Mittal, P. (2009, February). *SybilInfer: Detecting sybil nodes using social networks.* Paper presented at the 16th Annual Network & Distributed System Security Symposium, San Diego, CA.

Datta, R., Joshi, D., Li, J., & Wang, J. Z. (2008). Image retrieval: Ideas, influences, and trends of the new age. *ACM Computing Surveys, 40*(2), 5: 1-60.

De Capitani Di Vimercati, S., Foresti, S., Jajodia, S., & Samarati, P. (2007). Access control policies and languages in open environments. In *Secure Data Management in Decentralized Systems* (pp. 21–58). Springer. doi:10.1007/978-0-387-27696-0_2

Debatin, B., Lovejoy, J. P., Horn, A.-K., & Hughes, B. N. (2009). Facebook and online privacy: Attitudes, behaviors, and unintended consequences. *Journal of Computer-Mediated Communication, 15*(1), 83–108. doi:10.1111/j.1083-6101.2009.01494.x

Dellarocas, C. (2001). Analyzing the economic efficiency of eBay-like online reputation mechanisms. In *Proceedings of the 3rd ACM Conference on Electronic Commerce* (pp. 171-179). Tampa, Florida: ACM Press.

Dennis, J. B., & Van Horn, E. C. (1966). Programming semantics for multi-programmed computations. *Communications of the ACM, 9*(3), 143–155. doi:10.1145/365230.365252

Devriese, D., & Piessens, F. (2010). Noninterference through secure multi-execution. In *Proceedings of the IEEE Symposium on Security and Privacy* (pp. 109-124).

Dhanalakshmi, R., & Chellappan, C. (2012). Mitigating e-mail threats - a web content based. In S. I. Ao, O. Castillo, C. Douglas, D.D. Feng, & J. Lee (Eds.), *Proceedings of the International Multi Conference of Engineers and Computer Scientists* (pp. 632-637). Hong Kong, China: International Association of Engineers.

Didriksen, T. (1997). Rule based database access control: A practical approach. In *Proceedings of the second ACM workshop on role-based access control* (pp. 143–151). New York, NY: ACM.

Dinakar, K., Jones, B., Lieberman, H., Picard, R., Rose, C., Thoman, M., & Reichart, R. (2011, June). *You too?! Mixed-initiative LDA story matching to help teens in distress*. Paper presented at the Sixth International AAAI Conference on Weblogs and Social Media, Dublin, Ireland.

Dinakar, K., Jones, B., Havasi, C., Lieberman, H., & Picard, R. (in press). Commonsense reasoning for detection, prevention, and mitigation of cyberbullying. *ACM Transactions on Interactive Intelligent Systems*.

Ding, J., Cruz, I., & Li, C. (2009). *A formal model for building a social network*. SOLI.

Dingledine, R., Mathewson, N., & Syverson, P. (2004). Tor: The second-generation onion router. In *Proceedings of the 13th conference on USENIX Security Symposium, SSYM'04* (pp. 21–21). San Diego, CA: USENIX Association.

Donath, J. (2008). Signals in social supernets. *Journal of Computer-Mediated Communication, 13*(1), 231–251. doi:10.1111/j.1083-6101.2007.00394.x

Donath, J., & Boyd, D. (2004). Public displays of connection. *BT Technology Journal, 22*(4), 71–82. doi:10.1023/B:BTTJ.0000047585.06264.cc

Dooley, J. J., Pyzalski, J., & Cross, D. (2009). Cyberbullying versus face-to-face bullying: A theoretical and conceptual review. *The Journal of Psychology, 217*(4), 182–188. doi:10.1027/0044-3409.217.4.182

Dorigo, M., & Birattari, M. (2007). Swarm intelligence. *Scholarpedia, 2*(9), 1462. doi:10.4249/scholarpedia.1462

Dorigo, M., Bonabeau, E., & Theraulaz, G. (2000). Ant algorithms and stigmergy. *Future Generation Computer Systems, 16*(9), 851–871. doi:10.1016/S0167-739X(00)00042-X

Duckham, M., Mokbel, M., & Nittel, S. (2007). Special issue on privacy aware and location-based mobile services. *Journal of Location Based Services, 1*(3), 161–164. doi:10.1080/17489720802089489

Dutertre, B., & Moura, L. M. (2006). *A fast linear-arithmetic solver for DPLL(T). Computer Aided Verification* (pp. 81–94). CAV. doi:10.1007/11817963_11

Dwork, C. (2006). Differential privacy. *International Colloquium on Automata, Languages and Programming (ICALP)* (pp. 1-12).

Dwyer, C., Hiltz, S. R., & Passerini, K. (2007). Trust and privacy concern within social networking sites: A comparison of Facebook and MySpace. In *Proceedings of the Thirteenth Americas Conference on Information Systems*, Keystone, Colorado.

Dwyer, C., Hiltz, S. R., & Passerini, K. (2007). Trust and privacy concern within social networking sites: A comparison of Facebook and Myspace. In Hoxmeier, J. A., & Hayne, S. (Eds.), *AMCIS* (p. 339). Association for Information Systems.

Egele, M., Moser, A., Kruegel, C., & Kirda, E. (2011). PoX: Protecting users from malicious Facebook applications. In *Proceedings of the IEEE International Conference on Pervasive Computing and Communications Workshops (PERCOM)*.

Ellison, N. B., Steinfield, C., & Lampe, C. (2007). The benefits of Facebook 'friends': Social capital and college students' use of online social network sites. *Journal of Computer-Mediated Communication, 12*(4), 1143–1168. doi:10.1111/j.1083-6101.2007.00367.x

Ellison, N. B., Steinfield, C., & Lampe, C. (2011). Connection strategies: Social capital implications of Facebook-enabled communication practices. *New Media & Society, 13*(6), 873–892. doi:10.1177/1461444810385389

Englander, E. K. (2012). Spinning our wheels: Improving our ability to respond to bullying and cyberbullying. *Child and Adolescent Psychiatric Clinics of North America, 21*, 43–55. doi:10.1016/j.chc.2011.08.013

Enisa Europa. (2013). Website. Retrieved September 9, 2012, from http://www.enisa.europa.eu/

Entman, R. M. (1989). How the media affect what people think: An information processing approach. *The Journal of Politics, 51*(2), 347–370. doi:10.2307/2131346

Erlingsson, U., & Irm, F. B. S. (2000). IRM enforcement of java stack inspection. In *Proceedings of the 2000 IEEE Symposium on Security and Privacy*, 246–255. IEEE.

Evans, L. (2011). Location-based services: Transformation of the experience of space. *Journal of Location Based Services, 5*(3-4), 242–260. doi:10.1080/17489725.2011.637968

Facebook (2011). *Facebook statement of rights and responsibilities.* Retrieved September 26, 2012 from http://www.facebook.com/terms.php

Facebook (2012). *Key Facts.* Retrieved September 11, 2012, from http://newsroom.fb.com/content/default.aspx?NewsAreaId=22

Facebook 'linked to rise in syphilis'. (2010). *The Telegraph.* Retrieved September 11, 2012 from http://www.telegraph.co.uk/technology/facebook/7508945/Facebook-linked-to-rise-in-syphilis.html

Facebook Stat. Page. (2011). Website. Retrieved March, 2012, from http://www.socialtechnologyreview.com/articles/50-facebook-stats-every-marketer-should-know

Facebook. (2013). Website. Retrieved September 9, 2012, from http://www.facebook.com/note.php?note_id=%20322194465300

Feigenbaum, L., Herman, I., Hongsermeier, T., Neumann, E., & Stephens, S. (2007, December). The semantic web in action. *Scientific American, 297*, 90–97. doi:10.1038/scientificamerican1207-90

Felipe, M. T., García, S. D. O., Babarro, J. M., & Arias, R. M. (2011). Social characteristics in bullying typology: Digging deeper into description of bully-victim. *Procedia - Social and Behavioral Sciences, 29*, 869-878.

Felt, A., & Evans, D. (2008). Privacy protection for social networking platforms. In *Proceedings of the Workshop on Web 2.0 Security and Privacy (W2SP).*

Felt, A., & Evans, D. (2008). Privacy protection for social networking platforms. In *Proceedings of Web 2.0 Security and Privacy (W2SP 2008).*

Ferdig, R. E., Dawson, K., Black, E. W., Paradise Black, N. M., & Thompson, L. A. (2008). Medical students' and residents' use of online social networking tools: Implications for teaching professionalism in medical education. *First Monday, 13*(9). Retrieved September 11, 2012, from http://firstmonday.org/htbin/cgiwrap/bin/ojs/index.php/fm/article/viewArticle/2161/2026

Ferraiolo, D. F., & Kuhn, D. R. (1992). Role based access control. In *Proceedings of the 15th National Computer Security Conference* (pp. 554–563).

Finin, T., Ding, L., Zhou, L., & Joshi, A. (2005). Social networking on the semantic web. *The Learning Organization, 12*(5). doi:10.1108/09696470510611384

Fong, P. W. L. (2011). Relationship-based access control: protection model and policy language. In *Proceedings of the first ACM conference on data and application security and privacy* (pp. 191–202). New York, NY, USA: ACM.

Fong, P. W. L., & Siahaan, I. (2011). Relationship-based access control policies and their policy languages. In *Proceedings of the 16th ACM symposium on access control models and technologies* (pp. 51–60). New York, NY, USA: ACM.

Fong, P. W. L., Anwar, M. M., & Zhao, Z. (2009). *A privacy preservation model for facebook-style social network systems* (pp. 303–320). ESORICS. doi:10.1007/978-3-642-04444-1_19

Fox, S., Rainie, L., Horrigan, J., Lenhart, A., Spooner, T., & Carter, C. (2000). *Trust and privacy online: Why Americans want to rewrite the rules.* Pew Internet and American Life Project.

Franchi, E., & Tomaiuolo, M. (2012). Software agents for distributed social networking. In *Proceedings of the 13th Workshop Dagli Oggetti agli Agenti, WOA 2012* (pp. 1–5).

Freeman, L. C. (1979). Centrality in social networks conceptual clarification. *Social Networks, 1*(3), 215–239. doi:10.1016/0378-8733(78)90021-7

Fuller, A. (2006, January 20). Employers snoop on Facebook. *The Stanford Daily.* Retrieved May 15, 2012, from http://archive.stanforddaily.com/?p=1019651

Fusco, S. J., Michael, K., & Michael, M. G. (2010). *Using a social informatics framework to study the effects of location-based social networking on relationships between people: A review of literature*. Paper presented at the IEEE Symposium on Technology and Society, Wollongong, Australia.

Fusco, S. J., Michael, K., Aloudat, A., & Abbas, R. (2011). *Monitoring people using location-based social networking and its negative impact on trust: an exploratory contextual analysis of five types of "friend" relationships*. Paper presented at the International Symposium on Technology and Society, Chicago, IL.

Gandon, F. L., & Sadeh, N. M. (2004). Semantic web technologies to reconcile privacy and context awareness. *Journal of Web Semantics*, *1*(3), 241–260. doi:10.1016/j.websem.2003.07.008

Gao, H., Hu, J., Huang, T., Wang, J., & Chen, Y. (2011). Security issues in online social networks. *IEEE Internet Computing*, *15*(4), 56–63. doi:10.1109/MIC.2011.50

Garton, L., Haythornthwaite, C., & Wellman, B. (1997). Studying online social networks. *Journal of Computer-Mediated Communication*, *3*(1).

Gates, C. (2007). Access control requirements for Web 2.0 Security and Privacy. *IEEE Web*, *2*, 2–4.

Gest, S. D., Graham-bermann, S. A., & Hartup, W. W. (2001). Peer experience: Common and unique features of number of friendships, social network centrality, and sociometric status. *Social Development*, *10*(1), 23–40. doi:10.1111/1467-9507.00146

Gideon, J., Cranor, L., Egelman, S., & Acquisti, A. (2006). *Power strips, prophylactics, and privacy, oh my!* Paper presented at the Second Symposium on Usable Privacy and Security, Pittsburgh, PA.

Gilbert, E., & Karahalios, K. (2009). Predicting tie strength with social media. In *Proceedings of the 27th international conference on Human factors in computing systems* (pp. 187-196).

Gillespie, A. A. (2006). Cyber-bullying and harassment of teenagers: The legal response. *Journal of Social Welfare and Family Law*, *28*(2), 123–136. doi:10.1080/09649060600973772

Giunchiglia, F., Zhang, R., & Crispo, B. (2008). RELBAC: Relation based access control. In *Proceedings of the 2008 fourth international conference on semantics, knowledge and grid* (pp. 3–11). Washington, DC, USA: IEEE Computer Society.

Giunchiglia, F., Marchese, M., & Zaihrayeu, I. (2005). *Towards a theory of formal classification (Tech. Rep.)*. University of Trento.

Golbeck, J. (2006). Combining provenance with trust in social networks for semantic web content filtering. In *IPAW'06* (p. 101-108). Springer.

Golbeck, J. (2009). Trust and nuanced profile similarity in online social networks. *ACM Transactions on the Web*, *3*(4). *Article*, *12*, 1–33.

Goldschlag, D., Reed, M., & Syverson, P. (1999). Onion routing. *Communications of the ACM*, *42*(2), 39–41. doi:10.1145/293411.293443

Gould, C., Su, Z., & Devanbu, P. (2004). JDBC checker: A static analysis tool for SQL/JDBC applications. In *Proceedings of the 26th International Conference on Software Engineering*.

Goyal, V., Pandey, O., Sahai, A., & Waters, B. (2006). Attribute-based encryption for fine-grained access control of encrypted data. In *ACM Conference on Computer and Communications Security* (pp. 89–98). ACM.

Graffi, K., Groß, C., Mukherjee, P., Kovacevic, A., & Steinmetz, R. (2010). LifeSocial.KOM: A P2P-based platform for secure online social networks. In *Proceedings of the 10th IEEE International Conference on Peer-to-Peer Computing, IEEE P2P'10* (pp. 554–558). IEEE Computer Society.

Granovetter, M. S. (1973). The strength of weak ties. *American Journal of Sociology*, *78*(6), 1360–1380. doi:10.1086/225469

Granovetter, M. S. (1973, January). The strength of weak ties. JSTOR.*American Journal of Sociology*, *78*(6), 1360–1380. doi:10.1086/225469

Gross, R., & Acquisti, A. (2005). Information revelation and privacy in online social networks. In *Proceedings of the 2005 ACM workshop on privacy in the electronic society* (pp. 71–80). New York, NY: ACM.

Gross, R., & Acquisti, A. (2005). Information revelation and privacy in online social networks. In *ACM workshop on privacy in the electronic society* (pp. 71–80). Alexandria, VA, USA: ACM. doi:10.1145/1102199.1102214

Groves, T. (1973). Incentives in teams. *Econometrica, 41*, 617–631. doi:10.2307/1914085

Gudivada, V. N., & Raghavan, V. V. (1995). Content-based image retrieval systems. *IEEE Computer, 28*(9), 18–31. doi:10.1109/2.410145

Guha, S., Tang, K., & Francis, P. (2008). NOYB: Privacy in online social networks. In *Proceedings of the 1st Workshop on Online Social Networks (WOSN 2008)* (pp. 49–54).

Gutfraind, A. (2010). Optimizing topological cascade resilience based on the structure of terrorist networks. *PLoS ONE, 5*(11), e13448. doi:10.1371/journal.pone.0013448

Guy, I., Jacovi, M., Shahar, E., Meshulam, N., Soroka, V., & Farrell, S. (2008). *Harvesting with SONAR: the value of aggregating social network information.* Paper presented at the 26th annual SIGCHI conference on Human factors in computing systems, Florence, Italy.

Hadjidj, R., Debbabi, M., Lounis, H., & Iqbal, F. (2009). Towards an integrated email forensic. *Digital Investigation, 5*(3-4), 124–137. doi:10.1016/j.diin.2009.01.004

Haferkamp, N., Eimler, S. C., Papadakis, A.-M., & Kruck, J. V. (2012). Men are from Mars, women are from Venus? Examining gender differences in self-presentation on social networking sites. *CyberPsychology. Behavior and Social Networking, 15*(2), 91–98. doi:10.1089/cyber.2011.0151

Hafez Ninggal, M. I., & Abawajy, J. (2011). *Attack vector analysis and privacy-preserving social network data publishing. Trust, Security and Privacy in Computing and Communications (TrustCom)* (pp. 847–852). IEEE.

Halfond, W. G. J., & Orso, A. (2006). Preventing SQL injection attacks using AMNESIA. In *Proceedings of the 28th International Conference on Software Engineering.*

Halfond, W. G. J., Orso, A., & Manolios, P. (2006). Using positive tainting and syntax-aware evaluation to counter SQL injection attacks. In *Proceedings of the 14th ACM SIGSOFT International Symposium on Foundations of Software Engineering.*

Hamlen, K. W., Morrisett, G., & Schneider, F. B. (2006). Computability classes for enforcement mechanisms. *ACM Transactions on Programming Languages and Systems, 28*(1), 175–205. doi:10.1145/1111596.1111601

Hampton, K. N., Sessions Goulet, L., Rainie, L., & Purcell, K. (2011). *Social networking sites and our lives. How people's trust, personal relationships, and civic and political involvement are connected to their use of social networking sites and other technologies.* Pew Research Center's Internet & American Life Project.

Harvey, M., Treadway, D. C., & Heames, J. T. (2007). The occurrence of bullying in global organizations: A model and issues associated with social/emotional contagion. *Journal of Applied Social Psychology, 37*(11), 2576–2599. doi:10.1111/j.1559-1816.2007.00271.x

Haselager, G. J. T., Hartup, W. W., Lieshout, C. F. M. V., & Riksen-walraven, J. M. A. (1998). Similarities between friends and nonfriends in middle childhood. *Child Development, 69*(4), 1198–1208.

Hasib, A. (2009). Threats of online social networks. *International Journal of Computer Science and Network Security, 9*(11), 288–293.

Havlena, W. J., & DeSarbo, W. S. (1991). On the measurement of perceived consumer risk. *Decision Sciences, 22*(4), 927–939. doi:10.1111/j.1540-5915.1991.tb00372.x

Haythornthwaite, C. (1996). Social network analysis: An approach and technique for the study of information exchange. *Library & Information Science Research, 18*(4), 323–342. doi:10.1016/S0740-8188(96)90003-1

Haythornthwaite, C. (2005). Social networks and Internet connectivity effects. *Information Communication and Society, 8*(2), 125–147. doi:10.1080/13691180500146185

Heckmann, D. (2006). *Ubiquitous user modeling. Dissertations in Artificial Intelligence,* vol. 297. DISKI. IOS Press.

Hedin, D., & Sabelfeld, A. (2012). Information-flow security for a core of JavaScript. In *Proceedings of the IEEE Computer Security Foundations Symposium (CSF).*

Henderson, K., Gallagher, B., Li, L., Akoglu, L., Eliassi-Rad, T., Tong, H., & Faloutsos, C. (2011). It's who you know: Graph mining using recursive structural features. In *Proceedings of the 17th ACM SIGKDD International conference on knowledge discovery and data mining* (pp. 663-671). San Diego, California: ACM.

Herring, S. C. (2001). Computer-mediated discourse. In Schiffrin, D., Tannen, D., & Hamilton, H. (Eds.), *The handbook of discourse analysis* (pp. 612–634). Oxford, UK: Blackwell Publishers.

Hew, K. F. (2011). Students' and teachers' use of Facebook. *Computers in Human Behavior, 27*(2), 662–676. doi:10.1016/j.chb.2010.11.020

Hinduja, S., & Patchin, J. W. (2009). *Bullying beyond the schoolyard: Preventing and responding to cyberbullying*. Thousand Oaks, CA: Corwin Press.

Hinduja, S., & Patchin, J. W. (2010). Bullying, cyberbullying, and suicide. *Archives of Suicide Research, 41*(3), 206–221. doi:10.1080/13811118.2010.494133

Hoare, J. H., & Sanders, J. W. (1986). Data refinement refined. *European Symposium on Programming* (pp. 187-196).

Hobbs, R. (2010). *Digital and media literacy: A plan of action.* Knight Commission on the Information Needs of Communities in a Democracy, Aspen Institute, Washington DC. Retrieved September 11, 2012, from http://www.knightcomm.org/digital-and-media-literacy/

Hogben, G. (2009). Security issues in the future of social networking. In *W3C Workshop on the Future of Social Networking*, Barcelona, Spain. Position Paper.

Hogben, G. (Ed.). (2007). *Security issues and recommendations for online social networks.* ENISA Position Paper No.1.

Honjo, M., Hasegawa, T., Hasegawa, T., Suda, T., Mishima, K., & Yoshida, T. (2011). A framework to identify relationships among students in school bullying using digital communication media. In *Proceedings of the 3rd IEEE International Conference on Privacy, Security, Risk and Trust (PASSAT), and 2011 3rd IEEE International Conference on Social Computing (SOCIALCOM)* (pp. 1474–1479).

Huang, Y.-W., Yu, F., Hang, C., Tsai, C.-H., Lee, D.-T., & Kuo, S.-Y. (2004). *Securing web application code by static analysis and runtime protection.* Paper presented at the Proceedings of the 13th international conference on World Wide Web, New York, NY, USA.

Huber, M., Mulazzani, M., Weippl, E., Kitzler, G., & Goluch, S. (2011). Friend-in-the-middle attacks: Exploiting social networking sites for spam. *IEEE Internet Computing, 15*(3), 28–34. doi:10.1109/MIC.2011.24

Hu, H., Ahn, G.-J., & Jorgensen, J. (2012). Multiparty access control for online social networks: Model and mechanisms. *IEEE Transactions on Knowledge and Data Engineering*, 99.

Hu, H., Gail-Joon, A., & Jan, J. (2012). *Enabling collaborative data sharing in Google+ (Tech. Rep.).* Arizona State University.

Hussein, D., Ghada, A., & Hamad, A. (2009). Classifying Web 2.0 supported applications by pattern of usage: Functional & technical ISSUES. In *MCIS 2009 Proceedings*. Paper 94.

Huttunen, A., Salmivalli, C., & Lagerspetz, K. M. J. (2006). Friendship networks and bullying in schools. *Annals of the New York Academy of Sciences. Understanding Aggressive Behavior in Children, 794*, 355–359.

Identity Theft Resource Center. (2012). *ITRC fact sheet 138 - social networking and identity theft.* Retrieved September 11, 2012, from http://www.idtheftcenter.org/artman2/publish/v_fact_sheets/FS_138.shtml

IndraniBalasundaram, & Ramaraj. (2011). An approach to detect and prevent SQL injection attacks in database using web service. *International Journal of Computer Science and Network Security, 11*, 197–205.

Irani, D., Webb, S., Li, K., & Pu, C. (2011). Modeling unintended personal-information leakage from multiple online social networks. *IEEE Internet Computing, 15*(3), 13–19. doi:10.1109/MIC.2011.25

Jahid, S., Mittal, P., & Borisov, N. (2011). EASiER: Encryption-based access control in social networks with efficient revocation. In *Proceedings of the 6th ACM symposium on information, computer and communications security* (pp. 411–415). ACM.

Jahid, S., Nilizadeh, S., Mittal, P., Borisov, N., & Kapadia, A. (2012). DECENT: A decentralized architecture for enforcing privacy in online social networks. In *Proceedings of the IEEE International Conference on Pervasive Computing and Communications Workshops* (pp. 326–332).

Jessen, J., & Jørgensen, A. H. (2012). Aggregated trustworthiness: Redefining online credibility through social validation. *First Monday, 17*(1). Retrieved September 11, 2012, from http://www.firstmonday.org/htbin/cgiwrap/bin/ojs/index.php/fm/article/view/3731/3132

Jie, W., Phan, R. C. W., Whitley, J. N., & Parish, D. J. (2010). Research on Multi-Level Security Framework for OpenID. In *Third International Symposium on Electronic Commerce and Security*.

Joinson, A. N., Reips, U.-D., Buchanan, T., & Schofield, C. B. P. (2010). Privacy, trust, and self-disclosure online. *Human-Computer Interaction, 25*(1), 1–24. doi:10.1080/07370020903586662

Joshi, P., & Kuo, C.-C. J. (2011). Security and privacy in online social networks: A survey. In *Proceedings of the IEEE International Conference on Multimedia and Expo* (pp. 1–6).

Joshi, J. B. D., Aref, W. G., Ghafoor, A., & Spafford, E. H. (2001). Security models for web-based applications. *Communications of the ACM, 44*(2), 38–44. doi:10.1145/359205.359224

Joslyn, C., Rocha, L., Smith, S., Johnson, N. L., Rasmussen, S., & Kantor, M. (1998). Symbiotic intelligence: Self-organizing knowledge on distributed networks driven by human interaction. In Adami, C. (Eds.), *Artificial life VI*. Cambridge, MA: MIT Press.

Jun, X., & Wooyong, L. (2003). Sustaining availability of web services under distributed denial of service attacks. *IEEE Transactions on Computers, 52*(2), 195–208. doi:10.1109/TC.2003.1176986

Juvonen, J., Graham, S., & Schuster, M. A. (2003). Bullying among young adolescents the strong, the weak and the troubled. *Pediatrics, 112*(6), 1131–1137. doi:10.1542/peds.112.6.1231

Kamkar, S. (2005). *Technical explanation of the MySpace worm*. Retrieved May 15, 2012, from http://namb.la/popular/tech.html

Kessler, V. (1992). On the Chinese wall model. In *Proceedings of the second European symposium on research in computer security* (pp. 41–54). London, UK: Springer-Verlag.

Kirkpatrick, D. (2010). *The facebook effect: The inside story of the company that is connecting the world*. New York: Simon & Schuster.

Koestler, A. (1968). *The ghost in the machine*. New York: Macmillan.

Konrad, M., Vyleta, M. L., Theis, F. J., Stock, M., Tragust, S., Klatt, M., & Cremer, S. (2012). Social transfer of pathogenic fungus promotes active immunisation in ant colonies. *PLoS Biology, 10*(4), e1001300. doi:10.1371/journal.pbio.1001300

Kontostathis, A., Edwards, L., & Leatherman, A. (2009, May). *ChatCoder: Toward the tracking and categorization of internet predators*. Paper presented of the Text Mining Workshop held in conjunction with the Ninth Siam International Conference on Data Mining, Sparks, NV.

Korolova, A., Motwani, R., Nabar, S. U., & Xu, Y. (2008). Link privacy in social networks. In *Proceedings of the 17th ACM conference on Information and knowledge management* (pp. 289-298). Napa Valley, California: ACM.

Kowalski, R. M., & Limber, S. P. (2007). Electronic bullying among middle school students. *The Journal of Adolescent Health, 41*(6), S22–SS30. doi:10.1016/j.jadohealth.2007.08.017

Kowalski, R. M., Limber, S. P., & Agatston, P. W. (2008). *Cyber bullying: The new moral frontier*. Oxford, UK: Blackwell Publishing Ltd.doi:10.1002/9780470694176

Kramer, S., & Bradfield, J. C. (2010). A general definition of malware. *Journal in Computer Virology, 6*(2), 105–114. doi:10.1007/s11416-009-0137-1

Krasnova, H., Spiekerman, S., Koroleva, K., & Hildebrand, T. (2010). Online social networks: Why we disclose. *Journal of Information Technology, 25*, 109–125. doi:10.1057/jit.2010.6

Krawetz, N. (2004). Anti-honeypot technology. *IEEE Security & Privacy, 2*(1), 76–79. doi:10.1109/MSECP.2004.1264861

Krebs, V. (2001). Connecting the dots – tracking two identified terrorists. Retrieved September 11, 2012, from http://www.orgnet.com/prevent.html

Krishnamurthy, B., & Wills, C. (2009). *On the leakage of personally identifiable information via online social networks*. Paper presented at the 2nd ACM Workshop on Online Social Networks. New York: ACM.

Krishnamurthy, B., & Wills, C. E. (2008). Characterizing privacy in online social networks. In *Proceedings of the Workshop on Online Social Networks* (pp. 37–42).

Kruk, S. (2004). FOAF-realm-control your friends' access to the resource. *FOAF Workshop proceedings 186*. Retrieved March, 2012, from http://www.w3.org/2001/sw/Europe/events/foaf-galway/papers/fp/foaf realm/.

Kruk, S., Grzonkowski, S., Gzella, A., Woroniecki, T., & Choi, H. (2006). D-FOAF: Distributed identity management with access rights delegation. *The Semantic Web–ASWC 2006*(4), 140–154.

Kuhn, D. R., Coyne, E. J., & Weil, T. R. (2010). Adding attributes to role based access control. *IEEE Computer, 43*(6), 79–81. doi:10.1109/MC.2010.155

Kuo, I., Horng, S., Kao, T., Lin, T., Lee, C., Chen, Y., & Terano, T. (2010). A hybrid swarm intelligence algorithm for the travelling salesman problem. *Expert Systems: International Journal of Knowledge Engineering and Neural Networks, 27*(3), 166–179. doi:10.1111/j.1468-0394.2010.00517.x

Lampson, B. (1974). Protection. *ACM SIGOPS Operating Systems Review, 8*(1), 18–24. doi:10.1145/775265.775268

Laorden, C., Sanz, B., Alvarez, G., & Bringas, P. G. (2010). A threat model approach to threats and vulnerabilities in on-line social networks. *Advances in Intelligent and Soft Computing, 85*, 135–142. doi:10.1007/978-3-642-16626-6_15

Law, D. M., Shapka, J. D., Domene, J. F., & Gagné, M. H. (2012). Are cyberbullies really bullies? An investigation of reactive and proactive online aggression. *Computers in Human Behavior, 28*(2), 664–672. doi:10.1016/j.chb.2011.11.013

Lazen, M. (2012, April 5). Social media today: Demanding credibility in authorship. *Social Media Today*. Retrieved September 11, 2012, from http://socialmediatoday.com/node/484395

Leaves, G. T., Baker, A. L., & Ruby, C. (2006). *Preliminary design of JML: A behavioral interface specification language for Java* (pp. 1–38). Software Engineering Notes.

Leino, R. (2005). Efficient weakest preconditions. *Information Processing Letters (IPL)*, 281–288. doi:10.1016/j.ipl.2004.10.015

Lenhart, A. (2009). *Adults and social network websites*. Pew Research Center's Internet & American Life Project.

Lenhart, A., Madden, M., Smith, A., Purcell, K., Zickuhr, K., & Rainie, L. (2011). *Teens, kindness and cruelty on social network sites. How American teens navigate the new world of "digital citizenship."*. Pew Research Center's Internet & American Life Project.

Leskovec, J., Lang, K. J., Dasgupta, A., & Mahoney, M. W. (2008). Statistical properties of community structure in large social and information networks. In *Proceeding of the 17th International Conference on World Wide Web* (pp. 695–704).

Lesniewski-Laas, C. (2008). A Sybil-proof one-hop DHT. In *Proceedings of the 1st workshop on Social network systems* (pp. 19–24). ACM.

Levien, R. (2009). Attack-resistant trust metrics. In *Computing with social trust* (pp. 121–132). Springer. doi:10.1007/978-1-84800-356-9_5

Lewin, T. (2010, May 5). Teenage insults, scrawled on web, not on walls. *New York Times*. Retrieved October 1, 2012, from http://www.nytimes.com/2010/05/06/us/06formspring.html.

Lewis, K., Kaufman, J., & Christakis, N. (2008). The taste for privacy: An analysis of college student privacy settings in an online social network. *Journal of Computer-Mediated Communication, 14*(1), 79–100. doi:10.1111/j.1083-6101.2008.01432.x

Lewko, A., & Waters, B. (2011). Decentralizing attribute-based encryption. In *Advances in Cryptology – EUROCRYPT 2011* (*Vol. 6632*, pp. 568–588). Lecture Notes in Computer ScienceSpringer. doi:10.1007/978-3-642-20465-4_31

Lew, M. S., Sebe, N., Lifl, D. C., & Jain, R. (2006). Content-based multimedia information retrieval: State of the art and challenges. *ACM Transactions on Multimedia Computing, Communications, and Applications*, *2*(1), 1–19. doi:10.1145/1126004.1126005

Leyla, B., Thorsten, S., Davide, B., & Engin, K. (2009, April). All your contacts are belong to us: Automated identity theft attacks on social networks. In *18th international world wide web conference*. ACM.

Li, N. (2000). Local names in SPKI/SDSI. In *Proceedings of the 13th IEEE workshop on Computer Security Foundations, CSFW '00*. IEEE Computer Society.

Li, N., Mitchell, J. C., & Winsborough, W. H. (2002). Design of a role-based trust-management framework. In *Proceedings of the 2002 IEEE symposium on security and privacy* (pp. 114–130). Washington, DC, USA: IEEE Computer Society.

Li, Q. (2005, April). *Cyberbullying in schools: Nature and extent of Canadian adolescents' experience*. Paper presented at the Annual Meeting of the American Educational Research Association, Montreal, Canada.

Ligatti, J., Bauer, L., & Walker, D. (2005). Enforcing non-safety security policies with program monitors. *Computer Security ESORICS*, *3679*, 355–373.

Li, N., Grosof, B. N., & Feigenbaum, J. (2003, February). Delegation logic: A logic-based approach to distributed authorization. *ACM Transactions on Information and System Security*, *6*(1), 128–171. doi:10.1145/605434.605438

Li, N., Zhang, N., & Das, S. K. (2011). Preserving relation privacy in online social network data. *IEEE Internet Computing*, *15*(3), 35–42. doi:10.1109/MIC.2011.26

Lindamood, J., Heatherly, R., Kantarcioglu, M., & Thuraisingham, B. (2009, April). *Inferring private information using social network data*. Paper presented at the 18th international conference on World Wide Web, Madrid, Spain.

Lin, W., Sun, M., Poovendran, R., & Zhang, Z. (2010). Group event detection with a varying number of group members for video surveillance. *IEEE Transactions on Circuits and Systems for Video Technology*, *20*(8), 1057–1067. doi:10.1109/TCSVT.2010.2057013

Lipford, H. R., Besmer, A., & Watson, J. (2008). Understanding privacy settings in Facebook with an audience view. In *Proceedings of the 1st conference on usability, psychology, and security* (pp. 2:1–2:8). Berkeley, CA, USA: USENIX Association.

Li, Q. (2006). Cyberbullying in schools: A research of gender difference. *School Psychology International*, *27*(2), 157–170. doi:10.1177/0143034306064547

Li, Q. (2007). New bottle but old wine: A research of cyberbullying in schools. *Computers in Human Behavior*, *23*(4), 1777–1791. doi:10.1016/j.chb.2005.10.005

Li, T., & Li, N. (2009). On the tradeoff between privacy and utility in data publishing. In Elder, J. F. IV, Fogelman-Soulie, F., Flach, P. A., & Zaki, M. (Eds.), *KDD* (pp. 517–526). ACM. doi:10.1145/1557019.1557079

Livingstone, S. (2008). Taking risky opportunities in youthful content creation: Teenagers' use of social networking sites for intimacy, privacy, and self-expression. *New Media &. Society*, *10*(3), 393–411.

Livingstone, S., & Brake, D. R. (2010). On the rapid rise of social networking sites: New findings and policy implications. *Children & Society*, *24*(1), 75–83. doi:10.1111/j.1099-0860.2009.00243.x

Livne, A., Simmons, M. P., Adar, E., & Adamic, L. A. (2011). The party is over here: Structure and content in the 2010 election. In *Proceedings of the Fifth International Conference on Weblogs*.

Lucas, M. M., & Borisov, N. (2008). FlyByNight: Mitigating the privacy risks of social networking. In *Proceedings of 7th ACM Workshop on Privacy in the Electronic Society (WPES 2008)* (pp. 1–8).

Luo, W., Liu, J., Liu, J., & Fan, C. (2009). *An analysis of security in social network*. Paper presented at the 6th IEEE International conference on dependable, automatic and secure computing, Chengdu, China.

Luo, W., Xie, Q., & Hengartner, U. (2009). FaceCloak: An architecture for user privacy on social networking sites. In *Proceedings of the International Conference on Computational Science and Engineering, (CSE '09)* (vol. 3, pp. 26–33).

Luo, S., Xia, H., Yoshida, T., & Wang, Z. (2009). Toward collective intelligence of online communities: A primitive conceptual model. *Journal of Systems Science and Systems Engineering*, *18*, 203–221. doi:10.1007/s11518-009-5095-0

Macskassy, S. A., & Provost, F. (2003). A simple relational classifier. In *Proceedings of the Second Workshop on Multi-Relational Data Mining (MRDM-2003) at the Ninth ACM SIGKDD International Conference on Knowledge Discovery and Data Mining (KDD-2003)* (pp. 64-76). Washington, DC.

Macskassy, S. A., & Provost, F. (2005). Suspicion scoring based on guilt-by-association, collective inference, and focused data access. In *International Conference on Intelligence Analysis*.

Maheswaran, M., Tang, H. C., & Ghunaim, A. (2007). Towards a gravity- based trust model for social networking systems. In *Proceedings of the 27th international conference on distributed computing systems workshops* (pp. 24–24). Washington, DC, USA: IEEE Computer Society.

Majeski, M., Johnson, M., & Bellovin, S. M. (2011). *The failure of online social network privacy settings* (Tech. Rep. No. CUCS-010-11). Department of Computer Science, Columbia University.

Malhotra, N. K., Kim, S. S., & Agarwal, J. (2004). Internet users' information privacy concerns (IUIPC): The construct, the scale and a causal model. *Information Systems Research*, *15*(4), 336–355. doi:10.1287/isre.1040.0032

Mani, M., Nguyen, A., & Crespi, N. (2010). Scope: A prototype for spontaneous P2P social networking. In *Proceedings of the 8th IEEE International Conference on Pervasive Computing and Communications Workshops, PERCOM* (pp. 220–225). IEEE Computer Society.

Martin, M., Livshits, B., & Lam, M. S. (2005). Finding application errors and security flaws using PQL: A program query language. *ACM SIGPLAN Notices*, *40*(10), 365–383. doi:10.1145/1103845.1094840

Mas-Colell, A., Whinston, M. D., & Green, J. R. (1995). *Microeconomic theory - chapter 23*. Oxford University Press. Hardcover.

Masoumzadeh, A., & Joshi, J. (2010). OSNAC: An ontology-based access control model for social networking systems. In *Proceedings of the 2010 IEEE second international conference on social computing* (pp. 751–759). Washington, DC, USA: IEEE Computer Society.

Maurer, H., & Kolbitsch, J. (2006). The transformation of the web: How emerging communities shape the information we consume. *Journal of Universal Computing Science*, *12*(2), 187–213.

Mayer, R. C., Davis, J. H., & Schoorman, F. D. (1995). An integrative model of organizational trust. *Academy of Management Review*, *20*(3), 709–734.

Mazer, J. P., Murphy, R. E., & Simonds, C. J. (2007). I'll see you on 'Facebook': The effects of computer-mediated teacher self-disclosure on student motivation, affective learning, and classroom climate. *Communication Education*, *56*(1), 1–17. doi:10.1080/03634520601009710

Mazur, Z., Mazur, H., & Mendyk-Krajewska, T. (2009). Security of internet transactions. *Internet-Technical Development and Applications*, *64*, 243–251. doi:10.1007/978-3-642-05019-0_26

Mazzara, M., Marraffa, A., Biselli, L., & Chiarabini, L. (2011). Polidoxa: A synergic approach of a social network and a search engine to offer trustworthy news. In *International Workshop on TRUstworthy Service-Oriented Computing (INTRUSO 2011)*. Copenhagen, Denmark.

Mazzara, M., Marraffa, A., Biselli, L., & Chiarabini, L. (2011). The Polidoxa Shift: a New Approach to Social Networks. *Journal of Internet Services and Information Security (JISIS)*, *1*(4), 74–88.

McCallister, E., Grance, T., & Scarfone, K. A. (2010). Guide to protecting the confidentiality of personally identifiable information (PII). Retrieved September, 2012, from http://csrc.nist.gov/publications/nistpubs/800-122/sp800-122.pdf

McClure, R. A., & Krüger, I. H. (2005). SQL DOM: Compile time checking of dynamic SQL statements. In *27th International Conference on Software Engineering*.

Mccombs, M. (2004). *Setting the agenda: The mass media and public opinion*. New York: Blackwell Publishing.

Mccombs, M., & Shaw, D. (1972). The agenda-setting function of mass media. *Public Opinion Quarterly, 36*, 176–187. Chicago, IL: University of Chicago Press. doi:10.1086/267990

Merchant, G. (2012). Unravelling the social network: Theory and research. *Learning, Media and Technology, 37*(1), 4–19. doi:10.1080/17439884.2011.567992

Mesh, G. S. (2012). Is online trust and trust in social institutions associated with online disclosure of identifiable information online? *Computers in Human Behavior, 28*(4), 1471–1477. doi:10.1016/j.chb.2012.03.010

Metzger, M. J. (2006). Effects of site, vendor, and consumer characteristics on Web site trust and disclosure. *Communication Research, 33*(3), 155–179. doi:10.1177/0093650206287076

Metzger, M. J., & Flanagin, A. J. (Eds.). (2008). *Digital media, youth, and credibility*. Cambridge, MA: The MIT Press.

Mezzour, G., Perrig, A., Gligor, V. D., & Papadimitratos, P. (2009, December 12-14). Privacy-preserving relationship path discovery in social networks. In *8th international conference on cryptology and network security* (pp. 189-208). Kanazawa, Japan.

Michael, K., & Michael, M. G. (2011). The social and behavioural implications of location-based services. *Journal of Location Based Services, 5*(3-4), 121–137. doi:10.1080/17489725.2011.642820

Michael, M. G., & Michael, K. (2010). Towards a state of uberveillance. *IEEE Technology and Society Magazine, 29*(2), 9–16. doi:10.1109/MTS.2010.937024

Mika, P. (2005). Ontologies are us: A unified model of social networks and semantics. In Gil, Y., Motta, E., Benjamins, V. R., & Musen, M. A. (Eds.), *The Semantic Web - ISWC 2005* (pp. 522–536). Springer. doi:10.1007/11574620_38

Miller, M. S., Yee, K.-P., & Shapiro, J. (2011). *Capability myths demolished* (Tech. Rep.). Systems Research Laboratory, Johns Hopkins University. Retrieved March, 2012, from http://srl.cs.jhu.edu/pubs/SRL2003-02.pdf.

Miller, P. (2010). *Smart swarm: Using animal behaviour to organise our world*. Collins.

Mills, E. (2008, June 26). *Facebook suspends app that permitted peephole*. Retrieved October 6, 2012, from http://news.cnet.com/8301-10784_3-9977762-7.html

Milne, G. R., & Culnan, M. J. (2004). Strategies for reducing online privacy risks: Why consumers read (or don't read) online privacy notices. *Journal of Interactive Marketing, 18*(3), 15–29. doi:10.1002/dir.20009

Mishne, G. (2005, August). *Experiments with mood classification in blog posts*. Paper presented at the Workshop on Stylistic Analysis of Text for Information Access, Salvador, Brazil.

Mont, M. C., Pearson, S., & Bramhall, P. (2003). Towards accountable management of identity and privacy: Sticky policies and enforceable tracing services. *14th International Workshop on Database and Expert Systems Applications (DEXA'03), September 1-5, 2003, Prague, Czech Republic, (pp. 377-382)*. IEEE Computer Society.

Moore, K. N. (2011). *Cyberbullying: An exploratory study of adolescent girls' perspectives on technology's impact on relationships*. (Doctoral Thesis). State University of New Jersey Rutgers.

Moore, M. J., Nakano, T., Enomoto, A., & Suda, T. (2012). Anonymity and roles associated with aggressive posts in an online forum. *Computers in Human Behavior, 28*(3), 861–867. doi:10.1016/j.chb.2011.12.005

Moradi, F., Olovsson, T., & Tsigas, P. (2012). Towards modeling legitimate and unsolicited email traffic using social network properties. In *Proceedings of the Fifth Workshop on Social Network Systems (SNS '12)* (pp. 9:1-9:6). Bern, Switzerland: ACM.

Motoyama, M., McCoy, D., Levchenko, K., Savage, S., & Voelker, G. (2011, August). Dirty jobs: The role of freelance labor in web service abuse. In *Proceedings of the USENIX security symposium*. San Francisco, CA.

Mouttapa, M., Valente, T., Gallaher, P., Rohrbach, L. A., & Unger, J. B. (2004). Social network predictors of bullying and victimization. *Adolescence, 39*(154), 315–335.

Mustafaraj, E., & Metaxas, P. (2010). From obscurity to prominence in minutes: Political speech and real-time search. In *Websci10: Extending the frontiers of society on-line*. Raleigh, NC, US.

Nagurney, & Wakolbinger, T. (2005). Supernetworks: An introduction to the concept and its applications with a specific focus on knowledge supernetworks. *International Journal of Knowledge, Culture and Change Management.*

Nahar, V., Unankard, S., Li, X., & Pang, C. (2012). Sentiment analysis for effective detection of cyber bullying. *Web Technologies and Applications, 7235*, 764–774. doi:10.1007/978-3-642-29253-8_75

Naor, M., & Pinkas, B. (2001). Efficient trace and revoke schemes. In *Proceedings of the 4th international conference on Financial Cryptography, 9*(6), 1–20. London, UK: Springer-Verlag.

Naor, D., Naor, M., & Lotspiech, J. B. (2001). *Revocation and tracing schemes for stateless receivers. Advances in Cryptology—CRYPTO 2001* (pp. 41–62). Springer.

Narayanan, A., & Shmatikov, V. (2009). De-anonymizing social networks. In *Proceedings of the 30th IEEE Symposium on Security and Privacy* (pp.173–187).

New Myspace and Facebook worms target social networks. (2008). Website. Retrieved March, 2012, from http://www.darknet.org.uk/2008/08/new-myspace-and-facebook-worm-target-social-networks/

Nguyen-Tuong, A., Guarnieri, S., Greene, D., Shirley, J., & Evans, D. (2005). Automatically hardening web applications using precise tainting. *Security and Privacy in the Age of Ubiquitous Computing*, 295-307.

Ni, Q., Bertino, E., Lobo, J., Brodie, C., Karat, C.-M., Karat, J. et al. (2010, July). Privacy-aware role-based access control. *ACM Transactions of Information System Security, 13*(3), 24:1–24:31.

Nielsen. (2011). *State of the media: The social media report Q3 2011. NM incite.* Retrieved September 11, 2012, from http://blog.nielsen.com/nielsenwire/social/

Nissenbaum, H. F. (2004). Privacy as contextual integrity. *Washington Law Review (Seattle, Wash.), 79*(1), 119–157.

Noelle-Neumann, E. (1974). The spiral of silence: A theory of public opinion. *The Journal of Communication, 24*, 43–51. doi:10.1111/j.1460-2466.1974.tb00367.x

Norberg, P. A., Horne, D. R., & Horne, D. A. (2007). The privacy paradox: Personal information disclosure intentions versus behaviors. *The Journal of Consumer Affairs, 41*(1), 100–126. doi:10.1111/j.1745-6606.2006.00070.x

Oasis committee. XACML 2.0 specification. (2012). Website. Retrieved March, 2012, from http://www.oasisopen.org/committees/tchome.php?wgabbrev=xacmlXACML20

Ochoa, A., Ponce, J., Jaramillo, R., Ornelas, F., & Hernández, D. Eliasa, A., & Hernández, A. (2011, December). *Analysis of cyber-bullying in a virtual social networking.* Paper presented at the 11th International Conference on Hybrid Intelligent Systems, Malacca, Malaysia.

OGP - OpenGraph Protocol. (2012). Website. Retrieved September, 2012, from http://ogp.me

Olson, P. (2012). *We are anonymous: Inside the hacker world of lulzsec, anonymous, and the global cyber insurgency.* Little, Brown and Company.

Olweus, D. (1991). Bully/victim problems among schoolchildren: Basic facts and effects of a school based intervention program. In Pepler, D. J., & Rubin, K. H. (Eds.), *The development and treatment of childhood aggression* (pp. 411–448). Mahwah, NJ: Lawrence Erlbaum Associates, Inc.

Ong, E. Y. L., Ang, R. P., Ho, J. C. M., Lim, J. C. Y., Goh, D. H., Lee, C. S., & Chua, A. Y. K. (2011). Narcissism, extraversion and adolescents' self-presentation on Facebook. *Personality and Individual Differences, 50*(2), 180–185. doi:10.1016/j.paid.2010.09.022

Opsahl, K. (2010). *A bill of privacy rights for social network users.* Retrieved May 15, 2010, from https://www.eff.org/deeplinks/2010/05/bill-privacy-rights-social-network-users

OWASP – The Open Web Application Security Project Homepage. (2012). Website. Retrieved September, 2012, from http://www.owasp.org

OWASP. (2010). The top 10 most critical web application security risks. Retrieved April 2011, from owasp.org

Pakaslahti, L., & Keltikangas-järvinen, L. (2001). Peer-attributed prosocial behavior among aggressive/preferred, aggressive/non-preferred, non-aggressive/preferred and non-aggressive/non-preferred adolescents. *Personality and Individual Differences*, *30*(6), 903–916. doi:10.1016/S0191-8869(00)00082-9

Palen, L., & Dourish, P. (2003). Unpacking privacy for a networked world. In *Proceedings of CHI '03*. New York: ACM Press.

Pang, B., & Lee, L. (2008). Opinion mining and sentiment analysis. *Foundations and Trends in Information Retrieval*, *2*(1-2), 1–135. doi:10.1561/1500000011

Papic, M., & Noonan, S. (2011, February). *Social media as a tool for protest*. Retrieved May 15, 2012, from http://www.stratfor.com/weekly/20110202-social-media-tool-protest?utmsource=SWeekly&utmmedium=email&utmcampaign=110203&utmcontent=readmore&elq=8a864881cc2546359a7360759ab0cfb3

Paragina, F., Paragina, S., & Jipa, A. (2011, April). *The cyberbullying and the educational resources*. Paper presented at the 7th International Scientific Conference eLearning and Software for Education, Bucharest, Romania.

Parikka, J. (2010). *Insect media. An archaeology of animals and technology*. University of Minnesota Press.

Park, N., Kee, K., & Valenzuela, S. (2009). Being immersed in social networking environment: Facebook groups, uses and gratifications, and social outcomes. *Cyberpsychology & Behavior*, *12*(6), 729–733. doi:10.1089/cpb.2009.0003

Patchin, J. W., & Hinduja, S. (2006). Bullies move beyond the schoolyard: A preliminary look at cyberbullying. *Youth Violence and Juvenile Justice*, *4*(2), 148–169. doi:10.1177/1541204006286288

Pekárek, M., & Pötzsch, S. (2009). A comparison of privacy issues in collaborative workspaces and social networks. *Identity in the Information Society*, *2*(1), 81–93. doi:10.1007/s12394-009-0016-4

Pellegrini, A. D., Bartini, M., & Brooks, F. (1999). School bullies, victims, and aggressive victims: Factors relating to group affiliation and victimization in early adolescence. *Journal of Educational Psychology*, *91*(2), 216–224. doi:10.1037/0022-0663.91.2.216

Peng, C. S., Chen, S. K., Chung, J. Y., Roy-Chowdhury, A., & Srinivasan, V. (2010). Accessing existing business data from the World Wide Web. *IBM Systems Journal*, *37*(1), 115–132. doi:10.1147/sj.371.0115

Pepitone, J. (2011). *Facebook settles FTC charges over 2009 privacy breaches*. Retrieved October 5, 2012, from http://money.cnn.com/2011/11/29/technology/facebook_settlement/index.htm?iid=HP_LN

Perfitt, T., & Englert, B. (2010). Megaphone: Fault tolerant, scalable, and trustworthy P2P microblogging. In *Proceedings of the Fifth International Conference on Internet and Web Applications and Services, ICIW'10* (pp. 469–477). IEEE Computer Society.

Peter, J. P., Tarpey, S., & Lawrence, X. (1975, June). A comparative analysis of three consumer decision strategies. *The Journal of Consumer Research*, *2*(1), 29–37. doi:10.1086/208613

Pfeil, U., Arjan, R., & Zaphiris, P. (2009). Age differences in online social networking – A study of user profiles and the social capital divide among teenagers and older users in MySpace. *Computers in Human Behavior*, *25*(3), 643–654. doi:10.1016/j.chb.2008.08.015

Pham, A. (2011, September 9). Article. *LA Times*. Retrieved October 6, 2012, from http://latimesblogs.latimes.com/entertainmentnewsbuzz/2011/09/sims-social-surpasses-farmville-as-second-largest-facebook-game.html

Phillips, P., Scruggs, W., Toole, A., Flynn, P., Bowyer, K., Schott, C., & Sharpe, M. (2006). *FRVT 2006 and ICE 2006 large-scale results (NISTIR No. 7408). Gaithersburg, MD 20899*. USA: National Institute of Standards and Technology.

Pietraszek, T., & Berghe, C. (2006). Defending against injection attacks through context-sensitive string evaluation. In Valdes, A., & Zamboni, D. (Eds.), *Recent advances in intrusion detection* (*Vol. 3858*, pp. 124–145). Springer. doi:10.1007/11663812_7

Pilkington, E. (2007, July 16). Blackmail claim stirs fears over Facebook. *The Guardian*. Retrieved May 15, 2012, from http://www.guardian.co.uk/international/story/0,2127084,00.html

Pittaro, M. (2007). Cyber stalking: An analysis of online harassment and intimidation. *International Journal of Cyber Criminology*, *1*(2), 180–197.

Pranata, I., Skinner, G., & Athauda, R. (2011). A distributed community approach for protecting resources in digital ecosystem. In *International Conference on Advanced Computer Science and Information System, ICACSIS* (pp. 95–100).

Prensky, M. (2004). The emerging online life of the digital native. Retrieved August 05, 2012, from http://www.marcprensky.com/writing/Prensky-The_Emerging_Online_Life_of_the_Digital_Native-03.pdf

Ptaszynski, M., Dybala, P., Matsuba, T., Masui, F., Rzepka, R., & Araki, K. (2010, March). *Machine learning and affect analysis against cyberbullying*. Paper presented at the the Linguistic and Cognitive Approaches to Dialog Agents Symposium, Leicester, United Kingdom.

Putnam, R. D. (1995). Bowling alone: America's declining social capital. *Journal of Democracy*, *6*(1), 65–78. doi:10.1353/jod.1995.0002

Putnam, R. D. (2000). *Bowling alone: The collapse and revival of American community*. New York: Simon & Schuster. doi:10.1145/358916.361990

Rainie, L., Lenhart, A., & Smith, A. (2012). *The tone of life on social networking sites*. Pew Research Center's Internet & American Life Project.

Ranieri, M., Manca, S., & Fini, A. (2012). Why (and how) do teachers engage in social networks? An exploratory study of professional use of Facebook and its implications for lifelong learning. *British Journal of Educational Technology*, *43*(5), 754–769. doi:10.1111/j.1467-8535.2012.01356.x

Ratkiewicz, J., Conover, M., Meiss, M., Gonçalves, B., Flammini, A., & Menczer, F. (2011). Detecting and tracking political abuse in social media. In *Proceedings of the 5th International Conference on Weblogs and Social Media (ICWSM)*. Barcelona, Catalonia, Spain: The AAAI Press.

Ratkiewicz, J., Conover, M., Meiss, M., Gonçalves, B., Patil, S., Flammini, A., & Menczer, F. (2011). Truthy: Mapping the spread of astroturf in microblog streams. In *20th international conference companion on world wide web* (pp. 249-252). Hyderabad, India: ACM New York, NY, USA.

Reid, P., Monsen, J., & Rivers, I. (2004). Psychology's contribution to understanding and managing bullying within schools. *Educational Psychology in Practice*, *20*(3), 241–258. doi:10.1080/0266736042000251817

Reppler. (2013). Website. Retrieved September 9, 2012, from http://www.reppler.com/

Reppler. (2013). Managing your online image across social networks. Retrieved September 9, 2012, from http://blog.reppler.com/2011/09/27/managing-your-online-image-across-social-networks

Resnick, P., & Varian, H. (1997, March). Recommender systems. *Introduction to special section of Communications of the ACM, 40*(3).

Ressler, S. (2006). Social network analysis as an approach to combat terrorism: Past, present, and future research. *The Journal of the Naval Postgraduate School Center for Homeland Defense and Security*, *2*(2).

Reynolds, K., Kontostathis, A., & Edwards, L. (2011, December). *Using machine learning to detect cyberbullying*. Paper presented at the 10th International Conference on Machine Learning and Applications and Workshops, Honolulu, HI.

Rieh, S. Y., & Danielson, D. R. (2007). Credibility: A multidisciplinary framework. In Cronin, B. (Ed.), *Annual review of information science and technology* (Vol. 41, pp. 307–364). Medford, NJ: Information Today.

Rivers, I., & Noret, N. (2009). 'I h8 u': Findings from a five-year study of text and email bullying. *British Educational Research Journal*, *36*(4), 643–671. doi:10.1080/01411920903071918

Robinson, N., Graux, H., Botterman, M., & Valeri, L. (2009). *Review of the European Data Protection Directive*. Santa Monica, CA: RAND Corporation.

Rodriguez, E., Rodriguez, V., Carreras, A., & Delgado, J. (2009). A digital rights management approach to privacy in online social networks. In *Workshop on privacy and protection in web-based social networks (within ICAIL'09), Barcelona, Spain, 2009*. IDT Series, vol. 3, ISSN 2013-5017.

Rosalind, T. (1992). *Literacy and orality in Ancient Greece*. Cambridge, MA: Cambridge University Press.

Rosenberg, J., & Egbert, N. (2011). Online impression management: Personality traits and concerns for secondary goals as predictors of self-presentation tactics on Facebook. *Journal of Computer-Mediated Communication, 17*(1), 1–18. doi:10.1111/j.1083-6101.2011.01560.x

Rosenblum, D. (2007, May-June). What anyone can know: The privacy risks of social networking sites. *Security Privacy, IEEE, 5*(3), 40–49. doi:10.1109/MSP.2007.75

RSA. (2011). The current state of cybercrime and what to expect in 2011. USA: EMC corporation.

Ruedy, M. C. (2008). Repercussions of a MySpace teen suicide: Should anti-cyberbullying laws be created. *North Carolina Journal of Law and Technology, 9*(2), 323–346.

Russell, P. (1983). *The global brain: Speculations on the evolutionary leap to planetary consciousness*. Boston, MA: Houghton Mifflin.

Rzadca, K., Datta, A., & Buchegger, S. (2010). Replica placement in p2p storage: Complexity and game theoretic analyses. In *Proceedings of the International Conference on Distributed Computing Systems* (pp. 599–609). IEEE Computer Society.

Sabelfeld, A., & Myers, A. C. (2003). Language-based information-flow security. *IEEE Journal on Selected Areas in Communications (JASC)*, 5–19. doi:10.1109/JSAC.2002.806121

Sadeh, N., Hong, J., Cranor, L., Fette, I., Kelley, P., Prabaker, M., & Rao, J. (2009). Understanding and capturing people's privacy policies in a mobile social networking application. *Personal and Ubiquitous Computing, 13*(6), 401–412. doi:10.1007/s00779-008-0214-3

Sahai, A., & Waters, B. (2005). Fuzzy identity based encryption. In *Advances in Cryptology – Eurocrypt 2005* (*Vol. 3494*, pp. 557–557). Lecture Notes in Computer ScienceSpringer. doi:10.1007/11426639_27

Sahin, M. (2012). The relationship between the cyberbullying/cybervictmization and loneliness among adolescents. *Children and Youth Services Review, 34*, 834–837. doi:10.1016/j.childyouth.2012.01.010

Samarati, P., & Vimercati, S. D. C. D. (2001). Access control: Policies, models, and mechanisms. In *Revised versions of lectures given during the IFIP WG 1.7 international school on foundations of security analysis and design on foundations of security analysis and design: Tutorial lectures, 2171* (pp. 137–196). London, UK: Springer-Verlag.

Sampson, T. D. (2012). *Virality. Contagion theory in the age of networks*. University of Minnesota Press.

Sandhu, R. S., Coyne, E. J., Feinstein, H. L., & Youman, C. E. (1996). Role-based access control models. *IEEE Computer, 29*(2), 38–47. doi:10.1109/2.485845

Sandhu, R., Bhamidipati, V., & Munawer, Q. (1999). The ARBAC97 model for role-based administration of roles. *ACM Transactions on Information and System Security, 2*(1), 105–135. doi:10.1145/300830.300839

Sandler, D., Mislove, A., Post, A., & Druschel, P. (2005). Feedtree: Sharing web micronews with peer-to-peer event notification. In *Peer-to-Peer Systems IV* (*Vol. 3640*, pp. 141–151). Lecture Notes in Computer ScienceBerlin: Springer / Verlag. doi:10.1007/11558989_13

Sattikar, A. A., & Kulkarni, R. V. (2011). A review of security and privacy issues in social networking. *International Journal of Computer Science and Information Technologies, 2*(6), 2784–2787.

Schaad, A. (2001). Detecting conflicts in a role-based delegation model. *Seventeenth Annual Computer Security Applications Conference*, 117–126. IEEE Comput. Soc.

Schaffer, N. (2009). *HOW TO: Establish social media credibility in 7 easy steps*. Retrieved September 11, 2012, from, http://windmillnetworking.com/2009/09/01/how-to-establish-social-media-credibility-in-7-easy-steps/

Schoen, S. (2007, July 20). Harry Potter and digital fingerprints. *Deep Links News*. Retrieved May 15, 2012, from https://www.eff.org/deeplinks/2007/07/harry-potter-and-digital-fingerprints

Scott, J. (1991). *Social network analysis: A handbook*. Newbury Park, California: SAGE Publications.

Shamir, A. (1984). Identity-based cryptosystems and signature schemes. In *Lecture Notes in Computer Science, Vol. 196. Advances in Cryptology: Proceedings of CRYPTO 84* (pp. 47–53). Berlin: Springer/Verlag.

Shamir, A. (1979, November). How to share a secret. *Communications of the ACM*, *22*(11), 612–613. doi:10.1145/359168.359176

Shankland, S. (2010). *Facebook blocks contact exporting tool*. Retrieved September 26, 2012, from http://news.cnet.com/8301-30685_3-20076774-264/facebook-blocks-contact-exporting-tool/

Shariff, S. (2005). Cyber-dilemmas in the new millennium: School obligations to provide student safety in a virtual school environment. *McGill Journal of Education*, *40*(3), 467–487.

Shen, H.-B., & Hong, F. (2006). An attribute-based access control model for web services. In *Proceedings of the seventh international conference on parallel and distributed computing, applications and technologies* (pp. 74–79). Washington, DC, USA: IEEE Computer Society.

Shuangling, L., Haoxiang, X., Taketoshi, Y., & Zhongtuo, W. (2009). Toward collective intelligence of online communities: A primitive conceptual model. *Journal of Systems Science and Systems Engineering*.

Simon, H. A. (1982). Models of bounded rationality. Trustme: Anonymous management of trust relationships in decentralized P2P systems. In N. Shahmehri, R. L. Graham, & G. Caronni (Eds.), *Peer-to-peer computing* (p. 142-149). IEEE Computer Society.

Singh, K., Bhola, S., & Lee, W. (2009). xBook: Redesigning privacy control in social networking platforms. In *Proceedings of the USENIX Security Symposium* (pp. 249-266).

Singh, L., & Zhan, J. (2007, November). *Measuring topological anonymity in social networks*. Paper presented at the IEEE International Conference on Granular Computing, Silicon Valley, CA.

Sirivianos, M., Kim, K., & Yang, X. (2009). *FaceTrust: Assessing the credibility of online personas via social networks*. Paper presented at the Usenix Workshop on Hot Topics in Security (HotSec) 2009, Montreal, Canada.

Skeels, M., & Grudin, J. (2009). When social networks cross boundaries: A case study of workplace use of Facebook and Linked-In. In *Proceedings of the ACM 2009 international conference on Supporting group work* , *09*, 95–104. doi:10.1145/1531674.1531689

Slonje, R., & Smith, P. K. (2008). Cyberbullying: Another main type of bullying? *Scandinavian Journal of Psychology*, *49*, 147–154. doi:10.1111/j.1467-9450.2007.00611.x

Smith, A. (2011). *Why Americans use social media. Social networking sites are appealing as a way to maintain contact with close ties and reconnect with old friends*. Pew Research Center's Internet & American Life Project.

Smith, P. K. (2004). Bullying: Recent developments. *Child and Adolescent Mental Health*, *9*(3), 98–103. doi:10.1111/j.1475-3588.2004.00089.x

Smith, P. K., Cowie, H., Olafsson, R. F., & Liefooghe, A. P. D. (2002). Definitions of bullying: A comparison of terms used, and age and gender differences, in a fourteen-country international comparison. *Child Development*, *73*(4), 1119–1133. doi:10.1111/1467-8624.00461

Smith, P. K., Mahdavi, J., Carvalho, M., Fisher, S., Russell, S., & Tippett, N. (2008). Cyberbullying: Its nature and impact in secondary school pupils. *Journal of Child Psychology and Psychiatry, and Allied Disciplines*, *49*(4), 376–385. doi:10.1111/j.1469-7610.2007.01846.x

Solove, D. J. (2006). A taxonomy of privacy. *University of Pennsylvania Law Review*, *154*(3), 477–560. doi:10.2307/40041279

Sood, S. O., Antin, J., & Churchill, E. F. (2012). *Using crowdsourcing to improve profanity detection* (Technical Report, SS-12-06). Retrieved from http://www.aaai.org/ocs/index.php/SSS/SSS12/paper/download/4256/4698

Spencer, K. (2008, May 1). *Identity 'at risk' on Facebook*. Retrieved October 6, 2012, from http://news.bbc.co.uk/2/hi/programmes/click_online/7375772.stm

Spiekermann, S., Grossklags, J., & Berendt, B. (2001). E-privacy in 2nd generation E-commerce: Privacy preferences versus actual behavior. *World Wide Web Internet And Web Information Systems*, 38–47.

Squicciarini, A. C., Shehab, M., & Paci, F. (2009). Collective privacy management in social networks. In *Proceedings of the 17th International World Wide Web Conference* (pp. 461–484). New York: ACM Press.

Squicciarini, A., Trombetta, A., Bhargav-Spantzel, A., & Bertino, E. (2007). K-anonymous attribute-based access control. *E. International Conference on Information and Computer Security (ICICS'07)*.

Squicciarini, A. C., & Shehab, M. (2010). Privacy policies for shared content in social network sites. *The VLDB Journal, 19*, 777–796. doi:10.1007/s00778-010-0193-7

Squicciarini, A. C., & Sundareswaran, S. (2009, December). Web-traveler policies for images on social networks. *World Wide Web (Bussum), 12*, 461–484. doi:10.1007/s11280-009-0070-8

Squicciarini, A. C., Xu, H., & Zhang, X. (2011). CoPE: Enabling collaborative privacy management in online social networks. *Journal of the American Society for Information Science and Technology, 62*(3), 521–534.

Stacey, E. (2008). Coping with the cyberworld: Student perspectives on cybersafe learning environments. In Schubert, S., Davies, G., & Stacey, E. (Eds.), *LYICT 2008: ICT and Learning in the Net Generation* (pp. 224–236). Kuala Lumpur, Malaysia: Open University Malaysia.

Steel, E., & Fowler, G. A. (2010, October 18). Facebook in privacy breach: Top-ranked applications transmit personal IDs, a journal investigation finds. *The Wall Street Journal.* Retrieved October 6, 2012, from http://online.wsj.com/article/SB10001424052702304772804575558484075236968.html

Steiner, P. (1993, July 5). Cartoon. *The New Yorker.*

Steinfield, C., Ellison, N. B., & Lampe, C. (2008). Social capital, self-esteem, and use of online social network sites: A longitudinal analysis. *Journal of Applied Developmental Psychology, 29*(6), 434–445. doi:10.1016/j.appdev.2008.07.002

Steven, J. (2002). *Emergence: The connected lives of ants, brains, cities and software.* Penguin.

Stroud, D. (2008). Social networking: An age-neutral commodity — Social networking becomes a mature web application. *Journal of Direct. Data and Digital Marketing Practice, 9*(3), 278–292. doi:10.1057/palgrave.dddmp.4350099

Su, Z., & Wassermann, G. (2006). *The essence of command injection attacks in web applications.* Paper presented at the Conference record of the 33rd ACM SIGPLAN-SIGACT symposium on Principles of programming languages. Charleston, South Carolina, USA.

Suh, B., & Pirolli, P. (2011). *Finding credible information sources in social networks based on content and social structure.* Paper presented at the 3rd IEEE International Conference on Social Computing (SocialCom), Boston, MA.

Sun, J., Zhu, X., & Fang, Y. (2010). A privacy-preserving scheme for online social networks with efficient revocation. In *Proceedings of the 2010 IEEE INFOCOM* (pp. 1–9).

Sutton, J., & Smith, P. K. (1999). Bullying as a group process: An adaptation of the participant role approach. *Aggressive Behavior, 25*, 97–111. doi:10.1002/(SICI)1098-2337(1999)25:2<97::AID-AB3>3.0.CO;2-7

Sweeny, L. (2002). K-anonymity: A model for protecting privacy. *International Journal on Uncertainty, Fuzziness and Knowledge-based Systems, 10*(5), 557–570. doi:10.1142/S0218488502001648

Sweney, M. (2012). Facebook quarterly report reveals 83m profiles are fake. *The Guardian.* Retrieved September 11, 2012, from http://www.guardian.co.uk/technology/2012/aug/02/facebook-83m-profiles-bogus-fake

Taki, M., Slee, P., Hymel, S., Pepler, D., Sim, H., & Swearer, S. (2008). A new definition and scales for indirect aggression in schools: Results from the longitudinal comparative survey among five countries. *International Journal of Violence and School, 7*, 1.

Tanenbaum, A. S., & Steen, M. V. (2006). *Distributed systems: Principles and paradigms* (2nd ed.). Prentice Hall.

Tang, Y., Mao, C., Lai, H., & Zhu, J. (2009, December). Role based access control for social network sites. 2009 *Joint Conferences on Pervasive Computing (JCPC)*, 389–394.

Tanis, M., & Postmes, T. (2005). Short communication, a social identity approach to trust: Interpersonal perception, groups membership and trusting behaviour. *European Journal of Social Psychology, 35*(3), 413–424. doi:10.1002/ejsp.256

Tapiador, A., Carrera, D., & Joaquin, S. (2011). Tie-RBAC: An application of RBAC to social networks. *Web 2.0 security and privacy.* Oakland, California.

The Google+ project. (2011). Website. Retrieved March, 2012, from https://plus.google.com

The state of social media 2011: Social is the new normal. (2012). Website. Retrieved March, 2012, from http://www.briansolis.com/2011/10/ http://www.briansolis.com/2011/10/state-of-social-media-2011/

Thomas, R. K. (1997). Team-based access control (TMAC): A primitive for applying role-based access controls in collaborative environments. In *Second ACM workshop on role-based access control* (pp. 13–19). ACM.

Thomas, R. K., & Sandhu, R. S. (1994). Conceptual foundations for a model of task-based authorizations. In *7th IEEE computer security foundations workshop* (pp. 66–79). IEEE Computer Society Press.

Thomas, R. K., & Sandhu, R. S. (1998). Task-based authorization controls (TBAC): A family of models for active and enterprise-oriented authorization management. In *Proceedings of the IFIP TC11 WG11.3 eleventh international conference on database security xi: Status and prospects* (pp. 166–181). London, UK: Chapman & Hall, Ltd.

Thornberg, R. (2007). A classmate in distress: Schoolchildren as bystanders and their reasons for how they act. *Social Psychology of Education*, *10*(1), 5–28. doi:10.1007/s11218-006-9009-4

Tokunaga, R. S. (2010). Following you home from school: A critical review and synthesis of research on cyberbullying victimization. *Computers in Human Behavior*, *26*(3), 277–287. doi:10.1016/j.chb.2009.11.014

Tolone, W., Ahn, G.-J., Pai, T., & Hong, S.-P. (2005). Access control in collaborative systems. *ACM Computing Surveys*, *37*(1), 29–41. doi:10.1145/1057977.1057979

Torrano-Gimenez, C., Perez-Villegas, A., & Alvarez, G. (2010). WASAT-A new web authorization security analysis tool. *Web Application Security*, 39-49.

Trant, J. (2009). Studying social tagging and folksonomy: A review and framework. *Journal of Digital Information*, *10*(1), 1–44.

Travers, J., & Milgram, S. (1969). An experimental study of the small world problem. *Sociometry*, *32*, 425–443. doi:10.2307/2786545

Trend Micro. (2009). 2009's most persistent malware threats. Retrieved February 3, 2011, from http://us.trendmicro.com/imperia/md/content/us/trendwatch/researchandanalysis/2009s_most_persistent_malware_threats__march_2010_.pdf

Trusteer. (2009). Banking malware Zeus sucessfully bypasses anti-virus detection. Retrieved March, 2011, from http://www.ecommerce-journal.com/news/18221_zeus_increasingly_avoids_pcs_detection

Tschantz, M. C., & Wing, J. M. (2009). *Formal methods for privacy* (pp. 1–15). Formal Methods, FM.

Turkle, S. (1997). *Life on the screen: Identity in the age of the Internet.* New York: Simon & Schuster.

Tuunainen, V. K., Pitkanen, O., & Hovi, M. (2009). *Users' awareness of privacy on online social networking sites - case Facebook. 22nd Bled eConference eEnablement: Facilitating an Open, Effective and Representative eSociety.* Slovenia: Bled.

Twitter (2012). *Twitter terms of service.* Retrieved September 26, 2012, from http://twitter.com/tos

Twyman, K., Saylor, C., Taylor, L. A., & Comeaux, C. (2010). Comparing children and adolescents engaged in cyberbullying to matched peers. *Cyberpsychology, Behavior, and Social Networking*, *13*(2), 195–199. doi:10.1089/cyber.2009.0137

United States Department of Defense. (1983). *Trusted Computer System Evaluation Criteria (Orange Book).* D. of Defense.

Urdaneta, G., Pierre, G., & Steen, M. V. (2011). A survey of DHT security techniques. *ACM Computing Surveys*, *43*(2), 1–49. doi:10.1145/1883612.1883615

Utz, S., & Kramer, N. (2009). The privacy paradox on social network sites revisited: The role of individual characteristics and group norms. *Cyberpsychology: Journal of Psychosocial Research on Cyberspace*, 3(2), article 1. Retrieved September 11, 2012, from http://www.cyberpsychology.eu/view.php?cisloclanku=2009111001&article=1

Valenzuela, S., Park, N., & Kee, K. F. (2009). Is there social capital in a social network site?: Facebook use and college students' life satisfaction, trust, and participation. *Journal of Computer-Mediated Communication, 14*(4), 875–901. doi:10.1111/j.1083-6101.2009.01474.x

Valeur, F., Mutz, D., & Vigna, G. (2005). A learning-based approach to the detection of SQL attacks. In Julisch, K., & Kruegel, C. (Eds.), *Detection of intrusions and malware, and vulnerability assessment* (*Vol. 3548*, pp. 533–546). Springer. doi:10.1007/11506881_8

Valli, C., & Brand, M. (2008). *The malware analysis body of knowledge*. MABOK.

Van der Hoven, J. (2008). Information technology, privacy and the protection of personal data. In Weckert, J., & Hoven, J. (Eds.), *Information technology and moral philosophy* (pp. 301–321). Cambridge, MA: Cambridge University Press.

Vandebosch, H., & Cleemput, V. K. (2008). Defining cyberbullying: A qualitative research into the perceptions of youngsters. *Cyberpsychology & Behavior, 11*, 499–503. doi:10.1089/cpb.2007.0042

Vassileva, J. (2001). *Distributed user modelling for universal information access*. Paper presented at the 9th International Conference of Human–Computer Interaction, New Orleans, Louisiana, USA.

Veenstra, R., Lindenberg, S., Oldehinkel, A. J., Winter, A. F. D., Verhulst, F. C., & Ormel, J. (2005). Bullying and victimization in elementary schools: A comparison of bullies, victims, bully/victims, and uninvolved preadolescents. *Developmental Psychology, 41*(4), 672–682. doi:10.1037/0012-1649.41.4.672

Vella, K. J. (2007, Jun 11). Web applications: What are they? What about them? Retrieved 2011, from http://www.windowsecurity.com/articles/Web-Applications.html?printversion

Ven, T. M. V. (2011). *Motivations behind cyber bullying and online aggression: Cyber sanctions, dominance, and trolling online*. (Master's thesis). Ohio University.

Verhanneman, T., Piessens, F., De Win, B., & Joosen, W. (2005). Uniform application-level access control enforcement of organization wide policies. In *Proceedings of the 21st annual computer security applications conference* (pp. 431–440). Washington, DC, USA: IEEE Computer Society.

Vicente, C. R., Freni, D., Bettini, C., & Jensen, C. S. (2011). Location-related privacy in geo-social networks. *IEEE Internet Computing, 15*(3), 20–27. doi:10.1109/MIC.2011.29

Villegas, W., Ali, B., & Maheswaran, M. (2008). An access control scheme for protecting personal data. In *Proceedings of the 2008 sixth annual conference on privacy, security and trust* (pp. 24–35). Washington, DC, USA: IEEE Computer Society.

Villeneuve, N. (2010, November). *Koobface: Inside a crimeware network* (Technical Report No. JR04-2010). Munk School of Global Affairs.

Viswanath, B., Post, A., Gummadi, K. P., & Mislove, A. (2010). An analysis of social network-based Sybil defenses. *ACM SIGCOMM Computer Communication Review, 40*(4), 363–374. doi:10.1145/1851275.1851226

W3C (World Wide Web Consortium) - Incubator Group Report (2010). *A standards-based, open and privacy-aware social Web*. Retrieved September, 2012 from http://www.w3.org/2005/Incubator/socialweb/XGR-socialweb-20101206

W3C. (2009). *Status for resource description framework (RDF) model and syntax specification*. Retrieved March, 2012, from http://www.w3.org/1999/status/PR-rdf-syntax-19990105/status.

W3C. (2009). *W3C semantic web activity*. Retrieved March, 2012, from http://www.w3.org/2001/sw/

W3schools. (2011). Introduction to SQL. Retrieved April, 2011, from http://www.w3schools.com/sql/sql_intro.asp

Wagner, C., Mitter, S., Körner, C., & Strohmaier, M. (2012). When social bots attack: Modeling susceptibility of users in online social networks. In *Making sense of microposts* (pp. 41-48).

Wang, C., & Leung, H.-F. (2004). A secure and private Clarke tax voting protocol without trusted authorities. In *Proceedings of the 6th international conference on electronic commerce* (pp. 556–565). New York, NY, USA: ACM.

Wang, H., & Sun, L. (2010). Trust-involved access control in collaborative open social networks. In *Proceedings of the 2010 fourth international conference on network and system security* (pp. 239–246). Washington, DC, USA: IEEE Computer Society.

Wang, W. (2009). *Digital video forensics*. (Doctoral thesis). Dartmouth University.

Wang, J., Nansel, T. R., & Iannotti, R. J. (2010). Cyber and traditional bullying: Differential association. *The Journal of Adolescent Health, 48*, 415–417. doi:10.1016/j.jadohealth.2010.07.012

Wang, S. S., Moon, S.-Il, Kwon, K. H., Evans, C. A., & Stefanone, M. A. (2010). Face off: Implications of visual cues on initiating friendship on Facebook. *Computers in Human Behavior, 26*(2), 226–234. doi:10.1016/j.chb.2009.10.001

Wang, Y. D., & Emurian, H. H. (2005). An overview of online trust: Concepts, elements, and implications. *Computers in Human Behavior, 21*(1), 105–125. doi:10.1016/j.chb.2003.11.008

Wasserman, S., & Faust, K. (1994). *Social network analysis: Methods and applications*. Cambridge, UK: Cambridge University Press. doi:10.1017/CBO9780511815478

Waters, S., & Ackerman, J. (2011). Exploring privacy management on Facebook: Motivations and perceived consequences of voluntary disclosure. *Journal of Computer-Mediated Communication, 17*(1), 101–115. doi:10.1111/j.1083-6101.2011.01559.x

Websites 'keeping deleted photos'. (2009). Article. Retrieved from http://news.bbc.co.uk/2/hi/8060407.stm

Weeks, S. (2001). Understanding trust management systems. In *Proceedings of the 2001 IEEE symposium on security and privacy* (pp. 94–105). Washington, DC, USA: IEEE Computer Society.

Weitzner, D. J., Hendler, J., Berners-Lee, T., & Connolly, D. (2006). Creating a policy-aware web: Discretionary, rule-based access for the world wide web. In Ferrari, E., & Thuraisingham, B. (Eds.), *Web and information security* (pp. 1–31). Idea Group Inc.doi:10.4018/978-1-59140-588-7.ch001

White, D. M. (1950). The gate-keeper: A case study in the selection of news. *The Journalism Quarterly, 27*, 383–390.

Williams, K. R., & Guerra, N. G. (2007). Prevalence and predictors of internet bullying. *The Journal of Adolescent Health, 41*, S14–S21. doi:10.1016/j.jadohealth.2007.08.018

Windley, P. (2005). *Digital identity*. Sebastopol, CA: O'Reilly Media, Inc.

Winsborough, W. H., & Li, N. (2002). Towards practical automated trust negotiation. In *Proceedings of the Third International Workshop on Policies for Distributed Systems and Networks* (pp. 92–103). IEEE Computer Society.

Winter, S., Haferkamp, N., Stock, Y., & Kramer, N. C. (2011). The digital quest for love – The role of relationship status in self-presentation on social networking sites. *Cyberpsychology: Journal of Psychosocial Research on Cyberspace, 5*(2), article 3. Retrieved September 11, 2012, from http://cyberpsychology.eu/view.php?cisloclanku=2011121801&article=3

Wireshark, the Worlds Foremost Network Analyzer (2012). Website. Retrieved September, 2012, from http://www.wireshark.org

Wolak, J., Mitchell, K. J., & Finkelhor, D. (2007). Does online harassment constitute bullying? An exploration of online harassment by known peers and online-only contacts. *The Journal of Adolescent Health, 41*(6), S51–S58. doi:10.1016/j.jadohealth.2007.08.019

Wondracek, G., Holz, T., Kirda, E., Antipolis, S., & Kruegel, C. (2010). A practical attack to de-anonymize social network users. In *Proceedings of the 2010 IEEE Symposium on Security and Privacy* (pp. 223–238).

Wong, A. H. (2009). *The prevalence of ethnicity-related victimization in urban multiethnic schools*. (Master's Thesis). University of Toronto.

Wong, C. K., Gouda, M. G., & Lam, S. S. (1998). Secure group communications using key graphs. *ACM SIGCOMM Computer Communication Review, 28*(4), 68–79. doi:10.1145/285243.285260

Wong, D. S. W. (2004). School bullying and tackling strategies in Hong Kong. *International Journal of Offender Therapy and Comparative Criminology, 48*(5), 437–453. doi:10.1177/0306624X04263887

Xie, H., Farmer, T. W., & Cairns, B. D. (2003). Different forms of aggression among inner-city African–American children: Gender, configurations, and school social networks. *Journal of School Psychology, 41*(5), 355–375. doi:10.1016/S0022-4405(03)00086-4

Xiong, L., & Liu, L. (2004, July 8–10). Peertrust: Supporting reputation-based trust for peer-to-peer electronic communities. *IEEE Transactions on Knowledge and Data Engineering*, *16*(7), 843–857. doi:10.1109/TKDE.2004.1318566

Xu, J., Jun, K., Zhu, X., & Bellmore, A. (2012). Learning from bullying traces in social media. In *Proceedings of the Conference of the North American Chapter of the Association for Computational Linguistics: Human Language Technologies*. Stroudsburg, PA: The Association for Computational Linguistics.

Xu, T., Chen, Y., & Fu, X. (2010). Twittering by cuckoo: Decentralized and socio-aware online microblogging services. In *Proceedings of the ACM SIGCOMM 2010 Conference* (pp. 473–475). ACM.

Xu, T., Chen, Y., Zhao, J., & Fu, X. (2010). Cuckoo: Towards decentralized, socio-aware online microblogging services and data measurements. In *Proceedings of the 2nd ACM International Workshop on Hot Topics in Planet-scale Measurement* (pp. 4:1–4:6). ACM.

Yang, Z., Wilson, C., Wang, X., Gao, T., Zhao, B. Y., & Dai, Y. (2011). Uncovering social network sybils in the wild. In *Proceedings of the ACM SIGCOMM Internet Measurement Conference* (pp. 259-268). New York, NY: Association for Computing Machinery.

Yang, Y., Wang, Q., Woo, H. L., & Quek, C. L. (2011). Using Facebook for teaching and learning: A review of the literature. *International Journal of Continuing Engineering Education and Lifelong Learning*, *21*(1), 72–86. doi:10.1504/IJCEELL.2011.039695

Ybarra, M. L., Diener-west, M., & Leaf, P. J. (2007). Examining the overlap in Internet harassment and school bullying: Implications for school intervention. *The Journal of Adolescent Health*, *41*(6), S42–S50. doi:10.1016/j.jadohealth.2007.09.004

Ybarra, M. L., & Mitchell, K. J. (2004). Youth engaging in online harassment: Associations with caregiver–child relationships, Internet use, and personal characteristics. *Journal of Adolescence*, *27*(3), 319–3360. doi:10.1016/j.adolescence.2004.03.007

Ybarra, M. L., Mitchell, K. J., Wolak, J., & Finkelhor, D. (2006). Examining characteristics and associated distress related to internet harassment: Findings from the second youth internet safety survey. *Pediatrics*, *118*(4), e1169–e1177. doi:10.1542/peds.2006-0815

Yeung, C. A., Liccardi, I., Lu, K., Seneviratne, O., & Berners-Lee, T. (2009). Decentralization: The future of online social networking. *W3C Workshop on the Future of Social Networking*. Position Paper.

Yin, D., Davison, B. D., Xue, Z., Hong, L., Kontostathis, A., & Edwards, L. (2009, April). *Detection of harassment on Web 2.0*. Paper presented at the Content Analysis in the Web 2.0, Madrid, Spain.

Yu, W. D., Aravind, D., & Supthaweesuk, P. (2006). *Software vulnerability analysis for web services software systems*.

Yu, H., Kaminsky, M., Gibbons, P., & Flaxman, A. (2006). Sybilguard: Defending against sybil attacks via social networks. *ACM SIGCOMM Computer Communication Review*, *36*(4), 267–278. doi:10.1145/1151659.1159945

Zhang, C., Sun, J., Zhu, X., & Fang, Y. (2010). Privacy and security for online social networks: Challenges and opportunities. *IEEE Network*, *24*(4), 13–18. doi:10.1109/MNET.2010.5510913

Zheleva, E., & Getoor, L. (2009, April). *To join or not to join: The illusion of privacy in social networks with mixed public and private user profiles*. Paper presented at the 18th International conference on World Wide Web, Madrid, Spain.

Zwart, M. D., Lindsay, D., Henderson, M., & Phillips, M. (2011). *Teenagers, legal risks and social networking sites*. Victoria, Australia: Monash University.

Zwier, S., Araujo, T., Boukes, M., & Willemsen, L. (2011). Boundaries to the articulation of possible selves through social networking sites: The case of Facebook profilers' social connectedness. *CyberPsychology. Behavior and Social Networking*, *14*(10), 571–576. doi:10.1089/cyber.2010.0612

Zzz, & Schimmer, L. (2009). Peer profiling and selection in the I2P anonymous network. In *Proceedings of PET-CON 2009* (pp. 1–12). Dresden, Germany.

About the Contributors

Luca Caviglione is a Researcher at the Institute of Intelligent Systems for Automation (Istituto di Studi sui Sistemi Intelligenti per l'Automazione, ISSIA) of the Italian National Research Council (CNR). In 2007 he was with the Italian National Consortium for Telecommunications (CNIT), University of Genoa Research Unit. He has a PhD in Electronic and Computer Engineering from the University of Genoa, Italy. His research interests include peer-to-peer (p2p) systems, IPv6, social networks, wireless communications, and network security. He is author and co-author of over 80 academic publications, and several patents in the field of p2p. He has been involved in Research Projects funded by the ESA, the EU and MIUR. He is a Work Group Leader of the Italian IPv6 Task Force, a contract Professor in the field of p2p networking and a Professional Engineer. From 2011, he is an Associate Editor for the Transactions on Emerging Telecommunications Technologies, Wiley.

Mauro Coccoli received the Laurea Degree in Electronic Engineering from the University of Genoa, in 1995. He received the PhD in Electronic Engineering and Computer Science from the University of Genoa in 2000. He is Assistant Professor at the University of Genoa, since December 2005. Since 2012, he is with the DIBRIS (Department of Informatics, Bioengineering, Robotics, and Systems Engineering), formerly DIST (Department of Communications, Computer and Systems Science), where he was a temporary researcher since late 1995. He is course lecturer for: "Data Base and Information Systems" since 2005, "Laboratory of Computer Science" since 2007, and "Fundamentals of Computer Science" since 2008, at the University of Genoa, Department of Education Science. His research interests include e-learning, social networks, and multi-agent systems.

Alessio Merlo received his PhD in Computer Science from University of Genoa (Italy) where he worked on performance and access control issues related to Grid Computing. He is currently serving as a Researcher at E-Campus University, Department of Engineering. His research interests are focused on performance and security issues related to Web and distributed systems (Grid, Cloud). He is currently working on security issues related to Android platform.

* * *

Jemal Abawajy is a faculty member at Deakin University and has published more than 100 articles in refereed journals and conferences as well as a number of technical reports. He is on the editorial board of several international journals and edited several international journals and conference proceedings. He has also been a member of the organizing committee for over 60 international conferences and workshops serving in various capacities including best paper award chair, general co-chair, publication chair, vice-chair, and program committee. He is actively involved in funded research in building secure, efficient, and reliable infrastructures for large-scale distributed systems. Towards this vision, he is working in several areas including: pervasive and networked systems (mobile, wireless network, sensor networks, grid, cluster, and P2P), e-science and e-business technologies and applications, and performance analysis and evaluation.

Ammar Alazab is a PhD research student at the Deakin University in the school of Information technology, Australia, with thesis title 'Malware prevention and detection'. He received his Bachelor degree in Computer science from Al-Balqa Applied University in 2001. He has been actively involved in IT consulting projects involving technology platforms such as Java / C++, JSP, ASP, .NET, Wireless XML and Oracle Wireless suites. He has published research papers in different international conferences and journals. His current research interests focus on Cybercrime, Reverse Engineering, Malware Analysis, Computer Forensic, Computer Threats, Malware Forensics, Android, Mobile Security, Mobile Malware, Malware Profiling, Cryptography and Steganography, Fraud detection, Identity Theft, Database Security, Anomaly Detection, Machine Learning, Misuse Intrusion detections, E-Commerce, E-Services, E-Government, Host and network Intrusion Detection.

Luca Biselli is an Italian Designer with a Master of Science in Architectural Engineering at the Polytechnic University of Turin, Italy. In Italy he became a registered engineer and worked as a freelance designer on industrial design projects, competitions, restorations and urban requalification. He also developed several innovative projects such as the Italian Scientific Station in Antarctica by Pininfarina Design Extra and the renovation of "Italia '61" Monorail Station in Turin. After relocating to the UK he worked as a senior designer at Sadler Brown Architecture. He followed a number of challenging projects such as the Haymarket Hub and Underground Station in Newcastle upon Tyne, the renovation of Middlesborough Transporter Bridge and several innovative country houses. He has been a Visiting Tutor at Newcastle University School of Architecture, Planning and Landscape and a speaker at architectural events in Newcastle upon Tyne and London. He is currently an independent design consultant and researcher. His main areas of research include advanced technologies, biomimicry, industrial design, mechatronics, parametric and computational design in architectural and structural design. He is also interested in applied research on human potential, creativity and social intelligence.

Francesca Carmagnola is a short time researcher in Computer Science at the University of Turin. She received her PhD in 2007 in Communication Science (University of Turin), in the area of distributed and interoperable user models. Her current research activities address user modeling, personalization of adaptive hypermedia systems, personalization of ubiquitous systems, infrastructures for adaptive web-based systems, personalized digital television, semantic knowledge representation and reasoning, semantic web. She is the author of several papers published on scientific journals, books and proceedings of international conferences.

Néstor Cataño is an Assistant Professor at the University of Madeira, Portugal, where he teaches Software Engineering courses at graduate and undergraduate levels. He is part of CMU (Carnegie Mellon University) Portugal. In spring 2010, he was a Visiting Professor at the Institute of Software Research (ISR) and the Human Computer Interaction Institute (HCII) of CMU in Pittsburgh. His current research interests include refinement calculus and the B method for software development, the Java Modeling Language (JML), and Social Networks. Néstor Cataño is a formal methods tool developer. He has recently designed and implemented the EventB2Jml tool that translates Event-B machines into JML abstract class specifications, and the Poporo tool for verifying privacy policies of social networking sites. He is an enthusiastic and experienced user of formal methods tools such as Rodin, PVS and the wide range of JML tools. Néstor Cataño is the project coordinator of several research projects on formal methods, concurrent programming, and Software Engineering.

Periklis Chatzimisios serves as an assistant professor with the Computing Systems, Security and Networks (CSSN) Research Lab of the Department of Informatics at the Alexander Technological Educational Institute of Thessaloniki, Greece. He currently participates in several European and National research projects acting in research and management positions. Since 2010, Dr. Chatzimisios serves as a Member of the Standards Development Board for the IEEE Communication Society (ComSoc). Dr. Chatzimisios serves as Organizing/TPC member and co-Chair for several conferences and he holds editorial board positions for many IEEE and non-IEEE journals. He is the author of 8 books and more than 60 peer-reviewed papers and book chapters in the areas of multimedia communications (mainly Quality of Service and Quality of Experience), wireless communications (mainly in IEEE 802.11 and 802.16 protocols) and security. His published research work has received more than 600 citations by other researchers.

Dave Clarke is a professor in the Department of Computer Science at the Katholieke Universiteit Leuven, Belgium. He received his PhD in 2001 from the University of New South Wales in Sydney, Australia. He has also held positions at Microsoft Research, Sydney, and Utrecht University and CWI, The Netherlands. His research covers programming languages, type systems, automata and logics for improving the quality of software, in particular, with applications in coordination, software product line engineering, and secure software.

Willem De Groef is a PhD student in the Department of Computer Science at the KU Leuven under the supervision of Prof. Frank Piessens. Having a background in low-level software security, his current research is mainly focused on the development of security-increasing solutions for web scripts by applying information flow security techniques. He is also the main author of FlowFox, a web browser with flexible and precise information flow control built-in. His research has been presented and published at various conferences, including ACM CCS. He is a teaching assistant at the KU Leuven of several courses on programming languages and computer architectures.

Simona de Nicola, class 1983, achieved a degree in Communication and Semiotics at Alma Mater Studiorum University of Bologna. She worked as a researcher in the Web, Communication and Technology Department, Bologna University on a study investigating the 'Use of Social Media in Academic Field.' At the moment she is working as a freelancer on communication, new technologies and Web 2.0.

Dominique Devriese is a PhD student in the Department of Computer Science at the KU Leuven, under the supervision of Prof. Frank Piessens. Before starting his PhD, he has gained practical experience in a banking corporation, working on a security-critical J2EE web banking and ATM platform. In his research, he focuses on formal approaches to software security as well as type systems and functional programming languages. His research has been published at conferences and journals like IEEE Security and Privacy, ICFP and JFP, and he has mentored multiple successful master thesis students (including Willem De Groef and Tom Reynaert). He assists on the teaching of KU Leuven courses on formal systems and declarative programming languages.

Nicola Dragoni obtained an MSc Degree and a PhD in computer science, respectively in 2002 and 2006, both at University of Bologna, Italy. He visited the Knowledge Media Institute at the Open University (UK) in 2004 and the MIT Center for Collective Intelligence (USA) in 2006. In 2007 and 2008 he was post-doctoral research fellow at University of Trento, working on security for mobile systems. Between 2005 and 2008 he also worked as freelance IT consultant. In 2009 he joined Technical University of Denmark (DTU) as assistant professor in security and distributed systems and was promoted to associate professor in 2011.

Akihiro Enomoto received the BE in Industrial Chemistry from Kyoto University and the MSc in Applied Mathematics and Physics from Graduate School of Informatics, Kyoto University, Japan and the PhD in Computer Science from University of California, Irvine, US in 2000, 2002 and 2009, respectively. Currently, he is an assistant project researcher in the Department of Computer Sciences, University of California, Irvine, US. His research interests are the areas of biological computing, distributed computing systems and wireless communication. His current research includes design and implementation of a molecular communication system, design and analysis of a social interaction network, and radio frequency design and analysis for a wireless and cellular network.

Enrico Franchi received BSc in Mathematics and Computer Science and MSc in Computer Science from the University of Parma. He is currently enrolled in the PhD course in Information Technologies from the same University under the supervision of Prof. Agostino Poggi. His main interests are related to Multi-Agent and distributed systems, social networks, artificial intelligence and software engineering. He is currently investigating the mutual relationships between social networks and multi-agent systems, with a special regard to simulations.

Pier Paolo Greco graduated as a chemical engineer in 1999 and worked in a Corporation for two years in detergents' technology. He later moved to the UK to get his Master Degree in Clean Technology/Sustainable Development. His next professional role was as Product Manager for Water Technology Chemicals, operating in Europe, Middle and Far East for 6 years before going back to Academia. Pier Paolo is currently in his 3rd year's PhD at Newcastle University focusing on Micro Porous Materials.

Sorren Christoper Hanvey has previously been a research assistant at the Madeira Interactive Technologies Institute, where he worked on the research project WeSP: Web Security and Privacy. He holds a Bachelors of Science from the University of Pune, India and a Master's in Software Engineering from the University of York, UK. He is currently completing a PhD in Software engineering from Universidade da Madeira (University of Madeira), Portugal. His PhD research has been focused on a formal methods approach to social networking, resulting in the Poporo tool. Commercially he has worked for Critical Software Technologies Ltd. UK, wherein he gained experience in safety critical systems relating to automated self-steered public transport vehicles and design verification of the onboard software for earth observation satellites.

Michael Hobbs is a faculty member and a Senior Lecturer at the University of Deakin. He has published more than 100 articles in refereed journals and conferences as well as a number of technical reports. He has more than 15 years' experience in computer science. He has served as a Chair, Organizing Committee Member, and Technical Program Committee member in numerous international conferences/workshops. He is working in several areas such as Distributed and parallel computing, Algorithms, Architectures for Parallel Processing, Security and Privacy, Game programming, Cloud Computing, Internet Security. He has been teaching various computing courses.

Christos Ilioudis is an associate professor of the Informatics Department of the Alexander Technological Educational Institute (ATEI) of Thessaloniki, Greece. He holds a BSc in Computer Science from the University of Crete and a PhD in Internet Security from the Aristotle University of Thessaloniki (Greece). His research interests include the areas of Internet security, information systems security, and digital forensics. He has been working on several EU research projects on the security area. He is a member of the Hellenic Computer Society, as well as of IEEE and the ACM.

Stefania Manca is a researcher at the Institute of Educational Technology of the National Research Council of Italy. She has been active in the field of educational technology, technology-based learning, distance education, and e-learning since 1995. Her major interests include the analysis of social and cognitive processes in Computer Supported Collaborative Learning environments and the analysis of specific linguistic features used to express and construct social dimension in asynchronous-based learning environments. She is currently investigating the value of social networking sites for formal and informal learning purposes and for professional development. She is author of several papers in these fields and has co-edited some books on the topic of knowledge building supported by technology-enhanced learning environments.

Antonio Marraffa achieved his Master in Linguistics and German studies in 1998 at the University of Bari (Italy). In 2007 he has obtained a Master in Computational linguistics at the University of Munich LMU. Since 2004, he works in the field of search engines: ranking algorithms, configuration and implementation for enterprise search solutions and SEO. In this area he has been working for Lycos, Fast Search & Transfer, Scout24 Holding (a Deutsche Telekom company). He also has great expertise in location based services and mobile applications. Currently he is working as a freelance consultant for online business.

Manuel Mazzara achieved his Master in 2002 and his PhD in 2006 at the University of Bologna. His thesis was based on Formal Methods for Web Services Composition. During 2000 he was a Technical Assistant at Computer Science Laboratories (Bologna, Italy). In 2003 he worked as Software Engineer at Microsoft (Redmond, USA). In 2004 and 2005 he worked as a freelance consultant and teacher in

Italy. In 2006 he was an assistant professor at the University of Bolzano (Italy) and in 2007 a researcher and project manager at the Technical University of Vienna (Austria). From 2008 to 2012 he worked at Newcastle University (UK) on the DEPLOY project before taking his appointments at United Nations University International Institute for Software Technology in Macao (China). He is currently also a visiting researcher at Newcastle University.

Michael J. Moore received his PhD in Computer Science at UCI in 2009 and his BSc in Computer Science and BSc in Biology at UCI in 2000. He was a post-doctoral researcher at the University of California, Irvine (UCI) from 2009-2010. He is currently a researcher at Osaka University, Japan. His research interests are in communication systems in the areas of social networks, distributed computer networks, and nano to micro-scale communications. His current research is focused on interdisciplinary research in the area of characterizing and detecting cyberbullying and in the area of designing molecular communication protocols and systems.

Tadashi Nakano received the PhD degree in information systems engineering from Osaka University, Japan, in 2002. He later worked in the Department of Computer Science, Donald Bren School of Information and Computer Sciences, University of California, Irvine, where he was a Postdoctoral Research Scholar from 2002 to 2007 and an Assistant Adjunct Professor from 2007 to 2009. Since 2009, he has been with the Graduate School of Engineering, Osaka University, where he is currently an Associate Professor. His research interests are in the areas of network applications and distributed computing systems with particular emphasis on interdisciplinary approaches. His current research is focused on biological-ICT, including the design, implementation, and evaluation of biologically inspired systems and synthetic biological systems.

Francesco Osborne is a PhD student in Computer Science at the University of Turin. His research focuses on semantic web, semantic knowledge representation and reasoning, automatic generation of semantic relationships, user modeling and storytelling. He is author of several papers published in the proceedings of relevant international conferences.

Alexandros Papanikolaou is an adjunct lecturer at the Department of Computer Science and Telecommunications of the Technological Educational Institute (TEI) of Larissa, Greece. He holds a BSc in Computer Science and a PhD in Cryptography and Information Security, both from Aston University (Birmingham, UK). His research interests include the evolution of cryptographic techniques and their application, wireless sensor networks security and intrusion detection systems.

Frank Piessens is a professor in the Department of Computer Science at the KU Leuven, Belgium. His research field is software security, where he focuses on the development of high-assurance techniques to deal with implementation-level software vulnerabilities and bugs, including techniques such as software verification, run-time monitoring, type systems and programming language design. He has published at ACM CCS, IEEE Security & Privacy, ESORICS, POPL, ECOOP, OOPSLA and many other conferences and journals. He also teaches software security at the KU Leuven, and at various academic and industrial conferences.

Nafees Qamar has a doctorate in computing science (2011) from INRIA/LIG Grenoble (France). Prior to that, he obtained a master degree in Software Systems and Engineering (2007) from Muhammad Ali Jinnah University, Islamabad (Pakistan). He is currently working as a Postdoctoral Fellow at the United Nations University (UNU-IIST), Macau SAR China. His current research addresses the challenges of the security and privacy issues arising in software systems and in particular social networks and healthcare, by employing innovative software engineering and formal methods concepts.

Maria Ranieri, PhD in Telematics and Information Society, is an Aggregate Professor of Educational Methods and Technology at the Department of Education and Psychology, University of Florence, Italy. Since 2001, she has been working in the field of educational technology, technology-enhanced learning and e-learning. Her main research areas include theory and methodology relating to media and technology in education, as well as work around teachers' practices and students' learning. She is currently investigating the interplay between mobile learning and social networking in formal and informal contexts of learning. Her publications include some more than thirty papers/chapters on these topics and four books on learning methods and technologies. She is member of SIRD (Italian Association of Educational Research) and of the executive council of MED (The Italian Association of Media Education).

Tom Reynaert holds a Master in Computer Science. He studied at the Department of Computer Science at the KU Leuven and at the École Polytechnique Fédérale de Lausanne. He is particularly interested in the fields of privacy and security of computer software. This interest is reflected in the subject of his master thesis, performed under the supervision of Frank Piessens, Dominique Devriese and Willem De Groef, in which he has investigated the privacy issues in social application platforms. He also presented the design and implementation of a novel privacy preserving application platform called PESAP. For the work in his master thesis, Tom received the Alcatel Lucent Thesis Award 2012.

Camilo Rueda is a full professor in the Faculty of Engineering at Universidad Javeriana-Cali, Colombia. He is also chair of the Department of Science and Engineering of Computing and director of the Research group AVISPA.

Rula Sayaf is a PhD student in the Department of Computer Science at the KU Leuven, Belgium. Her current research is on privacy preservation and access control models in online social networks under the supervision of Professor Dave Clarke. She holds a master degree in Artificial Intelligence from KU Leuven.

Tatsuya Suda received the BE, ME, and DrE degrees in Applied Mathematics and Physics from Kyoto University, Kyoto, Japan, in 1977, 1979, and 1982, respectively. From 1982 to 1984, he was with the Department of Computer Science, Columbia University. From 1984 through 2010, he was with the Department of Computer Science, University of California, Irvine. He is currently with the University Netgroup Inc. He has been engaged in research in the fields of networks and application of biological and sociology concepts to networks. His research also includes molecular communication, a new paradigm for nano-scale communication among bio-nanomachines. He is a fellow of IEEE and a member of ACM.

Michele Tomaiuolo obtained an MEng in Computer Engineering and a PhD in Information Technologies from the University of Parma. Currently he is an assistant professor at the Department of Information Engineering, University of Parma. He has given lessons on Foundations of Informatics, Object-oriented Programming, Software Engineering, Computer Networks, Mobile Code and Security. He participated in various national and international research projects, including @lis TechNet, Anemone, Agentcities, Collaborator, Comma. His current research activity is focused on online social networking, with attention to security and trust management, multi-agent systems, semantic web, rule-based systems, peer-to-peer networks.

Ilaria Torre is a researcher at the University of Genoa, Department of Informatics, Bioengineering, Robotics and Systems Engineering (DIBRIS). She is a member of the Laboratory of ELearning and Knowledge Management (ELKM) and a member of the committee of the Doctoral School in Languages, Cultures and Information and Communication Technologies. In 2003 she got her PhD in Communication Science and Project at the University of Turin. Her research activity concerns the study and design of web-based adaptive systems and focuses on technologies for the semantic and social Web. Her interest in social Web concerns specifically online social networks as a target and a source for user modeling and user-adapted interaction. She is author of a volume and of about fifty papers, published on scientific journals, books and on the proceedings of international conferences. Over the years she has been involved in European and national projects on the above themes.

Vasileios Vlachos is a lecturer at the Department of Computer Science and Telecommunications of the Technological Educational Institute (TEI) of Larissa, Greece. He was a senior R&D engineer at the Research Academic Computer Technology Institute (Patras, Greece) and a member of the Digital Awareness and Response to Threats team of the Hellenic Ministry of Economy and Finance. He holds a BEng in Electronic & Computer Engineering from Technical University of Crete, an MSc in Integrated Hardware and Software Systems from the University of Patras and a PhD in Information Systems Security of Athens University of Economics and Business.

Index

E

F

G

H

I

J

K

L

M

O

W

X

Y

Z

CPSIA information can be obtained at www.ICGtesting.com
Printed in the USA
BVOW05*0745170813

328516BV00015B/379/P

9 781466 639263